HMH

GO MATH!

Middle School | Grade 7

Edward B. Burger • Juli K. Dixon
Timothy D. Kanold • Matthew R. Larson
Steven J. Leinwand • Martha E. Sandoval-Martinez

Cover Image Credits: ©Kim Karpeles/Axiom Photographic Agency/Getty Images

2018 Edition

Printed in the U.S.A.

ISBN 978-1-328-45968-8

2 3 4 5 6 7 8 9 10 0868 27 26 25 24 23 22 21 20 19 18

4500711233 B C D E F G

Authors

Edward B. Burger, Ph.D., is the president of Southwestern University, a former Francis Christopher Oakley Third Century Professor of Mathematics at Williams College, and a former vice provost at Baylor University. He has authored or coauthored more than sixty-five articles, books, and video series; delivered over five hundred addresses and workshops throughout the world; and made more than fifty radio and television appearances. He is a Fellow of the American Mathematical Society as well as having earned many national honors, including the Robert Foster Cherry Award for Great Teaching in 2010. In 2012, Microsoft Education named him a "Global Hero in Education."

Juli K. Dixon, Ph.D., is a Professor of Mathematics Education at the University of Central Florida. She has taught mathematics in urban schools at the elementary, middle, secondary, and post-secondary levels. She is an active researcher and speaker with numerous publications and conference presentations. Key areas of focus are deepening teachers' content knowledge and communicating and justifying mathematical ideas. She is a past chair of the NCTM Student Explorations in Mathematics Editorial Panel and member of the Board of Directors for the Association of Mathematics Teacher Educators.

Timothy D. Kanold, Ph.D., is an award-winning international educator, author, and consultant. He is a former superintendent and director of mathematics and science at Adlai E. Stevenson High School District 125 in Lincolnshire, Illinois. He is a past president of the National Council of Supervisors of Mathematics (NCSM) and the Council for the Presidential Awardees of Mathematics (CPAM). He has served on several writing and leadership commissions for NCTM during the past decade. He presents motivational professional development seminars with a focus on developing professional learning communities (PLC's) to improve the teaching, assessing, and learning of students. He has recently authored nationally recognized articles, books, and textbooks for mathematics education and school leadership, including *What Every Principal Needs to Know about the Teaching and Learning of Mathematics*.

Matthew R. Larson, Ph.D., is the K-12 mathematics curriculum specialist for the Lincoln Public Schools and served on the Board of Directors for the National Council of Teachers of Mathematics from 2010-2013. He is a past chair of NCTM's Research Committee and was a member of NCTM's Task Force on Linking Research and Practice. He is the author of several books on implementing the Common Core Standards for Mathematics. He has taught mathematics at the secondary and college levels and held an appointment as an honorary visiting associate professor at Teachers College, Columbia University.

Steven J. Leinwand is a Principal Research Analyst at the American Institutes for Research (AIR) in Washington, D.C., and has over 30 years in leadership positions in mathematics education. He is past president of the National Council of Supervisors of Mathematics and served on the NCTM Board of Directors. He is the author of numerous articles, books, and textbooks and has made countless presentations with topics including student achievement, reasoning, effective assessment, and successful implementation of standards.

Martha E. Sandoval-Martinez is a mathematics instructor at El Camino College in Torrance, California. She was previously a Math Specialist at the University of California at Davis and former instructor at Santa Ana College, Marymount College, and California State University, Long Beach. In her current and former positions, she has worked extensively to improve fundamental pre-algebra and algebra skills in students who have historically struggled with mathematics.

Program Reviewers

Sharon Brown
Instructional Staff Developer
Pinellas County Schools
St. Petersburg, FL

Maureen Carrion
Math Staff Developer
Brentwood UFSD
Brentwood, NY

Jackie Cruse
Math Coach
Ferrell GPA
Tampa, FL

John Esser
Secondary Mathematics
Coordinator
Racine Unified School District
Racine, WI

Donald Hoessler
Math Teacher
Discovery Middle School
Orlando, Florida

Becky (Rebecca) Jones, M.Ed.
NBCT EA-Math
Orange County Public Schools
Orlando, FL

Sheila D.P. Lea, MSA
Ben L. Smith High School
Greensboro, NC

Toni Lwanga
Newell Barney Jr. High
Queen Creek Unified School District
Queen Creek, AZ

Tiffany J. Mack
Charles A. Lindbergh Middle School
Peoria District #150
Peoria, IL

Jean Sterner
Thurgood Marshall Fundamental
Middle School
Pinellas County Schools
St. Petersburg, FL

Mona Toncheff
Math Content Specialist
Phoenix Union High School District
Phoenix, AZ

Kevin Voepel
Mathematics & Professional
Development Coordinator
Ferguson-Florissant School District
Florissant, MO

UNIT 1 The Number System

MODULE 1 Adding and Subtracting Integers

MODULE 2 Multiplying and Dividing Integers

MODULE 3 Rational Numbers

UNIT 2 Ratios and Proportional Relationships

MODULE 4 Rates and Proportionality

MODULE 5 Proportions and Percent

UNIT 3 Expressions, Equations, and Inequalities

MODULE 6 Expressions and Equations

MODULE 7 Inequalities

UNIT 4 Geometry

MODULE 8 Modeling Geometric Figures

MODULE 9 Circumference, Area, and Volume

UNIT 5

Statistics

MODULE 10 Random Samples and Populations

MODULE 11 Analyzing and Comparing Data

UNIT 6 Probability

MODULE 12 Experimental Probability

MODULE 13 Theoretical Probability and Simulations

Mathematics Objectives

for *HMH Go Math* Grade 7

Objective	Descriptor	Taught & Practiced
Unit 1 The Number System		
Module 1 Adding and Subtracting Integers		
7.1.1.1	Students will add integers with the same sign.	Lesson 1.1: pp. 7–12
7.1.1.2	Students will add integers with different signs.	Lesson 1.2: pp. 13–18
7.1.1.3	Students will subtract integers.	Lesson 1.3: pp. 19–24
7.1.1.4	Students will solve multistep problems involving addition and subtraction of integers.	Lesson 1.4: pp. 25–30
Module 2 Multiplying and Dividing Integers		
7.1.2.1	Students will multiply integers.	Lesson 2.1: pp. 37–42
7.1.2.2	Students will divide integers.	Lesson 2.2: pp. 43–48
7.1.2.3	Students will use integer operations to solve real-world problems.	Lesson 2.3: pp. 49–54
Module 3 Rational Numbers		
7.1.3.1	Students will convert a rational number to a decimal.	Lesson 3.1: pp. 61–66
7.1.3.2	Students will add rational numbers.	Lesson 3.2: pp. 67–74
7.1.3.3	Students will subtract rational numbers.	Lesson 3.3: pp. 75–82
7.1.3.4	Students will multiply rational numbers.	Lesson 3.4: pp. 83–88
7.1.3.5	Students will divide rational numbers.	Lesson 3.5: pp. 89–94
7.1.3.6	Students will use different forms of rational numbers and strategically choose tools to solve problems.	Lesson 3.6: pp. 95–100
Unit 2 Ratios and Proportional Relationships		
Module 4 Rates and Proportionality		
7.2.4.1	Students will find and use unit rates.	Lesson 4.1: pp. 117–122
7.2.4.2	Students will identify and represent proportional relationships.	Lesson 4.2: pp. 123–128
7.2.4.3	Students will use graphs to represent and analyze proportional relationships.	Lesson 4.3: pp. 129–134
Module 5 Proportions and Percent		
7.2.5.1	Students will use percents to describe change.	Lesson 5.1: pp. 141–146
7.2.5.2	Students will rewrite expressions to help solve markup and markdown problems.	Lesson 5.2: pp. 147–152
7.2.5.3	Students will use percents to solve problems.	Lesson 5.3: pp. 153–158

Objective	Descriptor	Taught & Practiced
Unit 3 Expressions, Equations, and Inequalities		
Module 6 Expressions and Equations		
7.3.6.1	Students will add, subtract, factor, and multiply algebraic expressions.	Lesson 6.1: pp. 173–178
7.3.6.2	Students will use one-step equations with rational coefficients to solve problems.	Lesson 6.2: pp. 179–184
7.3.6.3	Students will write a two-step equation.	Lesson 6.3: pp. 185–190
7.3.6.4	Students will solve a two-step equation.	Lesson 6.4: pp. 191–196
Module 7 Inequalities		
7.3.7.1	Students will write and solve one-step inequalities.	Lesson 7.1: pp. 203–210
7.3.7.2	Students will write a two-step inequality.	Lesson 7.2: pp. 211–216
7.3.7.3	Students will solve a two-step inequality.	Lesson 7.3: pp. 217–222
Unit 4 Geometry		
Module 8 Modeling Geometric Figures		
7.4.8.1	Students will use scale drawings to solve problems.	Lesson 8.1: pp. 237–242
7.4.8.2	Students will draw shapes that satisfy given conditions.	Lesson 8.2: pp. 243–246
7.4.8.3	Students will identify cross sections of three-dimensional figures.	Lesson 8.3: pp. 247–250
7.4.8.4	Students will use angle relationships to solve problems.	Lesson 8.4: pp. 251–258
Module 9 Circumference, Area, and Volume		
7.4.9.1	Students will find and use the circumference of a circle.	Lesson 9.1: pp. 265–270
7.4.9.2	Students will find the area of a circle.	Lesson 9.2: pp. 271–276
7.4.9.3	Students will find the area of composite figures.	Lesson 9.3: pp. 277–282
7.4.9.4	Students will find the surface area of a figure made up of cubes and prisms.	Lesson 9.4: pp. 283–288
7.4.9.5	Students will find the volume of a figure made of cubes and prisms.	Lesson 9.5: pp. 289–294
Unit 5 Statistics		
Module 10 Random Samples and Populations		
7.5.10.1	Students will use a sample to gain information about a population.	Lesson 10.1: pp. 311–316
7.5.10.2	Students will use a sample to make inferences about a population.	Lesson 10.2: pp. 317–322
7.5.10.3	Students will generate and use random samples to represent a population.	Lesson 10.3: pp. 323–328

Objective	Descriptor	Taught & Practiced
Module 11 Analyzing and Comparing Data		
7.5.11.1	Students will compare two sets of data displayed in dot plots.	Lesson 11.1: pp. 335–340
7.5.11.2	Students will compare two sets of data displayed in box plots.	Lesson 11.2: pp. 341–346
7.5.11.3	Students will use statistical measures to compare populations.	Lesson 11.3: pp. 347–352
Unit 6 Probability		
Module 12 Experimental Probability		
7.6.12.1	Students will describe the likelihood of an event.	Lesson 12.1: pp. 367–374
7.6.12.2	Students will find the experimental probability of a simple event.	Lesson 12.2: pp. 375–380
7.6.12.3	Students will find the experimental probability of a compound event.	Lesson 12.3: pp. 381–386
7.6.12.4	Students will make predictions using experimental probability.	Lesson 12.4: pp. 387–392
Module 13 Theoretical Probability and Simulations		
7.6.13.1	Students will find the theoretical probability of a simple event.	Lesson 13.1: pp. 399–404
7.6.13.2	Students will find the theoretical probability of a compound event.	Lesson 13.2: pp. 405–410
7.6.13.3	Students will make predictions using theoretical probability.	Lesson 13.3: pp. 411–416
7.6.13.4	Students will use technology simulations to estimate probabilities.	Lesson 13.4: pp. 417–422

Process	Descriptor	Citations
MP Mathematical Processes		*The mathematical processes are integrated throughout the book. See, for example, the citations below.*
MP.1	**Problem Solving** **Mathematically proficient students start by explaining to themselves the meaning of a problem and looking for entry points to its solution. They analyze givens, constraints, relationships, and goals. They make conjectures about the form and meaning of the solution and plan a solution pathway, rather than simply jumping into a solution attempt. They consider analogous problems and try special cases and simpler forms of the original problem in order to gain insight into its solution. They monitor and evaluate their progress and change course if necessary. Mathematically proficient students check their answers to problems using a different method, and they continually ask themselves, "Does this make sense?" and "Is my answer reasonable?" They understand the approaches of others to solving complex problems and identify correspondences between different approaches. Mathematically proficient students understand how mathematical ideas interconnect and build on one another to produce a coherent whole.**	**100, 155, 222, 282, 324, 389**
MP.2	**Abstract and Quantitative Reasoning** **Mathematically proficient students make sense of quantities and their relationships in problem situations. They bring two complementary abilities to bear on problems involving quantitative relationships: the ability to decontextualize—to abstract a given situation and represent it symbolically and manipulate the representing symbols as if they have a life of their own, without necessarily attending to their referents—and the ability to contextualize, to pause as needed during the manipulation process in order to probe into the referents for the symbols involved. Quantitative reasoning entails habits of creating a coherent representation of the problem at hand; considering the units involved; attending to the meaning of quantities, not just how to compute them; and knowing and flexibly using different properties of operations and objects.**	**94, 149, 218, 273, 347–348, 392**

Process	Descriptor	Citations
MP.3	**Use and Evaluate Logical Reasoning** Mathematically proficient students understand and use stated assumptions, definitions, and previously established results in constructing arguments. They make conjectures and build a logical progression of statements to explore the truth of their conjectures. They analyze situations by breaking them into cases and recognize and use counterexamples. They organize their mathematical thinking, justify their conclusions and communicate them to others, and respond to the arguments of others. They reason inductively about data, making plausible arguments that take into account the context from which the data arose. Mathematically proficient students are also able to compare the effectiveness of two plausible arguments, distinguish correct logic or reasoning from that which is flawed, and—if there is a flaw in an argument—explain what it is. They justify whether a given statement is true always, sometimes, or never. Mathematically proficient students participate and collaborate in a mathematics community. They listen to or read the arguments of others, decide whether they make sense, and ask useful questions to clarify or improve the arguments.	18, 134, 210, 258, 340, 404
MP.4	**Mathematical Modeling** Mathematically proficient students apply the mathematics they know to solve problems arising in everyday life, society, and the workplace using a variety of appropriate strategies. They create and use a variety of representations to solve problems and to organize and communicate mathematical ideas. Mathematically proficient students apply what they know and are comfortable making assumptions and approximations to simplify a complicated situation, realizing that these may need revision later. They are able to identify important quantities in a practical situation and map their relationships using such tools as diagrams, two-way tables, graphs, flowcharts and formulas. They analyze those relationships mathematically to draw conclusions. They routinely interpret their mathematical results in the context of the situation and reflect on whether the results make sense, possibly improving the model if it has not served its purpose.	12, 122, 193, 270, 322, 386

Process	Descriptor	Citations
MP.5	**Use Mathematical Tools** Mathematically proficient students consider the available tools when solving a mathematical problem. These tools might include pencil and paper, models, a ruler, a protractor, a calculator, a spreadsheet, a computer algebra system, a statistical package, or dynamic geometry software. Mathematically proficient students are sufficiently familiar with tools appropriate for their grade or course to make sound decisions about when each of these tools might be helpful, recognizing both the insight to be gained and their limitations. Mathematically proficient students identify relevant external mathematical resources, such as digital content, and use them to pose or solve problems. They use technological tools to explore and deepen their understanding of concepts and to support the development of learning mathematics. They use technology to contribute to concept development, simulation, representation, reasoning, communication and problem solving.	100, 147, 191, 243–246, 323, 422
MP.6	**Use Precise Mathematical Language** Mathematically proficient students communicate precisely to others. They use clear definitions, including correct mathematical language, in discussion with others and in their own reasoning. They state the meaning of the symbols they choose, including using the equal sign consistently and appropriately. They express solutions clearly and logically by using the appropriate mathematical terms and notation. They specify units of measure and label axes to clarify the correspondence with quantities in a problem. They calculate accurately and efficiently and check the validity of their results in the context of the problem. They express numerical answers with a degree of precision appropriate for the problem context.	62, 128, 190, 250, 346, 380

Process	Descriptor	Citations
MP.7	**See Structure** Mathematically proficient students look closely to discern a pattern or structure. They step back for an overview and shift perspective. They recognize and use properties of operations and equality. They organize and classify geometric shapes based on their attributes. They see expressions, equations, and geometric figures as single objects or as being composed of several objects.	97, 146, 175, 283, 349, 410
MP.8	**Generalize** Mathematically proficient students notice if calculations are repeated and look for general methods and shortcuts. They notice regularity in mathematical problems and their work to create a rule or formula. Mathematically proficient students maintain oversight of the process, while attending to the details as they solve a problem. They continually evaluate the reasonableness of their intermediate results.	61, 152, 203–204, 265, 290, 407

Succeeding with HMH Go Math

Actively participate in your learning with your write-in Student Edition. Explore concepts, take notes, answer questions, and complete your homework right in your textbook!

LESSON 5.1 **Percent Increase and Decrease**

7.2.5.1

Students will use p... describe change.

Essential Questions ensure that you know exactly what you are learning.

ESSENTIAL QUESTION

How do you use percents to describe change?

Explore Activities help you develop a deeper understanding of math concepts.

EXPLORE ACTIVITY Real World

Finding Percent Increase

Percents can be used to describe how an amount changes.

$$\text{Percent Change} = \frac{\text{Amount of Change}}{\text{Original Amount}}$$

The change may be an increase or a decrease. **Percent increase** describes how much a quantity increases in comparison to the original amount.

Math On the Spot my.hrw.com

Scan QR codes with your smartphone or device to watch **Math On the Spot** tutorial videos for every example in the book!

EXAMPLE 1 **Amber got a raise, and her hourly wage increased from \$8 to \$9.50. What is the percent increase?**

STEP 1 Find the amount of change.

Amount of Change = Greater Value − Lesser Value

Substitute values. = ☐ − ☐

Subtract. = ☐

STEP 2 Find the percent increase. Round to the nearest percent.

Percent Change $= \frac{\text{Amount of Change}}{\text{Original Amount}}$

Substitute values. $= \frac{\square}{8.00}$

Divide. = ______

Write as a percent and round. ≈ ______

Reflect

1. What does a 100% increase mean?

______

______

Your Turn exercises check your understanding of new concepts.

YOUR TURN

2. The price of a pair of shoes increases from \$52 to \$64. What is the percent increase to the nearest percent? ______

Personal Math Trainer Online Assessment and Intervention my.hrw.com

Lesson 5.1 **141**

Play strategy **Games and Activities** with classmates to practice using the concepts you have learned.

PERCENTO!

INSTRUCTIONS

Playing the Game

STEP 1 One student is the caller. This student gets the caller cards. Each caller card contains a percent problem and its answer.

STEP 2 Each player gets a *Percento!* board and 20–25 counters. The center is a free space. Players should cover the center square before play begins.

STEP 3 On each turn, the caller reads aloud a problem to the players. The caller does not read the answer.

18 is 75% of what number?

24

STEP 4 The players solve the problem read by the caller. Then they find the

Review concepts you will need to know before beginning each module.

Reading Start-Up

Visualize Vocabulary

Use the ✔ words to complete the triangle. Write the review word that fits the description in each section of the triangle.

a statement that two ratios are equivalent

compares a number to 100

a comparison of two numbers by division

Vocabulary

Review Words

- ✔ proportion *(proporción)*
- ✔ percent *(porcentaje)*
- rate *(tasa)*
- ✔ ratio *(razón)*
- unit rate *(tasa unitaria)*

Preview Words

- percent decrease *(porcentaje de disminución)*
- percent increase *(porcentaje de aumento)*
- principal *(capital)*
- simple interest *(interés simple)*

Understand Vocabulary

Complete the sentences using the preview words.

1. A fixed percent of the principal is ______________.
2. The original amount of money deposited or borrowed is the ______________.
3. A ______________ is the amount of increase divided by the original amount.

Active Reading

Tri-Fold Before beginning the module, create a tri-fold to help you learn the concepts and vocabulary in this module. Fold the paper into three sections. Label the columns "What I Know," "What I Need to Know," and "What I Learned." Complete the first two columns before you read. After studying the module, complete the third.

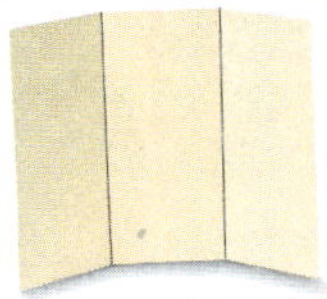

138 Unit 2

Get vocabulary, language, and note-taking support throughout the book.

Are YOU Ready?

Complete these exercises to review skills you will need for this module.

Personal Math Trainer — Online Assessment and Intervention — my.hrw.com

Percents and Decimals

EXAMPLE

$147\% = 100\% + 47\%$ — Write the percent as the sum of 1 whole and a percent remainder.

$= \frac{100}{100} + \frac{47}{100}$ — Write the percents as fractions.

$= 1 + 0.47$ — Write the fractions as decimals.

$= 1.47$ — Simplify.

Write each percent as a decimal.

1. 22% ______ 2. 75% ______ 3. 6% ______ 4. 189% ______

Write each decimal as a percent.

5. 0.59 ______ 6. 0.98 ______ 7. 0.02 ______ 8. 1.33 ______

Find the Percent of a Number

EXAMPLE

30% of 45 = ?

30% = 0.30 — Write the percent as a decimal.

$45 \times 0.3 = 13.5$ — Multiply.

Find the percent of each number.

9. 50% of 64 ______ 10. 7% of 30 ______ 11. 15% of 160 ______

12. 32% of 62 ______ 13. 120% of 4 ______ 14. 6% of 1...

Find out if you have mastered the concepts you learned in each module.

MODULE QUIZ

Ready to Go On?

Personal Math Trainer — Online Assessment and Intervention — my.hrw.com

4.1 Unit Rates

Find each unit rate. Round to the nearest hundredth, if necessary.

1. \$140 for 18 ft² ______ 2. 14 lb for \$2.99 ______

Circle the better deal in each pair. Then give the unit rate for the better deal.

3. $\frac{\$56}{25\text{ gal}}$ or $\frac{\$32.05}{15\text{ gal}}$ ______ 4. $\frac{\$160}{5\text{ g}}$ or $\frac{\$315}{9\text{ g}}$ ______

4.2 Constant Rates of Change

5. The table shows the amount of money Tyler earns for mowing lawns. Is the relationship a proportional relationship? Why or why not?

Number of Lawns	1	2	3	4
Amount Earned (\$)	15	30	48	64

6. On a recent day, 8 euros were worth \$9 and 24 euros were worth \$27. Write an equation of the form $y = kx$ to show the relationship between the number of euros and the value in dollars.

______, where y is dollars and x is euros

4.3 Proportional Relationships and Graphs

7. The graph shows the number of servings in different amounts of frozen yogurt listed on a carton. Write an equation that gives the number of servings y in x pints.

8. A refreshment stand makes 2 large servings of frozen yogurt from 3 pints. Add the line to the graph and write its equation.

ESSENTIAL QUESTION

9. How can you use rates to determine whether a situation is a proportional relationship?

Module 4 135

Apply new skills and concepts to solve real-world problems in Unit Performance Tasks and Careers in Math activities.

Unit 2 Performance Tasks

1. **CAREERS IN MATH** **Bicycle Tour Operator** Viktor is a bike tour operator and needs to replace two of his touring bikes. He orders two bikes from the sporting goods store for a total of \$2,000 and pays using his credit card. When the bill arrives, he reads the following information:

Balance: \$2,000
Annual interest rate: 14.9%
Minimum payment due: \$40
Late fee: \$10 if payment not received by 3/1/2013

a. To keep his good credit, Viktor promptly sends in a minimum payment of \$40. When the next bill arrives, it looks a lot like the previous bill.

Balance: \$1,984.34
Annual interest rate: 14.9%
Minimum payment due: \$40
Late fee: \$10 if payment not received by 4/1/2013

Explain how the credit card company calculated the new balance. Notice that the given interest rate is annual, but the payment is monthly.

b. Viktor was upset about the new bill, so he decided to send in \$150 for his April payment. The minimum payment on his bill is calculated as 2% of the balance (rounded to the nearest dollar) or \$20, whichever is greater. Fill out the details for Viktor's new bill.

Balance: ______
Annual interest rate: ______
Minimum payment due: ______
Late fee: \$10 if payment not received by ______

c. Viktor's bank offers a credit card with an introductory annual interest rate of 9.9%. He can transfer his current balance for a fee of \$40. After one year, the rate will return to the bank's normal rate, which is 13.9%. The bank charges a late fee of \$15. Give two reasons why Viktor should transfer the balance, and two reasons why he should not.

GO DIGITAL

my.hrw.com

Enhance Your Learning!

Interactive Student Editions provide additional multimedia resources to enhance your learning. You can enter in answers, watch videos, explore concepts with virtual manipulatives, and get homework help!

Real-World Videos show you how specific math topics can be used in all kinds of situations.

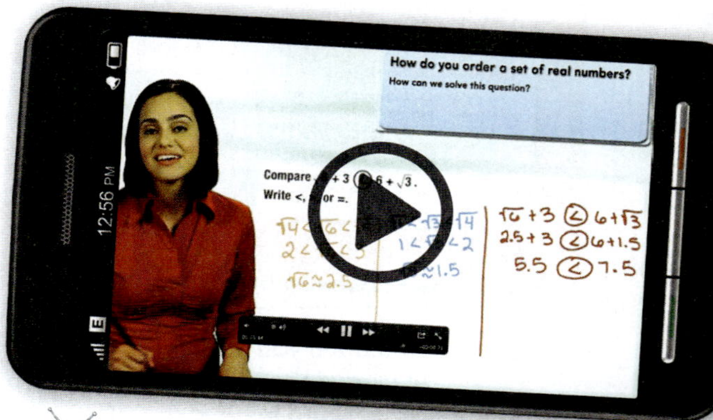

Math On the Spot video tutorials provide step-by-step instruction of the math concepts covered in each example.

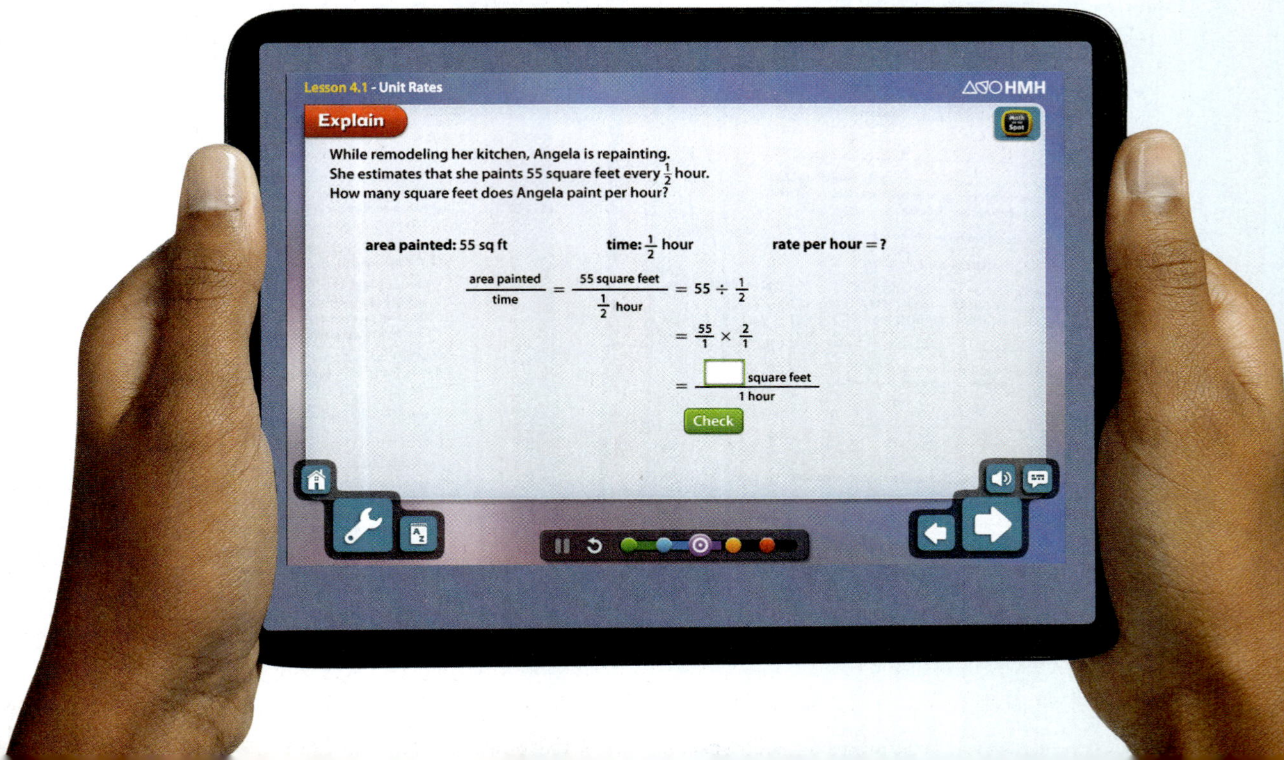

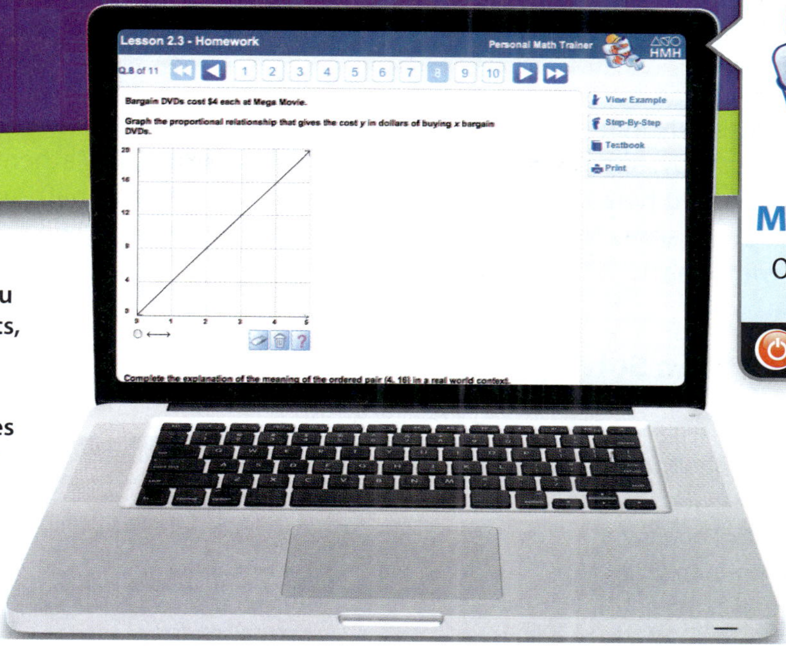

Personal Math Trainer lets you practice, take quizzes and tests, and get homework help with instant feedback!

Personal Math Trainer provides a variety of learning aids that develop and improve your understanding of math concepts, including videos, guided examples, and step-by-step solutions.

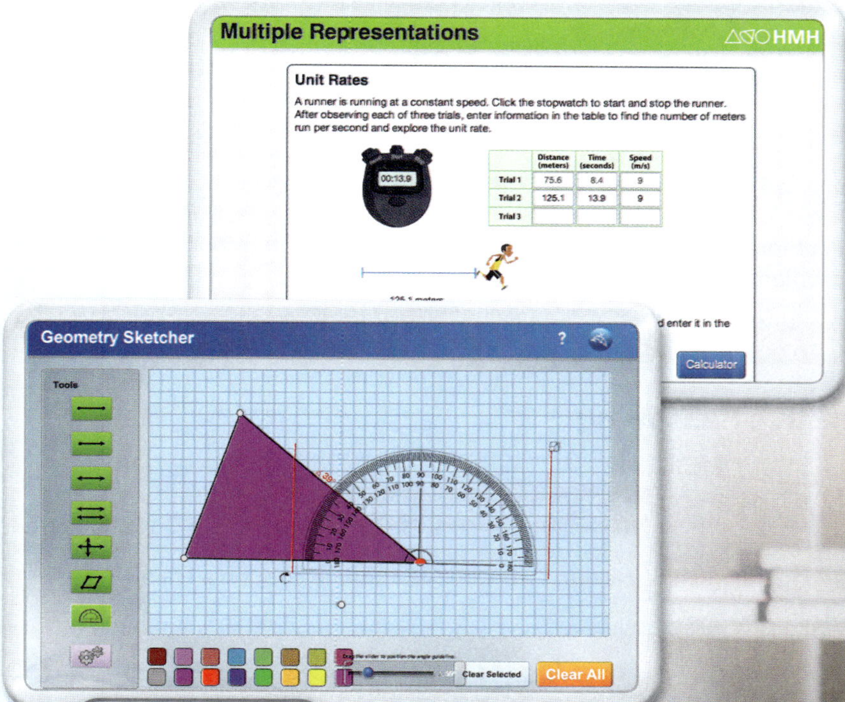

Animated Math activities and virtual manipulatives let you interactively explore and practice key math concepts and skills.

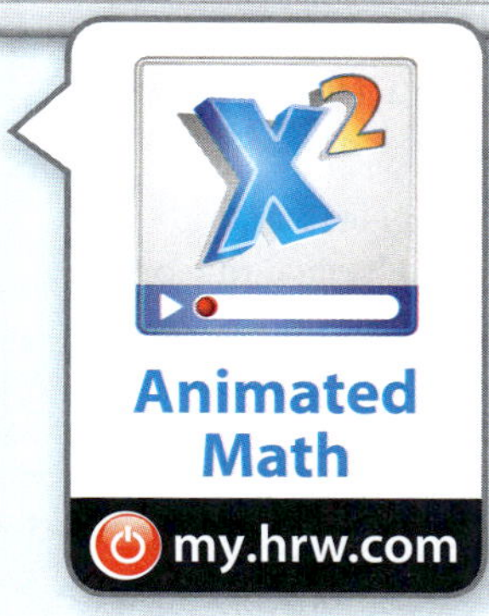

Mathematical Processes

The topics you study in mathematics will vary from year to year. However, the *way* you learn, study, and think about mathematics will not. The Mathematical Processes described here are skills that you will use in all of your math courses. These pages show some features of your book that will help you gain these skills and use them to master this year's topics.

MP.1 Problem Solving

Solving a problem often involves multiple steps. You must first understand the problem situation, analyze the given information, and identify the goal of the problem. Then you make a plan and implement that plan to solve the problem. Lastly, you check your solution and look back and analyze your solution method.

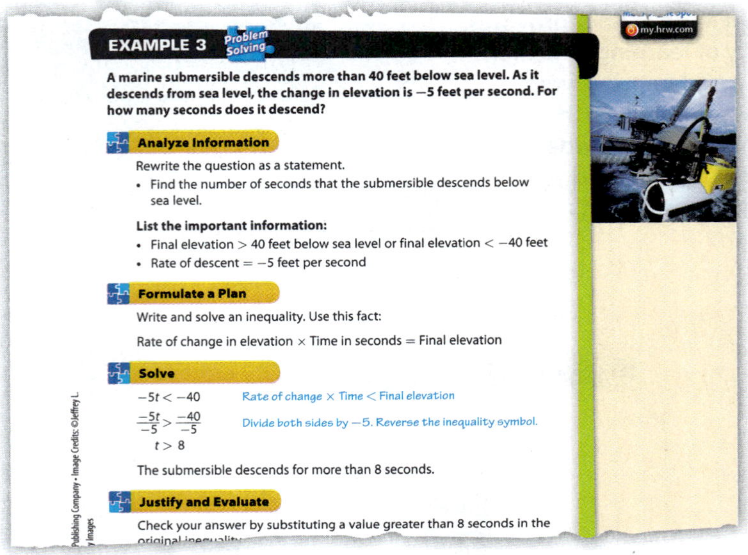
EXAMPLE 3 Problem Solving

A marine submersible descends more than 40 feet below sea level. As it descends from sea level, the change in elevation is −5 feet per second. For how many seconds does it descend?

Analyze Information

Rewrite the question as a statement.

- Find the number of seconds that the submersible descends below sea level.

List the important information:

- Final elevation > 40 feet below sea level or final elevation < −40 feet
- Rate of descent = −5 feet per second

Formulate a Plan

Write and solve an inequality. Use this fact:

Rate of change in elevation × Time in seconds = Final elevation

Solve

$-5t < -40$ Rate of change × Time < Final elevation

$\frac{-5t}{-5} > \frac{-40}{-5}$ Divide both sides by −5. Reverse the inequality symbol.

$t > 8$

The submersible descends for more than 8 seconds.

Justify and Evaluate

Check your answer by substituting a value greater than 8 seconds in the original inequality.

Problem-solving examples and exercises lead you through problem solving steps.

MP.2 Abstract and Quantitative Reasoning

When solving problems, you often need to represent a situation abstractly and work out a solution using a symbolic representation of the problem. At other times, you must refer back to the specific quantities the symbols represent in order to understand the meaning of your results.

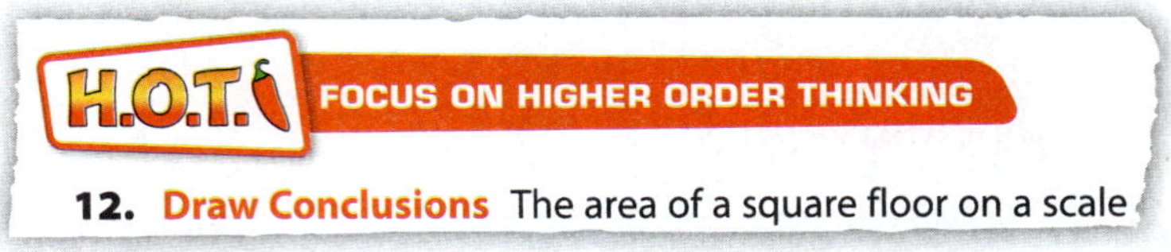
H.O.T. FOCUS ON HIGHER ORDER THINKING

12. Draw Conclusions The area of a square floor on a scale

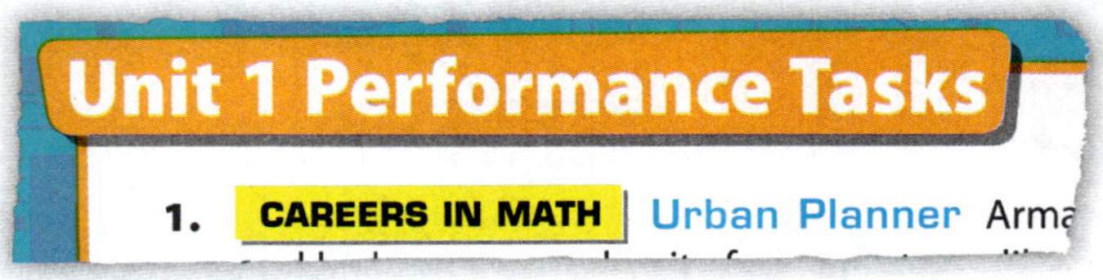
Unit 1 Performance Tasks

1. CAREERS IN MATH | Urban Planner Arma

Focus on Higher Order Thinking exercises in every lesson and **Performance Tasks** in every unit require you to use logical reasoning, represent situations symbolically, use mathematical models to solve problems, and state your answers in terms of a problem context.

MP.3 Use and Evaluate Logical Reasoning

Mathematics provides a unique opportunity to develop your logical reasoning capacities. You can do this by expressing your thoughts and justifying your conclusions. Soon you will recognize and correct flaws in reasoning.

Reflect

2. **Communicate Mathematical Ideas** What does the point (0, graph represent?

ESSENTIAL QUESTION CHECK-IN

Essential Question Check-in and **Reflect** in every lesson ask you to evaluate statements, explain relationships, apply mathematical principles, make conjectures, construct arguments, and justify your reasoning.

MP.4 Mathematical Modeling

You can use mathematics to solve problems in everyday life by learning how to represent real-world situations in mathematical terms.

EXAMPLE 2 Real World

A **During the day, the temperature increases by 4.5 degrees. At night, the temperature decreases by 7.5 degrees. What is the overall change in temperature?**

STEP 1 Use a positive number to represent the increase in temperature and a negative number to represent a decrease in temperature.

STEP 2 Find $4.5 + (-7.5)$.

STEP 3 Start at 4.5.

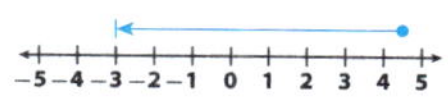

STEP 4 Move $|-7.5| = 7.5$ units to the *left* because the second addend is *negative*.

The result is -3.

The temperature decreased by 3 degrees overall.

© Houghton Mifflin Harcourt Publishing Company

Real-world examples and **mathematical modeling** apply mathematics to other disciplines and real-world contexts such as science and business.

MP.5 Use Mathematical Tools

Knowing when and how to use mathematical tools, ranging from rulers and protractors to graphing calculators and computer software, is a valuable skill. Used properly, tools can both simplify problem-solving and give you a deeper understanding of mathematical concepts.

EXPLORE ACTIVITY 2

Two Angles and Their Included Side

Use a ruler and a protractor to draw each triangle.

Triangle 1	Triangle 2
Angles: 30° and 80°	Angles: 55° and 50°
Length of included side: 2 inches	Length of included side: 1 inch

A Draw Triangle 1.

STEP 1 Use a ruler to draw a line that is 2 inches long. This will be the included side.

STEP 2 Place the center of the protractor on the left end of the 2-in. line. Then make a 30°-angle mark.

STEP 4 Repeat Step 2 on the right side of the triangle to construct the 80° angle.

Exploration Activities in lessons use concrete and technological tools, such as manipulatives or graphing calculators, to explore mathematical concepts.

MP.6 Use Precise Mathematical Language

To communicate your reasoning and results to others, you must use mathematical terms, symbols, and units precisely and consistently. Defining terms clearly and labeling diagrams appropriately are essential for writing clear explanations.

Reflect

2. **Communicate Mathematical Ideas** What does the point graph represent?

Key Vocabulary

rate *(tasa)*
A ratio that compares two quantities measured in different units.

Precision refers not only to the correctness of calculations but also to the proper use of mathematical language and symbols. **Communicate Mathematical Ideas** exercises and **Key Vocabulary** highlighted for each module and unit help you learn and use the language of math to communicate mathematics precisely.

MP.7 See Structure

Recognizing patterns and similarities in the structure of varied problems can help you both to solve problems and to understand the underlying mathematical concepts.

B Complete the table.

Time (sec)	1	2	3	4	5
Distance (in.)			10.5		

C For each column of the table, find the distance and the time. Write each fraction as a decimal. Put distance in the numerator and time in the denominator.

D What do you notice about the decimal forms of the fractions?

E **Conjecture** How do you think the distance a tortoise travels is related

Throughout the lessons, you will observe regularity in mathematical structures in order to make generalizations and make connections between related problems. For example, you can learn to recognize proportional relationships.

MP.8 Generalize

As you do similar calculations repeatedly, you can discover general methods and shortcuts for solving problems.

25. **Look for a Pattern** Find the next three terms in the pattern −11, ... Then describe the pattern.

27. **Look for a Pattern** Leroi and Sylvia both put $100 in a s Leroi decides he will put in an additional $10 each week. put in an additional 10% of the amount in the account e

a. Who has more money after the first additional depo

27. **Look for a Pattern** Solve $x + 1 > 10$, $x + 11 > 20$, and $x + 2$ Describe a pattern. Then use the pattern to predict the solut $x + 9{,}991 > 10{,}000$.

You will look for repeated calculations and mathematical patterns in examples and exercises. Recognizing patterns can help you make generalizations and obtain a better understanding of the underlying mathematics.

GRADE 6 PART 1

Review Test

Personal Math Trainer
Online Assessment and Intervention
my.hrw.com

Selected Response

1. Suppose you have developed a scale that indicates the brightness of sunlight. Each category in the table is 5 times brighter than the category above it. For example, a day that is dazzling is 5 times brighter than a day that is radiant. How many times brighter is a dazzling day than a dim day?

Sunlight Intensity	
Category	**Brightness**
Dim	2
Illuminated	3
Radiant	4
Dazzling	5

Ⓐ 125 times brighter

Ⓑ 625 times brighter

Ⓒ 3 times brighter

Ⓓ 25 times brighter

2. Patricia paid $584 for 8 nights at a hotel. Find the unit rate.

Ⓐ $\frac{\$146}{1 \text{ night}}$ Ⓒ $\frac{\$37}{1 \text{ night}}$

Ⓑ $\frac{\$584}{1 \text{ night}}$ Ⓓ $\frac{\$73}{1 \text{ night}}$

3. Valerie sold 6 tickets to the school play and Mark sold 16 tickets. What is the ratio of the number of tickets Valerie sold to the number of tickets Mark sold?

Ⓐ 16 to 6 Ⓒ 2 to 8

Ⓑ 2 to 3 Ⓓ 3 to 8

4. Grant and Pedro are comparing their stocks for the week. On Monday, their results were opposites. Explain how you would graph their results for Monday if Grant lost $4.

Ⓐ Grant's point is 4 units to the right of 0 on a number line, and Pedro's point is 4 units to the left of 0.

Ⓑ Grant's point is 4 units to the right of 0 on a number line, and Pedro's point is the same point.

Ⓒ Grant's loss is a point 4 units to the left of 0 on a number line, and Pedro's point is 4 units to the right of 0.

Ⓓ Grant's loss is a point 4 units to the left of 0 on a number line, and Pedro's point is the same point because it's already negative.

5. The fuel for a chain saw is a mix of oil and gasoline. The label says to mix 5 ounces of oil with 15 gallons of gasoline. How much oil would you use if you had 45 gallons of gasoline?

Ⓐ 21 ounces Ⓒ 15 ounces

Ⓑ 1.67 ounces Ⓓ 135 ounces

6. A stack of blocks is 12.3 inches tall. If there are 10 blocks stacked one on top of the other, how tall is each block?

Ⓐ 1.33 inches Ⓒ 2.3 inches

Ⓑ 1.13 inches Ⓓ 1.23 inches

7. Which temperature is warmest?

Ⓐ 16 °F Ⓒ −21 °F

Ⓑ −16 °F Ⓓ 21 °F

8. Each student needs a pencil and an eraser to take a test. If pencils come 8 in a box and erasers come 12 in a bag, what is the least number of boxes and bags needed for 24 students to each have a pencil and an eraser?

Ⓐ 3 boxes of pencils, 2 bags of erasers

Ⓑ 1 box of pencils, 1 bag of erasers

Ⓒ 8 boxes of pencils, 12 bags of erasers

Ⓓ 2 boxes of pencils, 3 bags of erasers

9. Find the quotient $7\frac{1}{6} \div \frac{5}{9}$.

Ⓐ 12 Ⓒ $12\frac{9}{10}$

Ⓑ $13\frac{1}{2}$ Ⓓ $1\frac{13}{30}$

10. Find the product 4.7×4.75.

Ⓐ 223.25 Ⓒ 22.325

Ⓑ 9.45 Ⓓ 2.2325

11. Carla is building a table out of boards that are 4.25 inches wide. She wants the table to be at least 36 inches wide. What is the least number of boards she can use?

Ⓐ 8 Ⓒ 9.5

Ⓑ 9 Ⓓ 153

12. How many centimeters are there in 740.2 millimeters?

Ⓐ 7402 cm Ⓒ 7.402 cm

Ⓑ 74.02 cm Ⓓ 0.7402 cm

Mini-Tasks

13. Jada is making lasagna and pizzas for a large party. Her lasagna recipe calls for $1\frac{1}{4}$ cups of tomato paste, and her pizza recipe uses $\frac{1}{2}$ cup of tomato paste per pizza. She will double her lasagna recipe and make 5 pizzas. Write and evaluate an expression for how many $\frac{3}{4}$-cup cans of tomato paste she will need in all.

____

14. Explain how you can use multiplication to find the quotient $\frac{3}{5} \div \frac{3}{15}$. Then evaluate the expression.

____

____

15. You are working as an assistant to a chef. The chef has 8 cups of berries and will use $\frac{2}{3}$ cup of berries for each dessert he makes. How many desserts can he make?

____

____

Performance Task

16. School A has 216 students and 12 classrooms. School B has 104 students and 4 classrooms.

Part A: What is the ratio of students to classrooms at School A?

Part B: What is the ratio of students to classrooms at School B?

Part C: How many students would have to transfer from School B to School A for the ratios of students to classrooms at both schools to be the same? Explain your reasoning.

____

____

____

____

____

____

____

____

____

____

____

GRADE 6 PART 2

Review Test

Personal Math Trainer
Online Assessment and Intervention
my.hrw.com

Selected Response

1. Kahlil is recording a beat for a song that he is working on. He wants the length of the beat to be more than 17 seconds long. His friend tells him the beat needs to be 9 seconds longer than that to match the lyrics he has written.

Write an inequality to represent the beat's length. Give three possible beat lengths that satisfy the inequality.

Ⓐ $t < 17$
8, 6, 5

Ⓑ $t > 26$
27, 35, 33

Ⓒ $t > 8$
27, 35, 33

Ⓓ $t < 26$
8, 6, 5

2. Write an expression for the missing value in the table.

Tom's Age	Kim's Age
11	14
12	15
13	16
a	?

Ⓐ $a + 16$

Ⓑ $a + 11$

Ⓒ $a + 1$

Ⓓ $a + 3$

3. A plant's height is 1.6 times its age. Write an equation for the situation. Tell what each variable you use represents.

Ⓐ h = plant's height; y = plant's age; $1.6 = hy$

Ⓑ h = plant's height; y = plant's age; $y = 1.6h$

Ⓒ h = plant's age; y = plant's height; $h = 1.6y$

Ⓓ h = plant's height; y = plant's age; $h = 1.6y$

4. A driveway is 162 feet long, 6 feet wide, and 4 inches deep. How many cubic feet of concrete will be required for the driveway?

Ⓐ 355 ft^3

Ⓑ 324 ft^3

Ⓒ 3,888 ft^3

Ⓓ 254 ft^3

5. Write the phrase as an algebraic expression.

6 less than a number times 11

Ⓐ $6y - 11y$

Ⓑ $11 \div y$

Ⓒ $11y - 6$

Ⓓ $11 + y$

6. Wilson bought gift cards for some lawyers and their assistants. Each lawyer got a gift card worth $\$\ell$. Each assistant got a gift card worth $\$a$. There are 14 lawyers. Each lawyer has three assistants. The expression for total cost of the gift cards is $14\ell + 42a$. Write an expression that is equivalent to the given expression.

Ⓐ $14(\ell + 2a)$

Ⓑ $14(\ell + 3a)$

Ⓒ $14(\ell + 42a)$

Ⓓ $42(\ell + 3a)$

7. At the beginning of the year, Jason had \$80 in his savings account. Each month, he added \$15 to his account. Write an expression for the amount of money in Jason's savings account each month. Then use the expression to find the amount of money in his account at the end of the year.

Month	January	February	March	m
Amount	\$95	\$110	\$125	\$?

Ⓐ $95 + 15m$; \$275

Ⓑ $95 + m$; \$107

Ⓒ $80 + 12m$; \$224

Ⓓ $15m + 80$; \$260

8. In a fish tank, $\frac{6}{7}$ of the fish have a red stripe on them. If 18 of the fish have red stripes, how many total fish are in the tank?

Ⓐ 26 fish
Ⓒ 23 fish
Ⓑ 21 fish
Ⓓ 25 fish

9. Solve the equation $s + 2.8 = 6.59$.

Ⓐ $s = 4.13$
Ⓒ $s = 9.39$
Ⓑ $s = 3.79$
Ⓓ $s = 3$

10. Which question is a statistical question?

Ⓐ How long is lunch period at your school?
Ⓑ How old is the oldest student in your class?
Ⓒ How many classrooms are there in your school?
Ⓓ What are the ages of all the people in your class?

11. In a box-and-whisker plot, the *interquartile range* is a measure of the spread of the middle half of the data. Find the interquartile range for the data set: 10, 3, 7, 6, 9, 12, 13.

Ⓐ 12
Ⓒ 6
Ⓑ 7
Ⓓ 8

12. Mike was in charge of collecting contributions for the Food Bank. He received contributions of \$50, \$80, \$60, \$50, and \$90. Find the mean and median of the contributions.

Ⓐ mean: \$66 median: \$60
Ⓒ mean: \$50 median: \$60
Ⓑ mean: \$50 median: \$66
Ⓓ mean: \$60 median: \$66

13. Which expression is NOT equivalent to the expression $11y + 5$?

Ⓐ $0.5(22y + 10)$
Ⓑ $5y + 11 + 6y - 6$
Ⓒ $5(2y + 1) + y$
Ⓓ $6y + 3 + 5y - 2$

Mini-Tasks

14. It costs \$9 to go to Pete's Pottery Place to make your own bowls for \$3 per bowl. Natalie goes to Pete's Pottery Place and makes *b* bowls. She decides to make bowls 5 days this month so she can sell them at a crafts fair.

Part A: Write an expression that will represent Natalie's total cost for this month.

Part B: If she makes 4 bowls each time she goes to Pete's Pottery Place, what will her total cost be?

____

____

15. To find the mileage, or how many miles per gallon a car can travel, you can use the expression $\frac{m}{g}$, where *m* is the distance in miles and *g* is the number of gallons of gas used. Find the mileage for a car that travels 576 miles on 18 gallons of gas.

____

Performance Task

16. ***Part A:*** Is $x = 6$ a solution of the equation $8x + 8 = 56$? Explain.

Part B: Suppose the solution $x = 6$ increases to $x = 9$, and the left side of the equation stays the same. How would the right side need to change if the solution is now $x = 9$?

____

____

____

____

____

____

____

____

GRADE 7 PART 1

Benchmark Test

Personal Math Trainer
my.hrw.com
Online Assessment and Intervention

Selected Response

1. Evaluate $a + b$ for $a = -46$ and $b = 34$.

Ⓐ -12 Ⓒ -80
Ⓑ 80 Ⓓ 12

2. A triangle has sides with lengths of $2x - 7$, $5x - 3$, and $2x - 2$. What is the perimeter of the triangle?

Ⓐ $9x - 12$ Ⓒ $-x - 6$
Ⓑ $5x - 12$ Ⓓ $-3x$

3. Which of the following ratios does *not* form a proportion?

Ⓐ $\frac{3}{7} \stackrel{?}{=} \frac{9}{21}$ Ⓒ $\frac{3}{7} \stackrel{?}{=} \frac{9}{28}$
Ⓑ $\frac{24}{56} \stackrel{?}{=} \frac{3}{7}$ Ⓓ $\frac{3}{7} \stackrel{?}{=} \frac{12}{28}$

4. For a sale, a store decreases its prices on all items by 20%. An item that cost \$120 before the sale now costs \$120 − 0.2(\$120). What is another expression for the sale price?

Ⓐ 0.2(\$120) Ⓒ 0.8(\$120)
Ⓑ \$120 − 80 Ⓓ \$120 − 20

5. Write an equation that models the situation and find its solution.

It's going to be Lindsay's birthday soon, and her friends Chris, Mikhail, Wolfgang, and Adrian have contributed equal amounts of money to buy her a present. They have \$27.00 to spend altogether. Determine how much each contributed.

Ⓐ $4x = \$27.00$; $x = \$7.75$ Ⓒ $4x = \$27.00$; $x = \$108.00$
Ⓑ $5x = \$27.00$; $x = \$5.40$ Ⓓ $4x = \$27.00$ $x = \$6.75$

6. Four sisters bought a present for their mother. They received a 10% discount on the original price of the gift. After the discount was taken, each sister paid \$9.00. What was the original price of the gift?

Ⓐ \$40.00 Ⓒ \$36.00
Ⓑ \$32.73 Ⓓ \$16.00

7. Jared is redoing his bathroom floor with tiles measuring 6 in. by 14 in. The floor has an area of 8,900 in^2. What is the least number of tiles he will need?

Ⓐ 105 tiles Ⓒ 445 tiles
Ⓑ 106 tiles Ⓓ 105.95 tiles

8. Iris wants to buy two necklaces, one for her sister and one for herself. The necklace for her sister costs \$42.00, and the necklace for herself costs \$28.00. The sales tax on the purchases is 8%. Find the total cost of Iris's purchases, including sales tax. If necessary, round your answer to the nearest cent.

Ⓐ \$64.40 Ⓒ \$75.60
Ⓑ \$5.60 Ⓓ \$70.00

9. One winter day, the temperature increased from a low of −5 °F to a high of 40 °F. By how many degrees did the temperature change?

Ⓐ 45 °F Ⓒ 25 °F
Ⓑ 35 °F Ⓓ 55 °F

10. Write the fraction $\frac{9}{50}$ as a decimal. If necessary, round your answer to the nearest hundredth.

Ⓐ 0.28 Ⓒ 0.5
Ⓑ 0.18 Ⓓ 0.09

11. Terry drove 366 miles in 6 hours at a constant speed. How long would it take him to drive 427 miles at the same speed?

Ⓐ 3 hours
Ⓑ 6.5 hours
Ⓒ 7 hours
Ⓓ 61 hours

12. Tell whether the data sets show a direct variation. If so, identify the constant of variation.

Number of Baskets	Cost
3	$12
5	$20
6	$24
8	$32
15	$60

Ⓐ not a direct variation
Ⓑ direct variation; $k = 9$
Ⓒ direct variation; $k = \frac{1}{4}$
Ⓓ direct variation; $k = 4$

13. Solve the equation $2(a - 5) - 5 = 3$.

Ⓐ $a = 9$
Ⓑ $a = 12$
Ⓒ $a = -9$
Ⓓ $a = -12$

Mini-Tasks

14. Find the unit price for each offer to determine which is the better buy: 6 paperback books for $19.00 or 8 paperback books for $26.00.

____

____

15. A vacation cabin has a water storage tank. In the first month (30 days) of the vacation season, the amount of water in the tank changed by an average of −36 gallons per day. At the end of the month, the tank contained 1,340 gallons of water. How much water was in the tank originally?

____

Performance Task

16. The graph shows the relationship between the total cost and the amount of rice purchased.

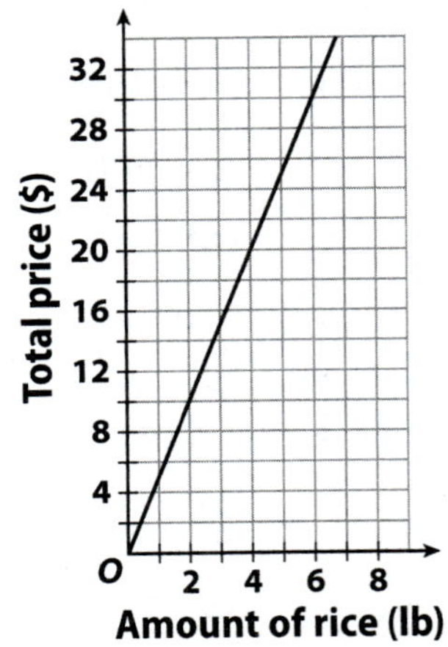

Part A: What does the ordered pair (6, 30) represent?

Part B: Which point on the graph represents the unit price?

Part C: How many pounds would you have to buy for the total cost to be $20? Explain how to find the answer.

____

____

____

____

____

____

____

____

____

____

____

Benchmark Test

Personal Math Trainer
my.hrw.com
Online Assessment and Intervention

Selected Response

1. What are the actual dimensions of the Books section?

Floor plan of library

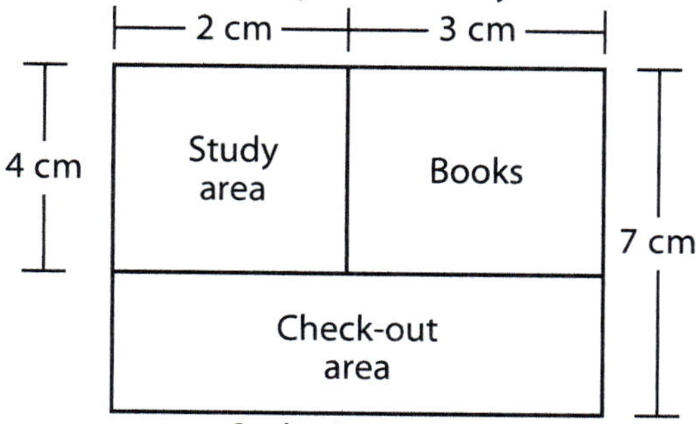

Scale: 1 cm : 5 m

Ⓐ 25 m × 35 m   Ⓒ 15 m × 35 m

Ⓑ 15 m × 20 m   Ⓓ 2 m × 4 m

2. For a history fair, a school is building a circular wooden stage. Find the area of the stage if the radius of the stage is 4 meters. Use 3.14 for π.

Ⓐ 25.12 m^2 Ⓒ 100.48 m^2

Ⓑ 50.24 m^2 Ⓓ 200.96 m^2

3. Find the area of the circle to the nearest tenth. Use 3.14 for π.

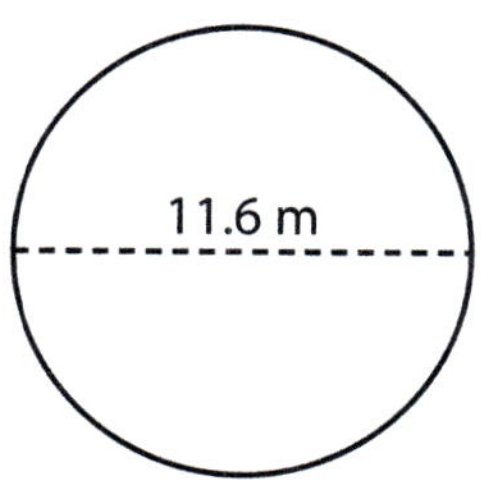

Ⓐ 105.6 m^2 Ⓒ 422.5 m^2

Ⓑ 36.4 m^2 Ⓓ 331.7 m^2

4. Find m$\angle ABC$.

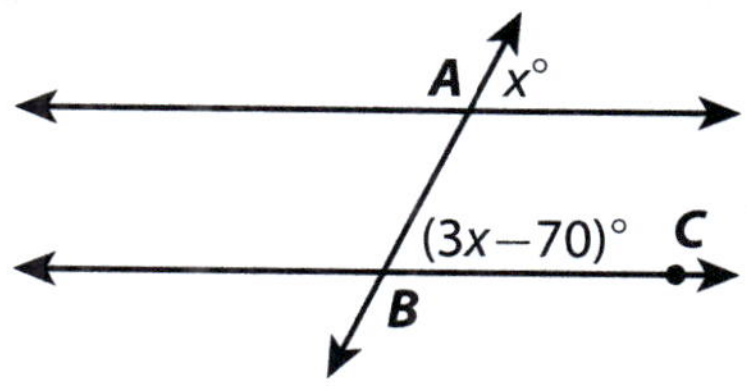

Ⓐ 40°   Ⓒ 35°

Ⓑ 45°   Ⓓ 50°

5. Ralph is an electrician. He charges an initial fee of $24, plus $24 per hour. If Ralph earned $144 on a job, how long did the job take?

Ⓐ 4 hours   Ⓒ 5 hours

Ⓑ 132 hours   Ⓓ 6.5 hours

6. Find the volume of the cylinder. Use 3.14 for π. Round your answer to the nearest tenth.

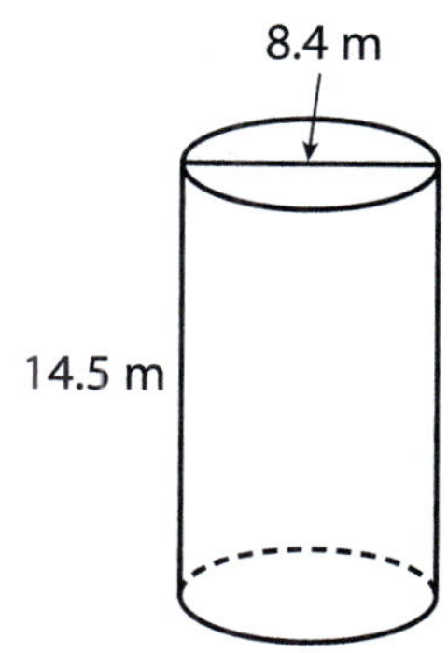

Ⓐ 3,212.6 m^3 Ⓒ 2,772.8 m^3

Ⓑ 382.5 m^3 Ⓓ 803.1 m^3

7. In a random sample of students at a middle school, 24 wanted to change the mascot, and 30 wanted to keep the current mascot. Which is the best prediction for how many of the total of 1,140 students want to keep the current mascot?

Ⓐ 507 students   Ⓒ 633 students

Ⓑ 600 students   Ⓓ 950 students

8. A coin-operated machine sells plastic rings. It contains 6 yellow rings, 11 blue rings, 15 green rings, and 3 black rings. Sarah puts a coin into the machine. Find the theoretical probability she gets a black ring. Express your answer as a decimal. If necessary, round your answer to the nearest thousandth.

Ⓐ 11.667
Ⓑ 0.171
Ⓒ 5.833
Ⓓ 0.086

9. Juan plays on the school baseball team. In the last 9 games, Juan was at bat 28 times and got 6 hits. What is the experimental probability that Juan will get a hit during his next time at bat? Express your answer as a fraction in simplest form.

Ⓐ $\frac{14}{3}$
Ⓑ $\frac{3}{14}$
Ⓒ $\frac{3}{11}$
Ⓓ $\frac{11}{14}$

10. An experiment consists of rolling two fair number cubes. What is the probability that the sum of the two numbers will be 4? Express your answer as a fraction in simplest form.

Ⓐ $\frac{11}{18}$
Ⓑ $\frac{1}{12}$
Ⓒ $\frac{12}{1}$
Ⓓ $\frac{11}{12}$

11. A manufacturer inspects a sample of 500 smartphones and finds that 496 of them have no defects. The manufacturer sent a shipment of 2000 smartphones to a distributor. Predict the number of smartphones in the shipment that are likely to have no defects.

Ⓐ 16
Ⓑ 1840
Ⓒ 496
Ⓓ 1984

Mini-Tasks

12. Two lines intersect in a plane and form four angles. One of the angles formed by this intersection is a 53° angle. What are the measures of the other three angles? Explain your answer.

13. A United States senator from Maine wants to find out the opinion of Maine voters on issues concerning education. The office of the senator sends out a survey to state residents who have contacted the senator in the past year. Is this sampling method random? Explain.

14. Using the following data, identify the errors in the box plot.

17, 13, 10, 15, 16, 12, 13, 20, 18

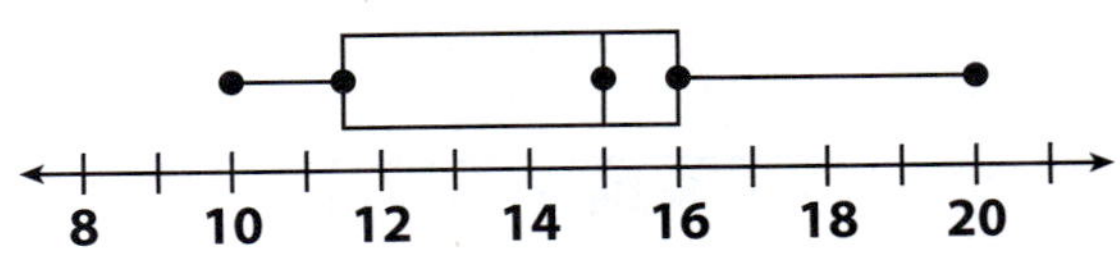

Performance Task

15. The number of goals scored by a soccer team in each of its first 10 games is shown below.

2, 6, 1, 2, 4, 1, 3, 2, 0, 4

Part A: Find the mean number of goals scored.

Part B: Find the mean absolute deviation (MAD) of the number of goals scored.

Part C: A second team in the same division scores a mean of 3.2 goals in its first 10 games, with the same MAD as the team above. Compare the difference in the teams' mean number of goals with the MAD in the number of goals scored.

UNIT 1

The Number System

CAREERS IN MATH

Urban Planner An urban planner creates plans for urban, suburban, and rural communities and makes recommendations about locations for infrastructure, such as buildings, roads, and sewer and water pipes. Urban planners perform cost-benefit analysis of projects, use measurement and geometry when they design the layout of infrastructure, and use statistics and mathematical models to predict the growth and future needs of a population.

If you are interested in a career as an urban planner, you should study these mathematical subjects:

- Algebra
- Geometry
- Trigonometry
- Statistics

Research other careers that require using measurement, geometry, and mathematical modeling.

Unit 1 Performance Task

At the end of the unit, check out how **urban planners** use math.

UNIT 1

Vocabulary Preview

Use the puzzle to preview key vocabulary from this unit. Unscramble the circled letters within found words to answer the riddle at the bottom of the page.

1. NIOARLTA MURNEB

2. GREITEN

3. PIRGENAET CMSEADIL

4. EADITIVD SENEIRV

5. TIIRANGTNEM SAELIDMC

1. Any number that can be written as a ratio of two integers. (Lesson 1.1)
2. A member of the set of whole numbers and their opposites. (Lesson 1.1)
3. Decimals in which one or more digits repeat infinitely. (Lesson 1.1)
4. The opposite of any number. (Lesson 1.3)
5. Decimals that have a finite number of digits. (Lesson 1.1)

Q: Why were the two fractions able to settle their differences peacefully?

A: They were both __ __ __ __ __ __ __ __!

Adding and Subtracting Integers

MODULE 1

ESSENTIAL QUESTION

How can you use addition and subtraction of integers to solve real-world problems?

Real-World Video

my.hrw.com

Death Valley contains the lowest point in North America, elevation −282 feet. The top of Mt. McKinley, elevation 20,320 feet, is the highest point in North America. To find the difference between these elevations, you can subtract integers.

GO DIGITAL
my.hrw.com

my.hrw.com
Go digital with your write-in student edition, accessible on any device.

Math On the Spot
Scan with your smart phone to jump directly to the online edition, video tutor, and more.

Animated Math
Interactively explore key concepts to see how math works.

Personal Math Trainer
Get immediate feedback and help as you work through practice sets.

Reading Start-Up

Visualize Vocabulary

Use the ✔ words to fill in the ovals on the graphic. You may put more than one word in each oval.

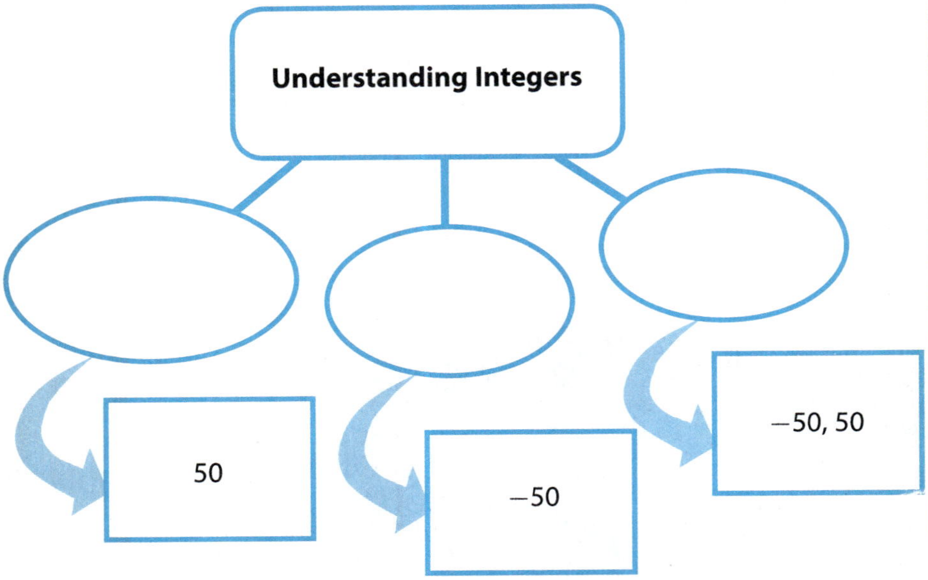

Vocabulary

Review Words

difference *(diferencia)*
integers *(enteros)*
✔ negative number *(número negativo)*
✔ opposites *(opuestos)*
✔ positive number *(número positivo)*
sum *(suma)*
✔ whole number *(número entero)*

Preview Words

absolute value *(valor absoluto)*
additive inverse *(inverso aditivo)*
expression *(expresión)*
model *(modelo)*

Understand Vocabulary

Complete the sentences using the preview words.

1. The ____________________ of a number gives its distance from zero.

2. The sum of a number and its ____________________ is zero.

Active Reading

Booklet Before beginning the module, create a booklet to help you learn the concepts in this module. Write the main idea of each lesson on each page of the booklet. As you study each lesson, write important details that support the main idea, such as vocabulary and processes. Refer to your finished booklet as you work on assignments and study for tests.

Are YOU Ready?

Complete these exercises to review skills you will need for this module.

Personal Math Trainer
Online Assessment and Intervention
my.hrw.com

Understand Integers

EXAMPLE A diver descended 20 meters.

Decide whether the integer is positive or negative:
descended → negative

−20

Write the integer.

Write an integer to represent each situation.

1. an elevator ride down 27 stories ________

2. a $700 profit ________

3. 46 degrees below zero ________

4. a gain of 12 yards ________

Whole Number Operations

EXAMPLE 245 − 28

```
   3 15
  2 4 5
−   2 8
  2 1 7
```

Think:
8 > 5
Regroup 1 ten as 10 ones.
1 ten + 5 ones = 15 ones
Subtract: 15 − 8 = 7

245 − 28 = 217

Find the sum or difference.

5. 183 + 78

6. 677 − 288

7. 1,188 + 902

8. 2,647 − 1,885

Locate Points on a Number Line

EXAMPLE

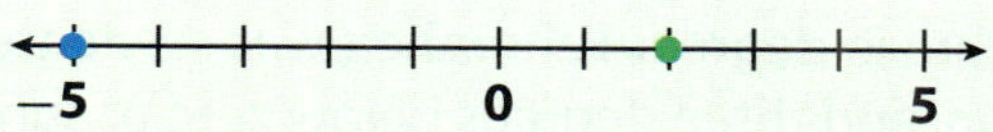

Graph +2 by starting at 0 and counting 2 units to the right.
Graph −5 by starting at 0 and counting 5 units to the left.

Graph each number on the number line.

9. 7

10. −4

11. −9

12. 4

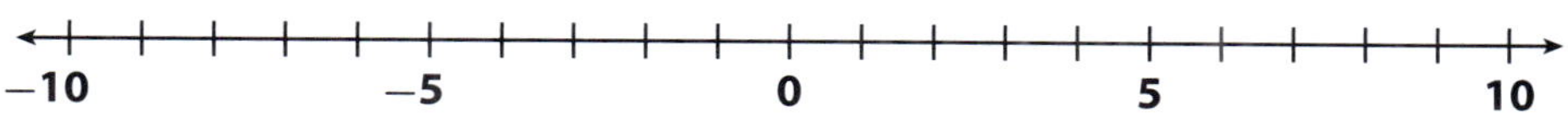

Are YOU Ready? *(cont'd)*

Complete these exercises to review skills you will need for this module.

Understand Integers

13. Parvana records the transactions for her bank account for the week. On Monday, she made a deposit of $45. On Tuesday, she used her debit card to pay $18 for a new shirt. On Thursday, she withdrew $7 from an ATM. Write an integer to represent each of Parvana's bank transactions.

Whole Number Operations

14. Lonnie made 1,200 dog collars to sell at the craft market. The table shows the number of collars he sold at the market over three weekends. How many collars does he have left? Show your work.

Lonnie's Dog Collars	
Weekend	**Number sold**
1	357
2	418
3	306

Locate Points on a Number Line

15. On a winter day, the temperature in degrees Fahrenheit was six degrees below zero at sunrise, four degrees at noon, and three degrees below zero at sunset. Graph each temperature on the number line. Explain how you chose each point.

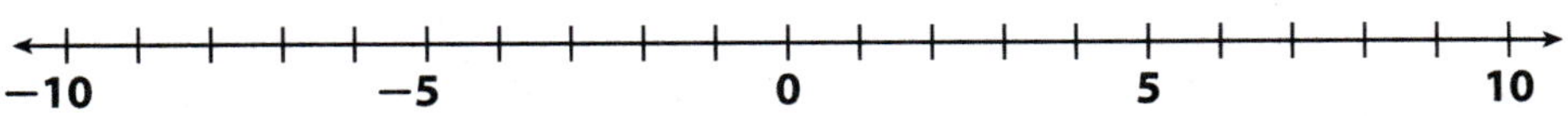

LESSON 1.1

Adding Integers with the Same Sign

7.1.1.1

Students will add integers with the same sign.

ESSENTIAL QUESTION

How do you add integers with the same sign?

EXPLORE ACTIVITY 1

Modeling Sums of Integers with the Same Sign

You can use colored counters to add positive integers and to add negative integers.

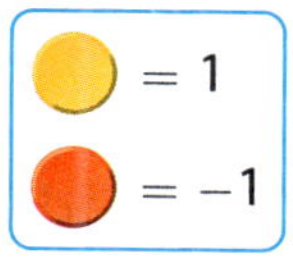

Model with two-color counters.

A $3 + 4$

How many counters are there in total? ________

What is the sum and how do you find it?

____

____

B $-5 + (-3)$

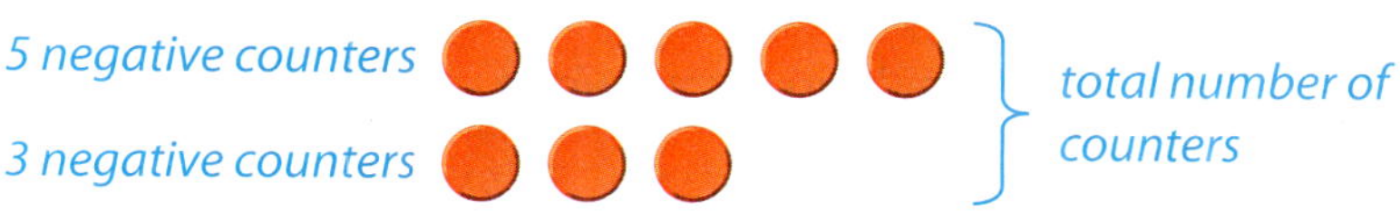

How many counters are there in total? ________

Since the counters are negative integers, what is the sum? ________

Math Talk
Mathematical Processes

What does the color of each row of counters represent?

Reflect

1. **Communicate Mathematical Ideas** When adding two numbers with the same sign, what sign do you use for the sum?

____

EXPLORE ACTIVITY 2 Real World

Adding on a Number Line

Positive and negative numbers can be represented by arrows on a number line. For instance, the arrow shown is for 4. The arrow is 4 units long and points in the positive direction. An arrow for −4 would be 4 units long and point in the negative direction.

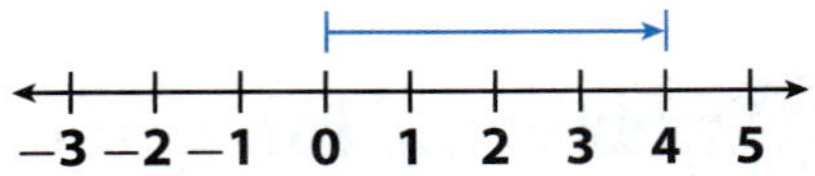

The temperature was 2 °F below zero. The temperature drops by 5 °F. What is the temperature now?

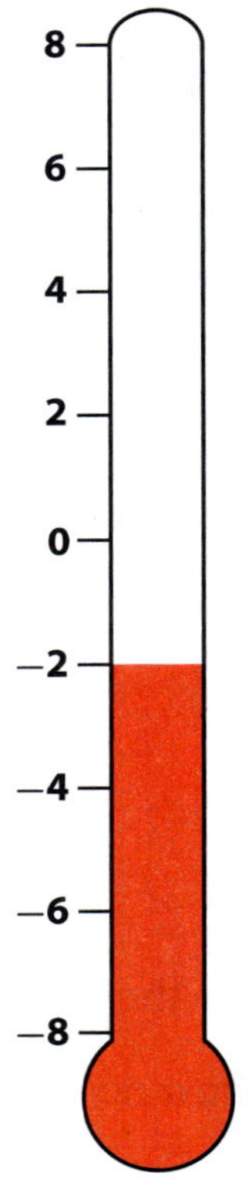

Temperature (°F)

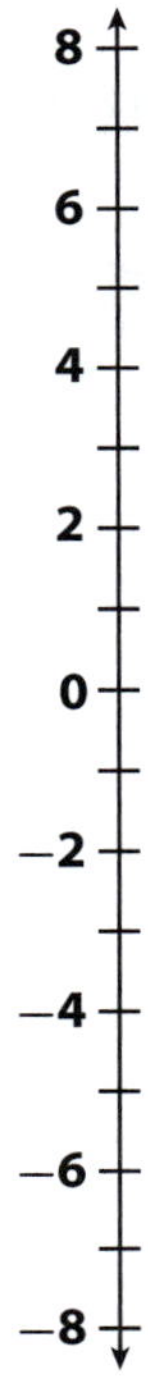

A What is the initial temperature written as an integer?

____

B Draw the arrow for the initial temperature on the number line.

C A drop in temperature of 5° is like adding −5° to the temperature.

To add −5, start at the tip of your first arrow, and draw an arrow representing −5. A single arrow from the start of your first arrow to the end of your second represents the sum.

D What is the temperature written as an integer?

____

The temperature is ________________ **above / below** zero.

Reflect

2. **Draw Conclusions** What is the length of the resulting arrow when you add two arrows pointing in the negative direction?

____

3. **What If?** Suppose the temperature is 1 °F and rises by 3 °F. Explain how to use the number line to find the new temperature. Then make a conclusion similar to the one you made in Question 2.

____

____

____

Adding Integers with a Common Sign

To add integers with the same sign, add the absolute values of the integers and use the sign of the integers for the sum.

EXAMPLE 1

Add $-7 + (-6)$.

The signs of both integers are the same.

STEP 1 Find the absolute values.

$|-7| = 7 \quad |-6| = 6$

The absolute value is always positive or zero.

STEP 2 Find the sum of the absolute values: $7 + 6 = 13$

STEP 3 Use the sign of the integers to write the sum.

$-7 + (-6) = -13$

The sign of each integer is negative.

Math On the Spot
my.hrw.com

Math Talk
Mathematical Processes

Can you use the same procedure you use to find the sum of two negative integers to find the sum of two *positive* numbers? Explain.

Reflect

4. **Communicate Mathematical Ideas** Does the Commutative Property of Addition apply when you add two negative integers? Explain.

____

____

5. **Critical Thinking** Choose any two negative integers. Is the sum of the integers less than or greater than the value of either of the integers? Will this be true no matter which integers you choose? Explain.

____

____

____

____

YOUR TURN

Find each sum.

6. $-8 + (-1) =$ ________
7. $-3 + (-7) =$ ________
8. $-48 + (-12) =$ ________
9. $-32 + (-38) =$ ________
10. $109 + 191 =$ ________
11. $-40 + (-105) =$ ________
12. $-150 + (-1500) =$ ________
13. $-200 + (-800) =$ ________

Personal Math Trainer
Online Assessment and Intervention
my.hrw.com

Guided Practice

Find each sum. (Explore Activity 1)

1. $-5 + (-1)$

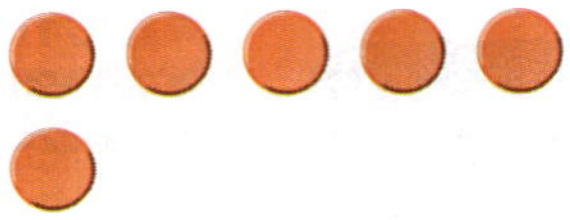

a. How many counters are there? ______

b. Do the counters represent positive or negative numbers? ______

c. $-5 + (-1) =$ ______

2. $-2 + (-7)$

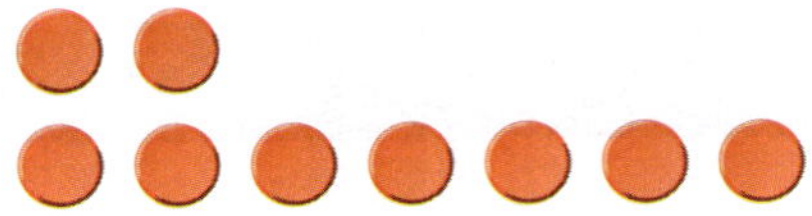

a. How many counters are there? ______

b. Do the counters represent positive or negative numbers? ______

c. $-2 + (-7) =$ ______

Model each addition problem on the number line to find each sum. (Explore Activity 2)

3. $-5 + (-2) =$ ______

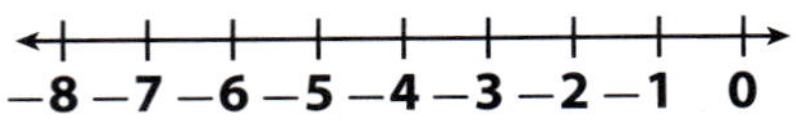

4. $-1 + (-3) =$ ______

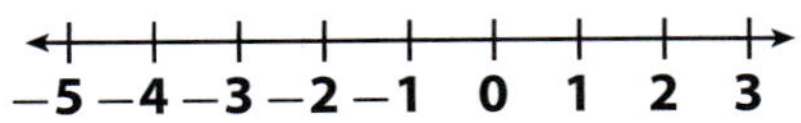

5. $-3 + (-4) =$ ______

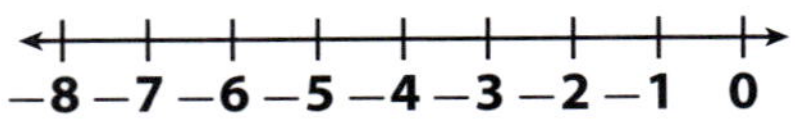

6. $-4 + (-1) =$ ______

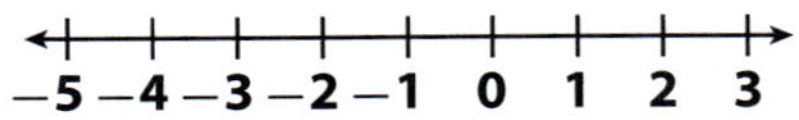

7. $-2 + (-2) =$ ______

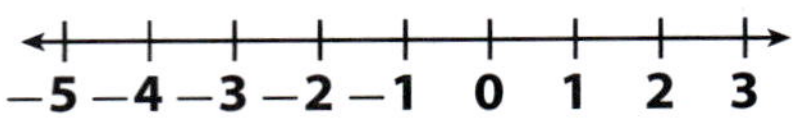

8. $-6 + (-8) =$ ______

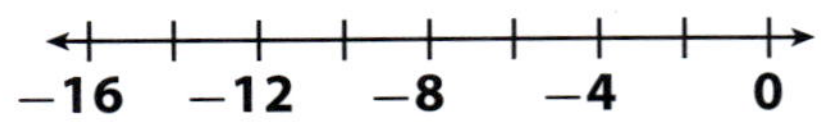

Find each sum. (Example 1)

9. $-5 + (-4) =$ ______

10. $-1 + (-10) =$ ______

11. $-9 + (-1) =$ ______

12. $-90 + (-20) =$ ______

13. $-52 + (-48) =$ ______

14. $5 + 198 =$ ______

15. $-4 + (-5) + (-6) =$ ______

16. $-50 + (-175) + (-345) =$ ______

ESSENTIAL QUESTION CHECK-IN

17. How do you add integers with the same sign?

______

______

Name ____________ Class ____________ Date ____________

1.1 Independent Practice

Personal Math Trainer
Online Assessment and Intervention
my.hrw.com

18. **Represent Real-World Problems** Jane and Sarah both dive down from the surface of a pool. Jane first dives down 5 feet, and then dives down 3 more feet. Sarah first dives down 3 feet, and then dives down 5 more feet.

a. **Multiple Representations** Use the number line to model the equation $-5 + (-3) = -3 + (-5)$.

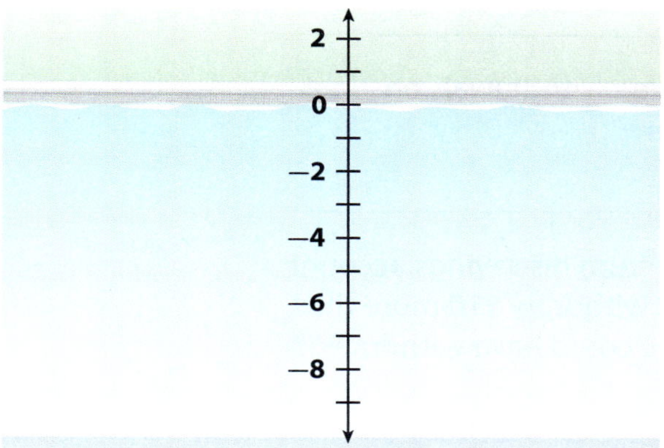

b. Does the order in which you add two integers with the same sign affect the sum? Explain.

____

____

c. Interpret the sum in context.

____

____

19. A golfer has the following scores for a four-day tournament.

Day	1	2	3	4
Score	−3	−1	−5	−2

What was the golfer's total score for the tournament?

____

20. A football team loses 3 yards on one play and 6 yards on another play. Write a sum of negative integers to represent this situation. Find the sum and explain how it is related to the problem.

____

____

21. When the quarterback is sacked, the team loses yards. In one game, the quarterback was sacked four times. What was the total sack yardage?

Sack	1	2	3	4
Sack yardage	−14	−5	−12	−23

____

22. **Multistep** The temperature in Jonestown and Cooperville was the same at 1:00. By 2:00, the temperature in Jonestown dropped 10 degrees, and the temperature in Cooperville dropped 6 degrees. By 3:00, the temperature in Jonestown dropped 8 more degrees, and the temperature in Cooperville dropped 2 more degrees.

a. Write and evaluate a sum to model the change to the temperature in Jonestown since 1:00.

____

b. Write and evaluate a sum to model the change to the temperature in Cooperville since 1:00.

____

c. Where is it colder at 3:00, Jonestown or Cooperville? Explain your reasoning.

____

____

23. **Represent Real-World Problems** Julio is playing a trivia game. On his first turn, he lost 100 points. On his second turn, he lost 75 points. On his third turn, he lost 85 points. Write a sum of three negative integers that models the change to Julio's score after his first three turns.

____

H.O.T. FOCUS ON HIGHER ORDER THINKING

Work Area

24. **Multistep** On Monday, Jan made withdrawals of \$25, \$45, and \$75 from her savings account. On the same day, her twin sister Julie made withdrawals of \$35, \$55, and \$65 from *her* savings account.

a. Write a sum of negative integers to show Jan's withdrawals on Monday. Find the total amount Jan withdrew.

____

b. Write a sum of negative integers to show Julie's withdrawals on Monday. Find the total amount Julie withdrew.

____

c. Julie and Jan's brother also withdrew money from his savings account on Monday. He made three withdrawals and withdrew \$10 more than Julie did. What are three possible amounts he could have withdrawn?

____

25. **Communicate Mathematical Ideas** Why might you want to use the Commutative Property to change the order of the integers in the following sum before adding?

$$-80 + (-173) + (-20)$$

____

____

26. **Critique Reasoning** The absolute value of the sum of two different integers with the same sign is 8. Pat says there are three pairs of integers that match this description. Do you agree? Explain.

____

____

____

____

____

LESSON 1.2 Adding Integers with Different Signs

7.1.1.2

Students will add integers with different signs.

ESSENTIAL QUESTION

How do you add integers with different signs?

EXPLORE ACTIVITY 1

Adding on a Number Line

When you add integers with different signs on a number line, one of the arrows "cancels out" at least part of the other. What remains is the sum.

$3 + (-2) = 1$

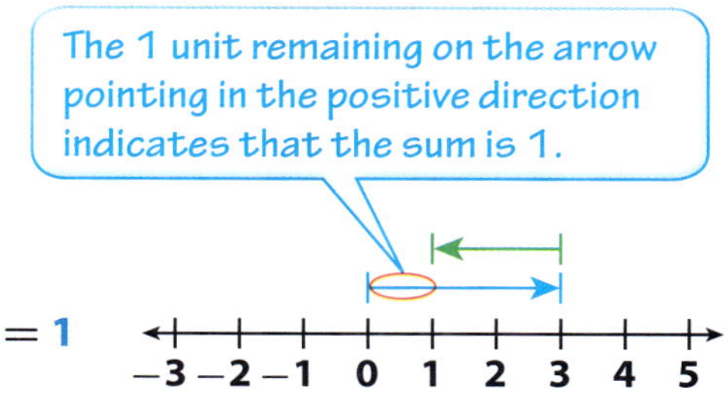

$-3 + 2 = -1$

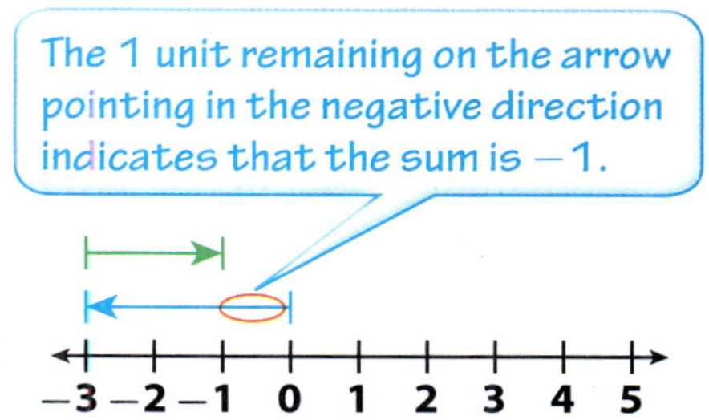

Model each sum on a number line.

A Use a model to find the sum: $4 + (-3) =$ ________

Start at 0. Draw the arrow for 4. Then, starting from directly above the tip of the arrow for 4, draw the arrow for −3.

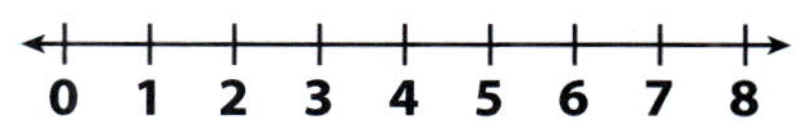

B Use a model to find the sum: $-7 + 5 =$ ________

Start at ________. Draw the arrow for ________.

Then, starting at ________, draw the arrow for ________.

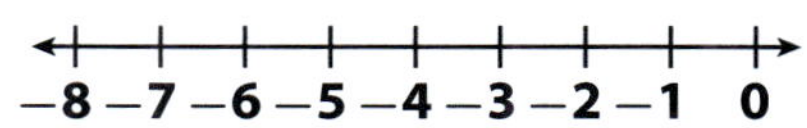

C Use a model to find the sum: $6 + (-6) =$ ________

Start at ________. Draw the arrow for ________.

Then, starting at ________, draw the arrow for ________.

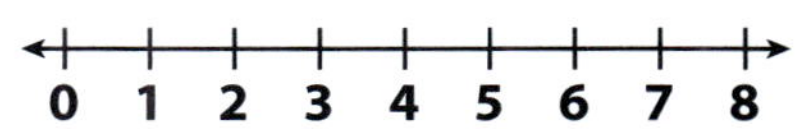

Reflect

1. **Make a Prediction** Predict the sum $-2 + 2$. Explain your prediction and check it using the number line.

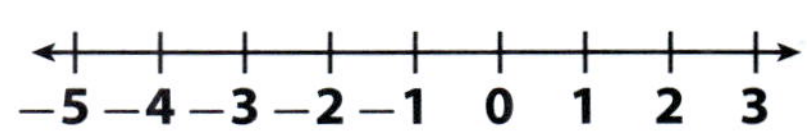

____

____

EXPLORE ACTIVITY 2

Modeling Sums of Integers with Different Signs

You can use colored counters to model adding integers with different signs. When you add a positive integer (yellow counter) and a negative integer (red counter), the result is 0. One red and one yellow counter form a *zero pair*.

$1 + (-1) = 0$

Model and find each sum using counters. Part A is modeled for you. For Part B, follow the steps to model and find the sum using counters.

A Model $3 + (-2)$.

Start with 3 positive counters to represent 3.

Add 2 negative counters to represent adding -2.

Form zero pairs.

What is left when you remove the zero pairs?

________ counter

Find the sum: $3 + (-2) =$ ________

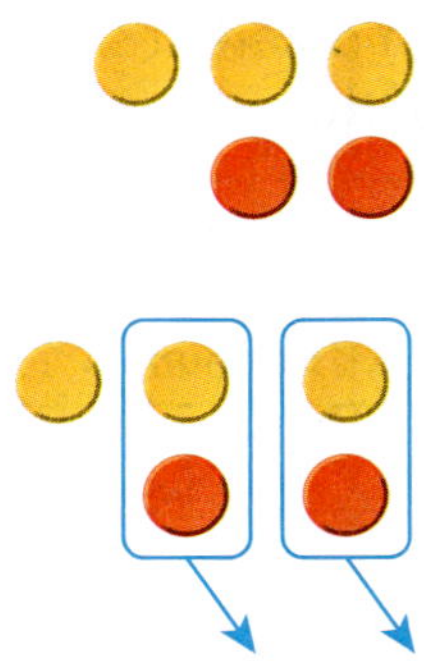

The value of a zero pair is 0. Adding or subtracting 0 to any number does not change its value.

B Model $-6 + 3$.

Start with ________ counters to represent ________.

Add ________ counters to represent adding ________.

Form zero pairs.

What is left when you remove the zero pairs?

________ counters

Find the sum: $-6 + 3 =$ ________

Reflect

2. **Make a Prediction** Kyle models a sum of two integers. He uses more negative (red) counters than positive (yellow) counters. What do you predict about the sign of the sum? Explain.

____

____

YOUR TURN

Model and find each sum using counters.

3. $5 + (-1)$ ____________ **4.** $4 + (-6)$ ____________

5. $1 + (-7)$ ____________ **6.** $3 + (-4)$ ____________

Personal Math Trainer
Online Assessment and Intervention
my.hrw.com

Adding Integers

You have learned how to add integers with the same signs and how to add integers with different signs. The table below summarizes the rules for adding integers.

	Adding Integers	Examples
Same Signs	Add the absolute values of the integers. Use the common sign for the sum.	$3 + 5 = 8$ $-2 + (-7) = -9$
Different Signs	Subtract the lesser absolute value from the greater absolute value. Use the sign of the integer with the greater absolute value for the sum.	$3 + (-5) = -2$ $-10 + 1 = -9$
Inverse Property of Addition	The opposite of any number is called its **additive inverse.** The sum of a number and its additive inverse is 0.	$4 + (-4) = 0$ $-11 + 11 = 0$

Math On the Spot
my.hrw.com

EXAMPLE 1

Find each sum.

A $-11 + 6$

$|-11| - |6| = 5$ *Subtract the lesser absolute value from the greater.*

$-11 + 6 = -5$ *Use the sign of the number with the greater absolute value.*

B $(-37) + 37$

$(-37) + 37 = 0$ *Inverse Property of Addition*

Math Talk
Mathematical Processes

Describe a real-world situation involving integers in which opposite quantities combine to make 0.

YOUR TURN

Find each sum.

7. $-51 + 23 =$ ____________ **8.** $10 + (-18) =$ ____________

9. $13 + (-13) =$ ____________ **10.** $25 + (-26) =$ ____________

Personal Math Trainer
Online Assessment and Intervention
my.hrw.com

Guided Practice

Use a number line to find each sum. (Explore Activity 1)

1. $7 + (-5) =$ ________

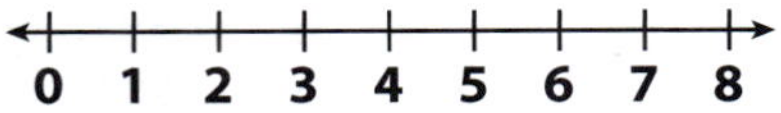

2. $-2 + 7 =$ ________

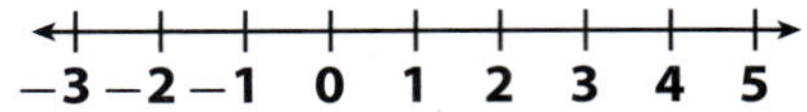

3. $-8 + 3 =$ ________

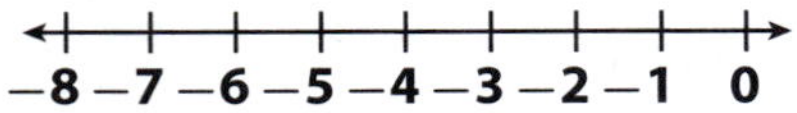

4. $1 + (-4) =$ ________

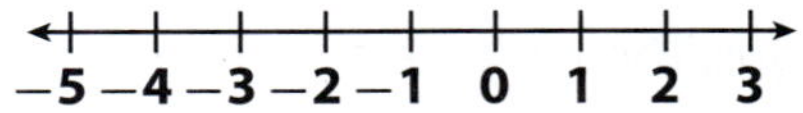

Circle the zero pairs in each model. Find the sum. (Explore Activity 2)

5. $-4 + 5 =$ ________

6. $-6 + 6 =$ ________

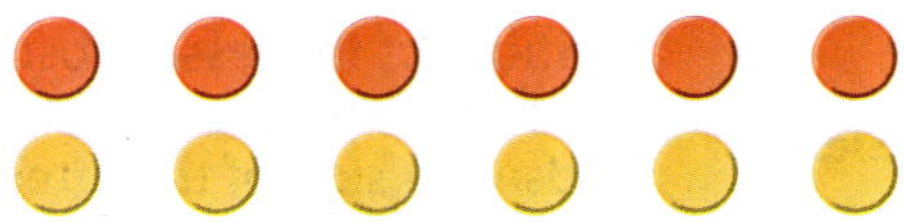

7. $2 + (-5) =$ ________

8. $-3 + 7 =$ ________

Find each sum. (Example 1)

9. $-8 + 14 =$ ________

10. $7 + (-5) =$ ________

11. $5 + (-21) =$ ________

12. $14 + (-14) =$ ________

13. $0 + (-5) =$ ________

14. $32 + (-8) =$ ________

ESSENTIAL QUESTION CHECK-IN

15. Describe how to find the sums $-4 + 2$ and $-4 + (-2)$ on a number line.

____

____

____

Name ____________________ Class ____________ Date ____________

1.2 Independent Practice

Personal Math Trainer
my.hrw.com
Online Assessment and Intervention

Find each sum.

16. $-15 + 71 =$ ____________

17. $-53 + 45 =$ ____________

18. $-79 + 79 =$ ____________

19. $-25 + 50 =$ ____________

20. $18 + (-32) =$ ____________

21. $5 + (-100) =$ ____________

22. $-12 + 8 + 7 =$ ____________

23. $-8 + (-2) + 3 =$ ____________

24. $15 + (-15) + 200 =$ ____________

25. $-500 + (-600) + 1200 =$ ____________

26. A football team gained 9 yards on one play and then lost 22 yards on the next. Write a sum of integers to find the overall change in field position. Explain your answer.

____

27. A soccer team is having a car wash. The team spent \$55 on supplies and earned \$275, including tips. The team's profit is the amount the team made after paying for supplies. Write a sum of integers that represents the team's profit.

____

28. Write and solve a problem involving a number and its opposite using the illustration shown. Identify any properties you use.

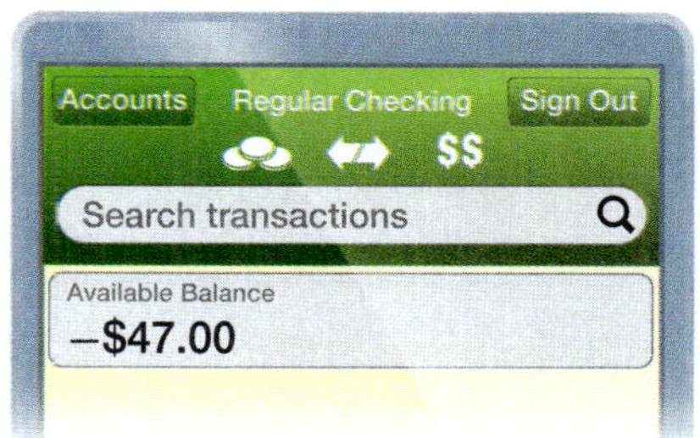

____

____

____

____

29. The sum of two integers with different signs is 8. Give two possible pairs of integers that fit this description.

____

30. **Multistep** Bart and Sam played a game in which each player earns or loses points in each turn. A player's total score after two turns is the sum of his points earned or lost. The player with the greater score after two turns wins. Bart earned 123 points and lost 180 points. Sam earned 185 points and lost 255 points. Which person won the game? Explain.

____

____

H.O.T. FOCUS ON HIGHER ORDER THINKING

Work Area

31. **Critical Thinking** Explain how you could use a number line to show that $-4 + 3$ and $3 + (-4)$ have the same value. Which property of addition states that these sums are equivalent?

32. **Represent Real-World Problems** Jim is standing beside a pool. He drops a weight from 4 feet above the surface of the water in the pool. The weight travels a total distance of 12 feet down before landing on the bottom of the pool. Explain how you can write a sum of integers to find the depth of the water.

33. **Communicate Mathematical Ideas** You are using counters to model the sum of two integers with different signs. Under what conditions will the model represent a positive sum?

34. **Analyze Relationships** You know that the sum of -5 and another integer is a positive integer. What can you conclude about the sign of the other integer? What can you conclude about the value of the other integer? Explain.

LESSON

1.3 Subtracting Integers

7.1.1.3

Students will subtract integers.

ESSENTIAL QUESTION

How do you subtract integers?

EXPLORE ACTIVITY 1

Modeling Integer Subtraction

You can use counters to find the difference of two integers. In some cases, you may need to add zero pairs.

$1 + (-1) = 0$

Model and find each difference using counters.

A Model $-4 - (-3)$.

Start with 4 negative counters to represent -4.

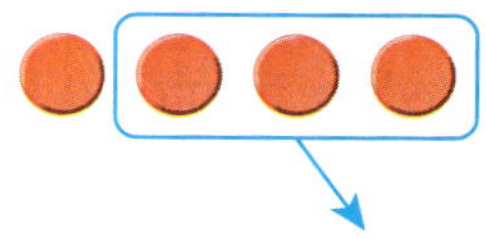

Take away 3 negative counters to represent subtracting -3.

What is left? ____________________

Find the difference: $-4 - (-3) =$ ____

B Model $6 - (-3)$.

Start with 6 positive counters to represent 6.

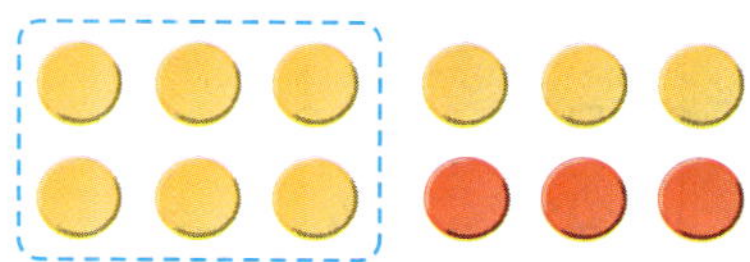

You need to take away 3 negative counters, so add 3 zero pairs.

Take away 3 negative counters to represent subtracting -3.

What is left? ____________________

Find the difference: $6 - (-3) =$ ____

C Model $-2 - (-5)$.

Start with ____________ counters.

You need to take away ____________ counters, so add ____ zero pairs.

Take away ____________ counters.

What is left? ____________________

Find the difference: $-2 - (-5) =$ ____

EXPLORE ACTIVITY 1 *(cont'd)*

Reflect

1. **Communicate Mathematical Ideas** Suppose you want to model the difference $-4 - 7$. Do you need to add zero pairs? If so, why? How many should you add? What is the difference?

____

____

____

EXPLORE ACTIVITY 2

Subtracting on a Number Line

You can think about modeling the difference $5 - 3$ on a horizontal number line by starting at 0 and moving 5 units to the right, then moving 3 units to the left. Notice that you model the sum $5 + (-3)$ in the same way. Subtracting 3 is the same as adding its opposite, -3.

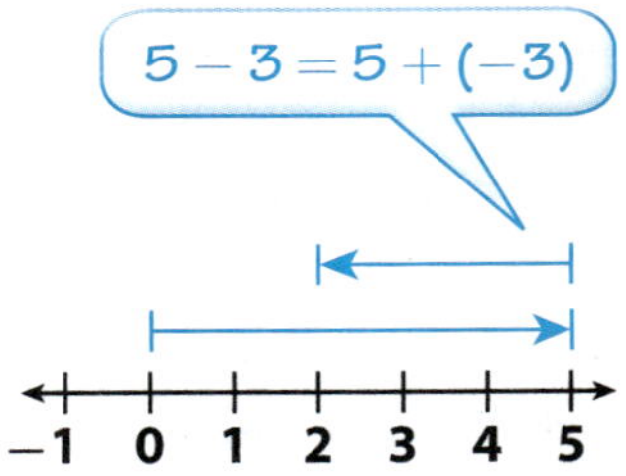

You can use the fact that subtracting a number is the same as adding its opposite to find a difference of two integers.

Find each difference on a number line.

A Find $-1 - 5$ on a number line.

Rewrite subtraction as addition of the opposite.

$-1 - 5 = -1 +$ _____

Start at _____. Draw the arrow for _____.

Then, starting at _____, draw the arrow for _____.

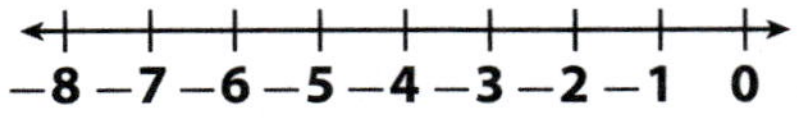

The difference is _____.

B Find $-7 - (-3)$.

Rewrite subtraction as addition of the opposite.

$-7 - (-3) = -7 +$ _____

Start at _____. Draw the arrow for _____.

Then, starting at _____, draw the arrow for _____.

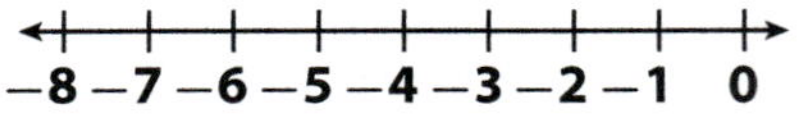

The difference is _____.

EXPLORE ACTIVITY 2 *(cont'd)*

Reflect

2. **Communicate Mathematical Ideas** Describe how to find $5 - (-8)$ on a number line. If you found the difference using counters, would you get the same result? Explain.

____

____

____

____

____

Subtracting Integers by Adding the Opposite

You can use the fact that subtracting an integer is the same as adding its opposite to solve problems.

Math On the Spot
my.hrw.com

Animated Math
my.hrw.com

EXAMPLE 1 Real World

The temperature on Monday was -5 °C. By Tuesday the temperature rose to -2 °C. Find the change in temperature.

STEP 1 Write a subtraction expression.

final temperature − Monday's temperature = change in temperature

$-2\ °C - (-5\ °C)$

STEP 2 Find the difference.

$-2 - (-5) = -2 + 5$ — To subtract -5, add its opposite, 5.

$-2 + 5 = 3$ — Use the rule for adding integers.

The temperature increased by 3 °C.

Math Talk
Mathematical Processes
Why does it make sense that the change in temperature is a positive number?

Reflect

3. **What If?** In Example 1, the temperature rose by 3 °C. Suppose it fell from -2 °C to -10 °C. Predict whether the change in temperature would be positive or negative. Then subtract to find the change.

____

____

Personal Math Trainer
Online Assessment and Intervention
my.hrw.com

YOUR TURN

Find each difference.

4. $-7 - 2 =$ ______

5. $-1 - (-3) =$ ______

6. $3 - 5 =$ ______

7. $-8 - (-4) =$ ______

Guided Practice

Explain how to find each difference using counters. (Explore Activity 1)

1. $5 - 8 =$ ______

______

______

______

______

2. $-5 - (-3) =$ ______

______

______

______

______

Use a number line to find each difference. (Explore Activity 2)

3. $-4 - 5 = -4 +$ ______ $=$ ______

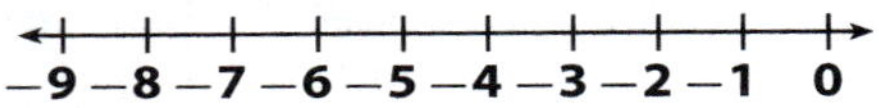

4. $1 - 4 = 1 +$ ______ $=$ ______

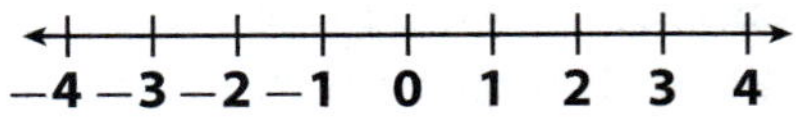

Solve. (Example 1)

5. $8 - 11 =$ ______

6. $-3 - (-5) =$ ______

7. $15 - 21 =$ ______

8. $-17 - 1 =$ ______

9. $0 - (-5) =$ ______

10. $1 - (-18) =$ ______

11. $15 - 1 =$ ______

12. $-3 - (-45) =$ ______

13. $19 - (-19) =$ ______

14. $-87 - (-87) =$ ______

ESSENTIAL QUESTION CHECK-IN

15. How do you subtract an integer from another integer without using a number line or counters? Give an example.

______

______

Name ____________ Class ____________ Date ____________

1.3 Independent Practice

Personal Math Trainer
Online Assessment and Intervention
my.hrw.com

16. Theo had a balance of −\$4 in his savings account. After making a deposit, he has \$25 in his account. What is the overall change to his account?

____

17. As shown, Suzi starts her hike at an elevation below sea level. When she reaches the end of the hike, she is still below sea level at −127 feet. What was the change in elevation from the beginning of Suzi's hike to the end of the hike?

____

18. The record high January temperature in Austin, Texas, is 90 °F. The record low January temperature is −2 °F. Find the difference between the high and low temperatures.

____

19. Cheyenne is playing a board game. Her score was −275 at the start of her turn, and at the end of her turn her score was −425. What was the change in Cheyenne's score from the start of her turn to the end of her turn?

____

20. A scientist conducts three experiments in which she records the temperature of some gases that are being heated. The table shows the initial temperature and the final temperature for each gas.

Gas	Initial Temperature	Final Temperature
A	−21 °C	−8 °C
B	−12 °C	12 °C
C	−19 °C	−15 °C

a. Write a difference of integers to find the overall temperature change for each gas.

Gas A: ______________________

Gas B: ______________________

Gas C: ______________________

b. **What If?** Suppose the scientist performs an experiment in which she cools the three gases. Will the changes in temperature be positive or negative for this experiment? Why?

____

21. **Analyze Relationships** For two months, Nell feeds her cat Diet Chow brand cat food. Then for the next two months, she feeds her cat Kitty Diet brand cat food. The table shows the cat's change in weight over 4 months.

	Cat's Weight Change (oz)
Diet Chow, Month 1	−8
Diet Chow, Month 2	−18
Kitty Diet, Month 3	3
Kitty Diet, Month 4	−19

Which brand of cat food resulted in the greatest weight loss for Nell's cat? Explain.

____

____

H.O.T. FOCUS ON HIGHER ORDER THINKING

Work Area

22. **Represent Real-World Problems** Write and solve a word problem that can be modeled by the difference −4 − 10.

____

____

____

23. **Explain the Error** When Tom found the difference −11 − (−4), he got −15. What might Tom have done wrong?

____

____

____

24. **Draw Conclusions** When you subtract one negative integer from another, will your answer be greater than or less than the integer you started with? Explain your reasoning and give an example.

____

____

____

____

25. **Look for a Pattern** Find the next three terms in the pattern 9, 4, −1, −6, −11, ... Then describe the pattern.

____

LESSON 1.4

Applying Addition and Subtraction of Integers

7.1.1.4

Students will solve multistep problems involving addition and subtraction of integers.

ESSENTIAL QUESTION

How do you solve multistep problems involving addition and subtraction of integers?

EXPLORE ACTIVITY 1 Real World

Solving a Multistep Problem

You can use what you know about adding and subtracting integers to solve a multistep problem.

Math On the Spot
my.hrw.com

EXAMPLE 1 **A seal is swimming in the ocean 5 feet below sea level. It dives down 12 feet to catch some fish. Then, the seal swims 8 feet up toward the surface with its catch. What is the seal's final elevation relative to sea level?**

STEP 1 Write an expression.

The seal starts at 5 feet below the surface, so its initial position is −5 feet. It swims 12 feet down, and then 8 feet up.

Starts	−	Distance down	+	Distance up
−5	−	_____	+	_____

STEP 2 Add or subtract from left to right to find the value of the expression.

$-5 - 12 + 8 =$ _____ $+ 8 =$ _____

This is reasonable because the seal swam farther down than up.

The seal's final elevation is _____ feet **above / below** sea level.

YOUR TURN

1. Anna is in a cave 40 feet below the cave entrance. She descends 13 feet, then ascends 18 feet. Write and evaluate an expression to find her new position relative to the cave entrance.

____

Personal Math Trainer
Online Assessment and Intervention
my.hrw.com

Math On the Spot
my.hrw.com

Applying Properties to Solve Problems

You can use properties of addition to solve problems involving integers.

EXAMPLE 2 Problem Solving

Irene has a checking account. On Monday she writes a $160 check for groceries. Then she deposits $125. Finally she writes another check for $40. What was the total change in the amount in Irene's account?

Analyze Information

When Irene deposits money, she adds that amount to the account. When she writes a check, that money is deducted from the account.

Formulate a Plan

Use a positive integer for the amount Irene added to the account. Use negative integers for the checks she wrote. Find the sum.

$-160 + 125 + (-40)$

Solve

Add the amounts to find the total change in the account. Use properties of addition to simplify calculations.

$$-160 + 125 + (-40) = -160 + (-40) + 125 \quad \text{Commutative Property}$$

$$= -200 + 125 \quad \text{Associative Property}$$

$$= -75$$

The amount in the account decreased by $75.

Justify and Evaluate

Irene's account has $75 less than it did before Monday. This is reasonable because she wrote checks for $200 but only deposited $125.

Reflect

2. **Communicative Mathematical Ideas** Describe a different way to find the change in Irene's account.

____

____

Personal Math Trainer
Online Assessment and Intervention
my.hrw.com

YOUR TURN

3. Alex wrote checks on Tuesday for $35 and $45. He also made a deposit in his checking account of $180. Find the overall change in the amount in his checking account.

____

Comparing Values of Expressions

Sometimes you may want to compare values obtained by adding and subtracting integers.

EXAMPLE 3 Problem Solving

Math On the Spot
my.hrw.com

The Tigers, a football team, must gain 10 yards in the next four plays to keep possession of the ball. The Tigers lose 12 yards, gain 5 yards, lose 8 yards, and gain 14 yards. Do the Tigers maintain possession of the ball?

Analyze Information

When the team gains yards, add that distance.

When the team loses yards, subtract that distance.

If the total change in yards is greater than or equal to 10, the team keeps possession of the ball.

Formulate a Plan

$-12 + 5 - 8 + 14$

Solve

$-12 + 5 - 8 + 14$

$-12 + 5 + (-8) + 14$ — *To subtract, add the opposite.*

$-12 + (-8) + 5 + 14$ — *Commutative Property*

$(-12 + (-8)) + (5 + 14)$ — *Associative Property*

$-20 + 19 = -1$

$-1 < 10$ — *Compare to 10 yards*

The Tigers gained less than 10 yards, so they do not maintain possession.

Justify and Evaluate

The football team gained 19 yards and lost 20 yards for a total of -1 yard.

Math Talk
Mathematical Processes

What does it mean that the football team had a total of -1 yard over four plays?

YOUR TURN

4. Jim and Carla are scuba diving. Jim started out 10 feet below the surface. He descended 18 feet, rose 5 feet, and descended 12 more feet. Then he rested. Carla started out at the surface. She descended 20 feet, rose 5 feet, and descended another 18 feet. Then she rested. Which person rested at a greater depth? Explain.

____

____

Personal Math Trainer
Online Assessment and Intervention
my.hrw.com

Guided Practice

Write an expression. Then find the value of the expression. (Explore Activity Example 1 and Example 2)

1. Tomas works as an underwater photographer. He starts at a position that is 15 feet below sea level. He rises 9 feet, then descends 12 feet to take a photo of a coral reef. Write and evaluate an expression to find his position relative to sea level when he took the photo.

____

2. The temperature on a winter night was −23 °F. The temperature rose by 5 °F when the sun came up. When the sun set again, the temperature dropped by 7 °F. Write and evaluate an expression to find the temperature after the sun set.

____

3. Jose earned 50 points in a video game. He lost 40 points, earned 87 points, then lost 30 more points. Write and evaluate an expression to find his final score in the video game.

____

Find the value of each expression. (Example 2)

4. $-6 + 15 + 15 =$ __________

5. $9 - 4 - 17 =$ __________

6. $50 - 42 + 10 =$ __________

7. $6 + 13 + 7 - 5 =$ __________

8. $65 + 43 - 11 =$ __________

9. $-35 - 14 + 45 + 31 =$ __________

Determine which expression has a greater value. (Example 3)

10. $-12 + 6 - 4$ or $-34 - 3 + 39$

____

11. $21 - 3 + 8$ or $-14 + 31 - 6$

____

ESSENTIAL QUESTION CHECK-IN

12. Explain how you can find the value of the expression $-5 + 12 + 10 - 7$.

____

____

Name ____________ Class ____________ Date ____________

1.4 Independent Practice

Personal Math Trainer
Online Assessment and Intervention
my.hrw.com

13. **Sports** Cameron is playing 9 holes of golf. He needs to score a total of at most 15 over par on the last four holes to beat his best golf score. On the last four holes, he scores 5 over par, 1 under par, 6 over par, and 1 under par.

a. Write and find the value of an expression that gives Cameron's score for 4 holes of golf.

____

b. Is Cameron's score on the last four holes over or under par?

____

c. Did Cameron beat his best golf score?

____

14. Herman is standing on a ladder that is partly in a hole. He starts out on a rung that is 6 feet under ground, climbs up 14 feet, then climbs down 11 feet. What is Herman's final position, relative to ground level?

____

15. **Explain the Error** Jerome tries to find the value of the expression $3 - 6 + 5$ by first applying the Commutative Property. He rewrites the expression as $3 - 5 + 6$. Explain what is wrong with Jerome's approach.

____

____

____

____

____

16. Lee and Barry play a trivia game in which questions are worth different numbers of points. If a question is answered correctly, a player earns points. If a question is answered incorrectly, the player loses points. Lee currently has -350 points.

a. Before the game ends, Lee answers a 275-point question correctly, a 70-point question correctly, and a 50-point question incorrectly. Write and find the value of an expression to find Lee's final score.

____

b. Barry's final score is 45. Which player had the greater final score?

____

17. **Multistep** Rob collects data about how many customers enter and leave a store every hour. He records a positive number for customers entering the store each hour and a negative number for customers leaving the store each hour.

	Entering	Leaving
1:00 to 2:00	30	−12
2:00 to 3:00	14	−8
3:00 to 4:00	18	−30

a. During which hour did more customers leave than arrive?

____

b. There were 75 customers in the store at 1:00. The store must be emptied of customers when it closes at 5:00. How many customers must leave the store between 4:00 and 5:00?

____

The table shows the changes in the values of two friends' savings accounts since the previous month.

	June	July	August
Carla	−18	22	−53
Leta	−17	−22	18

18. Carla had \$100 in her account in May. How much money does she have in her account in August? __________

19. Leta had \$45 in her account in May. How much money does she have in her account in August? __________

20. **Analyze Relationships** Whose account had the greatest decrease in value from May to August? __________

Work Area

H.O.T. FOCUS ON HIGHER ORDER THINKING

21. **Represent Real-World Problems** Write and solve a word problem that matches the diagram shown.

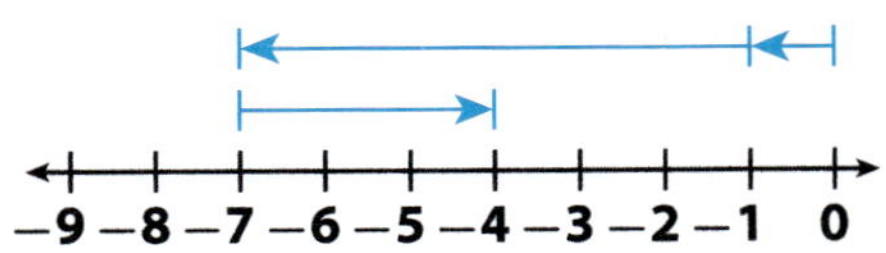

____

____

____

22. **Critical Thinking** Mary has \$10 in savings. She owes her parents \$50. She does some chores and her parents pay her \$12. She also gets \$25 for her birthday from her grandmother. Does Mary have enough money to pay her parents what she owes them? If not, how much more money does she need? Explain.

____

____

23. **Draw Conclusions** An expression involves subtracting two numbers from a given number. Under what circumstances will the value of the expression be negative? Give an example.

____

____

____

____

MODULE QUIZ

Ready to Go On?

Personal Math Trainer
Online Assessment and Intervention
my.hrw.com

1.1 Adding Integers with the Same Sign

Add.

1. $-8 + (-6)$ ________ **2.** $-4 + (-7)$ ________ **3.** $-9 + (-12)$ ________

1.2 Adding Integers with Different Signs

Add.

4. $5 + (-2)$ ________ **5.** $-8 + 4$ ________ **6.** $15 + (-8)$ ________

1.3 Subtracting Integers

Subtract.

7. $2 - 9$ ________ **8.** $-3 - (-4)$ ________ **9.** $11 - (-12)$ ________

1.4 Applying Addition and Subtraction of Integers

10. A bus makes a stop at 2:30, letting off 15 people and letting on 9. The bus makes another stop ten minutes later to let off 4 more people. How many more or fewer people are on the bus after the second stop compared to the number of people on the bus before the 2:30 stop?

____

11. Cate and Elena were playing a card game. The stack of cards in the middle had 24 cards in it to begin with. Cate added 8 cards to the stack. Elena then took 12 cards from the stack. Finally, Cate took 9 cards from the stack. How many cards were left in the stack? ________

ESSENTIAL QUESTION

12. Write and solve a word problem that can be modeled by addition of two negative integers.

____

____

____

MODULE 1 **MIXED REVIEW**

Assessment Readiness

Personal Math Trainer

my.hrw.com

Online Assessment and Intervention

Selected Response

1. Which expression has the same value as $-3 + (-5)$?

Ⓐ $-3 - (-5)$

Ⓑ $-3 + 5$

Ⓒ $-5 + (-3)$

Ⓓ $-5 - (-3)$

2. A diver's elevation is -30 feet relative to sea level. She dives down 12 feet. What is her elevation after the dive?

Ⓐ 12 feet

Ⓑ 18 feet

Ⓒ -30 feet

Ⓓ -42 feet

3. Which number line models the expression $-3 + 5$?

Ⓐ 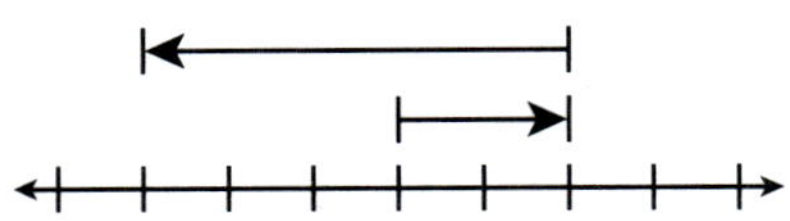

Ⓑ 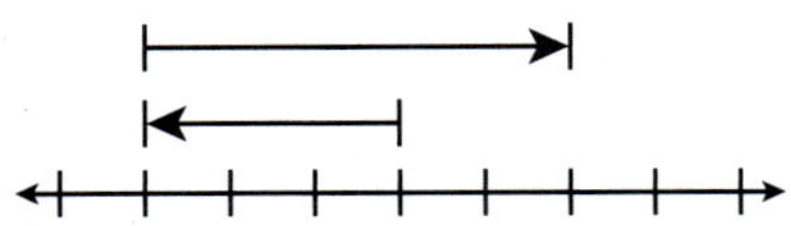

Ⓒ 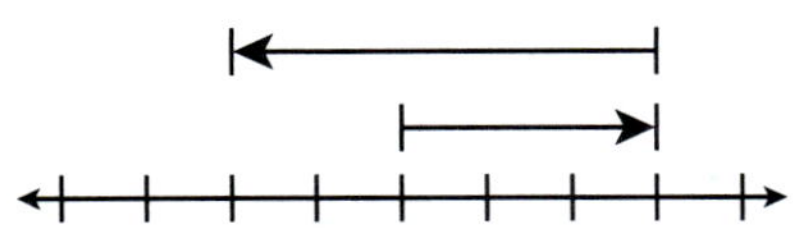

Ⓓ 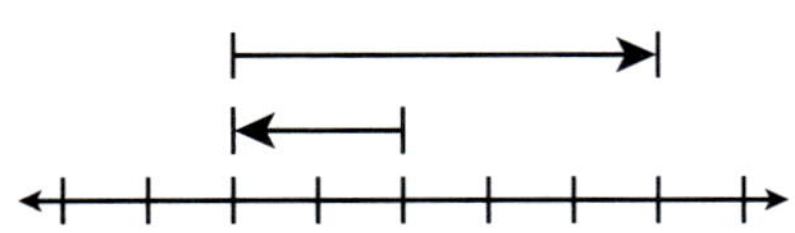

4. Which number can you add to 5 to get a sum of 0?

Ⓐ -10

Ⓑ -5

Ⓒ 0

Ⓓ 5

5. The temperature in the morning was $-3\,°F$. The temperature dropped 11 degrees by night. What was the temperature at night?

Ⓐ $-14\,°F$

Ⓑ $-8\,°F$

Ⓒ $8\,°F$

Ⓓ $14\,°F$

6. Which of the following expressions has the greatest value?

Ⓐ $3 - 7 + (-10)$

Ⓑ $3 + 7 - (-10)$

Ⓒ $3 - 7 - (-10)$

Ⓓ $3 + 7 + (-10)$

Mini-Task

7. At the end of one day, the value of a share of a certain stock was \$12. Over the next three days, the change in the value of the share was $-\$1$, then, $-\$1$, and then \$3.

a. Write an expression that describes the situation.

____

b. Evaluate the expression. ______________

c. What does your answer to part **b** mean in the context of the problem?

____

____

Multiplying and Dividing Integers

MODULE 2

ESSENTIAL QUESTION

How can you use multiplication and division of integers to solve real-world problems?

Real-World Video

my.hrw.com

The giant panda is an endangered animal. For some endangered species, the population has made a steady decline. This can be represented by multiplying integers with different signs.

GO DIGITAL
my.hrw.com

my.hrw.com
Go digital with your write-in student edition, accessible on any device.

Math On the Spot
Scan with your smart phone to jump directly to the online edition, video tutor, and more.

Animated Math
Interactively explore key concepts to see how math works.

Personal Math Trainer
Get immediate feedback and help as you work through practice sets.

Reading Start-Up

Visualize Vocabulary

Use the ✔ words to complete the chart. You may put more than one word in each box.

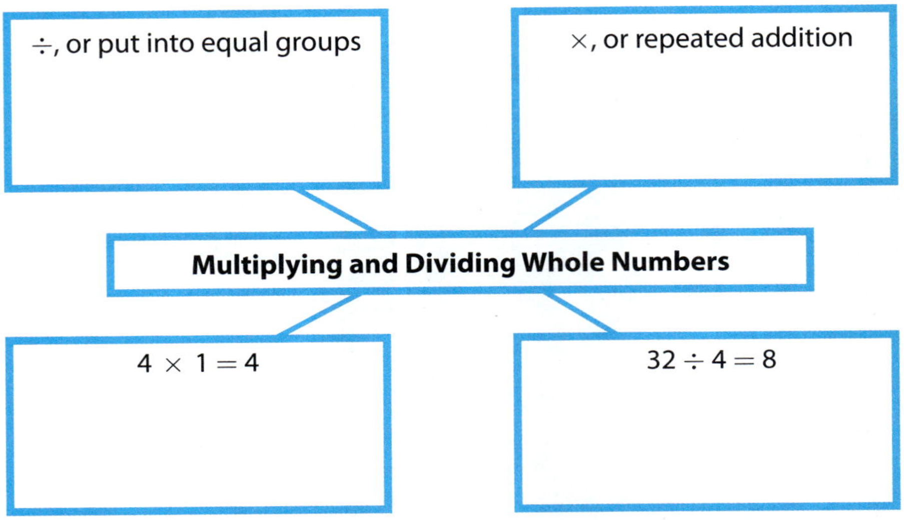

Understand Vocabulary

Complete the sentences using the review words.

1. A ______________________ is a number that is less than 0. A ______________________ is a number that is greater than 0.

2. Division problems have three parts. The part you want to divide into groups is called the ______________. The number that is divided into another number is called the ______________. The answer to a division problem is called the ______________.

3. ______________ are all whole numbers and their opposites.

Vocabulary

Review Words

- ✔ divide *(dividir)*
- ✔ dividend *(dividendo)*
- ✔ divisor *(divisor)*
- integers *(enteros)*
- ✔ multiply *(multiplicar)*
- negative number *(número negativo)*
- operation *(operación)*
- opposites *(opuestos)*
- positive number *(número positivo)*
- ✔ product *(producto)*
- ✔ quotient *(cociente)*

Active Reading

Double-Door Fold Create a double-door fold to help you understand the concepts in this module. Label one flap "Multiplying Integers" and the other flap "Dividing Integers." As you study each lesson, write important ideas under the appropriate flap. Include information that will help you remember the concepts later when you look back at your notes.

Are YOU Ready?

Complete these exercises to review skills you will need for this module.

Personal Math Trainer
my.hrw.com
Online Assessment and Intervention

Multiplication Facts

EXAMPLES $7 \times 9 = \blacksquare$

$7 \times 9 = 63$

Use patterns. When you multiply 9 by a number 1 through 9, the digits of the product add up to 9. $6 + 3 = 9$

$12 \times 10 = \blacksquare$

$12 \times 10 = 120$

Products of 10 end in 0.

Multiply.

1. 9×3 ______ **2.** 7×10 ______ **3.** 9×8 ______ **4.** 15×10 ______

5. 6×9 ______ **6.** 10×23 ______ **7.** 9×9 ______ **8.** 10×20 ______

Division Facts

EXAMPLE $48 \div 6 = \blacksquare$

Think: 6 times what number equals 48?
$6 \times 8 = 48$

$48 \div 6 = 8$

So, $48 \div 6 = 8$

Divide.

9. $54 \div 9$ ______ **10.** $42 \div 6$ ______ **11.** $24 \div 3$ ______ **12.** $64 \div 8$ ______

13. $90 \div 10$ ______ **14.** $56 \div 7$ ______ **15.** $81 \div 9$ ______ **16.** $110 \div 11$ ______

Order of Operations

EXAMPLE $32 - 2(10 - 7)^2$

$32 - 2(3)^2$ To evaluate, first operate within parentheses.

$32 - 2(9)$ Next, simplify exponents.

$32 - 18$ Then multiply and divide from left to right.

14 Finally add and subtract from left to right.

Evaluate each expression.

17. $12 + 8 \div 2$ ______ **18.** $15 - (4 + 3) \times 2$ ______ **19.** $18 - (8 - 5)^2$ ______

20. $6 + 7 \times 3 - 5$ ______ **21.** $9 + (2^2 + 3)^2 \times 2$ ______ **22.** $6 + 5 - 4 \times 3 \div 2$ ______

Are YOU Ready? *(cont'd)*

Complete these exercises to review skills you will need for this module.

Multiplication Facts

23. A chef ordered 400 pounds of potatoes in same-sized bags. Which expressions show the number of bags and number of pounds of potatoes per bag the chef may have ordered? Choose all that apply.

Ⓐ 80×5 Ⓑ 10×40 Ⓒ 20×2 Ⓓ 20×20 Ⓔ 50×80

Division Facts

24. Josh has 36 postcards from national parks he visited. He wants to put them in a binder. Each page in the binder holds 4 postcards. How many pages does he need for the binder? Explain.

Order of Operations

25. A coach bought 3 soccer balls on sale. They normally sell for \$26 each. They were on sale for \$7 off the original price. The total tax on the balls was \$4. The expression $4 + 3(26 - 7)$ can be used to find the total amount the coach paid. Tell why the expression represents the total amount paid. Then explain how to use the order of operations to find the total amount the coach paid for the soccer balls.

LESSON

2.1 Multiplying Integers

7.1.2.1

Students will multiply integers.

ESSENTIAL QUESTION

How do you multiply integers?

EXPLORE ACTIVITY 1

Multiplying Integers Using a Number Line

You can use a number line to see what happens when you multiply a positive number by a negative number.

A Henry made three withdrawals of $2 each from his savings account. What was the change in his balance?

Find 3(−2).

To show −2, you would draw an arrow from 0 to ______ .

3(−2) means (______) + (______) + (______).

To show 3(−2), you would draw the sum equivalent to 3(−2).

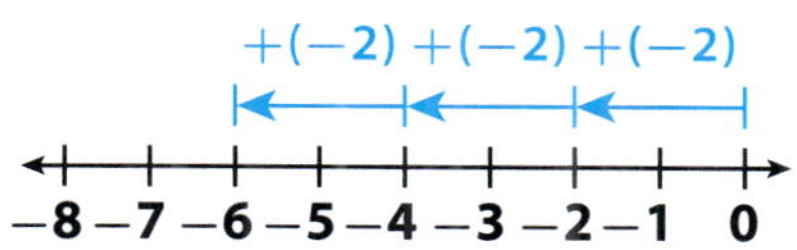

The result is ______.

The change in Henry's balance was ______.

B Lisa plays a video game in which she loses points. She loses 3 points 2 times. What is her score?

Find 2(−3).

2(−3) means (______) + (______).
Show this on the number line.

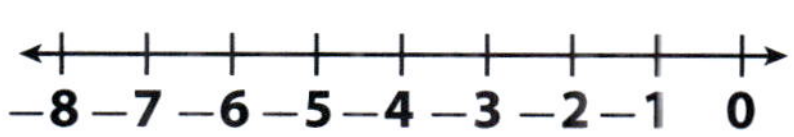

Lisa has a score of ______.

Reflect

1. What do you notice about the product of two integers with different signs?

____

____

EXPLORE ACTIVITY 2

Modeling Integer Multiplication

Counters representing positive and negative numbers can help you understand how to find the product of two negative integers.

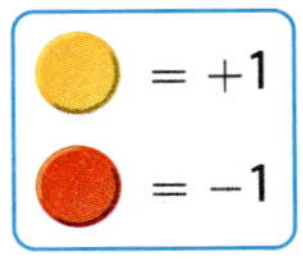

Find the product of −3 and −4.

Write $(-3)(-4)$ as $-3(-4)$, which means the *opposite* of $3(-4)$.

STEP 1 Use negative counters to model $3(-4)$.

STEP 2 Make the same model using positive counters to find the *opposite* of $3(-4)$.

STEP 3 Translate the model into a mathematical expression:

$(-3)(-4) =$ ______

The product of −3 and −4 is ______.

Reflect

2. What do you notice about the sign of the product of two negative integers?

____

3. **Make a Conjecture** What can you conclude about the sign of the product of two integers with the same sign?

____

____

____

____

Multiplying Integers

The product of two integers with opposite signs is negative. The product of two integers with the same sign is positive. The product of 0 and any other integer is 0.

Math On the Spot
my.hrw.com

Animated Math
my.hrw.com

EXAMPLE 1

A Multiply: (13)(−3).

STEP 1 Determine the sign of the product.

13 is positive and −3 is negative. Since the numbers have opposite signs, the product will be negative.

STEP 2 Find the absolute values of the numbers and multiply them.

$|13| = 13$ $|-3| = 3$

$13 \times 3 = 39$

STEP 3 Assign the correct sign to the product.

$13(-3) = -39$ *The product is −39.*

B Multiply: (−5)(−8).

STEP 1 Determine the sign of the product.

−5 is negative and −8 is negative. Since the numbers have the same sign, the product will be positive.

STEP 2 Find the absolute values of the numbers and multiply them.

$|-5| = 5$ $|-8| = 8$

$5 \times 8 = 40$

STEP 3 Assign the correct sign to the product.

$(-5)(-8) = 40$ *The product is 40.*

C Multiply: (−10)(0).

$(-10)(0) = 0$ *One of the factors is 0, so the product is 0.*

Math Talk
Mathematical Processes

Compare the rules for finding the product of a number and zero and finding the sum of a number and 0.

YOUR TURN

Find each product.

4. −3(5) ____________

5. (−10)(−2) ____________

6. 7(−6) ____________

7. 0(−22) ____________

8. (−15)(−3) ____________

9. 8(4) ____________

Personal Math Trainer
Online Assessment and Intervention
my.hrw.com

Guided Practice

Find each product. (Explore Activity 2 and Example 1)

1. $-1(9)$ ____________

2. $14(-2)$ ____________

3. $(-9)(-6)$ ____________

4. $(-2)(50)$ ____________

5. $(-4)(15)$ ____________

6. $-18(0)$ ____________

7. $(-7)(-7)$ ____________

8. $-15(9)$ ____________

9. $(8)(-12)$ ____________

10. $-3(-100)$ ____________

11. $0(-153)$ ____________

12. $-6(32)$ ____________

Solve. Show your work.

13. Flora made 7 withdrawals of $75 each from her bank account. What was the overall change in her account? (Example 1)

____

14. A football team lost 5 yards on each of 3 plays. Explain how you could use a number line to find the team's change in field position after the 3 plays. Then find and interpret the change in position. (Explore Activity 1)

____

____

15. The temperature dropped 2 °F every hour for 6 hours. What was the total number of degrees the temperature changed in the 6 hours? (Explore Activity 1)

____

16. The price of one share of Acme Company declined $5 per day for 4 days in a row. Find and interpret the total change in the price of one share after the 4 days. (Explore Activity 1)

____

17. A mountain climber climbed down a cliff 50 feet at a time. He did this 5 times in one day. What was the overall change in his elevation? (Explore Activity 1)

____

ESSENTIAL QUESTION CHECK-IN

18. Explain the process for finding the product of two integers.

____

____

____

Name ______________________ Class ______________ Date ______________

2.1 Independent Practice

Personal Math Trainer
Online Assessment and Intervention
my.hrw.com

19. **Critique Reasoning** Lisa used a number line to model −2(3). Does her number line make sense? Explain why or why not.

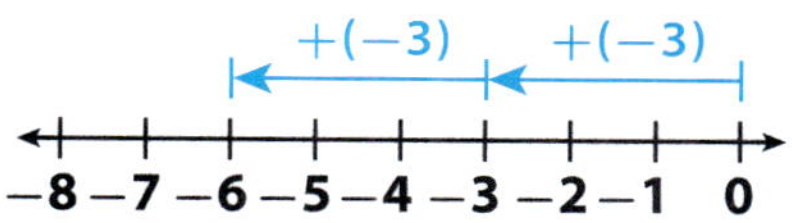

____

____

____

20. **Represent Real-World Problems** Mike got on an elevator and went down 3 floors. He meant to go to a lower level, so he stayed on the elevator and went down 3 more floors. How many floors did Mike go down altogether?

____

Solve. Show your work.

21. When Brooke buys lunch at the cafeteria, money is withdrawn from a lunch account. The table shows amounts withdrawn in one week. By how much did the amount in Brooke's lunch account change by the end of that week?

Lunch Account			
Week 1	**Lunch**	**Cost**	**Balance**
			$28
Monday	Pizza	$4	
Tuesday	Fish Tacos	$4	
Wednesday	Spaghetti	$4	
Thursday	Sandwich	$4	
Friday	Chicken	$4	

____

22. Adam is scuba diving. He descends 5 feet below sea level. He descends the same distance 4 more times. What is Adam's final elevation?

____

____

____

23. The price of jeans was reduced $6 per week for 7 weeks. By how much did the price of the jeans change over the 7 weeks?

____

____

____

24. Casey uses some of his savings on batting practice. The cost of renting a batting cage for 1 hour is $6. He rents a cage for 9 hours in each of two months. What is the change in Casey's savings after two months?

____

____

____

25. Volunteers at Sam's school use some of the student council's savings for a special project. They buy 7 backpacks for $8 each and fill each backpack with paper and pens that cost $5. By how much did the student council's savings change because of this project?

____

____

____

26. **Communicate Mathematical Ideas** Describe a real-world situation that can be represented by the product $8(-20)$. Then find the product and explain what the product means in terms of the real-world situation.

____

____

____

27. **What If?** The rules for multiplying two integers can be extended to a product of 3 or more integers. Find the following products by using the Associative Property to multiply 2 numbers at a time.

a. $3(3)(-3)$ ________ **b.** $3(-3)(-3)$ ________ **c.** $-3(-3)(-3)$ ________

d. $3(3)(3)(-3)$ ________ **e.** $3(3)(-3)(-3)$ ________ **f.** $3(-3)(-3)(-3)$ ________

g. **Make a Conjecture** Based on your results, complete the following statements:

When a product of integers has an odd number of negative factors, then the sign of the product is ________.

When a product of integers has an even number of negative factors, then the sign of the product is ________.

H.O.T. FOCUS ON HIGHER ORDER THINKING

Work Area

28. **Multiple Representations** The product of three integers is -3. Determine all of the possible values for the three factors.

____

29. **Analyze Relationships** When is the product of two nonzero integers less than or equal to both of the two factors?

____

____

30. **Justify Reasoning** The sign of the product of two integers with the same sign is positive. What is the sign of the product of three integers with the same sign? Explain your thinking.

____

____

____

____

____

LESSON

2.2 Dividing Integers

7.1.2.2

Students will divide integers.

ESSENTIAL QUESTION

How do you divide integers?

EXPLORE ACTIVITY Real World

A diver needs to descend to a depth of 100 feet. She wants to do it in 5 equal stages. Describe how she should travel at each stage.

A Use the number line at the right to help describe how the diver should travel at each of the 5 stages.

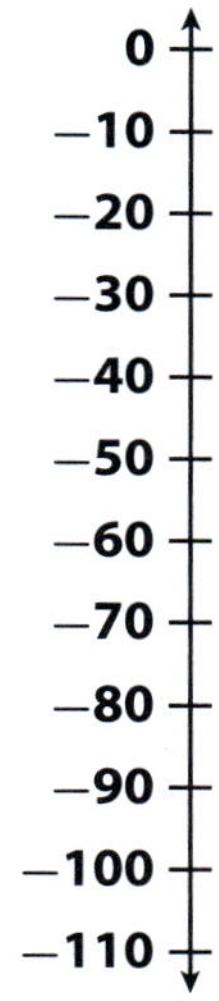

____

B To solve this problem, you can set up a division problem: $\frac{-100}{\square} = ?$

C Rewrite the division problem as a multiplication problem. Think: Some number multiplied by 5 equals −100.

__________ $\times\ ? = -100$

D Remember the rules for integer multiplication. If the product is negative, one of the factors must be negative. Since ________ is positive, the unknown factor must be **positive / negative.**

E You know that $5 \times$ ______ $= 100$. So, using the rules for integer multiplication you can say that $5 \times$ ________ $= -100$.

The diver should descend ________ feet at each stage.

F Use the process you just learned to find each of the quotients below.

$\frac{14}{-7} =$ ______ $\frac{-36}{-9} =$ ______ $\frac{-55}{11} =$ ______ $\frac{-45}{-5} =$ ______

Reflect

1. **Make a Conjecture** Make a conjecture about the quotient of two integers with different signs. Make a conjecture about the quotient of two integers with the same sign.

____

____

Math On the Spot
my.hrw.com

Dividing Integers

You used the relationship between multiplication and division to make conjectures about the signs of quotients of integers. As with multiplication, the quotient of two integers with different signs is negative, and the quotient of two integers with the same sign is positive.

You can use multiplication to understand why division by zero is not possible. Think about the division problem below and its related multiplication problem.

$$5 \div 0 = ? \qquad 0 \times ? = 5$$

The multiplication sentence says that there is some number times 0 that equals 5. You already know that 0 times any number equals 0. This means division by 0 is not possible, so we say that division by 0 is undefined.

My Notes

EXAMPLE 1

A Divide: $24 \div (-3)$

STEP 1 Determine the sign of the quotient.

24 is positive and -3 is negative. Since the numbers have opposite signs, the quotient will be negative.

STEP 2 Divide.

$24 \div (-3) = -8$

B Divide: $-6 \div (-2)$

STEP 1 Determine the sign of the quotient.

-6 is negative and -2 is negative. Since the numbers have the same sign, the quotient will be positive.

STEP 2 Divide: $-6 \div (-2) = 3$

C Divide: $0 \div (-9)$

STEP 1 Determine the sign of the quotient.

The dividend is 0 and the divisor is not 0. So, the quotient is 0.

STEP 2 Divide: $0 \div (-9) = 0$

Personal Math Trainer
Online Assessment and Intervention
my.hrw.com

YOUR TURN

Find each quotient.

2. $0 \div (-6)$ ______ **3.** $38 \div (-19)$ ______ **4.** $-13 \div (-1)$ ______

Using Integer Division to Solve Problems

You can use integer division to solve real-world problems. For some problems, you may need to perform more than one step. Be sure to check that the sign of the quotient makes sense for the situation.

Math On the Spot
my.hrw.com

EXAMPLE 2 Real World

Jake answers questions in two different online Olympic trivia quizzes. In each quiz, he loses points when he gives an incorrect answer. The table shows the score for each wrong answer in each quiz and Jake's total score for wrong answers in each quiz. In which quiz did he have more wrong answers?

Olympic Trivia Quiz	Score for each wrong answer	Total score for wrong answers
Winter Quiz	−3 points	−33 points
Summer Quiz	−7 points	−56 points

STEP 1 Find the number of incorrect answers Jake gave in the winter quiz.

$-33 \div (-3) = 11$ — *Divide the total score for wrong answers by the score for each wrong answer.*

STEP 2 Find the number of incorrect answers Jake gave in the summer quiz.

$-56 \div (-7) = 8$ — *Divide the total score for wrong answers by the score for each wrong answer.*

STEP 3 Compare the numbers of wrong answers.

$11 > 8$, so Jake had more wrong answers in the winter quiz.

Math Talk
Mathematical Processes

What is the sign of each quotient in Steps 1 and 2? Why does this make sense for the situation?

YOUR TURN

5. A penalty in Meteor-Mania is −5 seconds. A penalty in Cosmic Calamity is −7 seconds. Yolanda had penalties totaling −25 seconds in a game of Meteor-Mania and −35 seconds in a game of Cosmic Calamity. In which game did Yolanda receive more penalties? Justify your answer.

____

____

____

Personal Math Trainer
Online Assessment and Intervention
my.hrw.com

Guided Practice

Find each quotient. (Example 1)

1. $\frac{-14}{2}$ ______
2. $21 \div (-3)$ ______
3. $\frac{26}{-13}$ ______
4. $0 \div (-4)$ ______
5. $\frac{-45}{-5}$ ______
6. $-30 \div (10)$ ______
7. $\frac{-11}{-1}$ ______
8. $-31 \div (-31)$ ______
9. $\frac{0}{-7}$ ______
10. $\frac{-121}{-11}$ ______
11. $84 \div (-7)$ ______
12. $\frac{500}{-25}$ ______
13. $-6 \div (0)$ ______
14. $\frac{-63}{-21}$ ______

Write a division expression for each problem. Then find the value of the expression. (Example 2)

15. Clark made four of his truck payments late and was fined four late fees. The total change to his savings from late fees was −$40. How much was one late fee?

______

16. Jan received −22 points on her exam. She got 11 questions wrong out of 50 questions. How much was Jan penalized for each wrong answer?

______

17. Allen's score in a video game was changed by −75 points because he missed some targets. He got −15 points for each missed target. How many targets did he miss?

______

18. Louisa's savings change by −$9 each time she goes bowling. In all, it changed by −$99 during the summer. How many times did she go bowling in the summer?

______

ESSENTIAL QUESTION CHECK-IN

19. How is the process of dividing integers similar to the process of multiplying integers?

______

______

______

Name ______________________ Class ______________ Date ______________

2.2 Independent Practice

Personal Math Trainer
Online Assessment and Intervention
my.hrw.com

20. Walter buys a bus pass for \$30. Every time he rides the bus, money is deducted from the value of the pass. He rode 12 times and \$24 was deducted from the value of the pass. How much does each bus ride cost? ________

21. **Analyze Relationships** Elisa withdrew \$20 at a time from her bank account and withdrew a total of \$140. Francis withdrew \$45 at a time from his bank account and withdrew a total of \$270. Who made the greater number of withdrawals? Justify your answer.

____

____

____

22. **Multistep** At 7 p.m. last night, the temperature was 10 °F. At 7 a.m. the next morning, the temperature was -2 °F.

a. By how much did the temperature change from 7 p.m. to 7 a.m.?

____

b. The temperature changed by a steady amount overnight. By how much did it change each hour?

____

____

23. **Analyze Relationships** Nola hiked down a trail at a steady rate for 10 minutes. Her change in elevation was -200 feet. Then she continued to hike down for another 20 minutes at a different rate. Her change in elevation for this part of the hike was -300 feet. During which portion of the hike did she walk down at a faster rate? Explain your reasoning.

____

____

____

24. Write a real world description to fit the expression $-50 \div 5$.

____

____

____

25. **Communicate Mathematical Ideas** Two integers, a and b, have different signs. The absolute value of integer a is divisible by the absolute value of integer b. Find two integers that fit this description. Then decide if the product of the integers is greater than or less than the quotient of the integers. Show your work.

____

____

____

Determine if each statement is true or false. Justify your answer.

26. For any two nonzero integers, the product and quotient have the same sign.

____

____

____

27. Any nonzero integer divided by 0 equals 0.

____

____

H.O.T. FOCUS ON HIGHER ORDER THINKING

Work Area

28. **Multi-step** A perfect score on a test with 25 questions is 100. Each question is worth the same number of points.

a. How many points is each question on the test worth? ________

b. Fred got a score of 84 on the test. Write a division sentence using negative numbers where the quotient represents the number of questions Fred answered incorrectly. ________

29. **Persevere in Problem Solving** Colleen divided integer a by -3 and got 8. Then she divided 8 by integer b and got -4. Find the quotient of integer a and integer b. ________

30. **Justify Reasoning** The quotient of two negative integers results in an integer. How does the value of the quotient compare to the value of the original two integers? Explain.

____

____

____

LESSON 2.3

Applying Integer Operations

7.1.2.3

Students will use integer operations to solve real-world problems.

ESSENTIAL QUESTION

How can you use integer operations to solve real-world problems?

EXPLORE ACTIVITY Problem Solving

Using the Order of Operations with Integers

The order of operations applies to integer operations as well as positive number operations. Perform multiplication and division first, and then addition and subtraction. Work from left to right in the expression.

Math On the Spot

my.hrw.com

EXAMPLE 1 **Hannah made four withdrawals of $20 from her checking account. She also wrote a check for $215. By how much did the amount in her checking account change?**

Analyze Information

You need to find the total *change* in Hannah's account. Since withdrawals and writing a check represent a decrease in her account, use negative numbers to represent these amounts.

Formulate a Plan

Write a product to represent the four withdrawals. $-20 + (-20) + (-20) + (-20) = 4(\square)$

Add -215 to represent the check that Hannah wrote. $4(\square) + (\square)$

Solve

Evaluate the expression to find by how much the amount in the account changed.

Multiply first. Then add. $4(-20) - (215) = \square + (-215) = \square$

The amount in the account **increased / decreased** by $ ______.

Justify and Evaluate

The value -295 represents a decrease of 295 dollars. This makes sense, since withdrawals and writing checks remove money from the checking account.

EXPLORE ACTIVITY (cont'd)

YOUR TURN

1. Reggie lost 3 spaceships in level 3 of a video game. He lost 30 points for each spaceship. When he completed level 3, he earned a bonus of 200 points. By how much did his score change?

____

____

2. Simplify: $-6(13) - 21$ _______________

Personal Math Trainer
Online Assessment and Intervention
my.hrw.com

Math On the Spot
my.hrw.com

Using Negative Integers to Represent Quantities

You can use positive and negative integers to solve problems involving amounts that increase or decrease. Sometimes you may need to use more than one operation.

EXAMPLE 2 Real World

Three brothers each have their own savings. They borrow \$72 from their parents for concert tickets. Each brother must pay back an equal share of this amount. Also, the youngest brother owes his parents \$15. By how much will the youngest brother's savings change after he pays his parents?

STEP 1 Determine the signs of the values and the operations you will use. Write an expression.

Since the money is being paid back, it will *decrease* the amount in each brother's savings. Use -72 and -15.

Since an *equal share* of the \$72 will be paid back, use division to determine 3 equal parts of -72. Then add -15 to one of these equal parts.

Change to youngest brother's savings $= (-72) \div 3 + (-15)$

STEP 2 Evaluate the expression.

$(-72) \div 3 + (-15) = -24 + (-15)$ Divide.

$= -39$ Add.

The youngest brother's savings will decrease by \$39.

Math Talk
Mathematical Processes

Suppose the youngest brother has \$60 in savings. How much will he have left after he pays his parents what he owes?

Reflect

3. **What If?** Suppose there were four brothers in Example 2. How much would the youngest brother need to pay?

____

YOUR TURN

Simplify each expression.

4. $(-12) \div 6 + 2$ ________

5. $-87 \div (-3) - 9$ ________

6. $40 \div (-5) + 30$ ________

7. $-39 \div 3 - 15$ ________

Personal Math Trainer
Online Assessment and Intervention
my.hrw.com

Comparing Values of Expressions

Often, problem situations require making comparisons between two values. Use integer operations to calculate values. Then compare the values.

Math On the Spot
my.hrw.com

EXAMPLE 3 Real World

Jill and Tony play a board game in which they move counters along a board. Jill moves her counter back 3 spaces four times, and then moves her counter forward 6 spaces. Tony moves his counter back 2 spaces three times, and then moves his counter forward 3 spaces one time. Find each player's overall change in position. Who moved farther?

STEP 1 Find each player's overall change in position.

Jill: $4(-3) + 6 = -12 + 6 = -6$ *Jill moves back 6 spaces.*

Tony: $3(-2) + 3 = -6 + 3 = -3$ *Tony moves back 3 spaces.*

STEP 2 Compare the numbers of spaces moved by the players.

$|-6| > |-3|$ *Compare absolute values.*

Jill moves farther back than Tony.

Math Talk
Mathematical Processes
Why do you compare absolute values in Step 2?

YOUR TURN

8. Amber and Will are in line together to buy tickets. Amber moves back by 3 places three times to talk to friends. She then is invited to move 5 places up in line. Will moved back by 4 places twice, and then moved up in line by 3 places. Overall, who moved farther back in line?

____

Evaluate each expression. Circle the expression with the greater value.

9. $(-10) \div 2 - 2 =$ ________

$(-28) \div 4 + 1 =$ ________

10. $42 \div (-3) + 9 =$ ________

$(-36) \div 9 - 2 =$ ________

Personal Math Trainer
Online Assessment and Intervention
my.hrw.com

Guided Practice

Evaluate each expression. (Explore Activity Example 1)

1. $-6(-5) + 12$ ______
2. $3(-6) - 3$ ______
3. $-2(8) + 7$ ______
4. $4(-13) + 20$ ______
5. $(-4)(0) - 4$ ______
6. $-3(-5) - 16$ ______

Write an expression to represent the situation. Evaluate the expression and answer the question. (Example 2)

7. Bella pays 7 payments of \$5 each to a game store. She returns one game and receives \$20 back. What is the change to the amount of money she has?

______

8. Ron lost 10 points seven times playing a video game. He then lost an additional 100 points for going over the time limit. What was the total change in his score?

______

9. Ned took a test with 25 questions. He lost 4 points for each of the 6 questions he got wrong and earned an additional 10 points for answering a bonus question correctly. How many points did Ned receive or lose overall?

______

10. Mr. Harris has some money in his wallet. He pays the babysitter \$12 an hour for 4 hours of babysitting. His wife gives him \$10, and he puts the money in his wallet. By how much does the amount in his wallet change?

______

Compare the values of the two expressions using $<$, $=$, or $>$. (Example 3)

11. $-3(-2) + 3$ ______ $3(-4) + 9$
12. $-8(-2) - 20$ ______ $3(-2) + 2$
13. $-7(5) - 9$ ______ $-3(20) + 10$
14. $-16(0) - 3$ ______ $-8(-2) - 3$

ESSENTIAL QUESTION CHECK-IN

15. When you solve a problem involving money, what can a negative answer represent?

______

______

______

Name ________________ Class ________________ Date ________________

2.3 Independent Practice

Personal Math Trainer

Online Assessment and Intervention

my.hrw.com

Evaluate each expression.

16. $-12(-3) + 7$ ________________

17. $-42 \div (-6) + 5 - 8$ ________________

18. $10(-60) - 18$ ________________

19. $(-11)(-7) + 5 - 82$ ________________

20. $35 \div (-7) + 6$ ________________

21. $-13(-2) - 16 - 8$ ________________

22. **Multistep** Lily and Rose are playing a game. In the game, each player starts with 0 points and the player with the most points at the end wins. Lily gains 5 points two times, loses 12 points, and then gains 3 points. Rose loses 3 points two times, loses 1 point, gains 6 points, and then gains 7 points.

a. Write and evaluate an expression to find Lily's score.

____

b. Write and evaluate an expression to find Rose's score.

____

c. Who won the game?

____

Write an expression from the description. Then evaluate the expression.

23. 8 less than the product of 5 and -4

____

24. 9 more than the quotient of -36 and -4.

____

25. **Multistep** Arleen has a gift card for a local lawn and garden store. She uses the gift card to rent a tiller for 4 days. It costs $35 per day to rent the tiller. She also buys a rake for $9.

a. Find the change to the value on her gift card.

____

b. The original amount on the gift card was $200. Does Arleen have enough left on the card to buy a wheelbarrow for $50? Explain.

____

____

26. Carlos made up a game where, in a deck of cards, the red cards (hearts and diamonds) are negative and the black cards (spades and clubs) are positive. All face cards are worth 10 points, and number cards are worth their value.

a. Samantha has a king of hearts, a jack of diamonds, and a 3 of spades. Write an expression to find the value of her cards.

____

b. Warren has a 7 of clubs, a 2 of spades, and a 7 of hearts. Write an expression to find the value of his cards.

____

c. If the greater score wins, who won?

____

d. If a player always gets three cards, describe two different ways to receive a score of 7.

____

____

H.O.T. FOCUS ON HIGHER ORDER THINKING

Work Area

27. **Represent Real-World Problems** Write a problem that the expression $3(-7) - 10 + 25 = -6$ could represent.

____

____

____

28. **Critique Reasoning** Jim found the quotient of two integers and got a positive integer. He added another integer to the quotient and got a positive integer. His sister Kim says that all the integers Jim used to get this result must be positive. Do you agree? Explain.

____

____

____

29. **Persevere in Problem Solving** Lisa is standing on a dock beside a lake. She drops a rock from her hand into the lake. After the rock hits the surface of the lake, the rock's distance from the lake's surface changes at a rate of −5 inches per second. If Lisa holds her hand 5 feet above the lake's surface, how far from Lisa's hand is the rock 4 seconds after it hits the surface?

____

MODULE QUIZ

Ready to Go On?

Personal Math Trainer
Online Assessment and Intervention
my.hrw.com

2.1 Multiplying Integers

Find each product.

1. $(-2)(3)$ ________

2. $(-5)(-7)$ ________

3. $(8)(-11)$ ________

4. $(-3)(2)(-2)$ ________

5. The temperature dropped 3 °C every hour for 5 hours. Write an integer that represents the change in temperature. ________

2.2 Dividing Integers

Find each quotient.

6. $\frac{-63}{7}$ ________

7. $\frac{-15}{-3}$ ________

8. $0 \div (-15)$ ________

9. $96 \div (-12)$ ________

10. An elephant at the zoo lost 24 pounds over 6 months. The elephant lost the same amount of weight each month. Write an integer that represents the change in the elephant's weight each month. ________

2.3 Applying Integer Operations

Evaluate each expression.

11. $(-4)(5) + 8$ ________

12. $(-3)(-6) - 7$ ________

13. $-27 \div 9 - 11$ ________

14. $\frac{-24}{-3} - (-2)$ ________

ESSENTIAL QUESTION

15. Write and solve a real-world problem that can be represented by the expression $(-3)(5) + 10$.

____

____

____

____

MODULE 2 MIXED REVIEW

Assessment Readiness

Personal Math Trainer
my.hrw.com
Online Assessment and Intervention

Selected Response

1. A diver is at an elevation of -18 feet relative to sea level. The diver descends to an undersea cave that is 4 times as far from the surface. What is the elevation of the cave?

   Ⓐ -72 feet
   Ⓑ -22 feet
   Ⓒ -18 feet
   Ⓓ -14 feet

2. The football team lost 4 yards on 2 plays in a row. Which of the following could represent the change in field position?

   Ⓐ -12 yards
   Ⓑ -8 yards
   Ⓒ -6 yards
   Ⓓ -2 yards

3. Clayton climbed down 50 meters. He climbed down in 10-meter intervals. In how many intervals did Clayton make his climb?

   Ⓐ 5
   Ⓑ 10
   Ⓒ 40
   Ⓓ 500

4. Which expression results in a negative answer?

   Ⓐ a negative number divided by a negative number
   Ⓑ a positive number divided by a negative number
   Ⓒ a negative number multiplied by a negative number
   Ⓓ a positive number multiplied by a positive number

5. Clara played a video game before she left the house to go on a walk. She started with 0 points, lost 6 points 3 times, won 4 points, and then lost 2 points. How many points did she have when she left the house to go on the walk?

   Ⓐ -20
   Ⓑ -16
   Ⓒ 12
   Ⓓ 20

6. Which expression is equal to 0?

   Ⓐ $\frac{-24}{6} - 4$
   Ⓑ $\frac{-24}{-6} + 4$
   Ⓒ $\frac{24}{6} + 4$
   Ⓓ $\frac{-24}{-6} - 4$

Mini-Task

7. Rochelle and Denae started with the same amount of money in their bank accounts. Rochelle made three withdrawals of \$25 and then wrote a \$100 check. Denae deposited \$5 and then wrote a \$200 check.

   a. Find the total change in the amount of money in Rochelle's account.

   ____

   b. Find the total change in the amount of money in Denae's account.

   ____

   c. Compare the amounts of money the two women have in their accounts now.

   ____

   ____

   ____

Rational Numbers

MODULE 3

ESSENTIAL QUESTION

How can you use rational numbers to solve real-world problems?

Real-World Video

In many competitive sports, scores are given as decimals. For some events, the judges' scores are averaged to give the athlete's final score.

my.hrw.com

GO DIGITAL
my.hrw.com

my.hrw.com
Go digital with your write-in student edition, accessible on any device.

Math On the Spot
Scan with your smart phone to jump directly to the online edition, video tutor, and more.

Animated Math
Interactively explore key concepts to see how math works.

Personal Math Trainer
Get immediate feedback and help as you work through practice sets.

Reading Start-Up

Visualize Vocabulary

Use the ✔ words to complete the graphic. You can put more than one word in each section of the triangle.

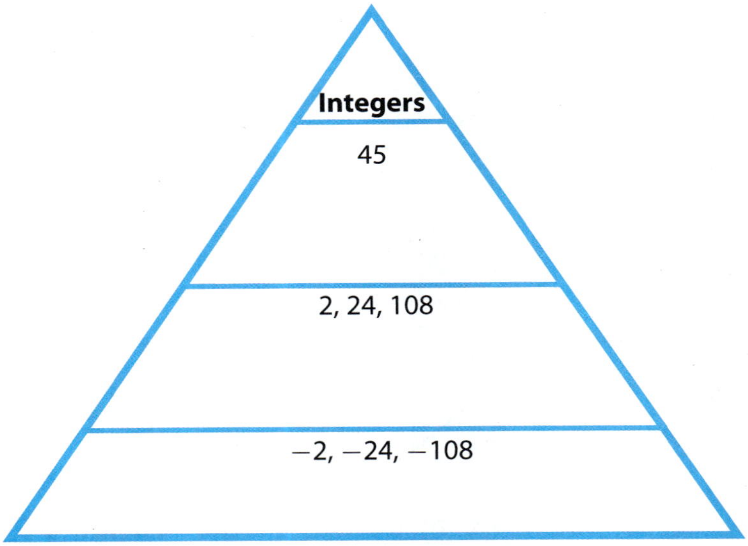

Vocabulary

Review Words

integers *(enteros)*
✔ negative numbers *(números negativos)*
pattern *(patrón)*
✔ positive numbers *(números positivos)*
✔ whole numbers *(números enteros)*

Preview Words

additive inverse *(inverso aditivo)*
opposite *(opuesto)*
rational number *(número racional)*
repeating decimal *(decimal periódico)*
terminating decimal *(decimal finito)*

Understand Vocabulary

Complete the sentences using the preview words.

1. A decimal number for which the decimals come to an end is a

_____________________ decimal.

2. The _____________________ , or ______________, of a number is the same distance from 0 on a number line as the original number, but on the other side of 0.

Active Reading

Layered Book Before beginning the module, create a layered book to help you learn the concepts in this module. At the top of the first flap, write the title of the module, "Rational Numbers." Label the other flaps "Adding," "Subtracting," "Multiplying," and "Dividing." As you study each lesson, write important ideas, such as vocabulary and processes, on the appropriate flap.

Are YOU Ready?

Complete these exercises to review skills you will need for this module.

Personal Math Trainer

my.hrw.com

Online Assessment and Intervention

Multiply Fractions

EXAMPLE $\frac{3}{8} \times \frac{4}{9}$

$\frac{3}{8} \times \frac{4}{9} = \frac{\cancel{3}^{1}}{\cancel{8}_{2}} \times \frac{\cancel{4}^{1}}{\cancel{9}_{3}}$ Divide by the common factors.

$= \frac{1}{6}$ Simplify.

Multiply. Write the product in simplest form.

1. $\frac{9}{14} \times \frac{7}{6}$ ______ **2.** $\frac{3}{5} \times \frac{4}{7}$ ______ **3.** $\frac{11}{8} \times \frac{10}{33}$ ______ **4.** $\frac{4}{9} \times 3$ ______

Operations with Fractions

EXAMPLE $\frac{2}{5} \div \frac{7}{10} = \frac{2}{5} \times \frac{10}{7}$ Multiply by the reciprocal of the divisor.

$= \frac{2}{\cancel{5}_{1}} \times \frac{^{2}\cancel{10}}{7}$ Divide by the common factors.

$= \frac{4}{7}$ Simplify.

Divide.

5. $\frac{1}{2} \div \frac{1}{4}$ ______ **6.** $\frac{3}{8} \div \frac{13}{16}$ ______ **7.** $\frac{2}{5} \div \frac{14}{15}$ ______ **8.** $\frac{4}{9} \div \frac{16}{27}$ ______

9. $\frac{3}{5} \div \frac{5}{6}$ ______ **10.** $\frac{1}{4} \div \frac{23}{24}$ ______ **11.** $6 \div \frac{3}{5}$ ______ **12.** $\frac{4}{5} \div 10$ ______

Order of Operations

EXAMPLE

$50 - 3(3 + 1)^2$ To evaluate, first operate within parentheses.

$50 - 3(4)^2$ Next simplify exponents.

$50 - 3(16)$ Then multiply and divide from left to right.

$50 - 48$ Finally add and subtract from left to right.

2

Evaluate each expression.

13. $21 - 6 \div 3$ ____ **14.** $18 + (7 - 4) \times 3$ ____ **15.** $5 + (8 - 3)^2$ ____

16. $9 + 18 \div 3 + 10$ ____ **17.** $60 - (3 - 1)^4 \times 3$ ____ **18.** $10 - 16 \div 4 \times 2 + 6$ ____

Are YOU Ready? *(cont'd)*

Complete these exercises to review skills you will need for this module.

Multiply Fractions

19. Brittany has a wooden plank that is $\frac{3}{4}$ foot long. She paints $\frac{2}{5}$ of the plank with yellow paint. How long is the part of the plank that is painted yellow? Show your work.

Operations with Fractions

20. To find the quotient $4 \div \frac{2}{5}$, Kim wrote the following. What was his error?

$$4 \div \frac{2}{5} = \frac{1}{4} \times \frac{2}{5}$$

$$= \frac{1}{\cancel{4}_{2}} \times \frac{\cancel{2}^{1}}{5}$$

$$= \frac{1}{10}$$

Order of Operations

21. Zooey says the expressions $6 + (7 + 2)^2$ and $6 + 7^2 + 2^2$ have the same value. Trey says the expressions do **not** have the same value. Who is correct? How do you know?

LESSON 3.1

Rational Numbers and Decimals

7.1.3.1

Students will convert a rational number to a decimal.

ESSENTIAL QUESTION

How can you convert a rational number to a decimal?

EXPLORE ACTIVITY

Describing Decimal Forms of Rational Numbers

A **rational number** is a number that can be written as a ratio of two integers *a* and *b*, where *b* is not zero. For example, $\frac{4}{7}$ is a rational number, as is 0.37 because it can be written as the fraction $\frac{37}{100}$.

A Use a calculator to find the equivalent decimal form of each fraction. Remember that numbers that repeat can be written as 0.333… or $0.\overline{3}$.

Fraction	$\frac{1}{4}$	$\frac{5}{8}$	$\frac{2}{3}$	$\frac{2}{9}$	$\frac{12}{5}$		
Decimal Equivalent						0.2	0.875

B Now find the corresponding fraction of the decimal equivalents given in the last two columns in the table. Write the fractions in simplest form.

C **Conjecture** What do you notice about the digits after the decimal point in the decimal forms of the fractions? Compare notes with your neighbor and refine your conjecture if necessary.

____

Reflect

1. Consider the decimal 0.101001000100001000001…. Do you think this decimal represents a rational number? Why or why not?

____

____

2. Do you think a negative sign affects whether or not a number is a rational number? Use $-\frac{8}{5}$ as an example.

____

____

EXPLORE ACTIVITY *(cont'd)*

3. Do you think a mixed number is a rational number? Explain.

____

____

____

Math On the Spot
my.hrw.com

Writing Rational Numbers as Decimals

You can convert a rational number to a decimal using long division. Some decimals are **terminating decimals** because the decimals come to an end. Other decimals are **repeating decimals** because one or more digits repeat infinitely.

EXAMPLE 1

Write each rational number as a decimal.

A $\frac{5}{16}$

Divide 5 by 16.
Add a zero after the decimal point.
Subtract 48 from 50.
Use the grid to help you complete the long division.

Add zeros in the dividend and continue dividing until the remainder is 0.

The decimal equivalent of $\frac{5}{16}$ is 0.3125.

		0.	3	1	2	5	
1	6)	5.	0	0	0	0	
		−4	8				
			2	0			
			−1	6			
				4	0		
				−3	2		
					8	0	
					−8	0	
						0	

B $\frac{13}{33}$

Divide 13 by 33.
Add a zero after the decimal point.
Subtract 99 from 130.
Use the grid to help you complete the long division.

You can stop dividing once you discover a repeating pattern in the quotient.

Write the quotient with its repeating pattern and indicate that the repeating numbers continue.

The decimal equivalent of $\frac{13}{33}$ is 0.3939…, or $0.\overline{39}$.

			0.	3	9	3	9	
3	3)	1	3.	0	0	0	0	
			−9	9				
			3	1	0			
			−2	9	7			
				1	3	0		
					−9	9		
					3	1	0	
					−2	9	7	
						1	3	

Math Talk
Mathematical Processes

Do you think that decimals that have repeating patterns always have the same number of digits in their pattern? Explain.

YOUR TURN

Write each rational number as a decimal.

4. $\frac{4}{7}$ ________ **5.** $\frac{1}{3}$ ________ **6.** $\frac{9}{20}$ ________

Personal Math Trainer
Online Assessment and Intervention
my.hrw.com

Writing Mixed Numbers as Decimals

You can convert a mixed number to a decimal by rewriting the fractional part of the number as a decimal.

Math On the Spot
my.hrw.com

EXAMPLE 2 Real World

Shawn rode his bike $6\frac{3}{4}$ miles to the science museum. Write $6\frac{3}{4}$ as a decimal.

My Notes

STEP 1 Rewrite the fractional part of the number as a decimal.

$$\begin{array}{r} 0.75 \\ 4\overline{)3.00} \\ -28 \\ \hline 20 \\ -20 \\ \hline 0 \end{array}$$

Divide the numerator by the denominator.

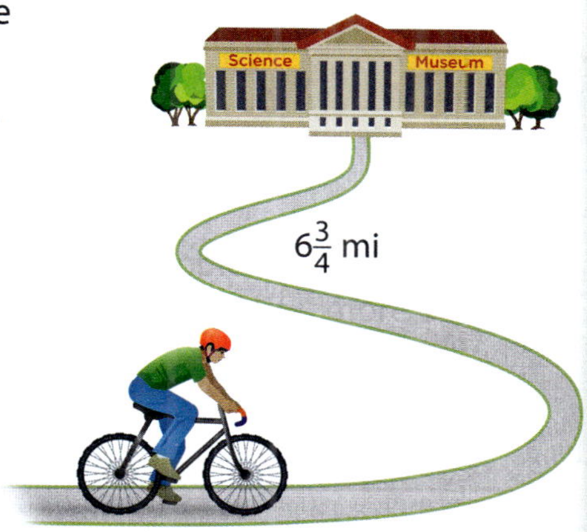

STEP 2 Rewrite the mixed number as the sum of the whole part and the decimal part.

$$6\frac{3}{4} = 6 + \frac{3}{4}$$
$$= 6 + 0.75$$
$$= 6.75$$

YOUR TURN

7. Yvonne made $2\frac{3}{4}$ quarts of punch. Write $2\frac{3}{4}$ as a decimal. $2\frac{3}{4} =$ ________

Is the decimal equivalent a terminating or repeating decimal?

____

8. Yvonne bought a watermelon that weighed $7\frac{1}{3}$ pounds. Write $7\frac{1}{3}$ as a decimal. $7\frac{1}{3} =$ ________________________________

Is the decimal equivalent a terminating or repeating decimal?

____

Personal Math Trainer
Online Assessment and Intervention
my.hrw.com

Guided Practice

Write each rational number as a decimal. Then tell whether each decimal is a terminating or a repeating decimal. (Explore Activity and Example 1)

1. $\frac{3}{5}=$ ____________

2. $\frac{89}{100}=$ ____________

3. $\frac{4}{12}=$ ____________

4. $\frac{25}{99}=$ ____________

5. $\frac{7}{9}=$ ____________

6. $\frac{9}{25}=$ ____________

7. $\frac{1}{25}=$ ____________

8. $\frac{25}{176}=$ ____________

9. $\frac{12}{1{,}000}=$ ____________

Write each mixed number as a decimal. (Example 2)

10. $11\frac{1}{6}=$ ____________

11. $2\frac{9}{10}=$ ____________

12. $8\frac{23}{100}=$ ____________

13. $7\frac{3}{15}=$ ____________

14. $54\frac{3}{11}=$ ____________

15. $3\frac{1}{18}=$ ____________

16. Maggie bought $3\frac{2}{3}$ lb of apples to make some apple pies. What is the weight of the apples written as a decimal? (Example 2)

$3\frac{2}{3}=$ ____________

17. Harry's dog weighs $12\frac{7}{8}$ pounds. What is the weight of Harry's dog written as a decimal? (Example 2)

$12\frac{7}{8}=$ ____________

ESSENTIAL QUESTION CHECK-IN

18. Tom is trying to write $\frac{3}{47}$ as a decimal. He used long division and divided until he got the quotient 0.0638297872, at which point he stopped. Since the decimal doesn't seem to terminate or repeat, he concluded that $\frac{3}{47}$ is not rational. Do you agree or disagree? Why?

____

Name ______________________ Class ______________ Date ____________

3.1 Independent Practice

Personal Math Trainer
Online Assessment and Intervention
my.hrw.com

Use the table for 19–23. Write each ratio in the form $\frac{a}{b}$ and then as a decimal. Tell whether each decimal is a terminating or a repeating decimal.

Team Sports	
Sport	**Number of Players**
Baseball	9
Basketball	5
Football	11
Hockey	6
Lacrosse	10
Polo	4
Rugby	15
Soccer	11

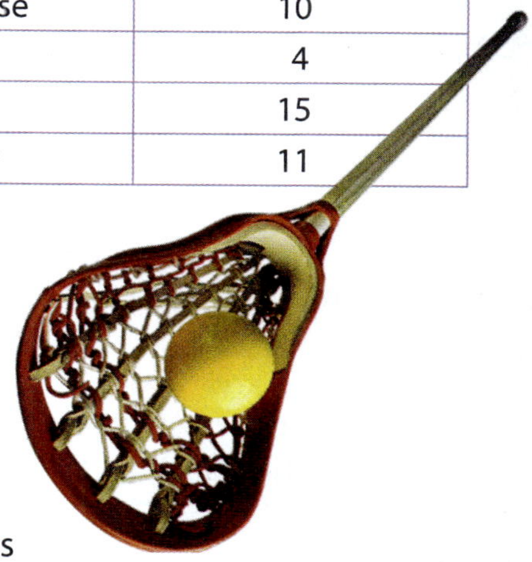

19. basketball players to football players

____

20. hockey players to lacrosse players

____

21. polo players to football players

____

22. lacrosse players to rugby players

____

23. football players to soccer players

____

24. **Look for a Pattern** Beth said that the ratio of the number of players in any sport to the number of players on a lacrosse team must always be a terminating decimal. Do you agree or disagree? Why?

____

____

____

____

25. Yvonne bought $4\frac{7}{8}$ yards of material to make a dress.

a. What is $4\frac{7}{8}$ written as an improper fraction? ____________

b. What is $4\frac{7}{8}$ written as a decimal? ____________

c. **Communicate Mathematical Ideas** If Yvonne wanted to make 3 dresses that use $4\frac{7}{8}$ yd of fabric each, explain how she could use estimation to make sure she has enough fabric for all of them.

____

____

____

26. **Vocabulary** A rational number can be written as the ratio of one ________________ to another and can be represented by a repeating or ________________ decimal.

Work Area

27. **Problem Solving** Marcus is $5\frac{7}{24}$ feet tall. Ben is $5\frac{5}{16}$ feet tall. Which of the two boys is taller? Justify your answer.

____

28. **Represent Real-World Problems** If one store is selling $\frac{3}{4}$ of a bushel of apples for \$9, and another store is selling $\frac{2}{3}$ of a bushel of apples for \$9, which store has the better deal? Explain your answer.

____

____

____

____

H.O.T. FOCUS ON HIGHER ORDER THINKING

29. **Analyze Relationships** You are given a fraction in simplest form. The numerator is not zero. When you write the fraction as a decimal, it is a repeating decimal. Which numbers from 1 to 10 could be the denominator?

____

____

30. **Communicate Mathematical Ideas** Julie got 21 of the 23 questions on her math test correct. She got 29 of the 32 questions on her science test correct. On which test did she get a higher score? Can you compare the fractions $\frac{21}{23}$ and $\frac{29}{32}$ by comparing 29 and 21? Explain. How can Julie compare her scores?

____

____

____

____

31. **Look for a Pattern** Look at the decimal 0.121122111222.... If the pattern continues, is this a repeating decimal? Explain.

____

____

____

LESSON 3.2

Adding Rational Numbers

7.1.3.2

Students will add rational numbers.

ESSENTIAL QUESTION

How can you add rational numbers?

EXPLORE ACTIVITY Real World

Adding Rational Numbers with the Same Sign

Math On the Spot
my.hrw.com

Previously, you used an arrow for each addend to add integers on a number line. You can also use a point for the first addend and movement in a positive or negative direction to represent adding the second addend.

EXAMPLE 1 **Use a number line to solve each problem.**

A **Malachi hikes for 2.5 miles and stops for lunch. Then he hikes for 1.5 more miles. How many miles did he hike altogether?**

Move right on a horizontal number line to add a positive number. Move left to add a negative number.

STEP 1 Use positive numbers to represent the distance Malachi hiked.

STEP 2 Find 2.5 + ______.

STEP 3 Start at ______.

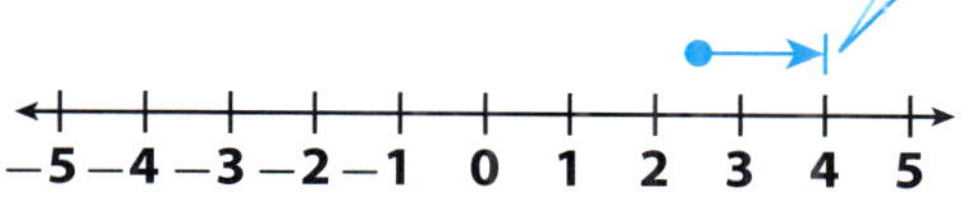

STEP 4 The second addend is *positive*. Move 1.5 units to the ______.

The result is ______. Malachi hiked ______ miles.

B **Kyle pours out $\frac{3}{4}$ liter of liquid from a beaker. Then he pours out another $\frac{1}{2}$ liter of liquid. What is the overall change in the amount of liquid in the beaker?**

STEP 1 Use negative numbers to represent the amount of change each time Kyle pours liquid from the beaker.

STEP 2 Find ☐ + (☐).

STEP 3 Start at ______.

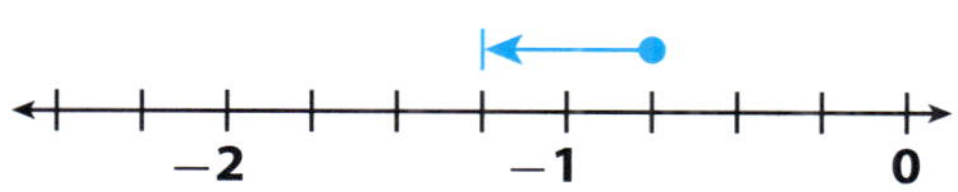

STEP 4 The second addend is negative. Move $\left|-\frac{1}{2}\right| = \frac{1}{2}$ unit to the left.

The result is ______.

The amount of liquid in the beaker has decreased by ______ liters.

EXPLORE ACTIVITY *(cont'd)*

Reflect

1. What do you notice about the signs of the sums and the signs of the addends in parts **A** and **B**?

____

____

YOUR TURN

Use a number line to find each sum.

2. $3 + 1\frac{1}{2} =$ ________

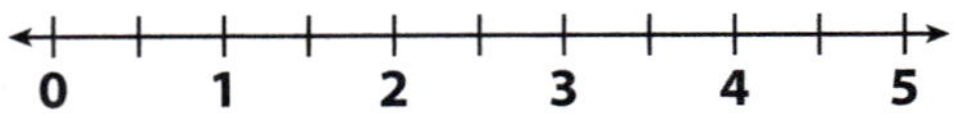

3. $-2.5 + (-4.5) =$ ________

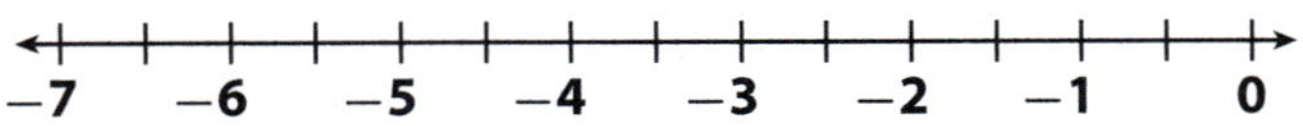

Personal Math Trainer
Online Assessment and Intervention
my.hrw.com

Math On the Spot
my.hrw.com

Adding Rational Numbers with Different Signs

You can also use a number line to add rational numbers with different signs. You start at the first number and move in the positive or negative direction by the absolute value of the second number, according to its sign.

EXAMPLE 2 Real World

A **During the day, the temperature increases by 4.5 degrees. At night, the temperature decreases by 7.5 degrees. What is the overall change in temperature?**

STEP 1 Use a positive number to represent the increase in temperature and a negative number to represent a decrease in temperature.

STEP 2 Find $4.5 + (-7.5)$.

STEP 3 Start at 4.5.

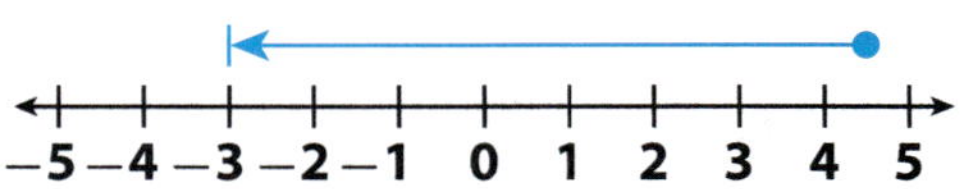

STEP 4 Move $|-7.5| = 7.5$ units to the *left* because the second addend is *negative*.

The result is -3.

The temperature decreased by 3 degrees overall.

Math Talk
Mathematical Processes
How can you tell that the answer is reasonable?

B **Ernesto writes a check for $2.50. Then he deposits $6 in his checking account. What is the overall increase or decrease in the account balance?**

STEP 1 Use a positive number to represent a deposit and a negative number to represent a withdrawal or a check.

STEP 2 Find $-2.5 + 6$.

STEP 3 Start at -2.5.

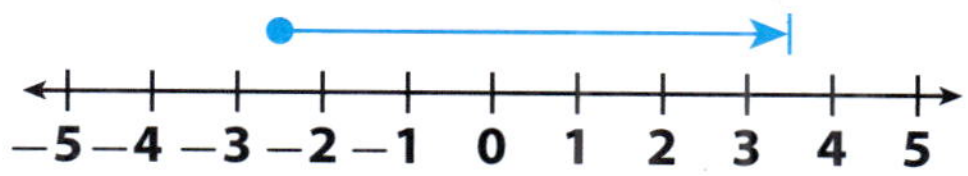

STEP 4 Move $|6| = 6$ units to the *right* because the second addend is *positive*.

The result is 3.5. The account balance will increase by $3.50.

Reflect

4. Do $-3 + 2$ and $2 + (-3)$ have the same sum? Does it matter if the negative number is the first addend or the second addend?

____

____

____

5. **Make a Conjecture** To add integers with different signs, you subtract the lesser absolute value from the greater absolute value and use the sign of the integer with the greater absolute value. Make a conjecture about adding any two rational numbers that have different signs. Explain using parts **A** and **B**.

____

____

____

____

YOUR TURN

Use a number line to find each sum.

6. $-8 + 5 =$ ________

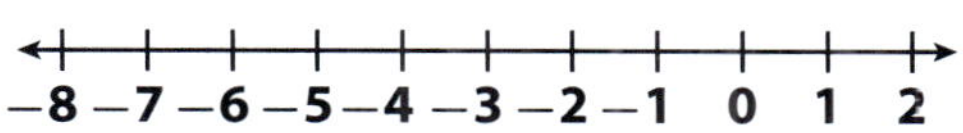

7. $\frac{1}{2} + \left(-\frac{3}{4}\right) =$ ________

8. $-1 + 7 =$ ________

Animated Math
my.hrw.com

My Notes

Personal Math Trainer
Online Assessment and Intervention
my.hrw.com

Math On the Spot
my.hrw.com

Additive Inverses of Rational Numbers

The opposite, or additive inverse, of a number is the same distance from 0 on a number line as the original number, but on the other side of 0. Recall the Inverse Property of Addition from your work with integers: The sum of a number and its additive inverse is 0. Zero is its own additive inverse.

EXAMPLE 3 Real World

A **A football team loses 3.5 yards on its first play. On the next play, it gains 3.5 yards. What is the overall increase or decrease in yards?**

STEP 1 Use a positive number to represent the gain in yards and a negative number to represent the loss in yards.

STEP 2 Find $-3.5 + 3.5$.

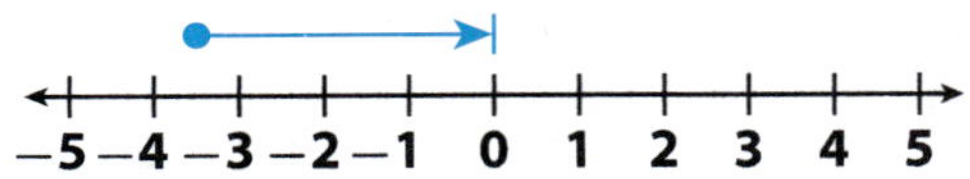

STEP 3 Start at -3.5.

STEP 4 Move $|3.5| = 3.5$ units to the *right*, because the second addend is *positive*.

The result is 0. This means the overall change is 0 yards.

B **Kendrick adds $\frac{3}{4}$ cup of broth to a pot. Then he removes $\frac{3}{4}$ cup. What is the overall increase or decrease in the amount of broth in the pot?**

STEP 1 Use a positive number to represent broth added to the pot and a negative number to represent broth removed from the pot.

STEP 2 Find $\frac{3}{4} + \left(-\frac{3}{4}\right)$.

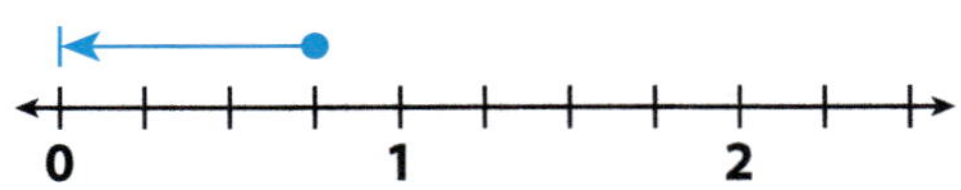

STEP 3 Start at $\frac{3}{4}$.

STEP 4 Move $\left|-\frac{3}{4}\right| = \frac{3}{4}$ units to the *left* because the second addend is *negative*.

The result is 0. This means the overall change is 0 cups.

Math Talk Mathematical Processes

Explain how to use a number line to find the additive inverse, or opposite, of -3.5.

My Notes

YOUR TURN

Use a number line to find each sum.

9. $2\frac{1}{2} + \left(-2\frac{1}{2}\right) =$ ________

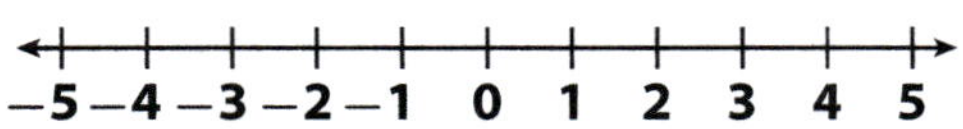

10. $-4.5 + 4.5 =$ ________

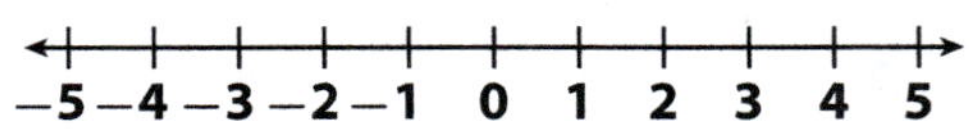

Personal Math Trainer
Online Assessment and Intervention
my.hrw.com

Adding Rational Numbers Using Rules

As you have seen in this lesson, the rules for adding integers also apply to adding rational numbers that are not integers.

Same signs: Add the absolute value of the numbers. Use the common sign for the sum.

Different signs: Subtract the lesser absolute value from the greater absolute value. Use the sign of the number with the greater absolute value.

Math On the Spot
my.hrw.com

EXAMPLE 4 Real World

Tina spent \$5.25 on craft supplies to make friendship bracelets. She made \$3.75 on Monday. On Tuesday, she sold an additional \$4.50 worth of bracelets. What was Tina's overall profit or loss?

Profit means the difference between income and costs is positive.

STEP 1 Use *negative* numbers to represent the amount Tina *spent* and *positive* numbers to represent the money Tina *earned*.

STEP 2 Find $-5.25 + 3.75 + 4.50$.

STEP 3 Group numbers with the same sign.

$-5.25 + (3.75 + 4.50)$ Associative Property of Addition

STEP 4 $-5.25 + 8.25$ Add the numbers inside the parentheses.

Find the difference of the absolute values: $8.25 - 5.25$.

3 Use the sign of the number with the greater absolute value. The sum is positive.

Tina earned a profit of \$3.00.

YOUR TURN

Find each sum.

11. $-1.5 + 3.5 + 2 =$ ______

12. $3\frac{1}{4} + (-2) + \left(-2\frac{1}{4}\right) =$ ______

13. $-2.75 + (-3.25) + 5 =$ ______

14. $15 + 8 + (-3) =$ ______

Personal Math Trainer
Online Assessment and Intervention
my.hrw.com

Guided Practice

Use a number line to find each sum. (Explore Activity Example 1 and Example 2)

1. $-3 + (-1.5) =$ __________

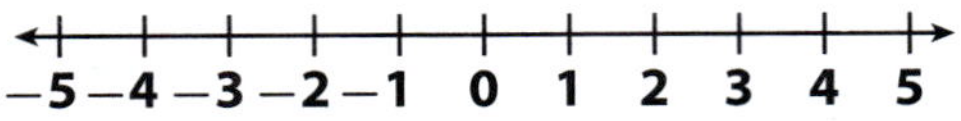

2. $1.5 + 3.5 =$ __________

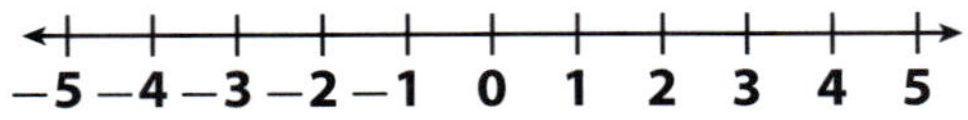

3. $\frac{1}{4} + \frac{1}{2} =$ __________

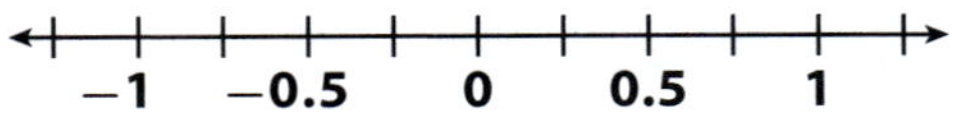

4. $-1\frac{1}{2} + \left(-1\frac{1}{2}\right) =$ __________

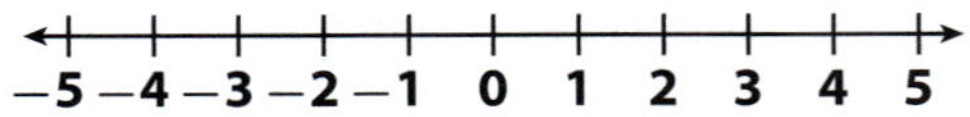

5. $3 + (-5) =$ __________

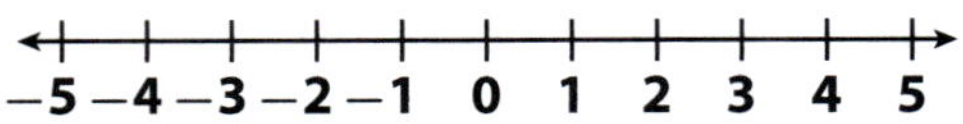

6. $-1.5 + 4 =$ __________

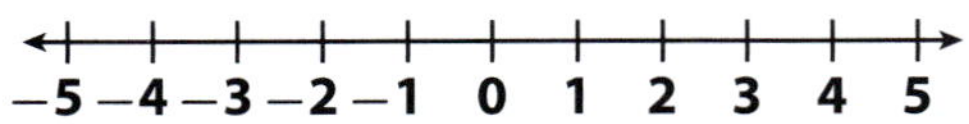

7. Victor borrowed $21.50 from his mother to go to the theater. A week later, he paid her $21.50 back. How much does he still owe her? (Example 3)

____

8. Sandra used her debit card to buy lunch for $8.74 on Monday. On Tuesday, she deposited $8.74 back into her account. What is the overall increase or decrease in her bank account? (Example 3)

____

Find each sum without using a number line. (Example 4)

9. $2.75 + (-2) + (-5.25) =$ __________

10. $-3 + \left(1\frac{1}{2}\right) + \left(2\frac{1}{2}\right) =$ __________

11. $-12.4 + 9.2 + 1 =$ __________

12. $-12 + 8 + 13 =$ __________

13. $4.5 + (-12) + (-4.5) =$ __________

14. $\frac{1}{4} + \left(-\frac{3}{4}\right) =$ __________

15. $-4\frac{1}{2} + 2 =$ __________

16. $-8 + \left(-1\frac{1}{8}\right) =$ __________

ESSENTIAL QUESTION CHECK-IN

17. How can you use a number line to find the sum of −4 and 6?

____

____

Name ______________________ Class ______________ Date ____________

3.2 Independent Practice

Personal Math Trainer
my.hrw.com
Online Assessment and Intervention

18. Samuel walks forward 19 steps. He represents this movement with a positive 19. How would he represent the opposite of this number? ____________

19. Julia spends \$2.25 on gas for her lawn mower. She earns \$15.00 mowing her neighbor's yard. What is Julia's profit? ____________

20. A submarine submerged at a depth of −35.25 meters dives an additional 8.5 meters. What is the new depth of the submarine? ____________

21. Renee hiked for $4\frac{3}{4}$ miles. After resting, Renee hiked back along the same route for $3\frac{1}{4}$ miles. How many more miles does Renee need to hike to return to the place where she started? ____________

22. **Geography** The average elevation of the city of New Orleans, Louisiana, is 0.5 m below sea level. The highest point in Louisiana is Driskill Mountain at about 163.5 m higher than New Orleans. How high is Driskill Mountain? ____________

23. **Problem Solving** A contestant on a game show has 30 points. She answers a question correctly to win 15 points. Then she answers a question incorrectly and loses 25 points. What is the contestant's final score?

____

Financial Literacy **Use the table for 24–26. Kameh owns a bakery. He recorded the bakery income and expenses in a table.**

Month	Income (\$)	Expenses (\$)
January	1,205	1,290.60
February	1,183	1,345.44
March	1,664	1,664.00
June	2,413	2,106.23
July	2,260	1,958.50
August	2,183	1,845.12

24. In which months were the expenses greater than the income? Name the month and find how much money was lost. ____________________

25. In which months was the income greater than the expenses? Name the months and find how much money was gained.

____

26. **Communicate Mathematical Ideas** If the bakery started with an extra \$250 from the profits in December, describe how to use the information in the table to figure out the profit or loss of money at the bakery by the end of August. Then calculate the profit or loss.

____

____

____

____

27. **Vocabulary** -2.9 is the ______________________ of 2.9.

28. The basketball coach made up a game to play where each player takes 10 shots at the basket. For every basket made, the player gains 10 points. For every basket missed, the player loses 15 points.

a. The player with the highest score sank 7 baskets and missed 3. What was the highest score?

____

b. The player with the lowest score sank 2 baskets and missed 8. What was the lowest score?

____

c. Write an expression using addition to find the score for a player who sank 5 baskets and missed 5 baskets. Interpret the result.

____

____

Work Area

H.O.T. FOCUS ON HIGHER ORDER THINKING

29. **Represent Real-World Problems** Write and solve a real-world addition problem involving the sum of a rational number and its additive inverse.

____

____

30. **Communicate Mathematical Ideas** Explain the different ways it is possible to add two rational numbers and get a negative number.

____

____

____

____

31. **Explain the Error** A student evaluated $-4 + x$ for $x = -9\frac{1}{2}$ and got an answer of $5\frac{1}{2}$. What might the student have done wrong?

____

____

32. **Draw Conclusions** How can you use mental math and the Inverse Property of Addition to find the sum $[5.5 + (-2.3)] + (-5.5 + 2.3)$?

____

____

LESSON 3.3
Subtracting Rational Numbers

7.1.3.3

Students will subtract rational numbers.

ESSENTIAL QUESTION

How do you subtract rational numbers?

EXPLORE ACTIVITY Real World

Math On the Spot
my.hrw.com

Subtracting Positive Rational Numbers

Recall that, on a horizontal number line, the positive direction is to the right, and the negative direction is to the left. On a vertical number line, the positive direction is up, and the negative direction is down.

You can use subtraction of a positive number to represent a decrease. To subtract a positive rational number on a number line, start at the first number and move in the negative direction.

EXAMPLE 1 **The temperature on a thermometer on Monday was 3.5 °C. The temperature on Thursday was 5.25 degrees less than the temperature on Monday. What was the temperature on Thursday?**

Subtract to find the temperature on Thursday.

STEP 1 Find 3.5 − ________.

STEP 2 Start at ________.

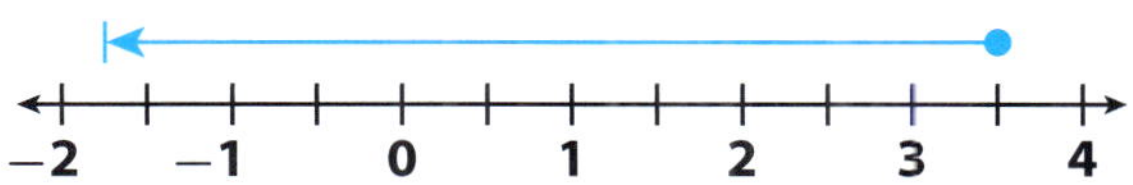

STEP 3 You are subtracting a positive number. Move |5.25| = 5.25 units to the ________.

The result is ________. The temperature on Thursday was ________ °C.

YOUR TURN

Use a number line to find each difference.

1. −6.5 − 2 = ______

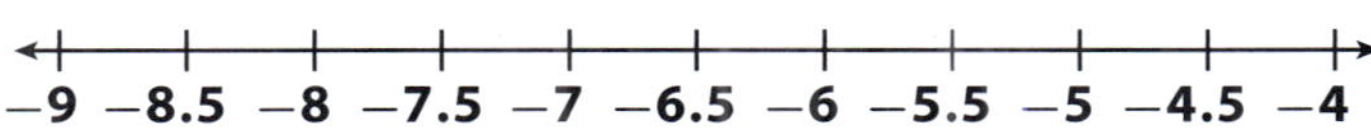

2. $1\frac{1}{2} - 2 =$ ________

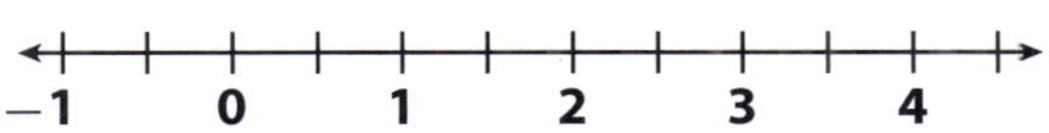

3. −2.25 − 5.5 = ______

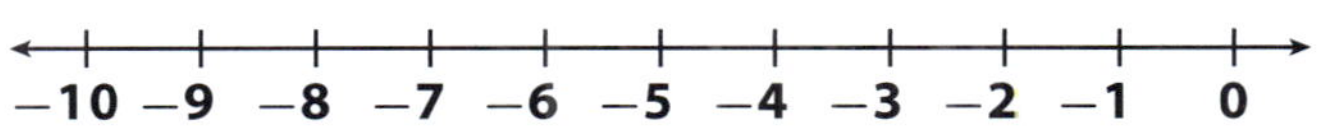

Personal Math Trainer
Online Assessment and Intervention
my.hrw.com

Subtracting Negative Rational Numbers

Math On the Spot
my.hrw.com

Subtracting a positive rational number is represented on a number line by movement in the *negative* direction. Subtracting a negative rational number is represented by movement in the opposite or *positive* direction.

EXAMPLE 2 Real World

During the hottest week of the summer, the water level of the Muskrat River was $\frac{5}{6}$ foot below normal. The following week, the level was $\frac{1}{3}$ foot below normal. What was the overall change in the water level?

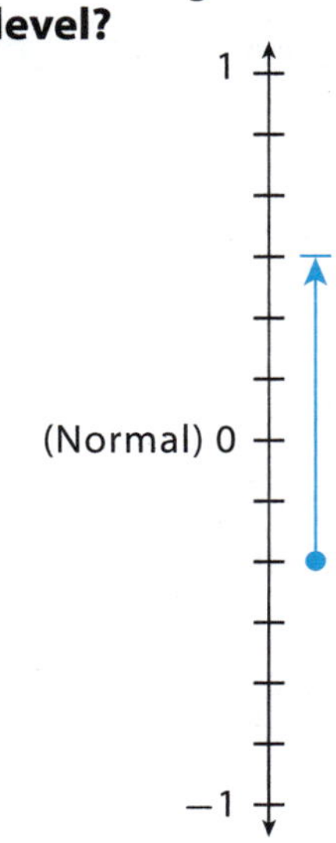

Subtract to find the difference in water levels.

STEP 1 Find $-\frac{1}{3} - \left(-\frac{5}{6}\right)$.

STEP 2 Start at $-\frac{1}{3}$.

STEP 3 Move $\left|-\frac{5}{6}\right| = \frac{5}{6}$ unit up because you are subtracting a *negative* number.

The result is $\frac{1}{2}$.

So, the water level increased by $\frac{1}{2}$ foot.

Math Talk
Mathematical Processes

How do you know the correct order for subtracting the numbers?

Reflect

4. Work with other students to compare addition of negative numbers on a number line to subtraction of negative numbers on a number line.

____

____

5. To subtract integers, you rewrote the difference as the sum of the first integer and the opposite of the second, and used the rules for adding integers. Apply the same method to the Activity and the Example. What do you notice?

____

____

YOUR TURN

Use a number line to find each difference.

6. $0.25 - (-1.50) =$ __________

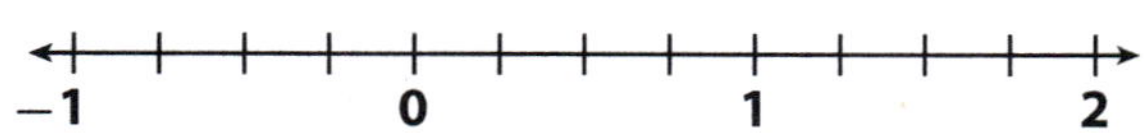

7. $-\frac{1}{2} - \left(-\frac{3}{4}\right) =$ ______

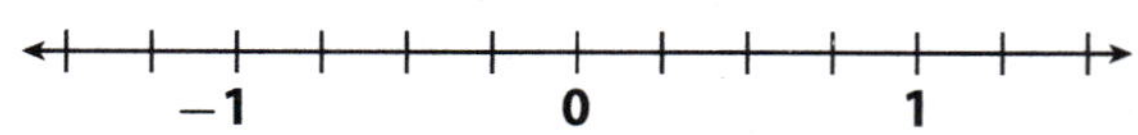

Personal Math Trainer
Online Assessment and Intervention
my.hrw.com

EXPLORE ACTIVITY 2 Real World

Adding the Opposite

Joe is diving $2\frac{1}{2}$ feet below sea level. He decides to descend $7\frac{1}{2}$ more feet. How many feet below sea level is he?

STEP 1 Use negative numbers to represent the number of feet below sea level.

STEP 2 Find $-2\frac{1}{2} - 7\frac{1}{2}$.

STEP 3 Start at $-2\frac{1}{2}$.

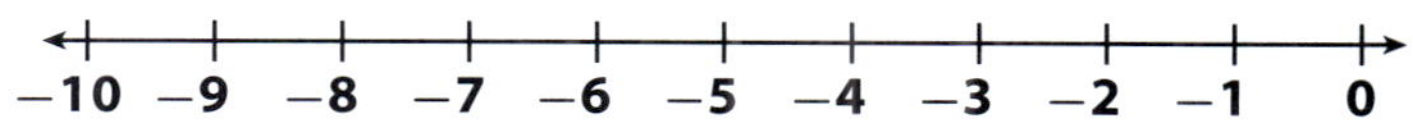

STEP 4 Move $\left|7\frac{1}{2}\right| = 7\frac{1}{2}$ units to the ____________

because you are subtracting a ____________ number.

The result is -10.

Joe is ____________ sea level.

You move left on a horizontal number line to add a negative number. You move the same direction to subtract a positive number.

Reflect

8. Use a number line to find each difference or sum.

a. $-3 - 3 =$ ________

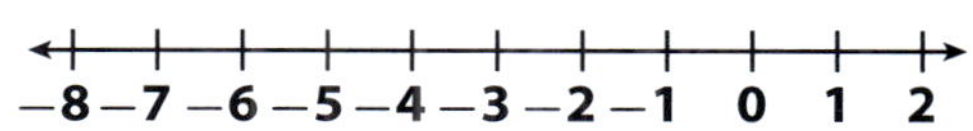

b. $-3 + (-3) =$ ________

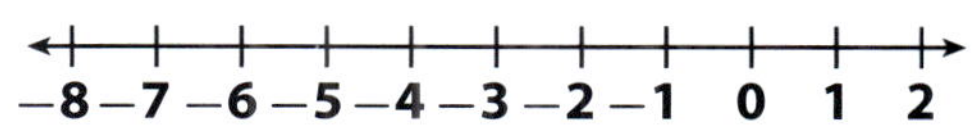

9. **Make a Conjecture** Work with other students to make a conjecture about how to change a subtraction problem into an addition problem.

____

____

____

Math Talk
Mathematical Processes
Compare the results from **8a** and **8b**.

Adding the Opposite

To subtract a number, add its opposite. This can also be written as $p - q = p + (-q)$.

You can use this property to subtract rational numbers. Rewrite subtracting a number as adding its opposite, or additive inverse.

EXPLORE ACTIVITY 3 Real World

Finding the Distance Between Two Numbers

A cave explorer climbed from an elevation of -11 meters to an elevation of -5 meters. What vertical distance did the explorer climb?

There are two ways to find the vertical distance.

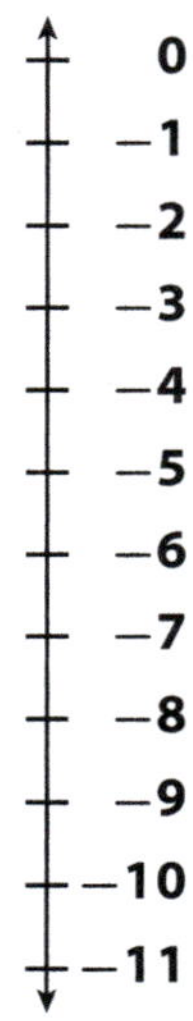

A Graph the numbers ________ and ________ as points on the number line to represent the elevations. Count the number of units between them.

The explorer climbed ________ meters.

This means that the vertical distance between

-11 meters and -5 meters is ________ meters.

B Find the difference between the two elevations and use absolute value to find the distance.

$-11 - (-5) =$ ________

Take the absolute value of the difference because distance traveled is always a nonnegative number.

$|-11 - (-5)| =$ ________

The vertical distance is ________meters.

Reflect

10. Does it matter which way you subtract the values when finding distance? Explain.

____

____

11. Would the same methods work if both the numbers were positive? What if one of the numbers were positive and the other negative?

____

Distance Between Two Numbers

The distance between two values a and b on a number line is represented by the absolute value of the difference of a and b.

Distance between a and $b = |a - b|$ or $|b - a|$.

Guided Practice

Use a number line to find each difference.
(Explore Activity Example 1, Example 2, and Explore Activity 3)

1. $5 - (-8) =$ ________

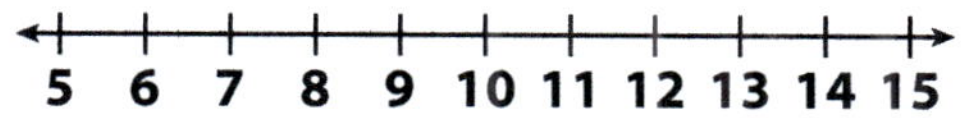

2. $-3\frac{1}{2} - 4\frac{1}{2} =$ ________

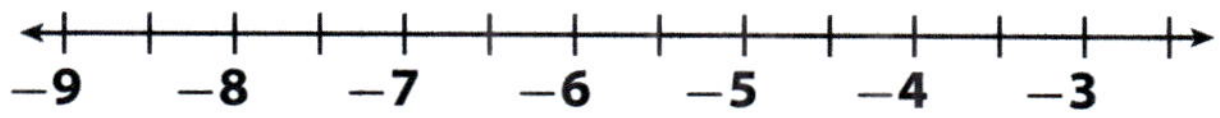

3. $-7 - 4 =$ ________

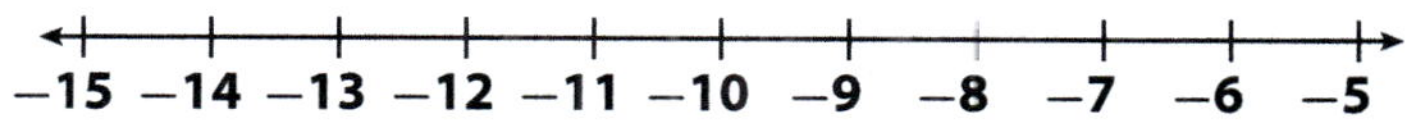

4. $-0.5 - 3.5 =$ ________

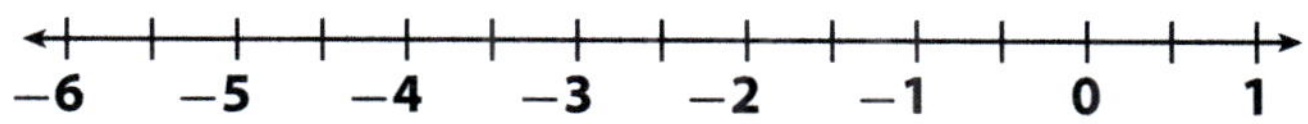

Find each difference. (Explore Activity 2)

5. $-14 - 22 =$ ________

6. $-12.5 - (-4.8) =$ ________

7. $\frac{1}{3} - \left(-\frac{2}{3}\right) =$ ________

8. $65 - (-14) =$ ________

9. $-\frac{2}{9} - (-3) =$ ________

10. $24\frac{3}{8} - \left(-54\frac{1}{8}\right) =$ ________

11. A girl is snorkeling 1 meter below sea level and then dives down another 0.5 meter. How far below sea level is the girl? (Explore Activity 2) ________

12. The first play of a football game resulted in a loss of $12\frac{1}{2}$ yards. Then a penalty resulted in another loss of 5 yards. What is the total loss or gain? (Explore Activity 2) ________

13. A climber starts descending from 533 feet above sea level and keeps going until she reaches 10 feet below sea level. How many feet did she descend? (Explore Activity 2) ________

14. Write two absolute-value expressions for the distance between −7 and 5 on a number line. Then give the distance between the numbers. (Explore Activity 3) ________ ________

ESSENTIAL QUESTION CHECK-IN

15. Mandy is trying to subtract 4 − 12, and she has asked you for help. How would you explain the process of solving the problem to Mandy, using a number line?

____

____

____

Name __________ Class __________ Date __________

3.3 Independent Practice

Personal Math Trainer
Online Assessment and Intervention
my.hrw.com

16. **Science** At the beginning of a laboratory experiment, the temperature of a substance is −12.6 °C. During the experiment, the temperature of the substance decreases 7.5 °C. What is the final temperature of the substance?

____

17. A diver went 25.65 feet below the surface of the ocean, and then 16.5 feet further down, he then rose 12.45 feet. Write and solve an expression to find the diver's new depth.

____

____

18. A city known for its temperature extremes started the day at −5 degrees Fahrenheit. The temperature increased by 78 degrees Fahrenheit by midday, and then dropped 32 degrees by nightfall.

a. What expression can you write to find the temperature at nightfall? __________

b. What expression can you write to describe the overall change in temperature? *Hint*: Do not include the temperature at the beginning of the day since you only want to know about how much the temperature changed. __________

c. What is the final temperature at nightfall? What is the overall change in temperature? __________

19. **Financial Literacy** On Monday, your bank account balance was −\$12.58. Because you didn't realize this, you wrote a check for \$30.72 for groceries.

a. What is the new balance in your checking account? __________

b. The bank charges a \$25 fee for paying a check on a negative balance. What is the balance in your checking account after this fee? __________

c. How much money do you need to deposit to bring your account balance back up to \$0 after the fee? __________

Astronomy **Use the table for problems 20–21.**

20. How much deeper is the deepest canyon on Mars than the deepest canyon on Venus?

____

Elevations on Planets

	Lowest (ft)	Highest (ft)
Earth	−36,198	29,035
Mars	−26,000	70,000
Venus	−9,500	35,000

21. **Persevere in Problem Solving** What is the difference between Earth's highest mountain and its deepest ocean canyon? What is the difference between Mars's highest mountain and its deepest canyon? Which difference is greater? How much greater is it?

____

22. Pamela is making the legs for a three-legged stool from two pieces of scrap wood. The lengths of the two pieces of wood are $36\frac{5}{8}$ inches and $21\frac{1}{8}$ inches. Each leg is $16\frac{1}{2}$ inches long.

    a. Pamela cuts one leg from each piece of wood. Write and evaluate two expressions to show how much of each piece of wood is left over.

    ____

    b. Will Pamela have enough wood for a third leg? Explain.

    ____

    ____

23. Jeremy is practicing some tricks on his skateboard. One trick takes him forward 5 feet, then he flips around and moves backward 7.2 feet, and then he moves forward again for 2.2 feet.

    a. What expression could be used to find how far Jeremy is from his starting position when he finishes the trick?

    ____

    b. How far from his starting point is he when he finishes the trick? Explain.

    ____

24. Tavia, Mitch, and Kate are playing a game. Players gain or lose points each round. The players' scores at the end of the first two rounds are shown in the table.

	Round 1	Round 2
Kate	$2\frac{1}{2}$	$-\frac{3}{4}$
Mitch	$-1\frac{3}{4}$	$1\frac{1}{2}$
Tavia	$-\frac{1}{2}$	$3\frac{3}{4}$

    a. How far apart are Mitch's and Tavia's scores after Round 1?

    ____

    b. Find the change in Kate's score from Round 1 to Round 2.

    ____

    c. When you subtract to find the answers in parts **a** and **b**, does the order of the numbers matter? Explain your reasoning.

    ____

    ____

    ____

    ____

H.O.T. FOCUS ON HIGHER ORDER THINKING

Work Area

25. **Look for a Pattern** Show how you could use the Commutative Property to simplify the evaluation of the expression $-\frac{7}{16} - \frac{1}{4} - \frac{5}{16}$.

26. **Problem Solving** The temperatures for five days in Kaktovik, Alaska, are given below.

−19.6 °F, −22.5 °F, −20.9 °F, −19.5 °F, −22.4 °F

Temperatures for the following week are expected to be twelve degrees lower every day. What are the highest and lowest temperatures expected for the corresponding 5 days next week?

27. **Make a Conjecture** Must the difference between two rational numbers be a rational number? Explain.

28. **Look for a Pattern** Evan said that the difference between two negative numbers must be negative. Was he right? Use examples to illustrate your answer.

Going Further 3.3

Identifying Operations

7.1.GF.3.3

Students will decide whether to model a real-world situation with addition or subtraction.

ESSENTIAL QUESTION

How do you decide whether to model a real-world situation with addition or subtraction?

EXPLORE ACTIVITY Real World

Applying Subtraction

A lab technician is studying the effect of storage temperatures on samples. Write and evaluate an expression for each situation using the rules for adding and subtracting rational numbers. Then explain the value in context.

A Sample A is stored at 1.25 °C. The technician lowers the temperature by 2.5 °C. What is the resulting temperature?

- The temperature is *decreasing*. Subtract the amount of change from the original temperature. $1.25 - \square$
- Rewrite the expression as addition of the opposite. $1.25 - \square = 1.25 + (\square)$
- The signs are different, so subtract the lesser absolute value from the greater absolute value. $|\square| - |1.25| = \square - 1.25$
  $= \square$
- Use the sign of the number with the greater absolute value. $1.25 - 2.5 = \square$

The resulting temperature is ________ °C, which is 1.25 degrees below 0 degrees Celsius.

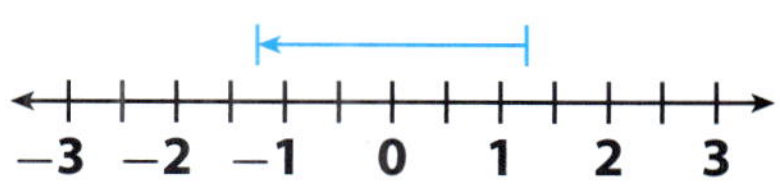

B The coldest temperature the lab technician used was −2.25 °C. The warmest temperature was 1.25 °C. What was the range in temperature?

- Find the absolute value of the difference between the two temperatures. $|1.25 - (\square)|$
- Rewrite the expression as addition of the opposite. $|1.25 - (\square)| = |1.25 + (\square)|$
- Evaluate the new expression. $= \square$

The value ________ means that the range in temperature was ________ °C.

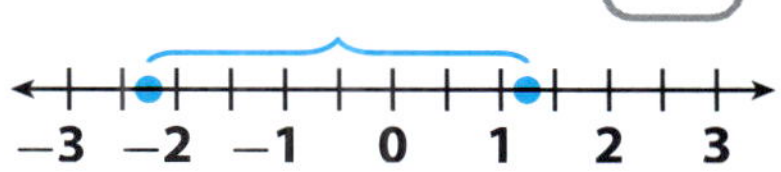

Practice

Match each situation to an expression. Then answer the question.

A $-15.5 + 12.5$ **B** $-15.5 - 12.5$ **C** $|-15.5 - 12.5|$

1. The temperature started at -15.5 °F and fell 12.5 °F. What was the temperature then? ______

2. A boater is at an elevation of 12.5 meters, directly above a diver at an elevation of -15.5 meters. How far apart are they? ______

3. Jo has a $-\$15.50$ balance on a credit card and pays \$12.50. What is her new balance? ______

Write and evaluate an expression for each situation using the rules for adding and subtracting rational numbers. Explain the value in context.

4. *Par* is the number of strokes an experienced golfer should need to complete a hole on a golf course, or the entire course. Par is represented by 0. Scores below par are negative and scores over par are positive.

   a. Hannah scored -3 on the first hole and 5 on the next. What was her total?

   ______

   b. Edwin scored -2 on the first hole. His total for that hole and the next was 1. What was his score on the second hole?

   ______

   ______

   c. Rachel scored 4 on the first hole. How many points apart were Rachel's and Hannah's scores on the first hole?

   ______

   ______

5. In an aquarium, a betta and a danio swim one above the other. The betta's elevation is $-8\frac{1}{4}$ inches. The danio's is $-16\frac{3}{4}$ inches.

   a. How far apart are the fish?

   ______

   b. Suppose the betta swam to the danio's elevation. What would be the change in the betta's elevation?

   ______

   ______

LESSON 3.4

Multiplying Rational Numbers

7.1.3.4

Students will multiply rational numbers.

ESSENTIAL QUESTION

How do you multiply rational numbers?

EXPLORE ACTIVITY Real World

Multiplying Rational Numbers with Different Signs

Math On the Spot my.hrw.com

The rules for the signs of products of rational numbers with different signs are summarized below. Let p and q be rational numbers.

Products of Rational Numbers

Sign of Factor p	Sign of Factor q	Sign of Product pq
+	−	−
−	+	−

You can also use the fact that multiplication is repeated addition.

EXAMPLE 1 **Gina hiked down a canyon and stopped each time she descended $\frac{1}{2}$ mile to rest. She hiked a total of 4 sections. What is her overall change in elevation?**

STEP 1 Use a negative number for the change in elevation.

STEP 2 Find $4(\square)$.

STEP 3 Start at 0. Move $\frac{1}{2}$ unit to the ________ 4 times.

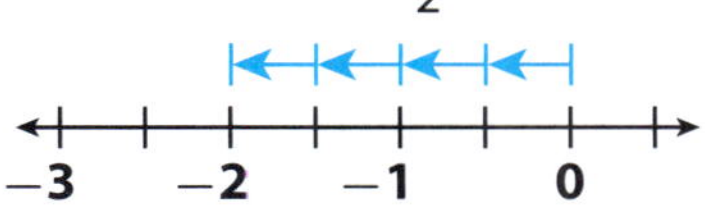

The result is ________. The overall change is ________ miles.

Check: Use the rules for multiplying rational numbers.

A negative times a positive is ________.

$$4\left(-\frac{1}{2}\right) = -\frac{\square}{2}$$

$$= \_\_\_\_\_\_ \checkmark$$

YOUR TURN

1. Use a number line to find 2(−3.5). ________

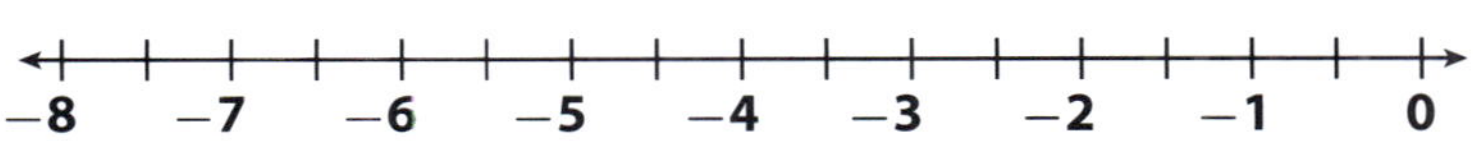

Personal Math Trainer

Online Assessment and Intervention

my.hrw.com

Math On the Spot
my.hrw.com

Multiplying Rational Numbers with the Same Sign

The rules for the signs of products with the same signs are summarized below.

Products of Rational Numbers

Sign of Factor p	Sign of Factor q	Sign of Product pq
+	+	+
−	−	+

You can also use a number line to find the product of rational numbers with the same signs.

My Notes

EXAMPLE 2

Multiply −2(−3.5).

STEP 1 First, find the product 2(−3.5).

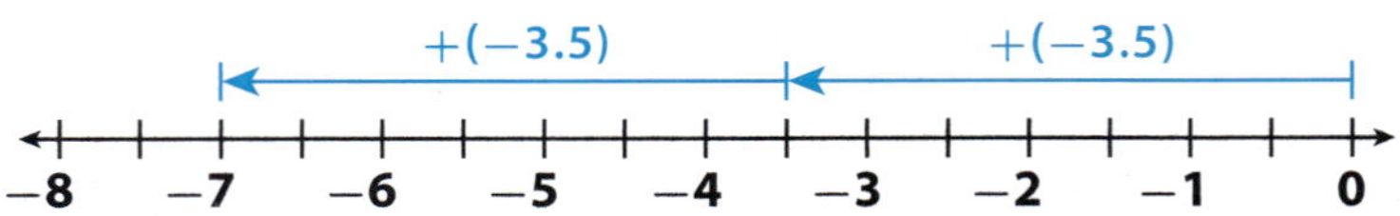

STEP 2 Start at 0. Move 3.5 units to the left two times.

STEP 3 The result is −7.

STEP 4 This shows that 2 groups of −3.5 equals −7.

So, −2 groups of −3.5 must equal the *opposite* of −7.

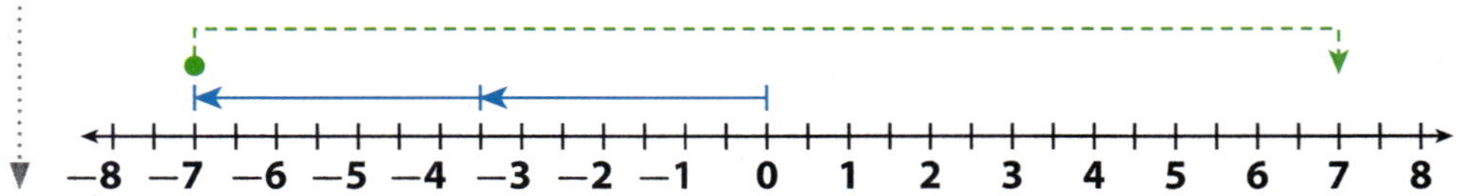

STEP 5 $-2(-3.5) = 7$

Check: Use the rules for multiplying rational numbers.

$-2(-3.5) = 7$ *A negative times a negative equals a positive.*

YOUR TURN

2. Find −3(−1.25). __________

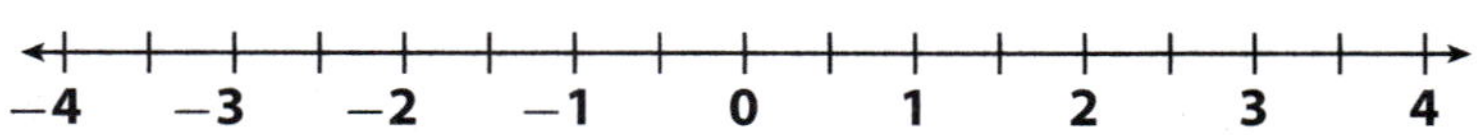

Personal Math Trainer
Online Assessment and Intervention
my.hrw.com

Multiplying More Than Two Rational Numbers

If you multiply three or more rational numbers, you can use a pattern to find the sign of the product.

Math On the Spot
my.hrw.com

EXAMPLE 3

Multiply $\left(-\frac{2}{3}\right)\left(-\frac{1}{2}\right)\left(-\frac{3}{5}\right)$.

STEP 1 First, find the product of the first two factors. Both factors are negative, so their product will be positive.

STEP 2 $\left(-\frac{2}{3}\right)\left(-\frac{1}{2}\right) = +\left(\frac{\cancel{2}}{3}\cdot\frac{1}{\cancel{2}}\right)$

$= \frac{1}{3}$

STEP 3 Now, multiply the result, which is positive, by the third factor, which is negative. The product will be negative.

STEP 4 $\frac{1}{3}\left(-\frac{3}{5}\right) = \frac{1}{\cancel{3}}\left(-\frac{\cancel{3}}{5}\right)$

STEP 5 $\left(-\frac{2}{3}\right)\left(-\frac{1}{2}\right)\left(-\frac{3}{5}\right) = -\frac{1}{5}$

Math Talk
Mathematical Processes
Suppose you find the product of several rational numbers, one of which is zero. What can you say about the product?

Reflect

3. **Look for a Pattern** You know that the product of two negative numbers is positive, and the product of three negative numbers is negative. Write a rule for finding the sign of the product of n negative numbers.

____

____

____

YOUR TURN

Find each product.

4. $\left(-\frac{3}{4}\right)\left(-\frac{4}{7}\right)\left(-\frac{2}{3}\right)$ _______________

5. $\left(-\frac{2}{3}\right)\left(-\frac{3}{4}\right)\left(\frac{4}{5}\right)$ _______________

6. $\left(\frac{2}{3}\right)\left(-\frac{9}{10}\right)\left(\frac{5}{6}\right)$ _______________

Personal Math Trainer
Online Assessment and Intervention
my.hrw.com

Guided Practice

Use a number line to find each product. (Explore Activity Example 1 and Example 2)

1. $5\left(-\frac{2}{3}\right) =$ ______

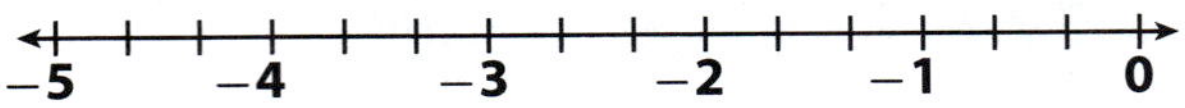

2. $3\left(-\frac{1}{4}\right) =$ ______

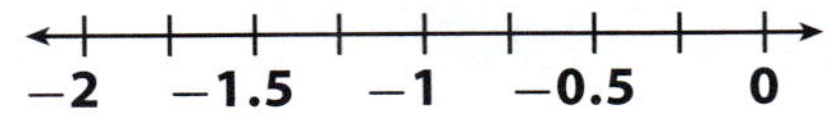

3. $-3\left(-\frac{4}{7}\right) =$ ______

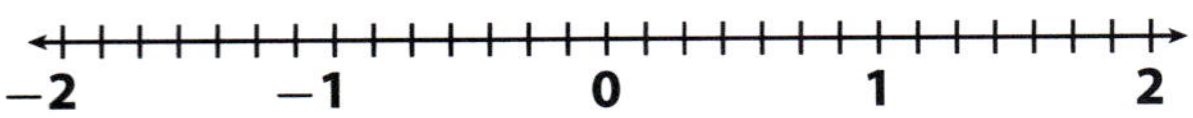

4. $-\frac{3}{4}(-4) =$ ______

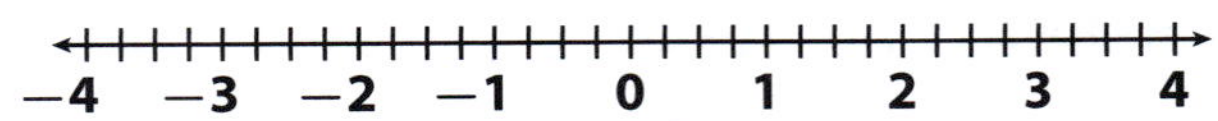

5. $4(-3) =$ ______

6. $-1.8(5) =$ ______

7. $-2\,(-3.4) =$ ______

8. $0.54(8) =$ ______

9. $-5(-1.2) =$ ______

10. $-2.4(3) =$ ______

Multiply. (Example 3)

11. $\frac{1}{2} \times \frac{2}{3} \times \frac{3}{4} = \square \times \frac{3}{4} =$ ______

12. $-\frac{4}{7}\left(-\frac{3}{5}\right)\left(-\frac{7}{3}\right) = \left(\square\right) \times \left(-\frac{7}{3}\right) =$ ______

13. $-\frac{1}{8} \times 5 \times \frac{2}{3} =$ ______

14. $-\frac{2}{3}\left(\frac{1}{2}\right)\left(-\frac{6}{7}\right) =$ ______

15. The price of one share of Acme Company stock declined $3.50 per day for 4 days in a row. What was the overall change in the price of one share? (Explore Activity Example 1)

______

16. In one day, 18 people each withdrew $100 from an ATM machine. What was the overall change in the amount of money in the ATM machine? (Explore Activity Example 1)

______

ESSENTIAL QUESTION CHECK-IN

17. Explain how you can find the sign of the product of two or more rational numbers.

______

______

______

Name ______________________ Class ______________ Date ______________

3.4 Independent Practice

Personal Math Trainer
Online Assessment and Intervention
my.hrw.com

18. **Financial Literacy** Sandy has \$200 in her bank account.

a. If she writes 6 checks for \$19.98 each, what expression describes the change in her bank account?

____

b. What is her account balance after the checks are cashed? Show your work.

____

19. **Communicating Mathematical Ideas** Explain, in words, how to find the product of $-4(-1.5)$ using a number line. Where do you end up?

____

20. Greg sets his watch for the correct time. Exactly one week later, he finds that his watch has lost $3\frac{1}{4}$ minutes. It loses time at the same rate for a total of 8 weeks. Write a multiplication expression that describes the situation. Find the product and explain how it is related to the problem.

____

21. A submarine dives below the surface, heading downward in three moves. If each move downward was 325 feet, where is the submarine after it is finished diving?

____

22. **Multistep** For home economics class, Sandra has 5 cups of flour. She made 3 batches of cookies that each used 1.5 cups of flour. Write and solve an expression to find the amount of flour Sandra has left after making the 3 batches of cookies.

____

23. **Critique Reasoning** In class, Matthew stated, "I think that a negative is like an opposite. That is why multiplying a negative times a negative equals a positive. The opposite of negative is positive, so it is just like multiplying the opposite of a negative twice, which is two positives." Do you agree or disagree with his reasoning? What would you say in response to him?

____

24. Kaitlin is on a long car trip. Every time she stops to buy gas, she loses 15 minutes of travel time. If she has to stop 5 times, how late will she be getting to her destination?

____

25. The table shows the scoring system for quarterbacks in Jeremy's fantasy football league. In one game, Jeremy's quarterback had 2 touchdown passes, 16 complete passes, 7 incomplete passes, and 2 interceptions. How many total points did Jeremy's quarterback score?

Quarterback Scoring	
Action	**Points**
Touchdown pass	6
Complete pass	0.5
Incomplete pass	−0.5
Interception	−1.5

____

Work Area

H.O.T. FOCUS ON HIGHER ORDER THINKING

26. **Represent Real-World Problems** The ground temperature at Brigham Airport is 12 °C. The temperature decreases by 6.8 °C for every increase of 1 kilometer above the ground. What is the temperature outside a plane flying at an altitude of 5 kilometers above Brigham Airport?

____

27. **Identify Patterns** The product of four numbers, *a*, *b*, *c*, and *d*, is a negative number. The table shows one combination of positive and negative signs of the four numbers that could produce a negative product. Complete the table to show the seven other possible combinations.

a	*b*	*c*	*d*
+	+	+	−

28. **Reason Abstractly** Find two integers whose sum is −7 and whose product is 12. Explain how you found the numbers.

____

____

____

____

LESSON 3.5

Dividing Rational Numbers

7.1.3.5

Students will divide rational numbers.

ESSENTIAL QUESTION

How do you divide rational numbers?

EXPLORE ACTIVITY

Placement of Negative Signs in Quotients

Quotients can have negative signs in different places.

Let p and q be rational numbers.

Quotients of Rational Numbers

Sign of Dividend p	Sign of Divisor q	Sign of Quotient $\frac{p}{q}$
+	−	−
−	+	−
+	+	+
−	−	+

Are the rational numbers $\frac{12}{-4}$, $\frac{-12}{4}$, and $-\left(\frac{12}{4}\right)$ equivalent?

A Find each quotient. Then use the rules in the table to make sure the sign of the quotient is correct.

$\frac{12}{-4} =$ ________ $\frac{-12}{4} =$ ________ $-\left(\frac{12}{4}\right) =$ ________

B What do you notice about each quotient?

____

C The rational numbers **are / are not** equivalent.

D **Conjecture** Explain how the placement of the negative sign in the rational number affects the sign of the quotients.

____

____

E If p and q are rational numbers and q is not zero, what do you know about $-\left(\frac{p}{q}\right)$, $\frac{-p}{q}$, and $\frac{p}{-q}$?

____

EXPLORE ACTIVITY *(cont'd)*

Reflect

Write two equivalent expressions for each quotient.

1. $\frac{14}{-7}$ __________, __________ **2.** $\frac{-32}{-8}$ __________, __________

Quotients of Rational Numbers

The rules for dividing rational numbers are the same as the rules for dividing integers.

Math On the Spot
my.hrw.com

EXAMPLE 1 Real World

Over 5 months, Carlos wrote 5 checks for a total of \$323.75 to pay for his cable TV service. His cable bill is the same amount each month. What was the change in Carlos's bank account each month to pay for cable?

Find the quotient: $\frac{-323.75}{5}$

STEP 1 Use a negative number to represent the withdrawal from his account each month.

STEP 2 Find $\frac{-323.75}{5}$.

STEP 3 Determine the sign of the quotient.

The quotient will be negative because the signs are different.

STEP 4 Divide.

$\frac{-323.75}{5} = -64.75$

Carlos withdrew \$64.75 each month to pay for cable TV.

Math Talk
Mathematical Processes

Describe another real-world problem that you solve by dividing a negative decimal by a positive number.

YOUR TURN

Find each quotient.

3. $\frac{2.8}{-4} =$ __________ **4.** $\frac{-6.64}{-0.4} =$ __________ **5.** $-\frac{5.5}{0.5} =$ __________

6. A diver descended 42.56 feet in 11.2 minutes. What was the diver's average change in elevation per minute?

____

Personal Math Trainer
Online Assessment and Intervention
my.hrw.com

Complex Fractions

A **complex fraction** is a fraction that has a fraction in its numerator, denominator, or both.

$$\frac{\frac{a}{b}}{\frac{c}{d}} = \frac{a}{b} \div \frac{c}{d}$$

Math On the Spot
my.hrw.com

EXAMPLE 2 Real World

A Find $\frac{\frac{7}{10}}{\frac{-1}{5}}$.

STEP 1 Determine the sign of the quotient.
The quotient will be negative because the signs are different.

STEP 2 Write the complex fraction as division: $\frac{\frac{7}{10}}{-\frac{1}{5}} = \frac{7}{10} \div -\frac{1}{5}$

STEP 3 Rewrite using multiplication: $\frac{7}{10} \times \left(-\frac{5}{1}\right)$ *Multiply by the reciprocal.*

STEP 4 $\frac{7}{10} \times \left(-\frac{5}{1}\right) = -\frac{35}{10}$ *Multiply.*

$= -\frac{7}{2}$ *Simplify.*

$$\frac{\frac{7}{10}}{-\frac{1}{5}} = -\frac{7}{2}$$

B Maya wants to divide a $\frac{3}{4}$-pound box of trail mix into small bags. Each bag will hold $\frac{1}{12}$ pound of trail mix. How many bags of trail mix can Maya fill?

STEP 1 Find $\frac{\frac{3}{4}}{\frac{1}{12}}$.

STEP 2 Determine the sign of the quotient.
The quotient will be positive because the signs are the same.

STEP 3 Write the complex fraction as division: $\frac{\frac{3}{4}}{\frac{1}{12}} = \frac{3}{4} \div \frac{1}{12}$.

STEP 4 Rewrite using multiplication: $\frac{3}{4} \times \frac{12}{1}$. *Multiply by the reciprocal.*

STEP 5 $\frac{3}{4} \times \frac{12}{1} = \frac{36}{4} = 9$ *Multiply.*

$\frac{\frac{3}{4}}{\frac{1}{12}} = 9$ *Simplify.*

Maya can fill 9 bags of trail mix.

YOUR TURN

7. $\frac{-\frac{5}{8}}{-\frac{6}{7}} =$ ________

8. $\frac{-\frac{5}{12}}{\frac{2}{3}} =$ ________

9. $\frac{-\frac{4}{5}}{\frac{1}{2}} =$ ________

Personal Math Trainer
Online Assessment and Intervention
my.hrw.com

Guided Practice

Find each quotient. (Explore Activities Example 1, and Example 2)

1. $\frac{0.72}{-0.9} =$ ______

2. $\left(\frac{-\frac{1}{5}}{\frac{7}{5}}\right) =$ ______

3. $\frac{56}{-7} =$ ______

4. $\frac{251}{4} \div \left(-\frac{3}{8}\right) =$ ______

5. $\frac{75}{-\frac{1}{5}} =$ ______

6. $\frac{-91}{-13} =$ ______

7. $\frac{-\frac{3}{7}}{\frac{9}{4}} =$ ______

8. $-\frac{12}{0.03} =$ ______

9. A water pail in your backyard has a small hole in it. You notice that it has drained a total of 3.5 liters in 4 days. What is the average change in water volume each day? (Example 1)

______

10. The price of one share of ABC Company declined a total of $45.75 in 5 days. What was the average change of the price of one share per day? (Example 1)

______

11. To avoid a storm, a passenger-jet pilot descended 0.44 mile in 0.8 minute. What was the plane's average change of altitude per minute? (Example 2)

______

ESSENTIAL QUESTION CHECK-IN

12. Explain how you would find the sign of the quotient $\frac{32 \div (-2)}{-16 \div 4}$.

______

Name ______________________ Class ______________ Date ______________

3.5 Independent Practice

Personal Math Trainer
Online Assessment and Intervention
my.hrw.com

13. $\frac{5}{-\frac{2}{8}} =$ ______________

14. $5\frac{1}{3} \div \left(-1\frac{1}{2}\right) =$ ______________

15. $\frac{-120}{-6} =$ ______________

16. $\frac{-\frac{4}{5}}{-\frac{2}{3}} =$ ______________

17. $1.03 \div (-10.3) =$ ______________

18. $\frac{-0.4}{80} =$ ______________

19. $1 \div \frac{9}{5} =$ ______________

20. $\frac{\frac{-1}{4}}{\frac{23}{24}} =$ ______________

21. $\frac{-10.35}{-2.3} =$ ______________

22. Alex usually runs for 21 hours a week, training for a marathon. If he is unable to run for 3 days, describe how to find out how many hours of training time he loses, and write the appropriate integer to describe how it affects his time.

____

23. The running back for the Bulldogs football team carried the ball 9 times for a total loss of $15\frac{3}{4}$ yards. Find the average change in field position on each run.

____

24. The 6:00 a.m. temperatures for four consecutive days in the town of Lincoln were −12.1 °C, −7.8 °C, −14.3 °C, and −7.2 °C. What was the average 6:00 a.m. temperature for the four days?

____

25. **Multistep** A seafood restaurant claims an increase of $1,750.00 over its average profit during a week where it introduced a special of baked clams.

a. If this is true, how much extra profit did it receive per day?

____

b. If it had, instead, lost $150 per day, how much money would it have lost for the week?

____

c. If its total loss was $490 for the week, what was its average daily change?

____

26. A hot air balloon descended 99.6 meters in 12 seconds. What was the balloon's average rate of descent in meters per second?

____

27. Sanderson is having trouble with his assignment. His shown work is as follows:

$$\frac{-\frac{3}{4}}{\frac{4}{3}} = -\frac{3}{4} \times \frac{4}{3} = -\frac{12}{12} = -1$$

However, his answer does not match the answer that his teacher gives him. What is Sanderson's mistake? Find the correct answer.

______

28. **Science** Beginning in 1996, a glacier lost an average of 3.7 meters of thickness each year. Find the total change in its thickness by the end of 2012.

______

H.O.T. FOCUS ON HIGHER ORDER THINKING

29. **Represent Real-World Problems** Describe a real-world situation that can be represented by the quotient $-85 \div 15$. Then find the quotient and explain what the quotient means in terms of the real-world situation.

______

30. **Construct an Argument** Divide 5 by 4. Is your answer a rational number? Explain.

______

31. **Critical Thinking** Should the quotient of an integer divided by a nonzero integer always be a rational number? Why or why not?

______

Work Area

Going Further 3.5

Applying Properties to Numerical Expressions

7.1.GF.3.5

Students will justify their steps when solving mathematical and real-world problems.

ESSENTIAL QUESTION

How can you justify your steps when solving mathematical and real-world problems?

EXPLORE ACTIVITY 1

Justifying That $(-1)(-1) = 1$

You can use properties of operations along with the order of operations to simplify expressions. When you solve a mathematical or real-world problem, you can use these properties and rules to justify that a step is valid.

Justify or complete each step to show that $(-1)(-1) = 1$.

Step	Justification
$(-1)(0) = 0$	Multiplication Property of ______
$(-1)(-1 + 1) = 0$	______
$(-1)(-1) + (-1)(1) = 0$	______
$(-1)(-1) + (\square) = 0$	Identity Property of ______
$(-1)(-1) + (-1) + \square = 0 + \square$	Addition Property of Equality
$(-1)(-1) + (-1 + 1) = 0 + 1$	______
$(-1)(-1) + \square = 0 + 1$	______ Property of Addition
$(-1)(-1) = \square$	______ Property of Addition

Reflect

1. How do you know which property justifies the first step?

______

______

2. How do you know which number to add to both sides of the equation in the step involving the Addition Property of Equality?

______

______

______

EXPLORE ACTIVITY 2 Real World

Applying Properties Strategically

The value of shares of stock varies as the price per share changes. Claire bought 8 shares of stock for \$5.65 per share. The price increased \$1.26 per share by midday and then decreased \$0.65 per share by day's end. What was the total value of Claire's shares at the end of the day? Did they gain or lose value during the day? Justify your steps.

A The **original / final** value of Claire's shares is equal to 8(5.65).

B The midday **gain / loss** in the value of her shares is equal to 8(1.26).

C The end-of-day loss in the value of **one of / all of** her shares is equal to 8(−0.65).

D Add the expressions. Simplify the sum and justify each step.

$8(5.65) + 8(1.26) + 8(-0.65)$

$8(5.65 + 1.26 + (-0.65))$ ____________________

$8(\square + \square + (-0.65))$ Commutative Property of Addition

$8(1.26 + [5.65 + (-0.65)])$ ____________________

$8(1.26 + \square)$ Add.

$8(6.26)$ ________

$\square$ Multiply.

E The value of Claire's 8 shares at the end of the day was ________. She paid ________ for the 8 shares, so they **gained / lost** value during the day.

Reflect

3. Interpret the expression $1.26 + (-0.65)$ in terms of the situation. Using the expression, represent the total change in value of the shares over the day if Claire had bought 20 shares. Interpret the change.

____

____

4. Write and evaluate an expression to show what the change in value per share would be if Claire's 8 shares were worth \$43.20 instead of \$50.08 at the end of the day. Interpret the result.

____

____

Practice

Simplify each expression. Justify each step.

1. $\left(-\frac{5}{2}\right)\left(-\frac{2}{5}\right)$ ______

2. $-132.59 + 0$ ______

3. $201.75 + (-201.75)$ ______

4. $\frac{1}{3}(1)$ ______

5. $3.6(2.5) + 3.6(-2.5)$

6. $\left(\frac{2}{3}\right)\left(-\frac{4}{3}\right)\left(\frac{3}{2}\right)$

7. $3\left(\frac{2}{3} + \left(-\frac{1}{3}\right)\right) + \frac{1}{2}(-4 + 2)$

Write an expression involving negative rational numbers to represent each situation. Evaluate the expression and explain the value in the context of the problem.

8. Experts say that when you buy a new car, the value decreases 9% when you drive the car off the lot. The Millers paid \$28,456 for a new car. How does the value of the car change after they drive it off the lot?

____

9. A bottle contains 68 teaspoons of solution. The solution drops out of the bottle at a constant rate during a 102-minute experiment. The bottle is completely empty just as the experiment ends. At what rate does the number of teaspoons of solution in the bottle change?

____

____

10. In golf, *par* on a hole is the number of strokes an experienced golfer should need to complete the hole. Par is represented by 0, scores under par are negative, and scores over par are positive. The table shows Michelle's scores and the number of times in an 18-hole game she got each score. Her game score is the sum of her scores for each hole. What was her game score?

Score	Number
−2	2
−1	3
0	12
+1	1

____

____

11. Ka'me and four friends go to a water park. Admission is \$31.50 per person. Ka'me uses a coupon for \$5 off each ticket for up to 4 people. Abby and Allen write expressions to represent the total amount Ka'me and his friends pay for admission.

Abby: $4(31.50 + (-5.00)) + 31.50$ **Allen:** $5(31.50) + 4(-5.00)$

Rewrite Abby's expression to show it is equal to Allen's expression. Justify each step.

Getting Ready 3.6

Estimation Strategies

7.1.GR.3.6

Students will use mental math and estimation to assess the reasonableness of calculations.

ESSENTIAL QUESTION

How can you use mental math and estimation to assess the reasonableness of calculations?

EXPLORE ACTIVITY

Compatible Numbers

You can use rounding, compatible numbers, and other strategies to help you estimate. *Compatible numbers* are numbers that make a calculation easier to do with mental math.

A Estimate the product using rounding and compatible numbers.

Round 92 and use a compatible fraction.

$\frac{11}{30} \times 92 \approx \frac{\square}{\square} \times \square = \square$

B The answer to Part A is an **overestimate / underestimate** because both factors were **rounded up / rounded down**.

C Estimate the sum using the front-end and adjust strategy.

$3.18
5.59
0.95
1.37
+2.79

$3 + \square + 1 + \square = \$\square$ — Add the front-end digits.

$0.18 + \square \approx \$1$

$0.37 + \square \approx \$1$

$\square \approx \$1$

Adjust by grouping cents amounts into dollars.

$\square + 3 = \$\square$ — Add the results.

D Is the answer to Part C an *overestimate* or an *underestimate?* Explain.

____

Reflect

1. **What if?** How would Parts C and D change if $3.18 changed to $3.46?

____

____

Reasonable Estimates

Estimation is helpful when you don't need an exact answer or when you want to check that an answer is reasonable. In a multistep problem, it might make sense to overestimate in some steps and underestimate in others.

EXAMPLE 1 Real World

Manuel earns a salary of $35,000 per year. He pays an income tax rate of 12%. He budgeted his weekly income after taxes to be $592.31. Use estimation to confirm that his budget is reasonable.

STEP 1 Use a compatible percent to estimate Manuel's annual income tax. 12% is close to 10%, so mentally multiply by 0.10 to estimate the tax.

$35{,}000 \times 0.10 = 3{,}500$ *$3,500 is an underestimate of the annual tax.*

STEP 2 Estimate how much of his annual income Manuel will keep after taxes. Since $3,500 is an underestimate, round up to the leading digit ($4,000) and subtract using mental math.

$35{,}000 - 4{,}000 = 31{,}000$ *He keeps about $31,000 per year.*

STEP 3 Estimate Manuel's weekly income, after taxes. There are 52 weeks in a year. So use 50 as the divisor and 30,000 as a compatible dividend.

$30{,}000 \div 50 = 600$ *His weekly after-tax income is about $600.*

Manuel's answer is reasonable, because $592.31 is close to $600.

Practice

1. Marta uses the expression $92 − 0.15($92) to find the sale price of an item and gets the answer $78.20. Show how to find an underestimate and an overestimate to explain why her answer is reasonable.

____

____

____

2. A club is planning a banquet. The club spends $60 for each table of 8 guests (dinner included). The club also spends $46 on decorations, $225 on a DJ, $150 on a photographer, and $760 for the hall. The club expects about 150 people to attend. Explain how to estimate the total cost.

____

____

____

____

LESSON 3.6

Applying Rational Number Operations

7.1.3.6

Students will use different forms of rational numbers and strategically choose tools to solve problems.

ESSENTIAL QUESTION

How do you use different forms of rational numbers and strategically choose tools to solve problems?

EXPLORE ACTIVITY Real World

Assessing Reasonableness of Answers

Math On the Spot
my.hrw.com

Even when you understand how to solve a problem, you might make a careless solving error. You should always check your answer to make sure that it is reasonable.

EXAMPLE 1 **Jon is hanging a picture. He wants to center it horizontally on the wall. The picture is $32\frac{1}{2}$ inches long, and the wall is $120\frac{3}{4}$ inches long. How far from each edge of the wall should he place the picture?**

STEP 1 Find the total length of the wall not covered by the picture.

Subtract the whole number parts. Then subtract the fractional parts.

$$120\frac{3}{4} - 32\frac{1}{2} = \square\frac{\square}{\square}$$

STEP 2 Find the length of the wall on each side of the picture.

Multiply by $\frac{1}{2}$.

$$\frac{1}{2}\left(\square\right) = \square\frac{\square}{\square}$$

Jon should place the picture ________ inches from each edge of the wall.

STEP 3 Check the answer for reasonableness.

The wall is about 120 inches long. The picture is about 30 inches long. The length of wall space left for *both* sides of the picture is about $120 - 30 = 90$ inches. The length left for *each* side is about $\frac{1}{2}(90) = 45$ inches.

The answer is reasonable because it is close to the estimate.

YOUR TURN

1. A 30-minute TV program consists of three commercials, each $2\frac{1}{2}$ minutes long, and four equal-length entertainment segments. How long is each entertainment segment? ____________

Personal Math Trainer
Online Assessment and Intervention
my.hrw.com

Math On the Spot

my.hrw.com

My Notes

Using Rational Numbers in Any Form

You have solved problems using integers, positive and negative fractions, and positive and negative decimals. A single problem may involve rational numbers in two or more of those forms.

EXAMPLE 2 Problem Solving

Alana uses $1\frac{1}{4}$ cups of flour for each batch of blueberry muffins she makes. She has a 5-pound bag of flour that cost \$4.49 and contains seventy-six $\frac{1}{4}$-cup servings. How many batches can Alana make if she uses all the flour? How much does the flour for one batch cost?

Analyze Information

Identify the important information.

- Each batch uses $1\frac{1}{4}$ cups of flour.
- Seventy-six $\frac{1}{4}$-cup servings of flour cost \$4.49.

Formulate a Plan

Use logical reasoning to solve the problem. Find the number of cups of flour that Alana has. Use that information to find the number of batches she can make. Use that information to find the cost of flour for each batch.

Solve

Number of cups of flour in bag:

76 servings $\times \frac{1}{4}$ cup per serving $=$ 19 cups

Number of batches Alana can make:

Write $1\frac{1}{4}$ as a decimal.

$$\text{total cups of flour} \div \frac{\text{cups of flour}}{\text{batch}} = 19 \text{ cups} \div \frac{1.25 \text{ cups}}{1 \text{ batch}}$$
$$= 19 \div 1.25$$
$$= 15.2$$

Alana cannot make 0.2 batch. The recipe calls for one egg, and she cannot divide one egg into tenths. So, she can make 15 batches.

Cost of flour for each batch: $\$4.49 \div 15 = \$0.299$, or about \$0.30.

Justify and Evaluate

A bag contains about 80 quarter cups, or about 20 cups. Each batch uses about 1 cup of flour, so there is enough flour for about 20 batches. A bag costs about \$5.00, so the flour for each batch costs about $\$5.00 \div 20 = \$0.25$. The answers are close to the estimates, so the answers are reasonable.

YOUR TURN

2. A 4-pound bag of sugar contains 454 one-teaspoon servings and costs \$3.49. A batch of muffins uses $\frac{3}{4}$ cup of sugar. How many batches can you make if you use all the sugar? What is the cost of sugar for each batch? (1 cup = 48 teaspoons) ______________________

Personal Math Trainer
Online Assessment and Intervention
my.hrw.com

Using Tools Strategically

A wide variety of tools are available to help you solve problems. Rulers, models, calculators, protractors, and software are some of the tools you can use in addition to paper and pencil. Choosing tools wisely can help you solve problems and increase your understanding of mathematical concepts.

Math On the Spot
my.hrw.com

EXAMPLE 3 Real World

The depth of Golden Trout Lake has been decreasing in recent years. Two years ago, the depth of the lake was 186.73 meters. Since then the depth has been changing at an average rate of $-1\frac{3}{4}$% per year. What is the depth of the lake today?

STEP 1 Convert the percent to a decimal.

$-1\frac{3}{4}\% = -1.75\%$ Write the fraction as a decimal.

$= -0.0175$ Move the decimal point two places left.

STEP 2 Find the depth of the lake after one year. Use a calculator to simplify the computations.

$186.73 \times (-0.0175) \approx -3.27$ meters Find the change in depth.

$186.73 - 3.27 = 183.46$ meters Find the new depth.

STEP 3 Find the depth of the lake after two years.

$183.46 \times (-0.0175) \approx -3.21$ meters Find the change in depth.

$183.46 - 3.21 = 180.25$ meters Find the new depth.

STEP 4 Check the answer for reasonableness.

The original depth was about 190 meters. The depth changed by about −2% per year. Because $(-0.02)(190) = -3.8$, the depth changed by about −4 meters per year or about −8 meters over two years. So, the new depth was about 182 meters. The answer is close to the estimate, so it is reasonable.

Math Talk
Mathematical Processes

How could you write a single expression for calculating the depth after 1 year? after 2 years?

Personal Math Trainer

Online Assessment and Intervention

my.hrw.com

YOUR TURN

3. Three years ago, Jolene bought \$750 worth of stock in a software company. Since then the value of her purchase has been increasing at an average rate of $12\frac{3}{5}$% per year. How much is the stock worth now? ________

Guided Practice

1. Mike hiked to Big Bear Lake in 4.5 hours at an average rate of $3\frac{1}{5}$ miles per hour. Pedro hiked the same distance at a rate of $3\frac{3}{5}$ miles per hour. How long did it take Pedro to reach the lake? (Explore Activity Example 1 and Example 2)

STEP 1 Find the distance Mike hiked.

4.5 h × ☐ miles per hour = ☐ miles

STEP 2 Find Pedro's time to hike the same distance.

☐ miles ÷ ☐ miles per hour = ☐ hours

2. Until this year, Greenville had averaged 25.68 inches of rainfall per year for more than a century. This year's total rainfall showed a change of $-2\frac{3}{8}$% with respect to the previous average. How much rain fell this year? (Example 3)

STEP 1 Use a calculator to find this year's decrease to the nearest hundredth.

☐ inches × ☐ ≈ ☐ inches

STEP 2 Find this year's total rainfall.

☐ inches − ☐ inches ≈ ☐ inches

ESSENTIAL QUESTION CHECK-IN

3. Why is it important to consider using tools when you are solving a problem?

____

____

____

Name ________________ Class ________________ Date ________________

3.6 Independent Practice

Personal Math Trainer
Online Assessment and Intervention
my.hrw.com

Solve, using appropriate tools.

4. Three rock climbers started a climb with each person carrying 7.8 kilograms of climbing equipment. A fourth climber with no equipment joined the group. The group divided the total weight of climbing equipment equally among the four climbers. How much did each climber carry? ________________

5. Foster is centering a photo that is $3\frac{1}{2}$ inches wide on a scrapbook page that is 12 inches wide. How far from each side of the page should he put the picture? ________________

6. Diane serves breakfast to two groups of children at a daycare center. One box of Oaties contains 12 cups of cereal. She needs $\frac{1}{3}$ cup for each younger child and $\frac{3}{4}$ cup for each older child. Today's group includes 11 younger children and 10 older children. Is one box of Oaties enough for everyone? Explain. ________________

7. The figure shows how the yard lines on a football field are numbered. The goal lines are labeled G. A referee was standing on a certain yard line as the first quarter ended. He walked $41\frac{3}{4}$ yards to a yard line with the same number as the one he had just left. How far was the referee from the nearest goal line? ________________

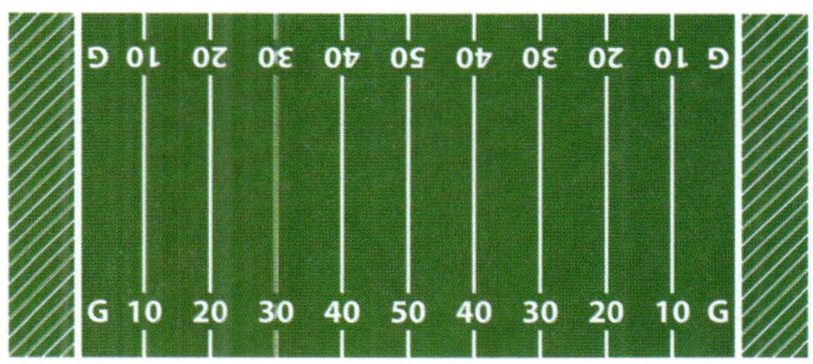

In 8–10, a teacher gave a test with 50 questions, each worth the same number of points. Donovan got 39 out of 50 questions right. Marci's score was 10 percentage points higher than Donovan's.

8. What was Marci's score? Explain.

____

9. How many more questions did Marci answer correctly? Explain.

____

10. Explain how you can check your answers for reasonableness.

____

____

____

For 11–13, use the expression $1.43 \times \left(-\frac{19}{37}\right)$.

11. **Critique Reasoning** Jamie says the value of the expression is close to -0.75. Does Jamie's estimate seem reasonable? Explain.

____

12. Find the product. Explain your method.

____

____

13. Does your answer to Exercise 12 justify your answer to Exercise 11?

____

H.O.T. FOCUS ON HIGHER ORDER THINKING

Work Area

14. **Persevere in Problem Solving** A scuba diver dove from the surface of the ocean to an elevation of $-79\frac{9}{10}$ feet at a rate of -18.8 feet per minute. After spending 12.75 minutes at that elevation, the diver ascended to an elevation of $-28\frac{9}{10}$ feet. The total time for the dive so far was $19\frac{1}{8}$ minutes. What was the rate of change in the diver's elevation during the ascent? __________

15. **Analyze Relationships** Describe two ways you could evaluate 37% of the sum of $27\frac{3}{5}$ and 15.9. Tell which method you would use and why.

____

____

____

____

____

____

16. **Represent Real-World Problems** Describe a real-world problem you could solve with the help of a yardstick and a calculator.

____

____

____

____

____

____

Game 3.6

Fraction Challenge

INSTRUCTIONS

Playing the Game

STEP 1 Have one student in your group shuffle the game cards and then place them face-down in a draw pile. Each game card shows a different positive or negative fraction.

STEP 2 Take turns drawing two cards from the draw pile. Wait to turn your cards over until all players, including the shuffler, have drawn two cards.

STEP 3 Look at your two fractions and the target value for the round on the scorecard shown below. Choose the operation (addition, subtraction, multiplication, or division) to perform on your fractions, in either order, that gets you as close as possible to the target value.

Write your expression and its simplified value on your scorecard.

Round	Target	Expression	Result	Points
1	Greatest number			
2	Least number			
3	Closest to 1			
4	Closest to 0			
5	Closest to -1			
			Total:	

STEP 4 Compare results with the other players in your group. Whoever is closest to the target value for the round receives 5 points. The other players receive 4, 3, and 2 points as their results get farther from the target.

For a tie, both players receive the same number of points, and the next point value is skipped, as shown below.

Player 1

Round	Target	Expression	Result	Points
5	Closest to -1	$-\frac{5}{4} - \left(-\frac{1}{2}\right)$	$-\frac{3}{4}$	5

Both players get 5 points because they are closest to and equally distar from -1.

Player 2

Round	Target	Expression	Result	Points
5	Closest to -1	$-\frac{5}{8} \times \frac{2}{1}$	$-1\frac{1}{4}$	5

Player 3

Round	Target	Expression	Result	Points
5	Closest to -1	$-\frac{3}{8} - \frac{1}{6}$	$-\frac{13}{24}$	3

No player gets 4 points. The next closest players get 3 points and points, respective

Player 4

Round	Target	Expression	Result	Points
5	Closest to -1	$-\frac{5}{6} \div \frac{8}{3}$	$-\frac{5}{16}$	2

STEP 5 Place your used game cards in a discard pile.

STEP 6 Repeat steps 2–5 for each round until the scorecard is filled in.

Winning the Game

The winner is the player with the most points. The maximum score per round is 5 points. So after 5 rounds, the player with the score closest to 25 points wins.

Player 1

Round	Target	Expression	Result	Points
5	Closest to -1	$-\frac{5}{4} - \left(-\frac{1}{2}\right)$	$-\frac{3}{4}$	5
			Total:	24

MODULE QUIZ

Ready to Go On?

Personal Math Trainer
Online Assessment and Intervention
my.hrw.com

3.1 Rational Numbers and Decimals

Write each mixed number as a decimal.

1. $4\frac{1}{5}$ ____________ **2.** $12\frac{14}{15}$ ____________ **3.** $5\frac{5}{32}$ ____________

3.2 Adding Rational Numbers

Find each sum.

4. $4.5 + 7.1 =$ ____________ **5.** $5\frac{1}{6} + \left(-3\frac{5}{6}\right) =$ ____________

3.3 Subtracting Rational Numbers

Find each difference.

6. $-\frac{1}{8} - \left(6\frac{7}{8}\right) =$ ____________ **7.** $14.2 - (-4.9) =$ ____________

3.4 Multiplying Rational Numbers

Multiply.

8. $-4\left(\frac{7}{10}\right) =$ ____________ **9.** $-3.2(-5.6)(4) =$ ____________

3.5 Dividing Rational Numbers

Find each quotient.

10. $-\frac{19}{2} \div \frac{38}{7} =$ ____________ **11.** $\frac{-32.01}{-3.3} =$ ____________

3.6 Applying Rational Number Operations

12. Luis bought stock at $83.60. The next day, the price increased $15.35. This new price changed by $-4\frac{3}{4}\%$ the following day. What was the final stock price? Is your answer reasonable? Explain.

____

____

ESSENTIAL QUESTION

13. How can you use negative numbers to represent real-world problems?

____

____

MODULE 3 MIXED REVIEW

Assessment Readiness

Personal Math Trainer

Online Assessment and Intervention

my.hrw.com

Selected Response

1. What is $-7\frac{5}{12}$ written as a decimal?

Ⓐ -7.25
Ⓑ $-7.333\ldots$
Ⓒ $-7.41666\ldots$
Ⓓ -7.512

2. Glenda began the day with a golf score of -6 and ended with a score of -10. Which statement represents her golf score for that day?

Ⓐ $-6 - (-10) = 4$
Ⓑ $-10 - (-6) = -4$
Ⓒ $-6 + (-10) = -16$
Ⓓ $-10 + (-6) = -16$

3. A submersible vessel at an elevation of -95 feet descends to 5 times that elevation. What is the vessel's new elevation?

Ⓐ -475 ft
Ⓑ -19 ft
Ⓒ 19 ft
Ⓓ 475 ft

4. The temperature at 7 P.M. at a weather station in Minnesota was -5 °F. The temperature began changing at the rate of -2.5 °F per hour. What was the temperature at 10 P.M.?

Ⓐ -15 °F
Ⓑ -12.5 °F
Ⓒ 2.5 °F
Ⓓ 5 °F

5. What is the sum of -2.16 and -1.75?

Ⓐ 0.41
Ⓑ 3.91
Ⓒ -0.41
Ⓓ -3.91

6. On Sunday, the wind chill temperature reached -36 °F. On Monday, the wind chill temperature only reached $\frac{1}{4}$ of Sunday's wind chill temperature. What was the lowest wind chill temperature on Monday?

Ⓐ -9 °F
Ⓑ $-36\frac{1}{4}$ °F
Ⓒ -40 °F
Ⓓ -144 °F

7. The level of a lake was 8 inches below normal. It decreased $1\frac{1}{4}$ inches in June and $2\frac{3}{8}$ inches more in July. What was the new level with respect to the normal level?

Ⓐ $-11\frac{5}{8}$ in.
Ⓑ $-10\frac{5}{8}$ in.
Ⓒ $-9\frac{1}{8}$ in.
Ⓓ $-5\frac{3}{8}$ in.

Mini-Task

8. The average annual rainfall for a town is 43.2 inches.

a. What is the average *monthly* rainfall?

____

b. The difference of a given month's rainfall from the average monthly rainfall is called the *deviation*. What is the deviation for each month shown?

Town's Rainfall in Last Three Months			
Month	May	June	July
Rain (in.)	$2\frac{3}{5}$	$\frac{7}{8}$	$4\frac{1}{4}$

____

c. The average monthly rainfall for the previous 9 months was 4 inches. Did the town exceed its average annual rainfall? If so, by how much?

____

UNIT 1

Study Guide Review

MODULE 1 Adding and Subtracting Integers

Key Vocabulary

additive inverse *(inverso aditivo)*

ESSENTIAL QUESTION

How can you use addition and subtraction of integers to solve real-world problems?

EXAMPLE 1

Add.

A. $-8 + (-7)$ — The signs of both integers are the same.

$8 + 7 = 15$ — Find the sum of the absolute values.

$-8 + (-7) = -15$ — Use the sign of integers to write the sum.

B. $-5 + 11$ — The signs of the integers are different.

$|11| - |-5| = 6$ — Greater absolute value – lesser absolute value.

$-5 + 11 = 6$ — 11 has the greater absolute value, so the sum is positive.

EXAMPLE 2

The temperature Tuesday afternoon was 3 °C. Tuesday night, the temperature was −6 °C. Find the change in temperature.

Find the difference $-6 - 3$.

Rewrite as $-6 + (-3)$. — -3 is the opposite of 3.

$-6 + (-3) = -9$

The temperature decreased 9 °C.

EXERCISES

Add. (Lessons 1.1, 1.2)

1. $-10 + (-5)$ ________ **2.** $9 + (-20)$ ________ **3.** $-13 + 32$ ________

Subtract. (Lesson 1.3)

4. $-12 - 5$ ________ **5.** $25 - (-4)$ ________ **6.** $-3 - (-40)$ ________

7. Antoine has $13 in his checking account. He buys some school supplies and ends up with $5 in his account. What was the overall change in Antoine's account? (Lesson 1.4) ________

MODULE 2

Multiplying and Dividing Integers

ESSENTIAL QUESTION

How can you use multiplication and division of integers to solve real-world problems?

EXAMPLE 1

Multiply.

A. (13)(−3)

Find the sign of the product. The numbers have different signs, so the product will be negative. Multiply the absolute values. Assign the correct sign to the product.

$13(-3) = -39$

B. (−5)(−8)

Find the sign of the product. The numbers have the same sign, so the product will be positive. Multiply the absolute values. Assign the correct sign to the product.

$(-5)(-8) = 40$

EXAMPLE 2

Christine received −25 points on her exam for 5 wrong answers. How many points did Christine receive for each wrong answer?

Divide −25 by 5.

$-25 \div 5 = -5$ — The signs are different. The quotient is negative.

Christine received −5 points for each wrong answer.

EXAMPLE 3

Simplify: 15 + (−3) × 8

$15 + (-24)$ — Multiply first.

-9 — Add.

EXERCISES

Multiply or divide. (Lessons 2.1, 2.2)

1. $-9 \times (-5)$ ______
2. $0 \times (-10)$ ______
3. $12 \times (-4)$ ______
4. $-32 \div 8$ ______
5. $-9 \div (-1)$ ______
6. $-56 \div 8$ ______

Simplify. (Lesson 2.3)

7. $-14 \div 2 - 3$ ______
8. $8 + (-20) \times 3$ ______
9. $36 \div (-6) \times -15$ ______

10. Tony bought 3 packs of pencils for $4 each and a pencil box for $7. Mario bought 4 binders for $6 each and used a coupon for $6 off. Write and evaluate expressions to find who spent more money. (Lesson 2.3)

______

MODULE 3 Rational Numbers

ESSENTIAL QUESTION

How can you use rational numbers to solve real-world problems?

Key Vocabulary

rational number *(número racional)*

repeating decimal *(decimal periódico)*

terminating decimal *(decimal finito)*

EXAMPLE 1

Eddie walked $1\frac{2}{3}$ miles on a hiking trail. Write $1\frac{2}{3}$ as a decimal. Use the decimal to classify $1\frac{2}{3}$ according to the number group(s) to which it belongs.

$1\frac{2}{3} = \frac{5}{3}$ — Write $1\frac{2}{3}$ as an improper fraction.

$$\begin{array}{r} 1.66 \\ 3\overline{)5.00} \\ -3 \\ \hline 2\,0 \\ -1\,8 \\ \hline 20 \\ -18 \\ \hline 2 \end{array}$$

Divide the numerator by the denominator.

The decimal equivalent of $1\frac{2}{3}$ is 1.66..., or $1.\overline{6}$. It is a repeating decimal, and therefore can be classified as a rational number.

EXAMPLE 2

Find each sum or difference.

A. $-2 + 4.5$

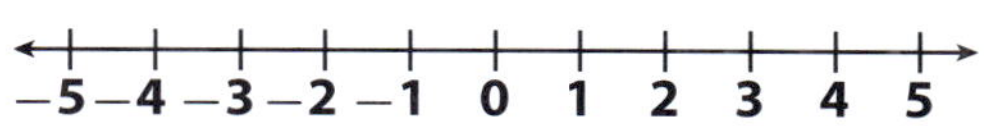

Start at -2 and move 4.5 units to the right: $-2 + 4.5 = 2.5$.

B. $-\frac{2}{5} - \left(-\frac{4}{5}\right)$

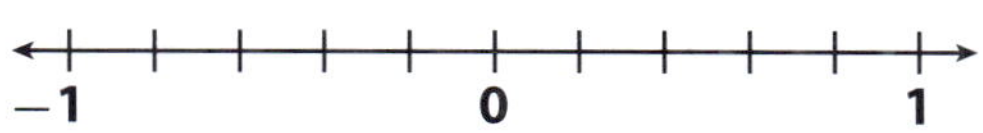

Start at $-\frac{2}{5}$. Move $\left|-\frac{4}{5}\right| = \frac{4}{5}$ unit to the right because you are subtracting a negative number: $-\frac{2}{5} - \left(-\frac{4}{5}\right) = \frac{2}{5}$.

EXAMPLE 3

Find the product: $3\left(-\frac{1}{6}\right)\left(-\frac{2}{5}\right)$.

$3\left(-\frac{1}{6}\right) = -\frac{1}{2}$ — Find the product of the first two factors. One is positive and one is negative, so the product is negative.

$-\frac{1}{\cancel{2}}\left(-\frac{\cancel{2}}{5}\right) = \frac{1}{5}$ — Multiply the result by the third factor. Both are negative, so the product is positive.

$3\left(-\frac{1}{6}\right)\left(-\frac{2}{5}\right) = \frac{1}{5}$

EXAMPLE 4

Find the quotient: $\frac{15.2}{-2}$.

$\frac{15.2}{-2} = -7.6$ The quotient is negative because the signs are different.

EXAMPLE 5

A lake's level dropped an average of $3\frac{4}{5}$ inches per day for 21 days. A heavy rain then raised the level 8.25 feet, after which it dropped $9\frac{1}{2}$ inches per day for 4 days. Jayden says that overall, the lake level changed about $-1\frac{1}{2}$ feet. Is this answer reasonable?

Yes; the lake drops about 4 inches, or $\frac{1}{3}$ foot, per day for 21 days, rises about 8 feet, then falls about $\frac{3}{4}$ foot for 4 days:
$-\frac{1}{3}(21) + 8 - \frac{3}{4}(4) = -7 + 8 - 3 = -2$ feet.

EXERCISES

Write each mixed number as a whole number or decimal. Classify each number according to the group(s) to which it belongs: rational numbers, integers, or whole numbers. (Lesson 3.1)

1. $\frac{3}{4}$ ______
2. $\frac{8}{2}$ ______
3. $\frac{11}{3}$ ______
4. $\frac{5}{2}$ ______

Find each sum or difference. (Lessons 3.2, 3.3)

5. $-5 + 9.5$ ______
6. $\frac{1}{6} + \left(-\frac{5}{6}\right)$ ______
7. $-0.5 + (-8.5)$ ______
8. $-3 - (-8)$ ______
9. $5.6 - (-3.1)$ ______
10. $3\frac{1}{2} - 2\frac{1}{4}$ ______

Find each product or quotient. (Lessons 3.4, 3.5)

11. $-9 \times (-5)$ ______
12. $0 \times (-7)$ ______
13. -8×8 ______
14. $\frac{-56}{8}$ ______
15. $\frac{-130}{-5}$ ______
16. $\frac{34.5}{1.5}$ ______
17. $-\frac{2}{5}\left(-\frac{1}{2}\right)\left(-\frac{5}{6}\right)$ ______
18. $\left(\frac{1}{5}\right)\left(-\frac{5}{7}\right)\left(\frac{3}{4}\right)$ ______
19. Lei withdrew \$50 from her bank account every day for a week. What was the change in her account in that week?

______

20. Dan is cutting 4.75 foot lengths of twine from a 240 foot spool of twine. He needs to cut 42 lengths, and says that 40.5 feet of twine will remain. Show that this is reasonable.

______

Unit 1 Performance Tasks

1. **CAREERS IN MATH** **Urban Planner** Armand is an urban planner, and he has proposed a site for a new town library. The site is between City Hall and the post office on Main Street.

The distance between City Hall and the post office is $6\frac{1}{2}$ miles. City Hall is $1\frac{1}{4}$ miles closer to the library site than it is to the post office.

a. Write $6\frac{1}{2}$ miles and $1\frac{1}{4}$ miles as decimals.

____

b. Let *d* represent the distance from City Hall to the library site. Write an expression for the distance from the library site to the post office.

____

c. Write an equation that represents the following statement: The distance from City Hall to the library site plus the distance from the library site to the post office is equal to the distance from City Hall to the post office.

____

d. Solve your equation from part **c** to determine the distance from City Hall to the library site, and the distance from the post office to the library site.

____

____

2. Sumaya is reading a book with 288 pages. She has already read 90 pages. She plans to read 20 more pages each day until she finishes the book.

a. Sumaya writes the equation $378 = -20d$ to find the number of days she will need to finish the book. Identify the errors that Sumaya made.

____

____

b. Write and solve an equation to determine how many days Sumaya will need to finish the book. In your answer, count part of a day as a full day. Show that your answer is reasonable.

____

____

c. Estimate how many days you would need to read a book about the same length as Sumaya's book. What information did you use to find the estimate?

3. Jackson works as a veterinary technician and earns \$12.20 per hour.

a. Jackson normally works 40 hours a week. In a normal week, what is his total pay before taxes and other deductions?

b. Last week, Jackson was ill and missed some work. His total pay before deductions was \$372.10. Write and solve an equation to find the number of hours Jackson worked.

c. Jackson records his hours each day on a time sheet. Last week when he was ill, his time sheet was incomplete. How many hours are missing? Show your work. Then show that your answer is reasonable.

Mon	Tues	Wed	Thurs	Fri
8	$7\frac{1}{4}$	$8\frac{1}{2}$		

d. When Jackson works more than 40 hours in a week, he earns 1.5 times his normal hourly rate for each of the extra hours. Jackson worked 43 hours one week. What was his total pay before deductions? Justify your answer.

e. What is a reasonable range for Jackson's expected yearly pay before deductions? Describe any assumptions you made in finding your answer.

UNIT 1 **MIXED REVIEW**

Assessment Readiness

Personal Math Trainer
Online Assessment and Intervention
my.hrw.com

Selected Response

1. What is $-6\frac{9}{16}$ written as a decimal?

Ⓐ -6.625

Ⓑ -6.5625

Ⓒ -6.4375

Ⓓ -6.125

2. Working together, 6 friends pick $14\frac{2}{5}$ pounds of pecans at a pecan farm. They divide the pecans equally among themselves. How many pounds does each friend get?

Ⓐ $20\frac{2}{5}$ pounds

Ⓑ $8\frac{2}{5}$ pounds

Ⓒ $2\frac{3}{5}$ pounds

Ⓓ $2\frac{2}{5}$ pounds

3. What is the value of $(-3.25)(-1.56)$?

Ⓐ -5.85

Ⓑ -5.07

Ⓒ 5.07

Ⓓ 5.85

4. Mrs. Rodriguez is going to use $6\frac{1}{3}$ yards of material to make two dresses. The larger dress requires $3\frac{2}{3}$ yards of material. How much material will Mrs. Rodriguez have left to use on the smaller dress?

Ⓐ $1\frac{2}{3}$ yards

Ⓑ $2\frac{1}{3}$ yards

Ⓒ $2\frac{2}{3}$ yards

Ⓓ $3\frac{1}{3}$ yards

5. Jaime had \$37 in his bank account on Sunday. The table shows his account activity for the next four days. What was the balance in Jaime's account after his deposit on Thursday?

Jamie's Bank Account		
Day	**Deposit**	**Withdrawal**
Monday	\$17.42	none
Tuesday	none	−\$12.60
Wednesday	none	−\$9.62
Thursday	\$62.29	none

Ⓐ \$57.49

Ⓑ \$59.65

Ⓒ \$94.49

Ⓓ \$138.93

6. A used motorcycle is on sale for \$3,600. Erik makes an offer equal to $\frac{3}{4}$ of this price. How much does Erik offer for the motorcycle?

Ⓐ \$4,800

Ⓑ \$2,700

Ⓒ \$2,400

Ⓓ \$900

7. Ruby ate $\frac{1}{3}$ of a pizza, and Angie ate $\frac{1}{5}$ of the pizza. How much of the pizza did they eat in all?

Ⓐ $\frac{1}{15}$ of the pizza

Ⓑ $\frac{1}{8}$ of the pizza

Ⓒ $\frac{3}{8}$ of the pizza

Ⓓ $\frac{8}{15}$ of the pizza

8. Winslow buys 1.2 pounds of bananas. The bananas cost \$1.29 per pound. To the nearest cent, how much does Winslow pay for the bananas?

Ⓐ \$1.08

Ⓑ \$1.20

Ⓒ \$1.55

Ⓓ \$2.49

9. The temperature was -10 °F and dropped by 16 °F. Which statement represents the resulting temperature in degrees Fahrenheit?

Ⓐ $-10 - (-16) = -6$

Ⓑ $-10 - 16 = -26$

Ⓒ $10 - (-16) = 26$

Ⓓ $-10 + 16 = 6$

10. A scuba diver at a depth of -12 ft (12 ft below sea level), dives down to a coral reef that is 3.5 times the diver's original depth. What is the diver's new depth?

Ⓐ -420 ft

Ⓑ -42 ft

Ⓒ 42 ft

Ⓓ about 3.4 ft

11. The school Spirit Club spent \$320.82 on food and took in \$643.59 selling the food. How much did the Spirit Club make?

Ⓐ $-$\$322.77

Ⓑ $-$\$964.41

Ⓒ \$322.77

Ⓓ \$964.41

12. Lila graphed the points -2 and 2 on a number line. What does the distance between these two points represent?

Ⓐ the sum of -2 and 2

Ⓑ the difference of 2 and -2

Ⓒ the difference of -2 and 2

Ⓓ the product of -2 and 2

Hot Tip! **Some answer choices, called distracters, may seem correct because they are based on common errors.**

13. What is a reasonable estimate of $-3\frac{4}{5} + (-5.25)$ and the actual value?

Ⓐ $-4 + (-5) = -9; -9\frac{1}{20}$

Ⓑ $-3 + (-5) = -8; -8\frac{1}{20}$

Ⓒ $-4 + (-5) = -1; -8\frac{9}{20}$

Ⓓ $-3 + (-5) = 8; 8\frac{1}{20}$

Mini-Task

14. Juanita is watering her lawn using the water stored in her rainwater tank. The water level in the tank drops $\frac{1}{3}$ inch every 10 minutes she waters.

a. What is the change in the tank's water level after 1 hour?

____

b. What is the expected change in the tank's water level after 2.25 hours?

____

c. If the tank's water level is 4 feet, how many days can Juanita water if she waters for 15 minutes each day?

____

UNIT 2

Ratios and Proportional Relationships

MODULE 4
Rates and Proportionality

MODULE 5
Proportions and Percents

CAREERS IN MATH

Bicycle Tour Operator A bike tour operator organizes cycling trips for tourists all over the world. Bike tour operators use math to calculate expenses, determine rates, and compute payroll information for their employees. If tours include travel in another country, operators must understand how to calculate currency exchange rates.

If you are interested in a career as a bicycle tour operator, you should study these mathematical subjects:

- Basic Math
- Business Math

Research other careers that require the understanding of business mathematics.

Unit 2 Performance Task

At the end of the unit, check out how **bicycle tour operators** use math.

UNIT 2

Vocabulary Preview

Use the puzzle to preview key vocabulary from this unit. Unscramble the circled letters within found words to answer the riddle at the bottom of the page.

1. A relationship between two quantities in which the rate of change or the ratio of one quantity to the other is constant. (Lesson 4.3)

(○) ___ ___ (○) ___ ___ ___ ___ ___ ___ ___ ___

(○) ___ ___ ___ ___ ___ (○) ___ ___ ___ ___ ___

2. Describes how much a quantity decreases in comparison to the original amount. (Lesson 5.1) ___ ___ (○) ___ ___ ___ ___

___ ___ ___ ___ ___ ___ ___ ___

3. A fixed percent of the principal. (Lesson 5.3)

___ ___ ___ ___ ___ ___   ___ (○) ___ ___ ___ ___ ___ (○)

4. The quantity k in a relationship described by an equation of the form $y = kx$. (Lesson 4.3)

___ (○) ___ ___ ___ ___ ___ ___ ___   ___ ___

___ ___ ___ ___ ___ ___ ___ ___ ___ ___ ___ ___ (○) ___ ___

5. A ratio that compares the amount of change in the dependent variable to the amount of change in the independent variable. (Lesson 4.2)

___ (○) ___ ___   (○) ___   ___ ___ ___ ___ ___ ___

Q: What did the athlete order when he needed a huge helping of mashed potatoes?

A: ___   ___ ___ ___ - ___ ___ ___ ___ ___ ___ ___!

Rates and Proportionality

MODULE 4

? **ESSENTIAL QUESTION**

How can you use rates and proportionality to solve real-world problems?

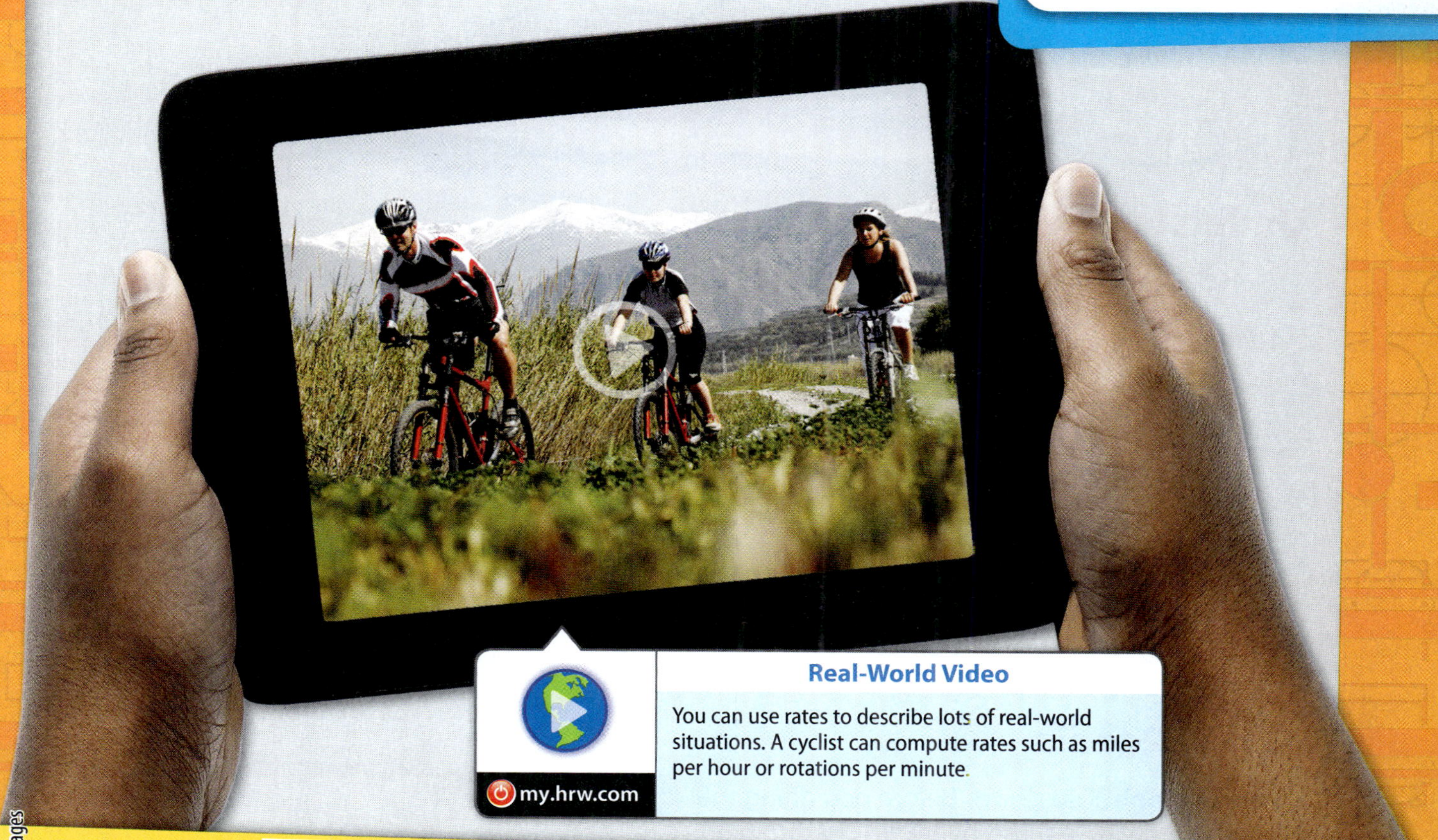

Real-World Video

You can use rates to describe lots of real-world situations. A cyclist can compute rates such as miles per hour or rotations per minute.

my.hrw.com

GO DIGITAL
my.hrw.com

my.hrw.com
Go digital with your write-in student edition, accessible on any device.

Math On the Spot
Scan with your smart phone to jump directly to the online edition, video tutor, and more.

Animated Math
Interactively explore key concepts to see how math works.

Personal Math Trainer
Get immediate feedback and help as you work through practice sets.

Reading Start-Up

Visualize Vocabulary

Use the ✔ words to complete the graphic. You can put more than one word in each bubble.

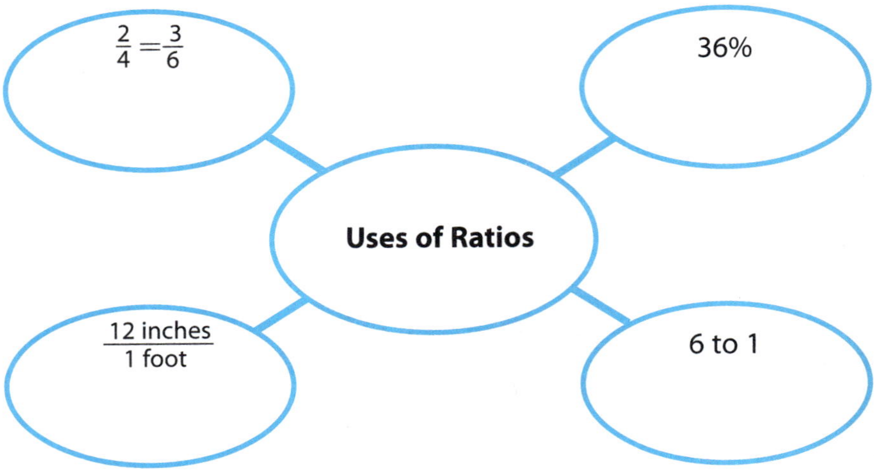

Understand Vocabulary

Match the term on the left to the definition on the right.

1. rate of change — **A.** Statement that two rates or ratios are equivalent.
2. proportion — **B.** A rate that describes how one quantity changes in relation to another quantity.
3. unit rate — **C.** Rate in which the second quantity is one unit.

Vocabulary

Review Words

constant *(constante)*
✔ conversion factor *(factor de conversión)*
✔ equivalent ratios *(razones equivalentes)*
✔ percent *(porcentaje)*
rate *(tasa)*
✔ ratio *(razón)*

Preview Words

complex fraction *(fracción compleja)*
constant of proportionality *(constante de proporcionalidad)*
proportion *(proporción)*
proportional relationship *(relación proporcional)*
rate of change *(tasa de cambio)*
unit rates *(tasas unitarias)*

Active Reading

Three-Panel Flip Chart Before beginning the module, create a three-panel flip chart to help you organize what you learn. Label each flap with one of the lesson titles from this module. As you study each lesson, write important ideas like vocabulary, properties, and formulas under the appropriate flap.

Are YOU Ready?

Complete these exercises to review skills you will need for this module.

Personal Math Trainer
my.hrw.com
Online Assessment and Intervention

Operations with Fractions

EXAMPLE

$$\frac{3}{10} \div \frac{5}{8} = \frac{3}{10} \times \frac{8}{5}$$ Multiply by the reciprocal of the divisor.

$$= \frac{3}{\cancel{10}_5} \times \frac{\cancel{8}^4}{5}$$ Divide by the common factors.

$$= \frac{12}{25}$$ Simplify.

Divide.

1. $\frac{3}{4} \div \frac{4}{5}$ ______ **2.** $\frac{5}{9} \div \frac{10}{11}$ ______ **3.** $\frac{3}{8} \div \frac{1}{2}$ ______ **4.** $\frac{16}{21} \div \frac{8}{9}$ ______

Ordered Pairs

EXAMPLE

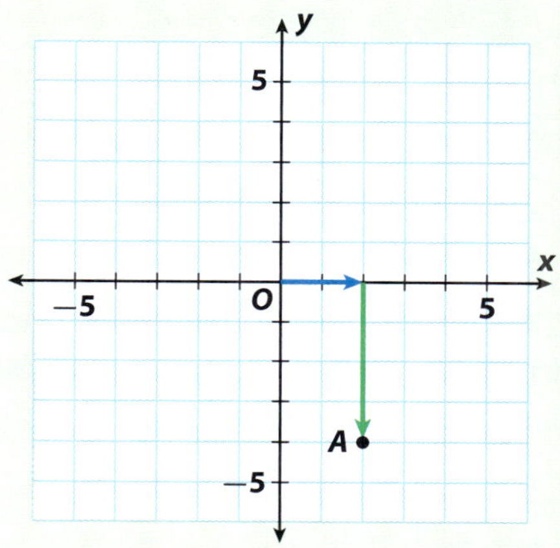

To write the ordered pair for A, start at the origin.
Move 2 units right.
Then move 4 units down.
The ordered pair for point A is $(2, -4)$.

Write the ordered pair for each point.

5. B ______ **6.** C ______

7. D ______ **8.** E ______

9. F ______ **10.** G ______

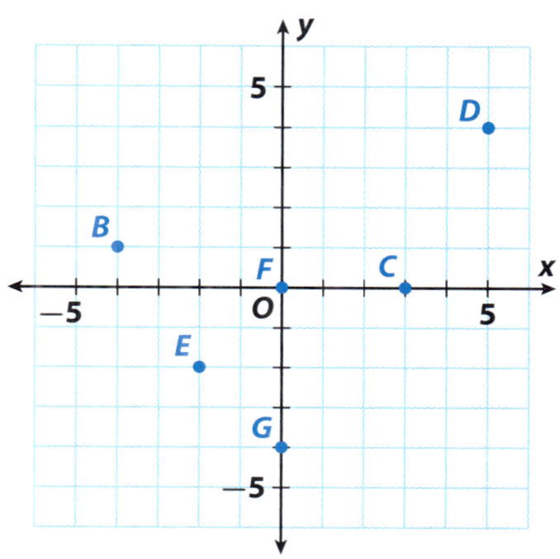

Are YOU Ready? *(cont'd)*

Complete these exercises to review skills you will need for this module.

Operations with Fractions

11. A track is $\frac{3}{4}$ mile long. The track is measured in units called furlongs. One furlong is equivalent to $\frac{1}{8}$ mile. How long is the track in furlongs? Show your work.

12. Which is greater: $\frac{1}{2} \div \frac{7}{10}$ or $\frac{1}{2} \div \frac{7}{8}$? How do you know?

Ordered Pairs

13. The origin on the coordinate grid represents Lincoln Middle School. Dora, Pedro, Naomi, and Rajeev live at the points represented by their initials. Write the ordered pair for each student's home with respect to the location of Lincoln Middle School.

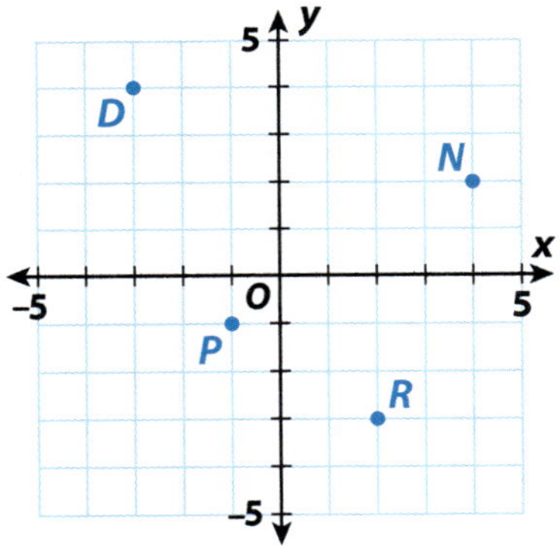

LESSON

4.1 Unit Rates

7.2.4.1

Students will find and use unit rates.

ESSENTIAL QUESTION

How do you find and use unit rates?

EXPLORE ACTIVITY Real World

Exploring Rates

Commonly used rates like miles per hour make it easy to understand and compare rates.

Jeff hikes $\frac{1}{2}$ mile every 15 minutes, or $\frac{1}{4}$ hour. Lisa hikes $\frac{1}{3}$ mile every 10 minutes, or $\frac{1}{6}$ hour. How far do they each hike in 1 hour? 2 hours?

A Use the bar diagram to help you determine how many miles Jeff hikes. How many $\frac{1}{4}$-hours are in 1 hour? How far does Jeff hike in 1 hour?

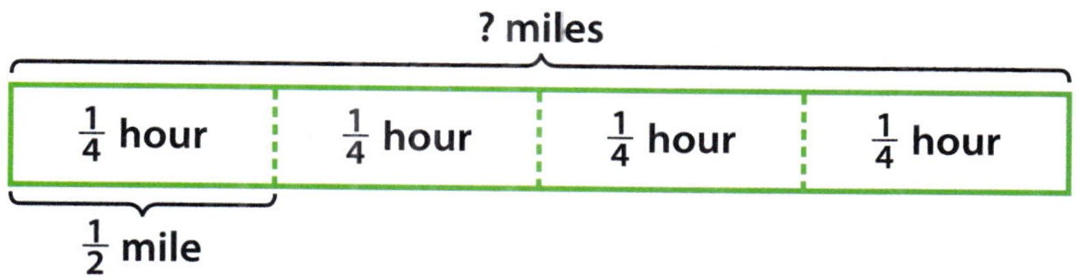

____

B Complete the table for Jeff's hike.

Distance (mi)	$\frac{1}{2}$				
Time (h)	$\frac{1}{4}$	$\frac{1}{2}$	$\frac{3}{4}$	1	2

C Complete the bar diagram to help you determine how far Lisa hikes. How many miles does she hike in 1 hour?

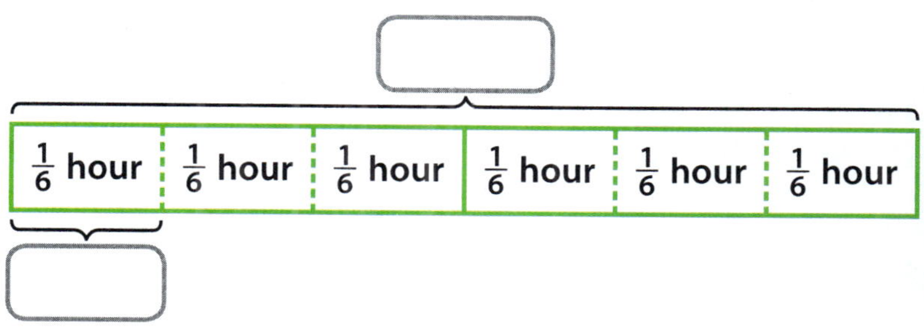

____

D Complete the table for Lisa's hike.

Distance (mi)	$\frac{1}{3}$				
Time (h)	$\frac{1}{6}$	$\frac{1}{3}$	$\frac{1}{2}$	1	2

EXPLORE ACTIVITY *(cont'd)*

Reflect

1. How did you find Jeff's distance for $\frac{3}{4}$ hour?

____

2. Which hiker walks farther in one hour? Which is faster?

____

Math On the Spot
my.hrw.com

Finding Unit Rates

A rate is a comparison of two quantities that have different units, such as miles and hours. Rates are often expressed as **unit rates**, that is, with a denominator of 1 unit.

$$\frac{60 \text{ miles} \div 2}{2 \text{ hours} \div 2} = \frac{30 \text{ miles}}{1 \text{ hour}}$$ This means 30 miles per hour.

When the two quantities being compared in the rate are both fractions, the rate is expressed as a *complex fraction*. A **complex fraction** is a fraction that has a fraction in its numerator, denominator, or both.

$$\frac{\frac{a}{b}}{\frac{c}{d}} = \frac{a}{b} \div \frac{c}{d}$$

EXAMPLE 1 Real World

While remodeling her kitchen, Angela is repainting. She estimates that she paints 55 square feet every half-hour. How many square feet does Angela paint per hour?

STEP 1 Determine the units of the rate.

The rate is **area in square feet** per **time in hours**.

STEP 2 Find Angela's rate of painting in area painted per time.

area painted: 55 sq ft **time:** $\frac{1}{2}$ hour

$$\frac{\text{area painted}}{\text{time}} = \frac{55 \text{ square feet}}{\frac{1}{2} \text{ hour}}$$

The fraction represents area in square feet per time in hours.

STEP 3 Find Angela's unit rate of painting in square feet per hour.

$\frac{55}{\frac{1}{2}} = 55 \div \frac{1}{2}$ Rewrite the fraction as division.

$= \frac{55}{1} \times \frac{2}{1}$ Multiply by the reciprocal.

$= \frac{110 \text{ square feet}}{1 \text{ hour}}$ The unit rate has a denominator of 1.

Angela paints 110 square feet per hour.

YOUR TURN

3. Paige mows $\frac{1}{6}$ acre in $\frac{1}{4}$ hour. How many acres does Paige mow per hour?

____

4. Greta uses 3 ounces of pasta to make $\frac{3}{4}$ of a serving of pasta. How many ounces of pasta are there per serving? ____________________

Personal Math Trainer
Online Assessment and Intervention
my.hrw.com

Using Unit Rates

You can use unit rates to simplify rates and ratios that appear complicated, such as those containing fractions in both the numerator and denominator.

Math On the Spot
my.hrw.com

EXAMPLE 2 Real World

Two pools are leaking. After 15 minutes, pool A has leaked $\frac{2}{3}$ gallon. After 20 minutes, pool B has leaked $\frac{3}{4}$ gallon. Which pool is leaking faster?

STEP 1 Find the rate in volume (gallons) per time (hours) at which each pool is leaking. First convert minutes to hours.

Pool A

$$\frac{\frac{2}{3}\text{ gal}}{15\text{ min}} = \frac{\frac{2}{3}\text{ gal}}{\frac{1}{4}\text{ h}}$$

15 min $= \frac{1}{4}$ h

Pool B

$$\frac{\frac{3}{4}\text{ gal}}{20\text{ min}} = \frac{\frac{3}{4}\text{ gal}}{\frac{1}{3}\text{ h}}$$

20 min $= \frac{1}{3}$ h

STEP 2 To find the unit rates, first rewrite the fractions.

Pool A

$$\frac{\frac{2}{3}\text{ gal}}{\frac{1}{4}\text{ h}} = \frac{2}{3} \div \frac{1}{4}$$

Pool B

$$\frac{\frac{3}{4}\text{ gal}}{\frac{1}{3}\text{ h}} = \frac{3}{4} \div \frac{1}{3}$$

STEP 3 To divide, multiply by the reciprocal.

Pool A

$$\frac{2}{3} \div \frac{1}{4} = \frac{2}{3} \times \frac{4}{1}$$
$$= \frac{8}{3}\text{, or } 2\tfrac{2}{3}\text{ gal per h}$$

Pool B

$$\frac{3}{4} \div \frac{1}{3} = \frac{3}{4} \times \frac{3}{1}$$
$$= \frac{9}{4}\text{, or } 2\tfrac{1}{4}\text{ gal per h}$$

STEP 4 Compare the unit rates.

Pool A **Pool B**

$$2\tfrac{2}{3} > 2\tfrac{1}{4}$$

So, Pool A is leaking faster.

My Notes

Math Talk
Mathematical Processes
How do you compare mixed numbers?

Personal Math Trainer
Online Assessment and Intervention
my.hrw.com

YOUR TURN

5. Jaylan makes limeade using $\frac{3}{4}$ cup water for every $\frac{1}{5}$ cup lime juice. Wanchen makes limeade using $\frac{2}{3}$ cup water for every $\frac{1}{6}$ cup lime juice. Find the unit rates of water (cups) per lime juice (cups). Whose limeade has a weaker lime flavor? Explain.

____

____

____

____

Guided Practice

1. Brandon enters bike races. He bikes $8\frac{1}{2}$ miles every $\frac{1}{2}$ hour. Complete the table to find how far Brandon bikes for each time interval. (Explore Activity)

Distance (mi)	$8\frac{1}{2}$				
Time (h)	$\frac{1}{2}$	1	$1\frac{1}{2}$	2	$2\frac{1}{2}$

Find each unit rate. (Example 1)

2. Julio walks $3\frac{1}{2}$ miles in $1\frac{1}{4}$ hours.

____

3. Kenny reads $\frac{5}{8}$ page in $\frac{2}{3}$ minute.

____

4. A garden snail moves $\frac{1}{6}$ foot in $\frac{1}{3}$ hour.

____

5. A machine covers $\frac{5}{8}$ square foot in $\frac{1}{4}$ hour.

____

Find each unit rate. Determine which is lower. (Example 2)

6. Brand A: 240 mg sodium for $\frac{1}{3}$ pickle
or Brand B: 325 mg sodium for $\frac{1}{2}$ pickle

____

____

7. Ingredient C: $\frac{1}{4}$ cup for $\frac{2}{3}$ serving
or Ingredient D: $\frac{1}{3}$ cup for $\frac{3}{4}$ serving

____

____

ESSENTIAL QUESTION CHECK-IN

8. How can you find a unit rate when given a rate?

____

____

Name ________________ Class ________________ Date ________________

4.1 Independent Practice

Personal Math Trainer
Online Assessment and Intervention
my.hrw.com

9. The information for two pay-as-you-go cell phone companies is given.

On Call	Talk Time
3.5 hours: $10	$\frac{1}{2}$ hour: $1.25

a. What is the unit rate in dollars per hour for each company?

b. **Analyze Relationships** Which company offers the best deal? Explain your answer.

c. **What If?** Another company offers a rate of $0.05 per minute. How would you find the unit rate per hour?

d. **Draw Conclusions** Is the rate in part **c** a better deal than On Call or Talk Time? Explain.

10. **Represent Real-World Problems** Your teacher asks you to find a recipe that includes two ingredients with a ratio of $\frac{\frac{1}{2}\text{ cup}}{\frac{1}{8}\text{ cup}}$.

a. Give an example of two ingredients in a recipe that would meet this requirement.

b. If you needed to triple the recipe, would the ratio change? Explain.

c. What is the unit rate of the two ingredients in part **a**?

11. A radio station requires DJs to play 2 commercials for every 10 songs they play. What is the unit rate of songs to commercials?

12. **Multistep** Terrance and Jesse are training for a long-distance race. Terrance trains at a rate of 6 miles every half hour, and Jesse trains at a rate of 2 miles every 15 minutes.

a. What is the unit rate in miles per hour for each runner?

b. How long will each person take to run a total of 50 miles at the given rates?

c. Sandra runs at a rate of 8 miles in 45 minutes. How does her unit rate compare to Terrance's and to Jesse's?

13. **Analyze Relationships** Eli takes a typing test and types all 300 words in $\frac{1}{10}$ hour. He takes the test a second time and types the words in $\frac{1}{12}$ hour. Was he faster or slower on the second attempt? Explain.

Work Area

H.O.T. FOCUS ON HIGHER ORDER THINKING

14. **Justify Reasoning** An online retailer sells two packages of protein bars.

Package	10-pack of 2.1 ounce bars	12-pack of 1.4 ounce bars
Cost ($)	15.37	15.35

a. Which package has the better price per bar?

b. Which package has the better price per ounce?

c. Which package do you think is a better buy? Justify your reasoning.

15. **Check for Reasonableness** A painter painted about half a room in half a day. Coley estimated the painter would paint 7 rooms in 7 days. Is Coley's estimate reasonable? Explain.

16. **Communicate Mathematical Ideas** If you know the rate of a water leak in gallons per hour, how can you find the number of hours it takes for 1 gallon to leak out? Justify your answer.

LESSON **4.2**

Constant Rates of Change

7.2.4.2

Students will identify and represent proportional relationships.

ESSENTIAL QUESTION

How can you identify and represent proportional relationships?

EXPLORE ACTIVITY Real World

Discovering Proportional Relationships

The bar diagram shows how far one tortoise walks on land over time.

A Use the bar diagram to determine how many inches the tortoise travels in the third second.

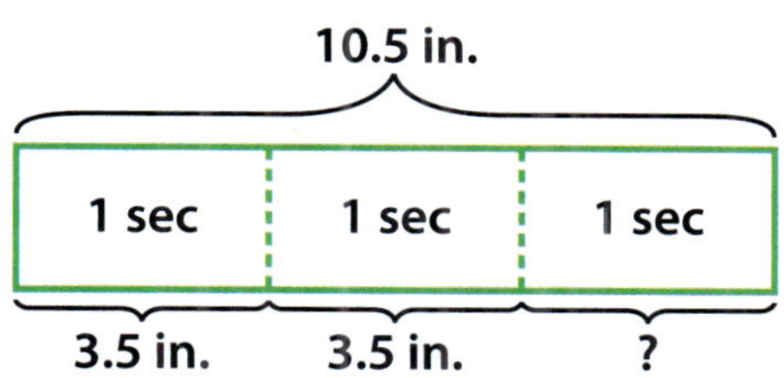

____

B Complete the table, assuming that the tortoise continues at a steady pace.

Time (sec)	1	2	3	4	5
Distance (in.)			10.5		

C For each column of the table, write a rate that compares the distance and the time. Put distance in the numerator and time in the denominator. Divide to write the rate as a decimal.

$\frac{\square}{\square} = \square$ $\quad \frac{\square}{\square} = \square$ $\quad \frac{\square}{\square} = \square$ $\quad \frac{\square}{\square} = \square$ $\quad \frac{\square}{\square} = \square$

D What do you notice about the decimal forms of the rates?

____

E Use a unit rate to describe how the distance the tortoise travels is related to time.

____

EXPLORE ACTIVITY *(cont'd)*

Reflect

1. Suppose the tortoise travels for 12 seconds at the same rate. Explain how you could find the distance the tortoise travels.

____

2. Explain why the tortoise's walking rate could be called *constant*.

____

Math On the Spot
my.hrw.com

Proportional Relationships

A **proportion** is a statement that two rates or ratios are equivalent. For example, $\frac{6\text{ mi}}{2\text{ h}} = \frac{3\text{ mi}}{1\text{ h}}$, or $\frac{2}{4} = \frac{1}{2}$.

A **proportional relationship** between two quantities is one in which the ratio of one quantity to the other is constant. A **rate of change** is a rate that describes how one quantity changes in relation to another quantity. In a proportional relationship, the rate of change is constant.

Proportional relationships are often described using words such as *per* or *for each*. For example, the rate $\frac{\$1.25}{1\text{ pound}}$ could be described as \$1.25 per pound or \$1.25 for each pound.

My Notes

EXAMPLE 1 Real World

Callie earns money by dog sitting. Based on the table, is the relationship between the amount Callie earns and the number of days a proportional relationship?

Number of Days	1	2	3	4	5
Amount Earned ($)	16	32	48	64	80

STEP 1 Write the rates.

$\frac{\text{Amount earned}}{\text{Number of days}} = \frac{\$16}{1\text{ day}}$

Put the amount earned in the numerator and the number of days in the denominator.

$\frac{\$32}{2\text{ days}} = \frac{\$16}{1\text{ day}}$

$\frac{\$48}{3\text{ days}} = \frac{\$16}{1\text{ day}}$

Each rate is equal to $\frac{\$16}{1\text{ day}}$, or \$16 per day.

$\frac{\$64}{4\text{ days}} = \frac{\$16}{1\text{ day}}$

$\frac{\$80}{5\text{ days}} = \frac{\$16}{1\text{ day}}$

STEP 2 Compare the rates. The rates are all equal. This means the rate is constant, so the relationship is proportional.

The constant rate of change is \$16 per day.

Math Talk
Mathematical Processes

How can you use the constant rate to find how much Callie earns for 10 days of dog sitting?

YOUR TURN

3. The table shows the distance Allison drove on one day of her vacation. Is the relationship between the distance and the time a proportional relationship? Did she drive at a constant speed? Explain.

Time (h)	1	2	3	4	5
Distance (mi)	65	120	195	220	300

____

Personal Math Trainer
Online Assessment and Intervention
my.hrw.com

Writing an Equation for a Proportional Relationship

If there is a proportional relationship between x and y, you can describe that relationship using the equation $y = kx$. The variable x is the independent variable and y is the dependent variable. The variable k is called the **constant of proportionality**, and it represents the constant rate of change or constant ratio between x and y. The value of k is represented by the equation $k = \frac{y}{x}$.

Math On the Spot
my.hrw.com

EXAMPLE 2 Real World

Two pounds of the cashews shown cost $19, and 8 pounds cost $76. Show that the relationship between the number of pounds of cashews and the cost is a proportional relationship. Then write an equation for the relationship. Describe the proportional relationship in words.

STEP 1 Make a table relating cost in dollars to pounds.

Number of Pounds	2	3	8
Cost ($)	19	28.50	76

STEP 2 Write the rates as fractions. Put the dependent variable, cost, in the numerator. Then write each rate as a decimal.

$$\frac{\text{Cost}}{\text{Number of Pounds}} \longrightarrow \frac{19}{2} = 9.50 \qquad \frac{28.50}{3} = 9.50 \qquad \frac{76}{8} = 9.50$$

The rates are all equal to $9.50 per pound. They are constant, so the relationship is proportional. The constant rate of change is $9.50 per pound.

STEP 3 To write an equation, first tell what the variables represent.

- Let x represent the number of pounds of cashews.
- Let y represent the cost in dollars.
- Use the decimal form of the constant rate of change as the constant of proportionality.

The equation for the relationship is $y = 9.5x$.

The cost is $9.50 per pound.

Math Talk
Mathematical Processes
How can you use your equation to find the cost of 6 pounds of cashews?

Personal Math Trainer
Online Assessment and Intervention
my.hrw.com

YOUR TURN

4. The table shows the number of adults required for a given number of students for a school field trip. Show that the relationship between the number of adults and the number of students is a proportional relationship. Then write an equation for the relationship.

Number of students	12	36	60
Number of adults	1	3	5

____

____

Guided Practice

1. The table shows the relationship between the age and height of a student. Use unit rates to determine if the relationship is a proportional relationship. (Explore Activity and Example 1)

Age (years)	6	7	8	9
Height (inches)	48	49	52	54

$\frac{\text{Height}}{\text{Age}}$: $\frac{48}{6} = \square$ $\frac{\square}{\square} = \square$ $\frac{\square}{\square} = \square$ $\frac{\square}{\square} = \square$

The relationship **is/ is not** proportional.

Find the constant of proportionality *k*. Then write an equation for the relationship between *x* and *y*. (Example 2)

2.

x	2	4	6	8
y	10	20	30	40

____

3.

x	8	16	24	32
y	2	4	6	8

____

ESSENTIAL QUESTION CHECK-IN

4. How can you represent a proportional relationship using an equation?

____

____

Name ____________ Class ____________ Date ____________

4.2 Independent Practice

Personal Math Trainer
Online Assessment and Intervention
my.hrw.com

Information on three car-rental companies is given.

Rent-All				
Days	3	4	5	6
Total Cost ($)	55.50	74.00	92.50	111.00

A-1 Rentals
The cost y of renting a car for x days is $10.99 for each half day.

Car Town
The cost of renting a car from us is just $19.25 per day!

5. Write an equation that gives the cost y of renting a car for x days from Rent-All. ____________

6. What is the cost per day of renting a car from A-1? ____________

7. **Analyze Relationships** Which company offers the best deal? Why?

____

____

8. **Critique Reasoning** A skydiver jumps out of an airplane. After 0.8 second, she has fallen 100 feet. After 3.1 seconds, she has fallen 500 feet. Emtiaz says that the skydiver should fall about 187.5 feet in 1.5 seconds. Is his answer reasonable? Explain.

____

____

____

Steven earns extra money babysitting. He charges $31.25 for 5 hours and $50 for 8 hours.

9. Explain why the relationship between how much Steven charges and time is a proportional relationship.

____

10. **Interpret the Answer** Explain what the constant rate of change means in the context.

____

11. Write an equation to represent the relationship. Tell what the variables represent.

____

____

12. How much would Steven charge for 3 hours? ____________

A submarine dives 300 feet every 2 minutes, and 6,750 feet every 45 minutes.

13. Find the constant rate at which the submarine dives. Give your answer in feet per minute and in feet per hour.

____

14. Let x represent the time of the dive. Let y represent the depth of the submarine. Write an equation for the proportional relationship using the rate in feet per minute.

____

15. **Draw Conclusions** If you wanted to find the depth of a submarine during a dive, would it be more reasonable to use an equation with the rate in feet per minute or feet per hour? Explain your reasoning.

____

H.O.T. FOCUS ON HIGHER ORDER THINKING

Work Area

16. **Critique Reasoning** Jack is 12 and his sister Sophia is 16. Jack says that the relationship between his age and Sophia's is proportional and the constant of proportionality is $\frac{12}{16}$. Do you agree? Explain.

____

____

17. **Make a Conjecture** There is a proportional relationship between your distance from a thunderstorm and the time from when you see lightning until you hear thunder. If that time is 9 seconds, the storm is about 3 kilometers away. If that time doubles, do you think the distance also doubles? Justify your reasoning.

____

____

18. **Communicate Mathematical Ideas** Luke's turkey chili recipe calls for 1.5 pounds of ground turkey for every 6 servings. How many servings can he make if he has 5 pounds of ground turkey? Show your work.

____

____

____

____

LESSON **4.3**

Proportional Relationships and Graphs

7.2.4.3

Students will use graphs to represent and analyze proportional relationships.

ESSENTIAL QUESTION

How can you use graphs to represent and analyze proportional relationships?

EXPLORE ACTIVITY Real World

Graphing Proportional Relationships

You can use a graph to explore proportional relationships.

The equation $y = 5x$ represents the relationship between the number of gallons of water used (y) and the number of minutes (x) for most showerheads manufactured before 1994.

A Explain why the relationship is proportional. Describe the relationship in words.

____

____

B Complete the table.

Time (min)	1	2	3		10
Water Used (gal)	5			35	

Substitute 2 for x in the equation $y = 5x$ and evaluate to find water used in 2 minutes.

C Write the data in the table as ordered pairs (time, water used).

(1, 5), (2, ____), (3, ____), (__ , 35), (10, ____)

D Plot the ordered pairs.

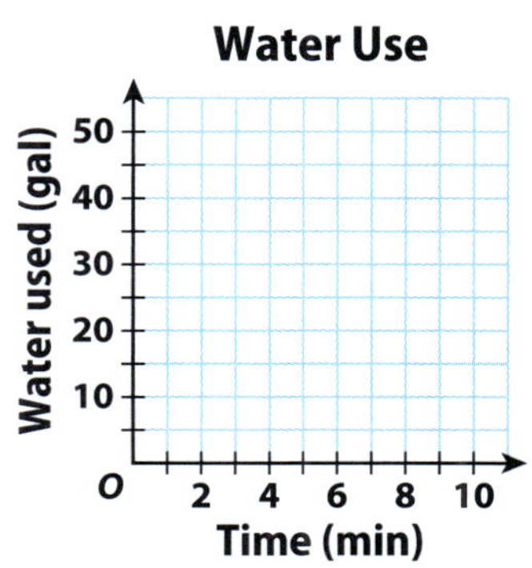

E If the showerhead is used for 0 minutes, how many gallons of water will be used? What ordered pair represents this situation? What is this location called? _______________________

F If the showerhead is used for 1 minute, how many gallons of water will be used? What ordered pair represents this situation? Why is this ordered pair significant?

____

G **Draw Conclusions** If you continued the table to include 23 minutes, would the point (23, 125) be on this graph? Why or why not?

____

Math On the Spot
my.hrw.com

Animated Math
my.hrw.com

Math Talk
Mathematical Processes

How does the table show a proportional relationship?

Identifying Proportional Relationships

In addition to using a table to determine if a relationship is proportional, you also can use a graph. A relationship is a proportional relationship if its graph is a straight line through the origin.

EXAMPLE 1 Real World

The table shows the relationship between the amount charged by a house cleaning company ($) and the amount of time worked (hours). Is the relationship a proportional relationship? Explain.

Time (h)	1	2	3	5	8
Total cost ($)	45	90	135	225	360

STEP 1 Write the data in the table as ordered pairs (time, cost).

(1, 45), (2, 90), (3, 135), (5, 225), (8, 360)

STEP 2 Graph the ordered pairs.

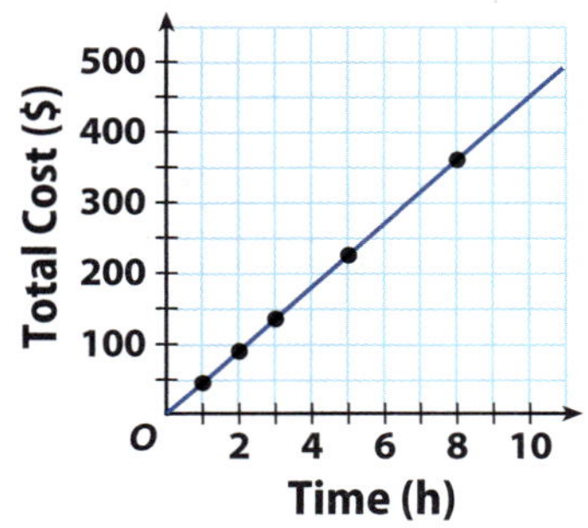

Place time on the x-axis and total cost on the y-axis.

Plot each point.

Notice that the points are on a line.

The graph is a line that goes through the origin.

The relationship is proportional. The point (1, 45) on the graph shows that the constant of proportionality (unit rate) is $45 per hour.

The housecleaning company charges $45 per hour.

YOUR TURN

1. Jared rents bowling shoes for $6 and pays $5 per bowling game. Is the relationship a proportional relationship? Explain.

Games	1	2	3	4
Total Cost ($)	11	16	21	26

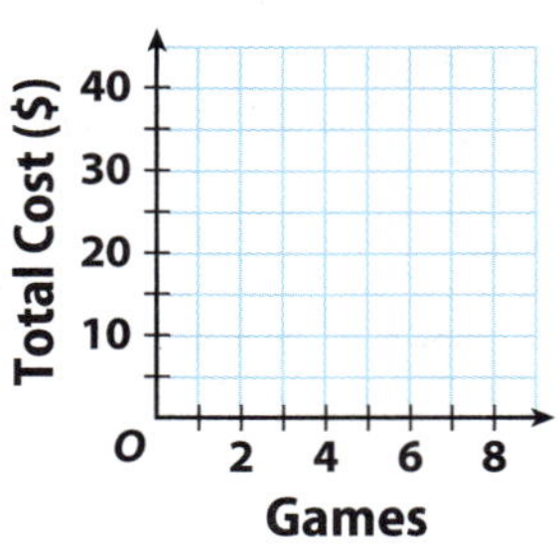

____

____

Personal Math Trainer
Online Assessment and Intervention
my.hrw.com

Analyzing Graphs

Recall that you can describe a proportional relationship with the equation $y = kx$. The constant of proportionality k tells you how steep the graph of the relationship is. The greater the absolute value of k, the steeper the line.

Math On the Spot
my.hrw.com

EXAMPLE 2 Real World

The graph shows the relationship between time in minutes and the number of miles Damon runs. Write an equation for this relationship.

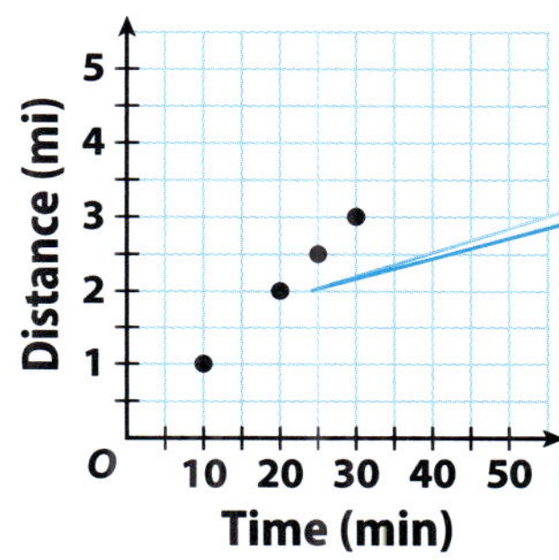

The points appear to form a line through the origin so the relationship is proportional.

STEP 1 Choose a point on the graph and tell what the point represents.

The point (25, 2.5) represents the distance (2.5 miles) that Damon runs in 25 minutes.

STEP 2 What is the constant of proportionality?

Because $\frac{\text{distance}}{\text{time}} = \frac{2.5 \text{ mi}}{25 \text{ min}} = \frac{1}{10}$, the constant of proportionality is $\frac{1}{10}$.

STEP 3 Write an equation in the form $y = kx$.

$y = \frac{1}{10}x$

Reflect

2. What do the points (0, 0) and $(1, \frac{1}{10})$ on the graph tell you?

____

3. **What If?** Suppose you drew a graph representing the relationship $y = \frac{1}{8}x$ between time in minutes and the number of miles Esther runs. How would the graph compare to the one for Damon? Explain.

____

4. Use your equation to find how far Damon runs in 40 minutes. How much time would it take him to run 7.5 miles? ____________

Math Talk
Mathematical Processes

What is the meaning of the point on the graph in Exercise 5 with x-coordinate 1?

YOUR TURN

5. The graph shows the relationship between the distance a bicyclist travels and the time in hours.

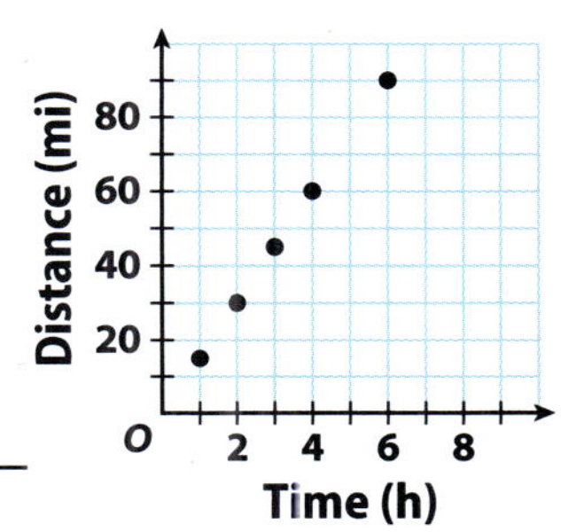

a. What does the point (4, 60) represent?

____

b. What is the constant of proportionality? ____________

c. Write an equation in the form $y = kx$ for this relationship. ____________

Personal Math Trainer
Online Assessment and Intervention
my.hrw.com

Guided Practice

For each situation, tell whether the relationship is a proportional relationship. Explain why or why not. If it is, identify the unit rate. (Explore Activity)

1. The table shows the number of pages a student reads in various amounts of time.

Time (h)	3	5	9	10
Pages	195	325	585	650

____

____

2. The double number line diagram shows the rate at which a babysitter is paid.

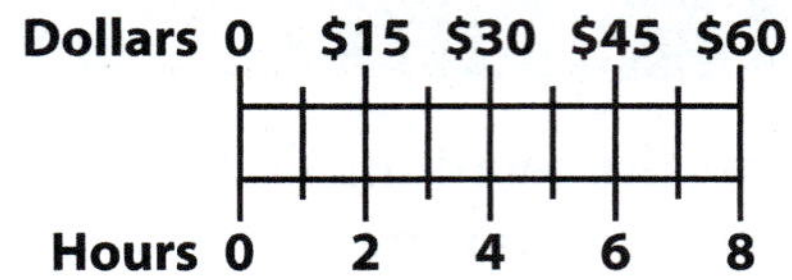

____

____

Tell whether the relationship is a proportional relationship. Explain why or why not. (Explore Activity and Example 1)

3.

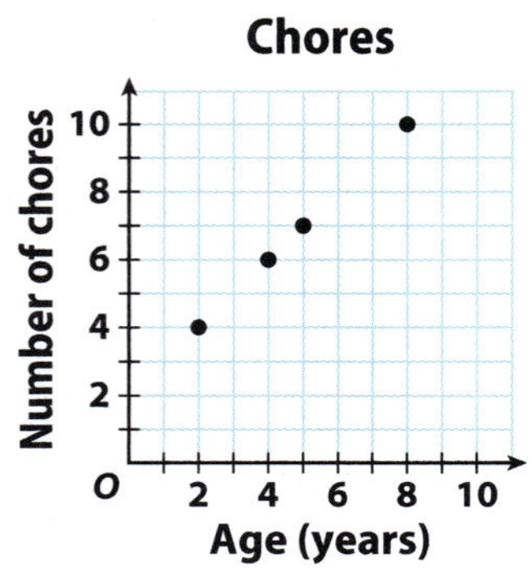

____

____

4.

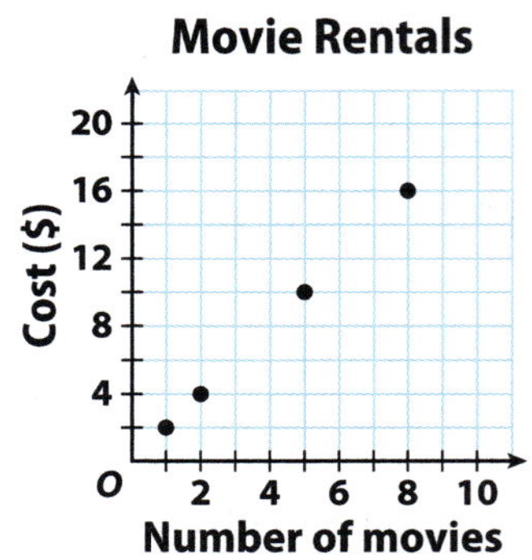

____

____

Write an equation of the form $y = kx$ for the relationship shown in each graph. (Example 2)

5.

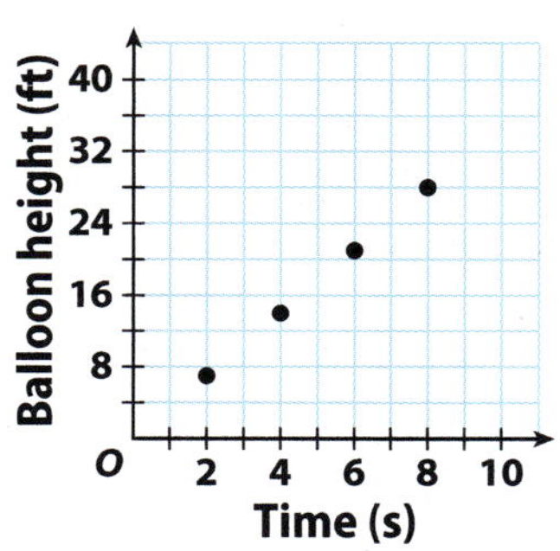

____

6.

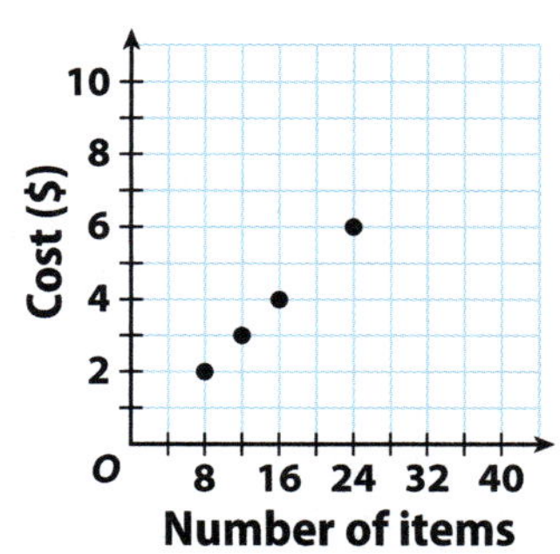

____

ESSENTIAL QUESTION CHECK-IN

7. How does a graph show a proportional relationship?

____

Name ________________ Class ________________ Date ________________

4.3 Independent Practice

Personal Math Trainer
Online Assessment and Intervention
my.hrw.com

For Exercises 8–12, the graph shows the relationship between time and distance run by two horses.

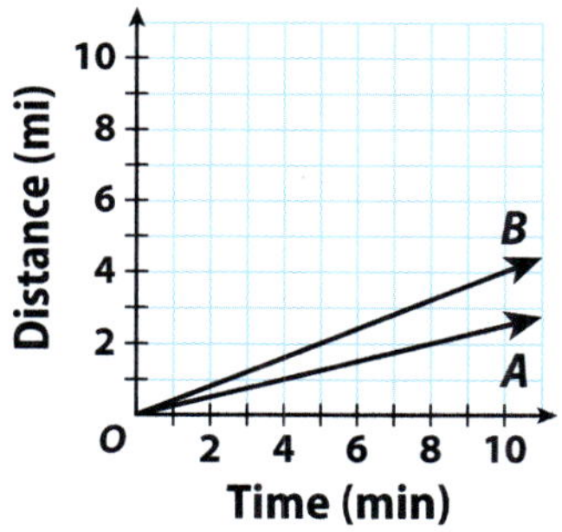

8. Explain the meaning of the point (0, 0).

____

____

9. How long does it take each horse to run a mile?

____

____

10. **Multiple Representations** Write an equation for the relationship between time and distance for each horse.

____

11. **Draw Conclusions** At the given rates, how far would each horse run in 12 minutes?

____

____

12. **Analyze Relationships** Draw a line on the graph representing a horse that runs faster than horses A and B.

____

____

13. A bullet train can travel at 170 miles per hour. Will a graph representing distance in miles compared to time in hours show a proportional relationship? Explain.

____

____

____

____

14. **Critical Thinking** For the equations $y = 3.5x$ and $y = 25x + 40.50$, x represents time in hours and y represents cost in dollars. Which equation is **not** the equation of a proportional relationship? Explain.

____

____

____

15. **Multiple Representations** Bargain DVDs cost $5 each at Mega Movie.

a. Graph the proportional relationship that gives the cost y in dollars of buying x bargain DVDs.

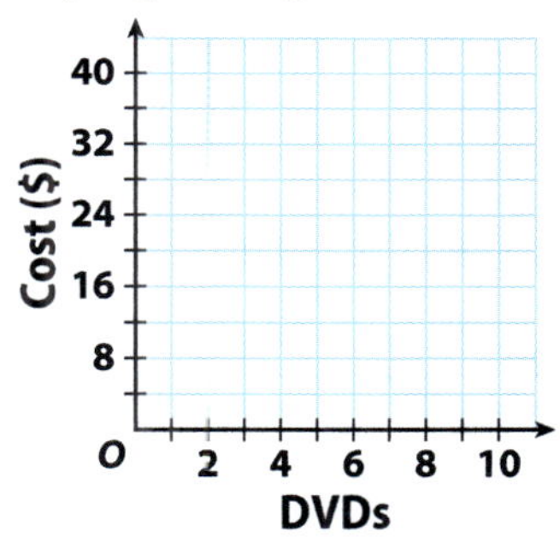

b. Give an ordered pair on the graph and explain its meaning in the real world context.

____

____

The graph shows the relationship between distance and time as Glenda swims.

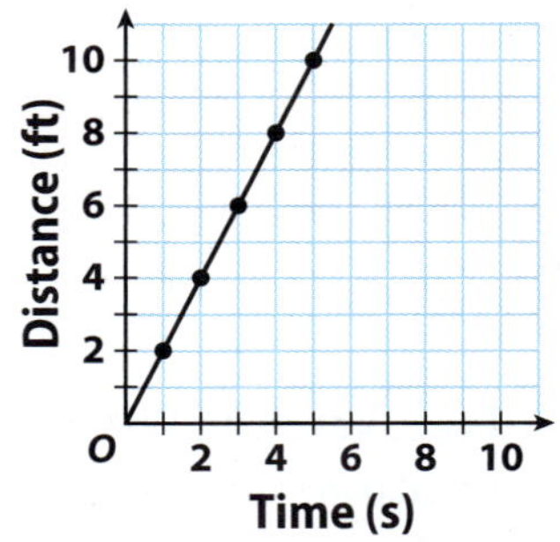

16. How far did Glenda swim in 4 seconds? ______________

17. **Communicate Mathematical Ideas** Is this a proportional relationship? Explain your reasoning.

____

18. **Multiple Representations** Write an equation that shows the relationship between time and distance. Use your equation to find how long it would take in minutes for Glenda to swim $\frac{1}{2}$ mile at this rate. ______________

Work Area

H.O.T. FOCUS ON HIGHER ORDER THINKING

19. **Make a Conjecture** If you know that a relationship is proportional and are given one ordered pair that is not (0, 0), how can you find another pair?

____

____

____

____

The tables show the distance traveled by three cars.

Car 1		Car 2		Car 3	
Time (h)	Distance (mi)	Time (h)	Distance (mi)	Time (h)	Distance (mi)
0	0	0	0	0	0
2	120	5	200	1	65
3	180	10	400	2	85
5	300	15	600	3	105
6	360	20	800	4	125

20. **Communicate Mathematical Ideas** Which car is not traveling at a constant speed? Explain your reasoning.

____

____

21. **Make a Conjecture** Car 4 is traveling at twice the rate of speed of car 2. How will the table values for car 4 compare to the table values for car 2?

____

____

____

Going Further 4.3

Assessing Proportionality

7.2.GF.4.3

Students will tell whether a relationship between two quantities is or is not proportional.

ESSENTIAL QUESTION

How can you tell whether a relationship between two quantities is or is not proportional?

EXPLORE ACTIVITY Real World

Examining Relationships

You can use logical reasoning and facts about proportional relationships to decide whether a relationship between two quantities is proportional.

Examine each relationship to tell whether it is proportional. Explain. If it is proportional, find the constant of proportionality.

A **Max and Meena volunteered to clean windows in a community center. Each student worked at the same rate. Together, the 2 students finished the job in 3 hours.**

If the relationship were proportional, doubling the number of students would _________ the number of hours to finish the job, to keep the ratio of time to students constant. However, common sense indicates that if twice as many people work on the same job at the same rate, it will take _________ the time.

The relationship **is / is not** proportional.

B **The Tranhs pay a $40 entry fee at a theme park and $5.00 for every book of tickets for rides. The graph shows the relationship between the number of books of tickets and the total cost of entry and tickets.**

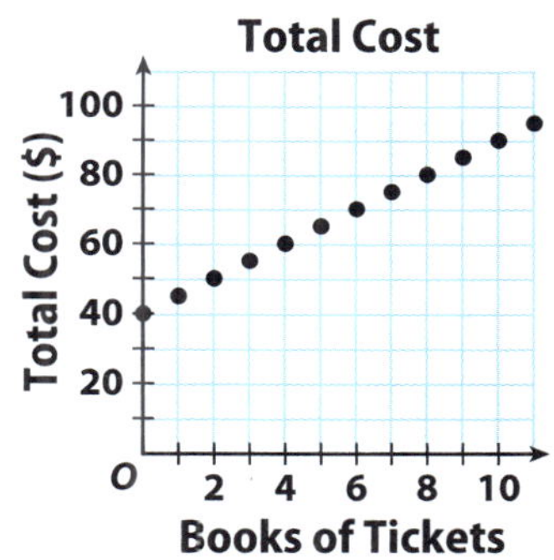

Although the points lie on a line, the graph does not go through the _________, therefore you can tell that the relationship **is / is not** proportional.

Reflect

1. In Part A, what fraction of the job does each student complete in an hour? _________________

2. In Part B, is the relationship between the cost of tickets and the number of books of tickets proportional? If so, what is the constant of proportionality? _________________

Practice

For Exercises 1–4, examine each relationship to tell whether it is proportional. Explain. If it is proportional, find the constant of proportionality.

1. The table below shows the number of pies Ned baked and the number of apples used.

Pies	5	7	8	10
Apples	22	35	48	50

2. The table indicates the amount of water for cooking different amounts of one type of pasta.

Packages	$\frac{1}{3}$	$\frac{1}{2}$	1
Water (qt)	2	3	5

3. The diagram shows the number of pages of a book Eleanor read during the 45 minutes between the end of school and her music lesson, during another 1.25 hours before dinner, and during another half hour before bed.

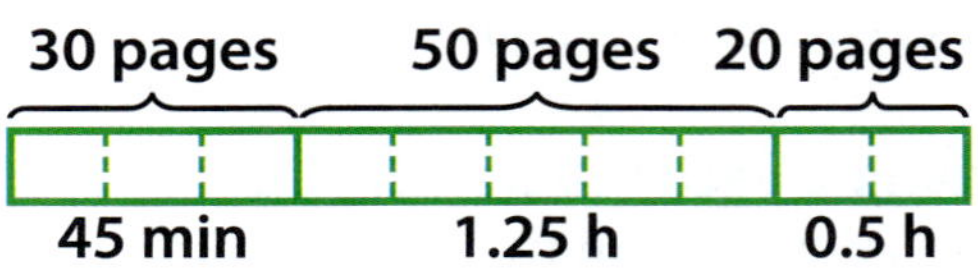

4. An apartment manager needs to hire workers to paint 50 apartments. Suppose they all paint at the same rate. The relationship between the number of workers x and the number of days y it takes to complete the job is given by the equation $y = \frac{300}{x}$.

5. **Critical Thinking** The graph shows the relationship between your earnings y and the time x you spend mowing the lawn.

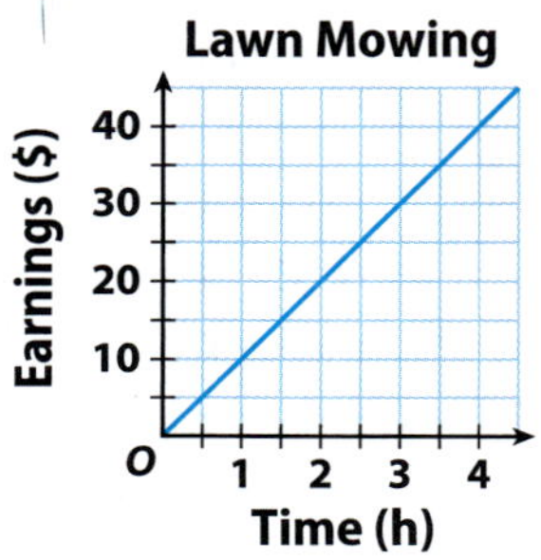

a. Is the relationship between time spent mowing and earnings proportional? Explain. If so, write an equation in the form $y = kx$ for the relationship.

b. Suppose you triple the number of hours spent mowing. Will the number of dollars triple? Explain.

c. Suppose you increase your mowing time by 3 hours. Will your pay increase by $3? Explain.

Activity 4.3

Proportional or Not Proportional?

That Is the Question

INSTRUCTIONS

STEP 1 Working with a partner, read one game card at a time and decide if the relationship on the card is proportional or not. Relationships are represented using tables, equations, graphs, verbal descriptions, or diagrams. You are not expected to write equations for relationships.

STEP 2 Separate the cards into a group labeled *Proportional* and a group labeled *Not Proportional*.

Proportional

Not Proportional

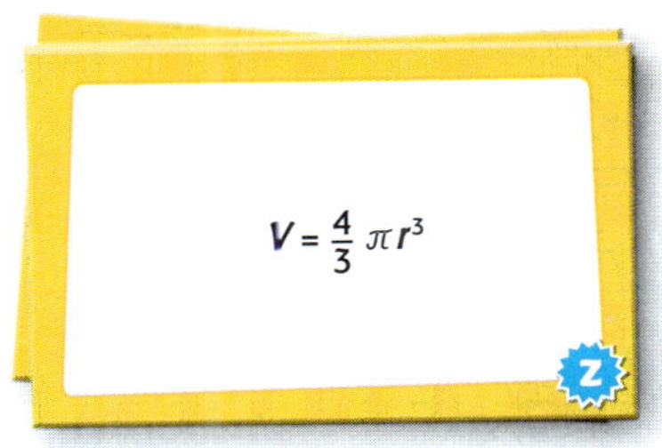

STEP 3 For the cards in the proportional group, write the card letters in alphabetical order in the first column of the table on the next page.

Card Letter	Independent Variable	Dependent Variable	Constant of Proportionality
Y	Number of shirts	Price ($)	20

STEP 4 Complete the remaining columns of the table for each card. You should complete the Independent Variable and Dependent Variable columns with the variable or the name of the quantity, and you should include units if applicable.

Card Letter	Independent Variable	Dependent Variable	Constant of Proportionality

Work Area

Game 4.3

Match the Proportional Relationships

INSTRUCTIONS

Playing the Game

STEP 1 Have one student in your group shuffle the game cards. Each card uses a table, equation, graph, or verbal description to portray a proportional relationship. Arrange the cards face-down in a 4-by-4 grid.

STEP 2 Take turns. When it is your turn, turn two cards face-up in their places in the grid.

STEP 3 If the two cards demonstrate the same proportional relationship, remove them from the grid and keep the matching pair. If the two cards do not demonstrate the same proportional relationship, turn the cards back face-down in their original positions. This ends your turn whether or not you turn over a matching pair.

STEP 4 Pass play to the next player.

STEP 5 The game ends when players have collected all of the pairs. (There will be no cards left over.)

Winner!

Winning the Game

The student with the most pairs of relationship cards when the game ends is the winner.

MODULE QUIZ

Ready to Go On?

Personal Math Trainer
Online Assessment and Intervention
my.hrw.com

4.1 Unit Rates

Find each unit rate. Round to the nearest hundredth, if necessary.

1. \$140 for 18 ft^2 ____________

2. 14 lb for \$2.99 ____________

Circle the better deal in each pair. Then give the unit rate for the better deal.

3. $\frac{\$56}{25\text{ gal}}$ or $\frac{\$32.05}{15\text{ gal}}$ ____________

4. $\frac{\$160}{5\text{ g}}$ or $\frac{\$315}{9\text{ g}}$ ____________

4.2 Constant Rates of Change

5. The table shows the amount of money Tyler earns for mowing lawns. Is the relationship a proportional relationship? Why or why not?

Number of Lawns	1	2	3	4
Amount Earned (\$)	15	30	48	64

____

6. On a recent day, 8 euros were worth \$9 and 24 euros were worth \$27. Write an equation of the form $y = kx$ to show the relationship between the number of euros and the value in dollars.

____________, where y is dollars and x is euros

4.3 Proportional Relationships and Graphs

7. The graph shows the number of servings in different amounts of frozen yogurt listed on a carton. Write an equation that gives the number of servings y in x pints.

____

Frozen Yogurt

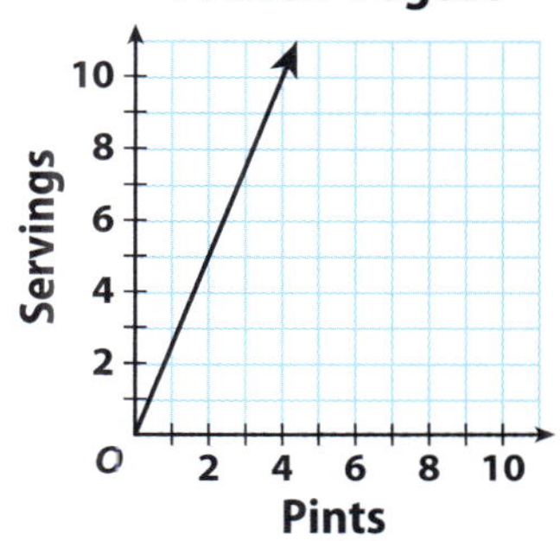

8. A refreshment stand makes 2 large servings of frozen yogurt from 3 pints. Add the line to the graph and write its equation.

____

ESSENTIAL QUESTION

9. How can you use rates to determine whether a situation is a proportional relationship?

____

____

MODULE 4 MIXED REVIEW

Assessment Readiness

Personal Math Trainer

my.hrw.com

Online Assessment and Intervention

Selected Response

1. Kori spent \$46.20 on 12 gallons of gasoline. What was the price per gallon?

Ⓐ \$8. 35 Ⓒ \$2.59

Ⓑ \$3.85 Ⓓ \$0.26

2. A rabbit can run short distances at a rate of 35 miles per hour. A fox can run short distances at a rate of 21 miles per half hour. Which animal is faster, and by how much?

Ⓐ The rabbit; 7 miles per hour

Ⓑ The fox; 7 miles per hour

Ⓒ The rabbit; 14 miles per hour

Ⓓ The fox; 14 miles per hour

3. A pet survey found that the ratio of dogs to cats is $\frac{2}{5}$. Which proportion shows the number of dogs if the number of cats is 140?

Ⓐ $\frac{2 \text{ dogs}}{5 \text{ cats}} = \frac{140 \text{ dogs}}{350 \text{ cats}}$

Ⓑ $\frac{2 \text{ dogs}}{5 \text{ cats}} = \frac{140 \text{ cats}}{350 \text{ dogs}}$

Ⓒ $\frac{2 \text{ dogs}}{5 \text{ cats}} = \frac{28 \text{ dogs}}{140 \text{ cats}}$

Ⓓ $\frac{2 \text{ dogs}}{5 \text{ cats}} = \frac{56 \text{ dogs}}{140 \text{ cats}}$

4. What is the cost of 2 kilograms of flour if 3 kilograms cost \$4.86 and the unit price for each package of flour is the same?

Ⓐ \$0.81 Ⓒ \$3.24

Ⓑ \$2.86 Ⓓ \$9.72

5. One gallon of paint covers about 450 square feet. How many square feet will 1.5 gallons of paint cover?

Ⓐ 300 ft^2 Ⓒ 675 ft^2

Ⓑ 451.5 ft^2 Ⓓ 900 ft^2

6. The graph shows the relationship between the late fines the library charges and the number of days late.

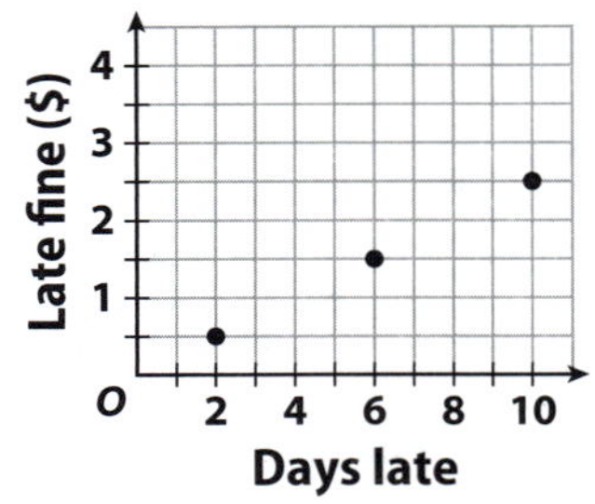

What is an equation for the relationship?

Ⓐ $y = 0.25x$ Ⓒ $y = 0.50x$

Ⓑ $y = 0.40x$ Ⓓ $y = 0.75x$

Mini-Task

7. School is 2 miles from home along a straight road. The table shows your distance from home as you walk home at a constant rate.

Time (min)	10	20	30
Distance from home (mi)	1.5	1	0.5

a. Is the relationship in the table proportional?

____

b. Find your distance from school for each time in the table.

____

c. Write an equation representing the relationship between the distance from school and time walking.

____

Proportions and Percent

MODULE 5

ESSENTIAL QUESTION

How can you use proportional relationships and percent to solve real-world problems?

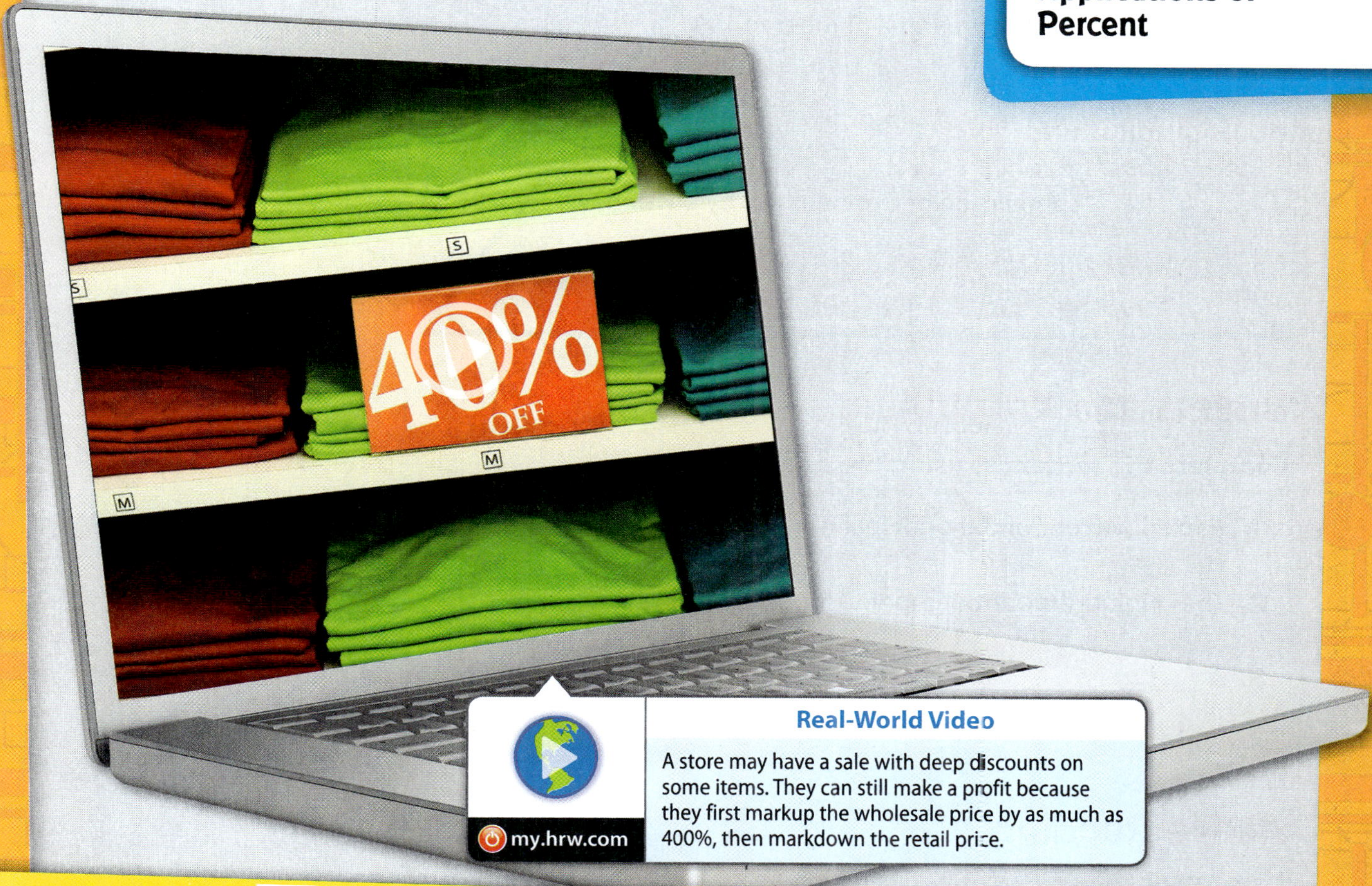

Real-World Video

A store may have a sale with deep discounts on some items. They can still make a profit because they first markup the wholesale price by as much as 400%, then markdown the retail price.

my.hrw.com

GO DIGITAL
my.hrw.com

my.hrw.com
Go digital with your write-in student edition, accessible on any device.

Math On the Spot
Scan with your smart phone to jump directly to the online edition, video tutor, and more.

Animated Math
Interactively explore key concepts to see how math works.

Personal Math Trainer
Get immediate feedback and help as you work through practice sets.

Reading Start-Up

Visualize Vocabulary

Use the ✔ words to complete the triangle. Write the review word that fits the description in each section of the triangle.

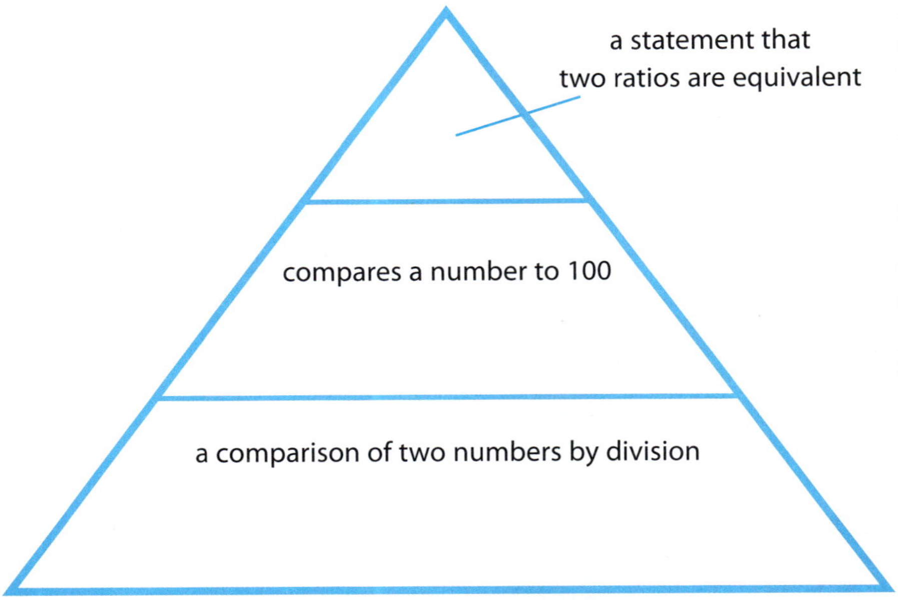

Vocabulary

Review Words

- ✔ proportion *(proporción)*
- ✔ percent *(porcentaje)*
- rate *(tasa)*
- ✔ ratio *(razón)*
- unit rate *(tasa unitaria)*

Preview Words

- percent decrease *(porcentaje de disminución)*
- percent increase *(porcentaje de aumento)*
- principal *(capital)*
- simple interest *(interés simple)*

Understand Vocabulary

Complete the sentences using the preview words.

1. A fixed percent of the principal is ____________________.

2. The original amount of money deposited or borrowed is the ____________________.

3. A ____________________ is the amount of increase divided by the original amount.

Active Reading

Tri-Fold Before beginning the module, create a tri-fold to help you learn the concepts and vocabulary in this module. Fold the paper into three sections. Label the columns "What I Know," "What I Need to Know," and "What I Learned." Complete the first two columns before you read. After studying the module, complete the third.

Are YOU Ready?

Complete these exercises to review skills you will need for this module.

Personal Math Trainer
my.hrw.com
Online Assessment and Intervention

Percents and Decimals

EXAMPLE

$147\% = 100\% + 47\%$	*Write the percent as the sum of 1 whole and a percent remainder.*
$= \frac{100}{100} + \frac{47}{100}$	*Write the percents as fractions.*
$= 1 + 0.47$	*Write the fractions as decimals.*
$= 1.47$	*Simplify.*

Write each percent as a decimal.

1. 22% ________ **2.** 75% ________ **3.** 6% ________ **4.** 189% ________

Write each decimal as a percent.

5. 0.59 ________ **6.** 0.98 ________ **7.** 0.02 ________ **8.** 1.33 ________

Find the Percent of a Number

EXAMPLE

30% of $45 = ?$

$30\% = 0.30$ *Write the percent as a decimal.*

$$\begin{array}{r} 45 \\ \times 0.3 \\ \hline 13.5 \end{array}$$

Multiply.

Find the percent of each number.

9. 50% of 64 ________ **10.** 7% of 30 ________ **11.** 15% of 160 ________

12. 32% of 62 ________ **13.** 120% of 4 ________ **14.** 6% of 1,000 ________

Are YOU Ready? (cont'd)

Complete these exercises to review skills you will need for this module.

Percents and Decimals

15. A company's profits this year were 128% of last year's profits. Drew recorded this year's profits as 12.8 times last year's profits. What mistake, if any, did Drew make?

16. Carlos puts 0.3 of his monthly income into savings. What percent of his monthly income is **not** put into savings? How do you know?

Find the Percent of a Number

17. In a school with 300 students, 18% of the students take violin lessons, and 6% of the students take clarinet lessons.

a. Find the number of students who take each type of lesson.

b. How many more students take violin lessons than take clarinet lessons?

18. A jacket costs $45. The sales tax on the jacket is 6%. Julia has $48. Does she have enough money to buy the jacket? Explain.

Game 5.1

PERCENTO!

INSTRUCTIONS

Playing the Game

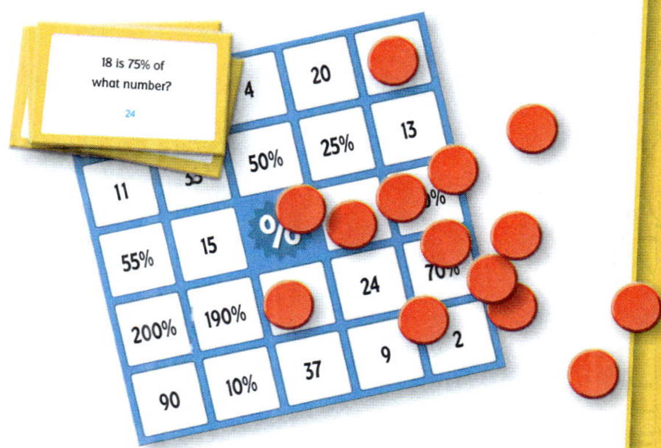

STEP 1 One student is the caller. This student gets the caller cards. Each caller card contains a percent problem and its answer.

STEP 2 Each player gets a *Percento!* board and 20–25 counters. The center is a free space. Players should cover the center square before play begins.

STEP 3 On each turn, the caller reads aloud a problem to the players. The caller does not read the answer.

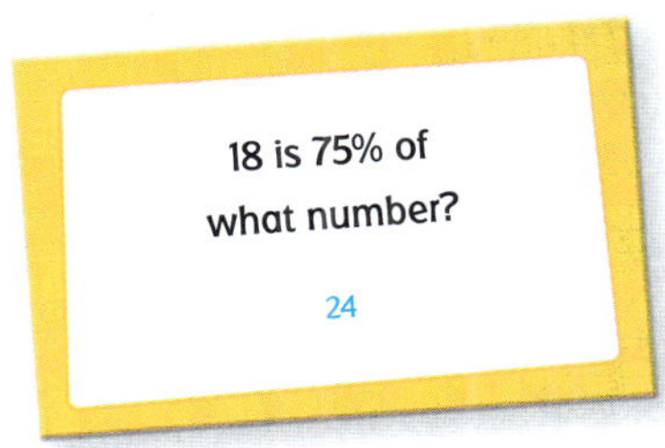

STEP 4 The players solve the problem read by the caller. Then they find the answer on their *Percento!* board and cover that square.

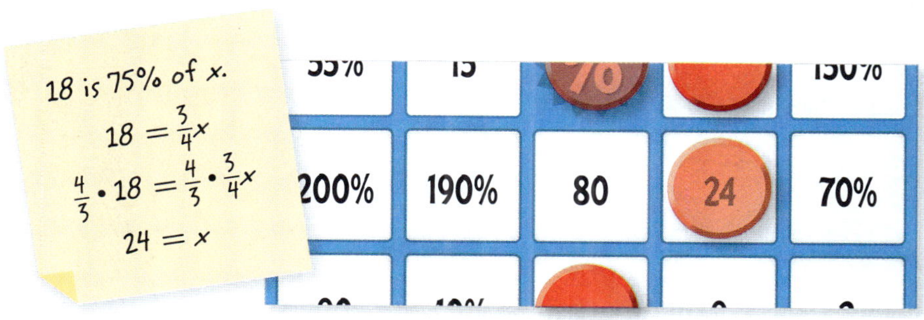

STEP 5 The caller places the cards that have been read in a discard pile.

Winning the Game

A player who covers five squares in a row horizontally, vertically, or diagonally says, "Percento!" The caller uses the cards in the discard pile to check that this player has calculated correctly. If so, that player is the winner. If not, play continues until someone else says, "Percento!"

LESSON 5.1
Percent Increase and Decrease

7.2.5.1

Students will use percents to describe change.

ESSENTIAL QUESTION

How do you use percents to describe change?

EXPLORE ACTIVITY Real World

Finding Percent Increase

Percents can be used to describe how an amount changes.

$$\text{Percent Change} = \frac{\text{Amount of Change}}{\text{Original Amount}}$$

The change may be an increase or a decrease. **Percent increase** describes how much a quantity increases in comparison to the original amount.

Math On the Spot
my.hrw.com

EXAMPLE 1 **Amber got a raise, and her hourly wage increased from \$8 to \$9.50. What is the percent increase?**

STEP 1 Find the amount of change.

Amount of Change = Greater Value − Lesser Value

Substitute values. = ______ − ______

Subtract. = ______

STEP 2 Find the percent increase. Round to the nearest percent.

$$\text{Percent Change} = \frac{\text{Amount of Change}}{\text{Original Amount}}$$

Substitute values. $= \frac{\square}{8.00}$

Divide. = ______

Write as a percent and round. ≈ ______

Reflect

1. What does a 100% increase mean?

____

____

YOUR TURN

2. The price of a pair of shoes increases from \$52 to \$64. What is the percent increase to the nearest percent? ______

Personal Math Trainer
Online Assessment and Intervention
my.hrw.com

Finding Percent Decrease

When the change in the amount decreases, you can use a similar approach to find percent decrease. **Percent decrease** describes how much a quantity decreases in comparison to the original amount.

Math On the Spot
my.hrw.com

EXAMPLE 2 Real World

David moved from a house that is 89 miles away from his workplace to a house that is 51 miles away from his workplace. What is the percent decrease in the distance from his home to his workplace?

STEP 1 Find the amount of change.

Amount of Change = Greater Value − Lesser Value

$= 89 - 51$ Substitute values.

$= 38$ Subtract.

STEP 2 Find the percent decrease. Round to the nearest percent.

$$\text{Percent Change} = \frac{\text{Amount of Change}}{\text{Original Amount}}$$

$= \frac{38}{89}$ Substitute values.

≈ 0.427 Divide.

$= 43\%$ Write as a percent and round.

Math Talk
Mathematical Processes

How can you use the benchmark fractions $\frac{1}{3}$ and $\frac{1}{2}$ to check that the answer is reasonable?

Reflect

3. **Critique Reasoning** David considered moving even closer to his workplace. He claims that if he had done so, the percent of decrease would have been more than 100%. Is David correct? Explain your reasoning.

____

____

____

YOUR TURN

4. The number of students in a chess club decreased from 18 to 12. What is the percent decrease? Round to the nearest percent. ______________

5. Officer Brimberry wrote 16 tickets for traffic violations last week, but only 10 tickets this week. What is the percent decrease? ______________

Personal Math Trainer
Online Assessment and Intervention
my.hrw.com

Using Percent of Change

Given an original amount and a percent increase or decrease, you can use the percent of change to find the new amount.

Math On the Spot
my.hrw.com

EXAMPLE 3 Real World

The grizzly bear population in Yellowstone National Park in 1970 was about 270. Over the next 35 years, it increased by about 115%. What was the population in 2005?

STEP 1 Find the amount of change.

$1.15 \times 270 = 310.5$ Find 115% of 270. Write 115% as a decimal.

≈ 311 Round to the nearest whole number.

STEP 2 Find the new amount.

New Amount = Original Amount + Amount of Change

$= 270 + 311$ Substitute values.

$= 581$ Add.

Add the amount of change because the population increased.

The population in 2005 was about 581 grizzly bears.

Reflect

6. Why will the percent of change always be represented by a positive number?

____

7. **Draw Conclusions** If an amount of $100 in a savings account increases by 10%, then increases by 10% again, is that the same as increasing by 20%? Explain.

____

YOUR TURN

A TV has an original price of $499. Find the new price after the given percent of change.

8. 10% increase __________ **9.** 30% decrease __________

Personal Math Trainer
Online Assessment and Intervention
my.hrw.com

Guided Practice

Find each percent increase. Round to the nearest percent. (Explore Activity Example 1)

1. From $5 to $8 ______
2. From 20 students to 30 students ______
3. From 86 books to 150 books ______
4. From $3.49 to $3.89 ______
5. From 13 friends to 14 friends ______
6. From 5 miles to 16 miles ______
7. Nathan usually drinks 36 ounces of water per day. He read that he should drink 64 ounces of water per day. If he starts drinking 64 ounces, what is the percent increase? Round to the nearest percent. (Explore Activity Example 1) ______

Find each percent decrease. Round to the nearest percent. (Example 2)

8. From $80 to $64 ______
9. From 95 °F to 68 °F ______
10. From 90 points to 45 points ______
11. From 145 pounds to 132 pounds ______
12. From 64 photos to 21 photos ______
13. From 16 bagels to 0 bagels ______
14. Over the summer, Jackie played video games 3 hours per day. When school began in the fall, she was only allowed to play video games for half an hour per day. What is the percent decrease? Round to the nearest percent. (Example 2) ______

Find the new amount given the original amount and the percent of change. (Example 3)

15. $9; 10% increase ______
16. 48 cookies; 25% decrease ______
17. 340 pages; 20% decrease ______
18. 28 members; 50% increase ______
19. $29,000; 4% decrease ______
20. 810 songs; 130% increase ______
21. Adam currently runs about 20 miles per week, and he wants to increase his weekly mileage by 30%. How many miles will Adam run per week? (Example 3) ______

ESSENTIAL QUESTION CHECK-IN

22. What process do you use to find the percent change of a quantity?

______

______

Name ______________________ Class ______________ Date ____________

5.1 Independent Practice

Personal Math Trainer
Online Assessment and Intervention
my.hrw.com

23. Complete the table.

Item	Original Price	New Price	Percent Change	Increase or Decrease
Bike	$110	$96		
Scooter	$45	$56		
Tennis Racket	$79		5%	Increase
Skis	$580		25%	Decrease

24. **Multiple Representations** The bar graph shows the number of hurricanes in the Atlantic Basin from 2006–2011.

a. Find the amount of change and the percent of decrease in the number of hurricanes from 2008 to 2009 and from 2010 to 2011. Compare the amounts of change and percents of decrease.

____

____

____

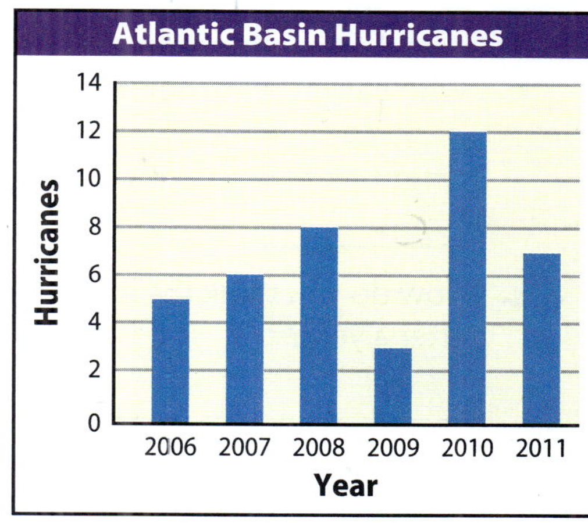

b. Between which two years was the percent of change the greatest? What was the percent of change during that period?

____

25. **Represent Real-World Problems** Cheese sticks that were previously priced at "5 for $1" are now "4 for $1". Find each percent of change and show your work.

a. Find the percent decrease in the number of cheese sticks you can buy for $1.

____

b. Find the percent increase in the price per cheese stick.

____

____

26. Percent error calculations are used to determine how close to the true values, or how accurate, experimental values really are. The formula is similar to finding percent of change.

$$\text{Percent Error} = \frac{|\text{Experimental Value} - \text{True Value}|}{\text{True Value}} \times 100$$

In chemistry class, Charlie records the volume of a liquid as 13.3 milliliters. The true volume is 13.6 milliliters. What is his percent error? Round to the nearest percent. ____________________

Work Area

H.O.T. FOCUS ON HIGHER ORDER THINKING

27. Look for a Pattern Leroi and Sylvia both put $1,000 in a savings account. Leroi decides he will put in an additional $100 each month. Sylvia decides to put in an additional 10% of the amount in the account each month.

a. Who has more money after the first additional deposit? Explain.

____

____

b. Who has more money after the second additional deposit? Explain.

____

____

c. How do you think the amounts in the two accounts will compare after a year?

____

____

____

28. Critical Thinking Suppose an amount increases by 50%, then decreases by 50%. Will the amount after the decrease be the same as the original amount? Explain your reasoning.

____

____

____

29. Look for a Pattern Ariel deposited $600 into a bank account. Each Friday she will withdraw 10% of the money in the account to spend. Ariel thinks her account will be empty after 10 withdrawals. Do you agree? Explain.

____

____

____

LESSON 5.2

Rewriting Percent Expressions

7.2.5.2

Students will rewrite expressions to help solve markup and markdown problems.

ESSENTIAL QUESTION

How can you rewrite expressions to help you solve markup and markdown problems?

EXPLORE ACTIVITY Real World

Calculating Markups

Math On the Spot
my.hrw.com

A *markup* is one kind of percent increase. You can use a bar model to represent the *retail price* of an item, that is, the total price including the markup.

EXAMPLE 1 **To make a profit, stores mark up the prices on the items they sell. A store manager buys skateboards from a supplier for s dollars. What is the retail price for skateboards that the manager buys for \$35 and \$56 after a 42% markup?**

STEP 1 Draw a bar for the cost of the skateboard s.

Then draw a bar that shows the markup: ________% of s, or $0.42s$.

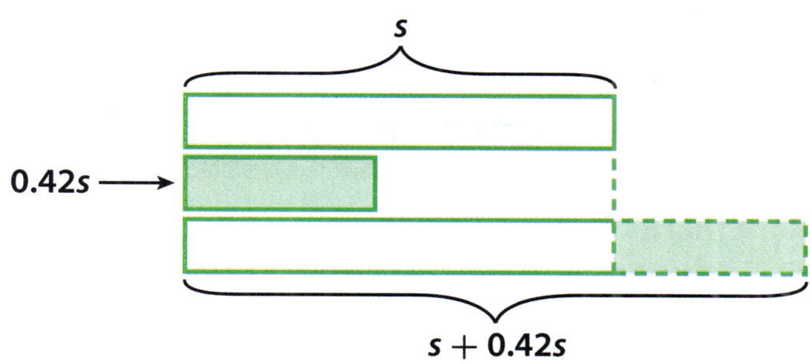

These bars together represent the cost plus the markup, $s +$ ________.

STEP 2 Retail price = Original cost + Markup

$= s + 0.42s$

$= 1s + 0.42s$ Identity Property of Multiplication

$=$ ________ Distributive Property

STEP 3 Use the expression to find the retail price of each skateboard.

$s = \$35$ → Retail price $= 1.42(\$35) =$ ☐

$s = \$56$ → Retail price $= 1.42(\$$☐$) =$ ☐

Reflect

1. Write an equation showing that the relationship between the supplier price, s, and the retail price, r, is proportional. What is the constant of proportionality? ________

EXPLORE ACTIVITY (cont'd)

YOUR TURN

2. Rick buys remote control cars to resell. He applies a markup of 10%.

   a. Write two expressions that represent the retail price of the cars.

   ____

   b. If Rick buys a remote control car for $28.00, what is his selling price?

   ____

3. An exclusive clothing boutique triples the price of the items it purchases for resale.

   a. What is the boutique's markup percent? ______________

   b. Write two expressions that represent the retail price of the clothes.

   ____

Personal Math Trainer
Online Assessment and Intervention
my.hrw.com

Math On the Spot
my.hrw.com

Calculating Markdowns

An example of a percent decrease is a *discount*, or *markdown*. A price after a markdown may be called a sale price. You can also use a bar model to represent the price of an item including the markdown.

EXAMPLE 2 Real World

A discount store marks down all of its holiday merchandise by 20% off the regular selling price. Find the discounted price of decorations that regularly sell for $16 and $23.

Animated Math
my.hrw.com

STEP 1 Use a bar model.

Draw a bar for the regular price p.

Then draw a bar that shows the discount: 20% of p, or $0.2p$.

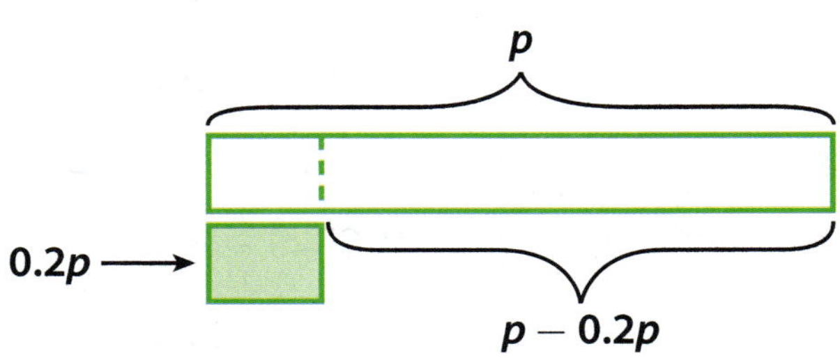

The difference between these two bars represents the price minus the discount, $p - 0.2p$.

STEP 2 Sale price = Original price − Markdown

$= p - 0.2p$

$= 1p - 0.2p$ Identity Property of Multiplication

$= 0.8p$ Distributive Property

STEP 3 Use the expression to find the sale price of each decoration.

$p = \$16 \longrightarrow$ Retail price $= 0.8(\$16) = \$12.80$

$p = \$23 \longrightarrow$ Retail price $= 0.8(\$23) = \$18.40$

Math Talk
Mathematical Processes

How do the expressions $1p - 0.2p$ and $0.8p$ for the sale price shed light on the problem?

Reflect

4. **Analyze Relationships** Is the relationship between the original price p and the retail price r proportional? Justify your answers.

____

____

YOUR TURN

5. A bicycle shop marks down each bicycle's selling price b by 24% for a holiday sale.

a. Draw a bar model to represent the problem.

b. What is a single term expression for the sale price? ____________

6. Jane sells pillows. For a sale, she marks them down 5%.

a. Write two expressions that represent the sale price of the pillows.

____

b. If the original price of a pillow is $15.00, what is the sale price?

____

Personal Math Trainer
Online Assessment and Intervention
my.hrw.com

Guided Practice

1. Dana buys dress shirts from a clothing manufacturer for s dollars each, and then sells the dress shirts in her retail clothing store at a 35% markup. (Explore Activity Example 1)

a. Write the markup using a decimal. ______

b. Write an expression for the retail price of the dress shirt. ______

c. What is the retail price of a dress shirt that Dana purchased for $32.00? ______

d. How much was added to the original price of the dress shirt? ______

List the markup and retail price of each item. Round to two decimal places when necessary. (Explore Activity Example 1)

	Item	Price	Markup %	Markup	Retail Price
2.	**Hat**	\$18	15%		
3.	**Book**	\$22.50	42%		
4.	**Shirt**	\$33.75	75%		
5.	**Shoes**	\$74.99	33%		
6.	**Clock**	\$48.60	100%		
7.	**Painting**	\$185.00	125%		

Find the sale price of each item. Round to two decimal places when necessary. (Example 2)

8. Original price: \$45.00; Markdown: 22%

______

9. Original price: \$89.00; Markdown: 33%

______

10. Original price: \$23.99; Markdown: 44%

______

11. Original price: \$279.99, Markdown: 75%

______

ESSENTIAL QUESTION CHECK-IN

12. How can you determine the sale price if you are given the regular price and the percent of markdown?

______

______

Name ______________________ Class ______________ Date ____________

5.2 Independent Practice

Personal Math Trainer

my.hrw.com

Online Assessment and Intervention

13. A bookstore manager marks down the price of older hardcover books, which originally sell for *b* dollars, by 46%.

a. Write the markdown using a decimal. ______________

b. Write an expression for the sale price of the hardcover book.

____

c. What is the sale price of a hardcover book for which the original retail price was $29.00? ______________

d. If you buy the book in part **c**, how much do you save by paying the sale price? ______________

14. Raquela's coworker made price tags for several items that are to be marked down by 35%. Match each Regular Price to the correct Sale Price, if possible. Not all sales tags match an item.

Regular Price $3.29	Regular Price $4.19	Regular Price $2.79	Regular Price $3.09	Regular Price $3.77

Sale Price $2.01	Sale Price $2.45	Sale Price $1.15	Sale Price $2.72	Sale Price $2.24

15. **Communicate Mathematical Ideas** For each situation, give an example that includes the original price and final price after markup or markdown.

a. A markdown that is greater than 99% but less than 100%

____

b. A markdown that is less than 1%

____

c. A markup that is more than 200%

____

16. **Represent Real-World Problems** Harold works at a men's clothing store, which marks up its retail clothing by 27%. The store purchases pants for $74.00, suit jackets for $325.00, and dress shirts for $48.00. How much will Harold charge a customer for two pairs of pants, three dress shirts, and a suit jacket? Use estimation to explain why your answer is reasonable.

17. **Analyze Relationships** Your family needs a set of 4 tires. Which of the following deals would you prefer? Explain.

(I) Buy 3, get one free **(II)** 20% off **(III)** $\frac{1}{4}$ off

H.O.T. FOCUS ON HIGHER ORDER THINKING

18. **Critique Reasoning** Margo purchases bulk teas from a warehouse and marks up those prices by 20% for retail sale. When teas go unsold for more than two months, Margo marks down the retail price by 20%. She says that she is *breaking even*, that is, she is getting the same price for the tea that she paid for it. Is she correct? Explain.

19. **Problem Solving** Grady marks down some $2.49 pens to $1.99 for a week and then marks them back up to $2.49. Find the percent of increase and the percent of decrease to the nearest tenth. Are the percents of change the same for both price changes? If not, which is a greater change?

20. **Persevere in Problem Solving** At Danielle's clothing boutique, if an item does not sell for eight weeks, she marks it down by 15%. If it remains unsold after that, she marks it down an additional 5% each week until she can no longer make a profit. Then she donates it to charity.

Rafael wants to buy a coat originally priced $150, but he can't afford more than $110. If Danielle paid $100 for the coat, during which week(s) could Rafael buy the coat within his budget? Justify your answer.

Work Area

LESSON 5.3 Applications of Percent

7.2.5.3

Students will use percents to solve problems.

ESSENTIAL QUESTION

How do you use percents to solve problems?

EXPLORE ACTIVITY Real World

Finding an Original or Final Amount

Sales tax, which is the tax on the sale of an item or service, is a percent of the purchase price that is collected by the seller. The relationship between an original amount and the amount after a percent change is a proportional relationship. For a given sales tax rate, you can use proportional reasoning to find the total cost if you know the price, or the price if you know the total cost.

EXAMPLE 1 **Marcus bought a varsity jacket. The total cost, including an 8% sales tax, was \$86.40. What was the price p of the jacket?**

You can draw a bar model to visualize the problem.

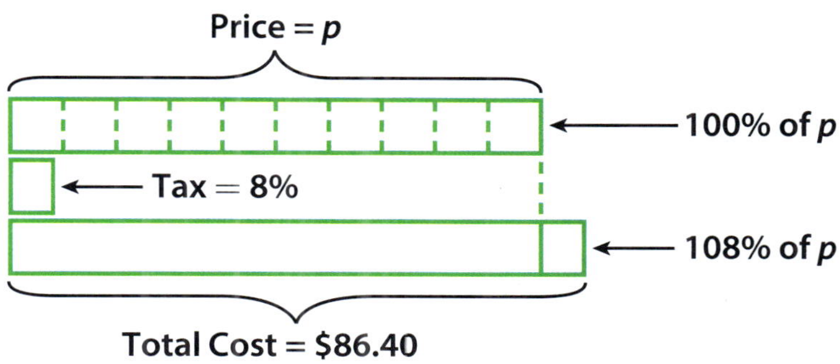

Because 100% is not evenly divisible by 8%, you can more easily use a proportion or an equation to solve the problem.

Method 1 Use a proportion comparing ratios of price to total cost.

percent **dollars**

$$\frac{100}{108} = \frac{p}{\boxed{}}$$

$$86.40 \times \frac{100}{108} = 86.40 \times \frac{p}{86.40}$$

$$\frac{\boxed{}}{108} = p$$

$$\_\_\_\_\_\_ = p$$

Method 2 Use an equation relating price and total cost.

Total Cost = 108% of Price

$$\_\_\_\_\_\_ = 1.08p$$

$$\frac{86.40}{1.08} = \frac{1.08p}{1.08}$$

$$\_\_\_\_\_\_ = p$$

The price of the jacket, before sales tax, was \$______.

Check: If the jacket's price is \$80, the total cost with tax is

$1.08(80) = \$ \boxed{}$.

Math On the Spot
my.hrw.com

EXPLORE ACTIVITY (cont'd)

YOUR TURN

1. Sharon wants to buy a shirt that costs \$20. The sales tax is 5%. How much is the sales tax? What is her total cost for the shirt? ______________

Personal Math Trainer
Online Assessment and Intervention
my.hrw.com

Math On the Spot
my.hrw.com

Finding Simple Interest

When you deposit money in a savings account, your money usually earns interest. When you borrow money, you must pay back the original amount of the loan plus interest. **Simple interest** is a fixed percent of the *principal*. The **principal** is the original amount of money deposited or borrowed.

EXAMPLE 2 Real World

Terry deposits \$200 into a bank account that earns 3% simple interest per year. What is the total amount in the account after 2 years?

STEP 1 Find the amount of interest earned in one year. Then calculate the amount of interest for 2 years.

Write 3% as a decimal: 0.03

Interest Rate	×	Initial Deposit	=	Interest for 1 year
0.03	×	\$200	=	\$6

Interest for 1 year	×	2 years	=	Interest for 2 years
\$6	×	2	=	\$12

STEP 2 Add the interest for 2 years to the initial deposit to find the total amount in his account after 2 years.

Initial deposit	+	Interest for 2 years	=	Total
\$200	+	\$12	=	\$212

The total amount in the account after 2 years is \$212.

Math Talk
Mathematical Processes

Is interest I earned on \$200 proportional to time t in years? If so, write the equation.

Reflect

2. Write an equation relating the total amount a in Terry's account to the number of years, t. Is the relationship proportional? Explain.

____

3. Commission and interest problems have some similarities. A salesperson receives a percent of the selling price of the item(s) sold, called a commission. Nadia earns a salary of \$3,300 per month selling furniture, plus a 3.25% commission. Calculate Nadia's total earnings in a month when her sales totaled \$29,600. Show your work.

____

YOUR TURN

4. Ariane borrows \$400 on a 4-year loan. She is charged 5% simple interest per year. How much interest is she charged for 4 years? What is the total amount she has to pay back? ____________

Personal Math Trainer
Online Assessment and Intervention
my.hrw.com

Math On the Spot
my.hrw.com

Using Multiple Percents

Some situations require applying more than one percent to a problem. For example, when you dine at a restaurant, you might pay a tax on the meal, and pay a tip to the wait staff. The tip is usually paid on the amount before tax. When you pay tax on a sale item, you pay tax only on the discounted price.

EXAMPLE 3 Problem Solving

The Maxwell family goes out for dinner, and the price of the meal is \$60. The sales tax on the meal is 7%, and they also want to leave a 15% tip. What is the total cost of the meal?

Analyze Information

Identify the important information.

- The bill for the meal is \$60.
- The sales tax is 7%, or 0.07.
- The tip is 15%, or 0.15.

The total cost will be the sum of the bill for the meal, the sales tax, and the tip.

Formulate a Plan

Calculate the sales tax separately, then calculate the tip, and then add the products to the bill for the meal to find the total.

Solve

Sales tax: $0.07 \times \$60 = \$4.20$ Tip: $0.15 \times \$60 = \$9.00$

Meal + Sales tax + Tip = Total cost

$\$60 + \$4.20 + \$9 = \$73.20$

The total cost is \$73.20.

Justify and Evaluate

Estimate the sales tax and tip. Sales tax is about 10% plus 15% for tip gives 25%. Find 25% of the bill: $0.25 \times \$60 = \$15$. Add this to the bill: $\$60 + \$15 = \$75$. The total cost should be about \$75.

Math Talk
Mathematical Processes

Write an equation and a proportion you could use to find the total cost *c* given the price *p*.

Personal Math Trainer
Online Assessment and Intervention
my.hrw.com

YOUR TURN

5. Samuel orders four DVDs from an online music store. Each DVD costs \$9.99. He has a 20% discount code, and sales tax is 6.75%. What is the total cost of his order?

____

Guided Practice

1. 5% of \$30 = _______________

2. 15% of \$70 = _______________

3. 0.4% of \$100 = _______________

4. 150% of \$22 = _______________

5. 1% of \$80 = _______________

6. 200% of \$5 = _______________

7. Brandon buys a radio for \$43.99 in a state where the sales tax is 7%. (Explore Activity Example 1)

a. How much does he pay in taxes? _______________

b. What is the total Brandon pays for the radio? _______________

8. Luisa received \$108 for a necklace she sold on an online auction. The auction site took a fee of 10% of the selling price. What was the selling price of the necklace? (Explore Activity Example 1) _______________

9. Joe borrowed \$2,000 from the bank at a rate of 7% simple interest per year. How much interest did he pay in 5 years? (Example 2) _______________

10. Sonia works at a sporting goods store. She earns \$415 per week plus a 5.25% commission on her sales. One week, her sales are \$2,200. What is her total income for the week? (Example 2) _______________

11. Martin finds a shirt on sale for 10% off at a department store. The original price was \$20. Martin must also pay 8.5% sales tax. (Example 3)

a. How much is the shirt before taxes are applied? _______________

b. How much is the shirt after taxes are applied? _______________

12. Teresa's restaurant bill comes to \$29.99 before tax. If the sales tax is 6.25% and she tips the waiter 20%, what is the total cost of the meal? (Example 3) _______________

ESSENTIAL QUESTION CHECK-IN

13. How can you determine the total cost of an item including tax if you know the price of the item and the tax rate?

____

____

Name ______________________ Class ______________ Date ______________

5.3 Independent Practice

Personal Math Trainer
Online Assessment and Intervention
my.hrw.com

14. Emily takes her friend Darren out to eat for his birthday. She pays a total of $45, which includes a 20% tip. There is no tax. Find the cost of the meals before the tip.

____

15. The Jayden family eats at a restaurant that is having a 15% discount promotion. Their meal costs $78.65 before the discount, and they leave a 20% tip. If the tip applies to the cost of the meal before the discount, what is the total cost of the meal?

____

16. A jeweler buys a ring from a jewelry maker for $125. He marks up the price by 135% for sale in his store. What is the selling price of the ring with 7.5% sales tax?

____

17. Luis wants to buy a skateboard that usually sells for $79.99. All merchandise is discounted by 12%. What is the total cost of the skateboard if Luis has to pay a state sales tax of 6.75%?

____

18. Kedar earns a monthly salary of $2,200 plus a 3.75% commission on the amount of his sales at a men's clothing store. What would he earn this month if he sold $4,500 in clothing? Round to the nearest cent.

____

19. Danielle earns a 7.25% commission on everything she sells at the electronics store where she works. She also earns a base salary of $750 per week. What were her sales last week if her total earnings for the week were $1,076.25?

____

20. Francois earns a weekly salary of $475 plus a 5.5% commission on sales at a gift shop. How much would he earn in a week if he sold $700 in goods? Round to the nearest cent.

____

21. Sandra is 4 feet tall. Pablo is 10% taller than Sandra, and Michaela is 8% taller than Pablo.

a. Explain how to find Michaela's height with the given information.

____

____

____

____

____

____

b. What is Michaela's approximate height in feet and inches?

____

22. Troy is buying a car that costs $15,000. He plans to get a 5-year loan to pay for it. He can get a loan for $15,000 or he can pay $3,000 from his savings and get a loan for the rest. The savings account pays 2% simple interest per year. The simple interest rate for the loan is 0.5% per year.

a. How much interest over a 5-year period will Troy receive on his $3,000 if he does not withdraw that money from his savings account? ____________

b. How much more interest will he pay to borrow $15,000 than $12,000? Why is the $15,000 option reasonable?

____

23. **Multistep** Eric downloads the coupon shown and goes shopping at Gadgets Galore, where he buys a digital camera for \$95 and an extra battery for \$15.99.

a. What is the total cost if the coupon is applied to the digital camera?

____

b. What is the total cost if the coupon is applied to the extra battery?

____

c. To which item should Eric apply the discount? Explain.

____

d. Eric has to pay 8% sales tax after the coupon is applied. How much is his total bill?

____

24. Kim takes some furniture to a consignment store. The store sells used items and takes a fee of 20% of the selling price. The remaining percent of the selling price goes to the seller, Kim.

a. What percent of the selling price p is the amount the seller gets?

____

b. Kim receives a check from the consignment store for \$592. What was the selling price of the furniture?

____

H.O.T. FOCUS ON HIGHER ORDER THINKING

Work Area

25. **Analyze Relationships** Marcus can choose between a monthly salary of \$1,500 plus 5.5% of sales or \$2,400 plus 3% of sales. He expects sales between \$5,000 and \$10,000 a month. Which salary option should he choose? Explain.

____

____

____

26. **Multistep** In chemistry class, Bob recorded the volume of a liquid as 13.2 mL. The true volume was 13.7 mL. Use the formula to find the percent error of Bob's measurement to the nearest tenth of a percent.

$$\text{Percent Error} = \frac{|\text{Experimental Value} - \text{True Value}|}{\text{True Value}} \times 100$$

____

MODULE QUIZ

Ready to Go On?

Personal Math Trainer
Online Assessment and Intervention
my.hrw.com

5.1 Percent Increase and Decrease

Find the percent change from the first value to the second.

1. 36; 63 ________
2. 50; 35 ________
3. 40; 72 ________
4. 92; 69 ________

5.2 Markup and Markdown

Use the original price and the markdown or markup to find the retail price.

5. Original price: \$60; Markup: 15%; Retail price: ________
6. Original price: \$32; Markup: 12.5%; Retail price: ________
7. Original price: \$50; Markdown: 22%; Retail price: ________
8. Original price: \$125; Markdown: 30%; Retail price: ________

5.3 Applications of Percent

9. Mae Ling earns a weekly salary of \$325 plus a 6.5% commission on sales at a gift shop. How much would she make in a work week if she sold \$4,800 worth of merchandise? ________

10. Ramon earns \$1,735 each month and pays \$53.10 for electricity. To the nearest tenth of a percent, what percent of Ramon's earnings are spent on electricity each month? ________

11. James, Priya, and Siobhan work in a grocery store. James makes \$7.00 per hour. Priya makes 20% more than James, and Siobhan makes 5% less than Priya. How much does Siobhan make per hour? ________

12. The Hu family goes out for lunch, and the price of the meal is \$45. The sales tax on the meal is 6%, and the family also leaves a 20% tip on the pre-tax amount. What is the total cost of the meal? ________

ESSENTIAL QUESTION

13. Give three examples of how percents are used in the real-world. Tell whether each situation represents a percent increase or a percent decrease.

____

____

MODULE 5 MIXED REVIEW

Assessment Readiness

Personal Math Trainer
my.hrw.com
Online Assessment and Intervention

Selected Response

1. Zalmon walks $\frac{3}{4}$ of a mile in $\frac{3}{10}$ of an hour. What is his speed in miles per hour?

Ⓐ 0.225 miles per hour
Ⓑ 2.3 miles per hour
Ⓒ 2.5 miles per hour
Ⓓ 2.6 miles per hour

2. Find the percent change from 70 to 56.

Ⓐ 20% decrease   Ⓒ 25% decrease
Ⓑ 20% increase   Ⓓ 25% increase

3. The rainfall total this year was 10.2 inches, which is 20% less than last year's rainfall total. What was last year's rainfall total?

Ⓐ 8.16 inches   Ⓒ 12.75 inches
Ⓑ 12.24 inches   Ⓓ 20.4 inches

4. A pair of basketball shoes was originally priced at $80, but was marked up 37.5%. What was the retail price of the shoes?

Ⓐ $50   Ⓒ $110
Ⓑ $83   Ⓓ $130

5. The sales tax rate in Jan's town is 7.5%. If she buys 3 lamps for $23.59 each and a sofa for $769.99, how much sales tax does she owe?

Ⓐ $58.85   Ⓒ $67.26
Ⓑ $63.06   Ⓓ $71.46

6. The day after a national holiday, decorations were marked down 40%. Before the holiday, a patriotic banner cost $5.75. How much did the banner cost after the holiday?

Ⓐ $1.15   Ⓒ $3.45
Ⓑ $2.30   Ⓓ $8.05

7. Dustin makes $2,330 each month and pays $840 for rent. To the nearest tenth of a percent, what percent of Dustin's earnings are spent on rent?

Ⓐ 84.0%   Ⓒ 56.4%
Ⓑ 63.9%   Ⓓ 36.1%

8. A scuba diver is positioned at −30 feet. How many feet will she have to rise to change her position to −12 feet?

Ⓐ −42 ft   Ⓒ 18 ft
Ⓑ −18 ft   Ⓓ 42 ft

9. A bank offers an annual simple interest rate of 8% on home improvement loans. Tobias borrowed $17,000 over a period of 2 years. How much did he repay altogether?

Ⓐ $1,360   Ⓒ $18,360
Ⓑ $2,720   Ⓓ $19,720

Mini-Task

10. The granola Summer buys used to cost $6.00 per pound, but it has been marked up 15%.

a. How much did it cost Summer to buy 2.6 pounds of granola at the old price?

____

b. How much does it cost her to buy 2.6 pounds of granola at the new price?

____

c. Suppose Summer buys 3.5 pounds of granola. How much more does it cost at the new price than at the old price?

____

UNIT 2

Study Guide Review

MODULE 4 Rates and Proportionality

Key Vocabulary

complex fraction *(fracción compleja)*

constant of proportionality *(constante de proporcionalidad)*

proportion *(proporción)*

proportional relationship *(relación proporcional)*

rate of change *(tasa de cambio)*

unit rate *(tasa unitaria)*

ESSENTIAL QUESTION

How can you use rates and proportionality to solve real-world problems?

EXAMPLE 1

A store sells onions by the pound. Is the relationship between the cost of an amount of onions and the number of pounds proportional? If so, write an equation for the relationship, and represent the relationship on a graph.

Number of pounds	2	5	6
Cost ($)	3.00	7.50	9.00

Write the rates.

$\frac{\text{cost}}{\text{number of pounds}}: \frac{\$3.00}{2 \text{ pounds}} = \frac{\$1.50}{1 \text{ pound}}$

$\frac{\$7.50}{5 \text{ pounds}} = \frac{\$1.50}{1 \text{ pound}}$

$\frac{\$9.00}{6 \text{ pounds}} = \frac{\$1.50}{1 \text{ pound}}$

The rates are constant, so the relationship is proportional.

The constant rate of change is \$1.50 per pound, so the constant of proportionality is 1.5. Let x represent the number of pounds and y represent the cost.

The equation for the relationship is $y = 1.5x$.

Plot the ordered pairs (pounds, cost): (2, 3), (5, 7.5), and (6, 9).

Connect the points with a line.

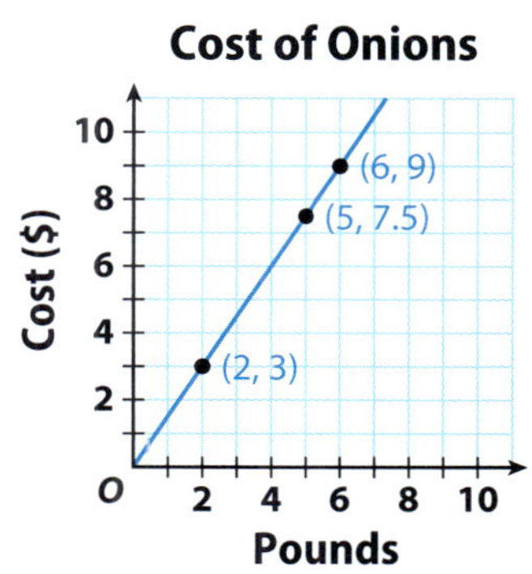

EXERCISES

1. Steve uses $\frac{8}{9}$ gallon of paint to paint 4 identical birdhouses. How many gallons of paint does he use for each birdhouse?

(Lesson 4.1) ________________

2. Ron walks 0.5 mile on the track in 10 minutes. Stevie walks 0.25 mile on the track in 6 minutes. Find the unit rate for each walker in miles per hour. Who is the faster walker?

(Lesson 4.1) ________________

____

3. The table below shows the proportional relationship between Juan's pay and the hours he works. Complete the table. Plot the data and connect the points with a line. (Lessons 4.2, 4.3)

Hours worked	2		5	6
Pay ($)	40	80		

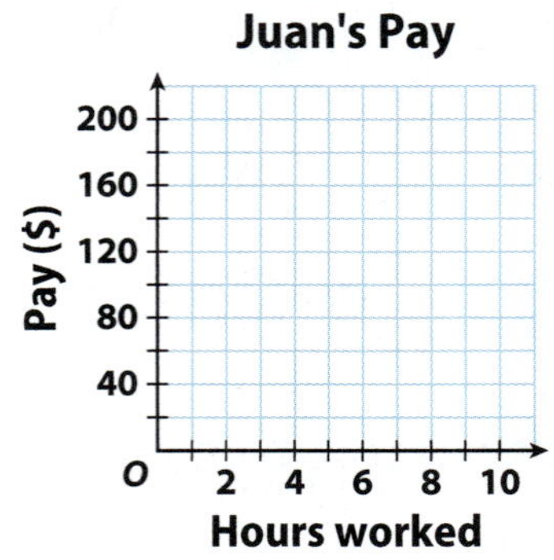

MODULE 5 Proportions and Percent

ESSENTIAL QUESTION

How can you use proportions and percent to solve real-world problems?

Key Vocabulary

percent decrease *(porcentaje de disminución)*

percent increase *(porcentaje de aumento)*

principal *(capital)*

simple interest *(interés simple)*

EXAMPLE 1

Donata had a 25-minute commute from home to work. Her company moved, and now her commute to work is 33 minutes long. Does this situation represent an increase or a decrease? Find the percent increase or decrease in her commute to work.

This situation represents an increase. Find the percent increase.

amount of change = greater value − lesser value

$33 - 25 = 8$

$$\text{percent increase} = \frac{\text{amount of change}}{\text{original amount}}$$

$\frac{8}{25} = 0.32 = 32\%$

Donata's commute increased by 32%.

1. Michelle purchased 25 audio files in January. In February she purchased 40 audio files. Find the percent increase. (Lesson 5.1) ________

2. Sam's dog weighs 72 pounds. The vet suggests that for the dog's health, its weight should decrease by 12.5 percent. According to the vet, what is a healthy weight for the dog? (Lesson 5.1) ________

3. The original price of a barbecue grill is $79.50. The grill is marked down 15%. What is the sale price of the grill? (Lesson 5.2) ________

4. A sporting goods store marks up the cost *s* of soccer balls by 250%. Write an expression that represents the retail cost of the soccer balls. The store buys soccer balls for $5.00 each. What is the retail price of the soccer balls? (Lesson 5.2) ________

Unit 2 Performance Tasks

1. **CAREERS IN MATH** **Bicycle Tour Operator** Viktor is a bike tour operator and needs to replace two of his touring bikes. He orders two bikes from the sporting goods store for a total of $2,000 and pays using his credit card. When the bill arrives, he reads the following information:

   Balance: $2,000
   Annual interest rate: 14.9%
   Minimum payment due: $40
   Late fee: $10 if payment not received by 3/1/2013

   a. To keep his good credit, Viktor promptly sends in a minimum payment of $40. When the next bill arrives, it looks a lot like the previous bill.

   Balance: $1,984.34
   Annual interest rate: 14.9%
   Minimum payment due: $40
   Late fee: $10 if payment not received by 4/1/2013

   Explain how the credit card company calculated the new balance. Notice that the given interest rate is annual, but the payment is monthly.

   ____

   ____

   ____

   b. Viktor was upset about the new bill, so he decided to send in $150 for his April payment. The minimum payment on his bill is calculated as 2% of the balance (rounded to the nearest dollar) or $20, whichever is greater. Fill out the details for Viktor's new bill.

   Balance: ______________

   Annual interest rate: ______________

   Minimum payment due: ______________

   Late fee: $10 if payment not received by ______________

   c. Viktor's bank offers a credit card with an introductory annual interest rate of 9.9%. He can transfer his current balance for a fee of $40. After one year, the rate will return to the bank's normal rate, which is 13.9%. The bank charges a late fee of $15. Give two reasons why Viktor should transfer the balance, and two reasons why he should not.

   ____

   ____

   ____

   ____

2. *Acceleration* is the rate at which the velocity of an object changes. Students in a science class study the acceleration of an object due to gravity. They perform an experiment in which they drop a ball from a balcony and measure the ball's velocity in meters per second at various times as it falls toward the ground. The table shows their measurements.

Time (s)	Velocity (m/s)	Acceleration(m/s^2)
0.00	0.00	—
0.05	0.49	
0.09	0.89	
0.14	1.37	

a. When velocity is measured in meters per second, acceleration is measured in *meters per second* per *second*, or *meters per second squared* (written m/s^2). Complete the third column of the table by finding the ratio of the change in velocity to the change in time from one row to the next.

b. Describe what you notice about the acceleration ratio in your table.

____

c. What is the average acceleration?

____

d. What does your answer to part **c** suggest about the rate of change in velocity over time for this situation?

____

e. Many things affect the acceleration due to gravity on Earth, including altitude, latitude, tides, and local gravity variations. Suppose that the accepted acceleration due to gravity in your location is 9.803 m/s^2. Use the formula below to find the percent error of the average acceleration due to gravity for this experiment. Give your answer to the nearest thousandth of a percent.

$$\frac{|\text{Experimental Value} - \text{True Value}|}{\text{True Value}} \times 100$$

____

f. Make a conjecture about a possible source of error in this experiment.

____

UNIT 2 **MIXED REVIEW**

Assessment Readiness

Personal Math Trainer

my.hrw.com

Online Assessment and Intervention

Selected Response

1. If the relationship between distance y in feet and time x in seconds is proportional, which rate is represented by $\frac{y}{x} = 0.6$?

Ⓐ 3 feet in 5 s

Ⓑ 3 feet in 9 s

Ⓒ 10 feet in 6 s

Ⓓ 18 feet in 3 s

2. The Baghrams make regular monthly deposits in a savings account. The graph shows the relationship between the number x of months and the amount y in dollars in the account.

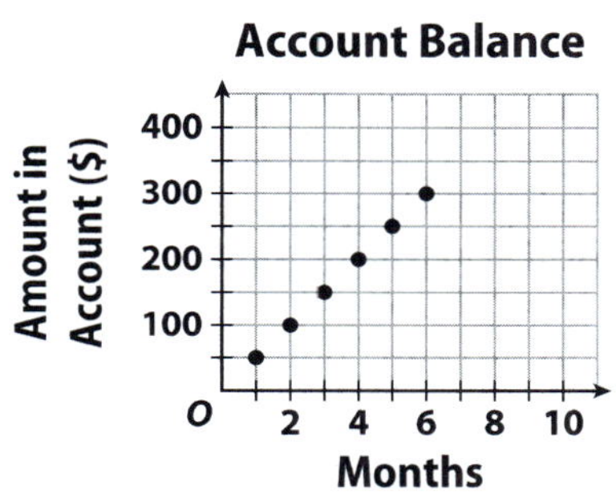

What is the equation for the deposit?

Ⓐ $\frac{y}{x} = \$25\text{/month}$

Ⓑ $\frac{y}{x} = \$40\text{/month}$

Ⓒ $\frac{y}{x} = \$50\text{/month}$

Ⓓ $\frac{y}{x} = \$75\text{/month}$

Hot Tip! **Read graphs and diagrams carefully. Look at the labels for important information.**

3. What is the decimal form of $-4\frac{7}{8}$?

Ⓐ −4.9375

Ⓑ −4.875

Ⓒ −4.75

Ⓓ −4.625

4. Find the percent change from 72 to 90.

Ⓐ 20% decrease

Ⓑ 20% increase

Ⓒ 25% decrease

Ⓓ 25% increase

5. A store had a sale on art supplies. The price p of each item was marked down 60%. Which expression represents the new price?

Ⓐ $0.4p$

Ⓑ $0.6p$

Ⓒ $1.4p$

Ⓓ $1.6p$

6. Clarke borrows $16,000 to buy a car. He pays simple interest at an annual rate of 6% over a period of 3.5 years. How much does he pay altogether?

Ⓐ $18,800

Ⓑ $19,360

Ⓒ $19,920

Ⓓ $20,480

7. To which set or sets does the number 37 belong?

Ⓐ integers only

Ⓑ rational numbers only

Ⓒ integers and rational numbers only

Ⓓ whole numbers, integers, and rational numbers

8. In which equation is the constant of proportionality 5?

Ⓐ $x = 5y$

Ⓑ $y = 5x$

Ⓒ $y = x + 5$

Ⓓ $y = 5 - x$

9. Suri charges by the day to walk a dog. She charges $6.25 for 5 days and $8.75 for 7 days. Which equation represents this relationship?

Ⓐ $y = 7x$

Ⓑ $y = 5x$

Ⓒ $y = 2.50x$

Ⓓ $y = 1.25x$

10. Randy walks $\frac{1}{2}$ mile in each $\frac{1}{5}$ hour. How far will Randy walk in one hour?

Ⓐ $\frac{1}{2}$ miles

Ⓑ 2 miles

Ⓒ $2\frac{1}{2}$ miles

Ⓓ 5 miles

11. On a trip to Spain, Sheila bought a piece of jewelry that cost $56.75. She paid for it with her credit card, which charges a foreign transaction fee of 3%. How much was the foreign transaction fee?

Ⓐ $0.17

Ⓑ $1.07

Ⓒ $1.70

Ⓓ $17.00

12. A baker is looking for a recipe that has the lowest unit rate for flour per batch of muffins. Which recipe should she use?

Ⓐ $\frac{1}{2}$ cup flour for $\frac{2}{3}$ batch

Ⓑ $\frac{2}{3}$ cup flour for $\frac{1}{2}$ batch

Ⓒ $\frac{3}{4}$ cup flour for $\frac{2}{3}$ batch

Ⓓ $\frac{1}{3}$ cup flour for $\frac{1}{4}$ batch

Mini-Task

13. Kevin was able to type 2 pages in 5 minutes, 3 pages in 7.5 minutes, and 5 pages in 12.5 minutes.

a. Make a table of the data.

b. Graph the relationship between the number of pages typed and the number of minutes.

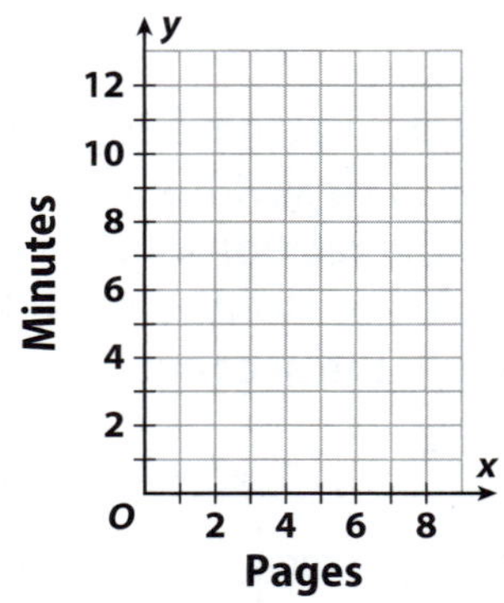

c. Describe how you know this is a proportional relationship.

____

____

____

____

d. Explain how to use the graph to find the unit rate.

____

____

____

____

____

____

UNIT 3

Expressions, Equations, and Inequalities

CAREERS IN MATH

Mechanical Engineer A mechanical engineer designs, develops, and manufactures mechanical devices and technological systems. Mechanical engineers use math to solve diverse problems, from calculating the strength of materials to determining energy consumption of a device.

If you are interested in a career in mechanical engineering, you should study these mathematical subjects:

- Algebra
- Geometry
- Trigonometry
- Statistics
- Calculus

Research other careers that require the daily use of mathematics to solve problems.

Unit 3 Performance Task

At the end of the unit, check out how **mechanical engineers** use math.

UNIT 3

Vocabulary Preview

Use the puzzle to preview key vocabulary from this unit. Unscramble the circled letters to answer the riddle at the bottom of the page.

An expression that contains at least one variable. (Lesson 6.1)

___ ___ ___ ___ ___ ___ ___ ___ ___

___ ___ ___ ___ ___ ___ ___ ___ ___ ___

An equation with more than one operation. (Lesson 6.3)

___ ___ ___   ___ ___ ___ ___   ___ ___ ___ ___ ___ ___ ___ ___

A variable whose value is less than zero. (Lesson 6.3)

___ ___ ___ ___ ___ ___ ___ ___   ___ ___ ___ ___ ___ ___ ___ ___

A variable whose value is greater than zero. (Lesson 6.3)

___ ___ ___ ___ ___ ___ ___ ___   ___ ___ ___ ___ ___ ___ ___ ___

A mathematical sentence that shows the relationship between quantities that are not equivalent. (Lesson 7.1)

___ ___ ___ ___ ___ ___ ___ ___ ___ ___

Q: Why does the sum of -4 and 3 complain more than the sum of -3 and 5?

A: It's the ___ ___ ___ ___ ___ ___ ___ ___   ___ ___ ___!

Expressions and Equations

MODULE 6

ESSENTIAL QUESTION

How can you use algebraic expressions and equations to solve real-world problems?

Real-World Video

When you take a taxi, you will be charged an initial fee plus a charge per mile. To describe situations like this, you can write a two-step equation.

my.hrw.com

GO DIGITAL
my.hrw.com

my.hrw.com
Go digital with your write-in student edition, accessible on any device.

Math On the Spot
Scan with your smart phone to jump directly to the online edition, video tutor, and more.

Animated Math
Interactively explore key concepts to see how math works.

Personal Math Trainer
Get immediate feedback and help as you work through practice sets.

Reading Start-Up

Vocabulary

Review Words

- algebraic expression *(expresión algebraica)*
- Distributive Property *(Propiedad distributiva)*
- ✔ equation *(ecuación)*
- factor *(factor)*
- ✔ operation *(operación)*
- ✔ solution *(solución)*
- ✔ variable *(variable)*

Visualize Vocabulary

Use the ✔ words to complete the graphic.

Identify the operation performed on the variable in the equation.

↓

Apply the inverse ____________ to both sides of the ____________.

↓

The ____________ in the equation is alone, and set equal to the ____________.

→

$$\begin{array}{rcl} x - 5.5 & = & 3 \\ \underline{+5.5} & & \underline{+5.5} \\ x & = & 8.5 \end{array}$$

Add 5.5 to both sides.
The solution is $x = 8.5$.

Understand Vocabulary

Complete the sentences using the review words.

1. A(n) ________________________ contains at least one variable.

2. A mathematical sentence that shows that two expressions are equivalent is called a(n) ____________________.

Active Reading

Tri-Fold Before beginning the module, create a tri-fold to help you learn the concepts and vocabulary in this module. Fold the paper into three sections. Label the columns "What I Know," "What I Need to Know," and "What I Learned." Complete the first two columns before you read. After studying the module, complete the third column.

Are YOU Ready?

Complete these exercises to review skills you will need for this chapter.

Personal Math Trainer
Online Assessment and Intervention
my.hrw.com

Words for Operations

EXAMPLE the difference of 2 and b — *Difference means subtraction.*

$2 - b$

the product of -8 and a number — *Product means multiplication.*

$(-8)x$ or $-8x$ — *Let x represent the unknown number.*

Write an algebraic expression for each word expression.

1. the sum of 5 and a number x ________

2. 11 decreased by n ________

3. the quotient of -9 and y ________

4. twice a number, minus 13 ________

Evaluate Expressions

EXAMPLE Evaluate $3x - 5$ for $x = -2$.

$3x - 5 = 3(-2) - 5$ — *Substitute the given value of x for x.*

$= -6 - 5$ — *Multiply.*

$= -11$ — *Subtract.*

Evaluate each expression for the given value of *x*.

5. $2x + 3$ for $x = 3$ ________

6. $-4x + 7$ for $x = -1$ ________

7. $1.5x - 2.5$ for $x = 3$ ________

8. $0.4x + 6.1$ for $x = -5$ ________

9. $\frac{2}{3}x - 12$ for $x = 18$ ________

10. $-\frac{5}{8}x + 10$ for $x = -8$ ________

Operations with Fractions

EXAMPLE $\frac{2}{5} \div \frac{7}{10}$

$\frac{2}{5} \div \frac{7}{10} = \frac{2}{5} \times \frac{10}{7}$ — *Multiply by the reciprocal of the divisor.*

$= \frac{2}{\cancel{5}_1} \times \frac{\cancel{10}^2}{7}$ — *Divide by the common factors.*

$= \frac{4}{7}$ — *Simplify.*

Divide.

11. $\frac{1}{2} \div \frac{1}{4}$ ________

12. $\frac{3}{8} \div \frac{13}{16}$ ________

13. $\frac{2}{5} \div \frac{14}{15}$ ________

14. $\frac{4}{9} \div \frac{16}{27}$ ________

Are YOU Ready? (cont'd)

Complete these exercises to review skills you will need for this module.

Words for Operations

15. Delia has two more than three times the number of model cars that Orlando has. If Orlando has c model cars, which algebraic expressions represent the number of model cars Delia has? Select all that apply.

Ⓐ $3(c + 2)$ Ⓑ $3c + 2$ Ⓒ $3c - 2$ Ⓓ $2 - 3c$ Ⓔ $2 + 3c$

Evaluate Expressions

16. Trent and Rita each did some hiking. The expression $2.5x - 1.5$ represents the number of miles each hiked this week. In the expression, x represents the number of miles each hiked last week. Trent hiked 4 miles last week and Rita hiked 3 miles last week.

a. How many miles did Trent hike this week? Show your work.

b. How many miles did Rita hike this week? Show your work. Last week, Rita hiked 1 mile less than Trent did. Did she also hike 1 less mile than Trent did this week?

Operations with Fractions

17. How are the quotients $\frac{3}{4} \div \frac{2}{3}$ and $\frac{2}{3} \div \frac{3}{4}$ related? Explain your thinking.

LESSON
6.1 Algebraic Expressions

7.3.6.1

Students will add, subtract, factor, and multiply algebraic expressions.

ESSENTIAL QUESTION

How do you add, subtract, factor, and multiply algebraic expressions?

EXPLORE ACTIVITY Real World

Simplifying Algebraic Expressions

When you simplify expressions using properties, you can combine like terms due to the Distributive Property: $a(b + c) = ab + ac$ and $a(b - c) = ab - ac$.

Math On the Spot
my.hrw.com

EXAMPLE 1 **Jill and Kyle get paid per project. Jill is paid a project fee of \$25 plus \$10.50 per hour. Kyle is paid a project fee of \$18 plus \$14.25 per hour. Write an expression to represent how much a company will pay to hire both to work the same number of hours on a project.**

STEP 1 Write expressions for how much the company will pay each person. Let h represent the number of hours they will work on the project.

Jill: \$25 + \$______h Kyle: \$18 + \$______h

STEP 2 Add the expressions, and simplify by combining like terms to represent the amount the company will pay to hire both.

Combine their pay. $25 + 10.50h + 18 + 14.25h$

Associative and Commutative Properties of Addition $= (25 + \_\_\_\_\_\_) + (10.50h + \_\_\_\_\_\_)$

Combine like terms. $= \_\_\_\_\_\_ + \_\_\_\_\_\_h$

The company will pay ______________ dollars to hire both Jill and Kyle.

Reflect

1. **Critical Thinking** What can you read directly from $43 + 24.75h$ that you cannot read directly from $25 + 10.50h + 18 + 14.25h$?

____

YOUR TURN

Simplify each expression.

2. $\left(3x + \frac{1}{2}\right) + \left(7x - 4\frac{1}{2}\right)$ ______________

3. $(-0.25x + 3) + (1.5x + 1.4)$ ______________

Personal Math Trainer
Online Assessment and Intervention
my.hrw.com

Math On the Spot
my.hrw.com

Simplifying More Complex Expressions

You can use the Distributive Property to remove parentheses when simplifying, or *expanding,* an algebraic expression, but be careful with negative signs and subtraction. Consider $-(x + 5)$. You can rewrite the expression as shown.

$$-(x+5) = (-1)(x+5) = (-1)(x) + (-1)(5) = -x + (-5) = -x - 5$$

Notice that you can get $-x - 5$ from $-(x + 5)$ by removing the parentheses and reversing the sign of each term. This process is called *distributing the negative*. It also applies when you distribute over subtraction, as shown.

$$-(x-5) = (-1)(x-5) = (-1)(x) - (-1)(5) = -x - (-5) = -x + 5$$

EXAMPLE 2

Simplify each expression.

A $5 - 3(7x + 8)$

$5 - 21x - 24$ — Use the Distributive Property to distribute −3.

$5 + (-21x) + (-24)$ — Rewrite subtraction as adding the opposite.

$5 + (-24) + (-21x)$ — Use the Commutative Property of Addition.

$-19 + (-21x)$ — Combine like terms.

$-19 - 21x$ — Simplify.

B $-9a - \frac{1}{3}\left(-\frac{3}{4} - \frac{2}{3}a + 12\right)$

$-9a + \frac{1}{4} + \frac{2}{9}a - 4$ — Use the Distributive Property to distribute $-\frac{1}{3}$.

$-9a + \frac{1}{4} + \frac{2}{9}a + (-4)$ — Rewrite subtraction as adding the opposite.

$-9a + \frac{2}{9}a + \frac{1}{4} + (-4)$ — Use the Commutative Property of Addition.

$-8\frac{7}{9}a - 3\frac{3}{4}$ — Use the Associative Property of Addition and combine like terms.

Math Talk
Mathematical Processes
In Part A, why is it helpful to write subtraction as adding the opposite?

Reflect

4. Why is the Associative Property of Addition applied in Part B?

____

YOUR TURN

Simplify each expression.

5. $0.2(3b - 15c)$ ____________

6. $5x - 3(x - 2) - x$ ____________

7. $8.3 + 3.4y - 0.5(12y - 7)$ ____________

Personal Math Trainer
Online Assessment and Intervention
my.hrw.com

EXPLORE ACTIVITY 2

Factoring Expressions

A factor is a number that is multiplied by another number to get a product. To **factor** is to write a number or an algebraic expression as a product.

Factor $4x + 8$.

A Model the expression with algebra tiles.

Use ______ positive x-tiles and ______ $+1$-tiles.

B Arrange the tiles to form a rectangle. The total area represents $4x + 8$.

C Since the length multiplied by the width equals the area, the length and the width of the rectangle are the factors of $4x + 8$. Find the length and width.

The length is __ x-tile and __ $+1$-tiles, or ______.

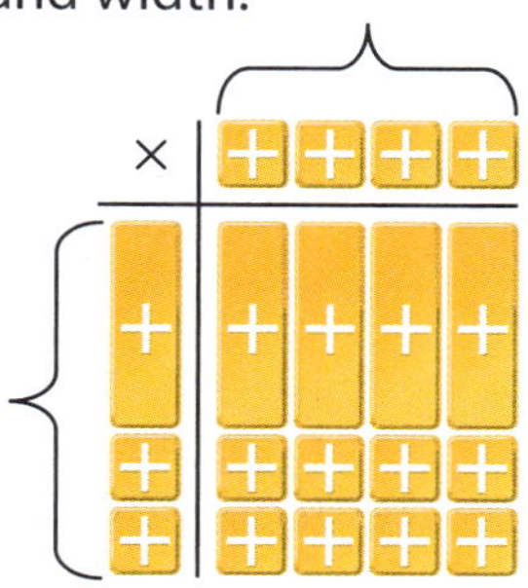

The width is __ $+1$-tiles, or __.

D Use the expressions for the length and width of the rectangle to write the area of the rectangle, $4x + 8$, in factored form. __________

Reflect

8. **Communicate Mathematical Ideas** How could you use the Distributive Property to check your factoring?

____

YOUR TURN

Factor each expression.

9. $2x + 2$ ________ **10.** $3x + 9$ ________ **11.** $5x + 15$ ________ **12.** $4x + 16$ ________

Personal Math Trainer
Online Assessment and Intervention
my.hrw.com

Guided Practice

1. The manager of a summer camp has 14 baseballs and 23 tennis balls. The manager buys some boxes of baseballs with 12 baseballs to a box and an equal number of boxes of tennis balls with 16 tennis balls to a box. Write an expression to represent the total number of balls. (Explore Activity Example 1)

STEP 1 Write expressions for the total number of baseballs and tennis balls. Let n represent the number of boxes of each type.

baseballs: ______ + (______)n tennis balls: ______ + (______)n

STEP 2 Find an expression for the total number of balls.

______ + ______ + ______ + ______ *Combine the two expressions.*

______ + ______ + ______ + ______ *Use the Commutative Property.*

______ + ______ *Combine like terms.*

So, the total number of baseballs and tennis balls is ______ + ______.

2. Use the expression you found above to find the total number of baseballs and tennis balls if the manager bought 9 boxes of each type. (Explore Activity Example 1) ______

Simplify each expression. (Example 2)

3. $0.5(12m - 22n)$

$0.5(12m - 22n) = 0.5($______$) - 0.5($______$)$ *Use the Distributive Property.*

$=$ ______ $-$ ______ *Multiply.*

4. $2(x - 3) - (6x - 4)$

______ $- 6 -$ ______ $+ 4 =$ ______ $+$ ______ $+ (-6) + 4 =$ ______ $-$ ______

Factor each expression. (Explore Activity 2)

5. $2x + 12$ ______

6. $12x + 24$ ______

7. $7x + 35$ ______

ESSENTIAL QUESTION CHECK-IN

8. What is the relationship between multiplying and factoring?

______

______

______

Name ______________________ Class ______________ Date ______________

6.1 Independent Practice

Personal Math Trainer
Online Assessment and Intervention
my.hrw.com

Write and simplify an expression for each situation.

9. A company rents out 15 food booths and 20 game booths at the county fair. The fee for a food booth is \$100 plus \$5 per day. The fee for a game booth is \$50 plus \$7 per day. The fair lasts for *d* days, and all the booths are rented for the entire time. Write and simplify an expression for the amount in dollars that the company is paid.

____

10. A rug maker is using a pattern that is a rectangle with a length of 96 inches and a width of 60 inches. The rug maker wants to increase each dimension by a different amount. Let ℓ and w be the increases in inches of the length and width. Write and simplify an expression for the perimeter of the new pattern.

____

In 11–12, identify the two factors that were multiplied together to form the array of tiles. Then identify the product of the two factors.

11.  ____________________

12.  ____________________

13. Explain how the figure illustrates that $6(9) = 6(5) + 6(4)$.

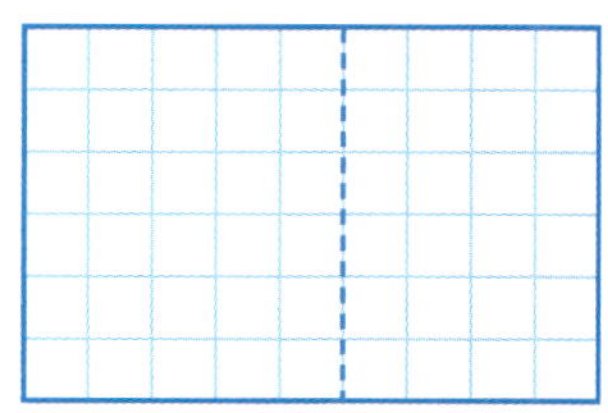

____

____

____

____

In 14–15, the perimeter of the figure is given. Find the length of the indicated side.

14.

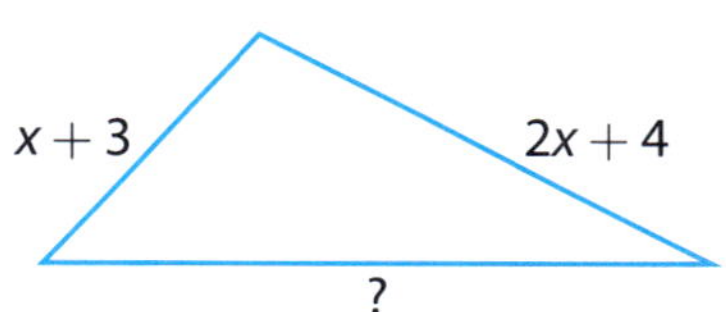

Perimeter $= 6x$ ____________

15.

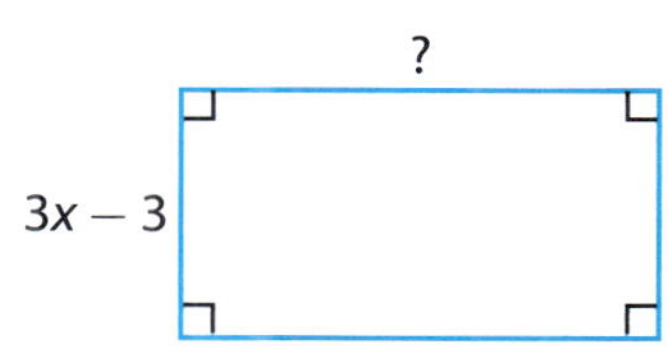

Perimeter $= 10x + 6$ ____________

16. **Persevere in Problem Solving** The figures show the dimensions of a tennis court and a basketball court given in terms of the width, x (in feet), of the tennis court.

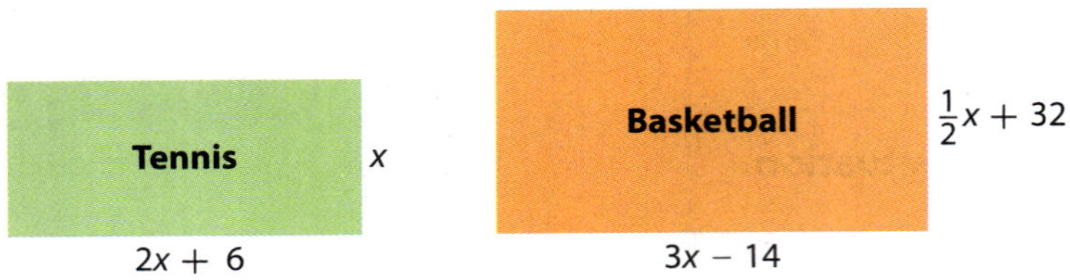

a. Write an expression for the perimeter of each court. ________________

b. Write an expression that describes how much greater the perimeter of the basketball court is than the perimeter of the tennis court. ________________________________

c. Suppose the tennis court is 36 feet wide. Find all dimensions of the two courts. ________________________________

Work Area

H.O.T. FOCUS ON HIGHER ORDER THINKING

17. **Draw Conclusions** Use the figure to find the product $(x + 3)(x + 2)$. (*Hint*: Find the area of each small square or rectangle, then add.)

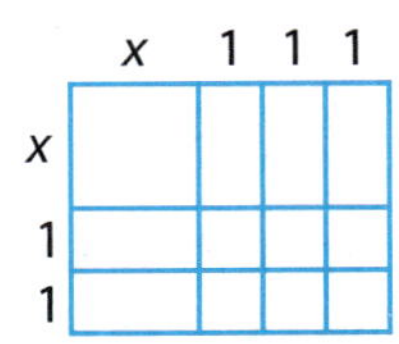

$(x + 3)(x + 2) =$ ________________

18. **Explain the Error** Andy and Sylvie each incorrectly simplified the expression $-3 - 4(2x - 3)$. Andy wrote $-14x + 21$ and Sylvie wrote $-8x - 6$. Explain their errors and give the correct answer.

____

____

____

____

____

19. **Justify Reasoning** Describe two different ways that you could find the product 8×997 using mental math. Find the product and explain why your methods work.

____

____

____

____

Going Further 6.1

Applying Properties to Algebraic Expressions

7.3.GF.6.1

Students will use the properties of operations to justify their work when simplifying algebraic expressions.

ESSENTIAL QUESTION

How can using the properties of operations to justify your work help you simplify algebraic expressions?

EXPLORE ACTIVITY

Applying Properties to Simplify

Using properties of operations can help you avoid errors when simplifying.

Justify each step in simplifying the expression $4x - 3(2x - 5) - (x + 4)$.

$4x - 3(2x - 5) - (x + 4)$	
$4x - 6x + 15 - x - 4$	________________
$4x + (-6x) + 15 + (-x) + (-4)$	Rewrite subtraction as ________ the opposite.
$[4x + (-6x) + (-x)] + [15 + (-4)]$	Commutative and ________ Properties of Addition
$-3x + 11$	Combine like terms.

Reflect

1. What is the coefficient of $-x$? ________________

Applying Properties to Factor

You can use the Distributive Property to factor a linear expression like $30x - 42$. To factor it completely, use the greatest common factor of the coefficient of the variable and the constant as one of the factors.

EXAMPLE

Factor the expression $30x - 42$ completely.

STEP 1 Find the greatest common factor of 30 and 42.

Factors of 30: 1, 2, 3, 5, (6), 10, 15, 30

Factors of 42: 1, 2, 3, (6), 7, 14, 21, 42

The GCF of 30 and 42 is 6.

STEP 2 Factor out the greatest common factor.

$30x - 42 = 6(5x) - 6(7)$ Factor each term using the GCF.

$= 6(5x - 7)$ Distributive Property

The expression $30x - 42$ factored completely is $6(5x - 7)$.

Practice

1. Hoon simplified the expression below using the steps shown. Justify each step in his simplification. There may be more than one property for a step.

$8\frac{1}{2} - \frac{1}{2}(17 - 6x) + 2\left(\frac{1}{2} - x\right)$

$8\frac{1}{2} - 8\frac{1}{2} + 3x + 1 - 2x$ ____________________

$8\frac{1}{2} + \left(-8\frac{1}{2}\right) + 3x + 1 + (-2x)$ ____________________

$0 + 3x + 1 + (-2x)$ ____________________

$3x + 1 + (-2x)$ ____________________

$1 + 3x + (-2x)$ ____________________

$1 + [3x + (-2x)]$ ____________________

$1 + x$ ____________________

Find and correct the error in the student's work.

2. Carole wrote $100 - 10(4 + 2f) = 100 - 40 + 20f$.

3. Adiba wrote $12 - 4(3x - 2) = 12 - 4(2 - 3x)$.

4. **Critical Thinking** The perimeter of the rectangle is $3x + 2 + x + 3x + 2 + x$. Alix expressed the perimeter as $2(3x + 2) + 2x$. Babat expressed it as $8x + 4$. Describe in words how each expression represents the perimeter in terms of the length $3x + 2$, the width x, or both. Then identify one benefit of each form of the expression.

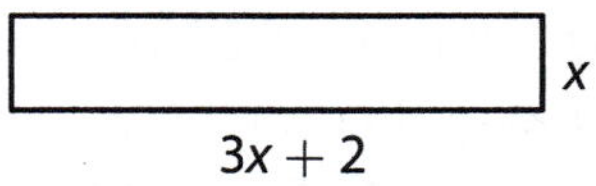

Factor each expression completely.

5. $4x - 16$

6. $52x + 13$

7. $8x + 14$

8. $16x - 24$

9. $-12x - 20$

10. $-20x + 50$

LESSON 6.2

One-Step Equations with Rational Coefficients

7.3.6.2

Students will use one-step equations with rational coefficients to solve problems.

ESSENTIAL QUESTION

How do you use one-step equations with rational coefficients to solve problems?

EXPLORE ACTIVITY

One-Step Equations

You have written and solved one-step equations involving whole numbers. Now you will learn to work with equations containing negative numbers.

Math On the Spot my.hrw.com

EXAMPLE 1 **Use inverse operations to solve each equation.**

A Begin with the equation $x + 3.2 = -8.5$.

Subtract 3.2 from both sides.

$$x + 3.2 = -8.5$$
$$-\square \qquad -\square$$
$$x = \square$$

B Begin with the equation $-\frac{2}{3} + y = 8$.

Add $\frac{2}{3}$ to both sides.

$$-\frac{2}{3} + y = 8$$
$$+\square \qquad = +\square$$
$$y = \square$$

C Begin with the equation $30 = -0.5a$.

Divide both sides by -0.5.

$$\frac{30}{\square} = \frac{-0.5a}{\square}$$
$$\square = a$$

D Begin with the equation $-\frac{q}{3.5} = 9.2$.

Multiply both sides by -3.5.

$$-\frac{q}{3.5} = 9.2$$
$$-\frac{q}{3.5}\left(\square\right) = 9.2\left(\square\right)$$
$$q = \square$$

YOUR TURN

Use inverse operations to solve each equation.

1. $4.9 + z = -9$ ________

2. $r - 17.1 = -4.8$ ________

3. $-3c = 36$ ________

Personal Math Trainer
Online Assessment and Intervention
my.hrw.com

Writing and Solving One-Step Addition and Subtraction Equations

Math On the Spot
my.hrw.com

Negative numbers often appear in real-world situations. For example, elevations below sea level are represented by negative numbers. When you increase your elevation, you are moving in a positive direction. When you decrease your elevation, you are moving in a negative direction.

EXAMPLE 2 Real World

A scuba diver is exploring at an elevation of −12.2 meters. As the diver rises to the surface, she plans to stop and rest briefly at a reef that has an elevation of −4.55 meters. Find the vertical distance that the diver will travel.

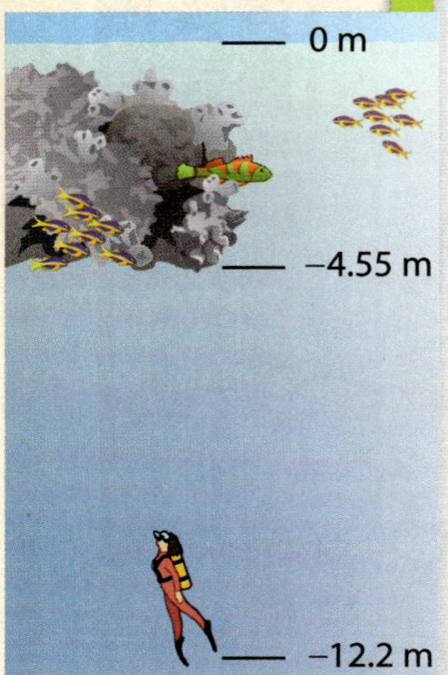

STEP 1 Write an equation. Let x represent the vertical distance between her initial elevation and the elevation of the reef.

$$-12.2 + x = -4.55$$

STEP 2 Solve the equation using an inverse operation.

$$\begin{aligned} -12.2 + x &= -4.55 \\ \underline{+12.2} \qquad & \underline{+12.2} \\ x &= 7.65 \end{aligned}$$

Add 12.2 to both sides.

The diver will travel a vertical distance of 7.65 meters.

Reflect

4. **Make a Prediction** Explain how you know whether the diver is moving in a positive or a negative direction before you solve the equation.

____

____

____

YOUR TURN

5. An airplane descends 1.5 miles to an elevation of 5.25 miles. Find the elevation of the plane before its descent.

____

____

Personal Math Trainer
Online Assessment and Intervention
my.hrw.com

Writing and Solving One-Step Multiplication and Division Problems

Temperatures can be both positive and negative, and they can increase or decrease during a given period of time. A decrease in temperature is represented by a negative number. An increase in temperature is represented by a positive number.

Math On the Spot
my.hrw.com

EXAMPLE 3 Real World

Between the hours of 10 P.M. and 6 A.M., the temperature decreases an average of $\frac{3}{4}$ of a degree per hour. How many minutes will it take for the temperature to decrease by 5 °F?

STEP 1 Write an equation. Let x represent the number of hours it takes for the temperature to decrease by 5 °F.

$$-\frac{3}{4}x = -5$$

STEP 2 Solve the equation using an inverse operation.

$$-\frac{3}{4}x = -5$$

$$-\frac{4}{3}\left(-\frac{3}{4}x\right) = -\frac{4}{3}(-5) \qquad \text{Multiply both sides by } -\frac{4}{3}.$$

$$x = \frac{20}{3}$$

STEP 3 Convert the number of hours to minutes.

$$\frac{20}{3} \text{ hours} \times \frac{60 \text{ minutes}}{1 \text{ hour}} = 400 \text{ minutes}$$

It takes 400 minutes for the temperature to decrease by 5 °F.

Math Talk
Mathematical Processes

Why is multiplying by $-\frac{4}{3}$ the inverse of multiplying by $-\frac{3}{4}$?

YOUR TURN

6. The value of a share of stock decreases in value at a rate of \$1.20 per hour during the first 3.5 hours of trading. Write and solve an equation to find the decrease in the value of the share of stock during that time.

____

7. After a power failure, the temperature in a freezer increased at an average rate of 2.5 °F per hour. The total increase was 7.5 °F. Write and solve an equation to find the number of hours until the power was restored.

____

Personal Math Trainer
Online Assessment and Intervention
my.hrw.com

Guided Practice

The table shows the average temperature in Barrow, Alaska, for three months during one year.

Month	Average Temperature (°F)
January	−13.4
June	34.0
November	−1.7

1. How many degrees warmer is the average temperature in November than in January?
(Explore Activity Example 1 and Example 2)

STEP 1 Write an equation. Let x represent ____________

____.

$x +$ ________ $=$ ________, or $x -$ ________ $=$ ________

STEP 2 Solve the equation. Show your work.

The average temperature in November

is ________ warmer.

2. Suppose that during one period of extreme cold, the average daily temperature decreased $1\frac{1}{2}$ °F each day. How many days did it take for the temperature to decrease by 9 °F?
(Explore Activity Example 1 and Example 3)

STEP 1 Write an equation. Let x represent ____________

____.

________ $x =$ ________

STEP 2 Solve the equation. Show your work.

It took ________ days for the temperature to decrease by 9 °F.

Use inverse operations to solve each equation. (Explore Activity Example 1)

3. $-2x = 34$

____

4. $y - 3.5 = -2.1$

____

5. $\frac{2}{3}z = -6$

____

ESSENTIAL QUESTION CHECK-IN

6. How does writing an equation help you solve a problem?

____

____

Name ______________________ Class ______________ Date ____________

6.2 Independent Practice

Personal Math Trainer
Online Assessment and Intervention
my.hrw.com

The table shows the elevation in feet at the peaks of several mountains. Use the table for 7–9.

Mountain	Elevation (feet)
Mt. McKinley	20,321.5
K2	28,251.31
Tupungato	22,309.71
Dom	14,911.42

7. Mt. Everest is 8,707.37 feet higher than Mt. McKinley. What is the elevation of Mt. Everest?

____

8. Liam descended from the summit of K2 to an elevation of 23,201.06 feet. How many feet did Liam descend? What was his change in elevation?

____

9. K2 is 11,194.21 feet higher than Mt. Kenya. Write and solve an equation to find the elevation of Mt. Kenya.

____

____

10. A hot air balloon begins its descent at a rate of $22\frac{1}{2}$ feet per minute. How long will it take for the balloon's elevation to change by −315 feet?

____

11. During another part of its flight, the balloon in Exercise 10 had a change in elevation of −901 feet in 34 minutes. What was its rate of descent?

____

The table shows the average temperatures in several states from January through March. Use the table for 12–14.

State	Average Temperature (°C)
Florida	18.1
Minnesota	−2.5
Montana	−0.7
Texas	12.5

12. Write and solve an equation to find how much warmer Montana's average 3-month temperature is than Minnesota's.

____

13. How much warmer is Florida's average 3-month temperature than Montana's?

____

14. How would the average temperature in Texas have to change to match the average temperature in Florida?

____

15. A football team has a net yardage of $-26\frac{1}{3}$ yards on a series of plays. The team needs a net yardage of 10 yards to get a first down. How many yards do they have to get on their next play to get a first down?

____

16. A diver begins at sea level and descends vertically at a rate of $2\frac{1}{2}$ feet per second. How long does the diver take to reach -15.6 feet? ___

17. **Analyze Relationships** In Exercise 16, what is the relationship between the rate at which the diver descends, the elevation he reaches, and the time it takes to reach that elevation?

___

18. **Check for Reasonableness** Jane withdrew money from her savings account in each of 5 months. The average amount she withdrew per month was \$45.50. How much did she withdraw in all during the 5 months? Show that your answer is reasonable.

___

___

H.O.T. FOCUS ON HIGHER ORDER THINKING

Work Area

19. **Justify Reasoning** Consider the two problems below. Which values in the problems are represented by negative numbers? Explain why.

(1) A diver below sea level ascends 25 feet to a reef at −35.5 feet. What was the elevation of the diver before she ascended to the reef?

(2) A plane descends 1.5 miles to an elevation of 3.75 miles. What was the elevation of the plane before its descent?

___

___

___

20. **Analyze Relationships** How is solving $-4x = -4.8$ different from solving $-\frac{1}{4}x = -4.8$? How are the solutions related?

___

___

___

21. **Communicate Mathematical Ideas** Flynn opens a savings account. In one 3-month period, he makes deposits of \$75.50 and \$55.25. He makes withdrawals of \$25.15 and \$18.65. His balance at the end of the 3-month period is \$210.85. Explain how you can find his initial deposit amount.

___

___

___

LESSON 6.3

Writing Two-Step Equations

7.3.6.3

Students will write a two-step equation.

ESSENTIAL QUESTION

How do you write a two-step equation?

EXPLORE ACTIVITY

Modeling Two-Step Equations

You can use algebra tiles to model two-step equations.

KEY

[+] = positive variable

[−] = negative variable

[+] = 1 [−] = −1

Use algebra tiles to model $3x - 4 = 5$.

A How can you model the left side of the equation?

____

B How can you model the right side of the equation?

____

C Use algebra tiles or draw them to model the equation on the mat.

Math Talk
Mathematical Processes

Why is the mat divided into two equal halves with a line?

Reflect

1. **What If?** How would you change the algebra tile model in the Explore Activity to model $-3x + 4 = 5$?

____

____

____

Math On the Spot
my.hrw.com

Writing Two-Step Equations

You can write two-step equations to represent real-world problems by translating the words of the problems into numbers, variables, and operations.

EXAMPLE 1 Real World

A one-year membership to Metro Gym costs $460. There is a fee of $40 when you join, and the rest is paid monthly. Write an equation to represent the situation that can help members find how much they pay per month.

STEP 1 Identify what you are trying to find. This will be the variable in the equation.

Let m represent the amount of money members pay per month.

STEP 2 Identify important information in the problem that can be used to help write an equation.

one-time joining fee: **$40**
fee charged for 1 year: **$12 \cdot m$**
total cost for the year: **$460**

Convert 1 year into 12 months to find how much members pay per month.

STEP 3 Use words in the problem to tie the information together and write an equation.

One-time joining fee	plus	12	times	monthly cost	equals	$460
↓	↓	↓	↓	↓	↓	↓
$40	+	12	·	m	=	$460

The equation $40 + 12m = 460$ can help members find out their monthly fee.

Reflect

2. **Multiple Representations** Why would this equation for finding the monthly fee be difficult to model with algebra tiles?

____

3. Can you rewrite the equation in the form $52m = 460$? Explain.

____

____

YOUR TURN

4. Billy has a gift card with a \$150 balance. He buys several video games that cost \$35 each. After the purchases, his gift card balance is \$45. Write an equation to help find out how many video games Billy bought.

____

Personal Math Trainer
Online Assessment and Intervention
my.hrw.com

Writing a Verbal Description of a Two-Step Equation

You can also write a verbal description to fit a two-step equation.

EXAMPLE 2 Real World

Math On the Spot
my.hrw.com

Write a corresponding real-world problem to represent $5x + 50 = 120$.

STEP 1 Analyze what each part of the equation means mathematically.

x is the solution of the problem, the quantity you are looking for.

$5x$ means that, for a reason given in the problem, the quantity you are looking for is multiplied by 5.

$+$ **50** means that, for a reason given in the problem, 50 is added to $5x$.

$=$ **120** means that after multiplying the solution x by 5 and adding 50 to it, the result is 120.

STEP 2 Think of some different situations in which a quantity x might be multiplied by 5.

You have x number of books, each weighing 5 pounds, and you want to know their total weight.	You save \$5 each week for x weeks and want to know the total amount you have saved.

STEP 3 Build on the situation and adjust it to create a verbal description that takes all of the information of the equation into account.

- A publisher ships a package of x number of books each weighing 5 pounds, plus a second package weighing 50 pounds. The total weight of both packages is 120 pounds. How many books are being shipped?
- Leon receives a birthday gift of \$50 from his parents and decides to save it. Each week he adds \$5 to his savings. How many weeks will it take for him to save \$120?

My Notes

Personal Math Trainer

Online Assessment and Intervention

my.hrw.com

YOUR TURN

5. Write a real-world problem that can be represented by $10x + 40 = 100$.

____

____

Guided Practice

Draw algebra tiles to model the given two-step equation. (Explore Activity)

1. $2x + 5 = 7$

2. $-3 = 5 - 4x$

3. A group of adults plus one child attend a movie at Cineplex 15. Tickets cost \$9 for adults and \$6 for children. The total cost for the movie is \$78. Write an equation to find the number of adults in the group. (Example 1) ______________

4. Break down the equation $2x + 10 = 16$ to analyze each part. (Example 2)

   x is ______________ of the problem.

   $2x$ is the quantity you are looking for ______________.

   $+ 10$ means 10 is ______________. **$= 16$** means the __________ is 16.

5. Write a corresponding real-world problem to represent $2x - 125 = 400$.

   (Example 2) ______________________________

   ____

ESSENTIAL QUESTION CHECK-IN

6. Describe the steps you would follow to write a two-step equation you can use to solve a real-world problem.

____

____

____

Name ______________________ Class ______________ Date ______________

6.3 Independent Practice

Personal Math Trainer
Online Assessment and Intervention
my.hrw.com

7. Describe how to model $-3x + 7 = 28$ with algebra tiles.

____

____

____

8. Val rented a bicycle while she was on vacation. She paid a flat rental fee of \$55.00, plus \$8.50 each day. The total cost was \$123. Write an equation you can use to find the number of days she rented the bicycle.

____

9. A restaurant sells a coffee refill mug for \$6.75. Each refill costs \$1.25. Last month Keith spent \$31.75 on a mug and refills. Write an equation you can use to find the number of refills that Keith bought.

____

10. A gym holds one 60-minute exercise class on Saturdays and several 45-minute classes during the week. Last week all of the classes lasted a total of 285 minutes. Write an equation you can use to find the number of weekday classes.

____

11. **Multiple Representations** There are 172 South American animals in the Springdale Zoo. That is 45 more than half the number of African animals in the zoo. Write an equation you could use to find n, the number of African animals in the zoo.

____

12. A school bought \$548 in basketball equipment and uniforms costing \$29.50 each. The total cost was \$2,023. Write an equation you can use to find the number of uniforms the school purchased.

____

13. **Financial Literacy** Heather has \$500 in her savings account. She withdraws \$20 per week for gas. Write an equation Heather can use to see how many weeks it will take her to have a balance of \$220.

____

14. **Critique Reasoning** For $9x + 25 = 88$, Deena wrote the situation "I bought some shirts at the store for \$9 each and received a \$25 discount. My total bill was \$88. How many shirts did I buy?"

a. What mistake did Deena make?

____

____

____

b. Rewrite the equation to match Deena's situation.

____

c. How could you rewrite the situation to make it fit the equation?

____

____

____

____

____

Work Area

15. **Multistep** Sandy charges each family that she babysits a flat fee of \$10 for the night and an extra \$5 per child. Kimmi charges \$25 per night, no matter how many children a family has.

a. Write a two-step equation that would compare what the two girls charge and find when their fees are the same. ________________

b. How many children must a family have for Sandy and Kimmi to charge the same amount? ________________

c. The Sanderson family has five children. Which babysitter should they choose if they wish to save some money on babysitting, and why?

____

____

H.O.T. FOCUS ON HIGHER ORDER THINKING

16. **Analyze Relationships** Each student wrote a two-step equation. Peter wrote the equation $4x - 2 = 10$, and Andres wrote the equation $16x - 8 = 40$. The teacher looked at their equations and asked them to compare them. Describe one way in which the equations are similar.

____

____

____

____

17. **What's the Error?** Damon has 5 dimes and some nickels in his pocket, worth a total of \$1.20. To find the number of nickels Damon has, a student wrote the equation $5n + 50 = 1.20$. Find the error in the student's equation.

____

____

____

18. **Represent Real-World Problems** Write a real-world problem you could answer by solving the equation $-8x + 60 = 28$.

____

____

____

____

LESSON 6.4

Solving Two-Step Equations

7.3.6.4

Students will solve a two-step equation.

ESSENTIAL QUESTION

How do you solve a two-step equation?

EXPLORE ACTIVITY

Modeling and Solving Two-Step Equations

You can solve two-step equations using algebra tiles.

Math On the Spot
my.hrw.com

EXAMPLE 1 **Use algebra tiles to model and solve $3n + 2 = 11$.**

STEP 1 Model the equation.

STEP 2 Remove, or subtract, an equal number of +1-tiles from both sides of the mat to help isolate the variable.

Remove _______ +1-tiles from each side of the mat.

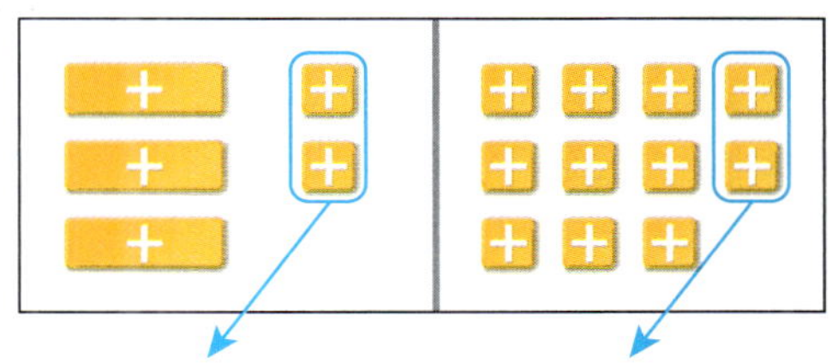

STEP 3 Divide each side into _______ equal groups.

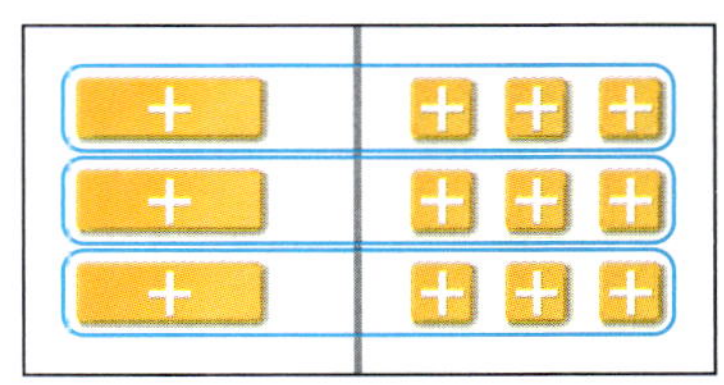

STEP 4 The solution is $n =$ _______.

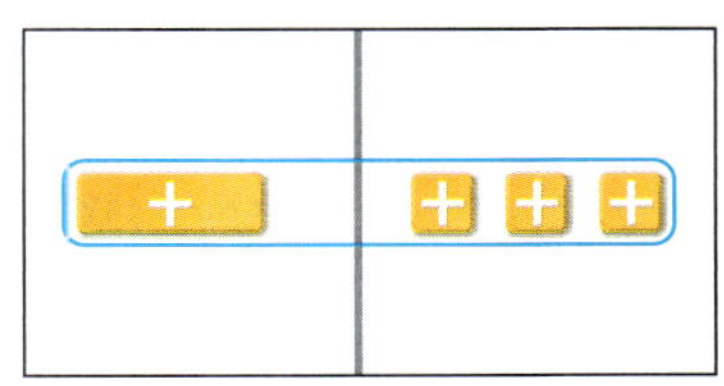

YOUR TURN

Use algebra tiles to model and solve each equation.

1. $2x + 5 = 11$ _______________

2. $3n - 1 = 8$ _______________

3. $2a - 3 = -5$ _______________

4. $-4y + 2 = -2$ _______________

Personal Math Trainer
Online Assessment and Intervention
my.hrw.com

Math On the Spot

my.hrw.com

Solving Two-Step Equations

You can use inverse operations to solve equations with more than one operation.

EXAMPLE 2 Real World

A dog sled driver added more gear to the sled, doubling its weight. This felt too heavy, so the driver removed 20 pounds to reach the final weight of 180 pounds. Write and solve an equation to find the sled's original weight.

STEP 1 Write an equation. Let w represent the original weight of the sled.

$2w - 20 = 180.$

STEP 2 Solve the equation.

$$2w - 20 = 180$$

$$+20 \quad +20 \qquad \text{Add 20 to both sides.}$$

$$2w = 200$$

$$\frac{2w}{2} = \frac{200}{2} \qquad \text{Divide both sides by 2.}$$

$$w = 100$$

The sled's original weight was 100 pounds.

Reflect

5. **Analyze Relationships** Describe how you could find the original weight of the sled using only arithmetic. Compare this method with the method shown in Example 2.

____

____

____

____

YOUR TURN

Solve each problem by writing and solving an equation.

6. The Wilsons have triplets and another child who is ten years old. The sum of the ages of their children is 37. How old are the triplets?

____

7. Five less than the quotient of a number and 4 is 15. What is the number?

____

Personal Math Trainer

Online Assessment and Intervention

my.hrw.com

Two-Step Equations with Negative Numbers

Many real-world quantities such as altitude or temperature involve negative numbers. You solve equations with negative numbers just as you did equations with positive numbers.

Math On the Spot
my.hrw.com

EXAMPLE 3 Real World

A **To convert a temperature from degrees Fahrenheit to degrees Celsius, first subtract 32. Then multiply the result by $\frac{5}{9}$. An outdoor thermometer showed a temperature of −10 °C. What was the temperature in degrees Fahrenheit?**

STEP 1 Write an equation. Let x represent the temperature in degrees Fahrenheit.

$$-10 = \frac{5}{9}(x - 32)$$

STEP 2 Solve the equation.

$$\frac{9}{5}(-10) = \frac{9}{5}\left(\frac{5}{9}(x - 32)\right) \qquad \text{Multiply both sides by } \frac{9}{5}.$$

$$-18 = x - 32$$

$$\underline{+32} \qquad \underline{+32} \qquad \text{Add 32 to both sides.}$$

$$14 = x$$

The temperature was 14 degrees Fahrenheit.

B **An airplane flies at an altitude of 38,000 feet. As it nears the airport, the plane begins to descend at a rate of 600 feet per minute. At this rate, how many minutes will the plane take to descend to 18,800 feet?**

STEP 1 Write an equation. Let m represent the number of minutes.

$$38{,}000 - 600m = 18{,}800$$

STEP 2 Solve the equation. Start by isolating the term that contains the variable.

$$38{,}000 - 600m = 18{,}800$$

$$\underline{-38{,}000} \qquad \underline{-38{,}000} \qquad \text{Subtract 38,000 from both sides.}$$

$$-600m = -19{,}200$$

$$\frac{-600m}{-600} = \frac{-19{,}200}{-600} \qquad \text{Divide both sides by } -600.$$

$$m = 32$$

The plane will take 32 minutes to descend to 18,800 feet.

Math Talk
Mathematical Processes
How can you check the solution?

Animated Math
my.hrw.com

Personal Math Trainer
Online Assessment and Intervention
my.hrw.com

YOUR TURN

Solve each problem by writing and solving an equation.

8. What is the temperature in degrees Fahrenheit of a freezer kept at -20 °C?

____

9. Jenny earned 92 of a possible 120 points on a test. She lost 4 points for each incorrect answer. How many incorrect answers did she have?

____

Guided Practice

The equation $2x + 1 = 9$ is modeled below. (Explore Activity Example 1)

1. To solve the equation with algebra tiles, first remove _______________.

Then divide each side into _______________.

2. The solution is $x =$ _______________.

Solve each problem by writing and solving an equation.

3. A rectangular picture frame has a perimeter of 58 inches. The height of the frame is 18 inches. What is the width of the frame? (Example 2)

____

4. A school store has 1200 pencils in stock, and sells an average of 25 pencils per day. The manager reorders when the number of pencils in stock is 500. In how many days will the manager have to reorder? (Example 3)

____

ESSENTIAL QUESTION CHECK-IN

5. How can you decide which operations to use to solve a two-step equation?

____

____

____

Name ____________ Class ____________ Date ____________

6.4 Independent Practice

Personal Math Trainer
my.hrw.com
Online Assessment and Intervention

Solve.

6. $9s + 3 = 57$

7. $4d + 6 = 42$

8. $-3y + 12 = -48$

9. $\frac{k}{2} + 9 = 30$

10. $\frac{g}{3} - 7 = 15$

11. $\frac{z}{5} + 3 = -35$

12. $-9h - 15 = 93$

13. $-3(n + 5) = 12$

14. $-17 + \frac{b}{8} = 13$

15. $7(c - 12) = -21$

16. $-3 + \frac{p}{7} = -5$

17. $46 = -6t - 8$

18. After making a deposit, Puja had $264 in her savings account. She noticed that if she added $26 to the amount originally in the account and doubled the sum, she would get the new amount. How much did she originally have in the account?

19. The current temperature in Smalltown is 20 °F. This is 6 degrees less than twice the temperature that it was six hours ago. What was the temperature in Smalltown six hours ago?

20. One reading at an Arctic research station showed that the temperature was -35 °C. What is this temperature in degrees Fahrenheit?

21. Artaud noticed that if he takes the opposite of his age and adds 40, he gets the number 28. How old is Artaud?

22. Sven has 11 more than twice as many customers as when he started selling newspapers. He now has 73 customers. How many did he have when he started?

23. Paula bought a ski jacket on sale for $6 less than half its original price. She paid $88 for the jacket. What was the original price?

24. The McIntosh family went apple picking. They picked a total of 115 apples. The family ate a total of 8 apples each day. After how many days did they have 19 apples left?

Use a calculator to solve each equation.

25. $-5.5x + 0.56 = -1.64$

26. $-4.2x + 31.5 = -65.1$

27. $\frac{k}{5.2} + 81.9 = 47.2$

28. Write a two-step equation that involves multiplication and subtraction, includes a negative coefficient, and has a solution of $x = 7$.

______

29. Write a two-step equation involving division and addition that has a solution of $x = -25$

______

30. **Explain the Error** A student's solution to the equation $3x + 2 = 15$ is shown. Describe and correct the error that the student made.

$3x + 2 = 15$ Divide both sides by 3.

$x + 2 = 5$ Subtract 2 from both sides.

$x = 3$

______

______

31. **Multiple Representations** Explain how you could use the work backward problem-solving strategy to solve the equation $\frac{x}{4} - 6 = 2$. Compare that method to an algebraic method.

______

______

______

______

______

H.O.T. FOCUS ON HIGHER ORDER THINKING

32. **Reason Abstractly** The formula $F = 1.8C + 32$ allows you to find the Fahrenheit (F) temperature for a given Celsius (C) temperature. Solve the equation for C to produce a formula for finding the Celsius temperature for a given Fahrenheit temperature.

______

33. **Reason Abstractly** The equation $P = 2(\ell + w)$ can be used to find the perimeter P of a rectangle with length ℓ and width w. Solve the equation for w to produce a formula for finding the width of a rectangle given its perimeter and length.

______

34. **Reason Abstractly** Solve the equation $ax + b = c$ for x.

______

Work Area

Going Further 6.4

Arithmetic and Algebraic Solutions

7.3.GF.6.4

Students will identify similarities and differences of arithmetic and algebraic solutions.

ESSENTIAL QUESTION

What are the similarities and differences of arithmetic and algebraic solutions?

EXPLORE ACTIVITY Real World

Comparing Solution Methods

Chris has a coupon for \$1.50 off the price of each T-shirt purchased. He uses the coupon and pays \$47.50 for five T-shirts. Complete Parts A and B to find the original price of a T-shirt without the coupon by two methods.

A Work backward using arithmetic to find the original price of a T-shirt.

$\$47.50 \div \square = \square$ Divide \$47.50 by ________ to find the purchase price of each T-shirt with a coupon.

$\square + \square = \square$ Add ________ to find the original price of each T-shirt without the coupon.

The original price of a T-shirt without the coupon is ________.

B Use algebra to find the original price of a T-shirt.

$5(p - 1.50) = 47.50$ Write an equation in which p is the original price.

$\frac{5(p - 1.50)}{\square} = \frac{47.50}{\square}$ Divide both sides by ________.

$p - 1.50 = 9.50$

$+\square \quad +\square$ Add ________ to both sides.

$p = \square$

The original price of a T-shirt without the coupon is ________.

Reflect

1. What was the sequence of operations you performed in Part A? How did this sequence compare to the sequence in Part B?

____

____

____

Practice

1. Layla buys a turkey and 3 cans of soup at the grocery store for a total of $20.75. The turkey costs $15.50. What is the cost of each can of soup?

   a. Show how to find the cost of each can of soup using arithmetic.

   b. Show how to find the cost *s* of each can of soup using algebra.

   c. Compare the solution methods in Parts **a** and **b**.

2. Carlos pays for dinner with a friend. He uses a coupon for $5 off the price of dinner, before taxes are applied. The tax rate is 8%. The total cost for dinner after the coupon and taxes is $30.78. What is the original price of dinner before the coupon and taxes?

   a. What operation would you do first to solve this problem using arithmetic? Why?

   b. Write an equation relating the original price of dinner *d* and the total cost after the coupon and taxes. Identify the first step you would use to solve the equation and the meaning of the result of that step.

   c. Show how to find the original price of dinner using any method.

3. Toby's bucket has a leak. The bucket starts with 5 gallons of water. After 7.5 minutes, there are only 2.5 gallons of water in the bucket. The equation $5 + 7.5r = 2.5$ represents this situation, where *r* is the rate of change of water in the bucket. Suppose you use arithmetic to find the rate of change. How can the equation help guide your steps? What are the steps and what does the result of each step represent?

Activity 6.4

Equality Property Sort

INSTRUCTIONS

STEP 1 At the top of the next page record the number of blue circles that appear in the top corner of each card in your set of activity cards.

STEP 2 Shuffle your activity cards. Working together, sort the activity cards to show the correct solutions of four different two-step equations and the properties that justify each step. An example is shown.

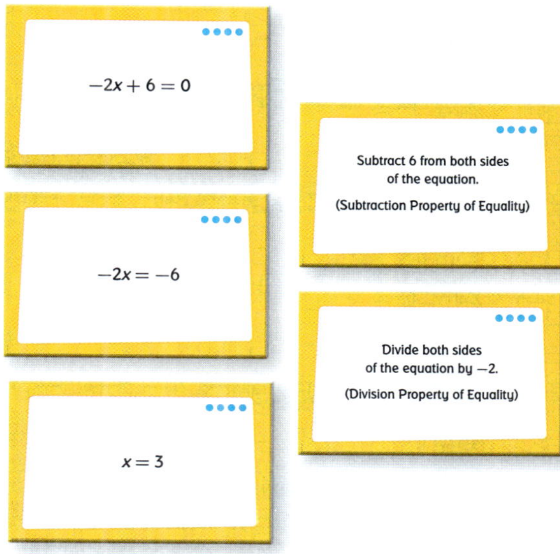

STEP 3 Check that the steps of each solution and the properties are in the correct order. Then record the steps and properties in the flow charts on the next page.

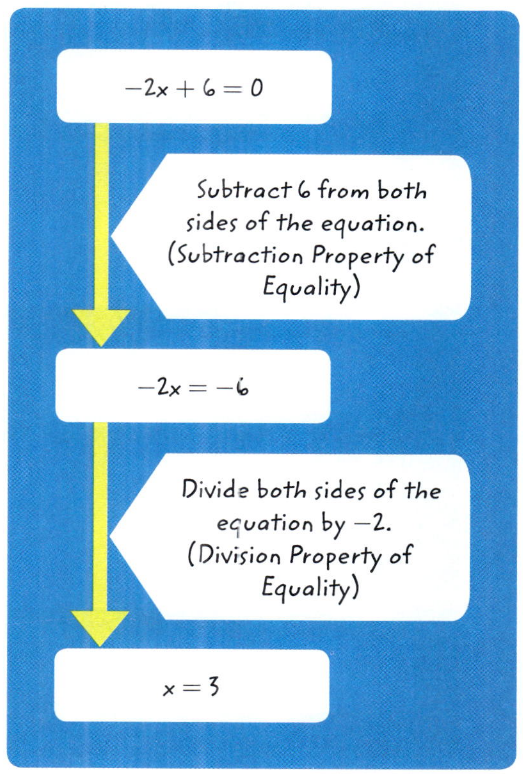

Number of blue circles ______________

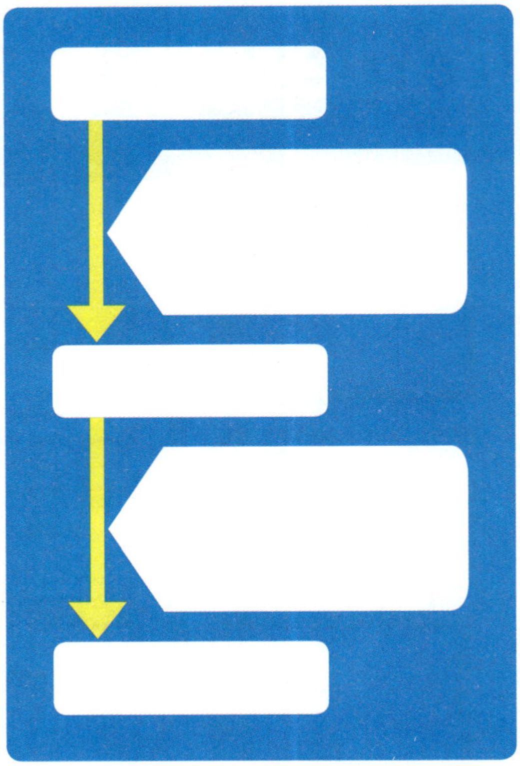

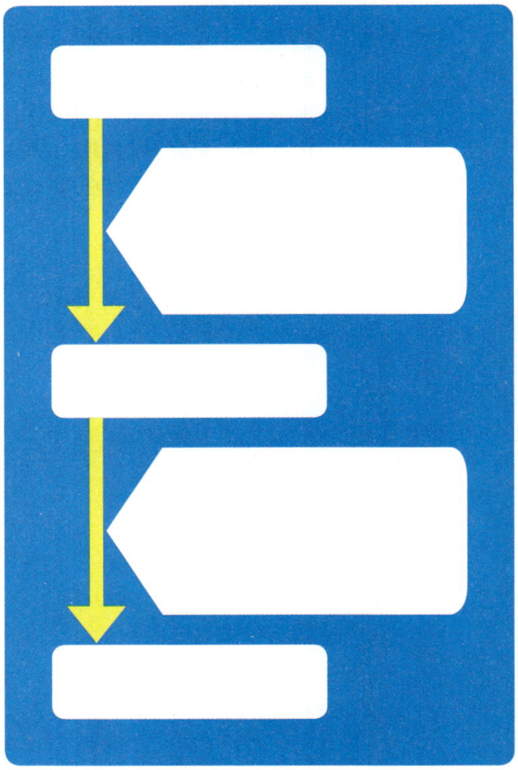

MODULE QUIZ

Ready to Go On?

Personal Math Trainer
Online Assessment and Intervention
my.hrw.com

6.1 Algebraic Expressions

1. The Science Club went on a two-day field trip. The first day the members paid \$60 for transportation plus \$15 per ticket to the planetarium. The second day they paid \$95 for transportation plus \$12 per ticket to the geology museum. Write an expression to represent the total cost for two days for the *n* members of the club. ___________

6.2 One-Step Equations with Rational Coefficients

Solve.

2. $h + 9.7 = -9.7$ ___________

3. $-\frac{3}{4} + p = \frac{1}{2}$ ___________

4. $-15 = -0.2k$ ___________

5. $\frac{y}{-3} = \frac{1}{6}$ ___________

6. $-\frac{2}{3}m = -12$ ___________

7. $2.4 = -\frac{t}{4.5}$ ___________

6.3 Writing Two-Step Equations

8. Jerry started doing sit-ups every day. The first day he did 15 sit-ups. Every day after that he did 2 more sit-ups than he had done the previous day. Today Jerry did 33 sit-ups. Write an equation that could be solved to find the number of days Jerry has been doing sit-ups, not counting the first day.

____

6.4 Solving Two-Step Equations

Solve.

9. $5n + 8 = 43$ ___________

10. $\frac{y}{6} - 7 = 4$ ___________

11. $8w - 15 = 57$ ___________

12. $\frac{g}{3} + 11 = 25$ ___________

13. $\frac{f}{5} - 22 = -25$ ___________

14. $-4p + 19 = 11$ ___________

ESSENTIAL QUESTION

15. How can you use two-step equations to represent and solve real-world problems?

____

____

MODULE 6 MIXED REVIEW

Assessment Readiness

Personal Math Trainer

Online Assessment and Intervention

my.hrw.com

Selected Response

1. A taxi cab costs \$1.50 for the first mile and \$0.75 for each additional mile. Which equation could be solved to find how many miles you can travel in a taxi for \$10, given that x is the number of additional miles?

Ⓐ $1.5x + 0.75 = 10$

Ⓑ $0.75x + 1.5 = 10$

Ⓒ $1.5x - 0.75 = 10$

Ⓓ $0.75x - 1.5 = 10$

2. Which is the solution of $\frac{t}{2.5} = -5.2$?

Ⓐ $t = -13$

Ⓑ $t = -2.08$

Ⓒ $t = 2.08$

Ⓓ $t = 13$

3. Which expression is equivalent to $5x - 30$?

Ⓐ $5(x - 30)$

Ⓑ $5(x - 6)$

Ⓒ $5x(x - 6)$

Ⓓ $x(5 - 30)$

4. In a science experiment, the temperature of a substance is changed from 42 °F to −54 °F at an average rate of −12 degrees per hour. Over how many hours does the change take place?

Ⓐ −8 hours

Ⓑ $\frac{1}{8}$ hour

Ⓒ 1 hour

Ⓓ 8 hours

5. Which statement best represents the distance on a number line between −14 and −5?

Ⓐ $-14 - (-5)$

Ⓑ $-14 + (-5)$

Ⓒ $-5 - (-14)$

Ⓓ $-5 + (-14)$

6. Which cereal costs the most per ounce?

Ⓐ \$4.92 for 12 ounces

Ⓑ \$4.25 for 10 ounces

Ⓒ \$5.04 for 14 ounces

Ⓓ \$3.92 for 8 ounces

Mini-Task

7. Casey bought 9 tickets to a concert. The total charge was \$104, including a \$5 service charge.

a. Write an equation you can solve to find c, the cost of one ticket.

____

b. Explain how you could estimate the solution of your equation.

____

____

____

____

c. Solve the equation. How much did each ticket cost?

____

Inequalities

MODULE 7

ESSENTIAL QUESTION

How can you use inequalities to solve real-world problems?

Real-World Video

Many school groups and other organizations hold events to raise money. Members can write and solve inequalities to represent the financial goals they are trying to achieve.

my.hrw.com

GO DIGITAL
my.hrw.com

my.hrw.com

Go digital with your write-in student edition, accessible on any device.

Math On the Spot

Scan with your smart phone to jump directly to the online edition, video tutor, and more.

Animated Math

Interactively explore key concepts to see how math works.

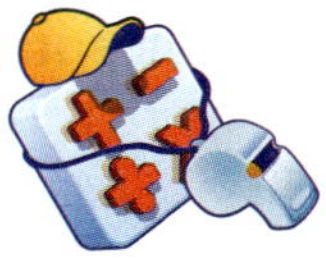

Personal Math Trainer

Get immediate feedback and help as you work through practice sets.

Reading Start-Up

Visualize Vocabulary

Use the ✔ words to complete the graphic. You may put more than one word in each box.

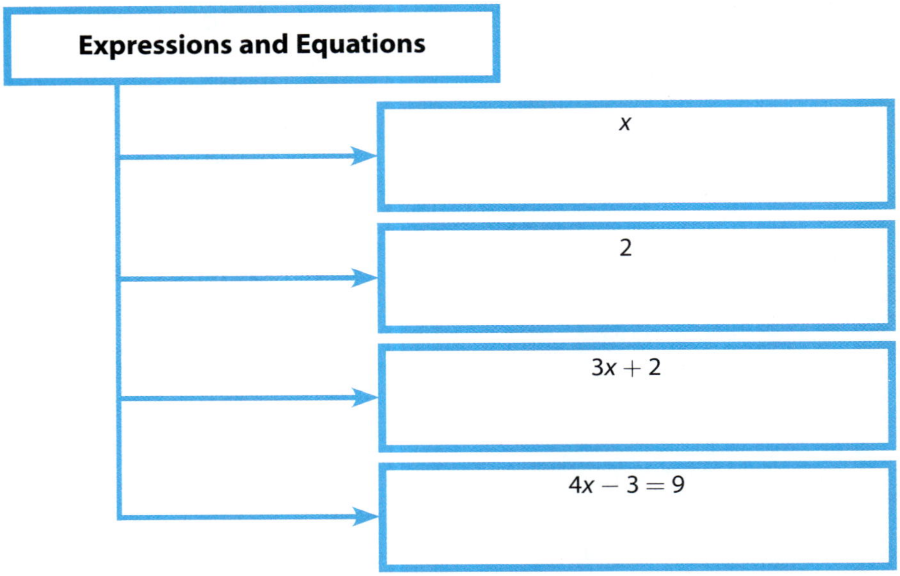

Vocabulary

Review Words

- ✔ algebraic expression *(expresión algebraica)*
- coefficient *(coeficiente)*
- ✔ constant *(constante)*
- ✔ equation *(ecuación)*
- greater than *(mayor que)*
- ✔ inequality *(desigualdad)*
- integers *(enteros)*
- less than *(menor que)*
- operations *(operaciones)*
- solution *(solución)*
- ✔ variable *(variable)*

Understand Vocabulary

Complete each sentence, using the review words.

1. A value of the variable that makes the equation true is a ________.
2. The set of all whole numbers and their opposites are __________.
3. An ____________________ is an expression that contains at least one variable.

Active Reading

Layered Book Before beginning the module, create a layered book to help you learn the concepts in this module. At the top of the first flap, write the title of the module, "Inequalities." Then label each flap with one of the lesson titles in this module. As you study each lesson, write important ideas, such as vocabulary and processes, under the appropriate flap.

Are YOU Ready?

Complete these exercises to review skills you will need for this module.

Personal Math Trainer
Online Assessment and Intervention
my.hrw.com

Inverse Operations

EXAMPLE

$3x = 24$ — *x is multiplied by 3.*

$\frac{3x}{3} = \frac{24}{3}$ — *Use the inverse operation, division. Divide both sides by 3.*

$x = 8$

$z + 6 = 4$ — *6 is added to z.*

$\underline{-6} = \underline{-6}$ — *Use the inverse operation, subtraction. Subtract 6 from both sides.*

$z = -2$

Solve each equation, using inverse operations.

1. $9w = -54$ ______ **2.** $b - 12 = 3$ ______ **3.** $\frac{n}{4} = -11$ ______

Locate Points on a Number Line

EXAMPLE

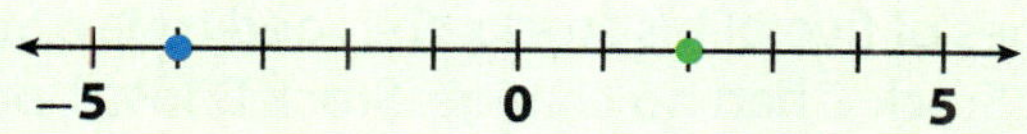

Graph +2 by starting at 0 and counting 2 units to the right.

Graph −4 by starting at 0 and counting 4 units to the left.

Graph each number on the number line.

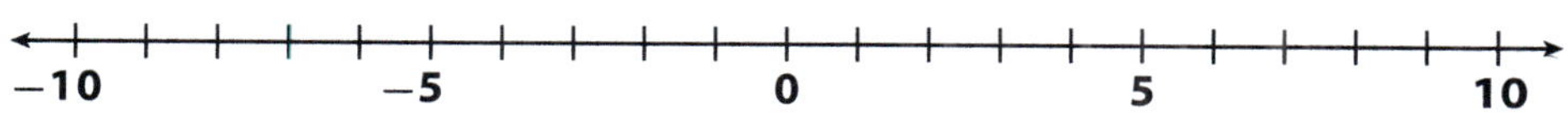

4. 3 **5.** −9 **6.** 7 **7.** −3

Integer Operations

EXAMPLE

$-7 - (-4) = -7 + 4$ — *To subtract an integer, add its opposite.*

$= |-7| - |4|$ — *The signs are different, so find the difference of the absolute values.*

$= 7 - 4, \text{ or } 3$

$= -3$ — *Use the sign of the number with the greater absolute value.*

8. $3 - (-5)$ ______ **9.** $-4 - 5$ ______ **10.** $6 - 10$ ______ **11.** $-5 - (-3)$ ______

12. $8 - (-8)$ ______ **13.** $9 - 5$ ______ **14.** $-3 - 9$ ______ **15.** $0 - (-6)$ ______

Are YOU Ready? (cont'd)

Complete these exercises to review skills you will need for this module.

Inverse Operations

16. In the equation $t - 3 = 12$, t represents the number of teachers at a karate dojo. In the equation $\frac{s}{8} = 16$, s represents the number of students enrolled in a camp at the dojo. Explain how to use inverse operations to find the number of teachers at the dojo and the number of students enrolled in the camp.

Locate Points on a Number Line

17. Martin checked how the values of five of his stocks changed today. Stock A fell 8 points. Stock B rose 3 points. Stock C had no change. Stock D lost 1 point. Stock E gained 7 points. On the number line below, plot how each of Martin's stocks changed and label each point with the letter of the stock.

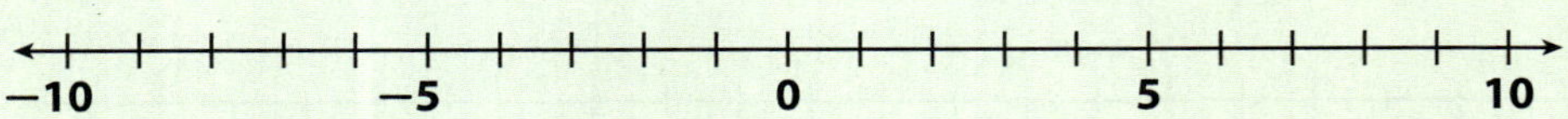

Integer Operations

18. At dusk, the temperature at the ski resort was −3 °C. By midnight, the temperature fell 8 °C. From midnight to dawn, the temperature rose 6 °C. Did the temperature ever rise above freezing (0 °C)? Justify your answer.

LESSON 7.1

Writing and Solving One-Step Inequalities

7.3.7.1

Students will write and solve one-step inequalities.

ESSENTIAL QUESTION

How do you write and solve one-step inequalities?

EXPLORE ACTIVITY

Investigating Inequalities

You know that when you perform any of the four basic operations on both sides of an equation, the resulting equation is still true. What effect does performing these operations on both sides of an *inequality* have?

A **Complete the table.**

Inequality	Add to both sides:	New Inequality	Is new inequality true or false?
$2 \geq -3$	**3**		
$-1 \leq 6$	**−1**		
$-8 > -10$	**−8**		

Reflect

1. **Make a Conjecture** When you add the same number to both sides of an inequality, is the inequality still true? Explain how you know that your conjecture holds for *subtracting* the same number.

____

B **Complete the table.**

Inequality	Divide both sides by:	New Inequality	Is new inequality true or false?
$4 < 8$	**4**		
$12 \geq -15$	**3**		
$-16 \leq 12$	**−4**		
$15 > 5$	**−5**		

What do you notice when you divide both sides of an inequality by the same negative number?

____

EXPLORE ACTIVITY *(cont'd)*

Reflect

2. **Make a Conjecture** What could you do to make the inequalities that are not true into true statements?

____

3. **Communicate Mathematical Ideas** Explain how you know that your conjecture holds for multiplying both sides of an inequality by a negative number.

____

Math On the Spot
my.hrw.com

Solving Inequalities Involving Addition and Subtraction

You can use properties of inequality to solve inequalities involving addition and subtraction with rational numbers.

Addition and Subtraction Properties of Inequality

Addition Property of Inequality	Subtraction Property of Inequality
You can add the same number to both sides of an inequality and the inequality will remain true.	You can subtract the same number from both sides of an inequality and the inequality will remain true.

EXAMPLE 1

Solve each inequality. Graph and check the solution.

A $x + 5 < -12$

STEP 1 Solve the inequality.

$x + 5 < -12$ — Use the Subtraction Property of Inequality.

$\underline{-5} \quad \underline{-5}$ — Subtract 5 from both sides.

$x \quad < -17$

STEP 2 Graph the solution.

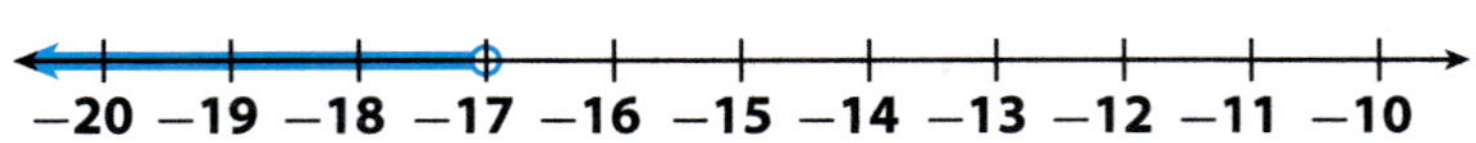

STEP 3 Check the solution. Substitute a solution from the shaded part of your number line into the original inequality.

$-18 + 5 \overset{?}{<} -12$ — Substitute −18 for *x* into $x + 5 < -12$.

$-13 < -12$ — The inequality is true.

B $8 \le y - 3$

STEP 1 Solve the inequality.

$$\begin{aligned} 8 &\le y - 3 \\ +3 & \quad\; +3 \\ \hline 11 &\le y \end{aligned}$$

Use the Addition Property of Inequality.
Add 3 to both sides.
You can rewrite $11 \le y$ as $y \ge 11$.

STEP 2 Graph the solution.

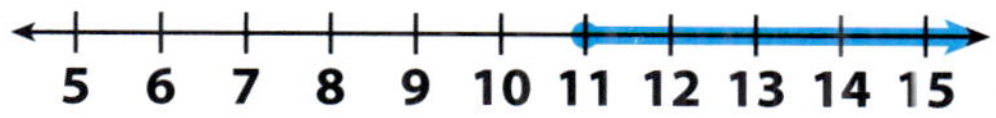

STEP 3 Check the solution. Substitute a solution from the shaded part of your number line into the original inequality.

$8 \overset{?}{\le} 12 - 3$ Substitute 12 for y in $8 \le y - 3$.

$8 \le 9$ The inequality is true.

Math Talk
Mathematical Processes

How does the true inequality you found by substituting 12 into the original inequality help you check the solution?

YOUR TURN

Solve each inequality. Graph and check the solution.

4. $y - 5 \ge -7$

____

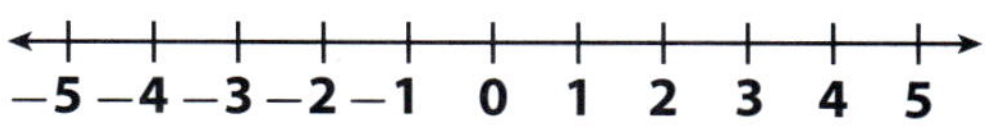

5. $21 > 12 + x$

____

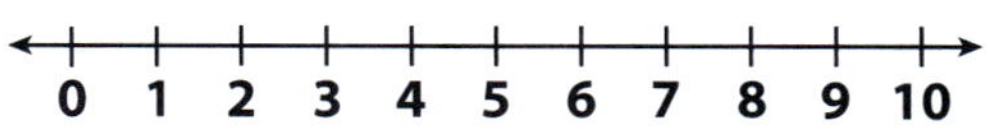

Personal Math Trainer
Online Assessment and Intervention
my.hrw.com

Solving Inequalities Involving Multiplication and Division

You can use properties of inequality to solve inequalities involving multiplication and division with rational numbers.

Math On the Spot
my.hrw.com

Multiplication and Division Properties of Inequality

- You can multiply or divide both sides of an inequality by the same positive number and the inequality will remain true.
- If you multiply or divide both sides of an inequality by the same negative number, you must reverse the inequality symbol for the statement to still be true.

EXAMPLE 2

My Notes

Solve each inequality. Graph and check the solution.

A $\frac{y}{3} \geq 5$

STEP 1 Solve the inequality.

$3\left(\frac{y}{3}\right) \geq 3(5)$ Multiply both sides by 3.

$y \geq 15$

STEP 2 Graph the solution.

Use a closed circle to show that 15 is a solution.

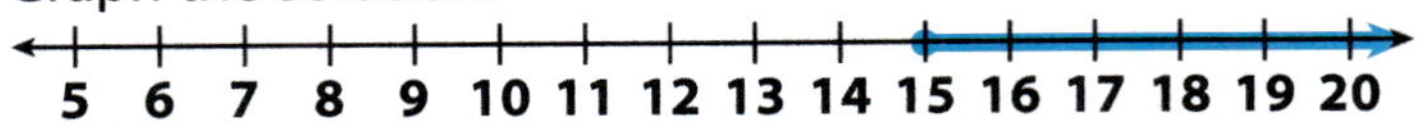

STEP 3 Check the solution by substituting a solution from the shaded part of the graph into the original inequality. For convenience, choose a multiple of 3.

$\frac{18}{3} \overset{?}{\geq} 5$ Substitute 18 for *x* in the original inequality.

$6 \geq 5$ The inequality is true.

B $-4x > 52$

STEP 1 Solve the inequality.

$-4x > 52$

$\frac{-4x}{-4} < \frac{52}{-4}$ Divide both sides by -4. Reverse the inequality symbol.

$x < -13$

STEP 2 Graph the solution.

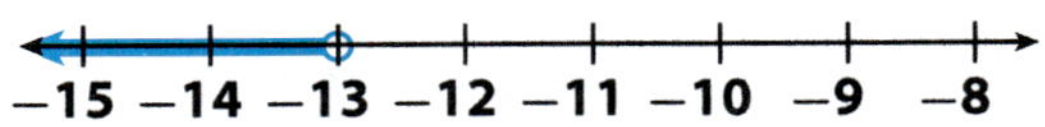

STEP 3 Check your answer using substitution.

$-4(-15) \overset{?}{>} 52$ Substitute -15 for *x* in $-4x > 52$.

$60 > 52$ The statement is true.

Personal Math Trainer
Online Assessment and Intervention
my.hrw.com

YOUR TURN

Solve each inequality. Graph and check the solution.

6. $-10y < 60$ ________________

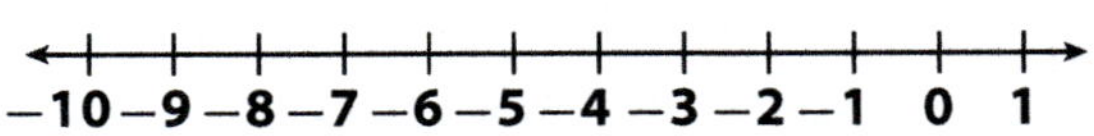

7. $7 \geq -\frac{t}{6}$ ________________

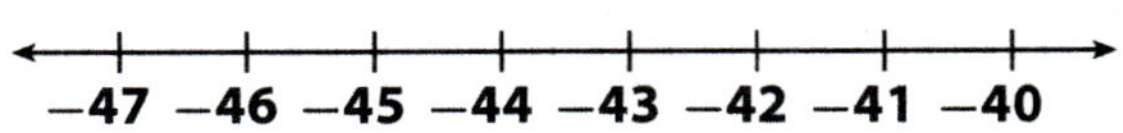

Solving a Real-World Problem

Although elevations below sea level are represented by negative numbers, we often use absolute values to describe these elevations. For example, -50 feet relative to sea level might be described as 50 feet below sea level.

Math On the Spot
my.hrw.com

EXAMPLE 3 Problem Solving

A marine submersible descends more than 40 feet below sea level. As it descends from sea level, the change in elevation is -5 feet per second. For how many seconds does it descend?

Analyze Information

Rewrite the question as a statement.

- Find the number of seconds that the submersible descends below sea level.

List the important information:

- Final elevation $>$ 40 feet below sea level or final elevation < -40 feet
- Rate of descent $= -5$ feet per second

Formulate a Plan

Write and solve an inequality. Use this fact:

Rate of change in elevation $\times$ Time in seconds $=$ Final elevation

Solve

$-5t < -40$ *Rate of change × Time < Final elevation*

$\frac{-5t}{-5} > \frac{-40}{-5}$ *Divide both sides by −5. Reverse the inequality symbol.*

$t > 8$

The submersible descends for more than 8 seconds.

Animated Math
my.hrw.com

Justify and Evaluate

Check your answer by substituting a value greater than 8 seconds in the original inequality.

$-5(9) \overset{?}{<} -40$ *Substitute 9 for t in the inequality −5t < −40.*

$-45 < -40$ *The statement is true.*

YOUR TURN

8. Every month, \$35 is withdrawn from Tony's savings account to pay for his gym membership. He has enough savings to withdraw no more than \$315. For how many months can Tony pay for his gym membership?

____

____

Personal Math Trainer
Online Assessment and Intervention
my.hrw.com

Guided Practice

Write the resulting inequality. (Explore Activity)

1. $-5 \le -2$; Add 7 to both sides ____________________

2. $-6 < -3$; Divide both sides by -3 ____________________

3. $7 > -4$; Subtract 7 from both sides ____________________

4. $-1 \ge -8$; Multiply both sides by -2 ____________________

Solve each inequality. Graph and check the solution. (Examples 1 and 2)

5. $n - 5 \ge -2$ ____________________

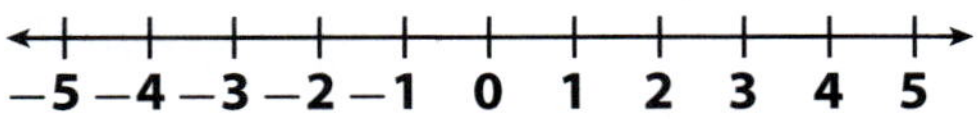

6. $3 + x < 7$ ____________________

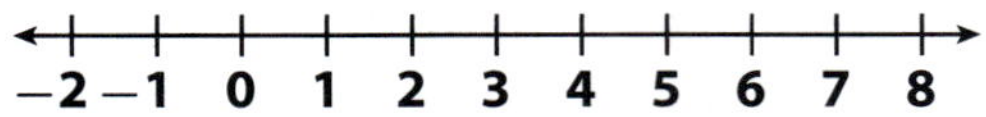

7. $-7y \le 14$ ____________________

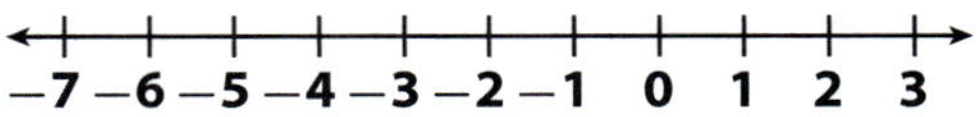

8. $\frac{b}{5} > -1$ ____________________

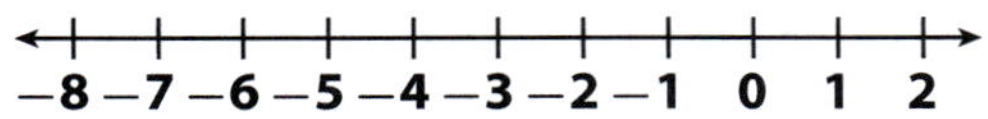

9. For a scientific experiment, a physicist must make sure that the temperature of a metal at 0 °C gets no colder than −80 °C. The physicist changes the metal's temperature at a steady rate of −4 °C per hour. For how long can the physicist change the temperature? (Example 3)

a. Let *t* represent temperature in degrees Celsius. Write an inequality. Use the fact that the rate of change in temperature times the number of hours equals the final temperature.

____

b. Solve the inequality in part **a**. How long can the physicist change the temperature of the metal?

____

c. The physicist has to repeat the experiment if the metal gets cooler than −80 °C. How many hours would the physicist have to cool the metal for this to happen?

____

ESSENTIAL QUESTION CHECK-IN

10. Suppose you are solving an inequality. Under what circumstances do you reverse the inequality symbol?

____

Name ______________________ Class ______________ Date ____________

7.1 Independent Practice

Personal Math Trainer
Online Assessment and Intervention
my.hrw.com

In 11–16, solve each inequality. Graph and check the solution.

11. $x - 35 > 15$ ________________

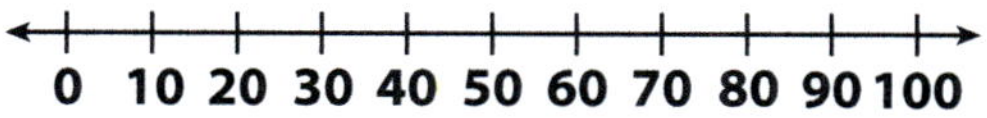

12. $193 + y \geq 201$ ________________

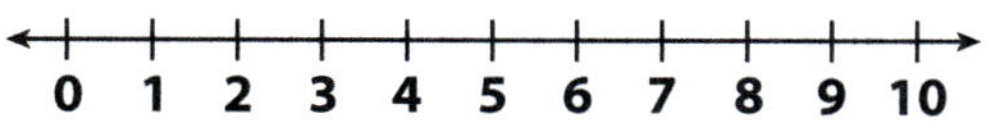

13. $-\frac{q}{7} \geq -1$ ________________

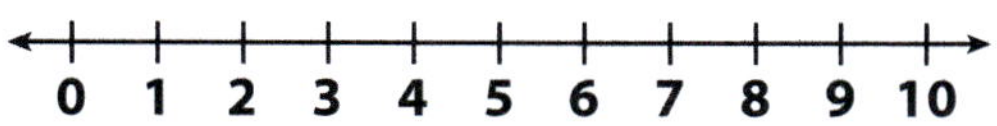

14. $-12x < 60$ ________________

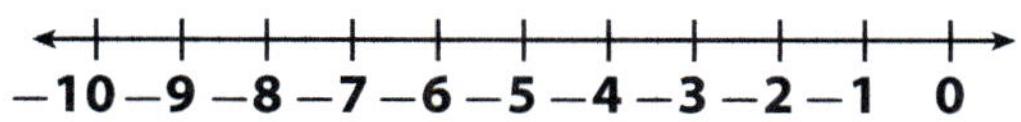

15. $5 > z - 3$ ________________

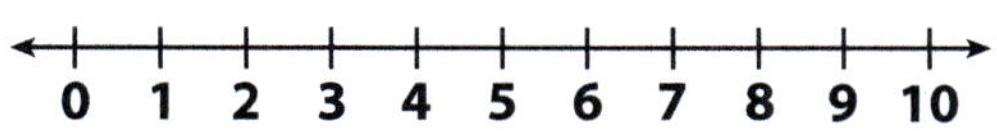

16. $0.5 \leq \frac{y}{8}$ ________________

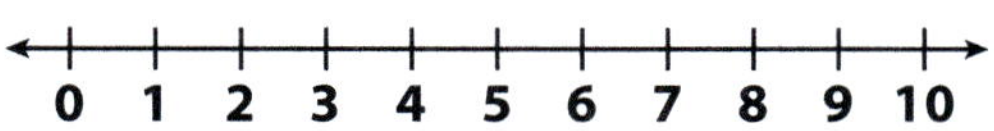

17. The vet says that Lena's puppy will grow to be at most 28 inches tall. Lena's puppy is currently 1 foot tall. How many more inches will the puppy grow?

____

18. In a litter of 7 kittens, each kitten weighs less than 3.5 ounces. Find all the possible values of the combined weights of the kittens.

____

19. **Geometry** The sides of the hexagon shown are equal in length. The perimeter of the hexagon is at most 42 inches. Find the possible side lengths of the hexagon.

____

20. To get a free meal at his favorite restaurant, Tom needs to spend \$50 or more at the restaurant. He has already spent \$30.25. How much more does Tom need to spend to get his free meal?

____

21. To cover a rectangular region of her yard, Penny needs at least 170.5 square feet of sod. The length of the region is 15.5 feet. What are the possible widths of the region?

____

22. **Draw Conclusions** A submarine descends from sea level to the entrance of an underwater cave. The elevation of the entrance is -120 feet. The rate of change in the submarine's elevation is less than -12 feet per second. Can the submarine reach the entrance to the cave in less than 10 seconds? Explain.

____

____

____

____

The sign shows some prices at a produce stand.

Produce	Price per Pound
Onions	$1.25
Yellow Squash	$0.99
Spinach	$3.00
Potatoes	$0.50

23. Selena has $10. What is the greatest amount of spinach she can buy?

____

24. Gary has enough money to buy at most 5.5 pounds of potatoes. How much money does Gary have?

____

25. Florence wants to spend no more than $3 on onions. Will she be able to buy 2.5 pounds of onions? Explain.

____

____

H.O.T. FOCUS ON HIGHER ORDER THINKING

Work Area

26. **Counterexamples** John says that if one side of an inequality is 0, you don't have to reverse the inequality symbol when you multiply or divide both sides by a negative number. Find an inequality that you can use to disprove John's statement. Explain your thinking.

____

____

____

____

27. **Look for a Pattern** Solve $x + 1 > 10$, $x + 11 > 20$, and $x + 21 > 30$. Describe a pattern. Then use the pattern to predict the solution of $x + 9{,}991 > 10{,}000$.

____

____

____

28. **Persevere in Problem Solving** The base of a rectangular prism has a length of 13 inches and a width of $\frac{1}{2}$ inch. The volume of the prism is less than 65 cubic inches. Find all possible heights of the prism. Show your work.

____

____

____

Activity 7.1

A Shared Solution

INSTRUCTIONS

STEP 1 Get an activity card from your teacher. Each card has a one-step inequality printed on it. Find the solution of the inequality.

STEP 2 Find and form a group with all other students whose inequalities have the same solution as your inequality.

STEP 3 Using one of the diagrams on the next page, work with the members of your group to write each one-step inequality in the rectangle labeled with the property used to solve it. Group members should fill in their own diagrams each round.

STEP 4 Complete the diagram by writing the common solution in the center rectangle.

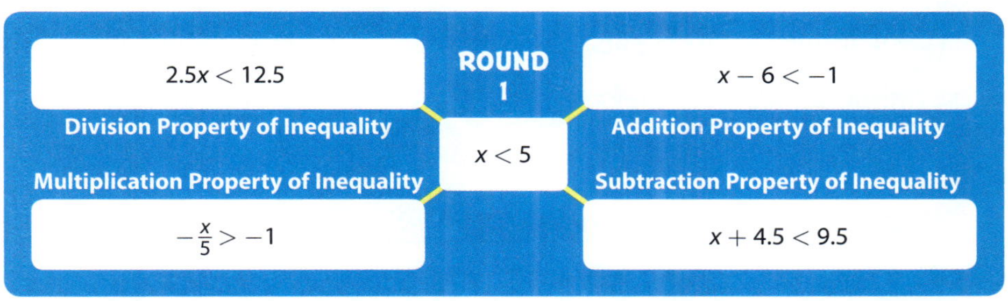

STEP 5 If you cannot form a complete group of four students, write your own one-step inequalities with the shared solution in any empty boxes. Highlight any inequalities that you write yourself.

STEP 6 Turn in the inequality cards to the teacher.

STEP 7 Repeat Steps 1–6 for each round.

ROUND 1

Division Property of Inequality

Multiplication Property of Inequality

Addition Property of Inequality

Subtraction Property of Inequality

ROUND 2

Division Property of Inequality

Multiplication Property of Inequality

Addition Property of Inequality

Subtraction Property of Inequality

ROUND 3

Division Property of Inequality

Multiplication Property of Inequality

Addition Property of Inequality

Subtraction Property of Inequality

ROUND 4

Division Property of Inequality

Multiplication Property of Inequality

Addition Property of Inequality

Subtraction Property of Inequality

ROUND 5

Division Property of Inequality

Multiplication Property of Inequality

Addition Property of Inequality

Subtraction Property of Inequality

LESSON 7.2

Writing Two-Step Inequalities

7.3.7.2

Students will write a two-step inequality.

ESSENTIAL QUESTION

How do you write a two-step inequality?

EXPLORE ACTIVITY

Modeling Two-Step Inequalities

You can use algebra tiles to model two-step inequalities.

Use algebra tiles to model $2k + 5 \geq -3$.

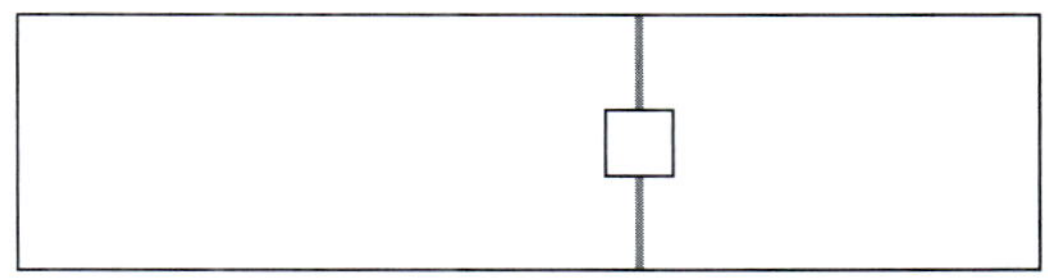

A Using the line on the mat, draw in the inequality symbol shown in the inequality.

B How can you model the left side of the inequality?

____

C How can you model the right side of the inequality?

____

D Use algebra tiles or draw them to model the inequality on the mat.

Reflect

1. **Multiple Representations** How does your model differ from the one you would draw to model the equation $2k + 5 = -3$?

____

____

____

2. Why might you need to change the inequality sign when you solve an inequality using algebra tiles?

____

____

____

Math On the Spot
my.hrw.com

Writing Two-Step Inequalities

You can write two-step inequalities to represent real-world problems by translating the words of the problems into numbers, variables, and operations.

EXAMPLE 1 Real World

A mountain climbing team is camped at an altitude of 18,460 feet on Mount Everest. The team wants to reach the 29,029-foot summit within 6 days. Write an inequality to find the average number of feet per day the team must climb to accomplish its objective.

STEP 1 Identify what you are trying to find. This will be the variable in the inequality.

Let d represent the average altitude the team must gain each day.

STEP 2 Identify important information in the problem that you can use to write an inequality.

starting altitude: **18,460 ft** target altitude: **29,029 ft**

number of days times altitude gained to reach target altitude: $6 \cdot d$

STEP 3 Use words in the problem to tie the information together and write an inequality.

starting altitude	+	number of days	times	altitude gain	is greater than or equal to	target altitude
↓	↓	↓	↓	↓	↓	↓
18,460	+	6	×	d	≥	29,029

$18{,}460 + 6d \geq 29{,}029$

Math Talk
Mathematical Processes

Why is the inequality sign ≥ used, rather than an equal sign?

YOUR TURN

3. The 45 members of the glee club are trying to raise $6,000 so they can compete in the state championship. They already have $1,240. What inequality can you write to find the amount each member must raise, on average, to meet the goal? ______________________

4. Ella has $40 to spend at the State Fair. Admission is $6 and each ride costs $3. Write an inequality to find the greatest number of rides she can go on.

____

Personal Math Trainer
Online Assessment and Intervention
my.hrw.com

Writing a Verbal Description of a Two-Step Inequality

You can also write a verbal description to fit a two-step inequality.

Math On the Spot
my.hrw.com

EXAMPLE 2 Real World

Write a corresponding real-world problem to represent $2x + 20 \leq 50$.

STEP 1 Analyze what each part of the inequality means mathematically.

x is the solution of the problem, the quantity you are looking for.

$2x$ means that, for a reason given in the problem, the quantity you are looking for is multiplied by 2.

$+ 20$ means that, for a reason given in the problem, 20 is added to $2x$.

≤ 50 means that after multiplying the solution x by 2 and adding 20 to it, the result can be no greater than 50.

STEP 2 Think of some different situations in which a quantity x is multiplied by 2.

You run x miles per day for 2 days. So, $2x$ is the total distance run.	You buy 2 items each costing x dollars. So, $2x$ is the total cost.

STEP 3 Build on the situation and adjust it to create a verbal description that takes all of the information into account.

- Tomas has run 20 miles so far this week. If he intends to run 50 miles or less, how many miles on average should he run on each of the 2 days remaining in the week?
- Manny buys 2 work shirts that are each the same price. After using a $20 gift card, he can spend no more than $50. What is the maximum amount he can spend on each shirt?

My Notes

YOUR TURN

Write a real-world problem for each inequality.

5. $3x + 10 > 30$

____

6. $5x - 50 \leq 100$

____

Personal Math Trainer
Online Assessment and Intervention
my.hrw.com

Guided Practice

Draw algebra tiles to model each two-step inequality. (Explore Activity)

1. $4x - 5 < 7$

2. $-3x + 6 > 9$

3. The booster club needs to raise at least $7,000 for new football uniforms. So far, they have raised $1,250. Write an inequality to find the average amounts each of the 92 members can raise to meet the club's objective. (Example 1)

Let *a* represent the amount each member must raise.

amount to be raised: ______ amount already raised: ______ number of members: ______

Use clues in the problem to write an equation.

[ ]	plus	[ ]	times	amount each member raises	[ ]	target amount
↓	↓	↓	↓	↓	↓	↓
1,250	+	[ ]	×	[ ]	≥	[ ]

The inequality that represents the situation is ______.

4. Analyze what each part of $7x - 18 \leq 32$ means mathematically. (Example 2)

x is ______. $7x$ is ______.

-18 means that ______.

≤ 32 means that ______

5. Write a real-world problem to represent $7x - 18 \leq 32$.

______

ESSENTIAL QUESTION CHECK-IN

6. Describe the steps you would follow to write a two-step inequality you can use to solve a real-world problem.

______

______

Name ______________________ Class ______________ Date ____________

7.2 Independent Practice

Personal Math Trainer
Online Assessment and Intervention
my.hrw.com

7. Three friends earned more than $200 washing cars. They paid their parents $28 for supplies and divided the rest of money equally. Write an inequality to find possible amounts each friend earned. Identify what your variable represents.

____

____

8. Nick has $7.00. Bagels cost $0.75 each, and a small container of cream cheese costs $1.29. Write an inequality to find the numbers of bagels Nick can buy. Identify what your variable represents.

____

____

9. Chet needs to buy 4 work shirts, all costing the same amount. After he uses a $25 gift certificate, he can spend no more than $75. Write an inequality to find the possible costs for a shirt. Identify what your variable represents.

____

____

10. Due to fire laws, no more than 720 people may attend a performance at Metro Auditorium. The balcony holds 120 people. There are 32 rows on the ground floor, each with the same number of seats. Write an inequality to find the numbers of people that can sit in a ground-floor row if the balcony is full. Identify what your variable represents.

____

____

11. Liz earns a salary of $2,100 per month, plus a commission of 5% of her sales. She wants to earn at least $2,400 this month. Write an inequality to find amounts of sales that will meet her goal. Identify what your variable represents.

____

____

12. Lincoln Middle School plans to collect more than 2,000 cans of food in a food drive. So far, 668 cans have been collected. Write an inequality to find numbers of cans the school can collect on each of the final 7 days of the drive to meet this goal. Identify what your variable represents.

____

____

13. Joanna joins a CD club. She pays $7 per month plus $10 for each CD that she orders. Write an inequality to find how many CDs she can purchase in a month if she spends no more than $100. Identify what your variable represents.

____

____

14. Lionel wants to buy a belt that costs $22. He also wants to buy some shirts that are on sale for $17 each. He has $80. What inequality can you write to find the number of shirts he can buy? Identify what your variable represents.

____

____

____

15. Write a situation for $15x - 20 \leq 130$ and solve.

____

____

____

Analyze Relationships **Write $>$, $<$, $\geq$, or $\leq$ in the blank to express the given relationship.**

16. m is at least 25 m ______ 25

17. k is no greater than 9 k ______ 9

18. p is less than 48 p ______ 48

19. b is no more than -5 b ______ -5

20. h is at most 56 h ______ 56

21. w is no less than 0 w ______ 0

22. **Critical Thinking** Marie scored 95, 86, and 89 on three science tests. She wants her average score for 6 tests to be at least 90. What inequality can you write to find the average scores that she can get on her next three tests to meet this goal? Use s to represent the lowest average score.

____

____

H.O.T. FOCUS ON HIGHER ORDER THINKING

Work Area

23. **Communicate Mathematical Ideas** Write an inequality that expresses the reason the lengths 5 feet, 10 feet, and 20 feet could not be used to make a triangle. Explain how the inequality demonstrates that fact.

____

____

____

____

____

24. **Analyze Relationships** The number m satisfies the relationship $m < 0$. Write an inequality expressing the relationship between $-m$ and 0. Explain your reasoning.

____

____

____

25. **Analyze Relationships** The number n satisfies the relationship $n > 0$. Write three inequalities to express the relationship between n and $\frac{1}{n}$.

____

LESSON 7.3

Solving Two-Step Inequalities

7.3.7.3

Students will solve a two-step inequality.

ESSENTIAL QUESTION

How do you solve a two-step inequality?

EXPLORE ACTIVITY

Modeling and Solving Two-Step Inequalities

Math On the Spot my.hrw.com

You can solve two-step inequalities using algebra tiles. The method is similar to the one you used to solve two-step equations.

EXAMPLE 1 **Use algebra tiles to model and solve $4d - 3 \geq 9$.**

STEP 1 Model the inequality. On the left side of the mat, place __________ positive variable tiles and __________ -1-tiles. On the right side, place __________ $+1$-tiles. Use a "$\geq$" symbol between the sides.

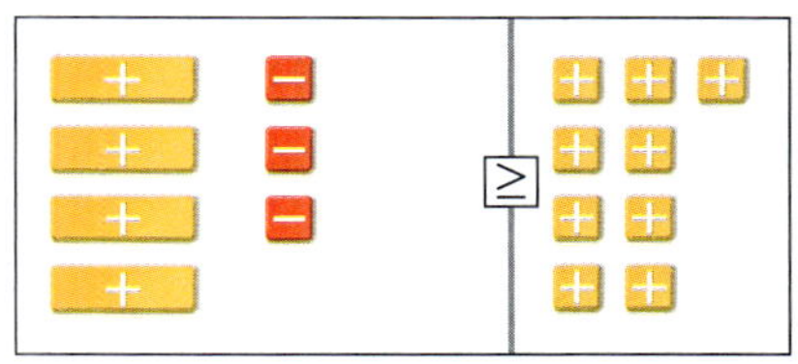

STEP 2 Add __________ $+1$-tiles to both sides of the mat to produce zero pairs with the three -1-tiles.

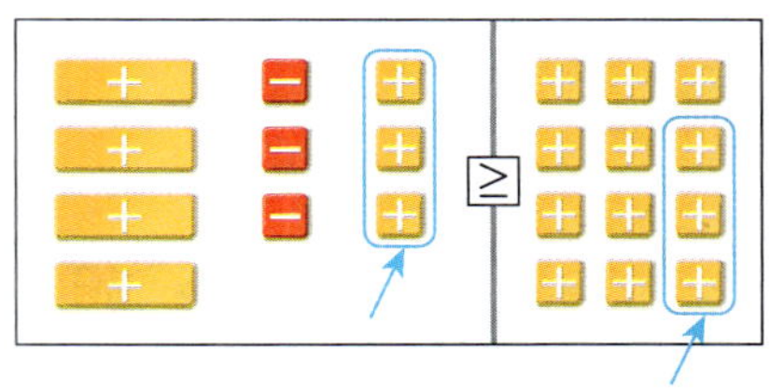

STEP 3 Remove __________ zero pairs from the left side of the mat.

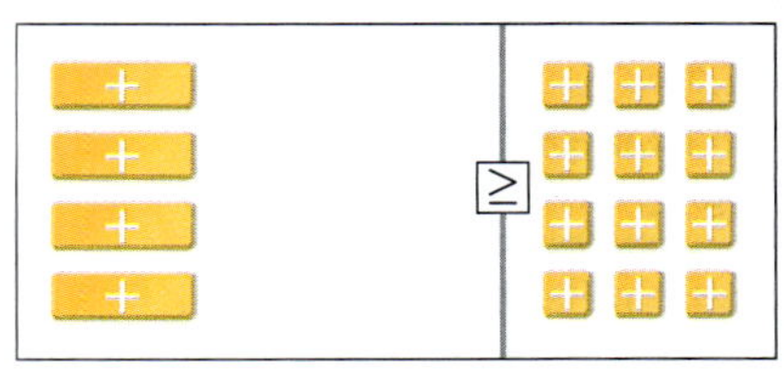

STEP 4 Divide each side into __________ equal groups.

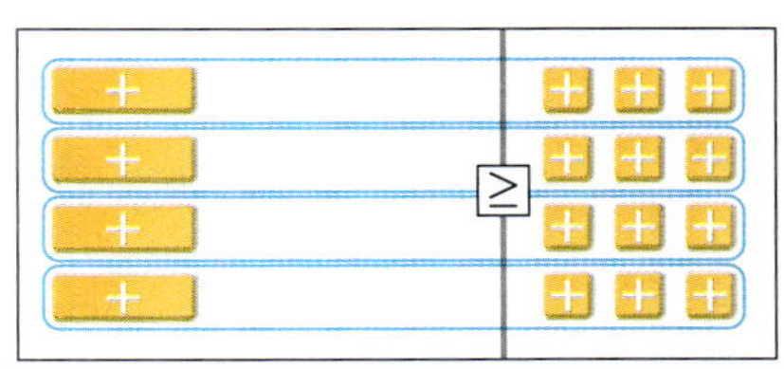

STEP 5 The solution is __________.

EXPLORE ACTIVITY *(cont'd)*

YOUR TURN

Use algebra tiles to model and solve each inequality.

1. $2x + 7 > 11$ ______________ **2.** $5h - 4 \geq 11$ ______________

Personal Math Trainer
Online Assessment and Intervention
my.hrw.com

Math On the Spot
my.hrw.com

Solving and Interpreting Solutions

You can apply what you know about solving two-step equations and one-step inequalities to solving two-step inequalities.

EXAMPLE 2 Real World

Serena wants to complete the first 3 miles of a 10-mile run in 45 minutes or less running at a steady pace. The inequality $10 - 0.75p \leq 7$ can be used to find p, the pace, in miles per hour, she can run to reach her goal. Solve the inequality. Then graph and interpret the solution.

STEP 1 Use inverse operations to solve the inequality.

$$10 - 0.75p \leq 7$$

$$\underline{-10} \qquad \underline{-10}$$ Subtract 10 from both sides.

$$-0.75p \leq -3$$

$$\frac{-0.75p}{-0.75} \geq \frac{-3}{-0.75}$$ Divide both sides by -0.75. Reverse the inequality symbol.

$$p \geq 4$$

STEP 2 Graph the inequality and interpret the circle and the arrow.

Serena can meet her goal by running at a pace of 4 miles per hour.

Serena can run at paces faster than 4 miles per hour and reach her goal.

Serena has to run at a steady pace of at least 4 miles per hour.

Math Talk
Mathematical Processes
In Example 2, how will the graph change if Serena's maximum pace is 12 miles per hour?

YOUR TURN

3. Joshua wants to complete the first mile of a 5-mile run in 10 minutes or less running at a steady pace. The inequality $5 - \frac{p}{6} \leq 4$ can be used to find p, the pace, in miles per hour, he can run to reach his goal. Solve the inequality. Then graph and interpret the solution.

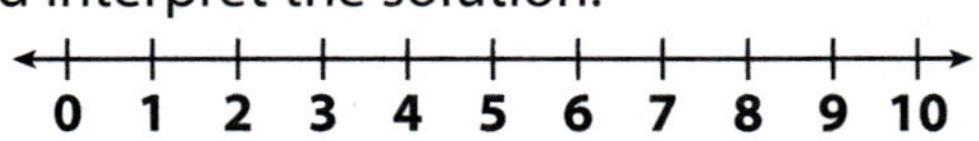

____

Personal Math Trainer
Online Assessment and Intervention
my.hrw.com

Determining if a Given Value Makes the Inequality True

You can use substitution to decide whether a given value is the solution of an inequality.

Math On the Spot
my.hrw.com

EXAMPLE 3 Real World

At Gas 'n' Wash, gasoline sells for \$4.00 a gallon and a car wash costs \$12. Harika wants to have her car washed and keep her total purchase under \$60. The inequality $4g + 12 < 60$ can be used to find g, the number of gallons of gas she can buy. Determine which, if any, of these values is a solution: $g = 10$; $g = 11$; $g = 12$.

STEP 1 Substitute each value for g in the inequality $4g + 12 < 60$.

$g = 10$	$g = 11$	$g = 12$
$4(10) + 12 < 60$	$4(11) + 12 < 60$	$4(12) + 12 < 60$

STEP 2 Evaluate each expression to see if a true inequality results.

$4(10) + 12 \overset{?}{<} 60$	$4(11) + 12 \overset{?}{<} 60$	$4(12) + 12 \overset{?}{<} 60$
$40 + 12 \overset{?}{<} 60$	$44 + 12 \overset{?}{<} 60$	$48 + 12 \overset{?}{<} 60$
$52 \overset{?}{<} 60$	$56 \overset{?}{<} 60$	$60 \overset{?}{<} 60$
true ✓	true ✓	*not* true ✗

So, Harika can buy 10 or 11 gallons of gas but not 12 gallons.

Check: Solve and graph the inequality.

$4g + 12 < 60$

$4g < 48$

$g < 12$

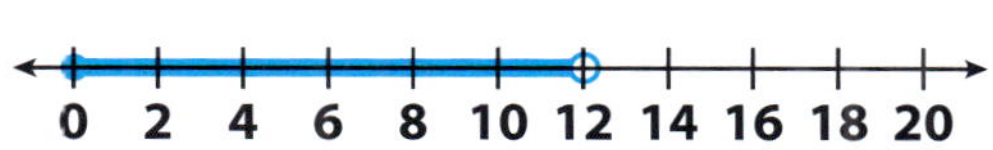

The closed circle at zero represents the minimum amount she can buy, zero gallons. She cannot buy a negative number of gallons. The open circle at 12 means that she can buy any amount up to but not including 12 gallons.

My Notes

Personal Math Trainer

Online Assessment and Intervention

my.hrw.com

YOUR TURN

Circle any given values that make the inequality true.

4. $3v - 8 > 22$

$v = 9$; $v = 10$; $v = 11$

5. $5h + 12 \leq -3$

$h = -3$; $h = -4$; $h = -5$

Guided Practice

1. Describe how to solve the inequality $3x + 4 < 13$ using algebra tiles. (Explore Activity Example 1)

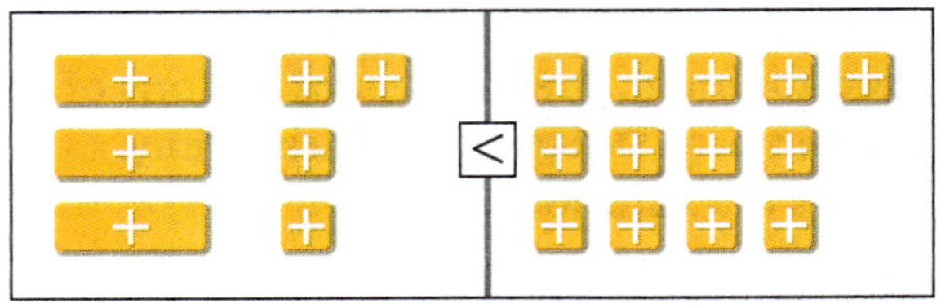

____

____

Solve each inequality. Graph and check the solution. (Example 2)

2. $5d - 13 < 32$ ____________________

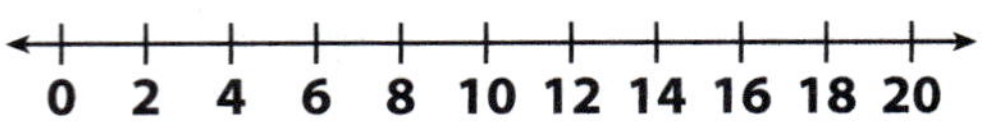

3. $-4b + 9 \leq -7$ ____________________

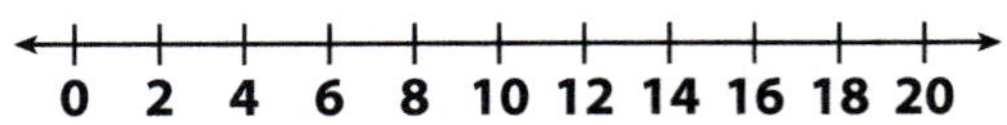

Circle any given values that make the inequality true. (Example 3)

4. $2m + 18 > -4$

$m = -12$; $m = -11$; $m = -10$

5. $-6y + 3 \geq 0$

$y = 1$; $y = \frac{1}{2}$; $y = 0$

6. Lizzy has 6.5 hours to tutor 4 students and spend 1.5 hours in a lab. She plans to tutor each student the same amount of time. The inequality $6.5 - 4t \geq 1.5$ can be used to find t, the amount of time in hours Lizzy could spend with each student. Solve the inequality. Graph and interpret the solution. Can Lizzy tutor each student for 1.5 hours? Explain. (Examples 2 and 3)

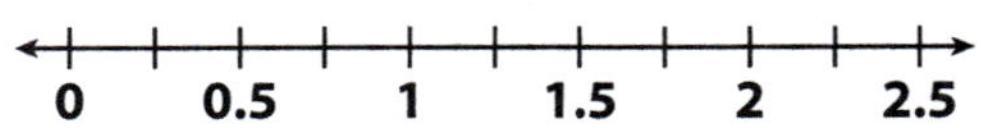

____

____

ESSENTIAL QUESTION CHECK-IN

7. How do you solve a two-step inequality?

____

____

____

Name ______________________ Class ______________ Date ____________

7.3 Independent Practice

Personal Math Trainer
Online Assessment and Intervention
my.hrw.com

Solve each inequality. Graph and check the solution.

8. $2s + 5 \geq 49$ ____________

10 12 14 16 18 20 22 24 26 28 30

9. $-3t + 9 \geq -21$ ____________

−10 −8 −6 −4 −2 0 2 4 6 8 10

10. $55 > -7v + 6$ ____________

−10 −9 −8 −7 −6 −5 −4 −3 −2 −1 0

11. $41 > 6m - 7$ ____________

0 1 2 3 4 5 6 7 8 9 10

12. $\frac{a}{-8} + 15 > 23$ ____________

−70 −69 −68 −67 −66 −65 −64 −63 −62 −61 −60

13. $\frac{f}{2} - 22 < 48$ ____________

100 105 110 115 120 125 130 135 140 145 150

14. $-25 + \frac{t}{2} \geq 50$ ____________

130 135 140 145 150 155 160 165 170 175 180

15. $10 + \frac{g}{-9} > 12$ ____________

−20 −19 −18 −17 −16 −15 −14 −13 −12 −11 −10

16. $25.2 \leq -1.5y + 1.2$ ____________

−20 −19 −18 −17 −16 −15 −14 −13 −12 −11 −10

17. $-3.6 \geq -0.3a + 1.2$ ____________

10 11 12 13 14 15 16 17 18 19 20

18. **What If?** The perimeter of a rectangle is at most 80 inches. The length of the rectangle is 25 inches. The inequality $80 - 2w \geq 50$ can be used to find w, the width of the rectangle in inches. Solve the inequality. Graph and interpret the solution. How will the solution change if the width must be at least 10 inches and a whole number?

0 2 4 6 8 10 12 14 16 18 20

____

____

____

19. **Interpret the Answer** Grace earns \$7 for each car she washes. She always saves \$25 of her weekly earnings. This week, she wants to have at least \$65 in spending money. How many cars must she wash? Write and solve an inequality to represent this situation. Interpret the solution in context.

____

____

H.O.T. FOCUS ON HIGHER ORDER THINKING

Work Area

20. **Critical Thinking** Is there any value of x with the property that $x < x - 1$? Explain your reasoning.

____

____

____

21. **Analyze Relationships** A *compound inequality* consists of two simple equalities joined by the word "*and*" or "*or*." Graph the solution sets of each of these compound inequalities.

   a. $x > 2$ and $x < 7$

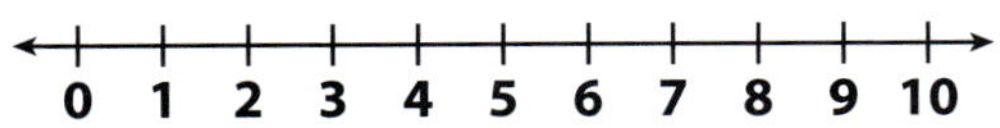

   b. $x < 2$ or $x > 7$

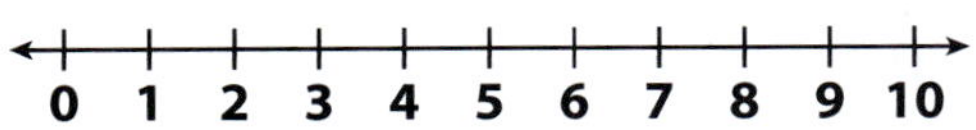

   c. Describe the solution set of the compound inequality $x < 2$ and $x > 7$.

   ____

   d. Describe the solution set of the compound inequality $x > 2$ or $x < 7$.

   ____

22. **Communicate Mathematical Ideas** Joseph used the problem-solving strategy Work Backward to solve the inequality $2n + 5 < 13$. Shawnee solved the inequality using the algebraic method you used in this lesson. Compare the two methods.

____

____

____

____

____

____

Activity 7.3

Inequalitrio

INSTRUCTIONS

STEP 1 The teacher will hand three students in your group a stack of Inequalitrio cards.

- If you are given cards with inequalities or graphs, first shuffle the cards. Then deal one card at a time face-down to each student in your group until all the cards are distributed.
- If you are given cards with real-world problems, wait until the other cards are dealt, then deal one card face-up to each student. Set aside any extras.

STEP 2 Examine your real-world problem and record the title of the problem on a piece of paper. Then write and solve an inequality that matches your problem situation. Let the variable be *x*.

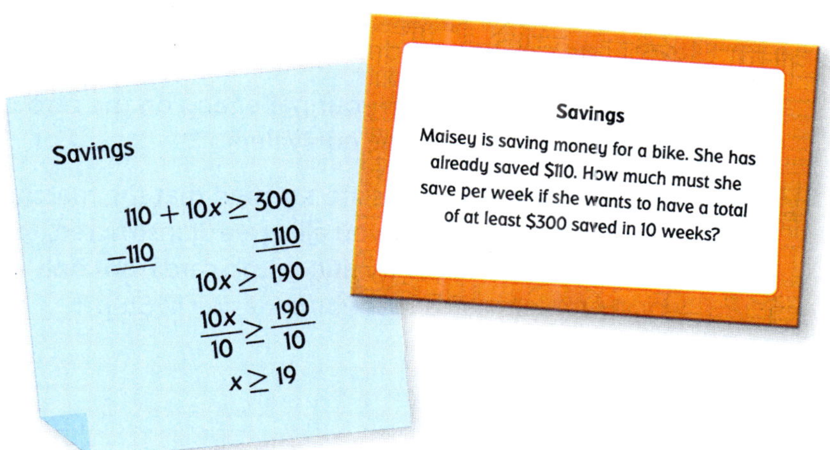

STEP 3 Turn your inequality and graph cards face-up.

STEP 4 Keep your real-world problem card, and, using your group members' papers to guide you, take turns distributing your inequality and graph cards to the group members with the matching problem situations. Set aside any inequality and graph cards that don't match any situation.

Continue until you each have a trio of cards—real-world problem, inequality, and graph—that all represent the same situation.

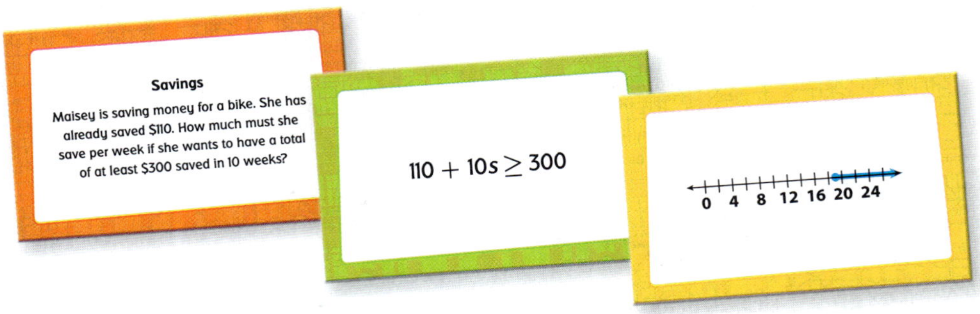

STEP 5 When you have completed your trios, work with another student in your group to verify that the cards in each of your trios match. If not, identify and correct any mistakes you made on your paper, or exchange cards as needed.

(Note: The inequality on your paper and on the card may not match exactly, but they must be equivalent.)

STEP 6 Once all group members are satisfied that the matches are correct, let your teacher know that you all agree. If instructed, repeat the activity using all of the inequality and graph cards, but only the unused real-world problem cards that you set aside in Step 1.

MODULE QUIZ

Ready to Go On?

Personal Math Trainer
Online Assessment and Intervention
my.hrw.com

7.1 Writing and Solving One-Step Inequalities

Solve each inequality.

1. $n + 7 < -3$ ________________

2. $5p \geq -30$ ________________

3. $14 < k + 11$ ________________

4. $\frac{d}{-3} \leq -6$ ________________

5. $c - 2.5 \leq 2.5$ ________________

6. $12 \geq -3b$ ________________

7. Jose has scored 562 points on his math tests so far this semester. To get an A for the semester, he must score at least 650 points. Write and solve an inequality to find the minimum number of points he must score on the remaining tests in order to get an A.

____

7.2 Writing Two-Step Inequalities

8. During a scuba dive, Lainey descended to a point 20 feet below the ocean surface. She continued her descent at a rate of 20 feet per minute. Write an inequality you could solve to find the number of minutes she can continue to descend if she does not want to reach a point more than 100 feet below the ocean surface.

____

7.3 Solving Two-Step Inequalities

Solve.

9. $2s + 3 > 15$ ________________

10. $-\frac{d}{12} - 6 < 1$ ________________

11. $-6w - 18 \geq 36$ ________________

12. $\frac{z}{4} + 22 \leq 38$ ________________

13. $\frac{b}{9} - 34 < -36$ ________________

14. $-2p + 12 > 8$ ________________

ESSENTIAL QUESTION

15. How can you recognize whether a real-world situation should be represented by an equation or an inequality?

____

____

MODULE 7 MIXED REVIEW

Assessment Readiness

Personal Math Trainer
my.hrw.com
Online Assessment and Intervention

Selected Response

1. Which graph models the solution of the inequality $-6 \leq -3x$?

Ⓐ 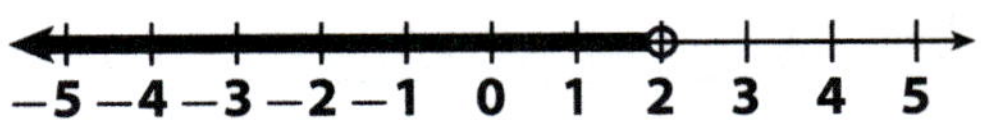

Ⓑ 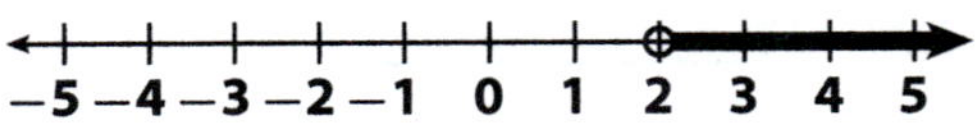

Ⓒ 

Ⓓ 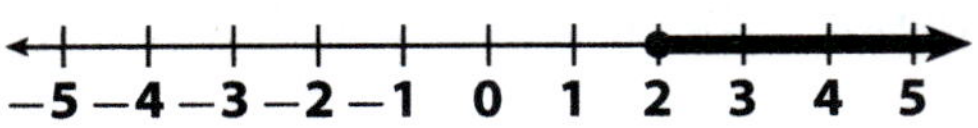

2. A taxi cab costs \$1.75 for the first mile and \$0.75 for each additional mile. You have \$20 to spend on your ride. Which inequality could be solved to find how many miles you can travel, if *n* is the number of additional miles?

Ⓐ $1.75n + 0.75 \geq 20$

Ⓑ $1.75n + 0.75 \leq 20$

Ⓒ $0.75n + 1.75 \geq 20$

Ⓓ $0.75n + 1.75 \leq 20$

3. The inequality $\frac{9}{5}C + 32 < -40$ can be used to find Celsius temperatures that are less than −40° Fahrenheit. What is the solution of the inequality?

Ⓐ $C < 40$　　Ⓒ $C < -40$

Ⓑ $C < -\frac{40}{9}$　　Ⓓ $C < -\frac{72}{5}$

4. The 30 members of a choir are trying to raise at least \$1,500 to cover travel costs to a singing camp. They have already raised \$600. Which inequality could you solve to find the average amounts each member can raise that will at least meet the goal?

Ⓐ $30x + 600 > 1{,}500$

Ⓑ $30x + 600 \geq 1{,}500$

Ⓒ $30x + 600 < 1{,}500$

Ⓓ $30x + 600 \leq 1{,}500$

5. Which represents the solution for the inequality $3x - 7 > 5$?

Ⓐ $x < 4$　　Ⓒ $x > 4$

Ⓑ $x \leq 4$　　Ⓓ $x \geq 4$

6. Which inequality has the following graphed solution?

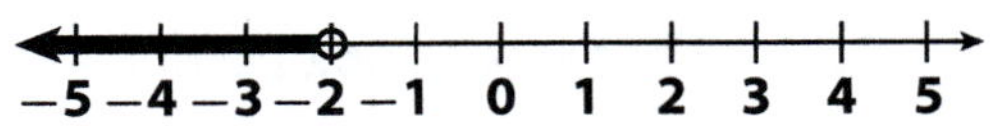

Ⓐ $3x + 8 \leq 2$　　Ⓒ $2x + 5 \leq 1$

Ⓑ $4x + 12 < 4$　　Ⓓ $3x + 6 < 3$

7. Divide: $-36 \div 6$.

Ⓐ 30　　Ⓒ −6

Ⓑ 6　　Ⓓ −30

8. Eleni bought 2 pounds of grapes at a cost of \$3.49 per pound. She paid with a \$10 bill. How much change did she get back?

Ⓐ \$3.02　　Ⓒ \$6.51

Ⓑ \$4.51　　Ⓓ \$6.98

Mini-Task

9. In golf, the lower your score, the better. Negative scores are best of all. Teri scored +1 on each of the first three holes at a nine-hole miniature golf course. Her goal is a total score of −9 or better after she has completed the final six holes.

a. Let *h* represent the score Teri must average on each of the last six holes in order to meet her goal. Write a two-step inequality you can solve to find *h*.

____

b. Solve the inequality.

____

UNIT 3

Study Guide Review

MODULE 6 Expressions and Equations

Key Vocabulary

algebraic expression *(expresión algebraica)*

equation *(ecuación)*

ESSENTIAL QUESTION

How can you use equations to solve real-world problems?

EXAMPLE 1

Huang and Belita both repair computers. Huang makes \$50 a day plus \$25 per repair. Belita makes \$20 a day plus \$35 per repair. Write an expression for Huang and Belita's total daily earnings if they make the same number of repairs *r*.

Huang: $\$50 + \$25r$

Belita: $\$20 + \$35r$

Together: $(50 + 25r) + (20 + 35r) = 50 + 20 + 25r + 35r$

$$= 70 + 60r$$

Huang and Belita earn $\$70 + \$60r$ together.

EXAMPLE 2

A skydiver's parachute opens at a height of 2,790 feet. He then falls at a rate of $-15\frac{1}{2}$ feet per second. How long will it take the skydiver to reach the ground?

Let x represent the number of seconds it takes to reach the ground.

$$-15\tfrac{1}{2}x = -2{,}790$$

$$-\frac{31}{2}x = -2{,}790 \quad \text{Write as a fraction.}$$

$$\left(-\frac{2}{31}\right)\left(-\frac{31}{2}x\right) = \left(-\frac{2}{31}\right)(-2{,}790) \quad \text{Multiply both sides by the reciprocal.}$$

$$x = 180$$

It takes 180 seconds for the skydiver to reach the ground.

EXAMPLE 3

A clothing store sells clothing for 2 times the wholesale cost plus $10. The store sells a pair of pants for $48. How much did the store pay for the pants? Represent the solution on a number line.

Let *w* represent the wholesale cost of the pants, or the price paid by the store.

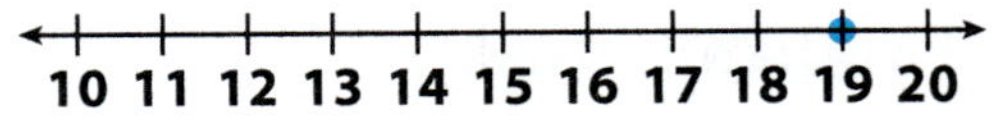

$2w + 10 = 48$

$2w = 38$ Subtract 10 from both sides.

$w = 19$ Divide both sides by 2.

The store paid $19 for the pants.

EXERCISES

Simplify each expression. (Lesson 6.1)

1. $(2x + 3\frac{2}{5}) + (5x - \frac{4}{5})$ ______________

2. $(-0.5x - 4) - (1.5x + 2.3)$ ______________

3. $9(3t + 4b)$ ______________

4. $0.7(5a - 13p)$ ______________

Factor each expression. (Lesson 6.1)

5. $8x + 56$ ______________

6. $3x + 57$ ______________

Use inverse operations to solve each equation. (Lesson 6.2)

7. $1.6 + y = -7.3$ ______________

8. $-\frac{2}{3}n = 12$ ______________

9. The cost of a ticket to an amusement park is $42 per person. For groups of up to 8 people, the cost per ticket decreases by $3 for each person in the group. Marcos's ticket cost $30. Write and solve an equation to find the number of people in Marcos's group. (Lesson 6.3, 6.4)

____

Solve each equation. Graph the solution on a number line. (Lesson 6.4)

10. $8x - 28 = 44$

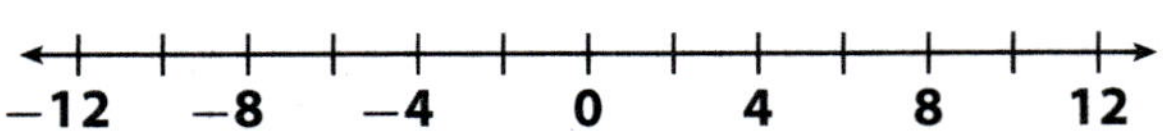

____

11. $-5z + 4 = 34$

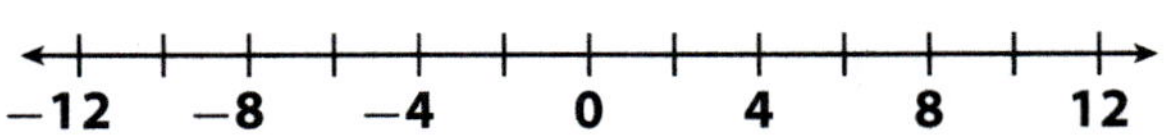

____

MODULE 7

Inequalities

Key Vocabulary
Inequalities
(desigualdad)

ESSENTIAL QUESTION

How can you use inequalities to solve real-world problems?

EXAMPLE 1

Amy is having her birthday party at a roller skating rink. The rink charges a fee of \$50 plus \$8 per person. If Amy wants to spend at most \$170 for the party at the rink, how many people can she invite to her party?

Let p represent the number of people skating at the party.

$50 + 8p \leq 170$

$8p \leq 120$ — Subtract 50 from both sides.

$\frac{8p}{8} \leq \frac{120}{8}$ — Divide both sides by 8.

$p \leq 15$

Up to 15 people can skate, so Amy can invite up to 14 people to her party.

EXAMPLE 2

Determine which, if any, of these values makes the inequality $-7x + 42 \leq 28$ true: $x = -1$, $x = 2$, $x = 5$.

$-7(-1) + 42 \leq 28$ $\quad -7(2) + 42 \leq 28$ $\quad -7(5) + 42 \leq 28$

Substitute each value for x in the inequality and evaluate the expression to see if a true inequality results.

$x = 2$ and $x = 5$

EXERCISES

1. Prudie needs \$90 or more to be able to take her family out to dinner. She has already saved \$30 and wants to take her family out to eat in 4 days. (Lesson 7.2)

a. Suppose that Prudie earns the same each day. Write an inequality to find how much she needs to earn each day.

____

b. Suppose that Prudie earns \$18 each day. Will she have enough money to take her family to dinner in 4 days? Explain.

____

Solve each inequality. Graph and check the solution. (Lesson 7.3)

2. $11 - 5y < -19$

____

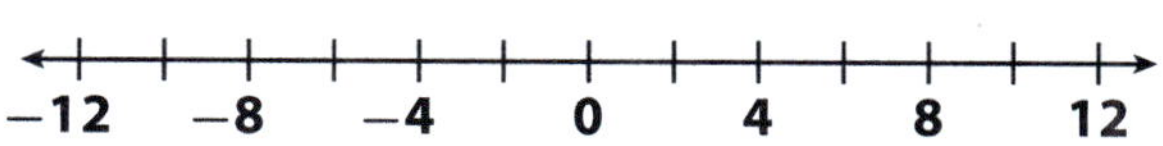

3. $7x - 2 \leq 61$

____

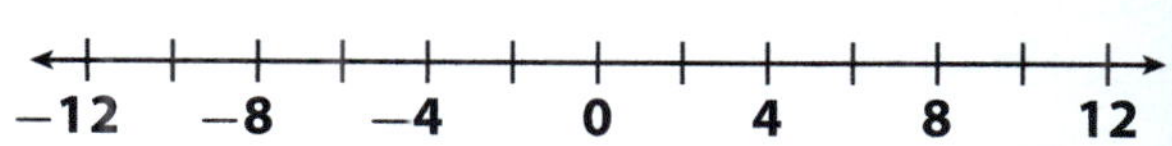

Unit 3 Performance Tasks

1. **CAREERS IN MATH** **Mechanical Engineer** A mechanical engineer is testing the amount of force needed to make a spring stretch by a given amount. The force y is measured in units called *Newtons*, abbreviated N. The stretch x is measured in centimeters. Her results are shown in the graph.

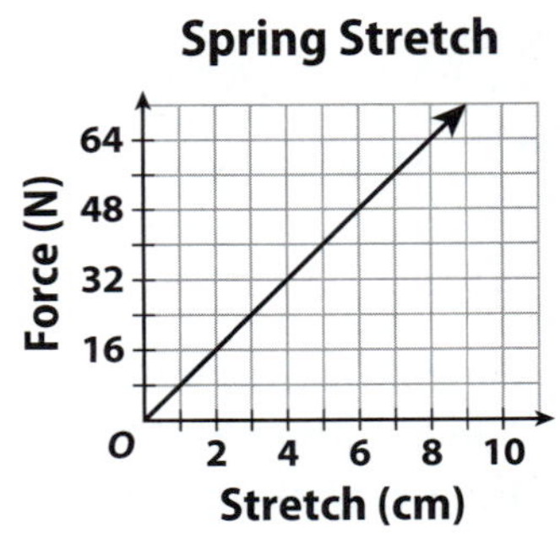

a. Write an equation for the line. Explain, using the graph and then using the equation, why the relationship is proportional.

b. Identify the rate of change and the constant of proportionality.

c. What is the meaning of the constant of proportionality in the context of the problem?

d. The engineer applies a force of 41.6 Newtons to the spring. Write and solve an equation to find the corresponding stretch in the spring.

2. A math tutor charges \$30 for a consultation, and then \$25 per hour. An online tutoring service charges \$30 per hour.

a. Does either service represent a proportional relationship? Explain.

b. Write an equation for the cost c of h hours of tutoring for either service. Which service charges less for 4 hours of tutoring? Show your work.

UNIT 3 **MIXED REVIEW**

Assessment Readiness

Personal Math Trainer
my.hrw.com
Online Assessment and Intervention

Selected Response

1. Which expression is equivalent to $(9x - 3\frac{1}{8}) - (7x + 1\frac{3}{8})$?

Ⓐ $2x - 4\frac{1}{2}$

Ⓑ $16x - 4\frac{1}{2}$

Ⓒ $2x - 1\frac{3}{4}$

Ⓓ $16x - 1\frac{3}{4}$

2. Timothy began the week with $35. He bought lunch at school, paying $2.25 for each meal. Let x be the number of meals he bought at school and y be the amount of money he had left at the end of the week. Which equation represents the relationship in the situation?

Ⓐ $y = 2.25x + 35$

Ⓑ $y = 35 - 2.25x$

Ⓒ $x = 35 - 2.25y$

Ⓓ $y = 2.25x - 35$

3. Which expression factors to $8(x + 2)$?

Ⓐ $8x + 2$

Ⓑ $8x + 10$

Ⓒ $16x$

Ⓓ $8x + 16$

4. Ramón's toll pass account has a value of $32. Each time he uses the toll road, $1.25 is deducted from the account. When the value drops below $10, he must add value to the toll pass. Which inequality represents how many times Ramón can use the toll road without having to add value to the toll pass?

Ⓐ $10 - 1.25t \geq 0$

Ⓑ $-1.25t + 32 < 10$

Ⓒ $32 - 1.25t \geq 10$

Ⓓ $32 - 10t \geq 1.25$

5. A taxi costs $1.65 for the first mile and $0.85 for each additional mile. Which equation could be solved to find the number x of additional miles traveled in a taxi given that the total cost of the trip is $20?

Ⓐ $1.65x + 0.85 = 20$

Ⓑ $0.85x + 1.65 = 20$

Ⓒ $1.65x - 0.85 = 20$

Ⓓ $0.85x - 1.65 = 20$

6. A sales tax of 6% is added to the price of an item. If Marisa buys an item, which expression indicates how much she will pay in all?

Ⓐ $n + 0.06$

Ⓑ $0.06n$

Ⓒ $n + 0.06n$

Ⓓ $0.06 + 0.06n$

7. Which equation has the solution $x = 12$?

Ⓐ $4x + 3 = 45$

Ⓑ $3x + 6 = 42$

Ⓒ $2x - 5 = 29$

Ⓓ $5x - 8 = 68$

8. The 23 members of the school jazz band are trying to raise at least $1,800 to cover the cost of traveling to a competition. The members have already raised $750. Which inequality could you solve to find the amount that each member should raise to meet the goal?

Ⓐ $23x + 750 > 1,800$

Ⓑ $23x + 750 \geq 1,800$

Ⓒ $23x + 750 < 1,800$

Ⓓ $23x + 750 \leq 1,800$

9. What is the solution of the inequality $2x - 9 < 7$?

Ⓐ $x < 8$

Ⓑ $x \leq 8$

Ⓒ $x > 8$

Ⓓ $x \geq 8$

10. Which inequality has the solution $n < 5$?

Ⓐ $4n + 11 > -9$

Ⓑ $4n + 11 < -9$

Ⓒ $-4n + 11 < -9$

Ⓓ $-4n + 11 > -9$

11. Which inequality has the solution shown?

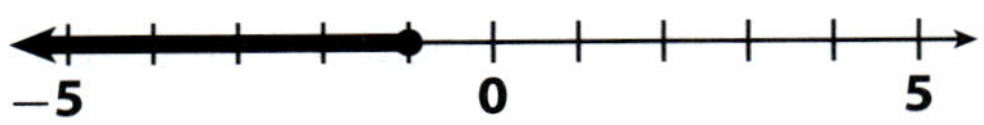

Ⓐ $3x + 5 < 2$

Ⓑ $4x + 12 < 4$

Ⓒ $2x + 5 \leq 1$

Ⓓ $3x + 6 \leq 3$

12. On a $4\frac{1}{2}$ hour trip, Leslie drove $\frac{2}{3}$ of the time. For how many hours did Leslie drive?

Ⓐ 3 hours

Ⓑ $3\frac{1}{2}$ hours

Ⓒ $3\frac{2}{3}$ hours

Ⓓ $3\frac{5}{6}$ hours

13. During a sale, the price of a sweater was changed from \$20 to \$16. What was the percent of decrease in the price of the sweater?

Ⓐ 4%

Ⓑ 20%

Ⓒ 25%

Ⓓ 40%

Mini-Task

14. Max wants to buy some shorts that are priced at \$8 each. He decided to buy a pair of sneakers for \$39, but the total cost of the shorts and the sneakers must be less than \$75.

a. Write an inequality to find out how many pairs of shorts Max can buy.

b. Suppose that Max wants to buy 6 pairs of shorts. Will he have enough money? Explain.

c. Solve the inequality to find the greatest number of pairs of shorts that Max can buy. Show your work.

UNIT 4

Geometry

MODULE 8
Modeling Geometric Figures

MODULE 9
Circumference, Area, and Volume

CAREERS IN MATH

Product Design Engineer A product design engineer works to design and develop manufactured products and equipment. A product design engineer uses math to design and modify models, and to calculate costs in producing their designs.

If you are interested in a career in product design engineering, you should study these mathematical subjects:

- Algebra
- Geometry
- Trigonometry
- Statistics
- Calculus

Research other careers that require the use of mathematics to design and modify products.

Unit 4 Performance Task

At the end of the unit, check out how **product design engineers** use math.

UNIT 4

Vocabulary Preview

Use the puzzle to preview key vocabulary from this unit. Unscramble the circled letters to answer the riddle at the bottom of the page.

1. NEONGTURC LANSEG

☐◯☐☐☐☐☐☐☐ ☐☐☐☐☐☐

2. LEOTECRAYMPMN SEGLAN

☐◯☐☐☐☐☐☐☐☐☐☐◯

☐☐◯☐☐☐

3. RIMEUCEEFNRCC

☐☐☐☐☐☐☐☐☐☐◯☐☐

4. LEARATL ERAA

☐☐☐☐☐☐◯ ☐☐☐☐

5. PIECOTMOS GUISEFR

☐☐☐◯☐☐☐☐☐ ☐☐☐☐☐☐☐

1. Angles that have the same measure. (Lesson 8.4)
2. Two angles whose measures have a sum of 90 degrees. (Lesson 8.4)
3. The distance around a circle. (Lesson 9.1)
4. The sum of the areas of the lateral faces of a prism. (Lesson 9.4)
5. A two-dimensional figure made from two or more geometric figures. (Lesson 9.3)

Q: What do you say when you see an empty parrot cage?

A: _ _ _ _ _ _ _!

Modeling Geometric Figures

MODULE 8

ESSENTIAL QUESTION

How can you use proportions to solve real-world geometry problems?

Real-World Video

my.hrw.com

Architects make blueprints and models of their designs to show clients and contractors. These scale drawings and scale models have measurements in proportion to those of the project when built.

GO DIGITAL
my.hrw.com

my.hrw.com

Go digital with your write-in student edition, accessible on any device.

Math On the Spot

Scan with your smart phone to jump directly to the online edition, video tutor, and more.

Animated Math

Interactively explore key concepts to see how math works.

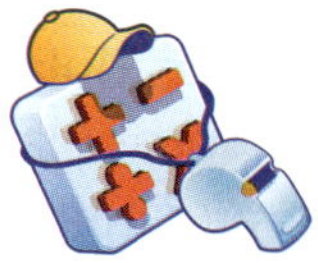

Personal Math Trainer

Get immediate feedback and help as you work through practice sets.

Reading Start-Up

Visualize Vocabulary

Use the ✔ words to complete the graphic. You may put more than one word on each line.

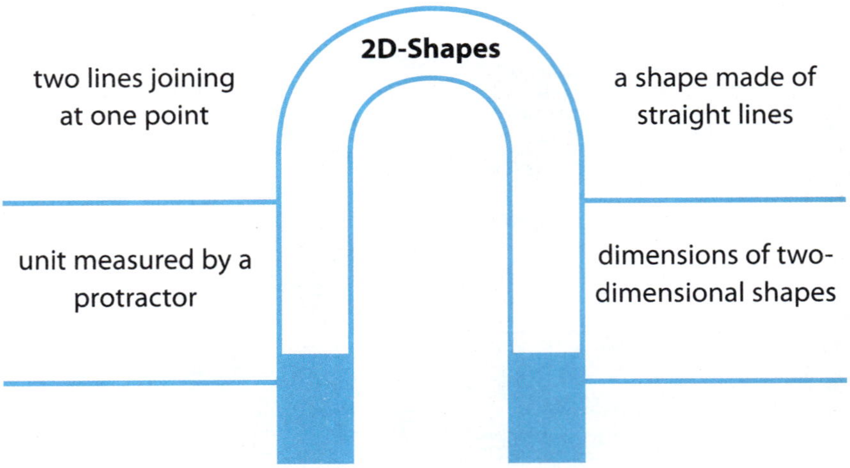

Vocabulary

Review Words

✔ angle *(ángulo)*
✔ degree *(grado)*
dimension *(dimensión)*
✔ length *(longitud)*
proportion *(proporción)*
✔ polygon *(polígono)*
ratio *(razón)*
✔ width *(ancho)*

Preview Words

adjacent angles *(ángulos adyacentes)*
complementary angles *(ángulos complementarios)*
congruent angles *(ángulos congruentes)*
cross section *(sección transversal)*
intersection *(intersección)*
scale *(escala)*
scale drawing *(dibujo a escala)*
supplementary angles *(ángulos suplementarios)*
vertical angles *(ángulos verticales)*

Understand Vocabulary

Complete each sentence using a preview word.

1. What is a proportional two-dimensional drawing of an object?

____

2. ____________________ are angles that have the same measure.

3. ________________________ are angles whose measures have a sum of 90°.

Active Reading

Key-Term Fold Before beginning the module, create a key-term fold to help you learn the vocabulary in this module. Write each highlighted vocabulary word on one side of a flap. Write the definition for each word on the other side of the flap. Use the key-term fold to quiz yourself on the definitions in this module.

Are YOU Ready?

Complete these exercises to review skills you will need for this module.

Personal Math Trainer
my.hrw.com
Online Assessment and Intervention

Solve Two-Step Equations

EXAMPLE

$5x + 3 = -7$

$5x + 3 - 3 = -7 - 3$ Subtract 3 from both sides.

$5x = -10$ Simplify.

$\frac{5x}{5} = \frac{-10}{5}$ Divide both sides by 5.

$x = -2$

Solve.

1. $3x + 4 = 10$ ______
2. $5x - 11 = 34$ ______
3. $-2x + 5 = -9$ ______
4. $-11 = 8x + 13$ ______
5. $4x - 7 = -27$ ______
6. $\frac{1}{2}x + 16 = 39$ ______
7. $12 = 2x - 16$ ______
8. $5x - 15 = -65$ ______

Solve Proportions

EXAMPLE

$\frac{a}{4} = \frac{27}{18}$

$a \times 18 = 4 \times 27$ Write the cross products.

$18a = 108$ Simplify.

$\frac{18a}{18} = \frac{108}{18}$ Divide both sides by 18.

$a = 6$

Solve for *x*.

9. $\frac{x}{5} = \frac{18}{30}$ ______
10. $\frac{x}{12} = \frac{24}{36}$ ______
11. $\frac{3}{9} = \frac{x}{3}$ ______
12. $\frac{14}{15} = \frac{x}{75}$ ______
13. $\frac{8}{x} = \frac{14}{7}$ ______
14. $\frac{14}{x} = \frac{2}{5}$ ______
15. $\frac{5}{6} = \frac{x}{15}$ ______
16. $\frac{81}{33} = \frac{x}{5.5}$ ______

Are YOU Ready? (cont'd)

Complete these exercises to review skills you will need for this module.

Solve Two-Step Equations

17. Danielle's aunt is 8 years younger than 3 times Danielle's age. Her aunt is 34. Write an equation that relates Danielle's age, *a*, to her aunt's age. Then find Danielle's age.

18. The formula $F = \frac{9}{5}C + 32$ can be used to convert between temperature in degrees Fahrenheit and temperature in degrees Celsius. Use the formula to find the temperature in degrees Celsius when the temperature is 95 °F. Show your work.

Solve Proportions

19. Which proportions have the same solution as the proportion $\frac{2}{8} = \frac{3}{x}$? Select all that apply.

Ⓐ $\frac{8}{2} = \frac{3}{x}$

Ⓑ $\frac{3}{x} = \frac{1}{4}$

Ⓒ $\frac{3}{8} = \frac{x}{2}$

Ⓓ $\frac{3}{2} = \frac{x}{8}$

20. Marcel earned \$32 for 4 hours of work. Show how to use a proportion to find how many hours, *h*, he must work to earn \$80.

LESSON 8.1 Similar Shapes and Scale Drawings

7.4.8.1

Students will use scale drawings to solve problems.

ESSENTIAL QUESTION

How can you use scale drawings to solve problems?

EXPLORE ACTIVITY 1 Real World

Scale Drawings and Proportional Reasoning

A blueprint is a technical drawing that usually displays architectural plans. Pete's blueprint shows a layout of a house. The table shows how the actual lengths in the house are related to the lengths in Pete's blueprint.

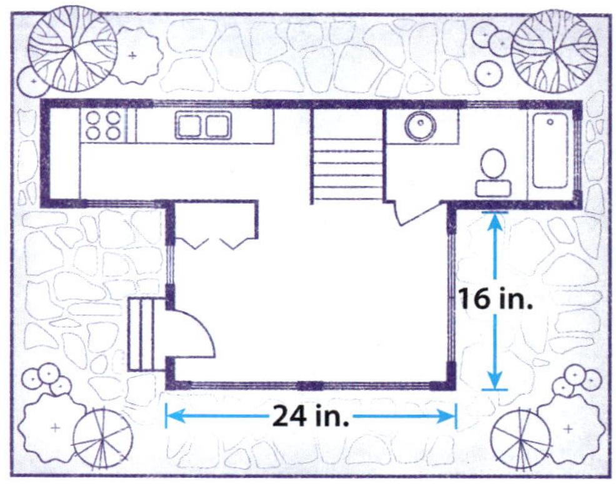

Blueprint length (in.)	4	8	12	16	20	24
Actual length (ft)	3	6	9	12	15	18

A Use the rates of actual length to blueprint length in the table to explain why the relationship between the two is proportional.

____

B Show how to use proportional reasoning to find the unit rate.

$$\frac{\text{Actual length}}{\text{Blueprint length}} = \frac{\square \div \square}{\square \div \square} = \frac{\square}{1 \text{ inch}}$$

C Write an equation for the relationship, where x is blueprint length, in inches, and y is actual length, in feet. Use the equation to find the actual length for a blueprint length of 21 inches and the blueprint length for an actual length of 7 feet.

____

Reflect

1. **Check for Reasonableness** Show that your answers to **C** are reasonable.

____

____

____

Finding Length, Width, and Area

A **scale drawing** is a proportional two-dimensional drawing of an object. Scale drawings can represent objects that are smaller or larger than the drawing.

A **scale** is a ratio between two sets of measurements. It shows how a dimension in a scale drawing is related to the actual object. Scales are usually shown as two numbers separated by a colon, such as 1:20 or 1 cm:1 m. Scales can be shown in the same unit or in different units.

You can solve scale-drawing problems by using proportional reasoning.

Math On the Spot
my.hrw.com

My Notes

EXAMPLE 1 Real World

The art class is planning to paint a mural on an outside wall. This figure is a scale drawing of the wall. What is the area of the actual wall?

28 in.

11 in.

2 in.:3 ft

STEP 1 Find the number of feet represented by 1 inch in the drawing.

$$\frac{2 \text{ in.} \div 2}{3 \text{ ft} \div 2} = \frac{1 \text{ in.}}{1.5 \text{ ft}}$$

1 inch in this drawing equals 1.5 feet on the actual wall.

STEP 2 Find the height of the actual wall labeled 11 inches in the drawing.

$$\frac{1 \text{ in.} \times 11}{1.5 \text{ ft} \times 11} = \frac{11 \text{ in.}}{16.5 \text{ ft}}$$

The height of the actual wall labeled 11 in. is 16.5 ft.

STEP 3 Find the length of the actual wall labeled 28 inches in the drawing.

$$\frac{1 \text{ in.} \times 28}{1.5 \text{ ft} \times 28} = \frac{28 \text{ in.}}{42 \text{ ft}}$$

The length of the actual wall is 42 ft.

STEP 4 Since area is length times width, the area of the actual wall is $16.5 \text{ ft} \times 42 \text{ ft} = 693 \text{ ft}^2$.

Math Talk
Mathematical Processes

What are two proportions you could use to find the actual length *L* and width *W*?

Reflect

2. **Analyze Relationships** Write the scale in Example 1 as a unit rate. Show that this unit rate is equal to the ratio of the height of the drawing to the actual height.

____

3. **Analyze Relationships** Write the ratio of the area of the drawing to the area of the actual wall. Write your answer as a unit rate. Show that this unit rate is equal to the square of the unit rate in Exercise 2.

____

YOUR TURN

4. Find the length and width of the actual room, shown in the scale drawing. Then find the area of the actual room. Round your answers to the nearest tenth.

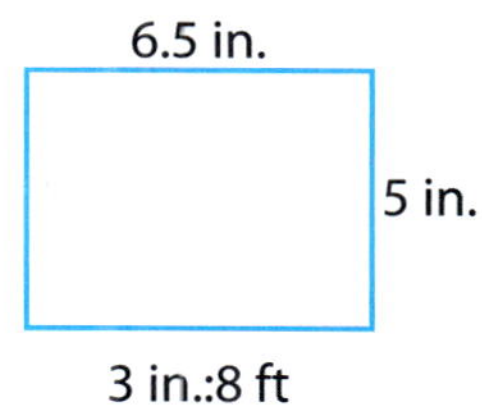

____

____

5. The drawing plan for an art studio shows a rectangle that is 13.2 inches by 6 inches. The scale in the plan is 3 in.:5 ft. Find the length and width of the actual studio. Then find the area of the actual studio.

____

Personal Math Trainer
Online Assessment and Intervention
my.hrw.com

EXPLORE ACTIVITY 2 Real World

Drawing in Different Scales

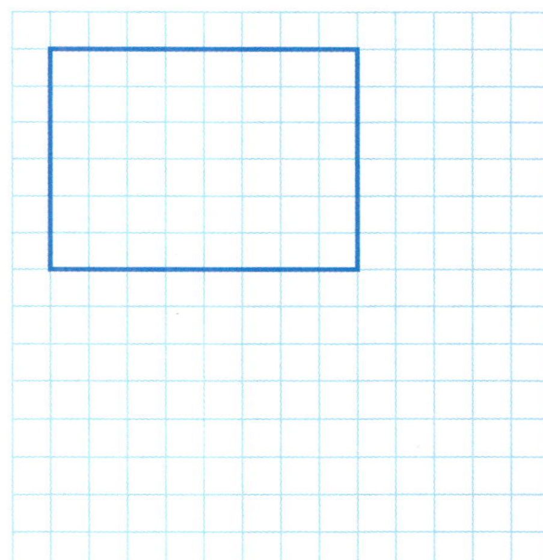

A A scale drawing of a meeting hall is drawn on centimeter grid paper as shown. The scale is 1 cm:3 m.

Suppose you redraw the rectangle on centimeter grid paper using a scale of 1 cm:6 m. In the new scale, 1 cm represents **more/less** than 1 cm in the old scale.

B Write and simplify the ratio of the new scale to the original scale.

$$\frac{\text{New scale}}{\text{Original scale}} = \frac{\square}{\frac{1\text{ cm}}{3\text{ m}}} = \frac{\square}{\square}$$

C The measurement of each side of the new drawing will be **twice/half** as long as the measurement of the original drawing.

D Draw the rectangle for the new scale 1 cm:6 m.

Reflect

6. Show how to find the actual length of each side of the hall using the original drawing and scale. Repeat using your new drawing and the new scale.

____

____

Guided Practice

1. The table compares actual lengths in a room to lengths in a blueprint of the room. (Explore Activity 1)

Blueprint length (in.)	3	6	9	12	15	18
Actual length (ft)	5	10	15	20	25	30

a. Write an equation for the relationship, where y is the actual length in feet. ______

b. The length of a wall on the blueprint is 10 inches. Find the actual length of the wall. ______

c. A window in the room has an actual width of 2.5 feet. Find the width of the window in the blueprint. ______

2. The scale in the drawing is 2 in. : 4 ft. What are the length, width, and area of the actual room? (Example 1)

Length = ______ feet, because $\frac{1 \text{ in.} \times 14}{\square \times \square} = \frac{14 \text{ in.}}{\square}$, width = ______ feet, and area = ______ square feet.

3. The scale in the drawing is 2 cm : 5 m. What are the length, width, and area of the actual room? (Example 1)

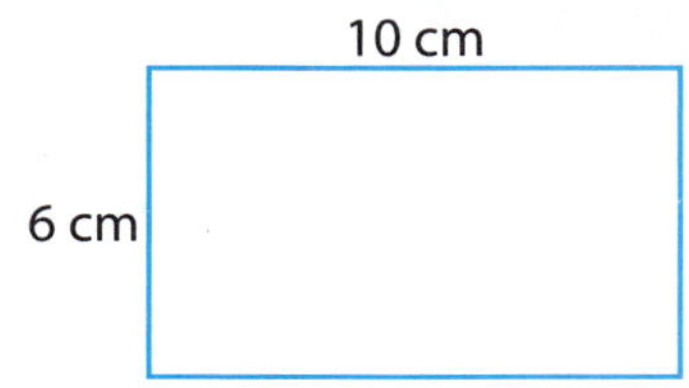

______

4. A scale drawing of a cafeteria is drawn on centimeter grid paper as shown. The scale is 1 cm : 4 m. (Explore Activity 2)

a. Redraw the rectangle on centimeter grid paper using a scale of 1 cm:6 m.

b. What are the actual length and width of the cafeteria using the original scale? What are the actual dimensions of the cafeteria using the new scale?

______

ESSENTIAL QUESTION CHECK-IN

5. If you have an accurate, complete scale drawing and the scale, which measurements of the object of the drawing can you find?

______

______

Name ____________________ Class ____________ Date ____________

8.1 Independent Practice

Personal Math Trainer
Online Assessment and Intervention
my.hrw.com

6. **Art** Marie has a small copy of Rene Magritte's famous painting, *The Schoolmaster*. Her copy has dimensions 2 inches by 1.5 inches. The scale of the copy is 1 in.:40 cm.

   a. Find the dimensions of the original painting.

   b. Find the area of the original painting.

   c. Since 1 inch is 2.54 centimeters, find the dimensions of the original painting in inches.

   d. Find the area of the original painting in square inches.

7. A game room has a floor that is 120 feet by 75 feet. A scale drawing of the floor on grid paper uses a scale of 1 unit:5 feet. What are the dimensions of the scale drawing?

8. **Multiple Representations** The length of a table is 6 feet. On a scale drawing, the length is 2 inches. Write three possible scales for the drawing.

9. **Analyze Relationships** A scale for a scale drawing is 10 cm:1 mm. Which is larger, the actual object or the scale drawing? Explain.

10. **Architecture** The scale model of a building is 5.4 feet tall.

    a. If the original building is 810 meters tall, what was the scale used to make the model?

    b. If the model is made out of tiny bricks each measuring 0.4 inch in height, how many bricks tall is the model?

11. You have been asked to build a scale model of your school out of toothpicks. Imagine your school is 30 feet tall. Your scale is 1 ft:1.26 cm.

a. If a toothpick is 6.3 cm tall, how many toothpicks tall will your model be?

____

b. Your mother is out of toothpicks, and suggests you use cotton swabs instead. You measure them, and they are 7.6 cm tall. How many cotton swabs tall will your model be?

____

H.O.T. FOCUS ON HIGHER ORDER THINKING

Work Area

12. **Draw Conclusions** The area of a square floor on a scale drawing is 100 square centimeters, and the scale of the drawing is 1 cm : 2 ft. What is the area of the actual floor? What is the ratio of the area in the drawing to the actual area?

____

13. **Multiple Representations** Describe how to redraw a scale drawing with a new scale.

____

____

____

____

____

____

14. The scale drawing of a room is drawn on a grid that represents quarter-inch grid paper. The scale is $\frac{1}{4}$ in. : 4 ft. Redraw the scale drawing of the same room using a different scale. What scale did you use? What are the length and width of the actual room? What is the area of the actual room?

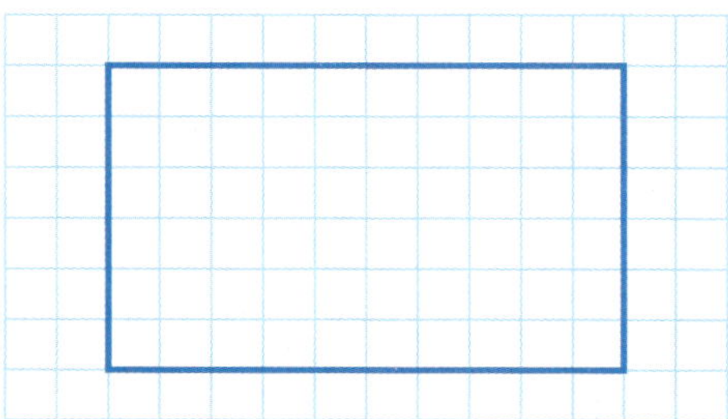

____

Going Further 8.1

Scale Drawings and Area

7.4.GF.8.1

Students will use the area of a figure on a scale drawing to find the corresponding area on the actual object.

ESSENTIAL QUESTION

How can you use the area of a figure on a scale drawing to find the corresponding area on the actual object?

EXPLORE ACTIVITY Real World

Using a Scale to Compute Area

The scale drawing is of a banner designed for Elmwood School's awards ceremony.

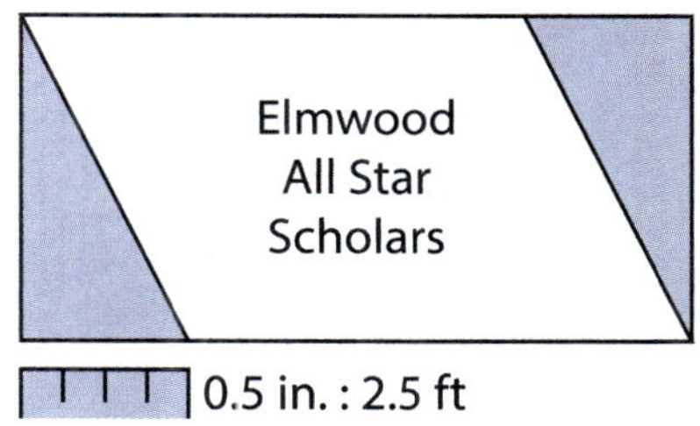

A The unit rate for the proportional relationship between dimensions x on the scale drawing and dimensions y on the banner is $\frac{\square \text{ ft}}{0.5 \text{ in.}} = \frac{\square \text{ ft}}{1 \text{ in.}}$ or ________ feet per inch. So an equation for the relationship is $y =$ ________.

B Measure the base and height of the white parallelogram on the scale drawing to the nearest half inch. Find the area of the parallelogram.

base = ________ in. height = ________ in. area = ________ in^2

C Use the equation from Part A and the base and height you found in Part B to find the base and height of the parallelogram on the banner. Then find the area of the parallelogram on the banner.

base = 5 × _____ = _____ ft height = 5 × _____ = _____ ft area = ______ ft^2

D The ratio of the area of the parallelogram on the banner to the area on the scale drawing is $\frac{\square \text{ ft}^2}{\square \text{ in}^2} = \frac{\square \text{ ft}^2}{1 \text{ in}^2} = \frac{\square^2 \text{ ft}^2}{1 \text{ in}^2}$.

E Show how to calculate the area of each triangle on the banner using the relationship described in Part D.

____

____

Reflect

1. **Focus on Modeling** Suppose the relationship between a length on a scale drawing d and the actual length a is $a = kd$. Write an equation of the relationship between an area x on the scale drawing and the corresponding actual area y. ________

Practice

For Exercises 1 and 2, use the scale drawing of a garden showing regions for different vegetables. Measure dimensions on the scale drawing to the nearest quarter of an inch.

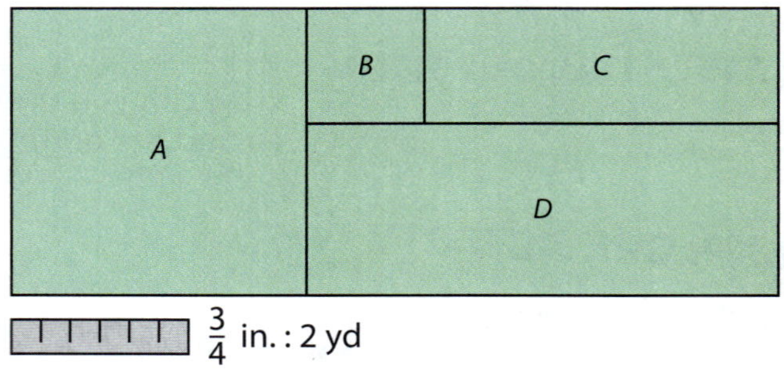

1. Use the scale to find the unit rate for the proportional relationship between dimensions on the scale drawing and dimensions in the garden in yards per inch.

____

2. Let x represent the area of a region on the scale drawing and y represent the corresponding area in the garden.

a. Write an equation for the relationship between x and y.

____

b. Find the area of regions A, B, C, and D in the garden.

____

3. Write an equation for the relationship between areas on the blueprint x and the actual areas in the room y. Use the equation to find the area of the actual living room. Then find the cost of carpeting the living room with carpeting that costs $6.52 for each square foot.

____

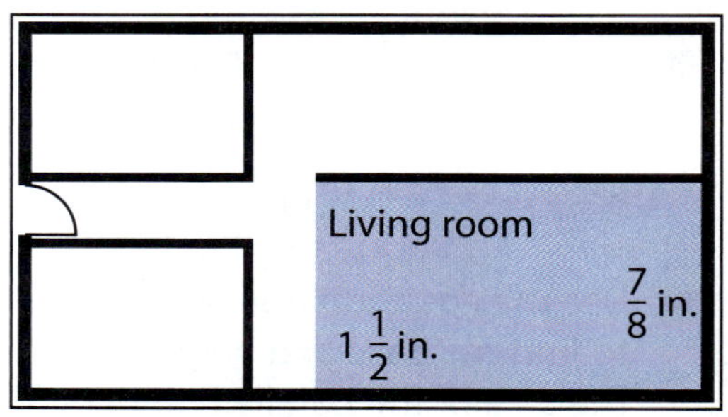

1 in. : 16 ft

4. **Estimation** The map shows a roughly parallelogram-shaped region formed by connecting the dots representing four cities. The map scale is shown as a bar representing distances.

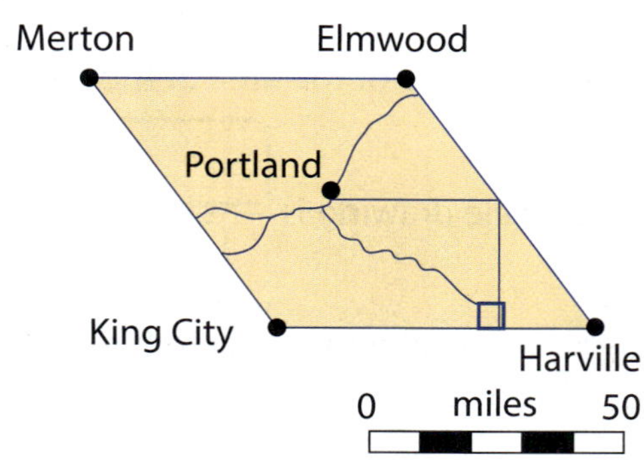

a. Use the scale to estimate the base and height of the region in miles. Then estimate the area of the region.

____

____

b. The signal of one Portland radio station can reach about 30 miles. Which of the four cities are likely to be able to receive the signal?

____

Activity 8.1

Scale a Comic

INSTRUCTIONS

STEP 1 Choose a single frame from the comic strip below or from another comic strip of your own. The comic strip below has three frames.

STEP 2 Carefully draw a 1 cm grid on the comic, starting at the bottom left corner of the frame.

STEP 3 Choose a scale that will enlarge the comic, but will allow the drawing to fit on an $8\frac{1}{2}$ in. × 11 in. sheet of quarter-inch graph paper. An example of a scale is 1 cm : 1.25 in. Record the scale below.

Scale ____________________

Visual Element	Original Measurement	Predicted Measurement	Scale Drawing Measurement

STEP 4 Measure four visual elements of your original comic and record the measurements in the table in Step 3.

STEP 5 Use your scale to predict corresponding measurements for the four visual elements on the scale drawing. Record the predicted measurements in the table.

STEP 6 Use your chosen scale and the grid lines to help you draw the scaled-up comic *square by square* on an $8\frac{1}{2}$ in. x 11 in. sheet of quarter-inch graph paper. Depending on the size of your comic, the scale you use, and the shape of the comic, the scaled-up comic may not fill the page.

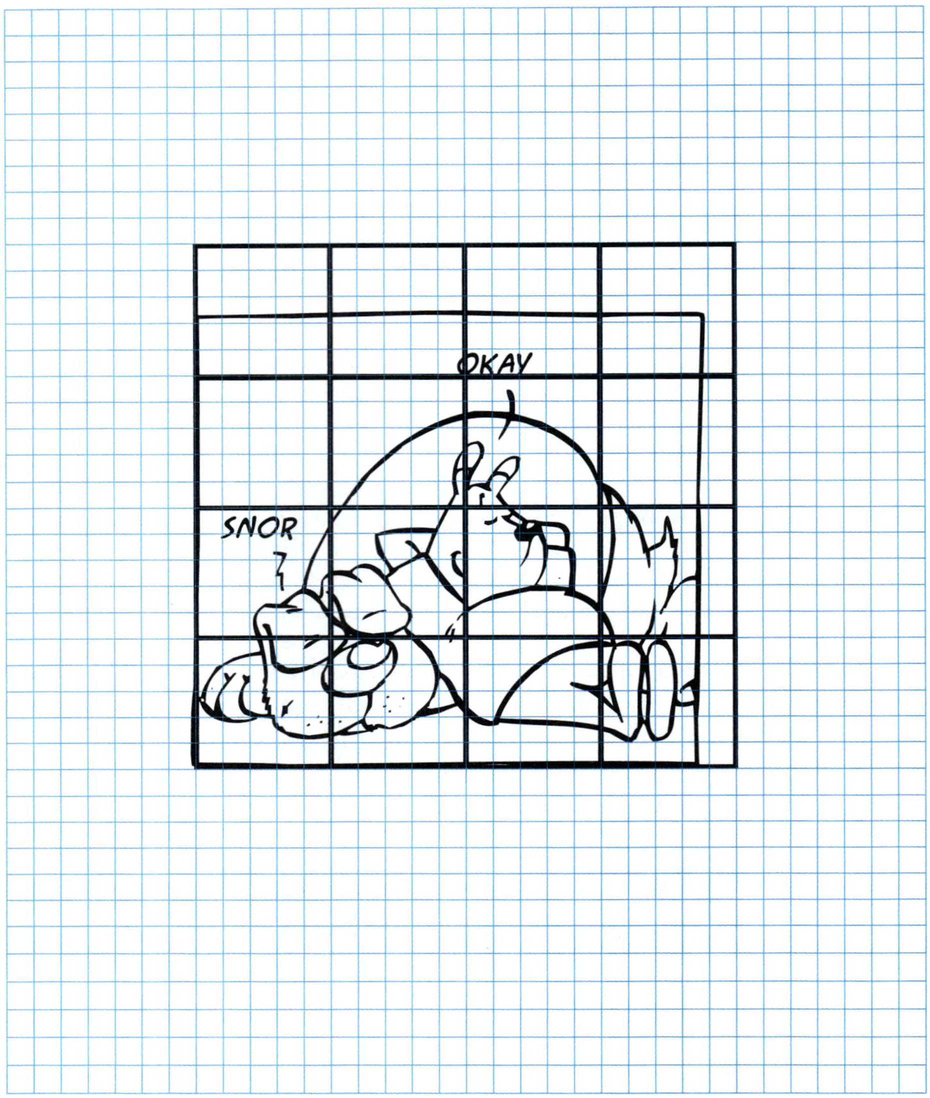

STEP 7 Measure corresponding lengths on the scaled-up drawing for the visual elements previously measured. Record the measurements in the last column of the table.

STEP 8 Compare your predicted measurements to the scale drawing measurements.

LESSON

8.2 Geometric Drawings

7.4.8.2

Students will draw shapes that satisfy given conditions.

ESSENTIAL QUESTION

How can you draw shapes that satisfy given conditions?

EXPLORE ACTIVITY 1

Drawing Three Sides

Use geometry software to draw a triangle whose sides have the following lengths: 2 units, 3 units, and 4 units.

A Draw the segments.

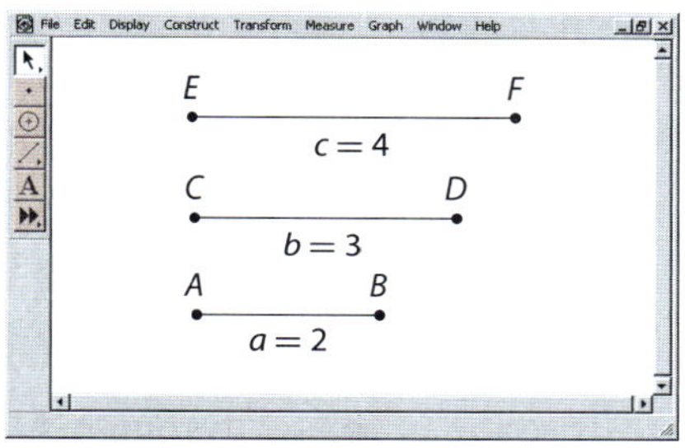

B Let $\overline{AB}$ be the base of the triangle. Place point *C* on top of point *B* and point *E* on top of point *A*.

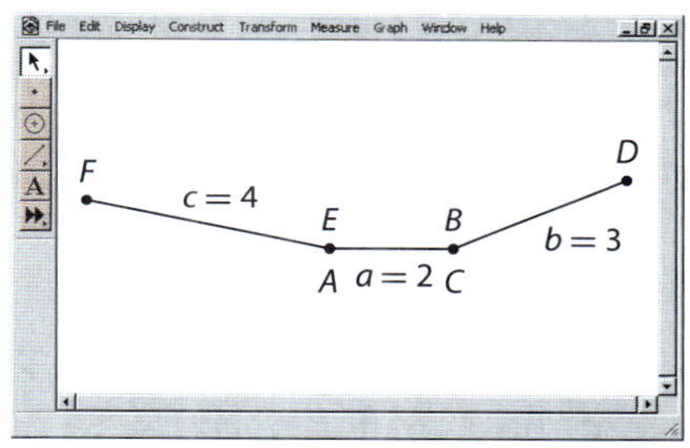

C Using the points *C* and *E* as fixed vertices, rotate points *F* and *D* to see if they will meet in a single point.

Note that the line segments form a triangle.

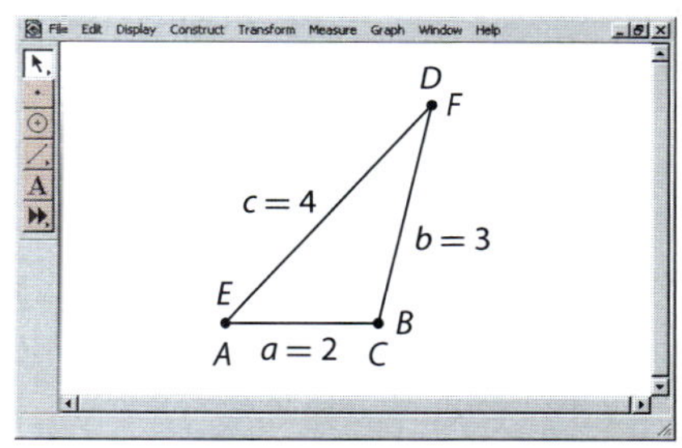

D Repeat **A** and **B**, but use a different segment as the base. Do the segments form a triangle? If so, is it the same as the original triangle?

____

E Use geometry software to draw a triangle with sides of length 2, 3, and 6 units, and one with sides of length 2, 3, and 5 units. Do the line segments form triangles? How does the sum of the lengths of the two shorter sides of each triangle compare to the length of the third side?

____

Animated Math
my.hrw.com

Reflect

1. **Conjecture** Do two segments of lengths *a* and *b* units and a longer segment of length *c* units form one triangle, more than one, or none?

____

EXPLORE ACTIVITY 2

Two Angles and Their Included Side

Use a ruler and a protractor to draw each triangle.

Triangle 1	Triangle 2
Angles: 30° and 80° Length of included side: 2 inches	Angles: 55° and 50° Length of included side: 1 inch

A Draw Triangle 1.

STEP 1 Use a ruler to draw a line that is 2 inches long. This will be the included side.

STEP 2 Place the center of the protractor on the left end of the 2-in. line. Then make a 30°-angle mark.

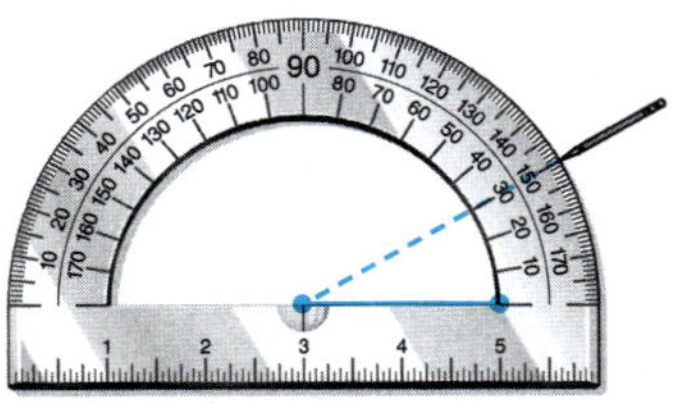

STEP 3 Draw a line connecting the left side of the 2-in. line and the 30°-angle mark. This will be the 30° angle.

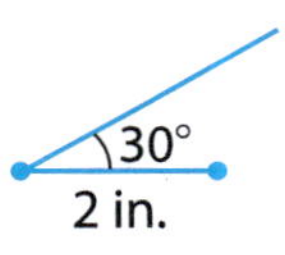

STEP 4 Repeat Step 2 on the right side of the triangle to construct the 80° angle.

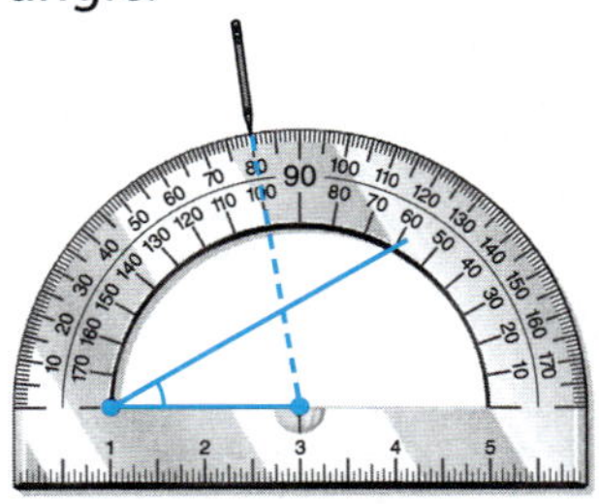

STEP 5 The side of the 80° angle and the side of the 30° angle will intersect. This is Triangle 1 with angles of 30° and 80° and an included side of 2 inches.

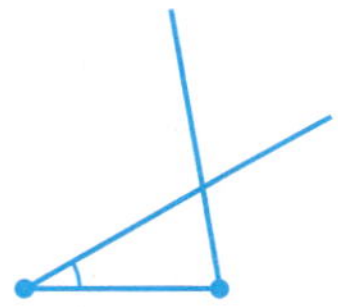

B Use the steps in A to draw Triangle 2.

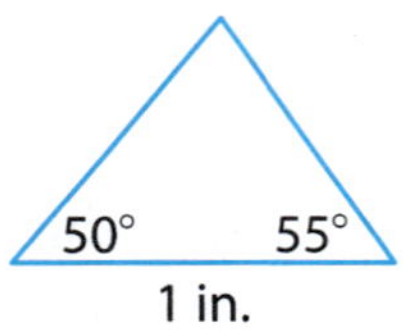

Reflect

2. **Conjecture** When you are given two angle measures and the length of the included side, do you get a unique triangle?

____

____

Name ____________ Class ____________ Date ____________

Guided Practice

Tell whether each figure creates the conditions to form a unique triangle, more than one triangle, or no triangle. (Explore Activities 1 and 2)

1. 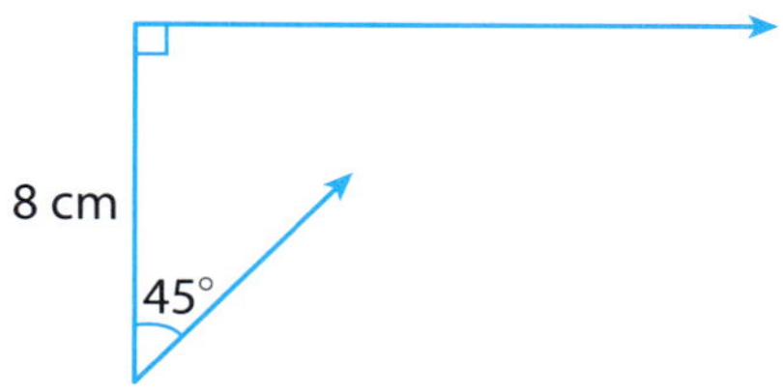

____

2. 

____

3. 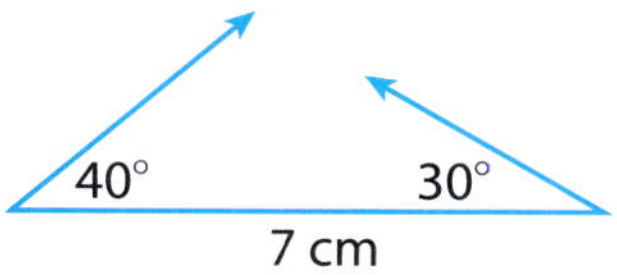

____

4. 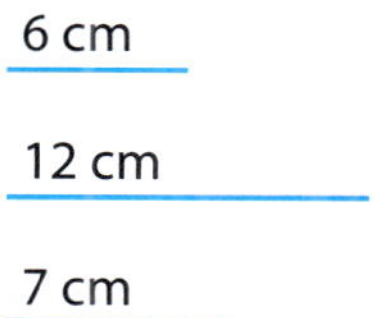

____

ESSENTIAL QUESTION CHECK-IN

5. Describe lengths of three segments that could **not** be used to form a triangle.

____

8.2 Independent Practice

6. On a separate piece of paper, try to draw a triangle with side lengths of 3 centimeters and 6 centimeters, and an included angle of 120°. Determine whether the given segments and angle produce a unique triangle, more than one triangle, or no triangle.

____

7. A landscape architect submitted a design for a triangle-shaped flower garden with side lengths of 21 feet, 37 feet, and 15 feet to a customer. Explain why the architect was not hired to create the flower garden.

____

____

8. **Make a Conjecture** The angles in an actual triangle-shaped traffic sign all have measures of 60°. The angles in a scale drawing of the sign all have measures of 60°. Explain how you can use this information to decide whether three given angle measures can be used to form a unique triangle or more than one triangle.

____

____

Work Area

H.O.T. FOCUS ON HIGHER ORDER THINKING

9. **Communicate Mathematical Ideas** The figure on the left shows a line segment 2 inches long forming a 45° angle with a dashed line whose length is not given. The figure on the right shows a compass set at a width of $1\frac{1}{2}$ inches with its point on the top end of the 2-inch segment. An arc is drawn intersecting the dashed line twice.

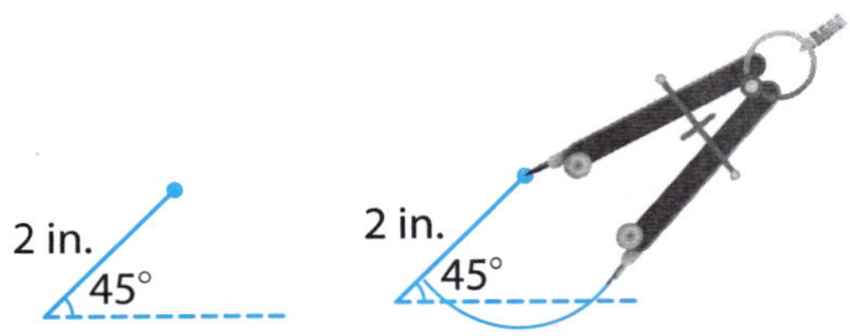

Explain how you can use this figure to decide whether two sides and an angle **not** included between them can be used to form a unique triangle, more than one triangle, or no triangle.

____

____

____

____

____

____

10. **Critical Thinking** Two sides of an isosceles triangle have lengths of 6 inches and 15 inches, respectively. Find the length of the third side. Explain your reasoning.

____

____

____

____

Activity 8.2

Draw a Triangle

INSTRUCTIONS

Part A: Two Angles Specified

STEP 1 Each member of your group should choose a different row of the table below. You will use the table to draw △*ABC* with two angles specified.

Triangle Number	Angle *A*	Angle *B*	Angle *C*	Sum of Angle Measures
1	45°	50°		
2	30°	90°		
3	25°	100°		

STEP 2 Using a ruler and protractor, draw and label angle *A* with your assigned angle measure on a sheet of paper or tracing paper. A sample is shown below.

STEP 3 Mark a separate point *B* on one side of angle *A*. Using a protractor, draw and label angle *B* with your assigned angle measure so that angles *A* and *B* form two angles of one triangle.

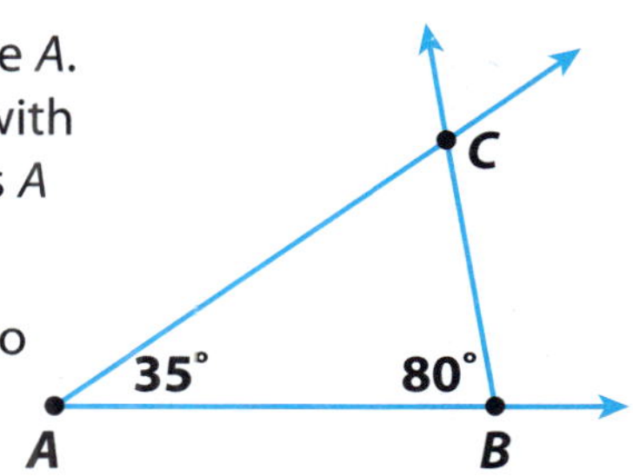

STEP 4 Extend the sides of your angles as needed to complete the triangle at point *C*. Label the point.

STEP 5 Measure angle *C* inside the triangle to the nearest degree, and work with your group to complete the remaining columns in your tables. What appears to be true about the sum of the angle measures for each triangle?

STEP 6 Compare the triangles drawn by your group with the triangles drawn by other groups. Does specifying two angles of a triangle determine a unique triangle? Explain.

INSTRUCTIONS

Part B: Two Angles and a Side Length Specified

STEP 1 Your teacher will assign your group a new $\triangle ABC$ and give you two of its angle measures. Record the information below.

Triangle Number	Angle *A*	Angle *B*	Side Length
			5 cm

STEP 2 Each of you will draw a triangle with these angle measures and one side that is 5 cm long. Make sure that $\overline{AB}$ is 5 cm long in one triangle, $\overline{AC}$ is 5 cm long in another, and $\overline{BC}$ is 5 cm long in the third.

STEP 3 Use a protractor and ruler to draw and label your $\triangle ABC$ on paper or tracing paper using the assigned angle measures and ensuring that the appropriate side is 5 cm in length. It might help to draw a copy of angle *B* on a separate piece of tracing paper to help guide you, as shown in blue in the example below, where $\overline{AC}$ is 5 cm long.

1) Draw angle *A*.
2) Draw point *C*.
3) Overlay a copy of angle *B* aligned with angle *A* and passing through point *C* as shown to locate point *B*.

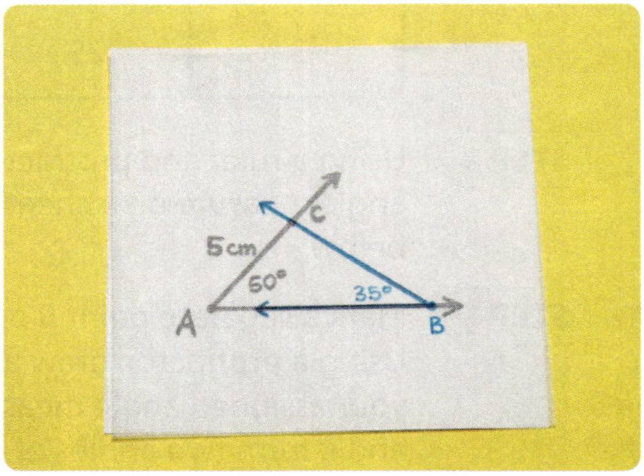

STEP 4 Compare your group's triangles. What do you observe? Did the measures you were given produce a unique triangle?

STEP 5 Find another group that was assigned the same triangle number as your group. Compare your triangles. Did your groups draw six unique triangles? Explain.

STEP 6 Discuss your results as a class. If you are given the measures of two specific angles of a triangle and the length of one specific side, does this determine a unique triangle? Explain.

LESSON

8.3 Cross Sections

7.4.8.3

Students will identify cross sections of three-dimensional figures.

ESSENTIAL QUESTION

How can you identify cross sections of three-dimensional figures?

EXPLORE ACTIVITY 1

Cross Sections of a Right Rectangular Prism

An **intersection** is a point or set of points common to two or more geometric figures. A **cross section** is the intersection of a three-dimensional figure and a plane. Imagine a plane slicing through the pyramid shown, or through a cone or a prism.

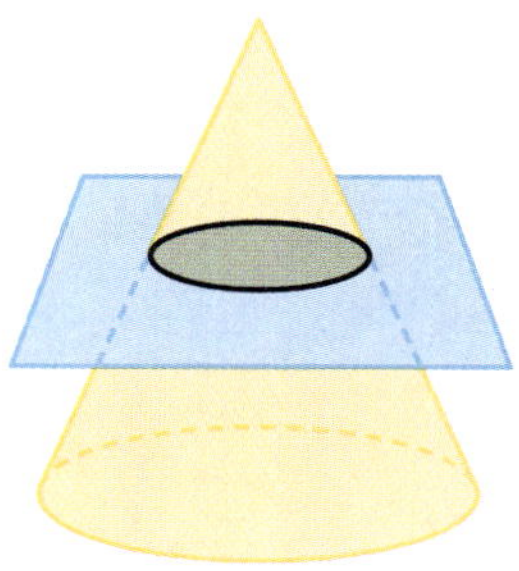

This figure shows the intersection of the cone and a plane. The cross section is a circle.

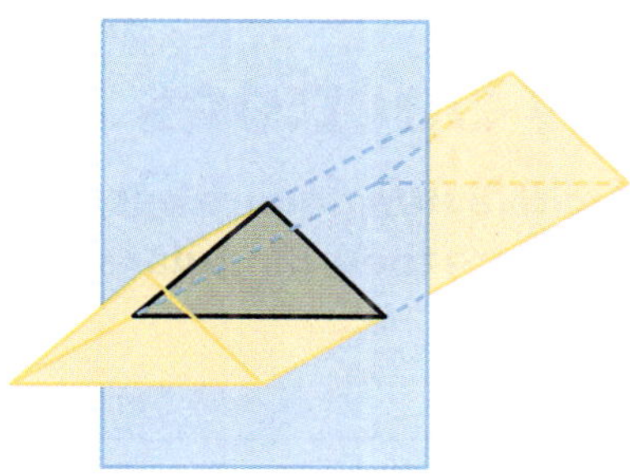

This figure shows the intersection of a triangular prism and a plane. The cross section is a triangle.

A three-dimensional figure can have several different cross sections depending on the position and the direction of the slice. For example, if the intersection of the plane and cone were vertical, the cross section would form a triangle.

Describe each cross section of the right rectangular prism with the name of its shape. (In a *right* prism, all the sides connecting the bases are rectangles at right angles with the base.)

A

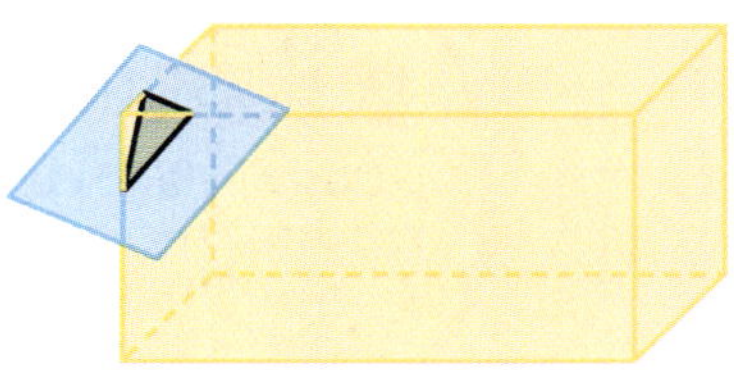

____

B

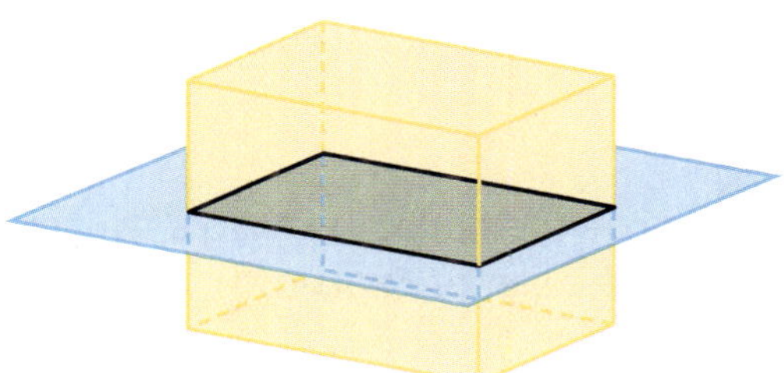

____

EXPLORE ACTIVITY 1 *(cont'd)*

C

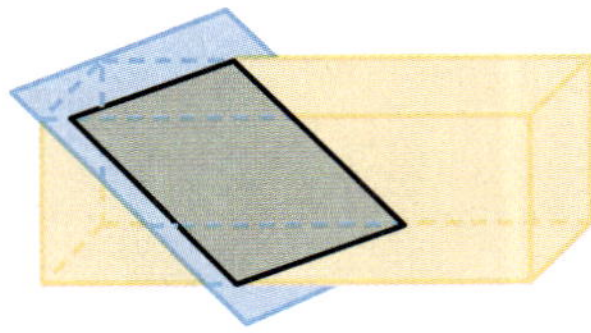

____

D

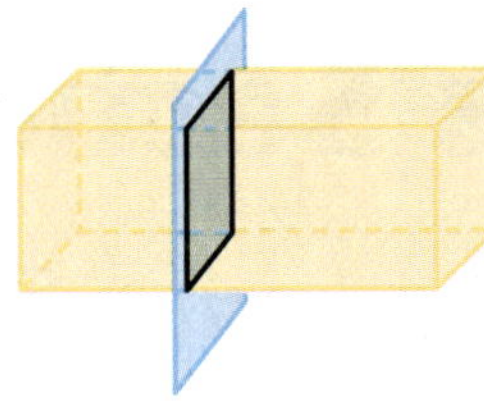

____

Reflect

1. **Conjecture** Is it possible to have a circular cross section in a right rectangular prism?

____

EXPLORE ACTIVITY 2

Describing Cross Sections

A right rectangular pyramid with a non-square base is shown. (In a *right* pyramid, the point where the triangular sides meet is centered over the base.)

A The shape of the base is a ______________________

The shape of each side is a ______________________

B Is it possible for a cross section of the pyramid to have each shape?

square	rectangle	triangle	circle	trapezoid
_____	_____	_____	_____	_____

C Sketch the cross sections of the right rectangular pyramid below.

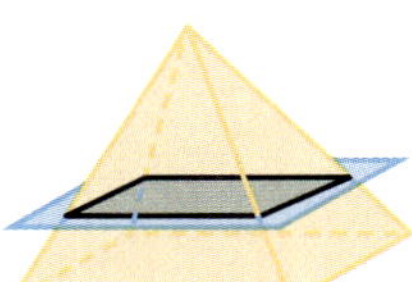

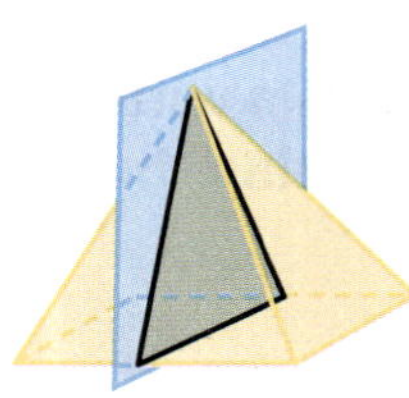

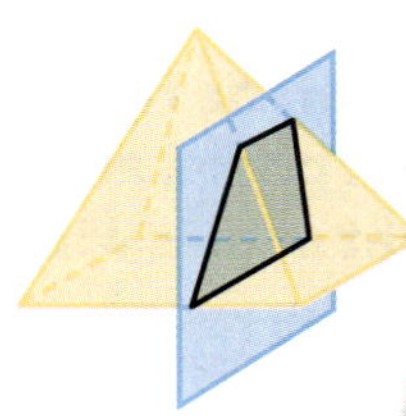

Math Talk
Mathematical Processes

Describe and compare the cross sections created when two horizontal planes intersect a right rectangular pyramid.

Reflect

2. **What If?** Suppose the figure in **B** had a square base. Would your answers in **B** be the same? Explain.

____

____

Name ______________________ Class ______________ Date ____________

Guided Practice

Describe each cross section.

1.

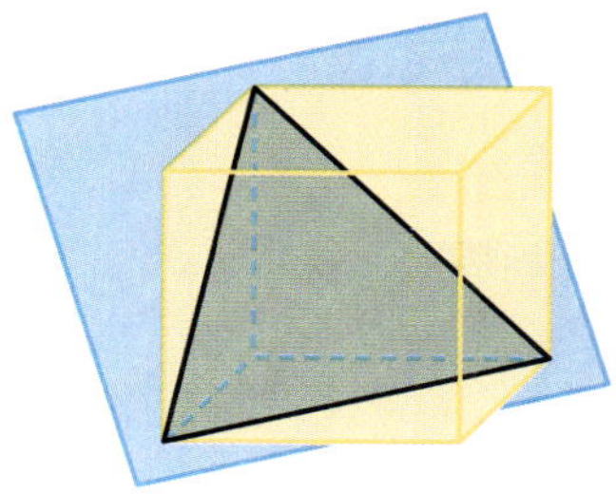

(Explore Activity 1)

____

2.

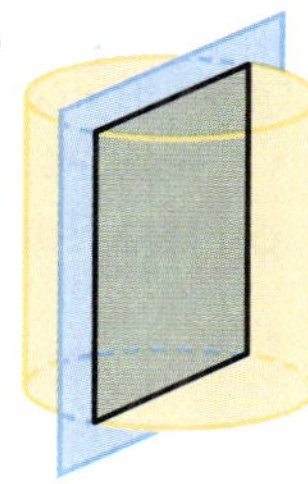

(Explore Activity 2)

____

3.

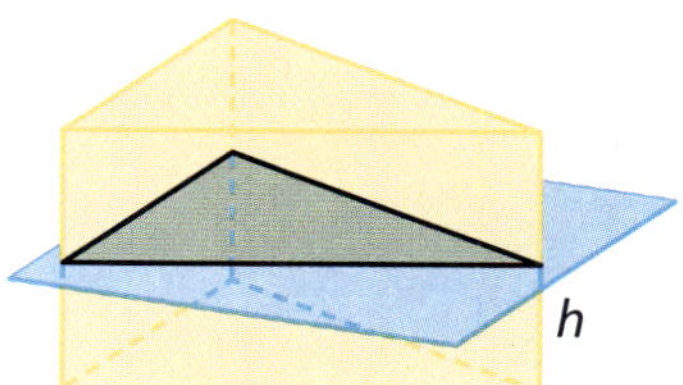

(Explore Activity 2)

____

4.

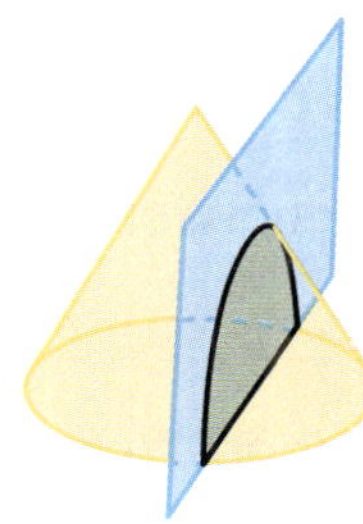

(Explore Activity 2)

____

ESSENTIAL QUESTION CHECK-IN

5. What is the first step in describing what figure results when a given plane intersects a given three-dimensional figure?

____

8.3 Independent Practice

Personal Math Trainer
Online Assessment and Intervention
my.hrw.com

6. Describe different ways in which a plane might intersect the cylinder, and the cross section that results.

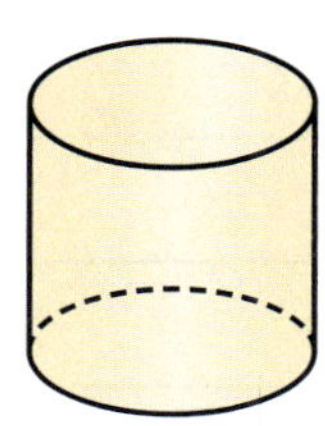

____

____

____

7. **Make a Conjecture** What cross sections might you see when a plane intersects a cone that you would **not** see when a plane intersects a pyramid or a prism? ______

Work Area

H.O.T. FOCUS ON HIGHER ORDER THINKING

8. **Critical Thinking** The two figures on the left below show that you can form a cross section of a cube that is a pentagon. Think of a plane cutting the cube at an angle in such a way as to slice through five of the cube's six faces. Draw dotted lines on the third cube to show how to form a cross section that is a hexagon.

9. **Analyze Relationships** A sphere has a radius of 12 inches. A horizontal plane passes through the center of the sphere.

 a. Describe the cross section formed by the plane and the sphere.

 ______

 b. Describe the cross sections formed as the plane intersects the interior of the sphere but moves away from the center.

 ______

 ______

 ______

10. **Communicate Mathematical Ideas** A right rectangular prism is intersected by a horizontal plane and a vertical plane. The cross section formed by the horizontal plane and the prism is a rectangle with dimensions 8 in. and 12 in. The cross section formed by the vertical plane and the prism is a rectangle with dimensions 5 in. and 8 in. Describe the faces of the prism, including their dimensions. Then find its volume.

 ______

 ______

11. **Represent Real-World Problems** Describe a real-world situation that could be represented by planes slicing a three-dimensional figure to form cross sections.

 ______

 ______

 ______

LESSON

8.4 Angle Relationships

7.4.8.4

Students will use angle relationships to solve problems.

ESSENTIAL QUESTION

How can you use angle relationships to solve problems?

EXPLORE ACTIVITY

Measuring Angles

It is useful to work with pairs of angles and to understand how pairs of angles relate to each other. **Congruent angles** are angles that have the same measure.

STEP 1 Using a ruler, draw a pair of intersecting lines. Label each angle from 1 to 4.

STEP 2 Use a protractor to help you complete the chart.

Angle	Measure of Angle
$m\angle 1$	
$m\angle 2$	
$m\angle 3$	
$m\angle 4$	
$m\angle 1 + m\angle 2$	
$m\angle 2 + m\angle 3$	
$m\angle 3 + m\angle 4$	
$m\angle 4 + m\angle 1$	

Reflect

1. **Make a Conjecture** Share your results with other students. Make a conjecture about pairs of angles that are opposite each other.

____

____

2. **Make a Conjecture** When two lines intersect to form four angles, what conjecture can you make about the pairs of angles that are next to each other?

____

____

Angle Pairs and One-Step Equations

Vertical angles are the opposite angles formed by two intersecting lines. Vertical angles are congruent because the angles have the same measure.

Adjacent angles are pairs of angles that share a *vertex* and one side but do not overlap. The **vertex** of an angle is the point where the sides meet.

Complementary angles are two angles whose measures have a sum of 90°.

Supplementary angles are two angles whose measures have a sum of 180°. You discovered in the Explore Activity that adjacent angles formed by two intersecting lines are supplementary.

Math On the Spot
my.hrw.com

EXAMPLE 1

Use the diagram.

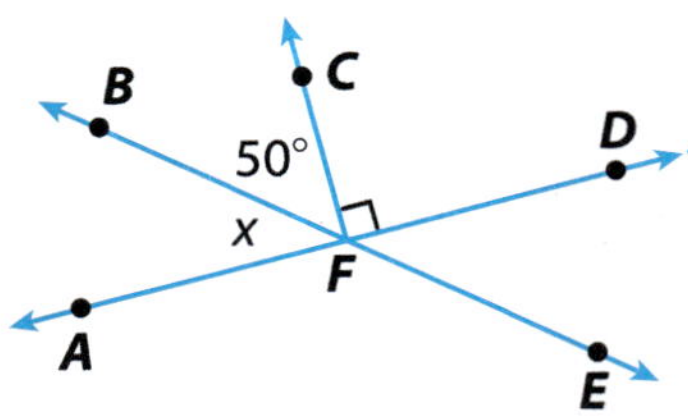

Recall that when multiple angles share a vertex, the angle is named by the vertex and one point on each side of the angle to avoid confusion. So the 50°-angle may be called ∠*BFC* or ∠*CFB*.

A **Name a pair of vertical angles.**

Vertical angles are opposite angles formed by intersecting lines.

∠*AFB* and ∠*DFE* are vertical angles.

B **Name a pair of adjacent angles.**

Adjacent angles share a vertex and a side but do not overlap.

∠*AFB* and ∠*BFD* are adjacent angles.

C **Name a pair of supplementary angles.**

Adjacent angles formed by intersecting lines are supplementary.

∠*AFB* and ∠*BFD* are supplementary angles.

D **Name two pairs of supplementary angles that include ∠*DFE*.**

Any angle that forms a line with ∠*DFE* is a supplementary angle to ∠*DFE*.

∠*DFE* and ∠*EFA* are supplementary angles, as are ∠*DFE* and ∠*DFB*.

Math Talk
Mathematical Processes
Are ∠*BFD* and ∠*AFE* vertical angles? Why or why not?

D **Find the measure of ∠*AFB*.**

Use the fact that ∠*AFB* and ∠*BFD* in the diagram are supplementary angles to find m∠*AFB*.

$$m\angle AFB + m\angle BFD = 180°$$ They are supplementary angles.

$$x + 140° = 180°$$ $m\angle BFD = 50° + 90° = 140°$

$$\underline{-140°} \quad \underline{-140°}$$ Subtract 140 from both sides.

$$x = 40°$$

The measure of ∠*AFB* is 40°.

Reflect

3. **Analyze Relationships** What is the relationship between ∠*AFB* and ∠*BFC*? Explain.

____

____

4. **Draw Conclusions** Are ∠*AFC* and ∠*BFC* adjacent angles? Why or why not?

____

____

YOUR TURN

Use the diagram.

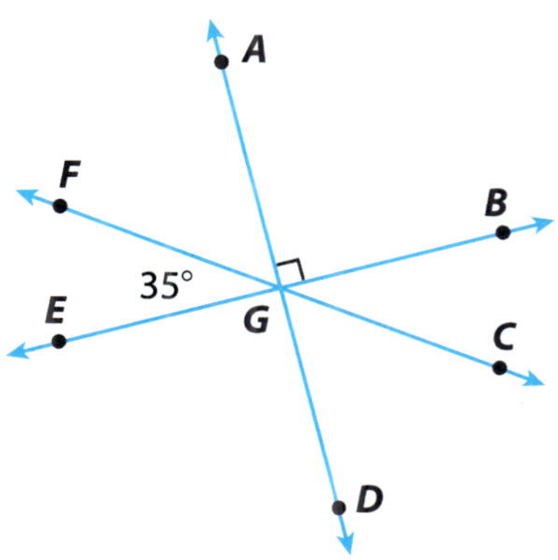

5. Name a pair of supplementary angles.

____

6. Name a pair of vertical angles.

____

7. Name a pair of adjacent angles.

____

8. Name a pair of complementary angles.

____

9. Find the measure of ∠*CGD*. _______________

My Notes

Personal Math Trainer
Online Assessment and Intervention
my.hrw.com

Math On the Spot
my.hrw.com

My Notes

Angle Pairs and Two-Step Equations

Sometimes solving an equation is only the first step in using an angle relationship to solve a problem.

EXAMPLE 2

A **Find the measure of $\angle EHF$.**

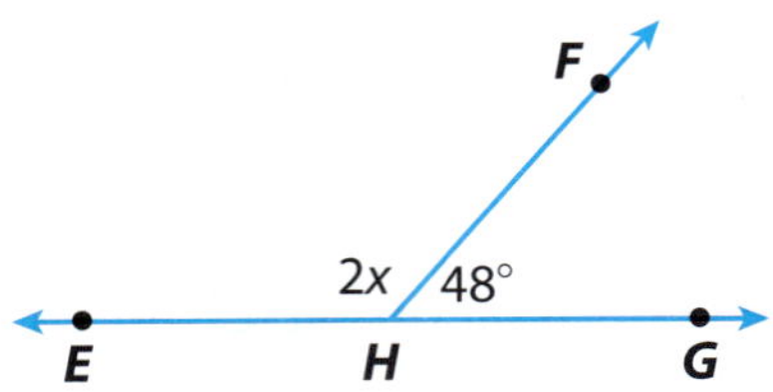

$\angle EHF$ and $\angle FHG$ form a straight line.

STEP 1 Identify the relationship between $\angle EHF$ and $\angle FHG$.

Since angles $\angle EHF$ and $\angle FHG$ form a straight line, the sum of the measures of the angles is 180°.

$\angle EHF$ and $\angle FHG$ are supplementary angles.

STEP 2 Write and solve an equation to find x.

$m\angle EHF + m\angle FHG = 180°$ — The sum of the measures of supplementary angles is 180°.

$$2x + 48° = 180°$$
$$\underline{-48°} \quad \underline{-48°}$$ — Subtract 48 from both sides.
$$2x = 132°$$ — Divide both sides by 2.
$$x = 66°$$

STEP 3 Find the measure of $\angle EHF$.

$m\angle EHF = 2x$

$= 2(66°)$ — Substitute 66° for x.

$= 132°$ — Multiply.

The measure of $\angle EHF$ is 132°.

Check Confirm that $\angle EHF$ and $\angle FHG$ are supplementary.

$$m\angle EHF + m\angle FHG \stackrel{?}{=} 180°$$
$$132° + 48° \stackrel{?}{=} 180°$$
$$180° = 180°$$

B **Find the measure of $\angle ZXY$.**

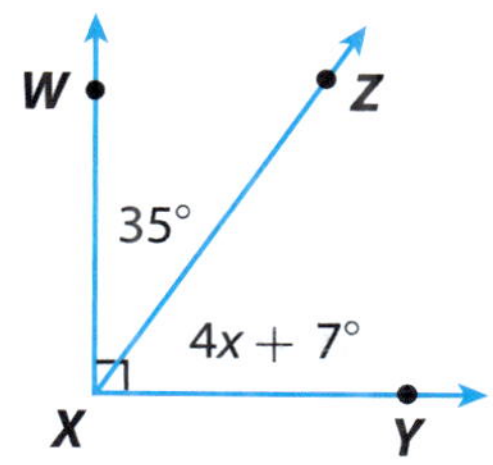

STEP 1 Identify the relationship between $\angle WXZ$ and $\angle ZXY$.

$\angle WXZ$ and $\angle ZXY$ are complementary angles.

STEP 2 Write and solve an equation to find x.

$m\angle WXZ + m\angle ZXY = 90°$	The sum of the measures of complementary angles is 90°.
$4x + 7° + 35° = 90°$	Substitute the values.
$4x + 42° = 90°$	Combine like terms.
$\underline{-42°} \quad \underline{-42°}$	Subtract 42 from both sides.
$4x = 48°$	Divide both sides by 4.
$x = 12°$	

STEP 3 Find the measure of $\angle ZXY$.

$m\angle ZXY = 4x + 7°$	
$= 4(12°) + 7°$	Substitute 12° for x.
$= 55°$	Use the Order of Operations.

The measure of $\angle ZXY$ is 55°.

Math Talk
Mathematical Processes
How can you check that your answer is reasonable?

YOUR TURN

10. Write and solve an equation to find the measure of $\angle JML$.

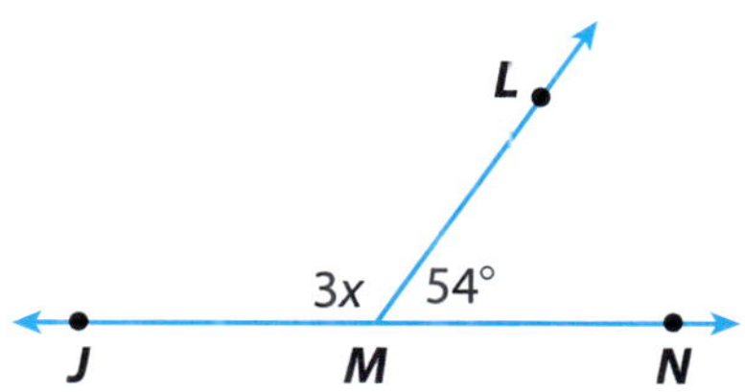

11. **Critique Reasoning** Cory says that to find $m\angle JML$ above, you can stop when you get to the solution step $3x = 126°$. Explain why this works.

____

____

____

Personal Math Trainer
Online Assessment and Intervention
my.hrw.com

Guided Practice

For 1–2, use the figure. (Example 1)

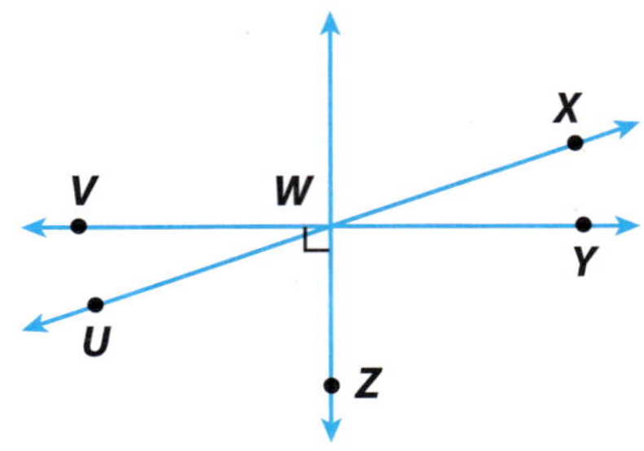

1. **Vocabulary** The sum of the measures of $\angle UWV$ and $\angle UWZ$ is 90°, so $\angle UWV$ and $\angle UWZ$ are

   ____________________ angles.

2. **Vocabulary** $\angle UWV$ and $\angle VWX$ share a vertex and one side. They do not overlap, so $\angle UWV$ and $\angle VWX$ are

   ____________________ angles.

For 3–4, use the figure.

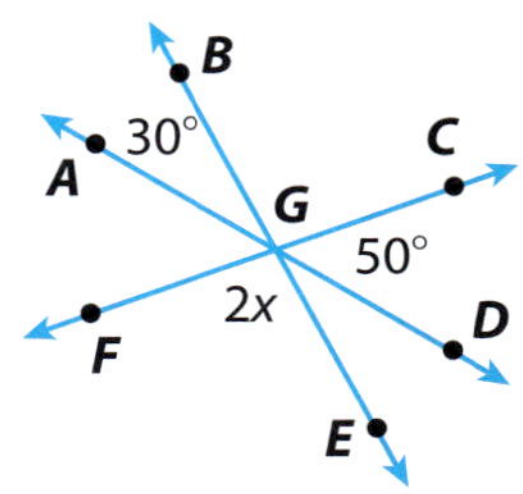

3. $\angle AGB$ and $\angle DGE$ are ____________________ angles,

   so $m\angle DGE =$ ____________________. (Example 1)

4. Find the measure of $\angle EGF$. (Example 2)

   $m\angle CGD + m\angle DGE + m\angle EGF = 180^\circ$

   ______ + ______ + ______ $= 180^\circ$

   ______ $+ 2x = 180^\circ$

   $2x =$ ________

   $m\angle EGF = 2x =$ ________

5. Find the value of x and the measure of $\angle MNQ$. (Example 2)

   $m\angle MNQ + m\angle QNP = 90^\circ$

   __________ + ______ $= 90^\circ$, so $3x +$ ______ $= 90^\circ$.

   Then $3x =$ ______, and $x =$ ______.

   $m\angle MNQ = 3x - 13^\circ = 3($______$) - 13^\circ$

   $=$ ______ $- 13^\circ$

   $=$ ______

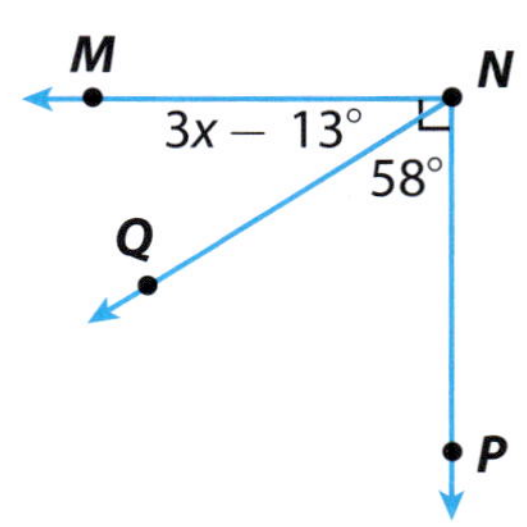

ESSENTIAL QUESTION CHECK-IN

6. Suppose that you know that $\angle T$ and $\angle S$ are supplementary, and that $m\angle T = 3(m\angle S)$. How can you find $m\angle T$?

   ____

   ____

Name ______________________ Class ______________ Date ______________

8.4 Independent Practice

Personal Math Trainer
Online Assessment and Intervention
my.hrw.com

For 7–11, use the figure.

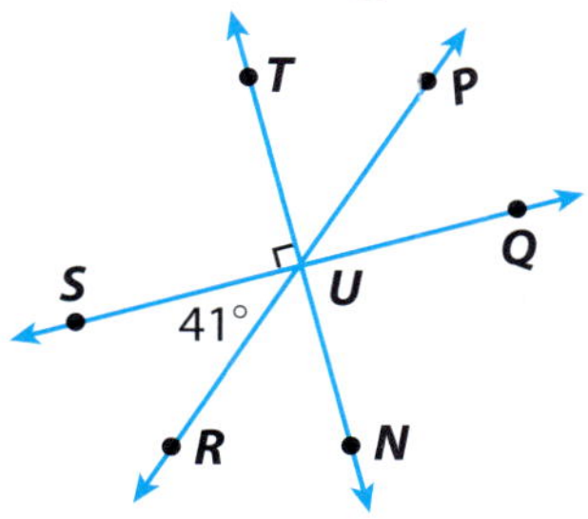

7. Name a pair of adjacent angles. Explain why they are adjacent.

____

____

____

8. Name a pair of acute vertical angles.

____

9. Name a pair of supplementary angles.

____

10. **Justify Reasoning** Find m∠*QUR*. Justify your answer.

____

____

____

____

____

11. **Draw Conclusions** Which is greater, m∠*TUR* or m∠*RUQ*? Explain.

____

____

____

____

____

For 12–13, use the figure. A bike path crosses a road as shown. Solve for each indicated angle measure or variable.

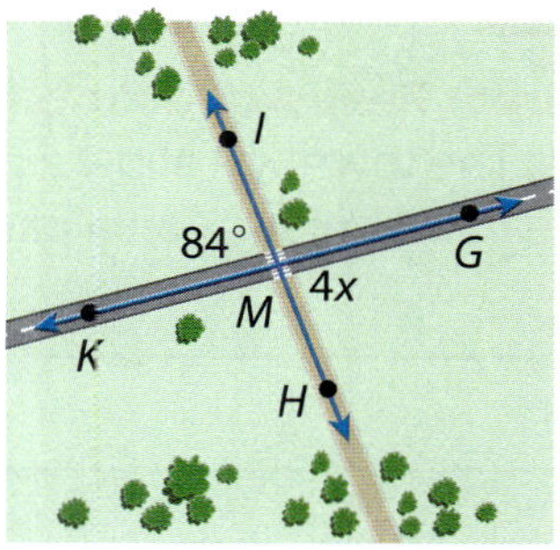

12. x ______________________

13. m∠*KMH* ______________________

For 14–16, use the figure. Solve for each indicated angle measure.

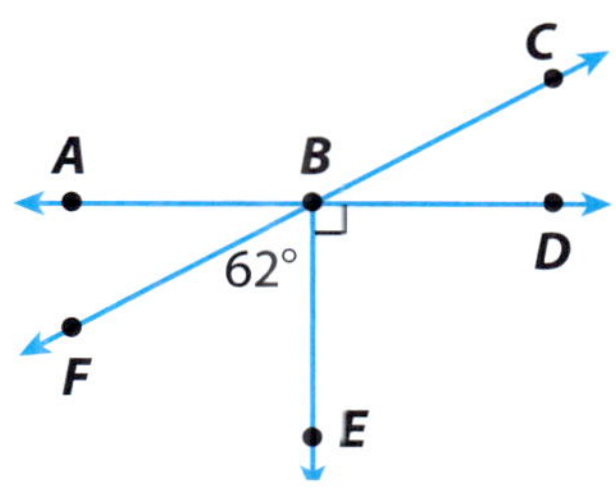

14. m∠*CBE* ______________________

15. m∠*ABF* ______________________

16. m∠*CBA* ______________________

17. The measure of ∠*A* is 4° greater than the measure of ∠*B*. The two angles are complementary. Find the measure of each angle.

____

18. The measure of ∠*D* is 5 times the measure of ∠*E*. The two angles are supplementary. Find the measure of each angle.

____

19. **Astronomy** Astronomers sometimes use angle measures divided into degrees, minutes, and seconds. One degree is equal to 60 minutes, and one minute is equal to 60 seconds. Suppose that $\angle J$ and $\angle K$ are complementary, and that the measure of $\angle J$ is 48 degrees, 26 minutes, 8 seconds. What is the measure of $\angle K$?

____

H.O.T. FOCUS ON HIGHER ORDER THINKING

20. **Represent Real-World Problems** The railroad tracks meet the road as shown. The town will allow a parking lot at angle K if the measure of angle K is greater than 38°. Can a parking lot be built at angle K? Why or why not?

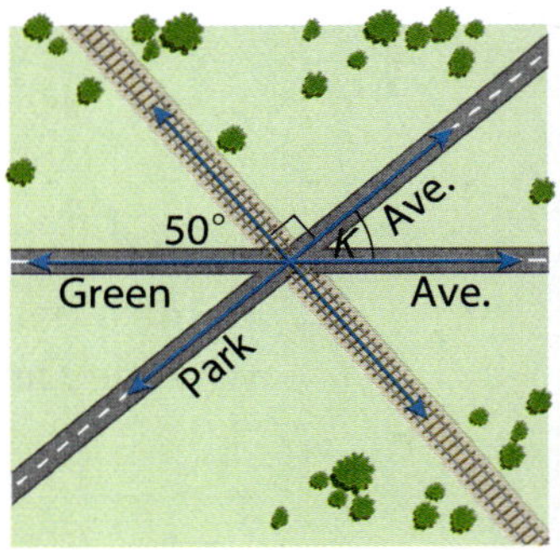

____

____

21. **Justify Reasoning** Kendra says that she can draw $\angle A$ and $\angle B$ so that m$\angle A$ is 119° and $\angle A$ and $\angle B$ are complementary angles. Do you agree or disagree? Explain your reasoning.

____

____

____

____

Work Area

22. **Draw Conclusions** If two angles are complementary, each angle is called a *complement* of the other. If two angles are supplementary, each angle is called a *supplement* of the other.

  a. Suppose m$\angle A = 77°$. What is the measure of a complement of a complement of $\angle A$? Explain.

____

____

____

  b. What conclusion can you draw about a complement of a complement of an angle? Explain.

____

____

____

____

____

MODULE QUIZ

Ready to Go On?

Personal Math Trainer
Online Assessment and Intervention
my.hrw.com

8.1 Similar Shapes and Scale Drawings

1. A house blueprint has a scale of 1 in. : 4 ft. The length and width of each room in the actual house are shown in the table. Complete the table by finding the length and width of each room on the blueprint.

	Living room	Kitchen	Office	Bedroom	Bedroom	Bathroom
Actual $\ell \times w$ (ft)	16×20	12×12	8×12	20×12	12×12	6×8
Blueprint $\ell \times w$ (in.)						

8.2 Geometric Drawings

2. Can a triangle be formed with the side lengths of 8 cm, 4 cm, and 12 cm? ______

3. A triangle has side lengths of 11 cm and 9 cm. Which could be the value of the third side, 20 cm or 15 cm? ______

8.3 Cross Sections

4. Name one possible cross section of a sphere. ______

5. Name at least two shapes that are cross sections of a cylinder.

______

8.4 Angle Relationships

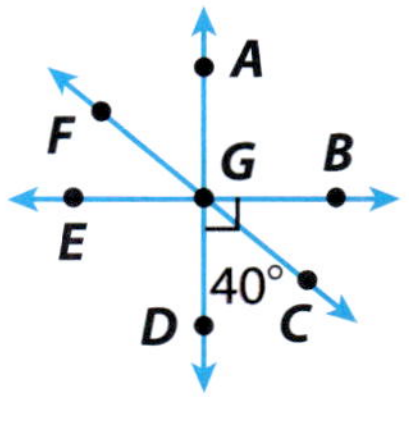

6. $\angle BGC$ and $\angle FGE$ are ______ angles, so $m\angle FGE =$ ______

7. Suppose you know that $\angle S$ and $\angle Y$ are complementary, and that $m\angle S = 2(m\angle Y) - 30°$. Find $m\angle Y$. ______

ESSENTIAL QUESTION

8. How can you model geometry figures to solve real-world problems?

______

______

MODULE 8 **MIXED REVIEW**

Assessment Readiness

Personal Math Trainer
Online Assessment and Intervention
my.hrw.com

Selected Response

1. Which number can you add to 15 to get a sum of 0?

Ⓐ −10 Ⓒ 0
Ⓑ −15 Ⓓ 15

2. Students are painting the backdrop for the school play. The backdrop is 15 feet wide and 10 feet high. Every 16 inches on the scale drawing represents 5 feet on the backdrop. What is the area of the scale drawing?

Ⓐ 150 in^2 Ⓒ 3,096
Ⓑ 6 in^2 Ⓓ 1,536 in^2

3. Two sides of a triangle measure 8 cm and 12 cm. Which of the following CANNOT be the measure of the third side?

Ⓐ 4 Ⓒ 8
Ⓑ 12 Ⓓ 16

4. A cross section is the intersection of a three-dimensional figure and a ___________.

Ⓐ point Ⓒ line
Ⓑ plane Ⓓ set

For 5–6, use the diagram.

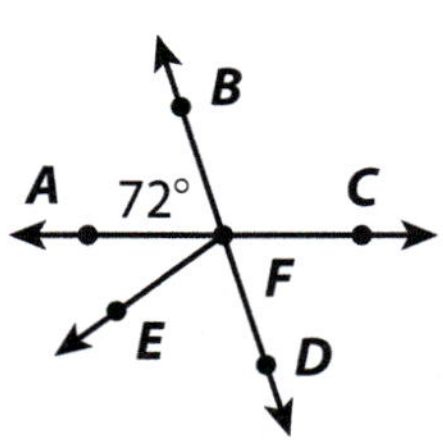

5. What is the measure of $\angle BFC$?

Ⓐ 18° Ⓒ 72°
Ⓑ 108° Ⓓ 144°

6. Which describes the relationship between $\angle BFA$ and $\angle CFD$?

Ⓐ adjacent angles
Ⓑ complementary angles
Ⓒ supplementary angles
Ⓓ vertical angles

7. All clothing is being marked down 15%. Which expression represents the new retail price?

Ⓐ $0.85x$ Ⓒ $1.85x$
Ⓑ $1.15x$ Ⓓ $0.15x$

Mini-Tasks

8. Ira built a model of the Great Pyramid in Egypt for a school project. The Great Pyramid has a square base with sides of length 756 feet. The height of the Great Pyramid is 481 feet. Ira made his model pyramid using a scale of 1 inch : 20 feet.

a. What is the length of each side of the base of Ira's pyramid?

____

b. What is the area of the base of Ira's pyramid?

____

c. What is the height of Ira's pyramid?

____

d. Ira built his model using cross sections that were cut parallel to the base. What shape was each cross section?

____

Circumference, Area, and Volume

MODULE 9

ESSENTIAL QUESTION

How can you apply geometry concepts to solve real-world problems?

Real-World Video

my.hrw.com

A 16-inch pizza has a diameter of 16 inches. You can use the diameter to find circumference and area of the pizza. You can also determine how much pizza in one slice of different sizes of pizzas.

GO DIGITAL
my.hrw.com

my.hrw.com
Go digital with your write-in student edition, accessible on any device.

Math On the Spot
Scan with your smart phone to jump directly to the online edition, video tutor, and more.

Animated Math
Interactively explore key concepts to see how math works.

Personal Math Trainer
Get immediate feedback and help as you work through practice sets.

Reading Start-Up

Vocabulary

Review Words

✔ area *(área)*
parallelogram *(paralelogramo)*
✔ perimeter *(perímetro)*
prism *(prisma)*
rectangle *(rectángulo)*
square *(cuadrado)*
trapezoid *(trapecio)*
triangle *(triángulo)*
✔ volume *(volumen)*

Preview Words

circumference *(circunferencia)*
composite figure *(figura compuesta)*
diameter *(diámetro)*
radius *(radio)*

Visualize Vocabulary

Use the ✔ words to complete the graphic. You will put one word in each oval. Then write examples of formulas in each rectangle.

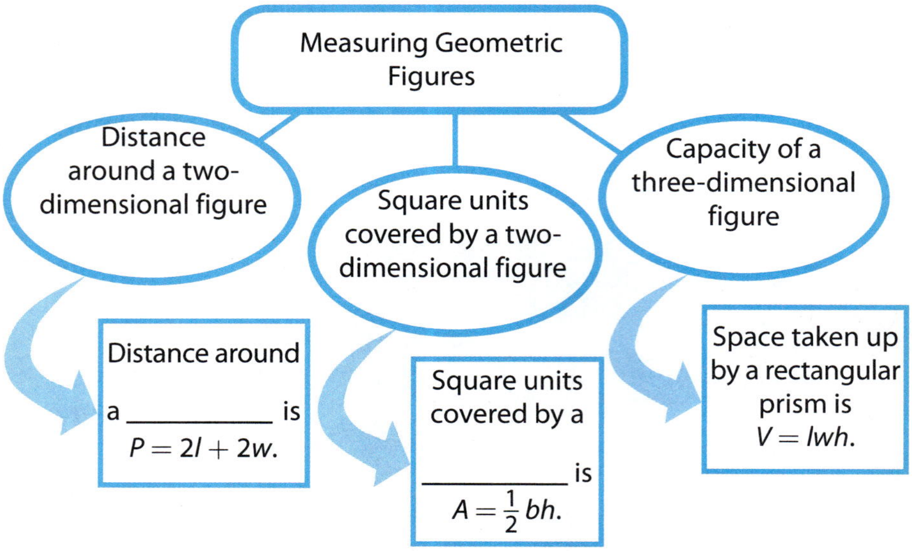

Understand Vocabulary

Match the term on the left to the correct expression on the right.

1. ____ circumference
2. ____ diameter
3. ____ radius

A. A line segment that passes through the center of a circle and has endpoints on the circle, or the length of that segment.

B. A line segment with one endpoint at the center of the circle and the other on the circle, or the length of that segment.

C. The distance around a circle.

Active Reading

Four-Corner Fold Before beginning the module, create a four-corner fold to help you organize what you learn. As you study this module, note important ideas, such as vocabulary, properties, and formulas, on the flaps. Use one flap each for circumference, area, surface area, and volume. You can use your FoldNote later to study for tests and complete assignments.

Are YOU Ready?

Complete these exercises to review skills you will need for this module.

Personal Math Trainer
my.hrw.com
Online Assessment and Intervention

Multiply with Fractions and Decimals

EXAMPLE

$$\begin{array}{r} 7.3 \\ \times\ 2.4 \\ \hline 292 \\ +\,146\ \ \\ \hline 17.52 \end{array}$$

Multiply as you would with whole numbers.
Count the total number of decimal places in the two factors.

Place the decimal point in the product so that there are the same number of digits after the decimal point.

Multiply.

1. $\begin{array}{r} 4.16 \\ \times\ 13 \\ \hline \end{array}$ ______

2. $\begin{array}{r} 6.47 \\ \times\ 0.4 \\ \hline \end{array}$ ______

3. $\begin{array}{r} 7.05 \\ \times\ 9.4 \\ \hline \end{array}$ ______

4. $\begin{array}{r} 25.6 \\ \times\ 0.49 \\ \hline \end{array}$ ______

Area of Squares, Rectangles, and Triangles

EXAMPLE

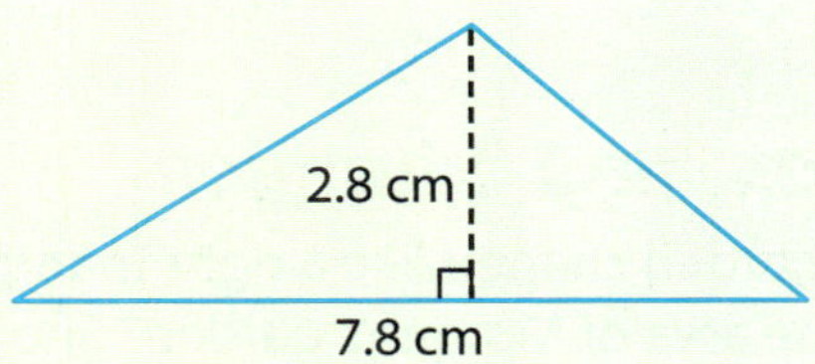

$A = \frac{1}{2}bh$ Use the formula for area of a triangle.

$= \frac{1}{2}(7.8)(2.8)$ Substitute for each variable.

$= 10.92\ \text{cm}^2$ Multiply.

Find the area of each figure.

5. triangle with base 14 in. and height 10 in. ______

6. square with sides of 3.5 ft ______

7. rectangle with length $8\frac{1}{2}$ in. and width 6 in. ______

8. triangle with base 12.5 m and height 2.4 m ______

Are YOU Ready? *(cont'd)*

Complete these exercises to review skills you will need for this module.

Multiply with Fractions and Decimals

9. Jon's car gets 35.5 miles per gallon in town. He used 0.3 gallon to drive to a meeting in town. How many miles did Jon drive?

10. Abby earns $9.95 per hour doing landscape work. She worked 8.5 hours last week. How much did she earn? Explain.

Area of Squares, Rectangles, and Triangles

11. In a corner of his yard, Morgan has a garden shaped like a right triangle. The garden has the dimensions shown. What is the area of Morgan's garden? Show your work.

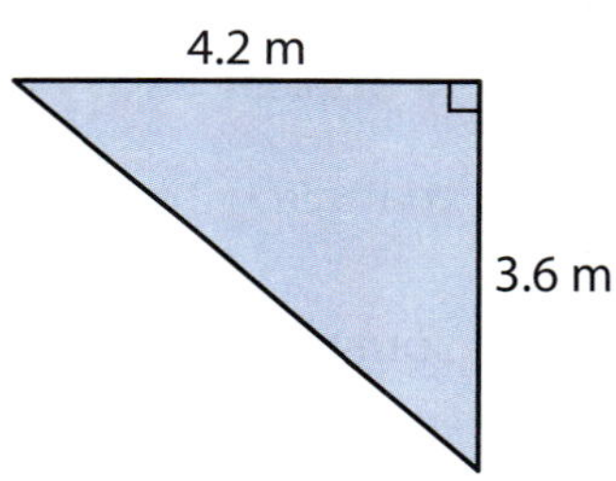

12. A rectangular sandbox is $10\frac{1}{2}$ feet long and 4 feet wide. What is the area of the sandbox? Show your work.

LESSON
9.1 Circumference

7.4.9.1

Students will find and use the circumference of a circle.

ESSENTIAL QUESTION

How do you find and use the circumference of a circle?

EXPLORE ACTIVITY

Exploring Circumference

A circle is a set of points in a plane that are a fixed distance from the center.

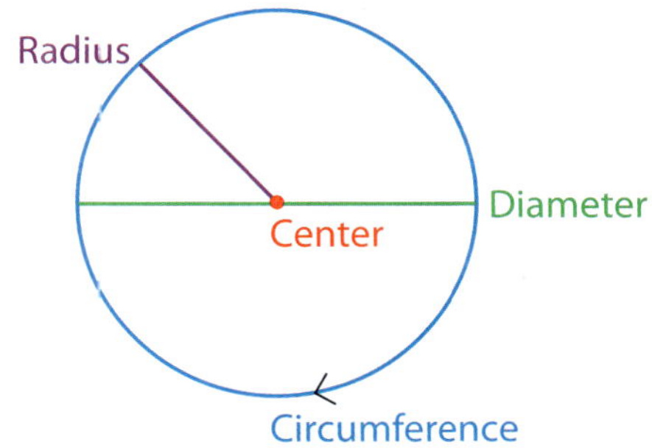

A **radius** is a line segment with one endpoint at the center of the circle and the other endpoint on the circle. The length of a radius is called the radius of the circle.

A **diameter** of a circle is a line segment that passes through the center of the circle and whose endpoints lie on the circle. The length of the diameter is twice the length of the radius. The length of a diameter is called the diameter of the circle.

The **circumference** of a circle is the distance around the circle.

A **Use a measuring tape to find the circumference of five circular objects. Then measure the distance across each item to find its diameter. Record the measurements of each object in the table.**

Object	Circumference C	Diameter d	$\frac{C}{d}$

B **Divide the circumference of each object by its diameter. Record your answer, rounded to the nearest hundredth, in the table above.**

Reflect

1. **Make a Conjecture** Describe what you notice about the ratio $\frac{C}{d}$ in your table. Does the relationship between the circumference and diameter of a circle appear to be proportional? Explain.

____

____

Math On the Spot
my.hrw.com

Finding Circumference

The ratio of the circumference to the diameter $\frac{C}{d}$ is the same for all circles. This ratio is called π or *pi*, and you can approximate it as 3.14 or as $\frac{22}{7}$. You can use π to find a formula for circumference.

For any circle, $\frac{C}{d} = \pi$. Solve the equation for C to give an equation for the circumference of a circle in terms of the diameter.

$\frac{C}{d} = \pi$ — The ratio of the circumference to the diameter is π.

$\frac{C}{d} \times d = \pi \times d$ — Multiply both sides by d.

$C = \pi d$ — Simplify.

The diameter of a circle is twice the radius. You can use the equation $C = \pi d$ to find a formula for the circumference C in terms of the radius r.

$C = \pi d = \pi(2r) = 2\pi r$

The two equivalent formulas for circumference are $C = \pi d$ and $C = 2\pi r$. These are proportional relationships. The constants of proportionality are π and 2π.

EXAMPLE 1 Real World

An irrigation sprinkler waters a circular region with a radius of 14 feet. Find the circumference of the region watered by the sprinkler. Use $\frac{22}{7}$ for π.

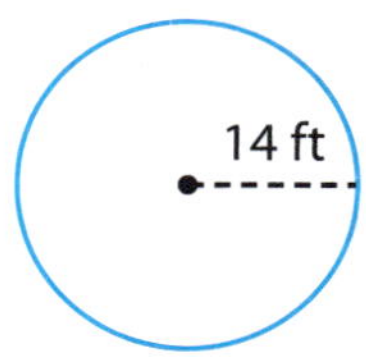

Use the formula.

$C = 2\pi r$ — The radius is 14 feet.

$C = 2\pi(14)$ — Substitute 14 for r.

$C \approx 2\left(\frac{22}{7}\right)(14)$ — Substitute $\frac{22}{7}$ for π.

$C \approx 88$ — Multiply.

The circumference of the region watered by the sprinkler is about 88 feet.

Reflect

2. **Analyze Relationships** When is it logical to use $\frac{22}{7}$ instead of 3.14 for π?

____

Personal Math Trainer
Online Assessment and Intervention
my.hrw.com

YOUR TURN

3. Find the circumference of the circle to the nearest hundredth.

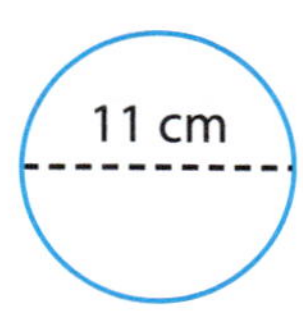

____

Using Circumference

Given the circumference of a circle, you can use the appropriate circumference formula to find the radius or the diameter of the circle. You can use that information to solve problems.

Math On the Spot
my.hrw.com

EXAMPLE 2 Real World

A circular pond has a circumference of 628 feet. A model boat is moving directly across the pond, along a radius, at a rate of 5 feet per second. How long does it take the boat to get from the edge of the pond to the center?

STEP 1 Find the radius of the pond.

$C = 2\pi r$ Use the circumference formula.

$628 \approx 2(3.14)r$ Substitute for the circumference and for π.

$\frac{628}{6.28} \approx \frac{6.28r}{6.28}$ Divide both sides by 6.28.

$100 \approx r$ Simplify.

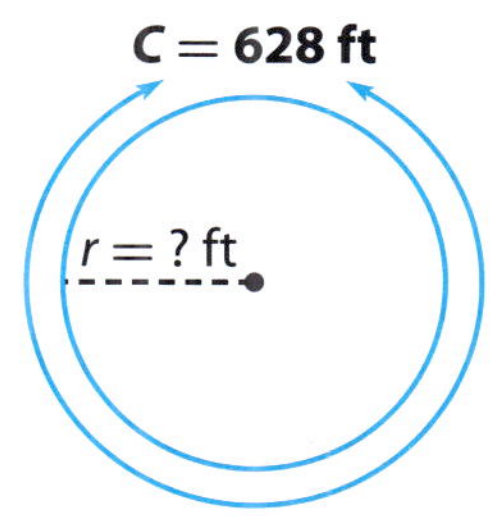

The radius is about 100 feet.

STEP 2 Find the time it takes the boat to get from the edge of the pond to the center along the radius. Divide the radius of the pond by the speed of the model boat.

$100 \div 5 = 20$

It takes the boat about 20 seconds to get to the center of the pond.

My Notes

Reflect

4. **Analyze Relationships** Dante checks the answer to Step 1 by multiplying it by 6 and comparing it with the given circumference. Explain why Dante's estimation method works. Use it to check Step 1.

____

5. **What If?** Suppose the model boat were traveling at a rate of 4 feet per second. How long would it take the model boat to get from the edge of the pond to the center? ____________________

Math Talk
Mathematical Processes
Would it be reasonable to solve Your Turn 6 using $\frac{22}{7}$ for π? Explain.

YOUR TURN

6. A circular garden has a circumference of 44 yards. Lars is digging a straight line along a diameter of the garden at a rate of 7 yards per hour. How many hours will it take him to dig across the garden?

____

Personal Math Trainer
Online Assessment and Intervention
my.hrw.com

Guided Practice

Find the circumference of each circle. (Example 1)

1. $C = \pi d$

$C \approx$ ____________

$C \approx$ ____________ inches

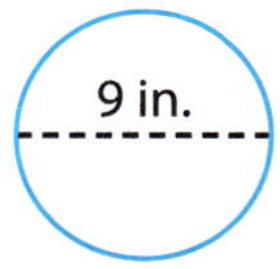

2. $C = 2\pi r$

$C \approx 2\left(\frac{22}{7}\right)$ (____________)

$C \approx$ ____________ cm

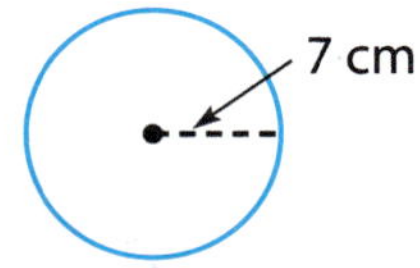

Find the circumference of each circle. Use 3.14 or $\frac{22}{7}$ for π. Round to the nearest hundredth, if necessary. (Example 1)

3.

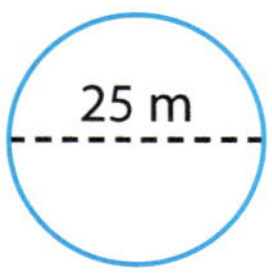

____

4.

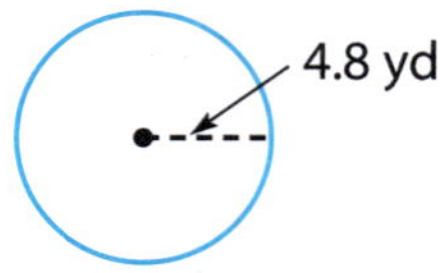

____

5.

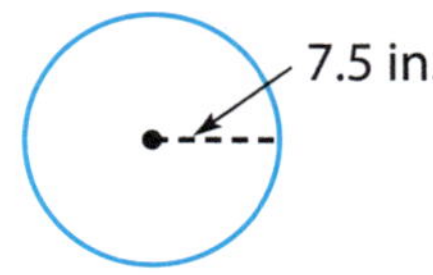

____

6. A round swimming pool has a circumference of 66 feet. Carlos wants to buy a rope to put across the diameter of the pool. The rope costs \$0.45 per foot, and Carlos needs 4 feet more than the diameter of the pool. How much will Carlos pay for the rope? (Example 2)

Find the diameter.

$C = \pi d$

________ $\approx 3.14d$

$\frac{\square}{3.14} \approx \frac{3.14d}{3.14}$

________ $\approx d$

Find the cost.

Carlos needs ____________ feet of rope.

________ $\times$ \$0.45 = ________

Carlos will pay ________ for the rope.

Find each missing measurement to the nearest hundredth. Use 3.14 for π. (Examples 1 and 2)

7. $r =$ ____________

$d =$ ____________

$C = \pi$ yd

8. $r \approx$ ____________

$d \approx$ ____________

$C = 78.8$ ft

9. $r \approx$ ____________

$d \approx 3.4$ in.

$C =$ ____________

ESSENTIAL QUESTION CHECK-IN

10. Norah knows that the diameter of a circle is 13 meters. How would you tell her to find the circumference?

____

____

Name ______________________ Class ______________ Date ______________

9.1 Independent Practice

Personal Math Trainer
my.hrw.com
Online Assessment and Intervention

For 11–13, find the circumference of each circle. Use 3.14 or $\frac{22}{7}$ for π. Round to the nearest hundredth, if necessary.

11.

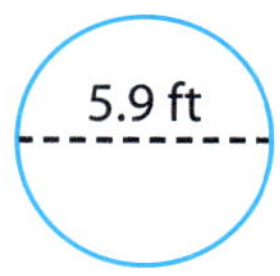

____

12.

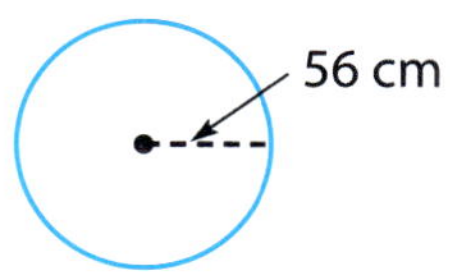

____

13.

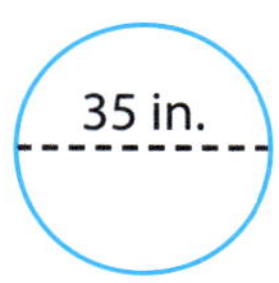

____

14. In Exercises 11–13, for which problems did you use $\frac{22}{7}$ for π? Explain your choice.

____

15. A circular fountain has a radius of 9.4 feet. Find its diameter and circumference to the nearest tenth.

____

16. Find the radius and circumference of a CD with a diameter of 4.75 inches.

____

17. A dartboard has a diameter of 18 inches. What are its radius and circumference?

____

18. **Multistep** Randy's circular garden has a radius of 1.5 feet. He wants to enclose the garden with edging that costs \$0.75 per foot. About how much will the edging cost? Explain.

____

19. **Represent Real-World Problems** The Ferris wheel shown makes 12 revolutions per ride. How far would someone travel during one ride?

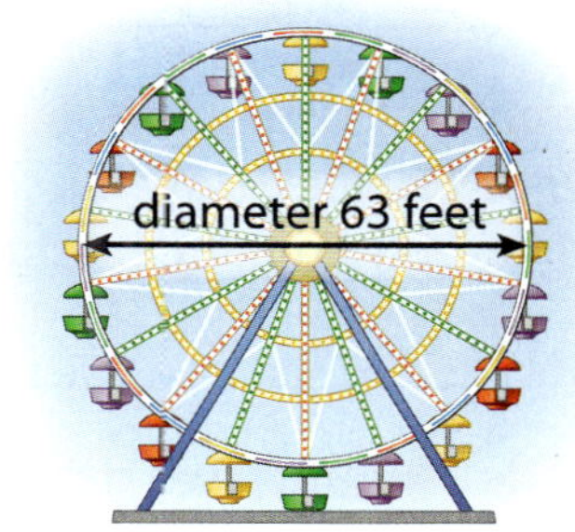

____

20. The diameter of a bicycle wheel is 2 feet. About how many revolutions does the wheel make to travel 2 kilometers? Explain. Hint: 1 km $\approx$ 3,280 ft

____

21. **Multistep** A map of a public park shows a circular pond. There is a bridge along a diameter of the pond that is 0.25 mi long. You walk across the bridge, while your friend walks halfway around the pond to meet you at the other side of the bridge. How much farther does your friend walk?

____

22. **Architecture** The Capitol Rotunda connects the House and the Senate sides of the U.S. Capitol. Complete the table. Round your answers to the nearest foot.

Capitol Rotunda Dimensions	
Height	180 ft
Circumference	301.5 ft
Radius	
Diameter	

H.O.T. FOCUS ON HIGHER ORDER THINKING

Work Area

23. **Multistep** A museum groundskeeper is creating a semicircular statuary garden with a diameter of 30 feet. There will be a fence around the garden. The fencing costs $9.25 per linear foot. About how much will the fencing cost altogether?

____

24. **Critical Thinking** Sam is placing rope lights around the edge of a circular patio with a diameter of 18 feet. The lights come in lengths of 54 inches. How many strands of lights does he need to surround the patio edge?

____

25. **Represent Real-World Problems** A circular path 2 feet wide has an inner diameter of 150 feet. How much farther is it around the outer edge of the path than around the inner edge?

____

26. **Critique Reasoning** Two gears on a bicycle have the shape of circles. Gear 1 has a diameter of 4 inches, and gear 2 has a diameter of 2 inches. Justin says that the circumference of gear 1 is 2 inches more than the circumference of gear 2. Do you agree? Explain your answer using proportional reasoning.

____

____

____

____

27. **Persevere in Problem Solving** Consider two circular swimming pools. Pool A has a radius of 12 feet, and Pool B has a diameter of 7.5 meters. Which pool has a greater circumference? How much greater? Justify your answers. (Use 1 foot $\approx$ 0.305 meter.)

____

____

____

____

LESSON

9.2 Area of Circles

7.4.9.2

Students will find the area of a circle.

ESSENTIAL QUESTION

How do you find the area of a circle?

EXPLORE ACTIVITY 1

Exploring Area of Circles

You can use what you know about circles and π to help find the formula for the area of a circle.

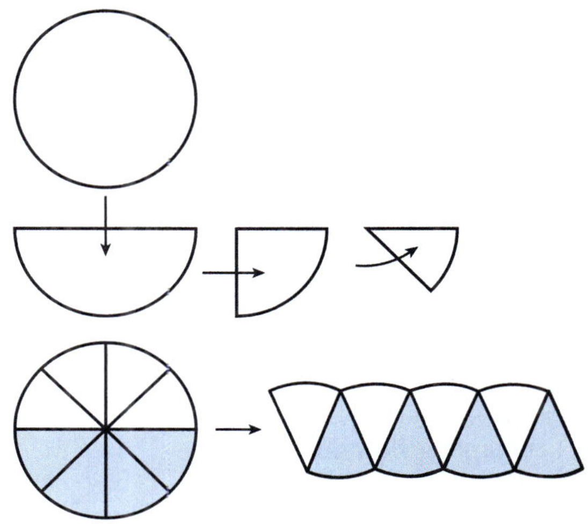

STEP 1 Use a compass to draw a circle and cut it out.

STEP 2 Fold the circle three times as shown to get equal wedges.

STEP 3 Unfold and shade one-half of the circle.

STEP 4 Cut out the wedges, and fit the pieces together to form a figure that looks like a parallelogram.

The base and height of the parallelogram relate to the parts of the circle.

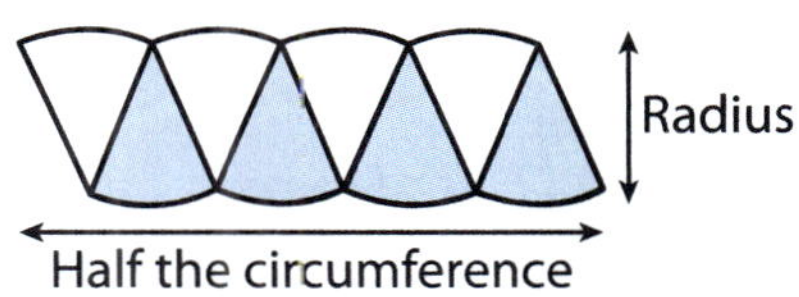

base $b = \frac{\square}{\square}$ the circumference of the circle, or ______

height $h =$ the __________ of the circle, or ______

Recall that the area A of a parallelogram is given by the formula $A = bh$. To find the area of the circle, substitute for b and h in the area formula.

$A = bh$

$A = \square\, h$ Substitute for *b*.

$A = \pi r \square$ Substitute for *h*.

$A = \pi \square$ Write using an exponent.

Reflect

1. How can you make the wedges look more like a parallelogram?

____

____

Math On the Spot
my.hrw.com

Finding the Area of a Circle

Area of a Circle

The area of a circle is equal to π times the radius squared.

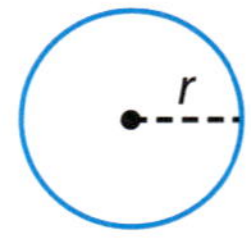

$$A = \pi r^2$$

Remember that area is given in square units.

EXAMPLE 1 Real World

A biscuit recipe calls for the dough to be rolled out and circles to be cut from the dough. The biscuit cutter has a radius of 4 cm. Find the area of the top of the biscuit once it is cut. Use 3.14 for π.

$A = \pi r^2$	Use the formula.
$A = \pi(4)^2$	Substitute. Use 4 for r.
$A \approx 3.14 \times 4^2$	Substitute. Use 3.14 for π.
$A \approx 3.14 \times 16$	Evaluate the power.
$A \approx 50.24$	Multiply.

The area of the biscuit is about 50.24 cm^2.

Math Talk
Mathematical Processes

If the radius increases by 1 centimeter, how does the area of the top of the biscuit change?

Reflect

2. Compare finding the area of a circle when given the radius with finding the area when given the diameter.

____

____

____

3. Why do you evaluate the power in the equation before multiplying by π?

____

____

Personal Math Trainer
Online Assessment and Intervention
my.hrw.com

YOUR TURN

4. A circular pool has a radius of 10 feet. What is the area of the *surface* of the water in the pool? Use 3.14 for π. ______________

EXPLORE ACTIVITY 2

Finding the Relationship between Circumference and Area

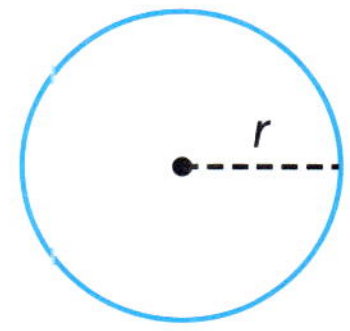

You can use what you know about circumference and area of circles to find a relationship between them.

Find the relationship between the circumference and area of a circle.

Start with a circle that has radius r.

Solve the equation $C = 2\pi r$ for r.

$$r = \frac{\square}{\square}$$

Substitute your expression for r in the formula for area of a circle.

$$A = \pi\left(\frac{\square}{\square}\right)^2$$

Remember: Because the exponent is outside the parentheses, you must apply it to the numerator and to each factor of the denominator.

Square the term in the parentheses.

$$A = \pi\left(\frac{\square^2}{\square^2 \cdot \square^2}\right)$$

Evaluate the power.

$$A = \frac{\square \cdot \square^2}{\square \cdot \square^2}$$

Simplify.

$$A = \frac{\square^2}{\square \cdot \square}$$

Solve for C^2.

$$C^2 = 4\,\square\,\square$$

The circumference of the circle squared is equal to

________________________________.

EXPLORE ACTIVITY 2 *(cont'd)*

Reflect

5. Does this formula work for a circle with a radius of 3 inches? Show your work.

Guided Practice

Find the area of each circle. Round to the nearest tenth if necessary. Use 3.14 for π. (Explore Activity 1)

1. 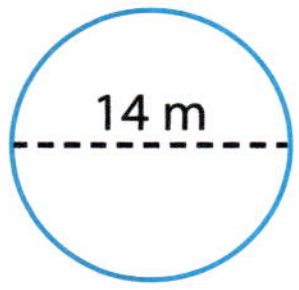

____

2. 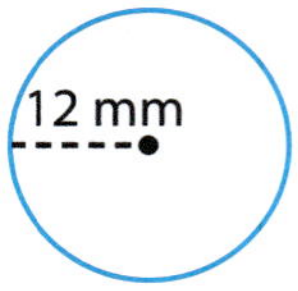

____

3. 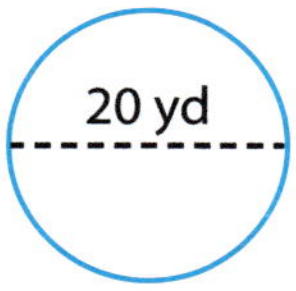

____

Solve. Use 3.14 for π. (Example 1)

4. A clock face has a radius of 8 inches. What is the area of the clock face? Round your answer to the nearest hundredth. __________

5. A DVD has a diameter of 12 centimeters. What is the area of the DVD? Round your answer to the nearest hundredth. __________

6. A company makes steel lids that have a diameter of 13 inches. What is the area of each lid? Round your answer to the nearest hundredth. __________

Find the area of each circle. Give your answers in terms of π. (Explore Activity 2)

7. $C = 4\pi$

$A =$ __________

8. $C = 12\pi$

$A =$ __________

9. $C = \frac{\pi}{2}$

$A =$ __________

10. A circular pen has an area of 64π square yards. What is the circumference of the pen? Give your answer in terms of π. (Explore Activity 2) __________

ESSENTIAL QUESTION CHECK-IN

11. What is the formula for the area A of a circle in terms of the radius r? __________

Name ______ Class ______ Date ______

9.2 Independent Practice

Personal Math Trainer
my.hrw.com
Online Assessment and Intervention

12. The most popular pizza at Pavone's Pizza is the 10-inch personal pizza with one topping. What is the area of a pizza with a diameter of 10 inches? Round your answer to the nearest hundredth.

______

13. A hubcap has a radius of 16 centimeters. What is the area of the hubcap? Round your answer to the nearest hundredth.

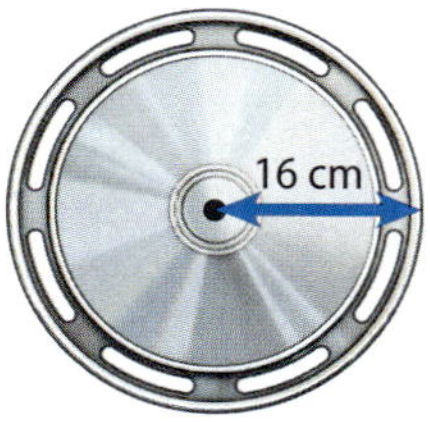

______

14. A stained glass window is shaped like a semicircle. The bottom edge of the window is 36 inches long. What is the area of the stained glass window? Round your answer to the nearest hundredth.

______

15. **Analyze Relationships** The point (3, 0) lies on a circle with the center at the origin. What is the area of the circle to the nearest hundredth?

______

16. **Multistep** A radio station broadcasts a signal over an area with a radius of 50 miles. The station can relay the signal and broadcast over an area with a radius of 75 miles. How much greater is the area of the broadcast region when the signal is relayed? Round your answer to the nearest square mile.

______

17. **Multistep** The sides of a square field are 12 meters. A sprinkler in the center of the field sprays a circular area with a diameter that corresponds to a side of the field. How much of the field is **not** reached by the sprinkler? Round your answer to the nearest hundredth.

______

18. **Justify Reasoning** A small silver dollar pancake served at a restaurant has a circumference of 2π inches. A regular pancake has a circumference of 4π inches. Is the area of the regular pancake twice the area of the silver dollar pancake? Explain.

______

19. **Analyze Relationships** A bakery offers a small circular cake with a diameter of 8 inches. It also offers a large circular cake with a diameter of 24 inches. Does the top of the large cake have three times the area of that of the small cake? If not, how much greater is its area? Explain.

______

20. **Communicate Mathematical Ideas** You can use the formula $A = \frac{C^2}{4\pi}$ to find the area of a circle given the circumference. Describe another way to find the area of a circle when given the circumference.

____

____

____

21. **Draw Conclusions** Mark wants to order a pizza. Which is the better deal? Explain.

Donnie's Pizza Palace		
Diameter (in.)	12	18
Cost ($)	10	20

____

____

____

22. **Multistep** A bear was seen near a campground. Searchers were dispatched to the region to find the bear.

a. Assume the bear can walk in any direction at a rate of 2 miles per hour. Suppose the bear was last seen 4 hours ago. How large an area must the searchers cover? Use 3.14 for π. Round your answer to the nearest square mile. ______________________

b. **What If?** How much additional area would the searchers have to cover if the bear were last seen 5 hours ago? ______________

H.O.T. FOCUS ON HIGHER ORDER THINKING

Work Area

23. **Analyze Relationships** Two circles have the same radius. Is the combined area of the two circles the same as the area of a circle with twice the radius? Explain.

____

____

24. **Look for a Pattern** How does the area of a circle change if the radius is multiplied by a factor of *n*, where *n* is a whole number? Explain.

____

____

25. **Represent Real World Problems** The bull's-eye on a target has a diameter of 3 inches. The whole target has a diameter of 15 inches. What part of the whole target is the bull's-eye? Explain.

____

LESSON 9.3

Area of Composite Figures

7.4.9.3

Students will find the area of composite figures.

ESSENTIAL QUESTION

How do you find the area of composite figures?

EXPLORE ACTIVITY Real World

Exploring Areas of Composite Figures

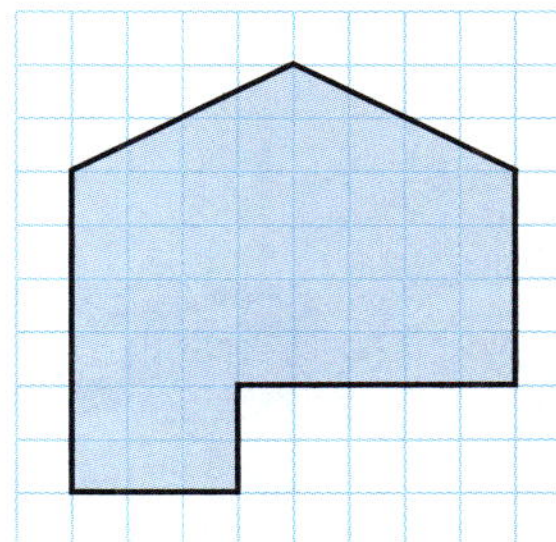

Aaron was plotting the shape of his garden on grid paper. While it was an irregular shape, it was perfect for his yard. Each square on the grid represents 1 square meter.

A Describe one way you can find the area of this garden.

____

____

____

B The area of the garden is __________ square meters.

C Compare your results with other students. What other methods were used to find the area?

____

____

____

D How does the area you found compare with the area found using different methods?

____

Reflect

1. Use dotted lines to show two different ways Aaron's garden could be divided up into simple geometric figures.

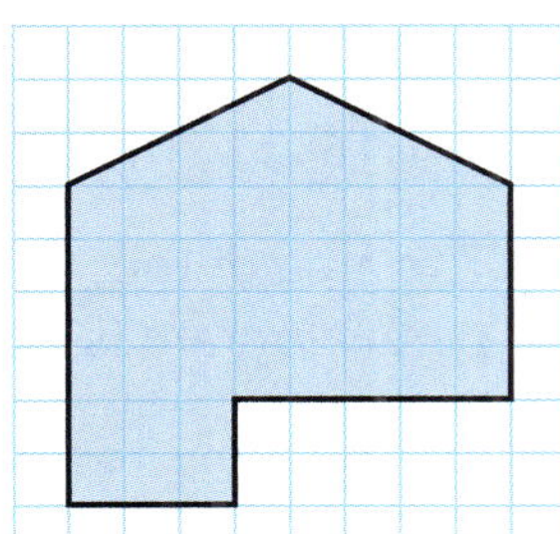

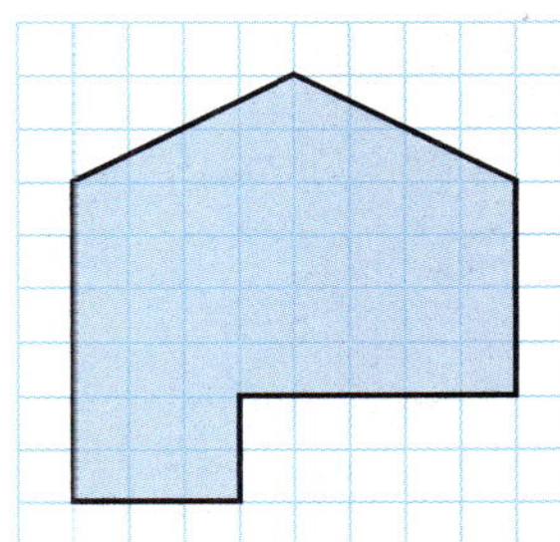

Math On the Spot
my.hrw.com

Finding the Area of a Composite Figure

A composite figure is made up of simple geometric shapes. To find the area of a composite figure or other irregular-shaped figure, divide it into simple, nonoverlapping figures. Find the area of each simpler figure, and then add the areas together to find the total area of the composite figure.

Use the chart below to review some common area formulas.

Shape	Area Formula
triangle	$A = \frac{1}{2}bh$
square	$A = s^2$
rectangle	$A = \ell w$
parallelogram	$A = bh$
trapezoid	$A = \frac{1}{2}h(b_1 + b_2)$

Animated Math
my.hrw.com

EXAMPLE 1 Real World

Find the area of the figure.

STEP 1 Separate the figure into smaller, familiar figures: a parallelogram and a trapezoid.

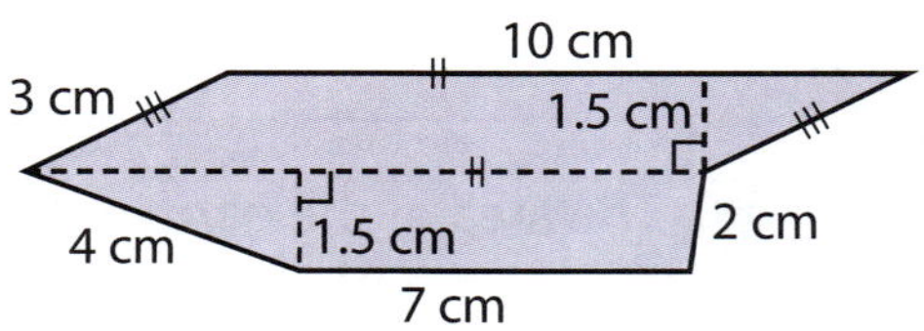

STEP 2 Find the area of each shape.

Area of the Parallelogram

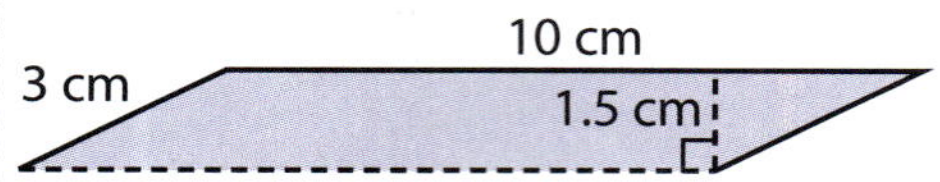

base = 10 cm

height = 1.5 cm

Use the formula.

$A = bh$

$A = 10 \cdot 1.5$

$A = 15$

The area of the parallelogram is 15 cm^2.

Area of the Trapezoid

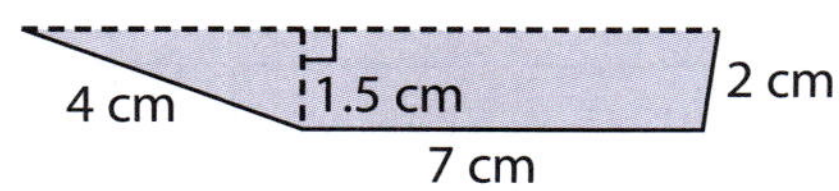

$base_1 = 7$ cm $base_2 = 10$ cm

height 1.5 cm

Use the formula.

$A = \frac{1}{2}h(b_1 + b_2)$

$A = \frac{1}{2}(1.5)(7 + 10)$

$A = \frac{1}{2}(1.5)(17) = 12.75$

The area of the trapezoid is 12.75 cm^2.

The top base of the trapezoid is 10 cm since it is the same length as the base of the parallelogram.

STEP 3 Add the areas to find the total area.

$A = 15 + 12.75 = 27.75$ cm^2

The area of the figure is 27.75 cm^2.

YOUR TURN

Find the area of each figure. Use 3.14 for π.

2.

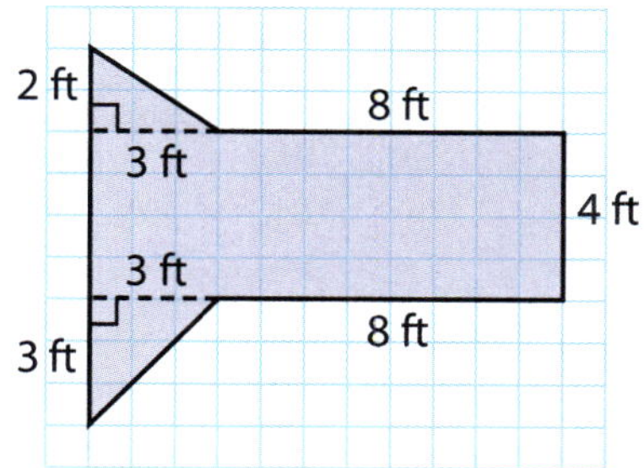

____

3.

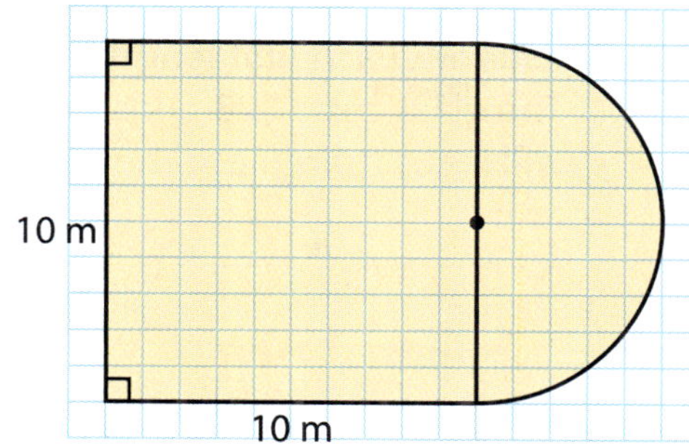

____

Personal Math Trainer
Online Assessment and Intervention
my.hrw.com

Using Area to Solve Problems

EXAMPLE 2 Real World

Math On the Spot
my.hrw.com

A banquet room is being carpeted. A floor plan of the room is shown at right. Each unit represents 1 yard. The carpet costs \$23.50 per square yard. How much will it cost to carpet the room?

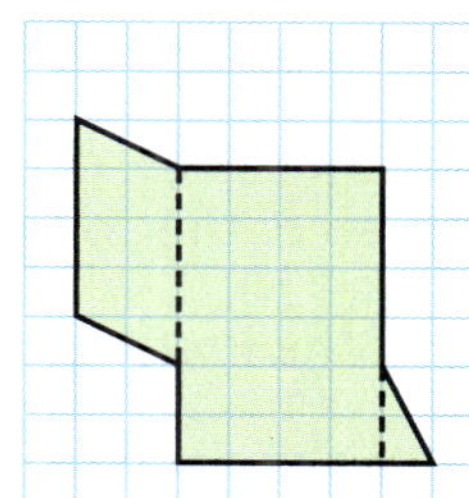

STEP 1 Separate the composite figure into simpler shapes as shown by the dashed lines: a parallelogram, a rectangle, and a triangle.

STEP 2 Find the area of the simpler figures. Count units to find the dimensions.

Parallelogram	Rectangle	Triangle
$A = bh$	$A = \ell w$	$A = \frac{1}{2}bh$
$A = 4 \cdot 2$	$A = 6 \cdot 4$	$A = \frac{1}{2}(1)(2)$
$A = 8 \text{ yd}^2$	$A = 24 \text{ yd}^2$	$A = 1 \text{ yd}^2$

STEP 3 Find the area of the composite figure.

$A = 8 + 24 + 1 = 33$ square yards

STEP 4 Calculate the cost to carpet the room.

Area · Cost per yard = Total cost

33 · \$23.50 = \$775.50

The cost to carpet the banquet room is \$775.50.

Math Talk
Mathematical Processes
Describe how you can estimate the cost to carpet the room.

Personal Math Trainer
Online Assessment and Intervention
my.hrw.com

YOUR TURN

4. A window is being replaced with tinted glass. The plan at the right shows the design of the window. Each unit length represents 1 foot. The glass costs \$28 per square foot. How much will it cost to replace the glass? Use 3.14 for π.

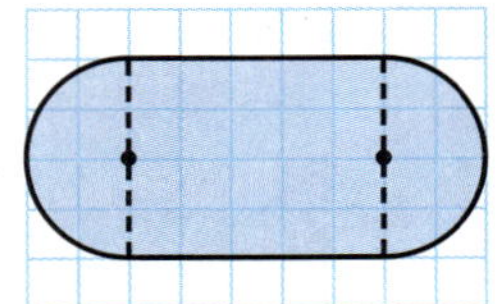

____

Guided Practice

1. A tile installer plots an irregular shape on grid paper. Each square on the grid represents 1 square centimeter. What is the area of the irregular shape? (Explore Activity, Example 2)

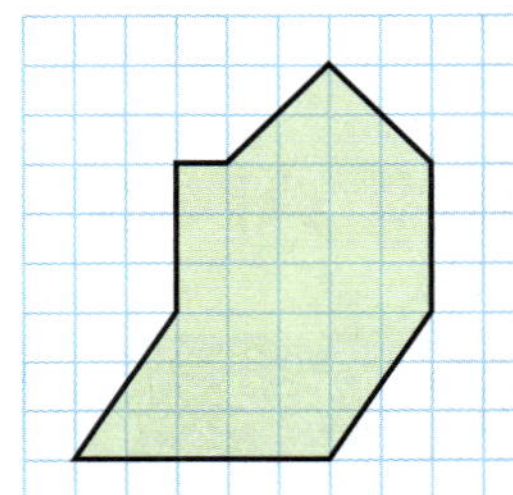

STEP 1 Separate the figure into a triangle, a ______________, and a parallelogram.

STEP 2 Find the area of each figure.

triangle: _____ cm^2; rectangle: _____ cm^2; parallelogram: _____ cm^2

STEP 3 Find the area of the composite figure: ____ + ____ + ____ = ____ cm^2

The area of the irregular shape is ____ cm^2.

2. Show two different ways to divide the composite figure. Find the area both ways. Show your work below. (Example 1)

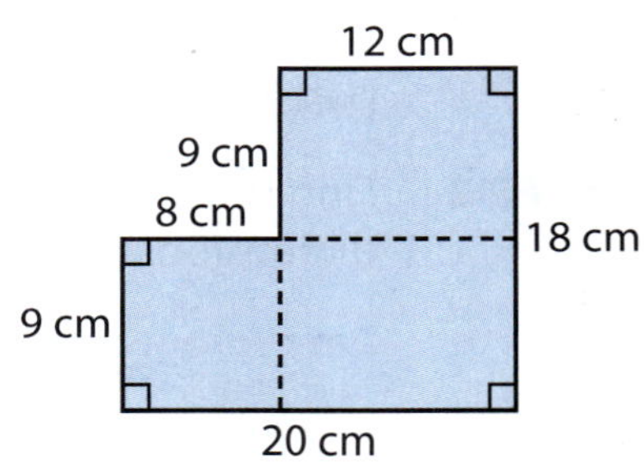

3. Sal is tiling his entryway. The floor plan is drawn on a unit grid. Each unit length represents 1 foot. Tile costs \$2.25 per square foot. How much will Sal pay to tile his entryway? (Example 2)

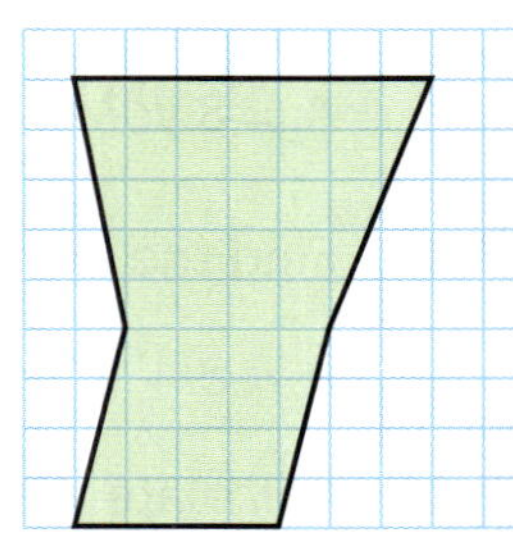

____

ESSENTIAL QUESTION CHECK-IN

4. What is the first step in finding the area of a composite figure?

____

Name ______________________ Class ______________ Date ______________

9.3 Independent Practice

Personal Math Trainer
Online Assessment and Intervention
my.hrw.com

5. A banner is made of a square and a semicircle. The square has side lengths of 26 inches. One side of the square is also the diameter of the semicircle. What is the total area of the banner? Use 3.14 for π.

____

6. **Multistep** Erin wants to carpet the floor of her closet. A floor plan of the closet is shown.

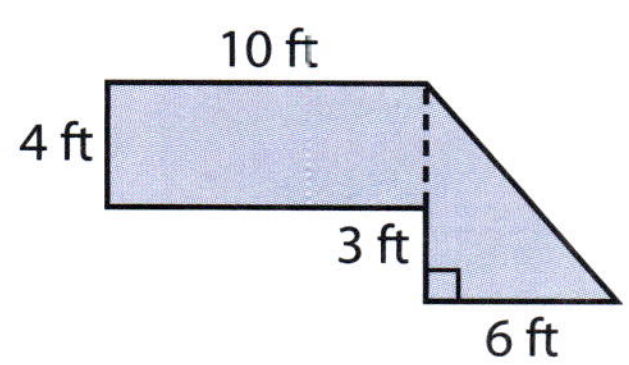

a. How much carpet does Erin need?

____

b. The carpet Erin has chosen costs $2.50 per square foot. How much will it cost her to carpet the floor?

____

7. **Multiple Representations** Hexagon *ABCDEF* has vertices $A(-2, 4)$, $B(0, 4)$, $C(2, 1)$, $D(5, 1)$, $E(5, -2)$, and $F(-2, -2)$. Sketch the figure on a coordinate plane. What is the area of the hexagon?

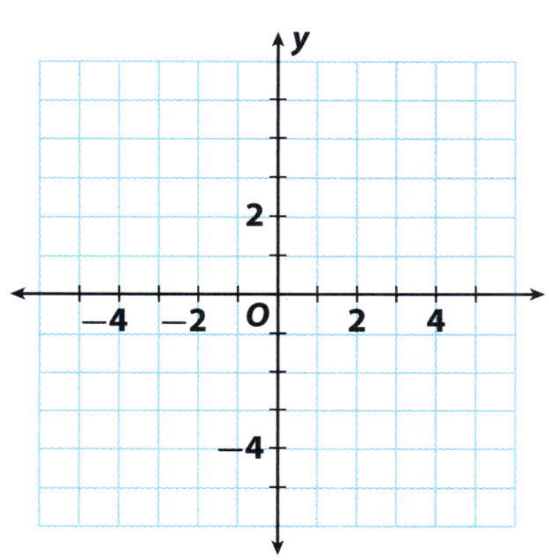

____

8. A field is shaped like the figure shown. What is the area of the field? Use 3.14 for π.

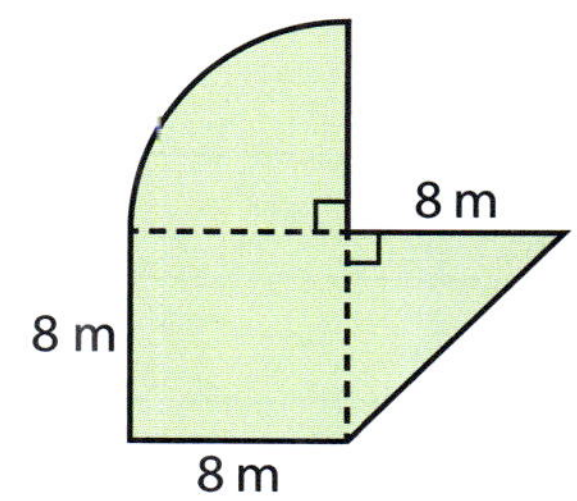

____

9. A bookmark is shaped like a rectangle with a semicircle attached at both ends. The rectangle is 12 cm long and 4 cm wide. The diameter of each semicircle is the width of the rectangle. What is the area of the bookmark? Use 3.14 for π.

____

10. **Multistep** Alex is making 12 pennants for the school fair. The pattern he is using to make the pennants is shown in the figure. The fabric for the pennants costs $1.25 per square foot. How much will it cost Alex to make 12 pennants?

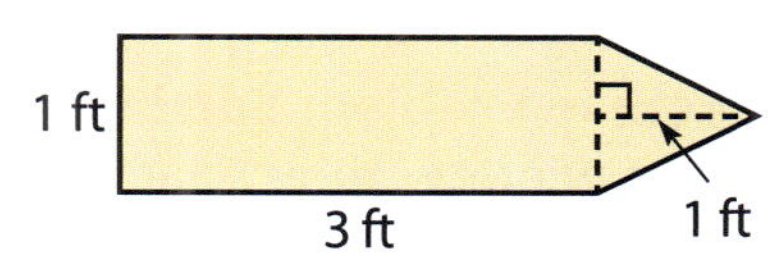

____

11. **Reasoning** A composite figure is formed by combining a square and a triangle. Its total area is 32.5 ft^2. The area of the triangle is 7.5 ft^2. What is the length of each side of the square? Explain.

____

____

____

____

H.O.T. FOCUS ON HIGHER ORDER THINKING

Work Area

12. **Represent Real-World Problems** Christina plotted the shape of her garden on graph paper. She estimates that she will get about 15 carrots from each square unit. She plans to use the entire garden for carrots. About how many carrots can she expect to grow? Explain.

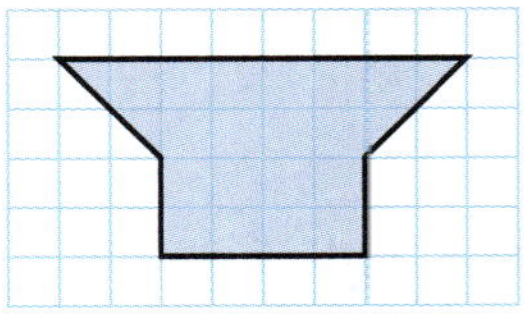

13. **Analyze Relationships** The figure shown is made up of a triangle and a square. The perimeter of the figure is 56 inches. What is the area of the figure? Explain.

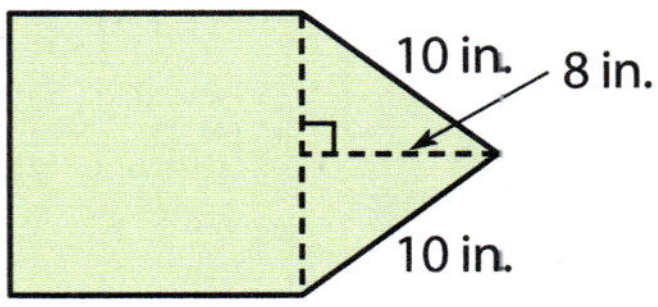

14. **Critical Thinking** The pattern for a scarf is shown at right. What is the area of the scarf? Use 3.14 for π.

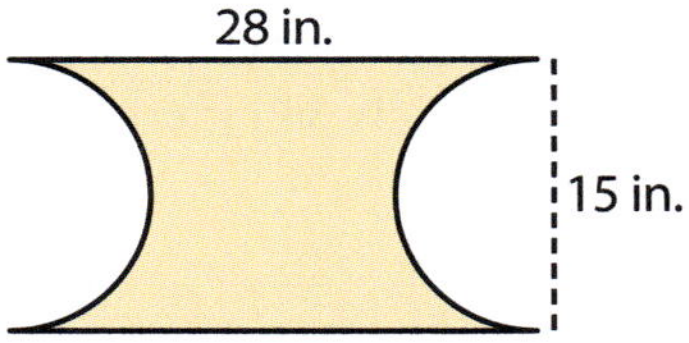

15. **Persevere in Problem Solving** The design for the palladium window shown includes a semicircular shape at the top. The bottom is formed by squares of equal size. A shade for the window will extend 4 inches beyond the perimeter of the window, shown by the dashed line around the window. Each square in the window has an area of 100 in^2.

a. What is the area of the window? Use 3.14 for π.

b. What is the area of the shade? Round your answer to the nearest whole number.

LESSON 9.4

Solving Surface Area Problems

7.4.9.4

Students will find the surface area of a figure made up of cubes and prisms.

ESSENTIAL QUESTION

How can you find the surface area of a figure made up of cubes and prisms?

EXPLORE ACTIVITY

Modeling Surface Area of a Prism

The surface area of a three-dimensional figure is the sum of the areas of all its surfaces. You know how to use the net of a figure to find its surface area. Now you will discover a formula that you can use.

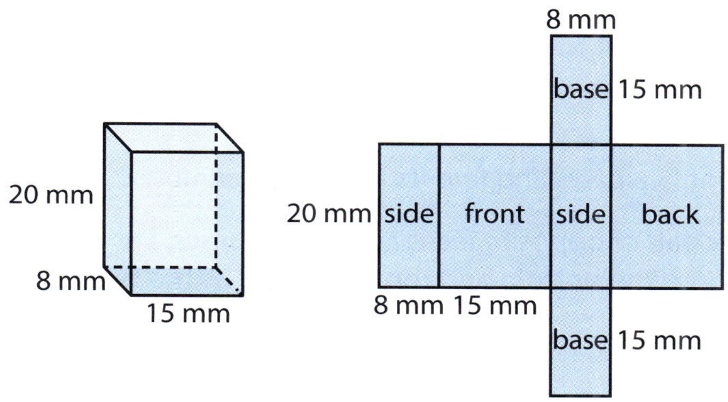

A The lateral area L of a prism is the area of all faces except the bases.

$L = 2(\_\_\_\_\_\_\_\_) + 2(\_\_\_\_\_\_\_\_) = \_\_\_\_\_\_\_\_$.

B The area B of each base is ________________.

C The surface area S of the prism is the sum of the lateral area L and the total area of the bases, or ________________.

Reflect

1. **Analyze Relationships** Use the net above.

a. How does the product of the perimeter P of the base of the prism and the height h of the prism compare to the lateral area L? ________________

b. How can you express the surface area S of the prism in terms of P, h, and B? ________________

2. A cube is a rectangular prism with six identical square faces. Rewrite your equation from **1b** for a cube with edge length e. Write the expression for the surface area in simplified form. ________________

Math On the Spot
my.hrw.com

Finding the Surface Area of a Prism

Given a prism's dimensions, you can use a formula to find the surface area.

Surface Area of a Prism

The surface area S of a prism with base perimeter P, height h, and base area B is $S = Ph + 2B$.

EXAMPLE 1 Real World

My Notes

Erin is making a jewelry box of wood in the shape of a rectangular prism. The jewelry box will have the dimensions shown. She plans to spray paint the exterior of the box. How many square inches will she have to paint?

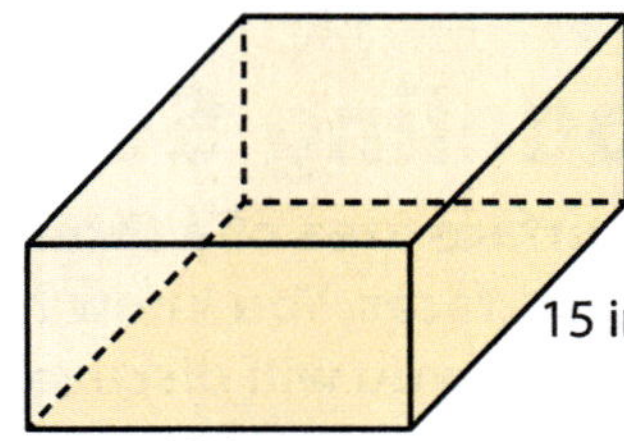

STEP 1 Make a sketch of the box. Drawing a diagram helps you understand and solve the problem.

STEP 2 Identify a base, and find its area and perimeter.

Any pair of opposite faces can be the bases. For example, you can choose the bottom and top of the box as the bases.

$B = \ell \times w$ $P = 2(12) + 2(15)$

$= 12 \times 15$ $= 24 + 30$

$= 180$ square inches $= 54$ inches

STEP 3 Identify the height, and find the surface area.

The height h of the prism is 6 inches. Use the formula to find the surface area.

$S = Ph + 2B$

$S = 54(6) + 2(180) = 684$ square inches

Erin will have to spray paint 684 square inches of wood.

Math Talk
Mathematical Processes

How can you express the formula for the surface area S of a rectangular prism in terms of its dimensions ℓ, w, and h?

YOUR TURN

3. A brand of uncooked spaghetti comes in a box that is a rectangular prism with a length of 9 inches, a width of 2 inches, and a height of $1\frac{1}{2}$ inches.

What is the surface area of the box? _______________

Personal Math Trainer
Online Assessment and Intervention
my.hrw.com

Finding the Surface Area of a Composite Solid

A composite solid is made up of two or more solid figures. To find the surface area of a composite solid, find the surface area of each figure. Subtract any area not on the surface.

Math On the Spot
my.hrw.com

EXAMPLE 2 Problem Solving

Daniel built the birdhouse shown. What was the surface area of the birdhouse before the hole was drilled?

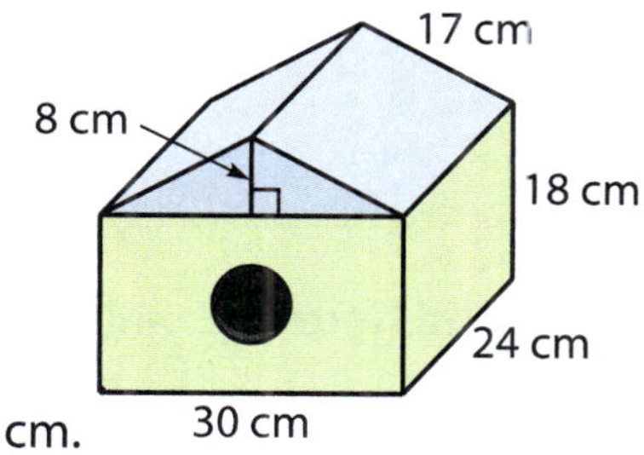

Analyze Information

Identify the important information.

- The top is a triangular prism with $h = 24$ cm. The base is a triangle with height 8 cm and base 30 cm.
- The bottom is a rectangular prism with $h = 18$ cm. The base is a 30 cm by 24 cm rectangle.
- One face of each prism is not on the surface of the figure.

Formulate a Plan

Find the surface area of each prism.

Add the surface areas. Subtract the areas of the parts not on the surface.

Solve

Find the surface area of the triangular prism.

Perimeter $= 17 + 17 + 30 = 64$ cm; Base area $= \frac{1}{2}(30)(8) = 120\text{ cm}^2$

Surface area $= Ph + 2B$

$= 64(24) + 2(120) = 1{,}776\text{ cm}^2$

Find the surface area of the rectangular prism.

Perimeter $= 2(30) + 2(24) = 108$ cm; Base area $= 30(24) = 720\text{ cm}^2$

Surface area $= Ph + 2B$

$= 108(18) + 2(720) = 3{,}384\text{ cm}^2$

Add. Then subtract the areas of the parts not on the surface.

Surface area $= 1{,}776 + 3{,}384 - 2(720) = 3{,}720\text{ cm}^2$

The surface area before the hole was drilled was $3{,}720\text{ cm}^2$.

Justify and Evaluate

You can check your work by using a net to find the surface areas.

Math Talk
Mathematical Processes

How could you find the surface area by letting the front and back of the prism be the bases?

Personal Math Trainer
Online Assessment and Intervention
my.hrw.com

YOUR TURN

4. Dara is building a plant stand. She wants to stain the plant stand, except for the bottom of the larger prism. Find the surface area of the part of the plant stand she will stain. __________

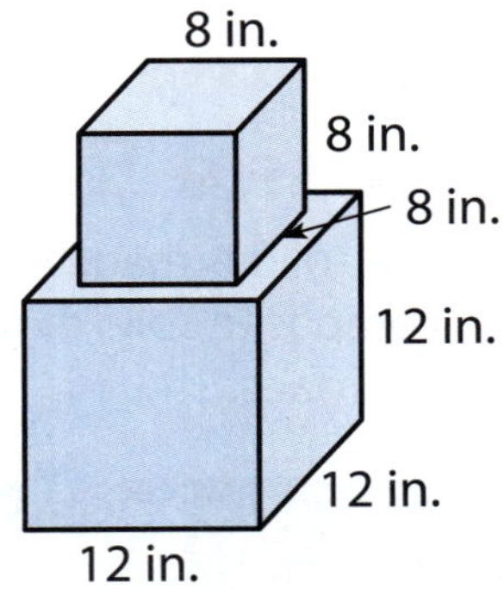

Guided Practice

Find the surface area of each solid figure. (Examples 1 and 2)

1.

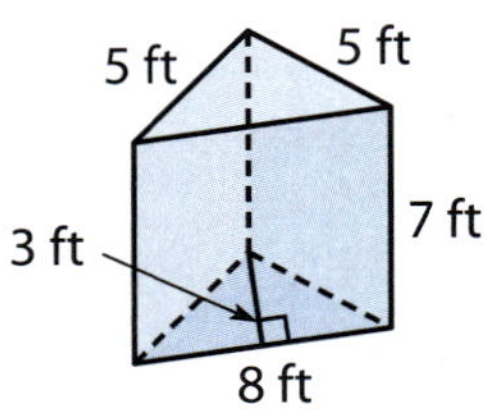

Perimeter of base = ________

Height = ________

Base area = ________

Surface area:

S = (________)(________) + 2(________)

= ________

2.

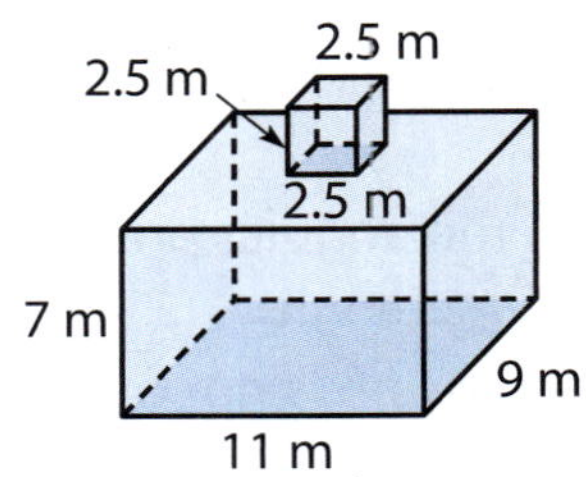

Surface area of cube:

S = __________

Surface area of rectangular prism:

S = __________

Overlapping area: A = __________

Surface area of composite figure:

= ________ + ________ − 2 (________) =

________ m^2

ESSENTIAL QUESTION CHECK-IN

3. How can you find the surface area of a composite solid made up of prisms?

____

____

____

Name ____________________ Class ____________ Date ____________

9.4 Independent Practice

Personal Math Trainer
Online Assessment and Intervention
my.hrw.com

4. Carla is wrapping a present in the box shown. How much wrapping paper does she need, not including overlap?

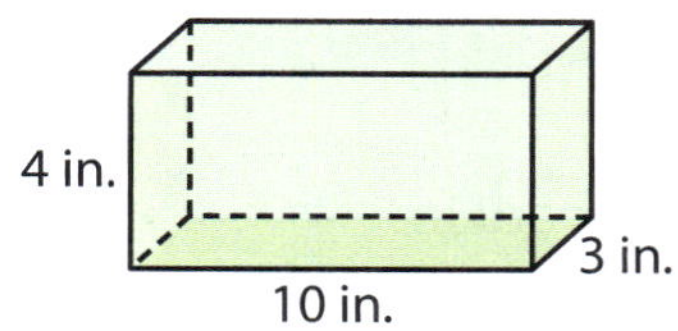

____

5. Dmitri wants to cover the top and sides of the box shown with glass tiles that are 5 mm square. How many tiles does he need?

____

6. Shera is building a cabinet. She is making wooden braces for the corners of the cabinet. Find the surface area of each brace.

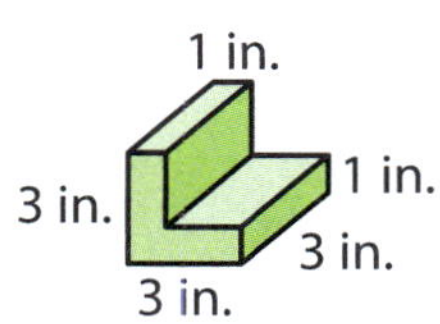

____

7. The doghouse shown has a floor, but no windows. Find the total surface area of the doghouse, including the door.

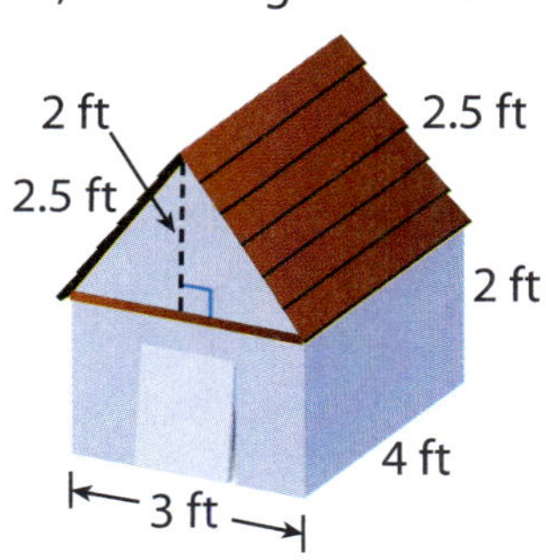

____

Eddie built the ramp shown to train his puppy to do tricks. Use the figure for 8–9.

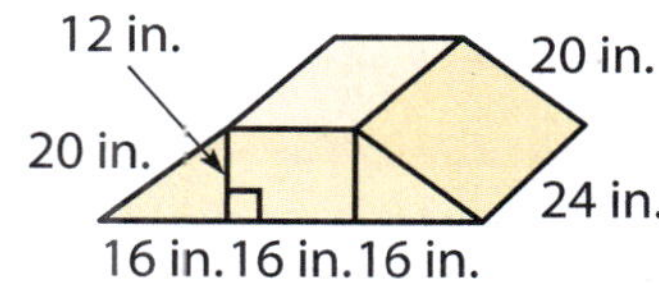

8. **Analyze Relationships** Describe two ways to find the surface area of the ramp.

____

____

____

____

9. What is the surface area of the ramp?

____

Marco and Elaine are building a stand like the one shown to display trophies. Use the figure for 10–11.

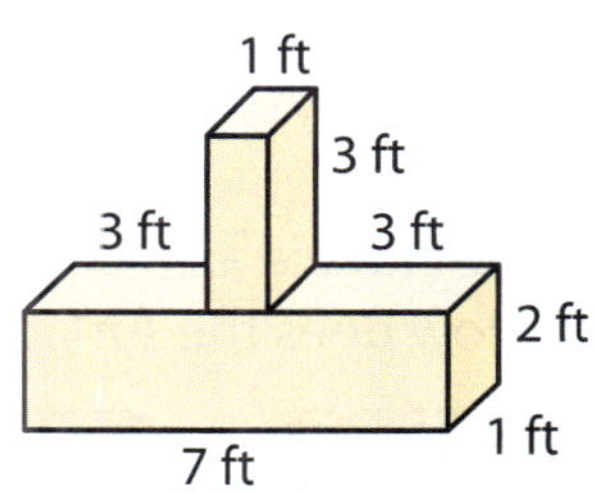

10. What is the surface area of the stand?

____

11. **Critique Reasoning** Marco and Elaine want to paint the entire stand silver. A can of paint covers 25 square feet and costs \$6.79. They set aside \$15 for paint. Is that enough? Explain.

____

____

12. Henry wants to cover the box shown with paper without any overlap. How many square centimeters will be covered with paper?

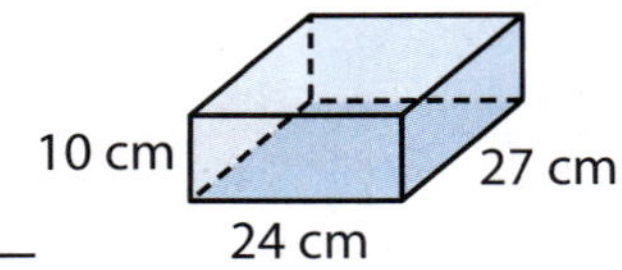

13. **What If?** Suppose the length and width of the box in Exercise 12 double. Does the surface area S double? Explain.

Work Area

H.O.T. FOCUS ON HIGHER ORDER THINKING

14. **Persevere in Problem Solving** Enya is building a storage cupboard in the shape of a rectangular prism. The rectangular prism has a square base with side lengths of 2.5 feet and a height of 3.5 feet. Compare the amount of paint she would use to paint all but the bottom surface of the prism to the amount she would use to paint the entire prism.

15. **Interpret the Answer** The oatmeal box shown is shaped like a cylinder. Use a net to find the surface area S of the oatmeal box to the nearest tenth. Then find the number of square feet of cardboard needed for 1,500 oatmeal boxes. Round your answer to the nearest whole number.

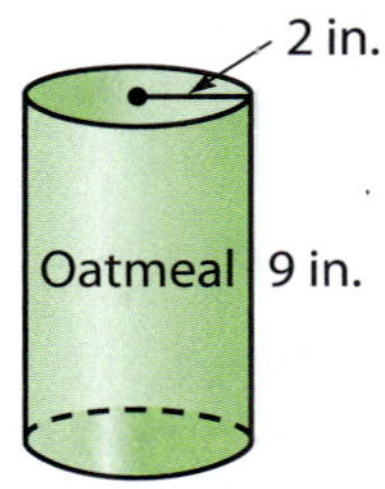

16. **Analyze Relationships** A prism is made of centimeter cubes. How can you find the surface area of the prism in Figure 1 without using a net or a formula? How does the surface area change in Figures 2, 3, and 4? Explain.

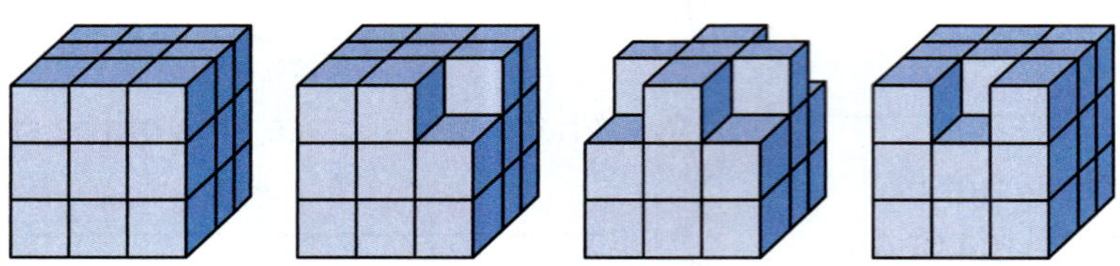

Figure 1 Figure 2 Figure 3 Figure 4

LESSON 9.5 Solving Volume Problems

7.4.9.5

Students will find the volume of a figure made of cubes and prisms.

ESSENTIAL QUESTION

How do you find the volume of a figure made of cubes and prisms?

EXPLORE ACTIVITY Real World

Volume of a Triangular Prism

The formula for the volume of a rectangular prism can be used for *any* prism.

Math On the Spot my.hrw.com

Volume of a Prism

The volume V of a prism is the area of its base B times its height h.

$$V = Bh$$

EXAMPLE 1 **Bradley's tent is in the shape of a triangular prism. How many cubic feet of space are in his tent?**

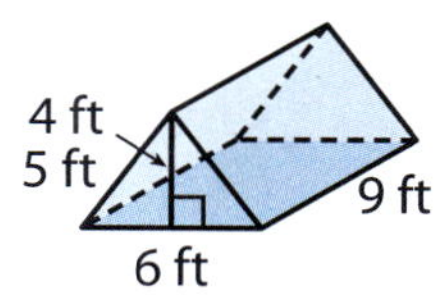

STEP 1 Find the base area B of the triangular prism.

Area of a triangle (b = base length, h = height) $B = \frac{1}{2}bh$

Substitute 6 for b and 4 for h. $= \frac{1}{2}(\square)(\square)$

Multiply to find the base area B. $= \square$ ft²

STEP 2 Find the volume of the prism.

Volume of a prism (B = base area, h = height) $V = Bh$

Substitute 12 for B and 9 for h. $= (\square)(\square)$

Multiply to find the volume. $= \square$ ft³

The volume of Bradley's tent is ________ ft³.

Reflect

1. **Analyze Relationships** For a prism that is **not** a rectangular prism, how do you determine which sides are the bases?

____

YOUR TURN

2. Find the volume of the prism. ________

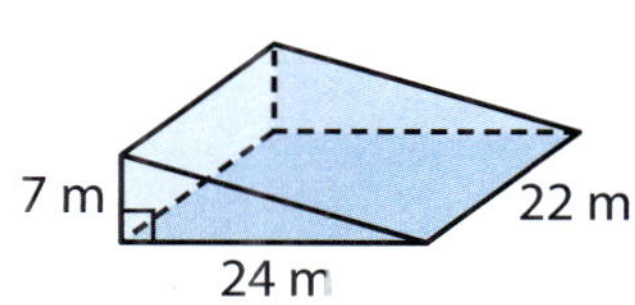

Personal Math Trainer
Online Assessment and Intervention
my.hrw.com

Volume of a Trapezoidal Prism

Prisms are named for the polygons that form their bases. In this lesson, you will focus on prisms whose bases are either triangles or quadrilaterals other than squares and rectangles.

Math On the Spot
my.hrw.com

EXAMPLE 2 Real World

Cherise is setting up her tent. Her tent is in the shape of a trapezoidal prism. How many cubic feet of space are in her tent?

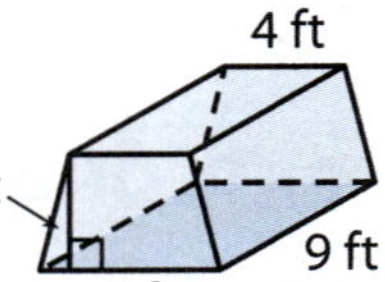

STEP 1 Find the base area B of the trapezoidal prism.

$B = \frac{1}{2}(b_1 + b_2)\,h$ — *Area of a trapezoid with bases of lengths b_1 and b_2 and height h*

$= \frac{1}{2}(6 + 4)4$ — *Substitute 6 for b_1, 4 for b_2, and 4 for h.*

$= \frac{1}{2}(10)4 = 20 \text{ ft}^2$

STEP 2 Find the volume of the prism.

$V = Bh$ — *Volume of a prism with base area B and height h*

$= (20)(9)$ — *Substitute 20 for B and 9 for h.*

$= 180 \text{ ft}^3$

The volume of Cherise's tent is 180 ft^3.

Math Talk
Mathematical Processes
Without calculating the volumes, how can you know whether Bradley's or Cherise's tent has a greater volume?

Reflect

3. **Look for a Pattern** How could you double the volume of the tent by doubling just one of its dimensions?

____

____

4. **What If?** How would doubling *all* the dimensions of the prism affect the volume of the tent?

____

YOUR TURN

5. Find the volume of the prism.

____

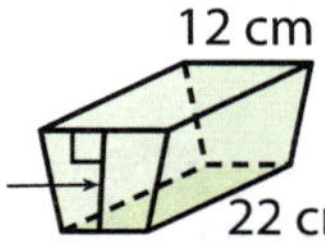

Personal Math Trainer
Online Assessment and Intervention
my.hrw.com

Volume of a Composite Solid

You can use the formula for the volume of a prism to find the volume of a composite figure that is made up of prisms.

Math On the Spot
my.hrw.com

EXAMPLE 3 Real World

Allie has two aquariums connected by a small square prism. Find the volume of the double aquarium.

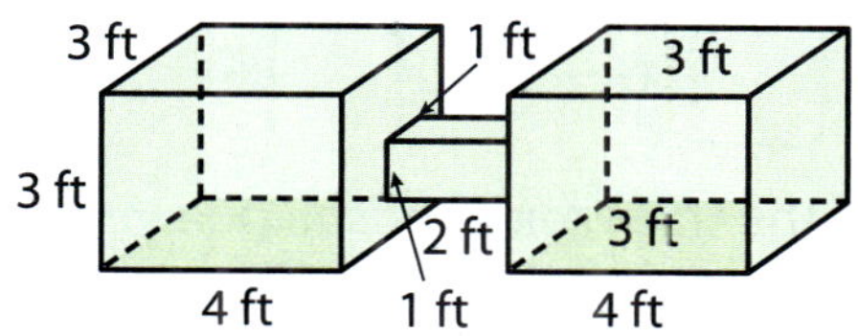

STEP 1 Find the volume of each of the larger aquariums.

$V = Bh$ *Volume of a prism*

$= (12)(3)$ *Substitute $3 \times 4 = 12$ for B and 3 for h.*

$= 36 \text{ ft}^3$

STEP 2 Find the volume of the connecting prism.

$V = Bh$ *Volume of a prism*

$= (1)(2)$ *Substitute $1 \times 1 = 1$ for B and 2 for h.*

$= 2 \text{ ft}^3$

STEP 3 Add the volumes of the three parts of the aquarium.

$V = 36 + 36 + 2 = 74 \text{ ft}^3$

The volume of the aquarium is 74 ft^3.

My Notes

Reflect

6. **What If?** Find the volume of one of the large aquariums on either end using another pair of opposite sides as the bases. Do you still get the same volume? Explain.

____

____

YOUR TURN

7. The figure is composed of a rectangular prism and a triangular prism. Find the volume of the figure.

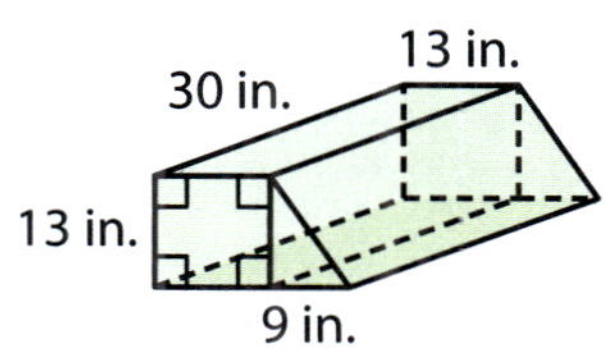

____

Personal Math Trainer
Online Assessment and Intervention
my.hrw.com

Guided Practice

1. Find the volume of the triangular prism. (Explore Activity Example 1)

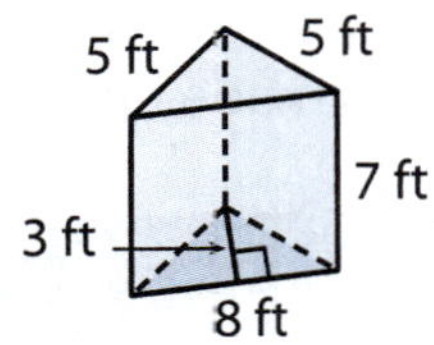

$B = \frac{1}{2}bh = \frac{1}{2}(8)(3) = 12 \text{ ft}^{\square}$

$V = Bh = (\square \times \square) \text{ ft}^{\square} = \square \text{ ft}^3$

2. Find the volume of the trapezoidal prism. (Example 2)

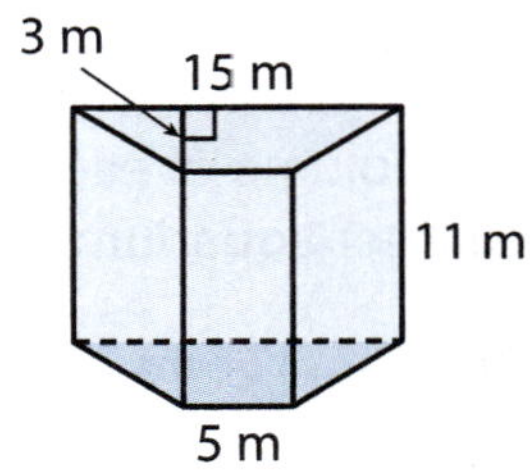

$B = \frac{1}{2}(b_1 + b_2)h = \frac{1}{2}(15 + 5)(3) = 30 \text{m}^{\square}$

$V = Bh = (\square \times \square) \text{ m}^{\square} = \square \text{ m}^3$

3. Find the volume of the composite figure. (Example 3)

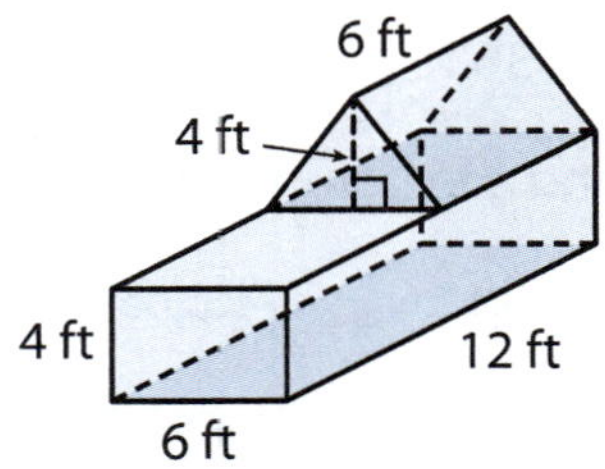

Volume of rectangular prism = ________________

Volume of triangular prism = ________________

Volume of composite figure = ________________

Find the volume of each figure. (Examples 2 and 3)

4. The figure shows a barn that Mr. Fowler is building for his farm.

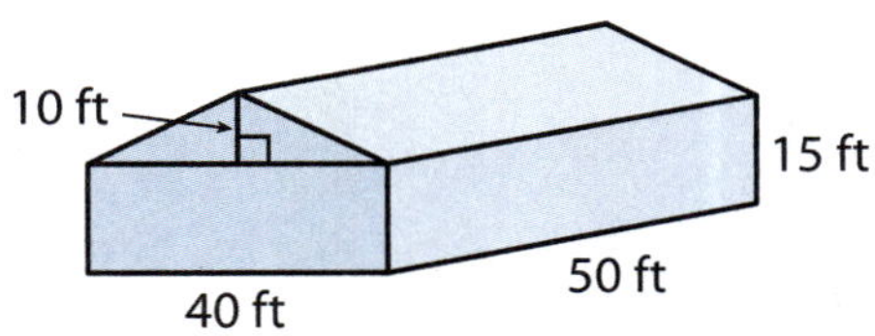

____

5. The figure shows a container, in the shape of a trapezoidal prism, that Pete filled with sand.

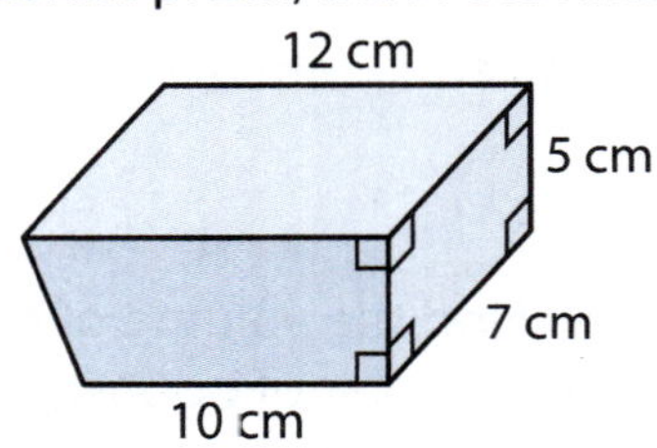

____

ESSENTIAL QUESTION CHECK-IN

6. How do you find the volume of a composite solid formed by two or more prisms?

____

____

Name ______________________ Class ______________ Date ______________

9.5 Independent Practice

Personal Math Trainer
Online Assessment and Intervention
my.hrw.com

7. A trap for insects is in the shape of a triangular prism. The area of the base is 3.5 in^2 and the height of the prism is 5 in. What is the volume of this trap?

____

8. Arletta built a cardboard ramp for her little brothers' toy cars. Identify the shape of the ramp. Then find its volume.

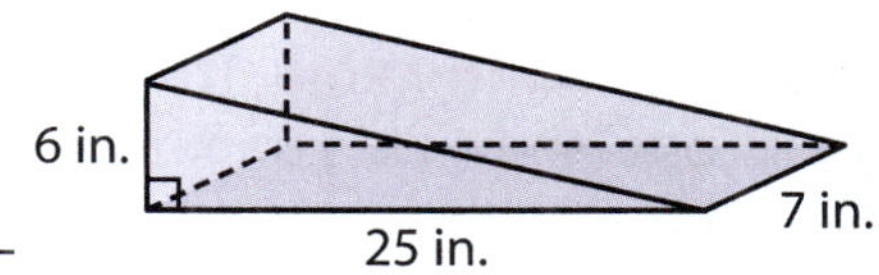

____

9. Alex made a sketch for a homemade soccer goal he plans to build. The goal will be in the shape of a triangular prism. The legs of the right triangles at the sides of his goal measure 4 ft and 8 ft, and the opening along the front is 24 ft. How much space is contained within this goal?

____

10. A gift box is in the shape of a trapezoidal prism with base lengths of 7 inches and 5 inches and a height of 4 inches. The height of the gift box is 8 inches. What is the volume of the gift box?

____

11. **Explain the Error** A student wrote this statement: "A triangular prism has a height of 15 inches and a base area of 20 square inches. The volume of the prism is 300 square inches." Identify and correct the error.

____

Find the volume of each figure. Round to the nearest hundredth if necessary.

12.

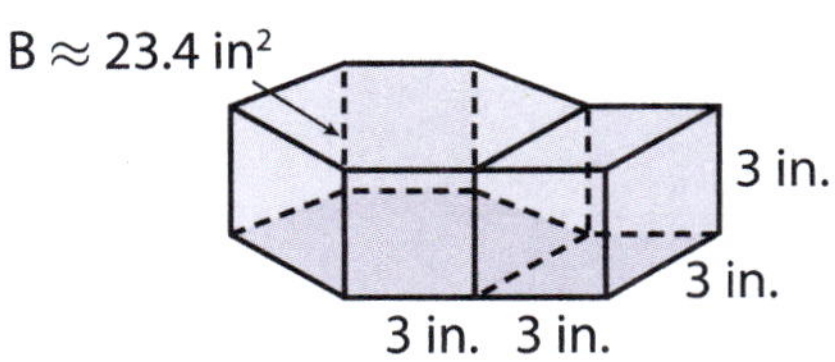

____

13.

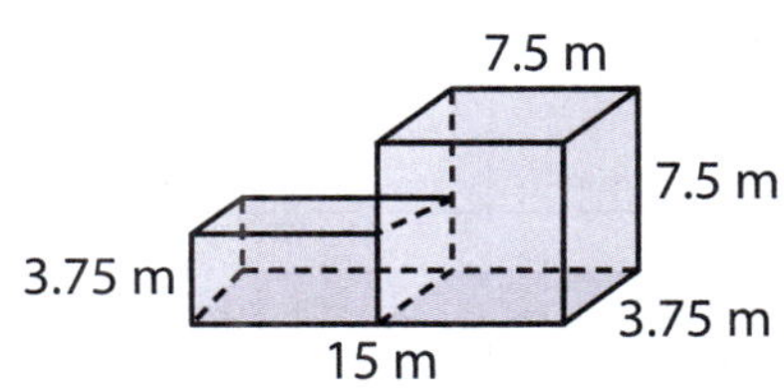

____

14. **Multi-Step** Josie has 260 cubic centimeters of candle wax. She wants to make a hexagonal prism candle with a base area of 21 square centimeters and a height of 8 centimeters. She also wants to make a triangular prism candle with a height of 14 centimeters. Can the base area of the triangular prism candle be 7 square centimeters? Explain.

____

15. A movie theater offers popcorn in two different containers for the same price. One container is a trapezoidal prism with a base area of 36 square inches and a height of 5 inches. The other container is a triangular prism with a base area of 32 square inches and a height of 6 inches. Which container is the better deal? Explain.

____

____

H.O.T. FOCUS ON HIGHER ORDER THINKING

Work Area

16. **Critical Thinking** The wading pool shown is a trapezoidal prism with a total volume of 286 cubic feet. What is the missing dimension?

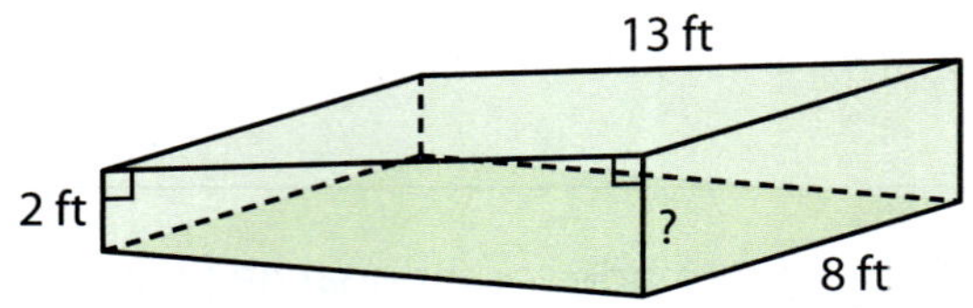

____

17. **Persevere in Problem Solving** Lynette has a metal doorstop with the dimensions shown. Each cubic centimeter of the metal in the doorstop has a mass of about 8.6 grams. Find the volume of the metal in the doorstop. Then find the mass of the doorstop.

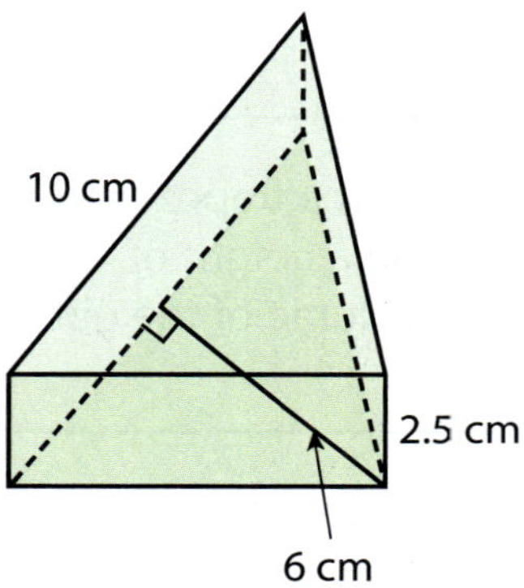

____

____

18. **Analyze Relationships** What effect would tripling all the dimensions of a triangular prism have on the volume of the prism? Explain your reasoning.

____

____

____

____

19. **Persevere in Problem Solving** Each of two trapezoidal prisms has a volume of 120 cubic centimeters. The prisms have no dimensions in common. Give possible dimensions for each prism.

____

____

____

____

MODULE QUIZ

Ready to Go On?

Personal Math Trainer
Online Assessment and Intervention
my.hrw.com

9.1, 9.2 Circumference and Area of Circles

Find the circumference and area of each circle. Use 3.14 for π. Round to the nearest hundredth if necessary.

1.

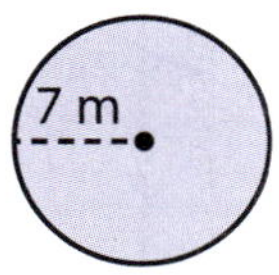

____

2.

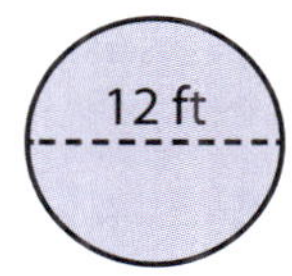

____

9.3 Area of Composite Figures

Find the area of each figure. Use 3.14 for π.

3.

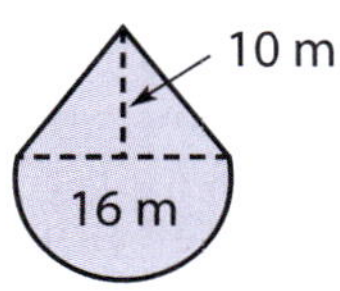

____

4.

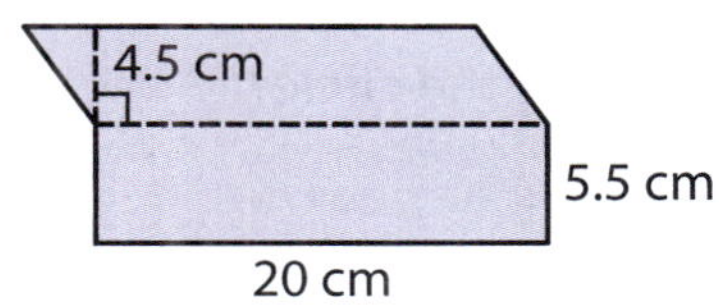

____

9.4, 9.5 Solving Surface Area and Volume Problems

Find the surface area and volume of each figure.

5.

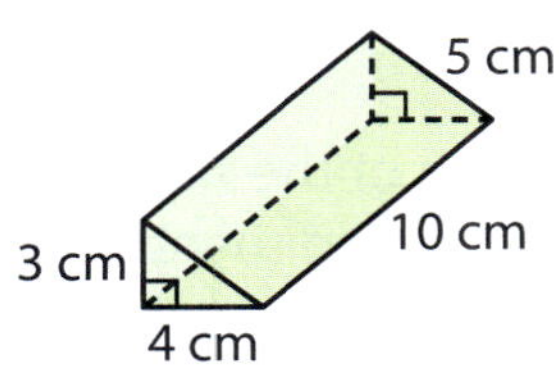

____

6.

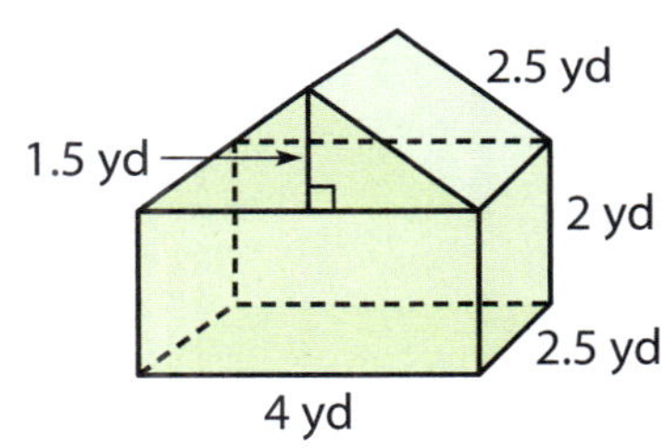

____

ESSENTIAL QUESTION

7. How can you use geometry figures to solve real-world problems?

____

____

MODULE 9 MIXED REVIEW
Assessment Readiness

Personal Math Trainer
my.hrw.com
Online Assessment and Intervention

Selected Response

1. What is the circumference of the circle?

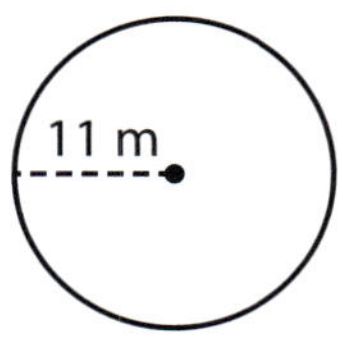

Ⓐ 34.54 m
Ⓑ 69.08 m
Ⓒ 379.94 m
Ⓓ 1,519.76 m

2. What is the area of the circle?

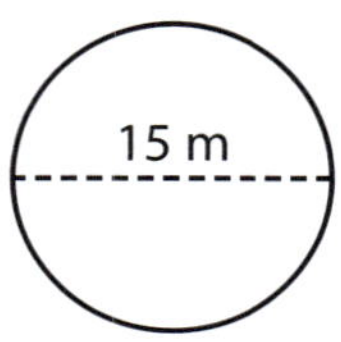

Ⓐ 23.55 m^2 Ⓒ 176.625 m^2
Ⓑ 47.1 m^2 Ⓓ 706.5 m^2

3. What is the area of the figure?

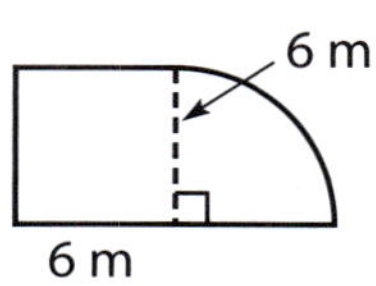

Ⓐ 28.26 m^2 Ⓒ 64.26 m^2
Ⓑ 36 m^2 Ⓓ 92.52 m^2

4. A one-year membership to a health club costs \$480. This includes a \$150 fee for new members that is paid when joining. Which equation represents the monthly cost x in dollars for a new member?

Ⓐ $12x + 150 = 480$
Ⓑ $\frac{x}{12} + 150 = 480$
Ⓒ $12x + 480 = 150$
Ⓓ $\frac{x}{12} + 480 = 150$

5. What is the volume of the prism?

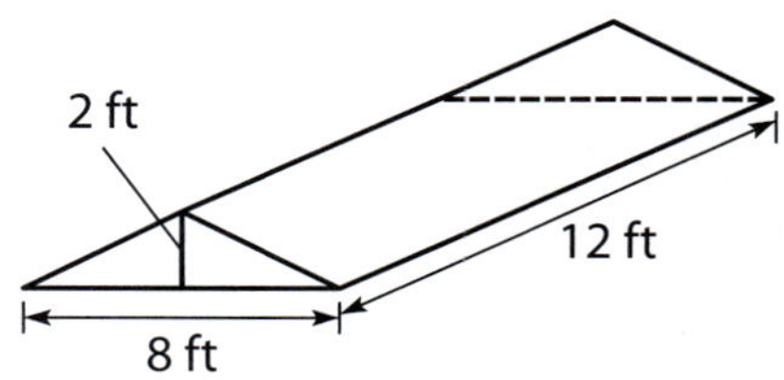

Ⓐ 192 ft^3 Ⓒ 69 ft^3
Ⓑ 48 ft^3 Ⓓ 96 ft^3

6. A school snack bar sells a mix of granola and raisins. The mix includes 2 pounds of granola for every 3 pounds of raisins. How many pounds of granola are needed for a mix that includes 24 pounds of raisins?

Ⓐ 16 pounds Ⓒ 48 pounds
Ⓑ 36 pounds Ⓓ 120 pounds

7. Find the percent change from \$20 to \$25.

Ⓐ 25% decrease Ⓒ 20% decrease
Ⓑ 25% increase Ⓓ 20% increase

Mini-Task

8. Each dimension of the smaller prism is half the corresponding dimension of the larger prism.

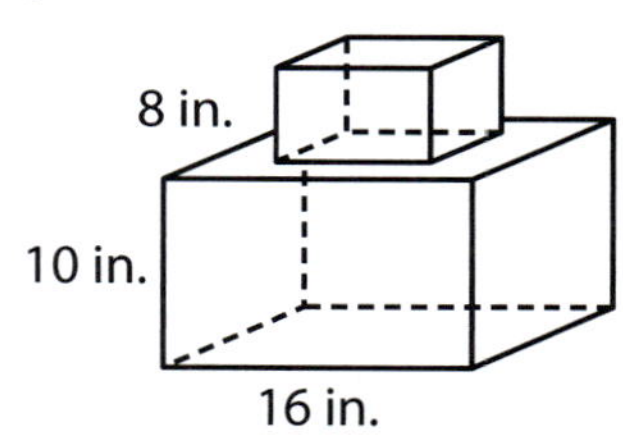

a. What is the surface area of the figure?

____

b. What is the volume of the figure?

____

UNIT 4

Study Guide Review

MODULE 8 Modeling Geometric Figures

ESSENTIAL QUESTION

How can you apply geometry concepts to solve real-world problems?

Key Vocabulary

adjacent angles *(ángulos adyacentes)*

complementary angles *(ángulos complementarios)*

congruent angles *(ángulos congruentes)*

cross section *(sección transversal)*

intersection *(intersección)*

scale *(escala)*

scale drawing *(dibujo a escala)*

supplementary angles *(ángulos suplementarios)*

vertical angles *(ángulos opuestos por el vértice)*

EXAMPLE 1

Use the scale drawing to find the perimeter of Tim's yard.

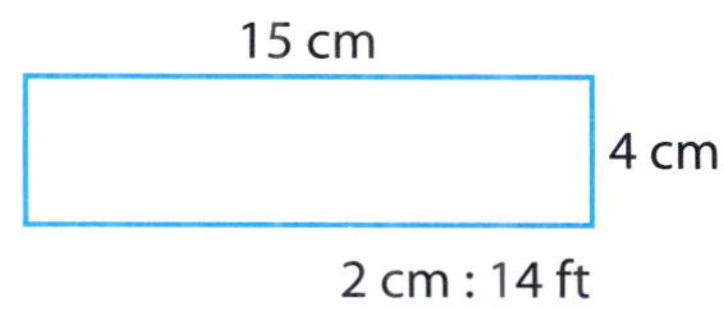

$\frac{2\text{ cm}}{14\text{ ft}} = \frac{1\text{ cm}}{7\text{ ft}}$ — 1 cm in the drawing equals 7 feet in the actual yard.

$\frac{1\text{ cm} \times 15}{7\text{ ft} \times 15} = \frac{15\text{ cm}}{105\text{ ft}}$ — 15 cm in the drawing equals 105 feet in the actual yard. Tim's yard is 105 feet long.

$\frac{1\text{ cm} \times 4}{7\text{ ft} \times 4} = \frac{4\text{ cm}}{28\text{ ft}}$ — 4 cm in the drawing equals 7 feet in the actual yard. Tim's yard is 28 feet wide.

Perimeter is twice the sum of the length and the width. So the perimeter of Tim's yard is $2(105 + 28) = 2(133)$, or 266 feet.

EXAMPLE 2

Find (a) the value of *x* and (b) the measure of $\angle APY$.

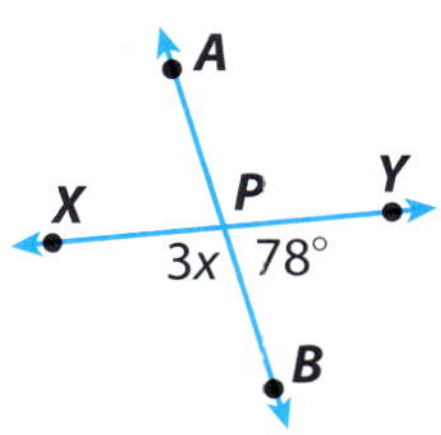

a. $\angle XPB$ and $\angle YPB$ are supplementary.

$3x + 78° = 180°$

$3x = 102°$

$x = 34°$

b. $\angle APY$ and $\angle XPB$ are vertical angles.

$m\angle APY = m\angle XPB = 3x = 102°$

EXERCISES

1. In the scale drawing of a park, the scale is 1 cm: 10 m. Find the area of the actual park.

(Lesson 8.1) ______________________

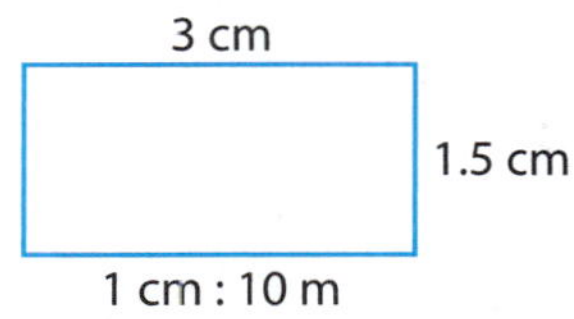

2. Find the value of y and the measure of $\angle YPS$ (Lesson 8.4)

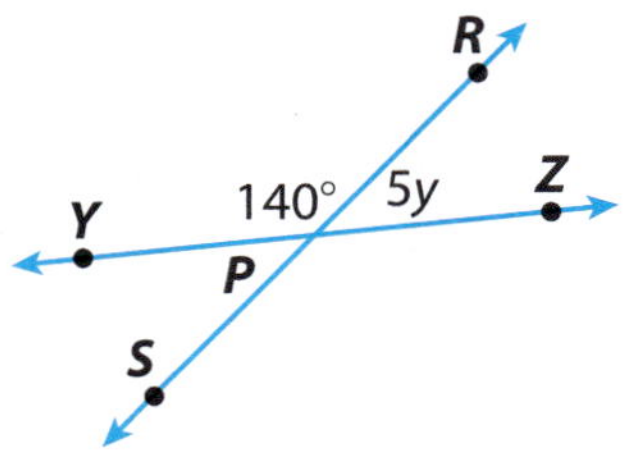

$y =$ ______________________

$m\angle YPS =$ ______________

3. Kanye wants to make a triangular flower bed using logs with the lengths shown below to form the border. Can Kanye form a triangle with the logs without cutting any of them? Explain. (Lesson 8.2)

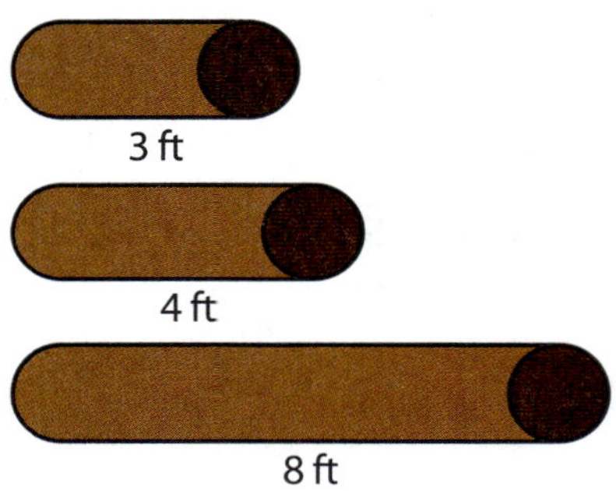

____

____

____

4. In shop class, Adriana makes a pyramid with a 4-inch square base and a height of 6 inches. She then cuts the pyramid vertically in half as shown. What is the area of each cut surface? (Lesson 8.3)

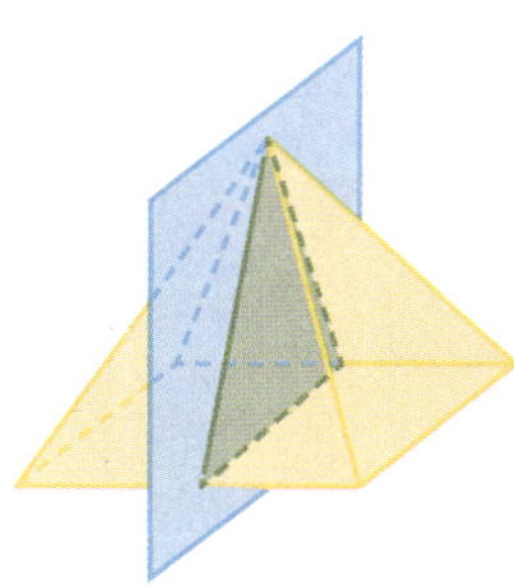

____

MODULE 9

Circumference, Area, and Volume

ESSENTIAL QUESTION

How can you use geometry concepts to solve real-world problems?

Key Vocabulary

circumference *(circunferencia)*
composite figure *(figura compuesta)*
diameter *(diámetro)*
radius *(radio)*

EXAMPLE 1

Find the area of the composite figure. It consists of a semicircle and a rectangle.

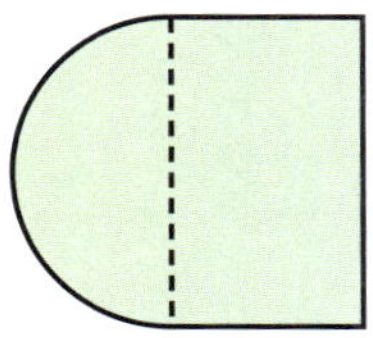

$$\text{Area of semicircle} = 0.5(\pi r^2)$$
$$\approx 0.5(3.14)25$$
$$\approx 39.25 \text{ cm}^2$$
$$\text{Area of rectangle} = \ell w$$
$$= 10(6)$$
$$= 60 \text{ cm}^2$$

The area of the composite figure is approximately 99.25 square centimeters.

EXAMPLE 2

Find the volume and surface area of the regular hexagonal prism hat box shown. Each side of the hexagonal base is 20 inches.

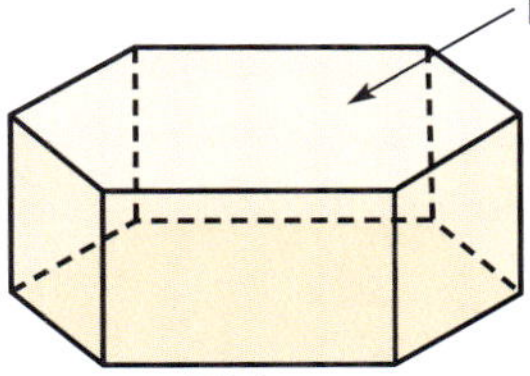

Use the formulas for volume and surface area of a prism.

$V = Bh$

$= 1{,}039(12)$

$= 12{,}468 \text{ in}^3$

$S = Ph + 2B$

$= 120(12) + 2(1{,}039)$

$= 1{,}440 + 2{,}078$

$= 3{,}518 \text{ in}^2$

Perimeter $= 6(20) = 120$ in.

Find the circumference and area of each circle. Round to the nearest hundredth. (Lessons 9.1, 9.2)

1.

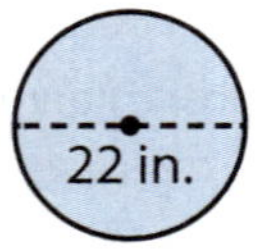

____

2.

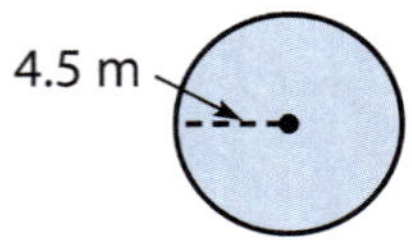

____

Find the area of each composite figure. Round to the nearest hundredth if necessary. (Lesson 9.3)

3.

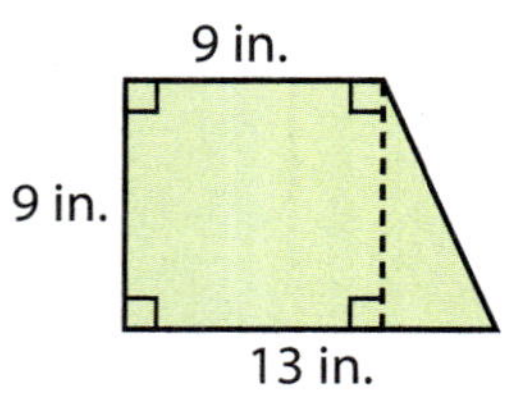

Area ________________________

4.

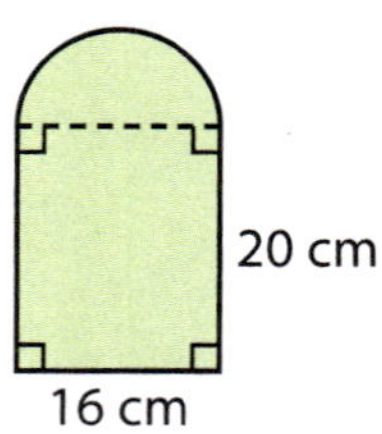

Area ________________________

Find the volume of the figure. (Lesson 9.5)

5.

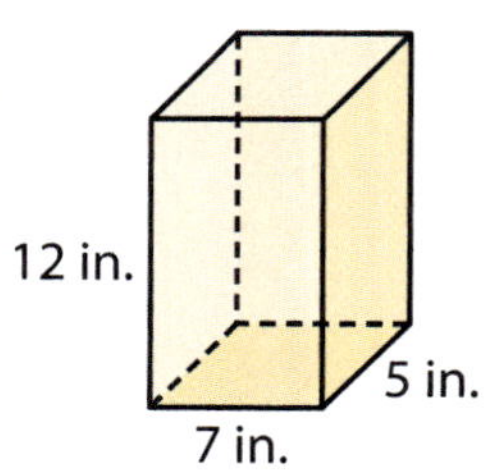

____

6. The volume of a triangular prism is 264 cubic feet. The area of a base of the prism is 48 square feet. Find the height of the prism.

(Lesson 9.5) ____________________

EXERCISES

A glass paperweight has a composite shape: a square pyramid fitting exactly on top of an 8 centimeter cube. The pyramid has a height of 3 cm. Each triangular face has a height of 5 centimeters. (Lessons 9.4, 9.5)

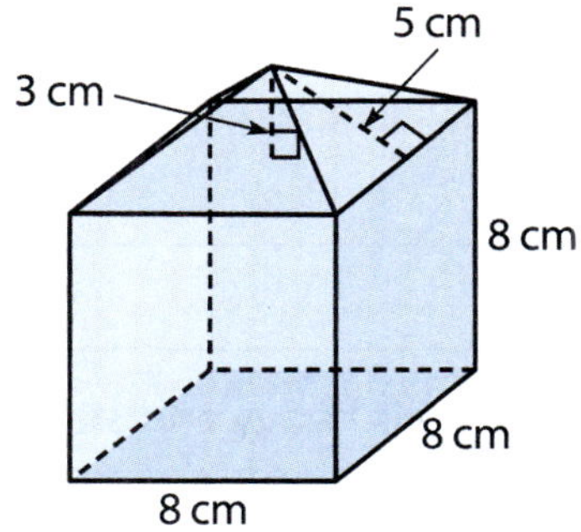

7. What is the volume of the paperweight? ________

8. What is the total surface area of the paperweight? ________

Unit 4 Performance Tasks

1. **CAREERS IN MATH** Product Design Engineer Miranda is a product design engineer working for a sporting goods company. She designs a tent in the shape of a triangular prism. The approximate dimensions of the tent are shown in the diagram.

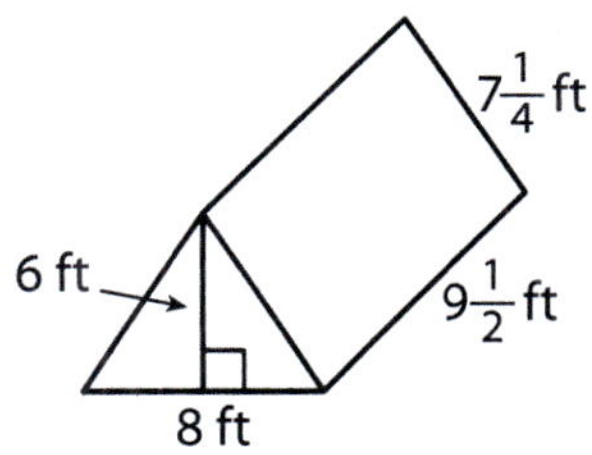

a. How many square feet of material does Miranda need to make the tent (including the floor)? Show your work.

____

____

b. What is the volume of the tent? Show your work.

____

c. Suppose Miranda wants to increase the volume of the tent by 10%. The specifications for the height (6 feet) and the width (8 feet) must stay the same. How can Miranda meet this new requirement? Explain.

____

____

2. Li is making a stand to display a sculpture made in art class. The stand will be 45 centimeters wide, 25 centimeters long, and 1.2 meters high.

a. What is the volume of the stand? Write your answer in cubic centimeters.

____

____

b. Li needs to fill the stand with sand so that it is heavy and stable. Each piece of wood is 1 centimeter thick. The boards are put together as shown in the figure, which is not drawn to scale. How many cubic centimeters of sand does she need to fill the stand? Explain how you found your answer.

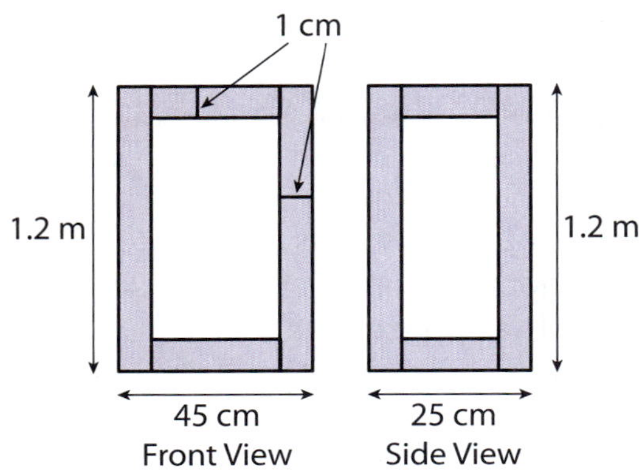

____

____

____

____

UNIT 4 MIXED REVIEW

Assessment Readiness

Personal Math Trainer

my.hrw.com

Online Assessment and Intervention

Selected Response

1. What is the value of x?

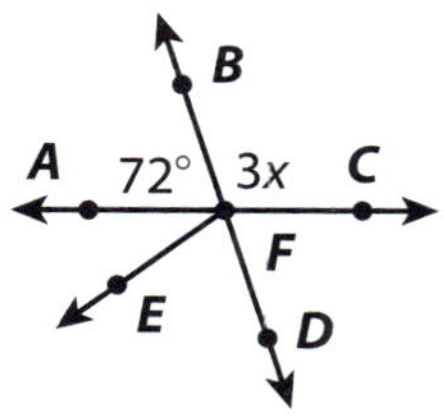

Ⓐ 108° Ⓒ 36°

Ⓑ 72° Ⓓ 18°

2. On a map with a scale of 2 cm = 1 km, the distance from Beau's house to the beach is 4.6 centimeters. What is the actual distance?

Ⓐ 2.3 km Ⓒ 6.5 km

Ⓑ 4.6 km Ⓓ 9.2 km

3. Lalasa and Yasmin are designing a triangular banner to hang in the school gymnasium. They first draw the design on paper. The triangle has a base of 5 inches and a height of 7 inches. If 1 inch on the drawing is equivalent to 1.5 feet on the actual banner, what will the area of the actual banner be?

Ⓐ 17.5 ft^2 Ⓒ 39.375 ft^2

Ⓑ 52.5 ft^2 Ⓓ 78.75 ft^2

4. Sonya has four straws of different lengths: 2 cm, 8 cm, 14 cm, and 16 cm. How many triangles can she make using the straws?

Ⓐ no triangle

Ⓑ one triangle

Ⓒ two triangles

Ⓓ more than two triangles

5. A one-topping pizza costs \$15.00. Each additional topping costs \$1.25. Let x be the number of additional toppings. You have \$20 to spend. Which equation can you solve to find the number of additional toppings you can get on your pizza?

Ⓐ $15x + 1.25 = 20$

Ⓑ $1.25x + 15 = 20$

Ⓒ $15x - 1.25 = 20$

Ⓓ $1.25x - 15 = 20$

6. A bank offers a home improvement loan with simple interest at an annual rate of 12%. J.T. borrows \$14,000 over a period of 3 years. How much will he pay back altogether?

Ⓐ \$15,680 Ⓒ \$19,040

Ⓑ \$17,360 Ⓓ \$20,720

7. What is the volume of a triangular prism that is 75 centimeters long and that has a base with an area of 30 square centimeters?

Ⓐ 2.5 cubic centimeters

Ⓑ 750 cubic centimeters

Ⓒ 1,125 cubic centimeters

Ⓓ 2,250 cubic centimeters

8. Consider the right circular cone shown.

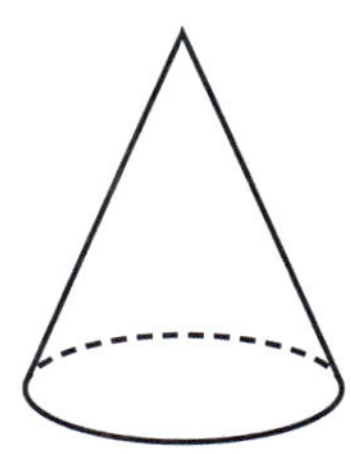

If a vertical plane slices through the cone to create two identical half cones, what is the shape of the cross section?

Ⓐ a rectangle Ⓒ a triangle

Ⓑ a square Ⓓ a circle

9. The radius of the circle is given in meters. What is the circumference of the circle? Use 3.14 for π.

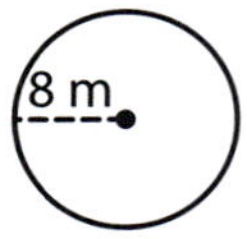

Ⓐ 25.12 meters

Ⓑ 50.24 meters

Ⓒ 200.96 meters

Ⓓ 803.84 meters

10. The dimensions of the figure are given in millimeters. What is the area of the two-dimensional figure?

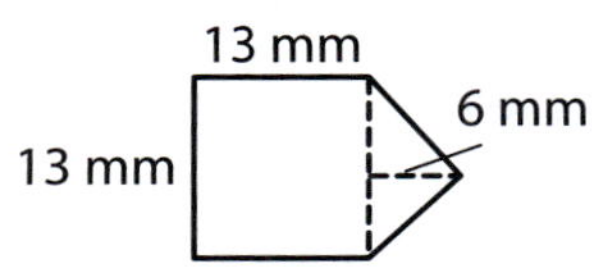

Ⓐ 39 square millimeters

Ⓑ 169 square millimeters

Ⓒ 208 square millimeters

Ⓓ 247 square millimeters

11. A forest ranger wants to determine the radius of the trunk of a tree. She measures the circumference to be 8.6 feet. What is the trunk's radius to the nearest tenth of a foot?

Ⓐ 1.4 ft Ⓑ 4.3 ft

Ⓒ 2.7 ft Ⓓ 17.2 ft

Hot Tip! **It is helpful to draw or redraw a figure. Answers to geometry problems may become clearer as you redraw the figure.**

12. What is the measure in degrees of an angle that is supplementary to a 74° angle?

Ⓐ 16°

Ⓑ 74°

Ⓒ 90°

Ⓓ 106°

13. What is the volume in cubic centimeters of a rectangular prism that has a length of 6.2 centimeters, a width of 3.5 centimeters, and a height of 10 centimeters?

Ⓐ 19.7 cm^3 Ⓒ 217.0 cm^3

Ⓑ 108.5 cm^3 Ⓓ 237.4 cm^3

14. A patio is the shape of a circle with diameter shown.

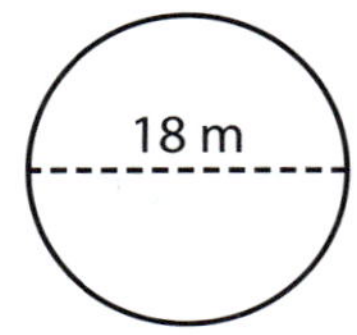

What is the area of the patio? Use 3.14 for π.

Ⓐ 9.00 m^2

Ⓑ 28.26 m^2

Ⓒ 254.34 m^2

Ⓓ 1,017.36 m^2

Mini-Tasks

15. Petra fills a small cardboard box with sand. The dimensions of the box are 3 inches by 4 inches by 2 inches.

a. What is the volume of the box?

____

b. Petra decides to cover the box by gluing on wrapping paper. How much wrapping paper does she need to cover all six sides of the box?

____

c. Petra has a second, larger box that is 6 inches by 8 inches by 4 inches. How many times larger is the volume of this second box? The surface area?

____

____

UNIT 5

Statistics

CAREERS IN MATH

Entomologist An entomologist is a biologist who studies insects. These scientists analyze data and use mathematical models to understand and predict the behavior of insect populations.

If you are interested in a career in entomology, you should study these mathematical subjects:

- Algebra
- Trigonometry
- Probability and Statistics
- Calculus

Research other careers that require the analysis of data and use of mathematical models.

Unit 5 Performance Task

At the end of the unit, check out how **entomologists** use math.

UNIT 5

Vocabulary Preview

Use the puzzle to preview key vocabulary from this unit. Unscramble the circled letters to answer the riddle at the bottom of the page.

Across

2. A sample in which every person, object, or event has an equal chance of being selected (2 words). (Lesson 10.1)

4. Part of a population chosen to represent the entire group. (Lesson 10.1)

5. A display in which each piece of data is represented by a dot above a number line (2 words). (Lesson 11.2)

6. An integer generated by chance, such as by rolling a number cube or using a graphing calculator. (Lesson 10.1)

Down

1. The entire group of objects, individuals, or events in a set of data. (Lesson 10.1)

3. A display that shows how the values in a data set are distributed (2 words). (Lesson 11.3)

Q: Where do cowboys who love statistics live?

A: on the ___ ___ ___ ___ ___!

Random Samples and Populations

MODULE 10

ESSENTIAL QUESTION

How can you use random samples and populations to solve real-world problems?

Real-World Video

my.hrw.com

Scientists study animals like dart frogs to learn more about characteristics such as behavior, diet, and communication.

GO DIGITAL
my.hrw.com

my.hrw.com
Go digital with your write-in student edition, accessible on any device.

Math On the Spot
Scan with your smart phone to jump directly to the online edition, video tutor, and more.

Animated Math
Interactively explore key concepts to see how math works.

Personal Math Trainer
Get immediate feedback and help as you work through practice sets.

Reading Start-Up

Visualize Vocabulary

Use the ✔ words to complete the right column of the chart.

Box Plots to Display Data	
Definition	**Review Word**
A display that uses values from a data set to show how the values are spread out.	
The middle value of a data set.	
The median of the lower half of the data.	
The median of the upper half of the data.	

Vocabulary

Review Words

✔ box plot *(diagrama de caja)*
data *(datos)*
dot plot *(diagrama de puntos)*
interquartile range *(rango entre cuartiles)*
✔ lower quartile *(cuartil inferior)*
✔ median *(mediana)*
spread *(dispersión)*
survey *(estudio)*
✔ upper quartile *(cuartil superior)*

Preview Words

biased sample *(muestra sesgada)*
population *(población)*
random sample *(muestra aleatoria)*
sample *(muestra)*

Understand Vocabulary

Complete each sentence, using the preview words.

1. An entire group of objects, individuals, or events is a

   ____________________.

2. A ____________________ is part of the population chosen to represent the entire group.

3. A sample that does not accurately represent the population is a

   ____________________.

Active Reading

Tri-Fold Before beginning the module, create a tri-fold to help you learn the concepts and vocabulary in this module. Fold the paper into three sections. Label the columns "What I Know," "What I Need to Know," and "What I Learned." Complete the first two columns before you read. After studying the module, complete the third column.

Are YOU Ready?

Complete these exercises to review skills you will need for this module.

Personal Math Trainer
my.hrw.com
Online Assessment and Intervention

Solve Proportions

EXAMPLE

$\frac{a}{1} = \frac{30}{1.5}$

$a \times 1.5 = 1 \times 30$ — Write the cross products.

$1.5a = 30$ — Simplify.

$\frac{1.5a}{1.5} = \frac{30}{1.5}$ — Divide both sides by 1.5.

$a = 20$

Solve for *x*.

1. $\frac{x}{16} = \frac{45}{40}$ ______ **2.** $\frac{x}{5} = \frac{1}{4}$ ______ **3.** $\frac{2.5}{10} = \frac{x}{50}$ ______ **4.** $\frac{x}{6} = \frac{2}{9}$ ______

Find the Range

EXAMPLE

29, 26, 21, 30, 32, 19 — Order the data from least to greatest.

19, 21, 26, 29, 30, 32

range $= 32 - 19$ — The range is the difference between the greatest and the least data items.

$= 13$

Find the range of the data.

5. 52, 48, 57, 47, 49, 60, 59, 51 ______

6. 5, 9, 13, 6, 4, 5, 8, 12, 12, 6 ______

7. 97, 106, 99, 97, 115, 95, 108, 100 ______

8. 27, 13, 35, 19, 71, 12, 66, 47, 39 ______

Find the Mean

EXAMPLE

21, 15, 26, 19, 25, 14

$\text{mean} = \frac{21 + 15 + 26 + 19 + 25 + 14}{6}$ — The mean is the sum of the data items divided by the number of items.

$= \frac{120}{6}$

$= 20$

Find the mean of each set of data.

9. 3, 5, 7, 3, 6, 4, 8, 6, 9, 5 ______

10. 8.1, 9.4, 11.3, 6.7, 6.2, 7.5 ______

Are YOU Ready? *(cont'd)*

Complete these exercises to review skills you will need for this module.

Solve Proportions

11. A designer uses 8 clay beads for every 12 wooden beads to make a necklace. The designer has 42 wooden beads. He sets up the proportion $\frac{8}{42} = \frac{x}{12}$ to find the number of clay beads he will need to make necklaces. Is the proportion correct? How many clay beads does the designer need? Explain.

Find the Range

12. Students recorded the temperature at noon each day for a 10-day period at their school. The temperatures, in °F, are 53, 48, 52, 67, 60, 55, 58, 46, 63, and 58. What is the range of the temperatures? Show your work.

Find the Mean

13. Rehan scored 87 on two history tests this term. His other history test scores were 79, 82, and 90. Find the mean of Rehan's history test scores.

LESSON 10.1

Populations and Samples

7.5.10.1

Students will use a sample to gain information about a population.

ESSENTIAL QUESTION

How can you use a sample to gain information about a population?

EXPLORE ACTIVITY Real World

Random and Non-Random Sampling

When information is being gathered about a group, the entire group of objects, individuals, or events is called the **population**. A **sample** is part of the population that is chosen to represent the entire group.

A vegetable garden has 36 tomato plants arranged in a 6-by-6 array as shown. The number in a given cell tells how many tomatoes are on that plant.

The gardener decides to find the average number of tomatoes on the plants based on a randomly chosen sample, because counting the number of tomatoes on all of the plants is too time-consuming.

To simulate a random selection: roll two number cubes a number of times. Let the first number cube represent the row, and the second represent the column. Record the number in each randomly selected cell. Do not count any cell more than once.

						Row
	8	9	13	18	24	15	**1**
	34	42	46	20	13	41	**2**
	29	21	14	45	27	43	**3**
	22	45	46	41	22	33	**4**
	12	42	44	17	42	11	**5**
	18	26	43	32	33	26	**6**
Column	**1**	**2**	**3**	**4**	**5**	**6**	

A Find the average number of tomatoes on 6 randomly selected plants. ________

B Find the average number of tomatoes on the plants in the first row. ________

C Find the average number of tomatoes on 12 randomly selected plants. ________

D A *representative* sample has the same characteristics as the population.

In which part, **A** or **B**, is the sample more likely representative? Explain.

____

____

E The samples in Parts **A** and **C** were both chosen randomly, but one is more likely to be representative. Which one is it? Explain.

____

____

EXPLORE ACTIVITY *(cont'd)*

Reflect

1. How do the averages you got with each sampling method compare to the average for the entire population, which is 28.25?

____

____

2. Why might selecting only the plants in the first row not give a close average?

____

____

Math On the Spot
my.hrw.com

Random Samples and Biased Samples

A sample in which every person, object, or event has an equal chance of being selected is called a **random sample**. A random sample is more likely to be representative of a population than a sample not chosen randomly. When a sample does not accurately represent the population, it is called a **biased sample**.

EXAMPLE 1 Real World

Identify the population. Determine whether each sample is a random sample or a biased sample. Explain your reasoning.

A Roberto wants to know the favorite sport of adults in his hometown. He surveys 50 adults at a baseball game.

The population is adults in Roberto's hometown.

Think: People who don't like baseball will not be represented in this sample.

The sample is biased.

B Paula wants to know the favorite type of music for students in her class. She puts the names of all students in a hat, draws 8 names, and surveys those students.

The population is students in Paula's class.

Think: Each student has an equal chance of being selected.

The sample is random.

Math Talk
Mathematical Processes
Why do you think samples are used? Why not survey each member of the population?

Reflect

3. **What if?** Suppose Paula draws 14 names for her random sample in Part **B**. Predict how this will affect the likelihood that the sample is representative.

____

____

YOUR TURN

4. For a survey, a company manager assigned a number to each of the company's 500 employees, and put the numbers in a bag. The manager chose 20 numbers and surveyed the employees with those numbers. Did the manager choose a random sample?

____

____

Personal Math Trainer
Online Assessment and Intervention
my.hrw.com

Bias in Survey Questions

Once you have selected a representative sample of the population, be sure that the data is gathered without bias. Make sure that the survey questions themselves do not sway people to respond a certain way.

Math On the Spot
my.hrw.com

EXAMPLE 2 Real World

In Madison County, residents were surveyed about a new skateboard park. Determine whether each survey question may be biased. Explain.

A Would you like to waste the taxpayers' money to build a frivolous skateboard park?

This question is biased. It discourages residents from saying yes to a new skateboard park by implying it is a waste of money.

B Do you favor a new skateboard park?

This question is not biased. It does not include an opinion on the skateboard park.

C Studies have shown that having a safe place to go keeps kids out of trouble. Would you like to invest taxpayers' money to build a skateboard park?

This question is biased. It leads people to say yes because it mentions having a safe place for kids to go and to stay out of trouble.

YOUR TURN

Determine whether each question may be biased. Explain.

5. When it comes to pets, do you prefer cats?

____

6. What is your favorite season?

____

____

Personal Math Trainer
Online Assessment and Intervention
my.hrw.com

Guided Practice

1. Follow each method described below to collect data to estimate the average shoe size of seventh grade boys. (Explore Activity)

Method 1

A Randomly select 6 seventh grade boys and ask each his shoe size. Record your results in a table like the one shown.

____

B Find the mean of this data. Mean:

____

Random Sample of Seventh Grade Male Students	
Student	Shoe Size

Method 2

A Find the 6 boys in your math class with the largest shoes and ask their shoe size. Record your results in a table like the one shown in Method 1.

____

B Find the mean of this data. Mean: _______________

2. Method 1 produces results that are **more / less** representative of the entire student population because it is a **random / biased** sample. (Example 1)

3. Method 2 produces results that are **more / less** representative of the entire student population because it is a **random / biased** sample. (Example 1)

4. Heidi decides to use a random sample to determine her classmates' favorite color. She asks, "Is green your favorite color?" Is Heidi's question biased? If so, give an example of an unbiased question that would serve Heidi better. (Example 2)

____

ESSENTIAL QUESTION CHECK-IN

5. How can you select a sample so that the information gained represents the entire population?

____

____

Name ________ Class ________ Date ________

10.1 Independent Practice

Personal Math Trainer
Online Assessment and Intervention
my.hrw.com

6. A school cafeteria is considering new menu options. The manager puts a comment box in the cafeteria where students can anonymously submit their choices. Is this a representative sample? Explain why or why not.

______

______

______

7. Nancy hears a report that the average price of gasoline is $2.82. She averages the prices of stations near her home. She finds the average price of gas to be $3.03. Why are the averages different?

______

______

______

For 8–10, determine whether each sample is a random sample or a biased sample. Explain.

8. Carol wants to find out the favorite foods of students at her middle school. She asks the boys' basketball team about their favorite foods.

______

______

9. Dallas wants to know what elective subjects the students at his school like best. He surveys students who are leaving band class.

______

______

______

10. To choose a sample for a survey of seventh graders, the student council puts pieces of paper with the names of all the seventh graders in a bag, and selects 20 names.

______

______

______

11. Members of a polling organization survey 700 of the 7,453 registered voters in a town by randomly choosing names from a list of all registered voters. Is their sample likely to be representative?

______

______

For 12–13, determine whether each question may be biased. Explain.

12. Joey wants to find out what sport seventh grade girls like most. He asks girls, "Is basketball your favorite sport?"

______

______

______

13. Jae wants to find out what type of art her fellow students enjoy most. She asks her classmates, "What is your favorite type of art?"

______

______

______

H.O.T. FOCUS ON HIGHER ORDER THINKING

Work Area

14. Draw Conclusions Determine which sampling method will better represent the entire population. Justify your answer.

Student Attendance at Football Games	
Sampling Method	**Results of Survey**
Collin surveys 78 students by randomly choosing names from the school directory.	63% attend football games.
Karl surveys 25 students that were sitting near him during lunch.	84% attend football games.

____

____

____

____

____

15. Multistep Barbara surveyed students in her school by looking at an alphabetical list of the 600 student names, dividing them into groups of 10, and randomly choosing one from each group.

a. How many students did she survey? What type of sample is this?

____

b. Barbara found that 35 of the survey participants had pets. About what percent of the students she surveyed had pets? Is it safe to believe that about the same percent of students in the school have pets? Explain your thinking.

____

____

____

16. Communicating Mathematical Ideas Carlo is shown the results of two surveys about the preferred practice day of all players in a soccer league. The surveys are based on two different samples, and the results are very different. What information about the samples and surveys might help Carlo decide which result is likely to be more accurate?

____

____

____

Getting Ready 10.2

Applying Proportional Reasoning

7.5.GR.10.2

Students will use proportional reasoning to solve multistep ratio problems.

ESSENTIAL QUESTION

How can you use proportional reasoning to solve multistep ratio problems?

EXPLORE ACTIVITY Real World

Proportional Reasoning in Recipes

Melinda uses 3 cups of salt for every 5 cups of flour to make modeling clay. How much flour will she use when she uses 30 cups of salt?

A Explain how you know that the dependent variable in the proportional relationship should represent the number of cups of salt.

____

____

B The unit rate for the relationship is ☐ cup of salt to 1 cup of flour.

C The graph helps you visualize the relationship. The triangles represent the fact that for each 1 cup increase in the amount of flour, the amount of salt increases by ☐ cup. For each triangle, the ratio of the height to the base is ☐, the constant of proportionality.

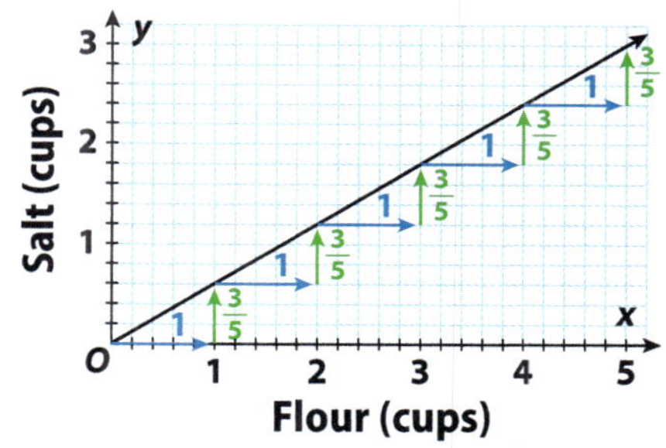

D An equation for the relationship is ________. When $y = 30$, $x =$ ______.

When Melinda uses 30 cups of salt, she uses ______ cups of flour.

Reflect

1. Melinda models the situation with the proportion $\frac{3}{5} = \frac{x}{30}$. Explain her error. Then show how to use the correct proportion to solve the problem.

____

____

Practice

1. Celine mixes raisins and peanuts to make a snack. She uses 0.75 cup of raisins for every 0.5 cup of peanuts. Write a proportion and use it to find the number of cups of raisins she uses if she uses 4.25 cups of peanuts.

2. Corey's salsa recipe calls for $2\frac{1}{2}$ cups of onions for every 4 pounds of tomatoes. Corey plans to use 10 pounds of tomatoes and wonders how many cups of onion he needs.

   a. Identify the quantities represented by the dependent and independent variables in the proportional relationship.

   b. **Explain the Error** Corey writes the equation $y = \frac{8}{5}x$ and finds that he needs 16 cups of onions. Describe and correct his error.

   c. **Focus on Reasoning** Explain why Corey should have known without calculating that the correct answer could not be 16 cups.

3. Neal makes a cleaning solution by mixing water and vinegar. He uses 7 cups of water for every 3 cups of vinegar. Write and use an equation to find how many more cups of vinegar he needs when he uses $7\frac{1}{2}$ cups of water than when he uses $4\frac{1}{2}$ cups of water. Define the variables.

4. **Explain the Error** In one middle school, there are 8 girls for every 7 boys. The total number of students is 330. Mischa wrote the proportion $\frac{8}{7} = \frac{x}{330}$ to find the number of girls in the school. Describe and correct her error.

LESSON 10.2

Making Inferences from a Random Sample

7.5.10.2

Students will use a random sample to make inferences about a population.

ESSENTIAL QUESTION

How can you use a random sample to make inferences about a population?

EXPLORE ACTIVITY 1 Real World

Using Dot Plots to Make Inferences

After obtaining a random sample of a population, you can make inferences about the population. Random samples are usually representative and support valid inferences.

Rosee asked students on the lunch line how many books they had in their backpacks. She recorded the data as a list: 2, 6, 1, 0, 4, 1, 4, 2, 2. Make a dot plot for the books carried by this sample of students.

STEP 1 Order the data from least to greatest. Find the least and greatest values in the data set.

STEP 2 Draw a number line from 0 to 6. Place a dot above each number on the number line for each time it appears in the data set.

Notice that the dot plot puts the data values in order.

Math Talk
Mathematical Processes
No students in Rosee's sample carry 3 books. Do you think this is true of all the students at the school? Explain.

Reflect

1. **Critical Thinking** How are the number of dots you plotted related to the number of data values?

____

2. **Draw Conclusions** Complete each qualitative inference about the population.

Most students have ____________ 1 book in their backpacks.

Most students have fewer than ____________ books in their backpacks.

Most students have between ____________ books in their backpacks.

3. **Analyze Relationships** What could Rosee do to improve the quality of her data?

____

EXPLORE ACTIVITY 2 Real World

Using Box Plots to Make Inferences

You can also analyze box plots to make inferences about a population.

The number of pets owned by a random sample of students at Park Middle school is shown below. Use the data to make a box plot.

9, 2, 0, 4, 6, 3, 3, 2, 5

STEP 1 Order the data from least to greatest. Then find the least and greatest values, the median, and the lower and upper quartiles.

STEP 2 The lower and upper quartiles can be calculated by finding the medians of each "half" of the number line that includes all the data.

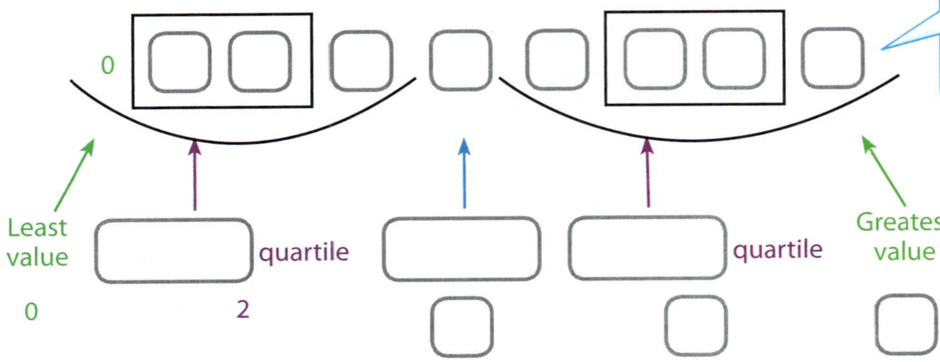

The lower quartile is the mean of 2 and 2. The upper quartile is the mean of 5 and 6.

Draw a number line that includes all the data values.

Plot a point for each of the values found in Step 1.

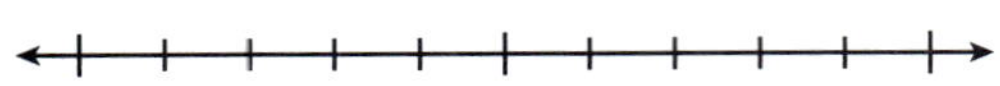

STEP 3 Draw a box from the lower to upper quartile. Inside the box, draw a vertical line through the median. Finally, draw the whiskers by connecting the least and greatest values to the box.

Math Talk
Mathematical Processes
What can you see from a box plot that is not readily apparent in a dot plot?

Reflect

4. **Draw Conclusions** Complete each qualitative inference about the population.

A good measure for the most likely number of pets is ______________.

50% of the students have between ______________ and 3 pets.

Almost every student in Parkview has at least ______________ pet.

Using Proportions to Make Inferences

If a sample is representative of the population, then the number of objects in the population with a given characteristic is proportional to the number of objects in the sample with that characteristic.

You can use data based on a random sample, along with proportional reasoning, to make inferences or predictions about the population.

Math On the Spot
my.hrw.com

EXAMPLE 1 Real World

A shipment to a warehouse consists of 3,500 MP3 players. The manager chooses a random sample of 50 MP3 players and finds that 3 are defective. How many MP3 players in the shipment are likely to be defective?

It is reasonable to make a prediction about the population because this sample is random.

STEP 1 Set up a proportion.

$$\frac{\text{defective MP3s in sample}}{\text{size of sample}} = \frac{\text{defective MP3s in population}}{\text{size of population}}$$

STEP 2 Substitute values into the proportion.

$$\frac{3}{50} = \frac{x}{3,500}$$

Substitute known values. Let x be the number of defective MP3 players in the population.

$$\frac{3 \cdot 70}{50 \cdot 70} = \frac{x}{3,500}$$

$50 \cdot 70 = 3,500$, so multiply the numerator and denominator by 70.

$$\frac{210}{3,500} = \frac{x}{3,500}$$

$$210 = x$$

Based on the sample, you can predict that 210 MP3 players in the shipment would be defective.

Animated Math
my.hrw.com

YOUR TURN

5. **What If?** How many MP3 players in the shipment would you predict to be damaged if 6 MP3s in the sample had been damaged?

____

Reflect

6. **Check for Reasonableness** How could you use estimation to check if your answer is reasonable?

____

____

Personal Math Trainer
Online Assessment and Intervention
my.hrw.com

Guided Practice

Patrons in the children's section of a local branch library were randomly selected and asked their ages. The librarian wants to use the data to infer the ages of all patrons of the children's section so he can select age appropriate activities. In 3–5, complete each inference. (Explore Activities 1 and 2)

7, 4, 7, 5, 4, 10, 11, 6, 7, 4

1. Make a dot plot of the sample population data.

2. Make a box plot of the sample population data.

3. The most common ages of children that use the library are ______ and ______.

4. The range of ages of children that use the library is from ______ to ______.

5. The median age of children that use the library is ______.

6. A manufacturer fills an order for 4,200 smart phones. The quality inspector selects a random sample of 60 phones and finds that 4 are defective. How many smart phones in the order are likely to be defective? (Example 1)

About __________ smart phones in the order are likely to be defective.

7. Part of the population of 4,500 elk at a wildlife preserve is infected with a parasite. A random sample of 50 elk shows that 8 of them are infected. How many elk are likely to be infected? (Example 1)

____

ESSENTIAL QUESTION CHECK-IN

8. How can you use a random sample of a population to make predictions?

____

____

____

____

____

Name ____________________ Class ____________ Date ____________

10.2 Independent Practice

Personal Math Trainer
Online Assessment and Intervention
my.hrw.com

9. A manager samples the receipts of every fifth person who goes through the line. Out of 50 people, 4 had a mispriced item. If 600 people go to this store each day, how many people would you expect to have a mispriced item?

____

10. Jerry randomly selects 20 boxes of crayons from the shelf and finds 2 boxes with at least one broken crayon. If the shelf holds 130 boxes, how many would you expect to have at least one broken crayon?

____

11. A random sample of dogs at different animal shelters in a city shows that 12 of the 60 dogs are puppies. The city's animal shelters collectively house 1,200 dogs each year. About how many dogs in all of the city's animal shelters are puppies?

____

12. Part of the population of 10,800 hawks at a national park are building a nest. A random sample of 72 hawks shows that 12 of them are building a nest. Estimate the number of hawks building a nest in the population.

____

13. In a wildlife preserve, a random sample of the population of 150 raccoons was caught and weighed. The results, given in pounds, were 17, 19, 20, 21, 23, 27, 28, 28, 28 and 32. Jean made the qualitative statement, "The average weight of the raccoon population is 25 pounds." Is her statement reasonable? Explain.

____

____

____

14. Greta collects the number of miles run each week from a random sample of female marathon runners. Her data are shown below. She made the qualitative statement, "25% of female marathoners run 13 or more miles a week." Is her statement reasonable? Explain. Data: 13, 14, 18, 13, 12, 17, 15, 12, 13, 19, 11, 14, 14, 18, 22, 12

____

____

____

15. A random sample of 20 of the 200 students at Garland Elementary is asked how many siblings each has. The data are ordered as shown. Make a dot plot of the data. Then make a qualitative statement about the population. Data: 0, 1, 1, 1, 1, 1, 1, 2, 2, 2, 2, 2, 3, 3, 3, 3, 4, 4, 4, 6

____

____

16. Linda collects a random sample of 12 of the 98 Wilderness Club members' ages. She makes an inference that most wilderness club members are between 20 and 40 years old. Describe what a box plot that would confirm Linda's inference should look like.

____

____

____

17. **What's the Error?** Kudrey was making a box plot. He first plotted the least and greatest data values. He then divided the distance into half, and then did this again for each half. What did Kudrey do wrong and what did his box plot look like?

H.O.T. FOCUS ON HIGHER ORDER THINKING

Work Area

18. **Communicating Mathematical Ideas** A dot plot includes all of the actual data values. Does a box plot include any of the actual data values?

19. **Make a Conjecture** Sammy counted the peanuts in several packages of roasted peanuts. He found that the bags had 102, 114, 97, 85, 106, 120, 107, and 111 peanuts. Should he make a box plot or dot plot to represent the data? Explain your reasoning.

20. **Represent Real-World Problems** The salaries for the eight employees at a small company are $20,000, $20,000, $22,000, $24,000, $24,000, $29,000, $34,000 and $79,000. Make a qualitative inference about a typical salary at this company. Would an advertisement that stated that the average salary earned at the company is $31,500 be misleading? Explain.

LESSON **10.3**

Generating Random Samples

7.5.10.3

Students will generate and use random samples to represent a population.

ESSENTIAL QUESTION

How can you generate and use random samples to represent a population?

EXPLORE ACTIVITY 1 Real World

Generating a Random Sample Using Technology

In an earlier lesson, you generated random samples by rolling number cubes. You can also generate random samples by using technology. In Explore Activity 1, you will generate samples using a graphing calculator.

Each of the 200 students in a school will have a chance to vote on one of two names, Tigers or Bears, for the school's athletic teams. A group of students decides to select a random sample of 20 students and ask them for which name they intend to vote. How can the group choose a random sample to represent the entire population of 200 students?

A One way to identify a random sample is to use a graphing calculator to generate random integers.

To simulate choosing 20 students at random from among 200 students:

- Press MATH, scroll right and select **PRB**, then select **5: randInt(**.
- Enter the least value, comma, greatest possible value.

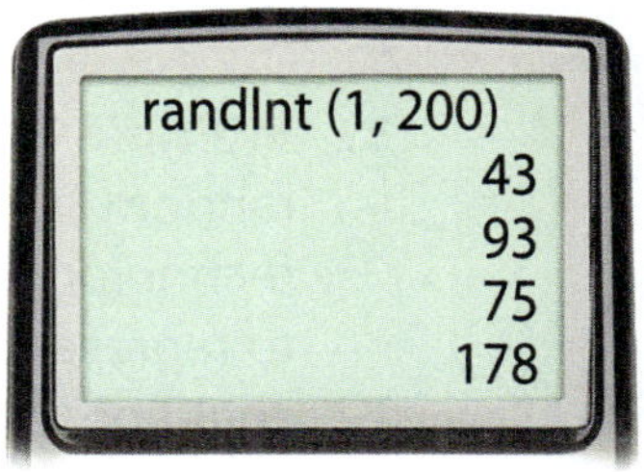

In this specific case, the students will enter **randInt** (☐, ☐)

because there are ________________ students in school.

- Hit ENTER ______ times to generate ______ random numbers.

The group gets a list of all the students in the school and assigns a number to each one. The group surveys the students with the given numbers.

Of the 20 students surveyed, 9 chose Tigers. The percent choosing

Tigers was ________. What might the group infer?

____

____

EXPLORE ACTIVITY 1 *(cont'd)*

B You can simulate multiple random samples to see how much statistical measures vary for different samples of size 20.

Assume that the 200 students are evenly divided among those voting for Tigers and those voting for Bears. You can generate random numbers and let each number represent a vote. Let numbers from 1 to 100 represent votes for Tigers, and numbers from 101 to 200 represent votes for Bears. For each simulated sample, use randInt(1, 200) and generate 20 numbers.

Perform the simulation 10 times and record how many numbers from 1 to 100 are generated. How many of the samples indicated that there were 9 or fewer votes for Tigers?

____

Combine your results with those of your classmates. Make a dot plot showing the number of numbers from 1 to 100 generated in each simulation.

____

Reflect

1. **Communicate Mathematical Reasoning** Assume that it was accurate to say that the 200 students are evenly divided among those voting for Tigers and those voting for Bears. Based on your results, does it seem likely that in a sample of size 20, there would be 9 or fewer votes for Tigers?

____

2. **Make a Prediction** Based on your answers, do you think it is likely that Tigers will win? Explain.

____

3. **Multiple Representations** Suppose you wanted to simulate a random sample for the situation in Explore Activity 1 without using technology. One way would be to use marbles of two different colors to represent students choosing the different names. Describe how you could perform a simulation.

____

____

____

____

____

____

EXPLORE ACTIVITY 2 Real World

Generating a Random Sample without Technology

A tree farm has a 100 acre square field arranged in a 10-by-10 array. The farmer wants to know the average number of trees per acre. Each cell in the table represents an acre. The number in each cell represents the number of trees on that acre.

22	24	27	29	31	24	27	29	30	25
37	22	60	53	62	42	64	53	41	62
61	54	57	34	44	66	39	60	65	40
45	33	64	36	33	51	62	66	42	42
37	34	57	33	47	43	66	33	61	66
66	45	46	67	60	59	51	46	67	48
53	46	35	35	55	56	61	46	38	64
55	51	54	62	55	58	51	45	41	53
61	38	48	48	43	59	64	48	49	47
41	53	53	59	58	48	62	53	45	59

The farmer decides to choose a random sample of 10 of the acres.

A To simulate the random selection, number the table columns 1–10 from left to right, and the rows 1–10 from top to bottom. Write the numbers 1–10 on identical pieces of paper. Place the pieces into a bag. Draw one at random, replace it, and draw another. Let the first number represent a table column, and the second represent a row. For instance, a draw of 2 and then 3 represents the cell in the second column and third row of the table, an acre containing 54 trees. Repeat this process 9 more times.

B Based on your sample, predict the average number of trees per acre. How does your answer compare with the actual mean number, 48.4?

____

____

C Compare your answer to **B** with several of your classmates' answers. Do they vary a lot? Is it likely that you can make a valid prediction about the average number of trees per acre? Explain.

____

EXPLORE ACTIVITY 2 *(cont'd)*

Reflect

4. **Communicate Mathematical Ideas** Suppose that you use the method in **A** to collect a random sample of 25 acres. Do you think any resulting prediction would be more or less reliable than your original one? Explain.

____

____

5. **Multiple Representations** How could you use technology to select the acres for your sample?

____

____

Guided Practice

A manufacturer gets a shipment of 600 batteries of which 50 are defective. The store manager wants to be able to test random samples in future shipments. She tests a random sample of 20 batteries in this shipment to see whether a sample of that size produces a reasonable inference about the entire shipment. (Explore Activities 1 and 2)

1. The manager selects a random sample using the formula

   randInt(☐, ☐) to generate ______ random numbers.

2. She lets numbers from 1 to ______ represent defective batteries, and

   ______ to ______ represent working batteries. She generates this list: 120, 413, 472, 564, 38, 266, 344, 476, 486, 177, 26, 331, 358, 131, 352, 227, 31, 253, 31, 277.

3. Does the sample produce a reasonable inference?

____

____

ESSENTIAL QUESTION CHECK-IN

4. What can happen if a sample is too small or is not random?

____

____

Name ________________ Class ________________ Date ________________

10.3 Independent Practice

Personal Math Trainer
Online Assessment and Intervention
my.hrw.com

Maureen owns three bagel shops. Each shop sells 500 bagels per day. Maureen asks her store managers to use a random sample to see how many whole-wheat bagels are sold at each store each day. The results are shown in the table. Use the table for 5–7.

	Total bagels in sample	Whole-wheat bagels
Shop A	50	10
Shop B	100	23
Shop C	25	7

5. If you assume the samples are representative, how many whole-wheat bagels might you infer are sold at each store?

____

6. Rank the samples for the shops in terms of how representative they are likely to be. Explain your rankings.

____

____

7. Which sample or samples should Maureen use to tell her managers how many whole-wheat bagels to make each day? Explain.

____

____

____

8. In a shipment of 1,000 T-shirts, 75 do not meet quality standards. The table below simulates a manager's random sample of 20 T-shirts to inspect. For the simulation, the integers 1 to 75 represent the below-standard shirts.

124	876	76	79	12	878	86	912	435	91
340	213	45	678	544	271	714	777	812	80

In the sample, how many of the shirts are below quality standards? ______

If someone used the sample to predict the number of below standard shirts in the shipment, how far off would the prediction be?

____

____

9. **Multistep** A 64-acre coconut farm is arranged in an 8-by-8 array. Mika wants to know the average number of coconut palms on each acre. Each cell in the table represents an acre of land. The number in each cell tells how many coconut palms grow on that particular acre.

56	54	40	34	44	66	43	65
66	33	42	36	33	51	62	63
33	34	66	33	47	43	66	61
46	35	48	67	60	59	52	67
46	32	64	35	55	47	61	38
45	51	53	62	55	58	51	41
48	38	47	48	43	59	64	54
53	67	59	59	58	48	62	45

a. The numbers in green represent Mika's random sample of 10 acres. What is the average number of coconut palms on the randomly selected acres?

____

b. Project the number of palms on the entire farm.

____

H.O.T. FOCUS ON HIGHER ORDER THINKING

Work Area

10. **Draw Conclusions** A random sample of 15 of the 78 competitors at a middle school gymnastics competition are asked their height. The data set lists the heights in inches: 55, 57, 57, 58, 59, 59, 59, 59, 59, 61, 62, 62, 63, 64, 66. What is the mean height of the sample? Do you think this is a reasonable prediction of the mean height of all competitors? Explain.

____

____

____

11. **Critical Thinking** The six-by-six grid contains the ages of actors in a youth Shakespeare festival. Describe a method for randomly selecting 8 cells by using number cubes. Then calculate the average of the 8 values you found.

12	15	16	9	21	11
9	10	14	10	13	12
16	21	14	12	8	14
16	20	9	16	19	18
17	14	12	15	10	15
12	20	14	10	12	9

____

____

____

____

____

____

12. **Communicating Mathematical Ideas** Describe how the size of a random sample affects how well it represents a population as a whole.

____

____

MODULE QUIZ

Ready to Go On?

Personal Math Trainer
Online Assessment and Intervention
my.hrw.com

10.1 Populations and Samples

1. A company uses a computer to identify their 600 most loyal customers from its database and then surveys those customers to find out how they like their service. Identify the population and determine whether the sample is random or biased.

____

____

10.2 Making Inferences from a Random Sample

2. A university has 30,330 students. In a random sample of 270 students, 18 speak three or more languages. Predict the number of students at the university who speak three or more languages.

____

10.3 Generating Random Samples

A store receives a shipment of 5,000 MP3 players. In a previous shipment of 5,000 MP3 players, 300 were defective. A store clerk generates random numbers to simulate a random sample of this shipment. The clerk lets the numbers 1 through 300 represent defective MP3 players, and the numbers 301 through 5,000 represent working MP3 players. The results are given.

13 2,195 3,873 525 900 167 1,094 1,472 709 5,000

3. Based on the sample, how many of the MP3 players might the clerk predict would be defective?

____

4. Can the manufacturer assume the prediction is valid? Explain.

____

ESSENTIAL QUESTION

5. How can you use random samples to solve real-world problems?

____

____

MODULE 10 MIXED REVIEW

Assessment Readiness

Personal Math Trainer

Online Assessment and Intervention

my.hrw.com

Selected Response

1. A farmer is using a random sample to predict the number of broken eggs in a shipment of 3,000 eggs. Using a calculator, the farmer generates the following random numbers. The numbers 1–250 represent broken eggs.

477	2,116	1,044	81	619	755
2,704	900	238	1,672	187	1,509

Based on this sample, how many broken eggs might the farmer expect?

Ⓐ 250 broken eggs

Ⓑ 375 broken eggs

Ⓒ 750 broken eggs

Ⓓ 900 broken eggs

2. A middle school has 490 students. Mae surveys a random sample of 60 students and finds that 24 of them have pet dogs. How many students are likely to have pet dogs?

Ⓐ 98

Ⓑ 196

Ⓒ 245

Ⓓ 294

3. A pair of shoes that normally costs $75 is on sale for $55. What is the percent decrease in the price, to the nearest whole percent?

Ⓐ 20%

Ⓑ 27%

Ⓒ 36%

Ⓓ 73%

4. Which of the following is a random sample?

Ⓐ A radio DJ asks the first 10 listeners who call in if they liked the last song.

Ⓑ 20 customers at a chicken restaurant are surveyed on their favorite food.

Ⓒ A polling organization numbers all registered voters, then generates 800 random integers. The polling organization interviews the 800 voters assigned those numbers.

Ⓓ Rebecca used an email poll to survey 100 students about how often they use the internet.

Mini-Task

5. Each cell in the table represents the number of people who work in one 25-square-block section of the town of Middleton. The mayor uses a random sample to estimate the average number of workers per block.

47	61	56	48	(56)
(60)	39	63	60	46
51	58	49	63	45
55	58	(50)	(43)	48
(62)	(53)	44	66	55

a. The circled numbers represent the mayor's random sample. What is the mean number of workers in this sample?

____

b. Predict the number of workers in the entire 25-block section of Middleton.

____

Analyzing and Comparing Data

MODULE 11

ESSENTIAL QUESTION

How can you solve real-world problems by analyzing and comparing data?

Real-World Video

Scientists place radio frequency tags on some animals within a population of that species. Then they track data, such as migration patterns, about the animals.

my.hrw.com

GO DIGITAL
my.hrw.com

my.hrw.com
Go digital with your write-in student edition, accessible on any device.

Math On the Spot
Scan with your smart phone to jump directly to the online edition, video tutor, and more.

Animated Math
Interactively explore key concepts to see how math works.

Personal Math Trainer
Get immediate feedback and help as you work through practice sets.

Reading Start-Up

Visualize Vocabulary

Use the ✔ words to complete the right column of the chart.

Statistical Data		
Definition	**Example**	**Review Word**
A group of facts.	Grades on history exams: 85, 85, 90, 92, 94	
The middle value of a data set.	85, 85, 90, 92, 94	
A value that summarizes a set of values, found through addition and division.	Results of the survey show that students typically spend 5 hours a week studying.	

Vocabulary

Review Words

✔ data *(datos)*
interquartile range *(rango entre cuartiles)*
✔ mean *(media)*
measure of center *(medida central)*
measure of spread *(medida de dispersión)*
✔ median *(mediana)*
survey *(encuesta)*

Preview Words

box plot *(diagrama de caja)*
dot plot *(diagrama de puntos)*
mean absolute deviation (MAD) *(desviación absoluta media, (DAM))*

Understand Vocabulary

Complete each sentence using the preview words.

1. A display that uses values from a data set to show how the values are spread out is a ____________________.

2. A ____________________ uses a number line to display data.

Active Reading

Layered Book Before beginning the module, create a layered book to help you learn the concepts in this module. Label the first flap with the module title. Label the remaining flaps with the lesson titles. As you study each lesson, write important ideas, such as vocabulary and formulas, under the appropriate flap. Refer to your finished layered book as you work on exercises from this module.

Are YOU Ready?

Complete these exercises to review skills you will need for this module.

Personal Math Trainer
my.hrw.com
Online Assessment and Intervention

Fractions, Decimals, and Percents

EXAMPLE Write $\frac{13}{20}$ as a decimal and a percent.

$$\begin{array}{r} 0.65 \\ 20\overline{)13.00} \\ \underline{-12\ 0} \\ 1\ 00 \\ \underline{-1\ 00} \\ 0 \end{array}$$

Write the fraction as a division problem.
Write a decimal point and zeros in the dividend.
Place a decimal point in the quotient.

$0.65 = 65\%$ Write the decimal as a percent.

Write each fraction as a decimal and a percent.

1. $\frac{7}{8}$ ________
2. $\frac{4}{5}$ ________
3. $\frac{1}{4}$ ________
4. $\frac{3}{10}$ ________
5. $\frac{19}{20}$ ________
6. $\frac{7}{25}$ ________
7. $\frac{37}{50}$ ________
8. $\frac{29}{100}$ ________

Find the Median and Mode

EXAMPLE 17, 14, 13, 16, 13, 11
11, 13, 13, 14, 16, 17 Order the data from least to greatest.

$\text{median} = \frac{13 + 14}{2} = 13.5$ The median is the middle item or the average of the two middle items.

$\text{mode} = 13$ The mode is the item that appears most frequently in the data.

Find the median and the mode of the data.

9. 11, 17, 7, 6, 7, 4, 15, 9 ________
10. 43, 37, 49, 51, 56, 40, 44, 50, 36 ________

Find the Mean

EXAMPLE 17, 14, 13, 16, 13, 11

$$\text{mean} = \frac{17 + 14 + 13 + 16 + 13 + 11}{6} = \frac{84}{6} = 14$$

The mean is the sum of the data items divided by the number of items.

Find the mean of the data.

11. 9, 16, 13, 14, 10, 16, 17, 9 ________
12. 108, 95, 104, 96, 97,106, 94 ________

Are YOU Ready? (cont'd)

Complete these exercises to review skills you will need for this module.

Fractions, Decimals, and Percents

13. A college basketball team won $\frac{21}{25}$ of its games. What is that fraction as a decimal and as a percent? Show your work.

Find the Median and Mode

14. The table shows the weekly total numbers of miles run by members of a running club. Find the median and the mode of the data.

Member	Bill	Thea	Roz	Hal	Ana	Nate	Jess	Marcos
Miles	18	15	10	12	17	14	12	20

Find the Mean

15. Three of the junior instructors at a tennis camp are 18 years old and two are 19 years old. The lead instructor is 28 years old. What is the mean age of the instructors? Explain your thinking.

LESSON 11.1

Comparing Data Displayed in Dot Plots

7.5.11.1

Students will compare two sets of data displayed in dot plots.

ESSENTIAL QUESTION

How do you compare two sets of data displayed in dot plots?

EXPLORE ACTIVITY Real World

Analyzing Dot Plots

You can use dot plots to analyze a data set, especially with respect to its center and spread.

People once used body parts for measurements. For example, an inch was the width of a man's thumb. In the 12th century, King Henry I of England stated that a yard was the distance from his nose to his outstretched arm's thumb. The dot plot shows the different lengths, in inches, of the "yards" for students in a 7th grade class.

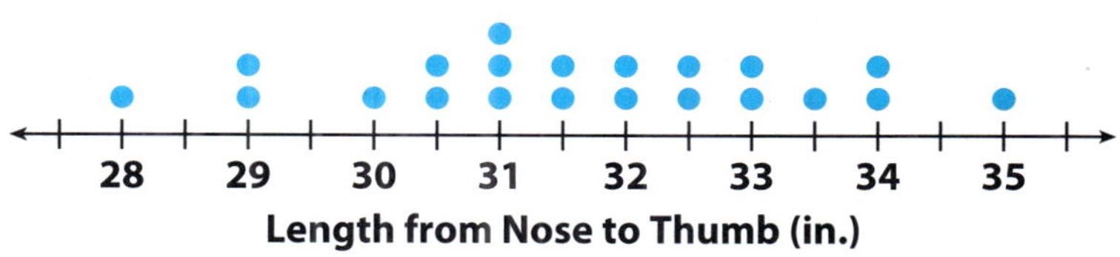

A Describe the shape of the dot plot. Are the dots evenly distributed or grouped on one side?

____

B Describe the center of the dot plot. What single dot would best represent the data?

____

____

C Describe the spread of the dot plot. Are there any outliers?

____

____

Reflect

1. Calculate the mean, median, and range of the data in the dot plot.

____

Math On the Spot
my.hrw.com

Comparing Dot Plots Visually

You can compare dot plots visually using various characteristics, such as center, spread, and shape.

EXAMPLE 1 Real World

The dot plots show the heights of 15 high school basketball players and the heights of 15 high school softball players.

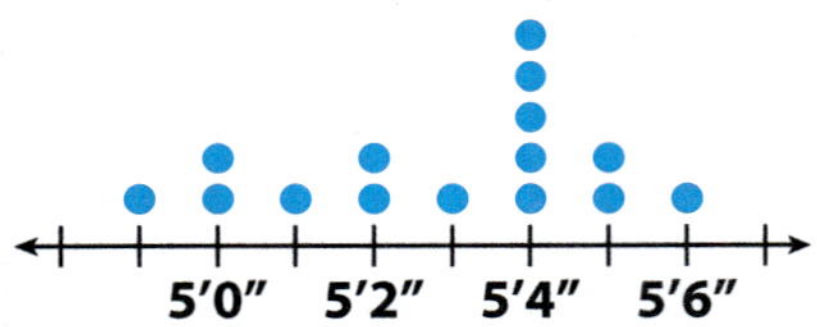

Softball Players' Heights

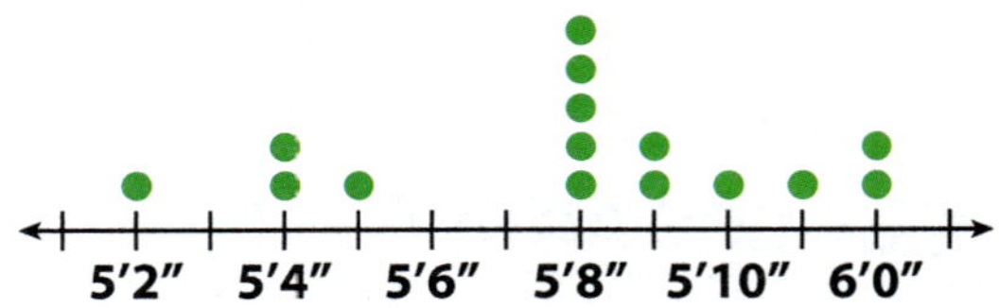

Basketball Players' Heights

A **Visually compare the shapes of the dot plots.**

Softball: All the data is 5′6″ or less.
Basketball: Most of the data is 5′8″ or greater.
As a group, the softball players are shorter than the basketball players.

B **Visually compare the centers of the dot plots.**

Softball: The data is centered around 5′4″.
Basketball: The data is centered around 5′8″.
This means that the most common height for the softball players is 5 feet 4 inches, and for the basketball players 5 feet 8 inches.

C **Visually compare the spreads of the dot plots.**

Softball: The spread is from 4′11″ to 5′6″.

Basketball: The spread is from 5′2″ to 6′0″.
There is a greater spread in heights for the basketball players.

Math Talk
Mathematical Processes

How do the heights of field hockey players compare with the heights of softball and basketball players?

YOUR TURN

2. Visually compare the dot plot of heights of field hockey players to the dot plots for softball and basketball players.

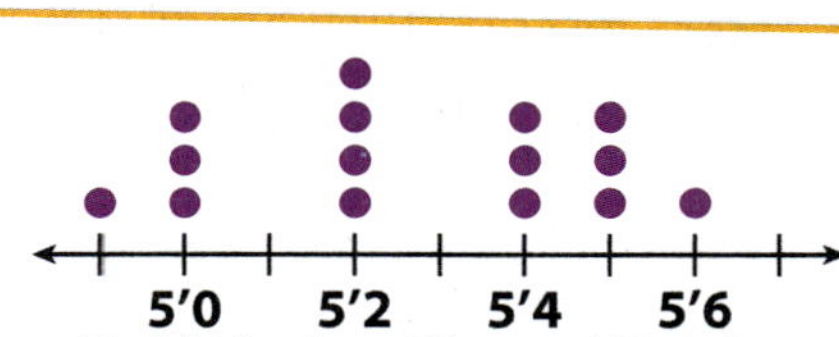

Field Hockey Players' Heights

Shape: ______________________________

____

Center: ______________________________

____

Spread: ______________________________

____

Personal Math Trainer
Online Assessment and Intervention
my.hrw.com

Comparing Dot Plots Numerically

You can also compare the shape, center, and spread of two dot plots numerically by calculating values related to the center and spread. Remember that outliers can affect your calculations.

Math On the Spot
my.hrw.com

EXAMPLE 2 Real World

Numerically compare the dot plots of the number of hours a class of students exercises each week to the number of hours they play video games each week.

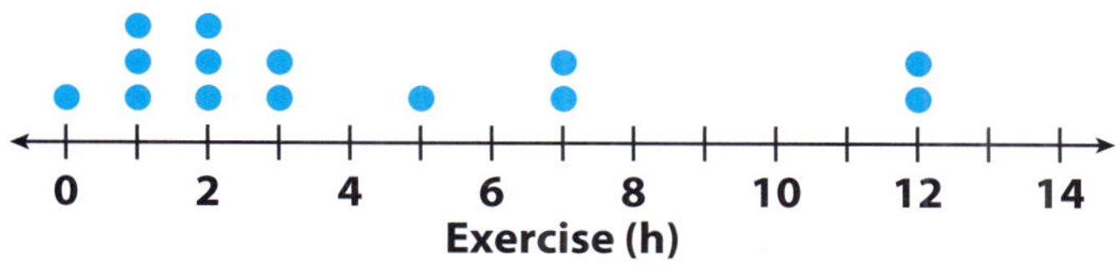

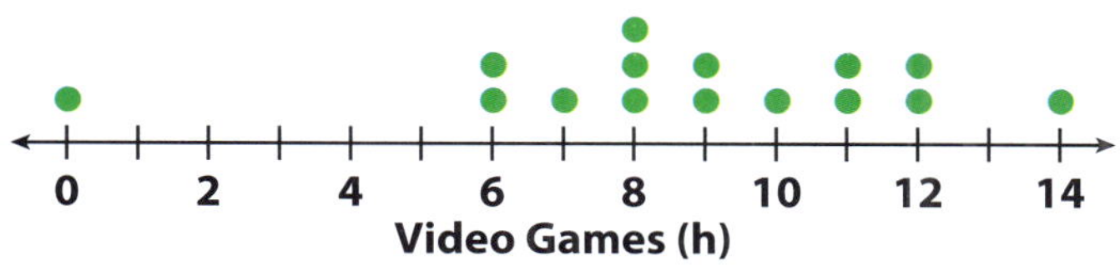

Animated Math
my.hrw.com

A **Compare the shapes of the dot plots.**

Exercise: Most of the data is less than 4 hours.
Video games: Most of the data is 6 hours or greater.

B **Compare the centers of the dot plots by finding the medians.**

Median for exercise: 2.5 hours. Even though there are outliers at 12 hours, most of the data is close to the median.
Median for video games: 9 hours. Even though there is an outlier at 0 hours, these values do not seem to affect the median.

Math Talk
Mathematical Processes
How do outliers affect the results of this data?

C **Compare the spreads of the dot plots by calculating the range.**

Exercise range with outlier: $12 - 0 = 12$ hours
Exercise range without outlier: $7 - 0 = 7$ hours
Video games range with outlier: $14 - 0 = 14$ hours
Video games range without outlier: $14 - 6 = 8$ hours

YOUR TURN

3. Calculate the median and range of the data in the dot plot. Then compare the results to the dot plot for Exercise in Example 2.

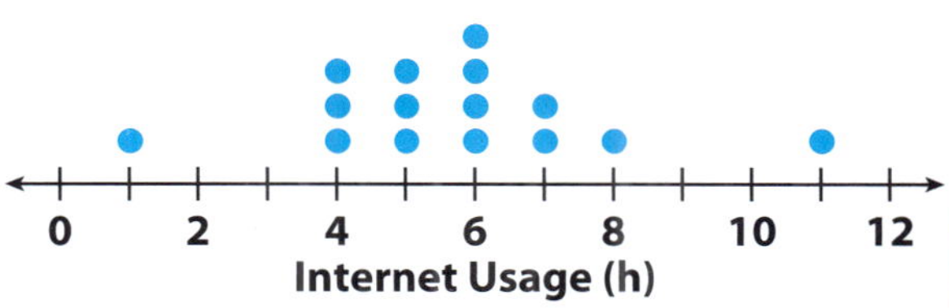

____

____

____

Personal Math Trainer
Online Assessment and Intervention
my.hrw.com

Guided Practice

The dot plots show the number of miles run per week for two different classes. For 1–5, use the dot plots shown.

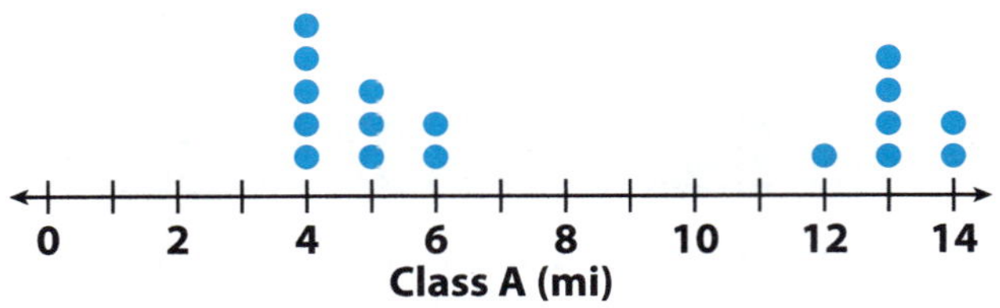

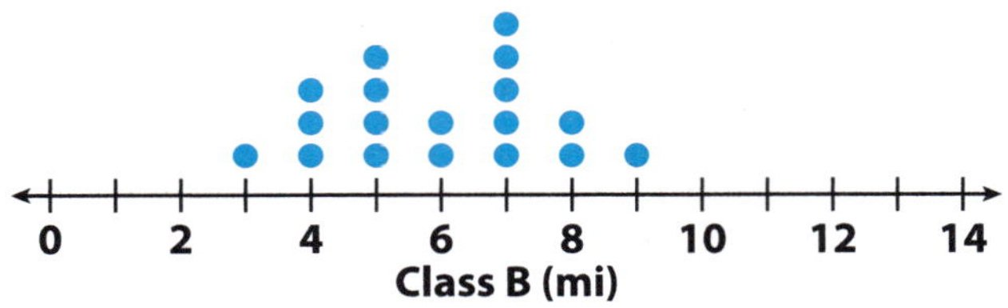

1. Compare the shapes of the dot plots.

____

____

2. Compare the centers of the dot plots.

____

____

3. Compare the spreads of the dot plots.

____

____

4. Calculate the medians of the dot plots.

____

5. Calculate the ranges of the dot plots.

____

ESSENTIAL QUESTION CHECK-IN

6. What do the medians and ranges of two dot plots tell you about the data?

____

____

____

Name ______________________ Class ______________ Date ____________

11.1 Independent Practice

Personal Math Trainer
Online Assessment and Intervention
my.hrw.com

The dot plot shows the number of letters in the spellings of the 12 months. Use the dot plot for 7–10.

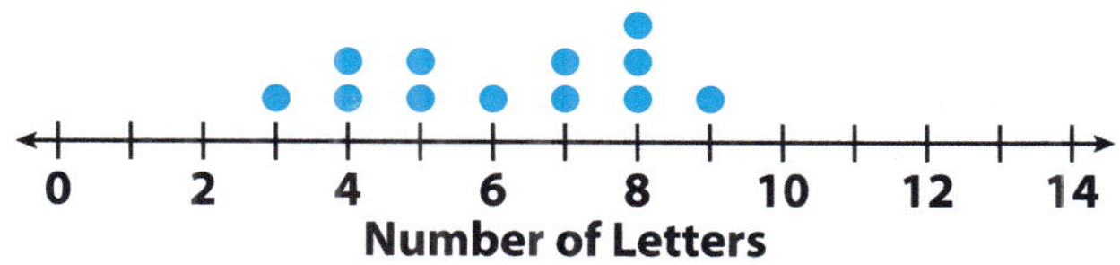

7. Describe the shape of the dot plot.

____

8. Describe the center of the dot plot.

____

9. Describe the spread of the dot plot.

____

10. Calculate the mean, median, and range of the data in the dot plot.

____

The dot plots show the mean number of days with rain per month for two cities.

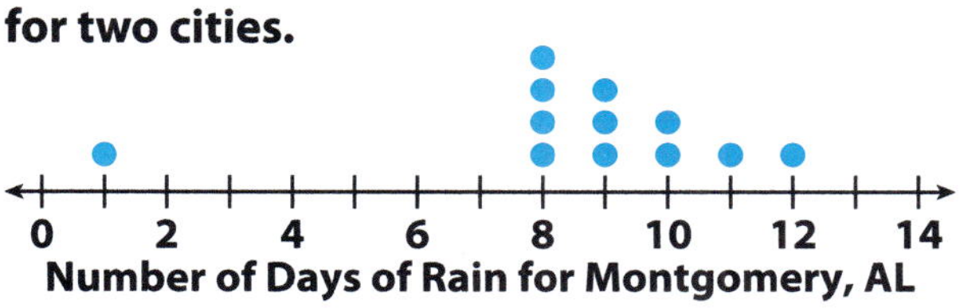

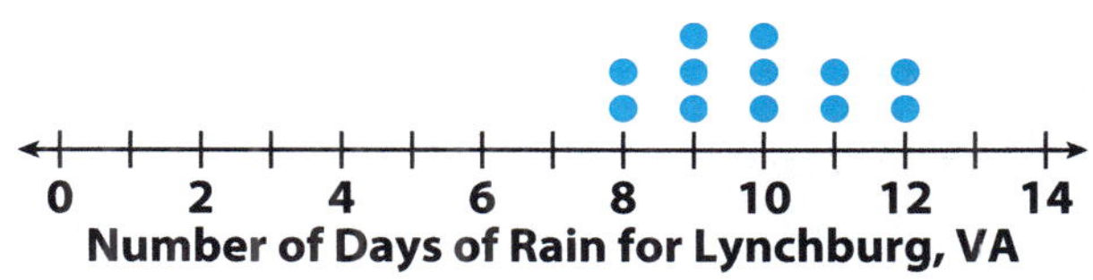

11. Compare the shapes of the dot plots.

____

____

12. Compare the centers of the dot plots.

____

____

13. Compare the spreads of the dot plots.

____

____

14. What do the dot plots tell you about the two cities with respect to their average monthly rainfall?

____

____

The dot plots show the shoe sizes of two different groups of people.

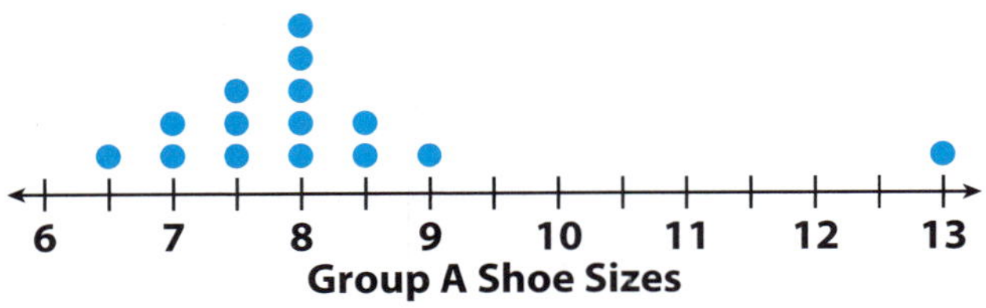

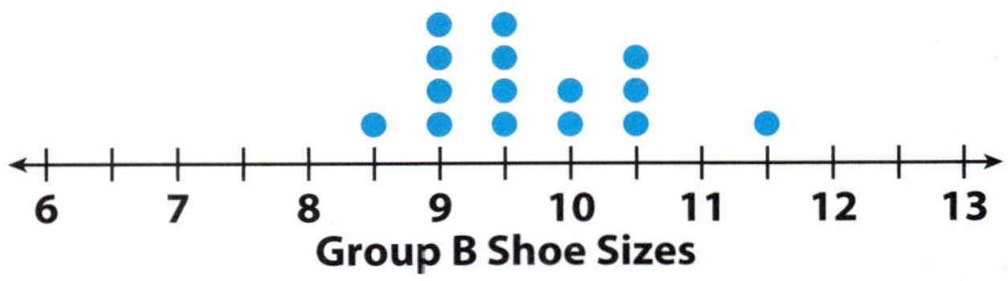

15. Compare the shapes of the dot plots.

____

____

16. Compare the medians of the dot plots.

____

17. Compare the ranges of the dot plots (with and without the outliers).

____

____

18. **Make A Conjecture** Provide a possible explanation for the results of the dot plots.

____

____

H.O.T. FOCUS ON HIGHER ORDER THINKING

Work Area

19. **Analyze Relationships** Can two dot plots have the same median and range but have completely different shapes? Justify your answer using examples.

____

____

____

____

____

20. **Draw Conclusions** What value is most affected by an outlier, the median or the range? Explain. Can you see these effects in a dot plot?

____

____

____

LESSON
11.2 Comparing Data Displayed in Box Plots

7.5.11.2

Students will compare two sets of data displayed in box plots.

ESSENTIAL QUESTION

How do you compare two sets of data displayed in box plots?

EXPLORE ACTIVITY Real World

Analyzing Box Plots

Box plots show five key values to represent a set of data, the least and greatest values, the lower and upper quartile, and the median. To create a box plot, arrange the data in order, and divide them into four equal-size parts or quarters. Then draw the box and the whiskers as shown.

The number of points a high school basketball player scored during the games he played this season are organized in the box plot shown.

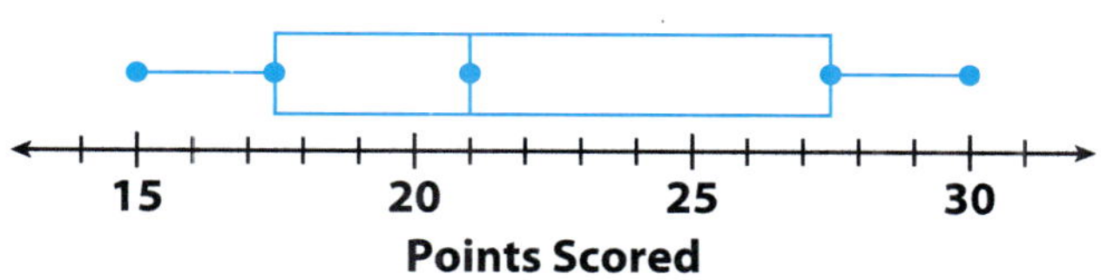

A Find the least and greatest values.

Least value: ________________ Greatest value: ________________

B Find the median and describe what it means for the data.

____

____

____

C Find and describe the lower and upper quartiles.

____

____

____

D The interquartile range is the difference between the upper and lower quartiles, which is represented by the length of the box. Find the interquartile range.

$Q_3 - Q_1 =$ ____________ − ____________ = ____________

Math Talk
Mathematical Processes

How do the lengths of the whiskers compare? Explain what this means.

EXPLORE ACTIVITY *(cont'd)*

Reflect

1. Why is one-half of the box wider than the other half of the box?

____

____

Math On the Spot
my.hrw.com

Box Plots with Similar Variability

You can compare two box plots numerically according to their centers, or medians, and their spreads, or variability. Range and interquartile range (IQR) are both measures of spread. Box plots with similar variability should have similar boxes and whiskers.

EXAMPLE 1 Real World

My Notes

The box plots show the distribution of times spent shopping by two different groups.

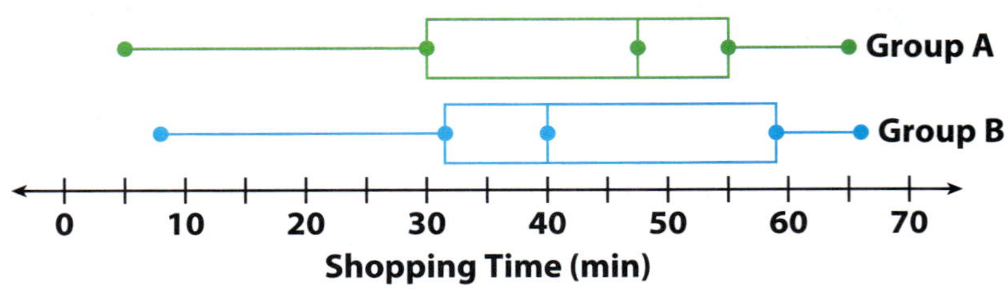

A Compare the shapes of the box plots.
The positions and lengths of the boxes and whiskers appear to be very similar. In both plots, the right whisker is shorter than the left whisker.

B Compare the centers of the box plots.
Group A's median, 47.5, is greater than Group B's, 40. This means that the median shopping time for Group A is 7.5 minutes more.

C Compare the spreads of the box plots.
The box shows the interquartile range. The boxes are similar.

Group A: $55 - 30 = 25$ min Group B: About $59 - 32 = 27$ min

The whiskers have similar lengths, with Group A's slightly shorter than Group B's.

Math Talk
Mathematical Processes
Which store has the shopper who shops longest? Explain how you know.

Reflect

2. Which group has the greater variability in the bottom 50% of shopping times? The top 50% of shopping times? Explain how you know.

____

____

YOUR TURN

3. The box plots show the distribution of weights in pounds of two different groups of football players. Compare the shapes, centers, and spreads of the box plots.

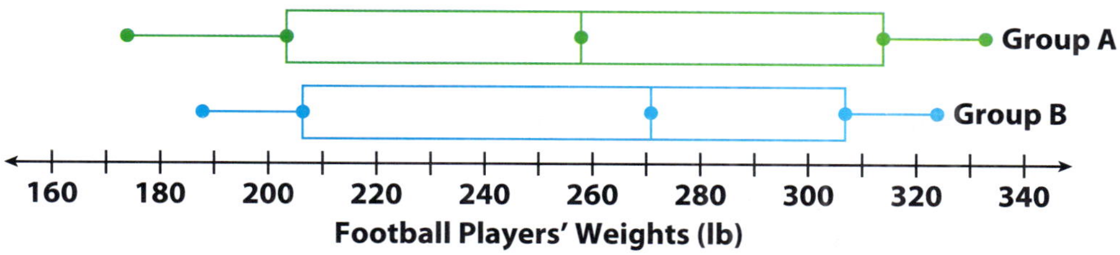

____

____

____

____

____

Personal Math Trainer

Online Assessment and Intervention

my.hrw.com

Box Plots with Different Variability

You can compare box plots with greater variability, where there is less overlap of the median and interquartile range.

Math On the Spot

my.hrw.com

EXAMPLE 2 Real World

The box plots show the distribution of the number of team wristbands sold daily by two different stores over the same time period.

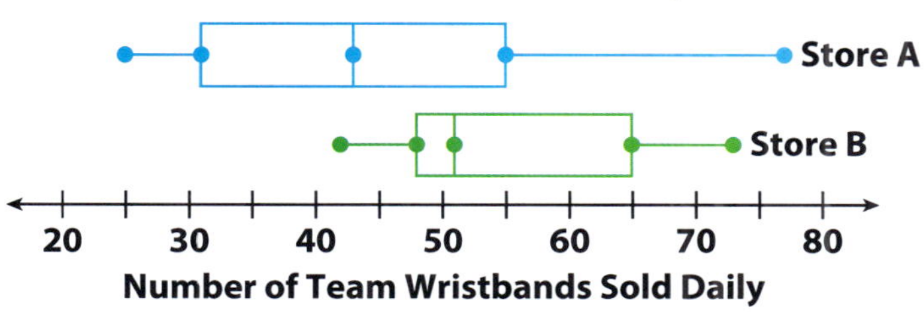

A Compare the shapes of the box plots.

Store A's box and right whisker are longer than Store B's.

B Compare the centers of the box plots.

Store A's median is about 43, and Store B's is about 51. Store A's median is close to Store B's minimum value, so about 50% of Store A's daily sales were less than sales on Store B's worst day.

C Compare the spreads of the box plots.

Store A has a greater spread. Its range and interquartile range are both greater. Four of Store B's key values are greater than Store A's corresponding value. Store B had a greater number of sales overall.

Personal Math Trainer
Online Assessment and Intervention
my.hrw.com

YOUR TURN

4. Compare the shape, center, and spread of the data in the box plot with the data for Stores A and B in the two box plots in Example 2.

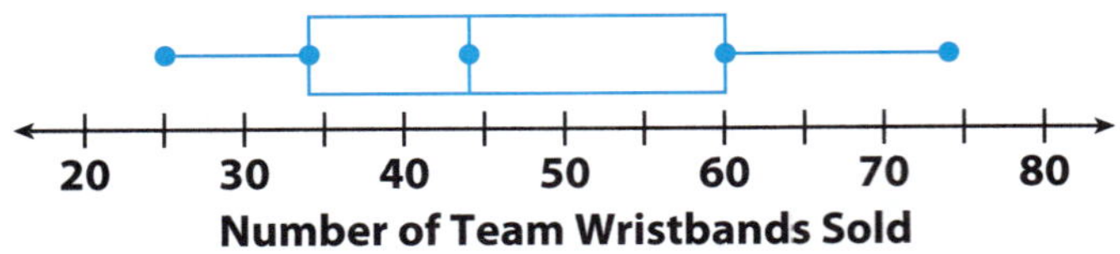

____

____

____

Guided Practice

For 1–3, use the box plot Terrence created for his math test scores. Find each value. (Explore Activity)

1. Minimum = ________ Maximum = ________

2. Median = __________

3. Range = __________ IQR = __________

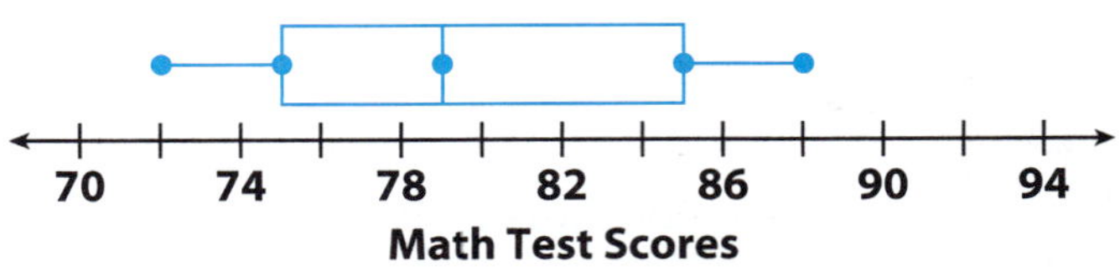

For 4–7, use the box plots showing the distribution of the heights of hockey and volleyball players. (Examples 1 and 2)

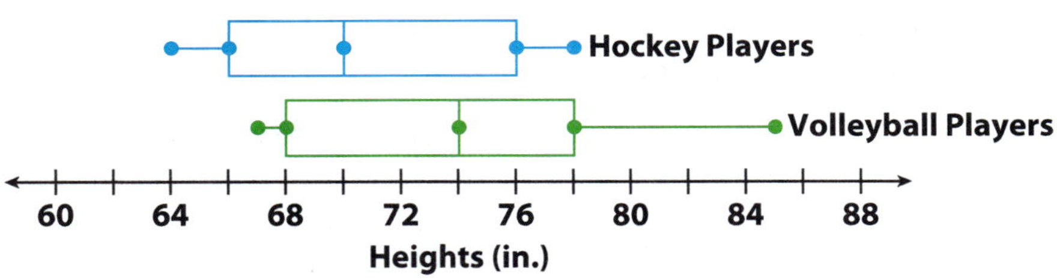

4. Which group has a greater median height? ______________________

5. Which group has the shortest player? ______________________

6. Which group has an interquartile range of about 10? ______________

ESSENTIAL QUESTION CHECK-IN

7. What information can you use to compare two box plots?

____

Name ______________________ Class ______________ Date ______________

11.2 Independent Practice

Personal Math Trainer
Online Assessment and Intervention
my.hrw.com

For 8–11, use the box plots of the distances traveled by two toy cars that were jumped from a ramp.

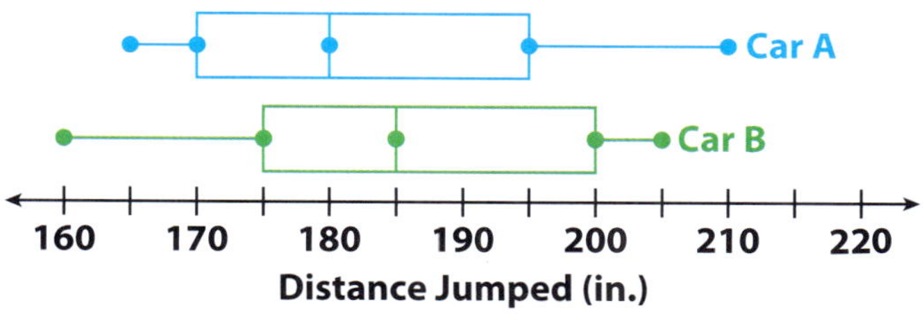

8. Compare the minimum, maximum, and median of the box plots.

____

9. Compare the ranges and interquartile ranges of the data in box plots.

____

10. What do the box plots tell you about the jump distances of two cars?

____

11. **Critical Thinking** What do the whiskers tell you about the two data sets?

____

For 12–14, use the box plots to compare the costs of leasing cars in two different cities.

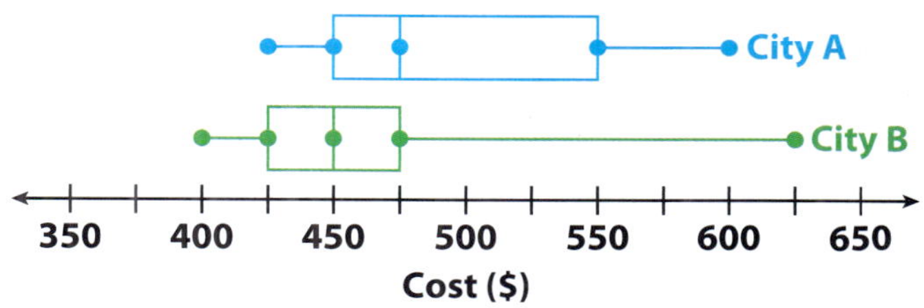

12. In which city could you spend the least amount of money to lease a car? The greatest?

____

13. Which city has a higher median price? How much higher is it?

____

14. **Make a Conjecture** In which city is it more likely to choose a car at random that leases for less than $450? Why?

____

15. **Summarize** Look back at the box plots for 12–14 on the previous page. What do the box plots tell you about the costs of leasing cars in those two cities?

____

____

____

____

H.O.T. FOCUS ON HIGHER ORDER THINKING

Work Area

16. **Draw Conclusions** Two box plots have the same median and equally long whiskers. If one box plot has a longer box than the other box plot, what does this tell you about the difference between the data sets?

____

____

17. **Communicate Mathematical Ideas** What you can learn about a data set from a box plot? How is this information different from a dot plot?

____

____

____

____

____

____

____

____

____

____

18. **Analyze Relationships** In mathematics, *central tendency* is the tendency of data values to cluster around some central value. What does a measure of variability tell you about the central tendency of a set of data? Explain.

____

____

____

LESSON
11.3 Using Statistical Measures to Compare Populations

7.5.11.3

Students will use statistical measures to compare populations.

ESSENTIAL QUESTION

How can you use statistical measures to compare populations?

EXPLORE ACTIVITY Real World

Math On the Spot
my.hrw.com

Comparing Differences in Centers to Variability

Recall that the mean and the mean absolute deviation (MAD) of a data set are measures of center and variability respectively. To find the MAD, first find the mean of the data. Next, take the absolute value of the difference between the mean and each data point. Finally, find the mean of those absolute values.

EXAMPLE 1 **The tables show the number of minutes per day students in a class spend exercising and playing video games. What is the difference of the means as a multiple of the mean absolute deviations?**

Minutes Per Day Exercising
0, 7, 7, 18, 20, 38, 33, 24, 22, 18, 11, 6

Minutes Per Day Playing Video Games
13, 18, 19, 30, 32, 46, 50, 34, 36, 30, 23, 19

STEP 1 Calculate the mean number of minutes per day exercising.

- Add: $0 + 7 + 7 + 18 + 20 + 38 + 33 + 24 + 22 + 18 + 11 + 6 =$ ___
- Divide the sum by the number of students: ___ $\div 12 =$ ___

STEP 2 Calculate the absolute deviations for the exercise data. Then find their mean.

$|0-17| = 17$ $|7-17| = 10$ $|7-17| = 10$ $|18-17| = 1$

$|20-17| = 3$ $|38-17| = 21$ $|33-17| = 16$ $|24-17| = 7$

$|22-17| =$ ___ $|18-17| =$ ___ $|11-$ ___ $| =$ ___ $|6-$ ___ $| =$ ___

Find the mean absolute deviation.

- Find the sum: $17 + 10 + 10 + 1 + 3 + 21 + 16 + 7 +$ ___ $+$ ___ $+$ ___ $+$ ___ $=$ ___
- Divide the sum by the number of students: ___ $\div 12 =$ ___

EXPLORE ACTIVITY *(cont'd)*

STEP 3 Calculate the mean number of minutes per day playing video games. Round to the nearest tenth.

- Add: $13 + 18 + 19 + 30 + 32 + 46 + 50 + 34 + 36 + 30 + 23 + 19 =$ □
- Divide the sum by the number of students: □ $\div$ □ $\approx$ □

STEP 4 Calculate the absolute deviations for the video game data. Then find their mean.

$\lvert 13 - 29.2 \rvert = 16.2$	$\lvert 18 - 29.2 \rvert = 11.2$	$\lvert 19 - 29.2 \rvert = 10.2$
$\lvert 30 - 29.2 \rvert = 0.8$	$\lvert 32 - 29.2 \rvert = 2.8$	$\lvert 46 - 29.2 \rvert = 16.8$
$\lvert 50 - 29.2 \rvert = 20.8$	$\lvert 34 - 29.2 \rvert = 4.8$	$\lvert 36 - 29.2 \rvert = 6.8$
|□ − 29.2| = □	|□ − 29.2| = □	|□ − 29.2| = □

Find the mean absolute deviation. Round to the nearest tenth.

- Add: $16.2 + 11.2 + 10.2 + 0.8 + 2.8 + 16.8 +$

  ______________________________ = □

- Divide the sum by the number of students:

  □ $\div$ □ $\approx$ □

STEP 5 Find the difference in the means.

- Subtract the lesser mean from the greater mean:

  □ $-$ □ $\approx$ □

STEP 6 Write the difference of the means as a multiple of the mean absolute deviations, which are similar but not identical. Round to the nearest tenth.

- Divide the difference of the means by the MAD:

  □ $\div$ □ $\approx$ □

The means of the two data sets differ by about _______ times the variability of the two data sets.

YOUR TURN

1. The high jumps in inches of the students on two intramural track and field teams are shown below. What is the difference of the means as a multiple of the mean absolute deviations?

High Jumps for Students on Team 1 (in.)
44, 47, 67, 89, 55, 76, 85, 80, 87, 69, 47, 58

High Jumps for Students on Team 2 (in.)
40, 32, 52, 75, 65, 70, 72, 61, 54, 43, 29, 32

____

Personal Math Trainer
Online Assessment and Intervention
my.hrw.com

Using Multiple Samples to Compare Populations

Many different random samples are possible for any given population, and their measures of center can vary. Using multiple samples can give us an idea of how reliable any inferences or predictions we make are.

Math On the Spot
my.hrw.com

EXAMPLE 2 Real World

A group of about 250 students in grade 7 and about 250 students in grade 11 were asked, "How many hours per month do you volunteer?" Responses from one random sample of 10 students in grade 7 and one random sample of 10 students in grade 11 are summarized in the box plots.

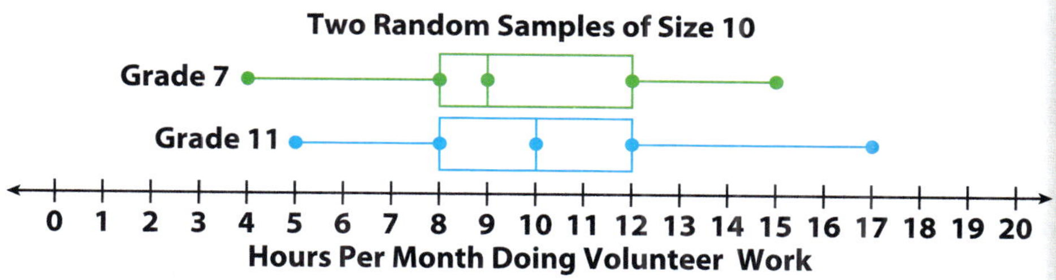

How can we tell if the grade 11 students do more volunteer work than the grade 7 students?

STEP 1 The median is higher for the students in grade 11. But there is a great deal of variation. To make an inference for the entire population, it is helpful to consider how the medians vary among multiple samples.

STEP 2 The box plots below show how the medians from 10 different random samples for each group vary.

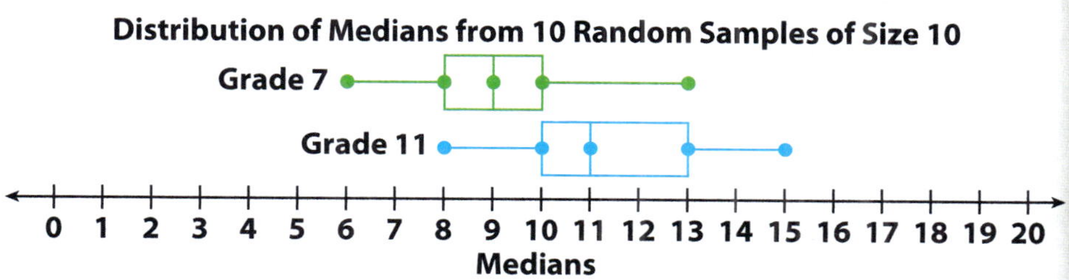

The medians vary less than the actual data. Half of the grade 7 medians are within 1 hour of 9. Half of the grade 11 medians are within 1 or 2 hours of 11. Although the distributions overlap, the middle halves of the data barely overlap. This is fairly convincing evidence that the grade 11 students volunteer more than the grade 7 students.

Math Talk
Mathematical Processes

Why doesn't the first box plot establish that students in grade 11 volunteer more than students in grade 7?

Personal Math Trainer
Online Assessment and Intervention
my.hrw.com

YOUR TURN

2. The box plots show the variation in the means for 10 different random samples for the groups in the example. Why do these data give less convincing evidence that the grade 11 students volunteer more?

Distribution of Means from 10 Random Samples of Size 10

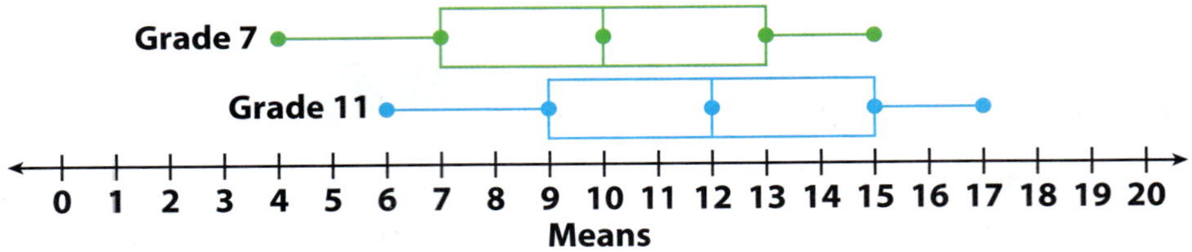

____

Guided Practice

The tables show the numbers of miles run by the students in two classes. Use the tables in 1–2. (Explore Activity Example 1)

Miles Run by Class 1 Students
12, 1, 6, 10, 1, 2, 3, 10, 3, 8, 3, 9, 8, 6, 8

Miles Run by Class 2 Students
11, 14, 11, 13, 6, 7, 8, 6, 8, 13, 8, 15, 13, 17, 15

1. For each class, what is the mean? What is the mean absolute deviation?

____

2. The difference of the means is about ____________ times the mean absolute deviations.

3. Mark took 10 random samples of 10 students from two schools. He asked how many minutes they spend per day going to and from school. The tables show the medians and the means of the samples. Compare the travel times using distributions of the medians and means. (Example 2)

School A
Medians: 28, 22, 25, 10, 40, 36, 30, 14, 20, 25
Means: 27, 24, 27, 15, 42, 36, 32, 18, 22, 29

School B
Medians: 22, 25, 20, 14, 20, 18, 21, 18, 26, 19
Means: 24, 30, 22, 15, 20, 17, 22, 15, 36, 27

____

____

ESSENTIAL QUESTION CHECK-IN

4. Why is it a good idea to use multiple random samples when making comparative inferences about two populations?

____

Name ________________ Class ________________ Date ________________

11.3 Independent Practice

Personal Math Trainer
Online Assessment and Intervention
my.hrw.com

Josie recorded the average monthly temperatures for two cities in the state where she lives. Use the data for 5–7.

Average Monthly Temperatures for City 1 (°F)
23, 38, 39, 48, 55, 56, 71, 86, 57, 53, 43, 31

Average Monthly Temperatures for City 2 (°F)
8, 23, 24, 33, 40, 41, 56, 71, 42, 38, 28, 16

5. For City 1, what is the mean of the average monthly temperatures? What is the mean absolute deviation of the average monthly temperatures?

____

6. What is the difference between each average monthly temperature for City 1 and the corresponding temperature for City 2? ________________

7. **Draw Conclusions** Based on your answers to Exercises 5 and 6, what do you think the mean of the average monthly temperatures for City 2 is? What do you think the mean absolute deviation of the average monthly temperatures for City 2 is? Give your answers without actually calculating the mean and the mean absolute deviation. Explain your reasoning.

____

____

8. What is the difference in the means as a multiple of the mean absolute deviations? ________________

9. **Make a Conjecture** The box plots show the distributions of mean weights of 10 samples of 10 football players from each of two leagues, A and B. What can you say about any comparison of the weights of the two populations? Explain.

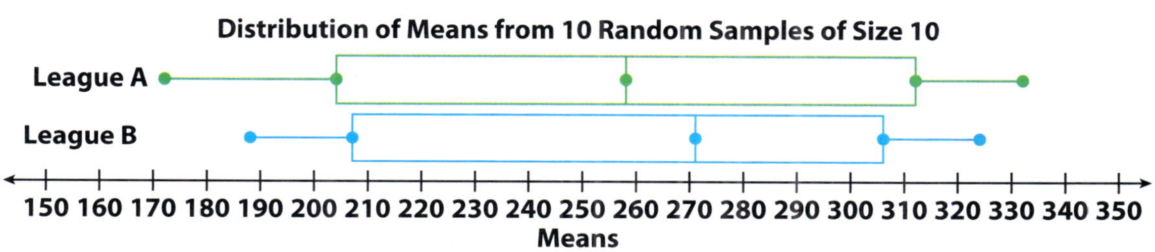

____

____

10. **Justify Reasoning** Statistical measures are shown for the ages of middle school and high school teachers in two states.

State A: Mean age of middle school teachers = 38, mean age of high school teachers = 48, mean absolute deviation for both = 6

State B: Mean age of middle school teachers = 42, mean age of high school teachers = 50, mean absolute deviation for both = 4

In which state is the difference in ages between members of the two groups more significant? Support your answer.

____

____

11. **Analyze Relationships** The tables show the heights in inches of all the adult grandchildren of two sets of grandparents, the Smiths and the Thompsons. What is the difference in the medians as a multiple of the ranges?

Heights of the Smiths' Adult Grandchildren (in.)
64, 65, 68, 66, 65, 68, 69, 66, 70, 67

Heights of the Thompsons' Adult Grandchildren (in.)
75, 80, 78, 77, 79, 76, 75, 79, 77, 74

____

H.O.T. FOCUS ON HIGHER ORDER THINKING

Work Area

12. **Critical Thinking** Jill took many samples of 10 tosses of a standard number cube. What might she reasonably expect the median of the medians of the samples to be? Why?

____

____

13. **Analyze Relationships** Elly and Ramon are both conducting surveys to compare the average numbers of hours per month that men and women spend shopping. Elly plans to take many samples of size 10 from both populations and compare the distributions of both the medians and the means. Ramon will do the same, but will use a sample size of 100. Whose results will probably produce more reliable inferences? Explain.

____

____

14. **Counterexamples** Seth believes that it is always possible to compare two populations of numerical values by finding the difference in the means of the populations as a multiple of the mean absolute deviations. Describe a situation that explains why Seth is incorrect.

____

____

MODULE QUIZ

Ready to Go On?

Personal Math Trainer
Online Assessment and Intervention
my.hrw.com

11.1 Comparing Data Displayed in Dot Plots

The two dot plots show the number of miles run by 14 students at the start and at the end of the school year. Compare each measure for the two dot plots. Use the data for 1–3.

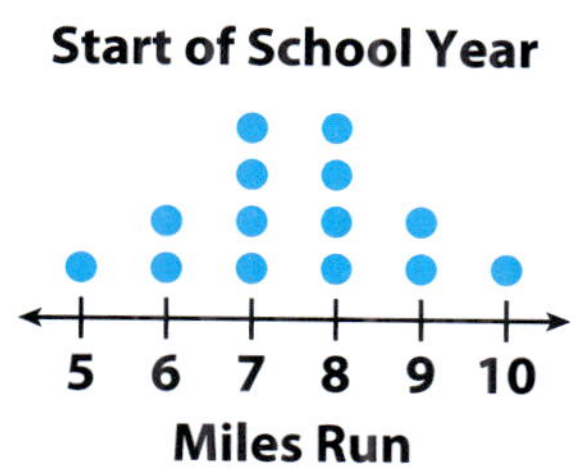

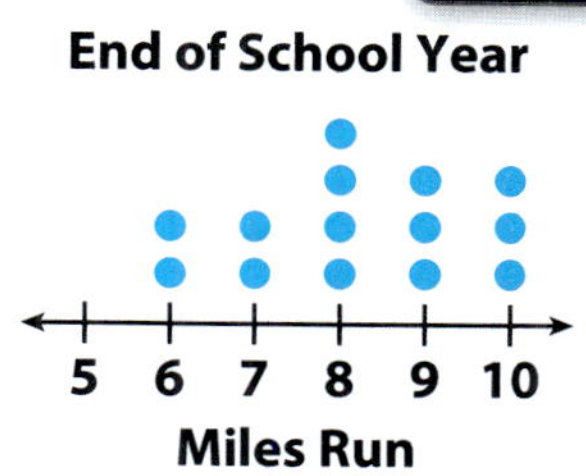

1. means ______

2. medians ______

3. ranges ______

11.2 Comparing Data Displayed in Box Plots

The box plots show lengths of flights in inches flown by two model airplanes. Use the data for 4–5.

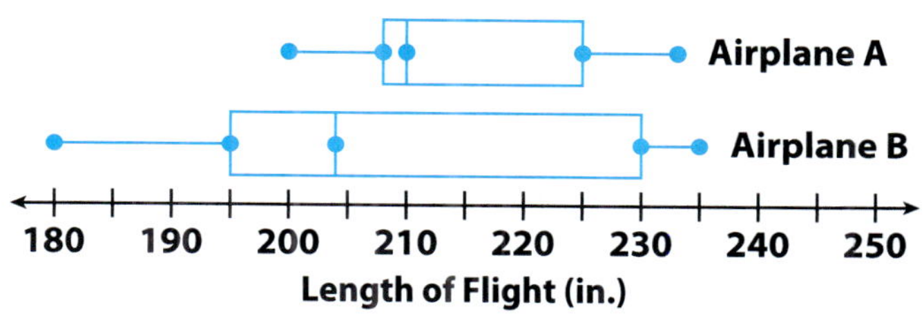

4. Which has a greater median flight length? ______

5. Which has a greater interquartile range? ______

11.3 Using Statistical Measures to Compare Populations

6. Roberta grows pea plants, some in shade and some in sun. She picks 8 plants of each type at random and records the heights.

Shade plant heights (in.)	7	11	11	12	9	12	8	10
Sun plant heights (in.)	21	24	19	19	22	23	24	24

Express the difference in the means as a multiple of their ranges.

______

ESSENTIAL QUESTION

7. How can you use and compare data to solve real-world problems?

______

MODULE 11 **MIXED REVIEW**

Assessment Readiness

Personal Math Trainer
Online Assessment and Intervention
my.hrw.com

Selected Response

1. Which statement about the data is true?

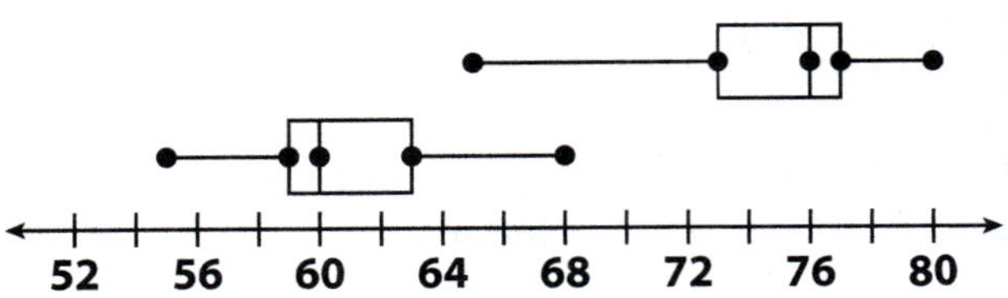

Ⓐ The difference between the medians is about 4 times the range.

Ⓑ The difference between the medians is about 4 times the IQR.

Ⓒ The difference between the medians is about 2 times the range.

Ⓓ The difference between the medians is about 2 times the IQR.

2. Which is a true statement based on the box plots below?

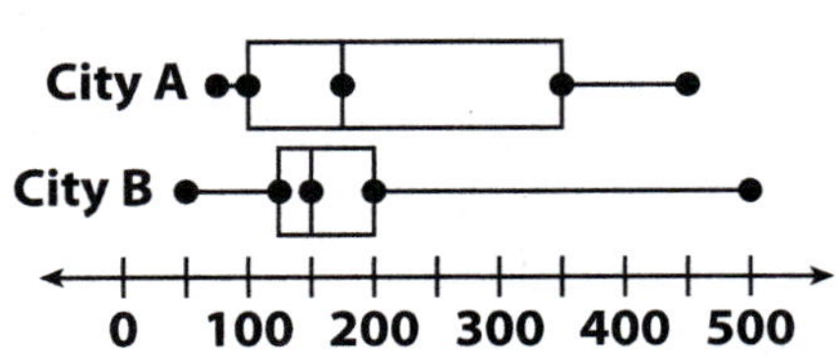

Ⓐ The data for City A has the greater range.

Ⓑ The data for City B is more symmetric.

Ⓒ The data for City A has the greater interquartile range.

Ⓓ The data for City B has the greater median.

3. What is $-3\frac{1}{2}$ written as a decimal?

Ⓐ -3.5

Ⓑ -3.05

Ⓒ -0.35

Ⓓ -0.035

4. Which is a true statement based on the dot plots below?

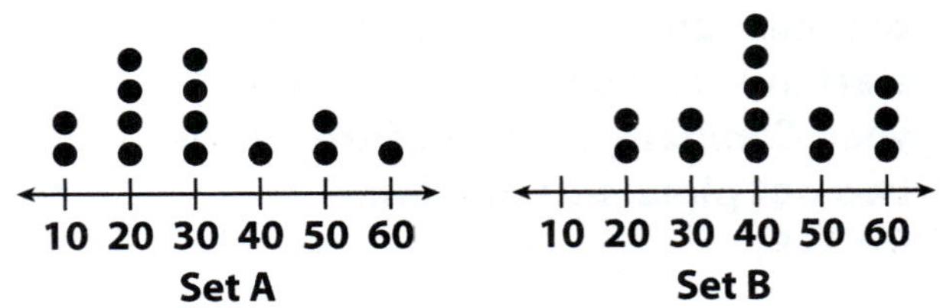

Ⓐ Set A has the lesser range.

Ⓑ Set B has the greater median.

Ⓒ Set A has the greater mean.

Ⓓ Set B is less symmetric than Set A.

Mini-Task

5. The dot plots show the lengths of a random sample of words in a fourth-grade book and a seventh-grade book.

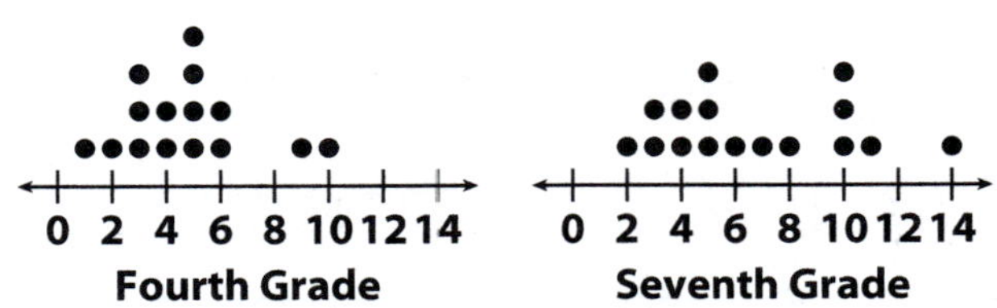

a. Compare the shapes of the plots.

____

____

____

b. Compare the ranges of the plots. Explain what your answer means in terms of the situation.

____

____

____

____

UNIT 5

Study Guide Review

MODULE 10 Random Samples and Populations

Key Vocabulary

biased sample *(muestra sesgada)*

population *(población)*

random sample *(muestra aleatoria)*

sample *(muestra)*

ESSENTIAL QUESTION

How can you use random samples and populations to solve real-world problems?

EXAMPLE 1

An engineer at a lightbulb factory chooses a random sample of 100 lightbulbs from a shipment of 2,500 and finds that 2 of them are defective. How many lightbulbs in the shipment are likely to be defective?

$$\frac{\text{defective lightbulbs}}{\text{size of sample}} = \frac{\text{defective lightbulbs in population}}{\text{size of population}}$$

$$\frac{2}{100} = \frac{x}{2{,}500}$$

$$\frac{2 \cdot 25}{100 \cdot 25} = \frac{x}{2{,}500}$$

$$x = 50$$

In a shipment of 2,500 lightbulbs, 50 are likely to be defective.

EXAMPLE 2

The 300 students in a school are about to vote for student body president. There are two candidates, Jay and Serena, and each candidate has about the same amount of support. Use a simulation to generate a random sample. Interpret the results.

Step 1: Write the digits 0 through 9 on 10 index cards, one digit per card. Draw and replace a card three times to form a 3-digit number. For example, if you draw 0-4-9, the number is 49. If you draw 1-0-8, the number is 108. Repeat this process until you have a sample of 30 3-digit numbers.

Step 2: Let the numbers from 1 to 150 represent votes for Jay and the numbers from 151 to 300 represent votes for Serena. For example:

Jay: 83, 37, 16, 4, 127, 93, 9, 62, 91, 75, 13, 35, 94, 26, 60, 120, 36, 73

Serena: 217, 292, 252, 186, 296, 218, 284, 278, 209, 296, 190, 300

Step 3: Notice that 18 of the 30 numbers represent votes for Jay. The results suggest that Jay will receive $\frac{18}{30} = 60\%$ of the 300 votes, or 180 votes.

Step 4: Based on this one sample, Jay will win the election. The results of samples can vary. Repeating the simulation many times and looking at the pattern across the different samples will produce more reliable results.

EXERCISES

1. Molly uses the school directory to select, at random, 25 students from her school for a survey on which sports people like to watch on television. She calls the students and asks them, "Do you think basketball is the best sport to watch on television?" (Lesson 10.1)

a. Did Molly survey a random sample or a biased sample of the students at her school?

____

b. Was the question she asked an unbiased question? Explain your answer.

____

____

2. There are 2,300 licensed dogs in Clarkson. A random sample of 50 of the dogs in Clarkson shows that 8 have ID microchips implanted. How many dogs in Clarkson are likely to have ID microchips implanted? (Lesson 10.2)

____

3. A store gets a shipment of 500 MP3 players. Twenty-five of the players are defective, and the rest are working. A graphing calculator is used to generate 20 random numbers to simulate a random sample of the players. (Lesson 10.3)

A list of 20 randomly generated numbers representing MP3 players is:

474	77	101	156	378	188	116	458	230	333
78	19	67	5	191	124	226	496	481	161

a. Let numbers 1 to 25 represent players that are ________________.

b. Let numbers 21 to 500 represent players that are ________________.

c. How many players in this sample are expected to be

defective? ________________

d. If 300 players are chosen at random from the shipment, how many are expected to be defective based on the sample? Does the sample provide a reasonable inference? Explain.

____

____

____

MODULE 11

Analyzing and Comparing Data

Key Vocabulary
mean absolute deviation (MAD) *(desviación absoluta media, (DAM))*

ESSENTIAL QUESTION

How can you solve real-world problems by analyzing and comparing data?

EXAMPLE

The box plots show amounts donated to two charities at a fundraising drive. Compare the shapes, centers and spreads of the box plots.

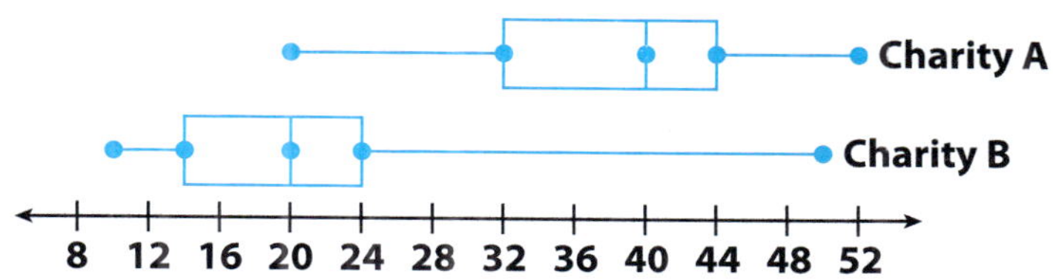

Shapes: The lengths of the boxes and overall plot lengths are fairly similar, but while the whiskers for Charity A are similar in length, Charity B has a very short whisker and a very long whisker.

Centers: The median for Charity A is \$40, and for Charity B is \$20.

Spreads: The interquartile range for Charity A is $44 - 32 = 12$. The interquartile range for Charity B is slightly less, $24 - 14 = 10$.

The donations varied more for Charity B and were lower overall.

EXERCISES

The dot plots show the number of hours a group of students spends online each week, and how many hours they spend reading. Compare the dot plots visually. (Lesson 11.1)

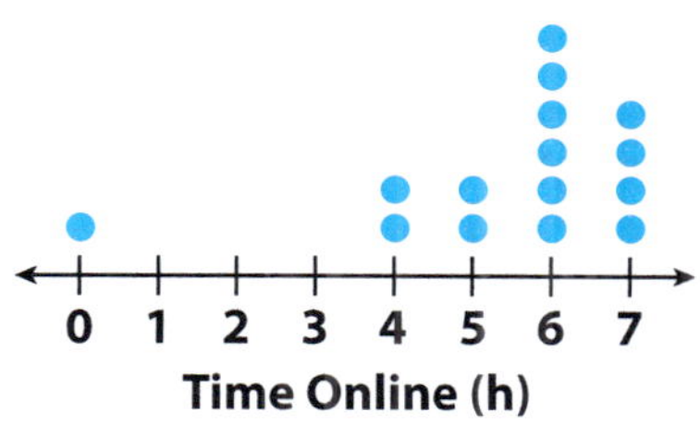

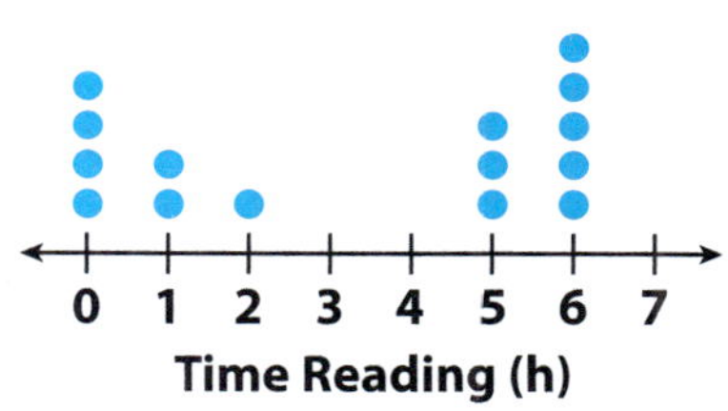

1. Compare the shapes, centers, and spreads of the dot plots.

Shape: ____________________

____

Center: ____________________

____

Spread: ____________________

____

2. Calculate the medians of the dot plots. ____________________

3. Calculate the ranges of the dot plots. ____________________

4. The average times (in minutes) a group of students spends studying and watching TV per school day are given. (Lesson 11.3)

Studying:	25, 30, 35, 45, 60, 60, 70, 75
Watching TV:	0, 35, 35, 45, 50, 50, 70, 75

a. Find the mean times for studying and for watching TV.

____

b. Find the mean absolute deviations (MADs) for each data set.

____

c. Find the difference of the means as a multiple of the MAD, to two decimal places.

____

Unit 5 Performance Tasks

1. **CAREERS IN MATH** Entomologist An entomologist is studying how two different types of flowers appeal to butterflies. The box-and-whisker plots show the number of butterflies that visited one of two different types of flowers in a field. The data were collected over a two-week period, for one hour each day.

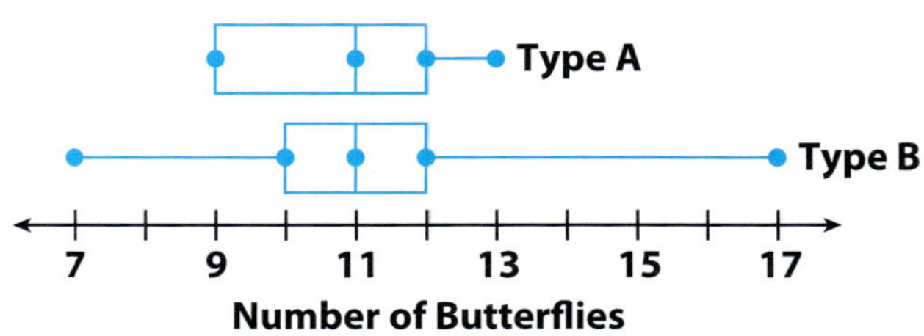

a. Find the median, range, and interquartile range for each data set.

____

____

b. Which measure makes it appear that flower type A had a more consistent number of butterfly visits? Which measure makes it appear that flower type B did? If you had to choose one flower as having the more consistent visits, which would you choose? Explain your reasoning.

____

____

____

____

UNIT 5 MIXED REVIEW
Assessment Readiness

Selected Response

1. Which is a true statement based on the dot plots below?

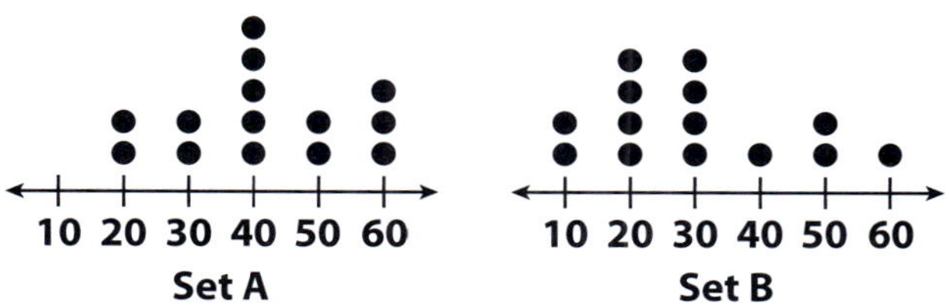

Ⓐ Set B has the greater range.

Ⓑ Set B has the greater median.

Ⓒ Set B has the greater mean.

Ⓓ Set A is less symmetric than Set B.

2. Which is a solution to the equation $7g - 2 = 47$?

Ⓐ $g = 5$

Ⓑ $g = 6$

Ⓒ $g = 7$

Ⓓ $g = 8$

3. Which is a true statement based on the box plots below?

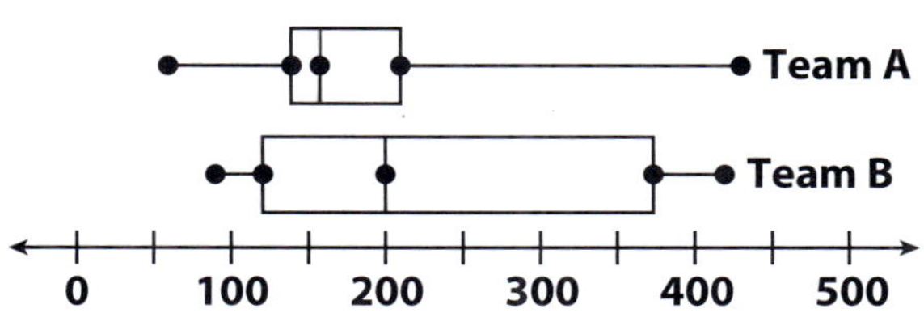

Ⓐ The data for Team B have the greater range.

Ⓑ The data for Team A are more symmetric.

Ⓒ The data for Team B have the greater interquartile range.

Ⓓ The data for Team A have the greater median.

4. Which is the best way to choose a random sample of people from a sold-out movie audience for a survey?

Ⓐ Survey all audience members who visit the restroom during the movie.

Ⓑ Assign each seat a number, write each number on a slip of paper, and then draw several slips from a hat. Survey the people in those seats.

Ⓒ Survey all of the audience members who sit in the first or last row of seats in the movie theater.

Ⓓ Before the movie begins, ask for volunteers to participate in a survey. Survey the first twenty people who volunteer.

5. Find the percent change from 84 to 63.

Ⓐ 30% decrease Ⓒ 25% decrease

Ⓑ 30% increase Ⓓ 25% increase

6. A survey asked 100 students in a school to name the temperature at which they feel most comfortable. The box plot below shows the results for temperatures in degrees Fahrenheit. Which could you infer based on the box plot below?

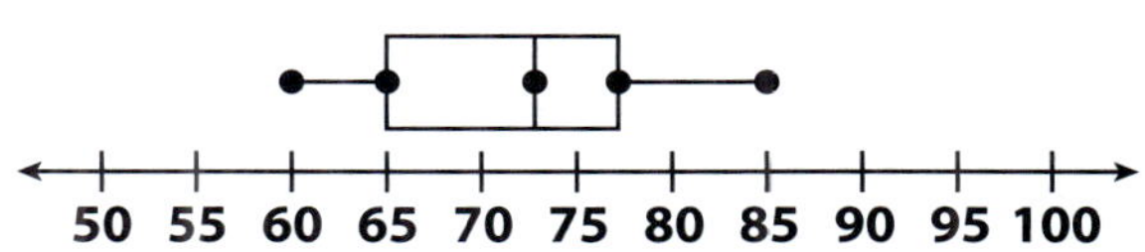

Ⓐ Most students prefer a temperature less than 65 degrees.

Ⓑ Most students prefer a temperature of at least 70 degrees.

Ⓒ Almost no students prefer a temperature of less than 75 degrees.

Ⓓ Almost no students prefer a temperature of more than 65 degrees.

7. The box plots below show data from a survey of students under 14 years old. They were asked on how many days in a month they read and draw. Based on the box plots, which is a true statement about students?

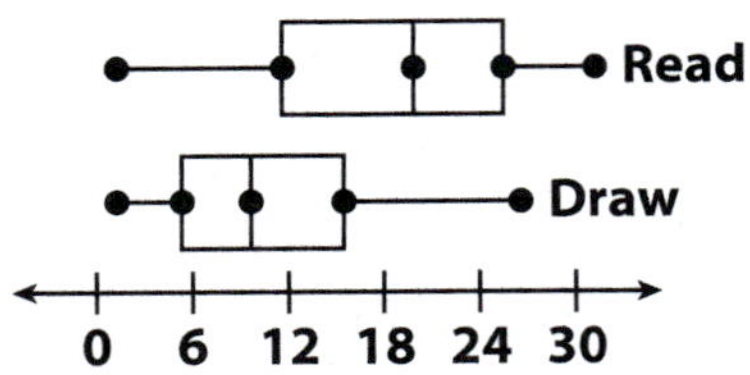

Ⓐ Most students draw at least 12 days a month.

Ⓑ Most students read less than 12 days a month.

Ⓒ Most students read more often than they draw.

Ⓓ Most students draw more often than they read.

Hot Tip! **Use logic to eliminate answer choices that are incorrect. This will help you to make an educated guess if you are having trouble with the question.**

8. Which describes the relationship between $\angle NOM$ and $\angle JOK$ in the diagram?

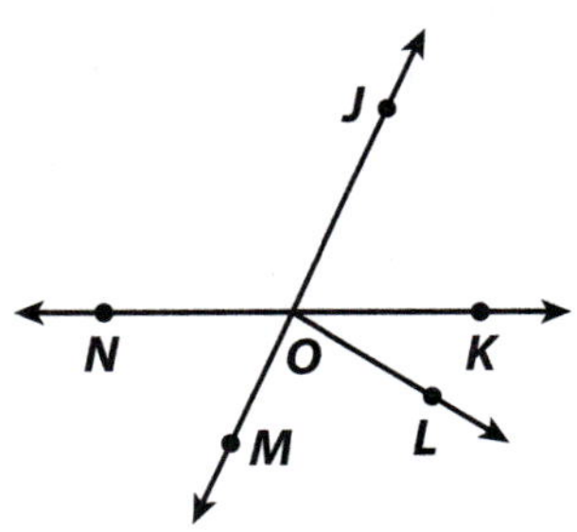

Ⓐ adjacent angles

Ⓑ complementary angles

Ⓒ supplementary angles

Ⓓ vertical angles

Mini-Task

9. The tables show the typical number of minutes spent exercising each week for a group of fourth-grade students and a group of seventh-grade students.

Weekly Exercising (minutes), 4th Grade
120, 75, 30, 30, 240, 90, 100, 180, 125, 300

Weekly Exercising (minutes), 7th Grade
410, 145, 240, 250, 125, 95, 210, 190, 245, 300

a. What is the mean number of minutes spent exercising for fourth graders? For seventh graders?

____

b. What is the mean absolute deviation of each data set?

____

c. Compare the two data sets with respect to their measures of center and their measures of variability.

____

____

____

____

d. How many times the MADs is the difference between the means, to the nearest tenth?

____

____

____

UNIT 6

Probability

MODULE 12
Experimental Probability

MODULE 13
Theoretical Probability and Simulations

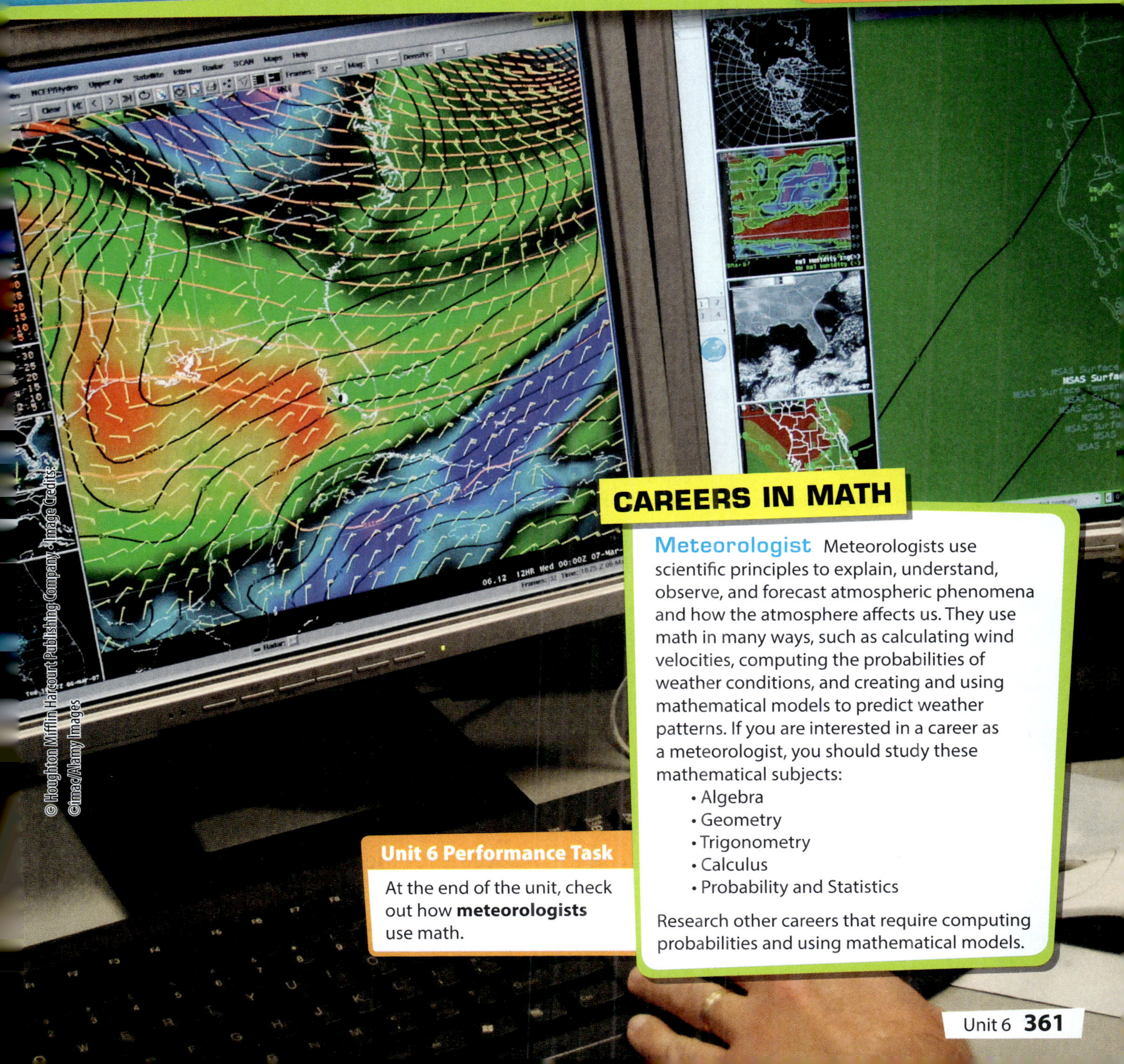

CAREERS IN MATH

Meteorologist Meteorologists use scientific principles to explain, understand, observe, and forecast atmospheric phenomena and how the atmosphere affects us. They use math in many ways, such as calculating wind velocities, computing the probabilities of weather conditions, and creating and using mathematical models to predict weather patterns. If you are interested in a career as a meteorologist, you should study these mathematical subjects:

- Algebra
- Geometry
- Trigonometry
- Calculus
- Probability and Statistics

Research other careers that require computing probabilities and using mathematical models.

Unit 6 Performance Task

At the end of the unit, check out how **meteorologists** use math.

UNIT 6

Vocabulary Preview

Use the puzzle to preview key vocabulary from this unit. Unscramble the circled letters within found words to answer the riddle at the bottom of the page.

Y	R	F	S	P	D	A	U	L	B	S	T	Y	C	P
(T)	N	U	E	A	G	V	V	X	I	Y	R	C	A	R
N	N	B	A	H	M	C	P	M	F	U	(I)	Y	H	O
R	E	E	X	C	K	P	P	L	O	O	A	A	X	(B)
K	V	H	M	H	O	(L)	L	D	G	H	L	T	O	A
Q	L	R	B	I	E	W	V	E	Z	V	I	W	S	(B)
L	F	E	B	E	(R)	X	E	X	S	I	F	Y	I	I
Q	V	I	V	T	N	E	M	E	L	P	M	(O)	C	L
Q	O	E	S	H	J	R	P	S	R	K	(A)	L	E	I
A	N	H	C	J	D	D	O	X	H	P	F	C	X	T
T	P	Z	K	V	Z	V	F	N	E	P	F	U	E	(Y)
U	V	K	S	(I)	M	U	L	A	T	I	O	N	P	J
K	X	O	L	P	M	O	M	S	U	Z	J	W	A	P
R	O	C	P	T	U	N	D	N	V	E	R	T	U	A
U	W	O	G	L	B	U	H	K	E	S	F	A	P	B

- An activity based on chance in which results are observed. (Lesson 12.1)
- The set of all outcomes that are not included in the event. (Lesson 12.1)
- Each observation of an experiment. (Lesson 12.1)
- A model of an experiment that would be difficult or too time-consuming to perform. (Lesson 12.2)
- Measures the likelihood that the event will occur. (Lesson 12.1)
- An event with only one outcome (2 words). (Lesson 12.2)
- A set of all possible outcomes for an event (2 words). (Lesson 12.1)

Q: Why was there little chance of success for the clumsy thieves?

A: Because they had low ___ ___ ___ – ___ ___ ___ ___ ___ ___ ___!

Experimental Probability

MODULE 12

ESSENTIAL QUESTION

How can you use experimental probability to solve real-world problems?

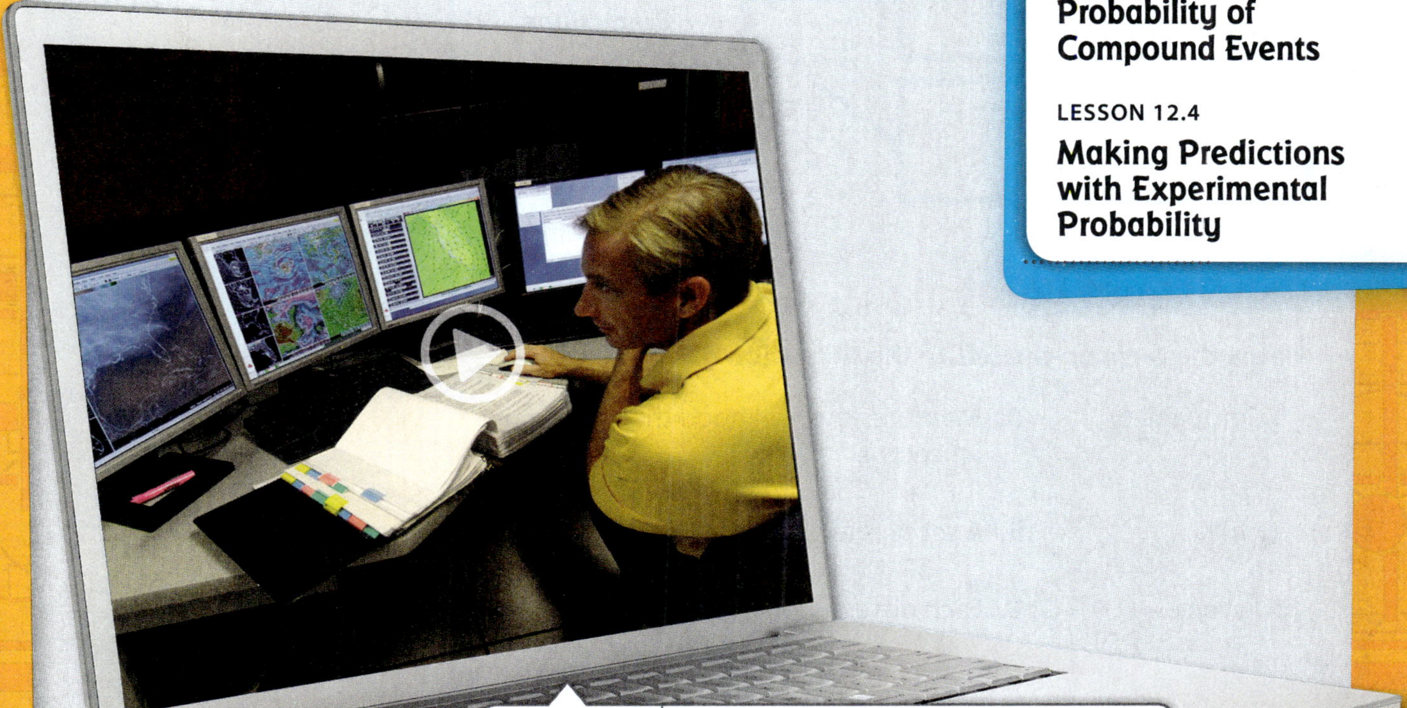

Real-World Video

my.hrw.com

Meteorologists use sophisticated equipment to gather data about the weather. Then they use experimental probability to forecast, or predict, what the weather conditions will be.

GO DIGITAL
my.hrw.com

my.hrw.com
Go digital with your write-in student edition, accessible on any device.

Math On the Spot
Scan with your smart phone to jump directly to the online edition, video tutor, and more.

Animated Math
Interactively explore key concepts to see how math works.

Personal Math Trainer
Get immediate feedback and help as you work through practice sets.

Reading Start-Up

Visualize Vocabulary

Use the ✔ words to complete the graphic. You can put more than one word in each box.

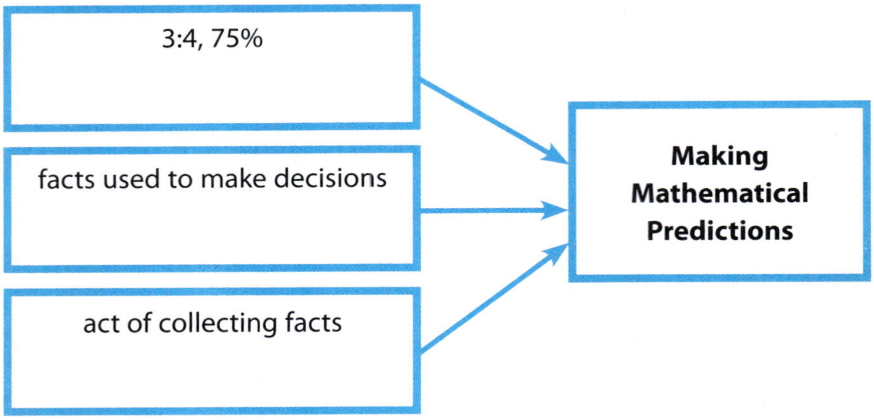

Understand Vocabulary

Match the term on the left to the definition on the right.

1. probability	**A.** Measures the likelihood that the event will occur.
2. trial	**B.** A set of one or more outcomes.
3. event	**C.** Each observation of an experiment.

Vocabulary

Review Words

✔ data *(datos)*
✔ observation *(observación)*
✔ percent *(porcentaje)*
✔ ratio *(razón)*

Preview Words

complement *(complemento)*
compound event *(suceso compuesto)*
event *(suceso)*
experiment *(experimento)*
experimental probability *(probabilidad experimental)*
outcome *(resultado)*
probability *(probabilidad)*
simple event *(suceso simple)*
simulation *(simulación)*
trial *(prueba)*

Active Reading

Pyramid Before beginning the module, create a rectangular pyramid to help you organize what you learn. Label each side with one of the lesson titles from this module. As you study each lesson, write important ideas, such as vocabulary, properties, and formulas, on the appropriate side.

Are YOU Ready?

Complete these exercises to review skills you will need for this module.

Personal Math Trainer
Online Assessment and Intervention
my.hrw.com

Simplify Fractions

EXAMPLE Simplify $\frac{12}{21}$.

12: 1, 2, (3), 4, 6, 12 — List all the factors of the numerator and denominator.
21: 1, (3), 7, 21 — Circle the greatest common factor (GCF).

$\frac{12 \div 3}{21 \div 3} = \frac{4}{7}$ — Divide the numerator and denominator by the GCF.

Write each fraction in simplest form.

1. $\frac{6}{10}$ ______ **2.** $\frac{9}{15}$ ______ **3.** $\frac{16}{24}$ ______ **4.** $\frac{9}{36}$ ______

5. $\frac{45}{54}$ ______ **6.** $\frac{30}{42}$ ______ **7.** $\frac{36}{60}$ ______ **8.** $\frac{14}{42}$ ______

Write Fractions as Decimals

EXAMPLE $\frac{13}{25} \rightarrow$

$$\begin{array}{r} 0.52 \\ 25\overline{)13.00} \\ -12.5 \\ \hline 50 \\ -50 \\ \hline 0 \end{array}$$

Write the fraction as a division problem.
Write a decimal point and a zero in the dividend.
Place a decimal point in the quotient.
Write more zeros in the dividend if necessary.

Write each fraction as a decimal.

9. $\frac{3}{4}$ ______ **10.** $\frac{7}{8}$ ______ **11.** $\frac{3}{20}$ ______ **12.** $\frac{19}{50}$ ______

Percents and Decimals

EXAMPLE

$$\begin{aligned} 109\% &= 100\% + 9\% \\ &= \frac{100}{100} + \frac{9}{100} \\ &= 1 + 0.09 \\ &= 1.09 \end{aligned}$$

Write the percent as the sum of 1 whole and a percent remainder.
Write the percents as fractions.
Write the fractions as decimals.
Simplify.

Write each percent as a decimal.

13. 67% ______ **14.** 31% ______ **15.** 7% ______ **16.** 146% ______

Write each decimal as a percent.

17. 0.13 ______ **18.** 0.55 ______ **19.** 0.08 ______ **20.** 1.16 ______

Are YOU Ready? *(cont'd)*

Complete these exercises to review skills you will need for this module.

Simplify Fractions

21. To simplify the fraction $\frac{24}{36}$, Felix divided both the numerator and the denominator by 4. He wrote the fraction $\frac{6}{9}$ as the simplest form of $\frac{24}{36}$. What error did Felix make? What is the simplest form of $\frac{24}{36}$?

Write Fractions as Decimals

22. Helena lives $\frac{9}{20}$ mile from her school and $\frac{5}{8}$ mile from the library. Write each distance as a decimal, then compare the distances. Does Helena live closer to the school or to the library?

Percents and Decimals

23. Wallace follows a budget each month.

a. Wallace budgets 7% of his income each month for clothing. Write 7% as a decimal.

b. Wallace budgets 0.2 of his income each month for savings. Write 0.2 as a percent.

c. Does Wallace budget more of his income for clothing or for savings? Explain.

LESSON

12.1 Probability

7.6.12.1

Students will describe the likelihood of an event.

ESSENTIAL QUESTION

How can you describe the likelihood of an event?

EXPLORE ACTIVITY

Finding the Likelihood of an Event

Each time you roll a number cube, a number from 1 to 6 lands face up. This is called an *event*.

Work with a partner to decide how many of the six possible results of rolling a number cube match the described event.

Then order the events from least likely (1) to most likely (9) by writing a number in each box to the right.

Rolling a number less than 7 ______ ☐

Rolling an 8 ______ ☐

Rolling a number greater than 4 ______ ☐

Rolling a 5 ______ ☐

Rolling a number other than 6 ______ ☐

Rolling an even number ______ ☐

Rolling a number less than 5 ______ ☐

Rolling an odd number ______ ☐

Rolling a number divisible by 3 ______ ☐

Reflect

1. Are any of the events impossible? ______

______

Math On the Spot
my.hrw.com

Describing Events

An **experiment** is an activity involving chance in which results are observed. Each observation of an experiment is a **trial**, and each result is an **outcome**. A set of one or more outcomes is an **event**.

The **probability** of an event, written *P*(event), measures the likelihood that the event will occur. Probability is a measure between 0 and 1 as shown on the number line, and can be written as a fraction, a decimal, or a percent.

If the event is not likely to occur, the probability of the event is close to 0. If an event is likely to occur, the event's probability is closer to 1.

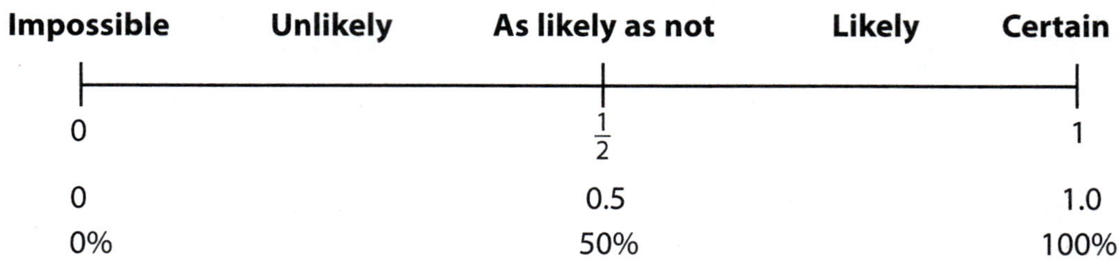

EXAMPLE 1 Real World

Tell whether each event is impossible, unlikely, as likely as not, likely, or certain. Then, tell whether the probability is 0, close to 0, $\frac{1}{2}$, close to 1, or 1.

A You roll a six-sided number cube and the number is 1 or greater.

This event is certain to happen. Its probability is 1.

Because you can roll the numbers 1, 2, 3, 4, 5, and 6 on a number cube, there are 6 possible outcomes.

B You roll two number cubes and the sum of the numbers is 3.

This event is unlikely to happen. Its probability is close to 0.

C A bowl contains disks marked with the numbers 1 through 10. You close your eyes and select a disk at random. You pick an odd number.

This event is as likely as not. The probability is $\frac{1}{2}$.

D A spinner has 8 equal sections marked 0 through 7. You spin and land on a prime number.

This event is as likely as not. The probability is $\frac{1}{2}$.

Remember that a prime number is a whole number greater than 1 and has exactly 2 divisors, 1 and itself.

Math Talk
Mathematical Processes
Is an event that is *not* certain an impossible event? Explain.

Reflect

2. The probability of event *A* is $\frac{1}{3}$. The probability of event *B* is $\frac{1}{4}$. What can you conclude about the two events?

YOUR TURN

3. A hat contains pieces of paper marked with the numbers 1 through 16. Tell whether picking an even number is impossible, unlikely, as likely as not, likely, or certain. Tell whether the probability is 0, close to 0, $\frac{1}{2}$, close to 1, or 1.

____

Personal Math Trainer
Online Assessment and Intervention
my.hrw.com

Finding Probability

A **sample space** is the set of all possible outcomes for an experiment. A sample space can be small, such as the 2 outcomes when a coin is flipped. Or a sample space can be large, such as the possible number of Texas Classic automobile license plates. Identifying the sample space can help you calculate the probability of an event.

Math On the Spot
my.hrw.com

Probability of An Event

$$P(\text{event}) = \frac{\text{number of outcomes in the event}}{\text{number of outcomes in the sample space}}$$

EXAMPLE 2 Real World

What is the probability of rolling an even number on a standard number cube?

STEP 1 Find the sample space for a standard number cube.

{1, 2, 3, 4, 5, 6} *There are 6 possible outcomes.*

STEP 2 Find the number of ways to roll an even number.

2, 4, 6 *The event can occur 3 ways.*

STEP 3 Find the probability of rolling an even number.

$$P(\text{even}) = \frac{\text{number of ways to roll an even number}}{\text{number of faces on a number cube}}$$

$$= \frac{3}{6} = \frac{1}{2}$$ *Substitute values and simplify.*

The probability of rolling an even number is $\frac{1}{2}$.

Personal Math Trainer
Online Assessment and Intervention
my.hrw.com

YOUR TURN

Find each probability. Write your answer in simplest form.

4. Picking a purple marble from a jar with 10 green and 10 purple marbles. ______________

5. Rolling a number greater than 4 on a standard number cube. ______________

Math On the Spot
my.hrw.com

Using the Complement of an Event

The **complement** of an event is the set of all outcomes in the sample space that are *not* included in the event. For example, in the event of rolling a 3 on a number cube, the complement is rolling any number other than 3, which means the complement is rolling a 1, 2, 4, 5, or 6.

An Event and Its Complement

The sum of the probabilities of an event and its complement equals 1.

$$P(\text{event}) + P(\text{complement}) = 1$$

You can apply probabilities to situations involving random selection, such as drawing a card out of a shuffled deck or pulling a marble out of a closed bag.

EXAMPLE 3 (Real World)

There are 2 red jacks in a standard deck of 52 cards. What is the probability of not getting a red jack if you select one card at random?

$$P(\text{event}) + P(\text{complement}) = 1$$

$$P(\text{red jack}) + P(\text{not a red jack}) = 1$$ The probability of getting a red jack is $\frac{2}{52}$.

$$\frac{2}{52} + P(\text{not a red jack}) = 1$$ Substitute $\frac{2}{52}$ for $P(\text{red jack})$.

$$\frac{2}{52} + P(\text{not a red jack}) = \frac{52}{52}$$ Subtract $\frac{2}{52}$ from both sides.

$$-\frac{2}{52} \qquad\qquad -\frac{2}{52}$$

$$P(\text{not a red jack}) = \frac{50}{52}$$

$$P(\text{not a red jack}) = \frac{25}{26}$$ Simplify.

The probability that you will not draw a red jack is $\frac{25}{26}$. It is likely that you will not select a red jack.

Reflect

6. Why do the probability of an event and the probability of its complement add up to 1?

____

____

____

____

____

YOUR TURN

7. A jar contains 8 marbles marked with the numbers 1 through 8. You pick a marble at random. What is the probability of not picking the marble marked with the number 5? __________

8. You roll a standard number cube. Use the probability of rolling an even number to find the probability of rolling an odd number. __________

Personal Math Trainer
Online Assessment and Intervention
my.hrw.com

Guided Practice

1. In a hat, you have index cards with the numbers 1 through 10 written on them. Order the events from least likely to happen (1) to most likely to happen (8) when you pick one card at random. In the boxes, write a number from 1 to 8 to order the eight different events. (Explore Activity)

Event	Order
You pick a number greater than 0.	☐
You pick an even number.	☐
You pick a number that is at least 2.	☐
You pick a number that is at most 0.	☐
You pick a number divisible by 3.	☐
You pick a number divisible by 5.	☐
You pick a prime number.	☐
You pick a number less than the greatest prime number.	☐

Guided Practice

Determine whether each event is impossible, unlikely, as likely as not, likely, or certain. Then, tell whether the probability is 0, close to 0, $\frac{1}{2}$, close to 1, or 1. (Example 1)

2. randomly picking a green card from a standard deck of playing cards

____

3. randomly picking a red card from a standard deck of playing cards

____

4. picking a number less than 15 from a jar with papers labeled from 1 to 12

____

5. picking a number that is divisible by 5 from a jar with papers labeled from 1 to 12

____

Find each probability. Write your answer in simplest form. (Example 2)

6. spinning a spinner that has 5 equal sections marked 1 through 5 and landing on an even number

____

7. picking a diamond from a standard deck of playing cards which has 13 cards in each of four suits: spades, hearts, diamonds and clubs

____

Use the complement to find each probability. (Example 3)

8. What is the probability of not rolling a 5 on a standard number cube?

____

9. A spinner has 3 equal sections that are red, white, and blue. What is the probability of not landing on blue?

____

10. A spinner has 5 equal sections marked 1 through 5. What is the probability of not landing on 4?

____

11. There are 4 queens in a standard deck of 52 cards. You pick one card at random. What is the probability of not picking a queen?

____

ESSENTIAL QUESTION CHECK-IN

12. Describe an event that has a probability of 0% and an event that has a probability of 100%.

____

____

____

Name ____________________ Class ____________ Date ____________

12.1 Independent Practice

Personal Math Trainer
Online Assessment and Intervention
my.hrw.com

13. There are 4 aces and 4 kings in a standard deck of 52 cards. You pick one card at random. What is the probability of selecting an ace or a king? Explain your reasoning.

____

____

14. There are 12 pieces of fruit in a bowl. Seven of the pieces are apples and two are peaches. What is the probability that a randomly selected piece of fruit will not be an apple or a peach? Justify your answer.

____

____

15. **Critique Reasoning** For breakfast, Clarissa can choose from oatmeal, cereal, French toast, or scrambled eggs. She thinks that if she selects a breakfast at random, it is likely that it will be oatmeal. Is she correct? Explain your reasoning.

____

____

____

16. **Draw Conclusions** A researcher's garden contains 90 sweet pea plants, which have either white or purple flowers. About 70 of the plants have purple flowers, and about 20 have white flowers. Would you expect that one plant randomly selected from the garden will have purple or white flowers? Explain.

____

____

____

____

17. The power goes out as Sandra is trying to get dressed. If she has 4 white T-shirts and 10 colored T-shirts in her drawer, is it likely that she will pick a colored T-shirt in the dark? What is the probability she will pick a colored T-shirt? Explain your answers.

____

____

18. James counts the hair colors of the 22 people in his class, including himself. He finds that there are 4 people with blonde hair, 8 people with brown hair, and 10 people with black hair. What is the probability that a randomly chosen student in the class does not have red hair? Explain.

19. **Persevere in Problem Solving** A bag contains 8 blue coins and 6 red coins. A coin is removed at random and replaced by three of the other color.

a. What is the probability that the removed coin is blue?

b. If the coin removed is blue, what is the probability of drawing a red coin after three red coins are put in the bag to replace the blue one?

c. If the coin removed is red, what is the probability of drawing a red coin after three blue coins are put in the bag to replace the red one?

H.O.T. FOCUS ON HIGHER ORDER THINKING

Work Area

20. **Draw Conclusions** Give an example of an event in which all of the outcomes are not equally likely. Explain.

21. **Critique Reasoning** A box contains 150 black pens and 50 red pens. Jose said the sum of the probability that a randomly selected pen will not be black and the probability that the pen will not be red is 1. Explain whether you agree.

22. **Communicate Mathematical Ideas** A spinner has 7 identical sections. Two sections are blue, 1 is red, and 4 of the sections are green. Suppose the probability of an event happening is $\frac{2}{7}$. What does each number in the ratio represent? What outcome matches this probability?

LESSON 12.2

Experimental Probability of Simple Events

7.6.12.2

Students will find the experimental probability of a simple event.

ESSENTIAL QUESTION

How do you find the experimental probability of a simple event?

EXPLORE ACTIVITY

Finding Experimental Probability

You can toss a paper cup to demonstrate *experimental probability*.

A Consider tossing a paper cup. Fill in the Outcome column of the table with the three different ways the cup could land.

B Toss a paper cup twenty times. Record your observations in the table.

Outcome	Number of Times

Reflect

1. Do the outcomes appear to be equally likely? ______________

2. Describe the three outcomes using the words *likely* and *unlikely*.

____

____

3. Use the number of times each event occurred to approximate the probability of each event.

4. **Make a Prediction** What do you think would happen if you performed more trials?

____

____

____

5. What is the sum of the probabilities in 3?

____

Outcome	Experimental Probability
Open-end up	$\frac{\text{open-end up}}{20} = \frac{\square}{20}$
Open-end down	$\frac{\text{open-end down}}{20} = \frac{\square}{20}$
On its side	$\frac{\text{on its side}}{20} = \frac{\square}{20}$

Math On the Spot
my.hrw.com

Animated Math
my.hrw.com

Calculating Experimental Probability

You can use *experimental probability* to approximate the probability of an event. An **experimental probability** of an event is found by comparing the number of times the event occurs to the total number of trials. When there is only one outcome for an event, it is called a **simple event**.

Experimental Probability

For a given experiment:

Experimental probability $= \frac{\text{number of times the event occurs}}{\text{total number of trials}}$

EXAMPLE 1 Real World

Martin has a bag of marbles. He removed one marble at random, recorded the color and then placed it back in the bag. He repeated this process several times and recorded his results in the table. Find the experimental probability of drawing each color.

Color	Frequency
Red	12
Blue	10
Green	15
Yellow	13

STEP 1 Identify the number of trials: $12 + 10 + 15 + 13 = 50$

STEP 2 Complete the table of experimental probabilities. Write each answer as a fraction in simplest form.

Color	Experimental Probability
Red	$\frac{\text{frequency of the event}}{\text{total number of trials}} = \frac{12}{50} = \frac{6}{25}$
Blue	$\frac{\text{frequency of the event}}{\text{total number of trials}} = \frac{10}{50} = \frac{1}{5}$
Green	$\frac{\text{frequency of the event}}{\text{total number of trials}} = \frac{15}{50} = \frac{3}{10}$
Yellow	$\frac{\text{frequency of the event}}{\text{total number of trials}} = \frac{13}{50}$

Substitute the results recorded in the table. You can also write each probability as a decimal or as a percent.

Reflect

6. **Communicate Mathematical Ideas** What are two different ways you could find the experimental probability of the event that Martin does **not** draw a red marble?

YOUR TURN

7. A spinner has three unequal sections: red, yellow, and blue. The table shows the results of Nolan's spins. Find the experimental probability of landing on each color. Write your answers in simplest form.

Color	Frequency
Red	10
Yellow	14
Blue	6

____

Math Talk
Mathematical Processes
Will everyone who does this experiment get the same results?

Making Predictions with Experimental Probability

A **simulation** is a model of an experiment that would be difficult or inconvenient to actually perform. You can use a simulation to find an experimental probability and make a prediction.

Math On the Spot
my.hrw.com

EXAMPLE 2 Real World

My Notes

A baseball team has a batting average of 0.250 so far this season. This means that the team's players get hits in 25% of their chances at bat. Use a simulation to predict the number of hits the team's players will have in their next 34 chances at bat.

STEP 1 Choose a model.

Batting average $= 0.250 = \frac{250}{1,000} = \frac{1}{4}$

A standard deck of cards has four suits, hearts, diamonds, spades, and clubs. Since $\frac{1}{4}$ of the cards are hearts, you can let hearts represent a "hit." Diamonds, clubs, and spades then represent "no hit."

STEP 2 Perform the simulation.

Draw a card at random from the deck, record the result, and put the card back into the deck. Continue until you have drawn and replaced 34 cards in all.

Since the team has 34 chances at bat, you must draw a card 34 times.

(H = heart, D = diamond, C = club, S = spade)

H D D S H C H S D H C D C C D H H
S D D H C C H C H H D S S S C H D

STEP 3 Make a prediction.

Count the number of hearts in the simulation.

Since there are 11 hearts, you can predict that the team will have 11 hits in its next 34 chances at bat.

Personal Math Trainer
Online Assessment and Intervention
my.hrw.com

YOUR TURN

8. A toy machine has equal numbers of red, white, and blue foam balls which it releases at random. Ross wonders which color ball will be released next. Describe how you could use a standard number cube to predict the answer.

____

____

____

____

____

Guided Practice

1. A spinner has four sections lettered A, B, C, and D. The table shows the results of several spins. Find the experimental probability of spinning each letter as a fraction in simplest form, a decimal, and a percent. (Explore Activity and Example 1)

Letter	A	B	C	D
Frequency	14	7	11	8

A: _______________ B: _______________

C: _______________ D: _______________

2. Rachel's free-throw average for basketball is 60%. She wants to predict how many times in the next 50 tries she will make a free throw. Describe how she could use 10 index cards to predict the answer. (Example 2)

____

____

____

ESSENTIAL QUESTION CHECK-IN

3. **Essential Question Follow Up** How do you find an experimental probability of a simple event?

____

____

Name ____________________ Class ____________________ Date ____________________

12.2 Independent Practice

Personal Math Trainer
my.hrw.com
Online Assessment and Intervention

4. Dree rolls a strike in 6 out of the 10 frames of bowling. What is the experimental probability that Dree will roll a strike in the first frame of the next game? Explain why a number cube would not be a good way to simulate this situation.

____

____

____

5. To play a game, you spin a spinner like the one shown. You win if the arrow lands in one of the areas marked "WIN". Lee played this game many times and recorded her results. She won 8 times and lost 40 times. Use Lee's data to explain how to find the experimental probability of winning this game.

____

____

6. The names of the students in Mr. Hayes' math class are written on the board. Mr. Hayes writes each name on an index card and shuffles the cards. Each day he randomly draws a card, and the chosen student explains a math problem at the board. What is the probability that Ryan is chosen today? What is the probability that Ryan is **not** chosen today?

Anna	Alisha	Kenna	Bridget
Meghan	Cody	Parker	Grace
Michael	Gabe	Taylor	Joel
Kate	Kaylee	Shaw	Tessa
Jon	Ryan	Morgan	Leo

____

7. **Critique Reasoning** A meteorologist reports an 80% chance of precipitation. Is this an example of experimental probability, written as a percent? Explain your reasoning.

____

8. Mica and Joan are on the same softball team. Mica got 8 hits out of 48 times at bat, while Joan got 12 hits out of 40 times at bat. Who do you think is more likely to get a hit her next time at bat? Explain.

9. **Make a Prediction** In tennis, Gabby serves an ace, a ball that can't be returned, 4 out of the 10 times she serves. What is the experimental probability that Gabby will serve an ace in the first match of the next game? Make a prediction about how many aces Gabby will have for the next 40 serves. Justify your reasoning.

10. **Represent Real-World Problems** Patricia finds that the experimental probability that her dog will want to go outside between 4 P.M. and 5 P.M. is $\frac{7}{12}$. About what percent of the time does her dog **not** want to go out between 4 P.M. and 5 P.M.?

H.O.T. FOCUS ON HIGHER ORDER THINKING

Work Area

11. **Explain the Error** Talia tossed a penny many times. She got 40 heads and 60 tails. She said the experimental probability of getting heads was $\frac{40}{60}$. Explain and correct her error.

12. **Communicate Mathematical Ideas** A high school has 438 students, with about the same number of males as females. Describe a simulation to predict how many of the first 50 students who leave school at the end of the day are female.

13. **Critical Thinking** For a scavenger hunt, Chessa put one coin in each of 10 small boxes. Four coins are quarters, 4 are dimes, and 2 are nickels. How could you simulate choosing one box at random? Would you use the same simulation if you planned to put these coins in your pocket and choose one? Explain your reasoning.

LESSON 12.3

Experimental Probability of Compound Events

7.6.12.3

Students will find the experimental probability of a compound event.

ESSENTIAL QUESTION

How do you find the experimental probability of a compound event?

EXPLORE ACTIVITY

Exploring Compound Probability

A **compound event** is an event that includes two or more simple events, such as flipping a coin *and* rolling a number cube. A compound event can include events that depend on each other or are independent. Events are independent if the occurrence of one event does not affect the probability of the other event, such as flipping a coin and rolling a number cube.

A What are the possible outcomes of flipping a coin once? ________________

B What are the possible outcomes of rolling a standard number cube once? ________________

C Complete the list for all possible outcomes for flipping a coin *and* rolling a number cube.

H1, H2, _____, _____, _____, _____, T1, _____, _____, _____, _____, _____

There are ________ possible outcomes for this compound event.

H1 would mean the coin landed on heads, and the number cube showed a 1.

D Flip a coin and roll a number cube 50 times. Use tally marks to record your results in the table.

	1	2	3	4	5	6
H						
T						

E Based on your data, which compound event had the greatest experimental probability and what was it? The least experimental probability? ________________________________

F **Draw Conclusions** Did you expect to have the same probability for each possible combination of flips and rolls? Why or why not?

____

____

Calculating Experimental Probability of Compound Events

The experimental probability of a compound event can be found using recorded data.

Math On the Spot
my.hrw.com

EXAMPLE 1 Real World

A food trailer serves chicken and records the order size and sides on their orders, as shown in the table. What is the experimental probability that the next order is for 3-pieces with cole slaw?

	Green Salad	Macaroni & Cheese	French Fries	Cole Slaw
2 pieces	33	22	52	35
3 pieces	13	55	65	55

STEP 1 Find the total number of trials, or orders.

$33 + 22 + 52 + 35 + 13 + 55 + 65 + 55 = 330$

STEP 2 Find the number of orders that are for 3 pieces with cole slaw: 55.

STEP 3 Find the experimental probability.

$P(3\text{ piece} + \text{slaw}) = \dfrac{\text{number of 3 piece} + \text{slaw}}{\text{total number of orders}}$

$= \dfrac{55}{330}$ Substitute the values.

$= \dfrac{1}{6}$ Simplify.

The experimental probability that the next order is for 3 pieces of chicken with cole slaw is $\frac{1}{6}$.

Math Talk
Mathematical Processes
Javier said the total number of orders is 8 and not 330. Is he correct? Explain.

YOUR TURN

1. Drink sales for an afternoon at the school carnival were recorded in the table. What is the experimental probability that the next drink is a small cocoa?

	Soda	Water	Cocoa
Small	77	98	60
Large	68	45	52

____

Personal Math Trainer
Online Assessment and Intervention
my.hrw.com

Using a Simulation to Make a Prediction

You can use a simulation or model of an experiment to find the experimental probability of compound events.

Math On the Spot
my.hrw.com

EXAMPLE 2 Real World

At a street intersection, a vehicle is classified either as a *car* or a *truck*, and it can turn *left*, *right*, or go *straight*. About an equal number of cars and trucks go through the intersection and turn in each direction. Use a simulation to find the experimental probability that the next vehicle will be a car that turns right.

STEP 1 Choose a model.

Use a coin toss to model the two vehicle types.
Let Heads = Car and Tails = Truck

Use a spinner divided into 3 equal sectors to represent the *three* directions as shown.

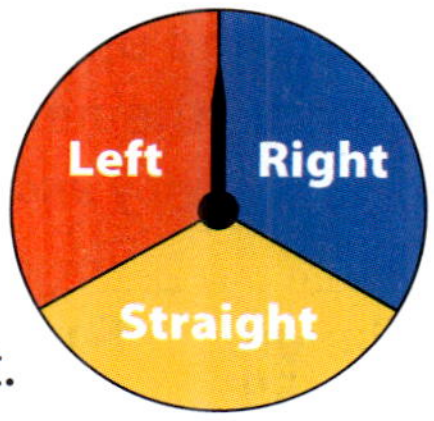

STEP 2 Find the sample space for the compound event.

There are 6 possible outcomes: CL, CR, CS, TL, TR, TS

STEP 3 Perform the simulation.

A coin was tossed and a spinner spun 50 times.
The results are shown in the table.

	Car	Truck
Left	8	9
Right	6	11
Straight	9	7

STEP 4 Find the experimental probability that a car turns right.

$$P(\text{Car turns right}) = \frac{\text{frequency of compound event}}{\text{total number of trials}}$$

$$= \frac{6}{50} \quad \text{Substitute the values.}$$

$$= \frac{3}{25} \quad \text{Simplify.}$$

Based on the simulation, the experimental probability is $\frac{3}{25}$ that the next vehicle will be a car that turns right.

Reflect

2. **Make a Prediction** Predict the number of cars that turn right out of 100 vehicles that enter the intersection. Explain your reasoning.

My Notes

Personal Math Trainer
Online Assessment and Intervention
my.hrw.com

YOUR TURN

3. A jeweler sells necklaces made in three sizes and two different metals. Use the data from a simulation to find the experimental probability that the next necklace sold is a 20-inch gold necklace.

	Silver	Gold
12 in.	12	22
16 in.	16	8
20 in.	5	12

____

Guided Practice

1. A dentist has 400 male and female patients that range in ages from 10 years old to 50 years old and up as shown in the table. What is the experimental probability that the next patient will be female and in the age range 22–39? (Explore Activity and Example 1)

	Range: 10–21	Range: 22–39	Range: 40–50	Range: 50+
Male	44	66	32	53
Female	36	50	45	74

____

2. At a car wash, customers can choose the type of wash and whether to use the interior vacuum. Customers are equally likely to choose each type of wash and whether to use the vacuum. Use a simulation to find the experimental probability that the next customer purchases a deluxe wash and no interior vacuum. Describe your simulation. (Example 2)

____

____

____

ESSENTIAL QUESTION CHECK-IN

3. How do you find the experimental probability of a compound event?

____

____

Name ____________________ Class ____________ Date ____________

12.3 Independent Practice

Personal Math Trainer
Online Assessment and Intervention
my.hrw.com

4. **Represent Real-World Problems** For the same food trailer mentioned in Example 1, explain how to find the experimental probability that the next order is two pieces of chicken with a green salad.

____

____

The school store sells spiral notebooks in four colors and three different sizes. The table shows the sales by size and color for 400 notebooks.

	Red	Green	Blue	Yellow
100 Pages	55	37	26	12
150 Pages	60	44	57	27
200 Pages	23	19	21	19

5. What is the experimental probability that the next customer buys a red notebook with 150 pages?

____

6. What is the experimental probability that the next customer buys any red notebooks?

____

7. **Analyze Relationships** How many possible combined page count and color choices are possible? How does this number relate to the number of page size choices and to the number of color choices?

____

____

A middle school English teacher polled random students about how many pages of a book they read per week.

	6th	7th	8th
75 Pages	24	18	22
100 Pages	22	32	24
150 Pages	30	53	25

8. **Critique Reasoning** Jennie says the experimental probability that a 7th grade student reads at least 100 pages per week is $\frac{16}{125}$. What is her error and the correct experimental probability?

____

9. **Analyze Relationships** Based on the data, which group(s) of students should be encouraged to read more? Explain your reasoning.

____

____

H.O.T. FOCUS ON HIGHER ORDER THINKING

Work Area

10. **Make a Conjecture** Would you expect the probability for the simple event "rolling a 6" to be greater than or less than the probability of the compound event "rolling a 6 and getting heads on a coin"? Explain.

____

____

11. **Critique Reasoning** Donald says he uses a standard number cube for simulations that involve 2, 3, or 6 equal outcomes. Explain how Donald can do this.

____

____

____

12. **Draw Conclusions** Data collected in a mall recorded the shoe styles worn by 150 male and for 150 female customers. What is the probability that the next customer is male and has an open-toe shoe (such as a sandal)? What is the probability that the next male customer has an open-toe shoe? Are the two probabilities the same? Explain.

	Male	Female
Open toe	11	92
Closed toe	139	58

____

____

____

13. **What If?** Suppose you wanted to perform a simulation to model the shoe style data shown in the table. Could you use two coins? Explain.

____

____

14. **Represent Real-World Problems** A middle school is made up of grades 6, 7, and 8, and has about the same number of male and female students in each grade. Explain how to use a simulation to find the experimental probability that the first 50 students who arrive at school are male and 7th graders.

____

____

____

____

LESSON 12.4

Making Predictions with Experimental Probability

7.6.12.4

Students will make predictions using experimental probability.

ESSENTIAL QUESTION

How do you make predictions using experimental probability?

EXPLORE ACTIVITY Real World

Using Experimental Probability to Make a Prediction

Math On the Spot
my.hrw.com

Scientists study data to make predictions. You can use probabilities to make predictions in your daily life.

EXAMPLE 1 **Danae found that the experimental probability of her making a bull's-eye when throwing darts is $\frac{2}{10}$, or 20%. Out of 75 throws, about how many bull's-eyes could she predict she would make?**

Method 1: Use a proportion.

Write a proportion. 2 out of 10 is how many out of 75? $\frac{2}{10} = \frac{x}{75}$

Since 10 times _______ is 75, multiply 2 times _______ to find the value of x.

$\frac{\square}{10} = \frac{\square}{75}$ (× ☐ on top, × ☐ on bottom)

$x = \square$

Method 2: Use a percent equation.

Write an equation to find 20% of 75. $\square \times 75 = x$

Multiply. $15 = x$

You can write probabilities as ratios, decimals, or percents.

Danae can predict that she will make about 15 bull's-eye throws out of 75.

YOUR TURN

1. A car rental company sells accident insurance to 24% of its customers. Out of 550 customers, about how many customers are predicted to purchase insurance? ____________________

Personal Math Trainer
Online Assessment and Intervention
my.hrw.com

Math On the Spot
my.hrw.com

Using Experimental Probability to Make a Qualitative Prediction

A prediction is something you reasonably expect to happen in the future. A qualitative prediction helps you decide which situation is more likely in general.

EXAMPLE 2 Real World

A doctor's office records data and concludes that, on average, 11% of patients call to reschedule their appointments per week. The office manager predicts that 23 appointments will be rescheduled out of the 240 total appointments during next week. Explain whether the prediction is reasonable.

Method 1: Use a proportion.

$$\frac{11}{100} = \frac{x}{240}$$ *Write a proportion. 11 out of 100 is how many out of 240?*

$$\frac{11}{100} \underset{\times 2.4}{=} \frac{x}{240}$$

$$\frac{11}{100} \overset{\times 2.4}{\underset{\times 2.4}{=}} \frac{26.4}{240}$$ *Since 100 times 2.4 is 240, multiply 11 times 2.4 to find the value of x.*

$$x = 26.4$$

26.4 is the average number of patients that would call to reschedule.

Method 2: Use a percent equation.

$0.11 \cdot 240 = x$ *Find 11% of 240.*

$26.4 = x$ *Solve for x.*

The prediction of 23 is reasonable but a little low, because 23 is a little less than 26.4.

Reflect

2. Does 26.4 make sense for the number of patients?

____

____

YOUR TURN

3. In emails to monthly readers of a newsletter 3% of the emails come back undelivered. The editor predicts that if he sends out 12,372 emails, he will receive 437 notices for undelivered email. Do you agree with his prediction?

Explain. ____

____

Personal Math Trainer
Online Assessment and Intervention
my.hrw.com

Making a Quantitative Prediction

You can use proportional reasoning to make quantitative predictions and compare options in real-world situations.

Math On the Spot
my.hrw.com

EXAMPLE 3 Problem Solving

An online poll for a movie site shows its polling results for a new movie. If a newspaper surveys 150 people leaving the movie, how many people can it predict will like the movie based on the online poll? Is the movie site's claim accurate if the newspaper has 104 people say they like the movie?

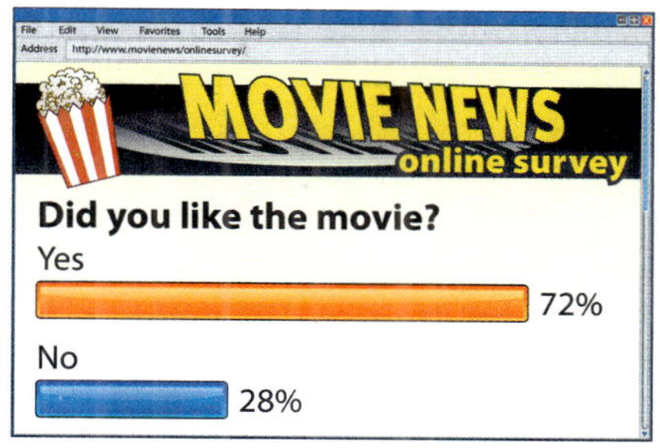

My Notes

Analyze Information

The **answer** is a prediction for how many people out of 150 will like the movie based on the online poll. Also tell whether the 104 people that say they like the movie is enough to support the movie site's claim.

List the important information:

- The online poll says 72% of movie goers like the new movie.
- A newspaper surveys 150 people.

Formulate a Plan

Use a proportion to calculate 72% of the 150 people surveyed.

Solve

$$\frac{72}{100} = \frac{x}{150}$$

Set up a proportion. 72 out of 100 is how many out of 150?

$$\frac{72}{100} = \frac{x}{150} \quad (\times 1.5)$$

$$\frac{72}{100} = \frac{108}{150} \quad (\times 1.5)$$

Since 100 times 1.5 is 150, multiply 72 times 1.5 to find the value of x.

$$x = 108$$

The newspaper can predict that 108 out of 150 people will say they like the movie, based on the online poll.

Justify and Evaluate

Since 108 is close to 104, the newspaper survey and the online poll show that about the same percent of people like the movie.

Personal Math Trainer
Online Assessment and Intervention
my.hrw.com

YOUR TURN

4. On average, 24% of customers who buy shoes in a particular store buy two or more pairs. One weekend, 350 customers purchased shoes. How many can be predicted to buy two or more pairs? If 107 customers buy more than two pairs, did more customers than normal buy two or more pairs?

Guided Practice

1. A baseball player reaches first base 30% of the times he is at bat. Out of 50 times at bat, about how many times will the player reach first base? (Explore Activity Example 1)

2. The experimental probability that it will rain on any given day in Houston, Texas, is about 15%. Out of 365 days, about how many days can residents predict rain? (Explore Activity Example 1)

3. A catalog store has 6% of its orders returned for a refund. The owner predicts that a new candle will have 812 returns out of the 16,824 sold. Do you agree with this prediction? Explain. (Example 2)

4. On a toy assembly line, 3% of the toys are found to be defective. The quality control officer predicts that 872 toys will be found defective out of 24,850 toys made. Do you agree with this prediction? Explain. (Example 2)

5. A light-rail service claims to be on time 98% of the time. Jeanette takes the light-rail 40 times one month, how many times can she predict she will be on time? Is the light-rail's claim accurate if she is late 6 times? (Example 3)

6. On average, a college claims to accept 18% of its applicants. If the college has 5,000 applicants, predict how many will be accepted. If 885 applicants are accepted, is the college's claim accurate? (Example 3)

ESSENTIAL QUESTION CHECK-IN

7. How do you make predictions using experimental probability?

Name ______________________ Class ______________ Date ____________

12.4 Independent Practice

Personal Math Trainer
Online Assessment and Intervention
my.hrw.com

The table shows the number of students in a middle school at the beginning of the year and the percentage that can be expected to move out of the area by the end of the year.

	6th	**7th**	**8th**
Number of Students	250	200	150
% Moves	2%	4%	8%

8. How many 7th grade students are expected to move by the end of the year? If 12 students actually moved, did more or fewer 7th grade students move than expected? Justify your answer.

____

____

9. **Critique Reasoning** The middle school will lose some of its funding if 50 or more students move away in any year. The principal claims he only loses about 30 students a year. Do the values in the table support his claim? Explain.

____

____

____

10. **Represent Real-World Problems** An airline knows that, on average, the probability that a passenger will not show up for a flight is 6%. If an airplane is fully booked and holds 300 passengers, how many seats are expected to be empty? If the airline overbooked the flight by 10 passengers, about how many passengers are expected to show up for the flight? Justify your answer.

____

____

____

____

11. **Draw Conclusions** In a doctor's office, an average of 94% of the clients pay on the day of the appointment. If the office has 600 clients per month, how many are expected not to pay on the day of the appointment? If 40 clients do not pay on the day of their appointment in a month, did more or fewer than the average not pay?

____

12. **Counterexamples** The soccer coach claimed that, on average, only 80% of the team come to practice each day. The table shows the number of students that came to practice for 8 days. If the team has 20 members, how many team members should come to practice to uphold the coach's claim? Was the coach's claim accurate? Explain your reasoning.

	1	2	3	4	5	6	7	8
Number of Students	18	15	18	17	17	19	20	20

____

____

13. **What's the Error?** Ronnie misses the school bus 1 out of every 30 school days. He sets up the proportion $\frac{1}{30} = \frac{180}{x}$ to predict how many days he will miss the bus in the 180-day school year. What is Ronnie's error?

____

H.O.T. FOCUS ON HIGHER ORDER THINKING

Work Area

14. **Persevere in Problem Solving** A gas pump machine rejects 12% of credit card transactions. If this is twice the normal rejection rate for a normal gas pump, how many out of 500 credit cards transactions would a normal gas pump machine reject? ____________________

15. **Make Predictions** An airline's weekly flight data showed a 98% probability of being on time. If this airline has 15,000 flights in a year, how many flights would you predict to arrive on time? Explain whether you can use the data to predict whether a specific flight with this airline will be on time.

____

____

____

____

16. **Draw Conclusions** An average response rate for a marketing letter is 4%, meaning that 4% of the people who receive the letter respond to it. A company writes a new type of marketing letter, sends out 2,400 of them, and gets 65 responses. Explain whether the new type of letter would be considered to be a success.

____

____

____

MODULE QUIZ

Ready to Go On?

Personal Math Trainer
Online Assessment and Intervention
my.hrw.com

12.1 Probability

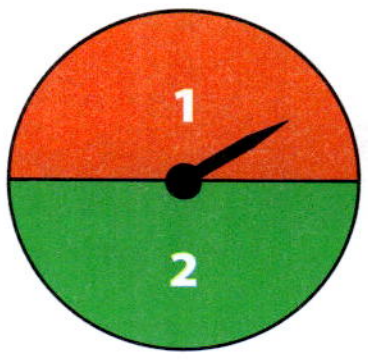

1. Josue tosses a coin and spins the spinner at the right. What are all the possible outcomes?

____

12.2 Experimental Probability of Simple Events

2. While bowling with friends, Brandy rolls a strike in 6 out of 10 frames. What is the experimental probability that Brandy will roll a strike in the first frame of the next game? __________

3. Ben is greeting customers at a music store. Of the first 20 people he sees enter the store, 13 are wearing jackets and 7 are not. What is the experimental probability that the next person to enter the store will be wearing a jacket? __________

12.3 Experimental Probability of Compound Events

4. Auden rolled two number cubes and recorded the results.

Roll #1	Roll #2	Roll #3	Roll #4	Roll #5	Roll #6	Roll #7
2, 1	4, 5	3, 2	2, 2	1, 3	6, 2	5, 3

What is the experimental probability that the sum of the next two numbers rolled is greater than 5? __________

12.4 Making Predictions with Experimental Probability

5. A player on a school baseball team reaches first base $\frac{3}{10}$ of the time he is at bat. Out of 80 times at bat, about how many times would you predict he will reach first base? __________

ESSENTIAL QUESTION

6. How is experimental probability used to make predictions?

____

____

____

MODULE 12 MIXED REVIEW

Assessment Readiness

Personal Math Trainer
Online Assessment and Intervention
my.hrw.com

Selected Response

1. A frozen yogurt shop offers scoops in cake cones, waffle cones, or cups. You can get vanilla, chocolate, strawberry, pistachio, or coffee flavored frozen yogurt. If you order a single scoop, how many outcomes are in the sample space?

Ⓐ 3
Ⓑ 5
Ⓒ 8
Ⓓ 15

2. A bag contains 7 purple beads, 4 blue beads, and 4 pink beads. What is the probability of **not** drawing a pink bead?

Ⓐ $\frac{4}{15}$
Ⓑ $\frac{7}{15}$
Ⓒ $\frac{8}{15}$
Ⓓ $\frac{11}{15}$

3. During the month of June, Ava kept track of the number of days she saw birds in her garden. She saw birds on 18 days of the month. What is the experimental probability that she will see birds in her garden on July 1?

Ⓐ $\frac{1}{18}$
Ⓑ $\frac{2}{5}$
Ⓒ $\frac{1}{2}$
Ⓓ $\frac{3}{5}$

4. A rectangle has a width of 4 inches and a length of 6 inches. A similar rectangle has a width of 12 inches. What is the length of the similar rectangle?

Ⓐ 8 inches
Ⓑ 12 inches
Ⓒ 14 inches
Ⓓ 18 inches

5. The experimental probability of hearing thunder on any given day in Ohio is 30%. Out of 600 days, on about how many days can Ohioans expect to hear thunder?

Ⓐ 90 days
Ⓑ 180 days
Ⓒ 210 days
Ⓓ 420 days

6. Isidro tossed two coins several times and then recorded the results in the table below.

Toss 1	Toss 2	Toss 3	Toss 4	Toss 5
H; T	T; T	T; H	H; T	H; H

What is the experimental probability that both coins will land on the same side on Isidro's next toss?

Ⓐ $\frac{1}{5}$
Ⓑ $\frac{2}{5}$
Ⓒ $\frac{3}{5}$
Ⓓ $\frac{4}{5}$

Mini-Task

7. Magdalena had a spinner that was evenly divided into sections of red, blue, and green. She spun the spinner and tossed a coin several times. The table below shows the results.

Trial 1	Trial 2	Trial 3	Trial 4	Trial 5
blue; T	green; T	green; H	red; T	blue; H

a. What are all the possible outcomes?

____

____

b. What experimental probability did Magdalena find for spinning blue? Give your answer as a fraction in simplest form, as a decimal, and as a percent.

____

c. Out of 90 trials, how many times should Magdalena predict she will spin green while tossing tails?

____

Theoretical Probability and Simulations

MODULE 13

ESSENTIAL QUESTION

How can you use theoretical probability to solve real-world problems?

Real-World Video

my.hrw.com

Many carnival games rely on theoretical probability to set the chance of winning fairly low. Understanding how the game is set up might help you be more likely to win.

GO DIGITAL
my.hrw.com

my.hrw.com

Go digital with your write-in student edition, accessible on any device.

Math On the Spot

Scan with your smart phone to jump directly to the online edition, video tutor, and more.

Animated Math

Interactively explore key concepts to see how math works.

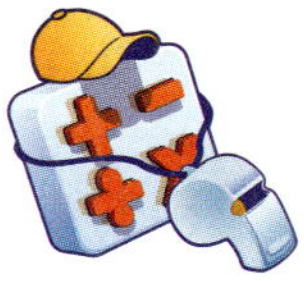

Personal Math Trainer

Get immediate feedback and help as you work through practice sets.

Reading Start-Up

Visualize Vocabulary

Use the ✔ words to complete the graphic.

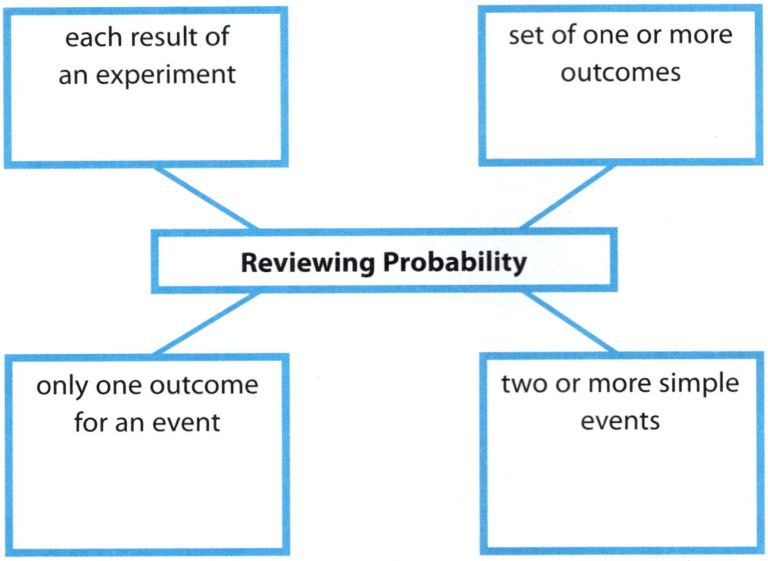

Vocabulary

Review Words

complement *(complemento)*

✔ compound event *(suceso compuesto)*

✔ event *(suceso)*

experiment *(experimento)*

✔ outcome *(resultado)*

✔ simple event *(suceso simple)*

probability *(probabilidad)*

Preview Words

theoretical probability *(probabilidad teórica)*

Understand Vocabulary

Match the term on the left to the correct expression on the right.

1. compound event

2. theoretical probability

3. complement

A. The set of all outcomes that are not the desired event.

B. An event made of two or more simple events.

C. The ratio of the number of equally likely outcomes in an event to the total number of possible outcomes.

Active Reading

Two-Panel Flip Chart Create a two-panel flip chart, to help you understand the concepts in this module. Label one flap "Simple Events" and the other flap "Compound Events." As you study each lesson, write important ideas under the appropriate flap. Include information that will help you remember the concepts later when you look back at your notes.

Are YOU Ready?

Complete these exercises to review skills you will need for this module.

Personal Math Trainer
Online Assessment and Intervention
my.hrw.com

Fractions, Decimals, and Percents

EXAMPLE Write $\frac{3}{8}$ as a decimal and a percent.

$$\begin{array}{r} 0.375 \\ 8\overline{)3.000} \\ -2\,4 \\ \hline 60 \\ -56 \\ \hline 40 \\ -40 \\ \hline 0 \end{array}$$

Write the fraction as a division problem.
Write a decimal point and zeros in the dividend.
Place a decimal point in the quotient.
Divide as with whole numbers.

$0.375 = 37.5\%$. Write the decimal as a percent.

Write each fraction as a decimal and a percent.

1. $\frac{3}{4}$ ______
2. $\frac{2}{5}$ ______
3. $\frac{9}{10}$ ______
4. $\frac{7}{20}$ ______
5. $\frac{7}{8}$ ______
6. $\frac{1}{20}$ ______
7. $\frac{19}{25}$ ______
8. $\frac{23}{50}$ ______

Operations with Fractions

EXAMPLE

$1 - \frac{7}{12} = \frac{12}{12} - \frac{7}{12}$ Use the denominator of the fraction to write 1 as a fraction.

$= \frac{12-7}{12}$ Subtract the numerators.

$= \frac{5}{12}$ Simplify.

Find each difference.

9. $1 - \frac{1}{5}$ ______
10. $1 - \frac{2}{9}$ ______
11. $1 - \frac{8}{13}$ ______
12. $1 - \frac{3}{20}$ ______

Multiply Fractions

EXAMPLE

$\frac{4}{15} \times \frac{5}{6} = \frac{\cancel{4}^{2}}{\cancel{15}_{3}} \times \frac{\cancel{5}^{1}}{\cancel{6}_{3}}$ Divide by the common factors.

$= \frac{2}{9}$ Simplify.

Multiply. Write each product in simplest form.

13. $\frac{8}{15} \times \frac{5}{8}$ ______
14. $\frac{2}{9} \times \frac{3}{4}$ ______
15. $\frac{9}{16} \times \frac{12}{13}$ ______
16. $\frac{7}{10} \times \frac{5}{28}$ ______

Are YOU Ready? *(cont'd)*

Complete these exercises to review skills you will need for this module.

Fractions, Decimals, and Percents

17. Lakshmi donated $\frac{2}{25}$ of her salary last week to an animal shelter. Write this fraction as a decimal and as a percent. Did she donate more or less than 10% of her salary?

Operations with Fractions

18. Kyle and his friends ordered a large pizza. They ate $\frac{7}{9}$ of the pizza. Kyle took the rest of the pizza home. What fraction of the pizza did Kyle take home?

Multiply Fractions

19. A costume designer has $\frac{9}{10}$ yard of silk. She uses $\frac{2}{3}$ of the silk to make a banner. How much silk does she use to make the banner? Explain your reasoning.

LESSON 13.1

Theoretical Probability of Simple Events

7.6.13.1

Students will find the theoretical probability of a simple event.

ESSENTIAL QUESTION

How can you find the theoretical probability of a simple event?

EXPLORE ACTIVITY 1 Real World

Finding Theoretical Probability

In previous lessons, you found probabilities based on observing data, or experimental probabilities. In this lesson, you will find *theoretical probabilities.*

Spinner A

Spinner B

At a school fair, you have a choice of spinning Spinner A or Spinner B. You win an MP3 player if the spinner lands on a section with a star in it. Which spinner should you choose if you want a better chance of winning?

A Complete the table.

	Spinner A	Spinner B
Total number of outcomes		
Number of sections with stars		
***P*(winning MP3)** $= \frac{\text{number of sections with stars}}{\text{total number of outcomes}}$		

B Compare the ratios for Spinner A and Spinner B.

The ratio for Spinner ________ is greater than the ratio for Spinner _______.

I should choose _________________ for a better chance of winning.

Math Talk
Mathematical Processes

Describe a way to change Spinner B to make your chances of winning equal to your chances of not winning. Explain.

Reflect

1. *Theoretical probability* is a way to describe how you found the chance of winning an MP3 player in the scenario above. Using the spinner example to help you, explain in your own words how to find the theoretical probability of an event.

___

___

___

Math On the Spot
my.hrw.com

Calculating Theoretical Probability of Simple Events

Theoretical probability is the probability that an event occurs when all of the outcomes of the experiment are equally likely.

Theoretical Probability

$$P(\text{event}) = \frac{\text{number of ways the event can occur}}{\text{total number of equally likely outcomes}}$$

Probability can be written as a fraction, a decimal, or a percent. For example, the probability you win with Spinner B is $\frac{5}{16}$. You can also write that as 0.3125 or as 31.25%.

EXAMPLE 1 Real World

A bag contains 6 red marbles and 12 blue ones. You select one marble at random from the bag. What is the probability that you select a red marble? Write your answer in simplest form.

STEP 1 Find the number of ways the event can occur, that is, the number of red marbles: 6

STEP 2 Add to find the total number of equally likely outcomes.

number of red marbles	+	number of blue marbles	=	total number of marbles
6	+	12	=	**18**

There are 18 possible outcomes in the sample space.

STEP 3 Find the probability of selecting a red marble.

$$P(\text{red marble}) = \frac{\text{number of red marbles}}{\text{total number of marbles}} = \frac{6}{\mathbf{18}}$$

The probability that you select a red marble is $\frac{6}{18}$, or $\frac{1}{3}$.

Math Talk
Mathematical Processes

Describe a situation that has a theoretical probability of $\frac{1}{4}$.

YOUR TURN

2. You roll a number cube one time. What is the probability that you roll a 3 or 4? Write your answer in simplest form.

$$P(\text{rolling a 3 or 4}) = \frac{\square}{\square} = \frac{\square}{\square} = \frac{\square}{\square}$$

3. How is the sample space for an event related to the formula for theoretical probability? ______________________________

____

Personal Math Trainer
Online Assessment and Intervention
my.hrw.com

EXPLORE ACTIVITY 2 Real World

Comparing Theoretical and Experimental Probability

Now that you have calculated theoretical probabilities, you may wonder how theoretical and experimental probabilities compare.

Six students are performing in a talent contest. You roll a number cube to determine the order of the performances.

STEP 1 You roll the number cube once. Complete the table of theoretical probabilities for the different outcomes.

Number	1	2	3	4	5	6
Theoretical probability						

STEP 2 Predict the number of times each number will be rolled out of 30 total rolls.

1: ☐ times 3: ☐ times 5: ☐ times

2: ☐ times 4: ☐ times 6: ☐ times

STEP 3 Roll a number cube 30 times. Complete the table for the frequency of each number and then find its experimental probability.

Number	1	2	3	4	5	6
Frequency						
Experimental probability						

STEP 4 Look at the tables you completed. How do the experimental probabilities compare with the theoretical probabilities?

____

____

STEP 5 **Conjecture** By performing more trials, you tend to get experimental results that are closer to the theoretical probabilities. Combine your table from **Step 3** with those of your classmates to make one table for the class. How do the class experimental probabilities compare with the theoretical probabilities?

____

____

EXPLORE ACTIVITY 2 *(cont'd)*

Reflect

4. Could the experimental probabilities ever be exactly equal to the theoretical probability? If so, how likely is it? If not, why not?

____

____

Guided Practice

At a school fair, you have a choice of randomly picking a ball from Basket A or Basket B. Basket A has 5 green balls, 3 red balls, and 8 yellow balls. Basket B has 7 green balls, 4 red balls, and 9 yellow balls. You can win a digital book reader if you pick a red ball. (Explore Activity 1)

	Basket A	Basket B
Total number of outcomes		
Number of red balls		
P(win) = $\frac{\text{number of red balls}}{\text{total number of outcomes}}$		

1. Complete the chart. Write each answer in simplest form.

2. Which basket should you choose if you want the better chance of winning? ______________

A spinner has 11 equal-sized sections marked 1 through 11. Find each probability. (Example 1)

3. You spin once and land on an odd number.

   $P(\text{odd}) = \frac{\text{number of \_\_\_\_\_ sections}}{\text{total number of \_\_\_\_\_}} = \frac{\square}{\square}$

4. You spin once and land on an even number.

   $P(\text{even}) = \frac{\text{number of \_\_\_\_\_ sections}}{\text{total number of \_\_\_\_\_}} = \frac{\square}{\square}$

You roll a number cube once.

5. What is the theoretical probability that you roll a 3 or 4? (Example 1) ______________

6. Suppose you rolled the number cube 199 more times. Would you expect the experimental probability of rolling a 3 or 4 to be the same as your answer to Exercise 5? (Explore Activity 2)

____

ESSENTIAL QUESTION CHECK-IN

7. How can you find the probability of a simple event if the total number of equally likely outcomes is 20?

____

Name ____________________ Class ____________ Date ____________

13.1 Independent Practice

Find the probability of each event. Write each answer as a fraction in simplest form, as a decimal to the nearest hundredth, and as a percent to the nearest whole number.

8. You spin the spinner shown. The spinner lands on yellow.

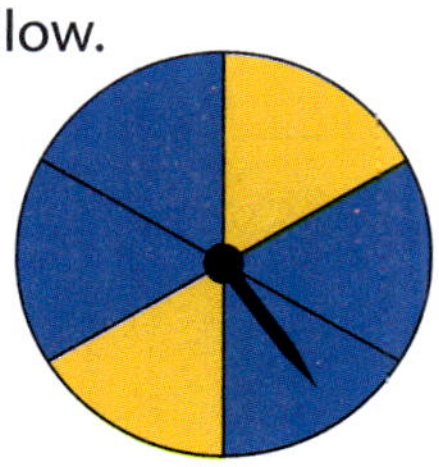

____

9. You spin the spinner shown. The spinner lands on blue or green.

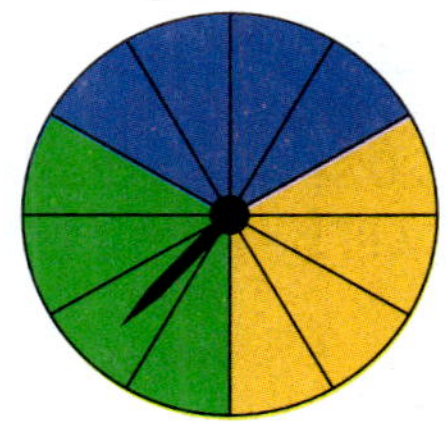

____

10. A jar contains 4 cherry cough drops and 10 honey cough drops. You choose one cough drop without looking. The cough drop is cherry. ____________

11. You pick one card at random from a standard deck of 52 playing cards. You pick a black card. ____________

12. There are 12 pieces of fruit in a bowl. Five are lemons and the rest are limes. You choose a piece of fruit without looking. The piece of fruit is a lime. ____________

13. You choose a movie disc at random from a case containing 8 comedy discs, 5 science fiction discs, and 7 adventure discs. The disc is **not** a comedy. ____________

14. You roll a number cube. You roll a number that is greater than 2 and less than 5. ____________

15. **Communicate Mathematical Ideas** The theoretical probability of a given event is $\frac{9}{13}$. Explain what each number represents.

____

____

____

16. Leona has 4 nickels, 6 pennies, 4 dimes, and 2 quarters in a change purse. Leona lets her little sister Daisy pick a coin at random. If Daisy is equally likely to pick each type of coin, what is the probability that her coin is worth more than five cents? Explain.

____

____

____

H.O.T. FOCUS ON HIGHER ORDER THINKING

Work Area

17. **Critique Reasoning** A bowl of flower seeds contains 5 petunia seeds and 15 begonia seeds. Riley calculated the probability that a randomly selected seed is a petunia seed as $\frac{1}{3}$. Describe and correct Riley's error.

____

____

____

____

18. There are 20 seventh graders and 15 eighth graders in a club. A club president will be chosen at random.

a. **Analyze Relationships** Compare the probabilities of choosing a seventh grader or an eighth grader.

____

____

b. **Critical Thinking** If a student from one grade is more likely to be chosen than a student from the other, is the method unfair? Explain.

____

____

A jar contains 8 red marbles, 10 blue ones, and 2 yellow ones. One marble is chosen at random. The color is recorded in the table, and then it is returned to the jar. This is repeated 40 times.

Red	Blue	Yellow
14	16	10

19. **Communicate Mathematical Ideas** Use proportional reasoning to explain how you know that for each color, the theoretical and experimental probabilities are not the same.

____

____

____

____

20. **Persevere in Problem Solving** For which color marble is the experimental probability closest to the theoretical probability? Explain.

____

____

LESSON 13.2

Theoretical Probability of Compound Events

7.6.13.2

Students will find the theoretical probability of a compound event.

ESSENTIAL QUESTION

How do you find the probability of a compound event?

EXPLORE ACTIVITY

Finding Probability Using a Table

Recall that a compound event consists of two or more simple events. To find the probability of a compound event, you write a ratio of the number of ways the compound event can happen to the total number of equally likely possible outcomes.

Jacob rolls two fair number cubes. Find the probability that the sum of the numbers he rolls is 8.

STEP 1 Use the table to find the sample space for rolling a particular sum on two number cubes. Each cell is the sum of the first number in that row and column.

	1	2	3	4	5	6
1						
2						
3						
4						
5						
6						

STEP 2 How many possible outcomes are in the sample space? ________

STEP 3 Circle the outcomes that give the sum of 8.

STEP 4 How many ways are there to roll a sum of 8? ________

STEP 5 What is the probability of rolling a sum of 8? ________

Reflect

1. Give an example of an event that is more likely than rolling a sum of 8.

____

2. Give an example of an event that is less likely than rolling a sum of 8.

____

Finding Probability Using a Tree Diagram

You can also use a tree diagram to calculate theoretical probabilities of compound events.

EXAMPLE 1 Real World

A deli prepares sandwiches with one type of bread (white or wheat), one type of meat (ham, turkey, or chicken), and one type of cheese (cheddar or Swiss). Each combination is equally likely. Find the probability of choosing a sandwich at random and getting turkey and Swiss on wheat bread.

STEP 1 Make a tree diagram to find the sample space for the compound event.

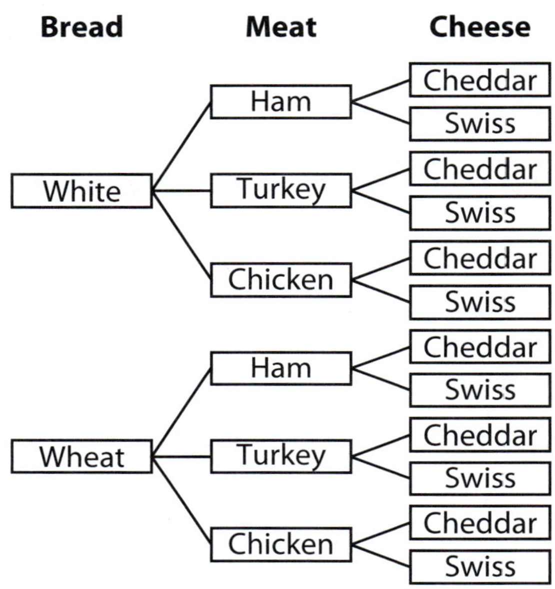

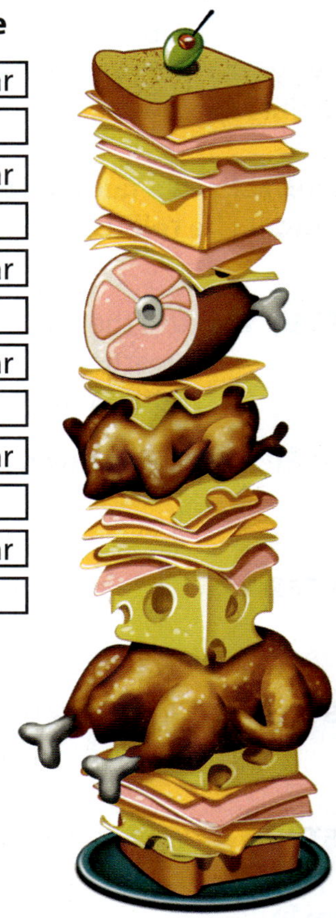

STEP 2 Find the number of possible outcomes in the sample space: **12**

STEP 3 Find the probability of choosing turkey and Swiss on wheat bread at random: $\frac{1}{12}$

Math Talk
Mathematical Processes
How many sandwich combinations are possible if one of the meat options is unavailable?

YOUR TURN

Use the diagram from Example 1 to find the given probabilities.

3. ham sandwich ____________________

4. sandwich containing Swiss cheese ____________________

Finding Probability Using a List

One way to provide security for a locker or personal account is to assign it an access code number known only to the owner.

Math On the Spot
my.hrw.com

EXAMPLE 2 Real World

The combination for Khiem's locker is a 3-digit code that uses the numbers 1, 2, and 3. Any of these numbers may be repeated. Find the probability that Khiem's randomly-assigned number is 222.

My Notes

Make an organized list to find the sample space.

STEP 1 List all the codes that start with 1 and have 1 as a second digit.

1	1	1
1	1	2
1	1	3

STEP 2 List all the codes that start with 1 and have 2 as a second digit.

1	2	1
1	2	2
1	2	3

STEP 3 List all the codes that start with 1 and have 3 as a second digit.

1	3	1
1	3	2
1	3	3

STEP 4 You have now listed all the codes that start with 1. Repeat Steps 1–3 for codes that start with 2, and then for codes that start with 3.

2	1	1
2	1	2
2	1	3

2	2	1
2	2	2
2	2	3

2	3	1
2	3	2
2	3	3

3	1	1
3	1	2
3	1	3

3	2	1
3	2	2
3	2	3

3	3	1
3	3	2
3	3	3

Notice that there are 3 possible first numbers, 3 possible second numbers, and 3 possible third numbers, or $3 \times 3 \times 3 = 27$ numbers in all.

STEP 5 Find the number of outcomes in the sample space by counting all the possible codes. There are **27** such codes.

STEP 6 Find the probability that Khiem's locker code is 222.

$$P(\text{Code } 222) = \frac{\text{number of favorable outcomes}}{\text{total number of possible outcomes}} = \frac{1}{27}$$

Math Talk
Mathematical Processes

How could you find the probability that Khiem's locker code includes exactly two 1s?

YOUR TURN

5. Martha types a 4-digit code into a keypad to unlock her car doors. The code uses the numbers 1 and 0. If the digits are selected at random, what is the probability of getting a code with exactly two 0s? ________

Personal Math Trainer
Online Assessment and Intervention
my.hrw.com

Guided Practice

Drake rolls two fair number cubes. (Explore Activity)

1. Complete the table to find the sample space for rolling a particular product on two number cubes.

2. What is the probability that the product of the two numbers Drake rolls is a multiple of 4? ________________

3. What is the probability that the product of the two numbers Drake rolls is less than 13? ________________

	1	2	3	4	5	6
1						
2						
3						
4						
5						
6						

You flip three coins and want to explore probabilities of certain events. (Examples 1 and 2)

4. Complete the tree diagram and make a list to find the sample space.

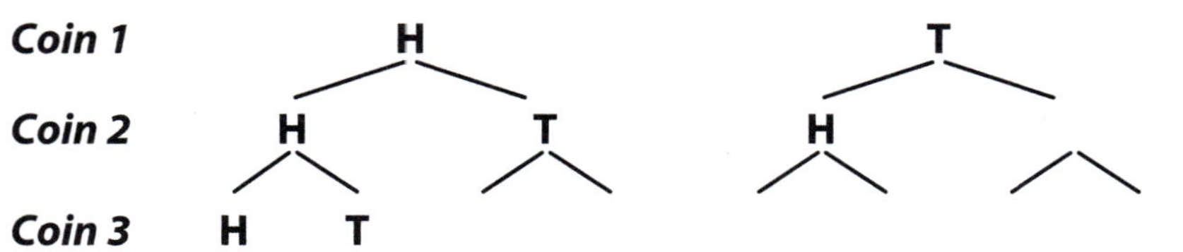

List: **HHH** **HHT** _____ _____ **T**____ **T**____ _____ _____

5. How many outcomes are in the sample space? ________

6. List all the ways to get three tails. ________

7. Complete the expression to find the probability of getting three tails.

$$P = \frac{\text{number of outcomes with } \square}{\text{total number of possible outcomes}} = \frac{\square}{\square}$$

The probability of getting three tails when three coins are flipped is ________.

8. What is the probability of getting exactly two heads?

There are ________ way(s) to obtain exactly two heads: HHT, ________________

$$P = \frac{\text{number of outcomes with } \square}{\text{total number of possible outcomes}} = \frac{\square}{\square}$$

ESSENTIAL QUESTION CHECK-IN

9. There are 6 ways a given compound event can occur. What else do you need to know to find the theoretical probability of the event?

____

Name ______________________ Class ______________ Date ____________

13.2 Independent Practice

Personal Math Trainer
my.hrw.com
Online Assessment and Intervention

In Exercises 10–12, use the following information. Mattias gets dressed in the dark one morning and chooses his clothes at random. He chooses a shirt (green, red, or yellow), a pair of pants (black or blue), and a pair of shoes (checkered or red).

10. Use the space below to make a tree diagram to find the sample space.

11. What is the probability that Mattias picks an outfit at random that includes red shoes? ______________

12. What is the probability that no part of Mattias's outfit is red? ______________

13. Rhee and Pamela are two of the five members of a band. Every week, the band picks two members at random to play on their own for five minutes. What is the probability that Rhee and Pamela are chosen this week? ______________

14. Ben rolls two number cubes. What is the probability that the sum of the numbers he rolls is less than 6? ______________

15. Nhan is getting dressed. He considers two different shirts, three pairs of pants, and three pairs of shoes. He chooses one of each of the articles at random. What is the probability that he will wear his jeans but not his sneakers?

Shirt	Pants	Shoes
collared	khakis	sneakers
T-shirt	jeans	flip-flops
	shorts	sandals

____

16. **Communicate Mathematical Ideas** A ski resort has 3 chair lifts, each with access to 6 ski trails. Explain how you can find the number of possible outcomes when choosing a chair lift and a ski trail without making a list, a tree diagram, or table.

____

____

____

____

17. **Explain the Error** For breakfast, Sarah can choose eggs, granola or oatmeal as a main course, and orange juice or milk for a drink. Sarah says that the sample space for choosing one of each contains $3^2 = 9$ outcomes. What is her error? Explain.

____

____

____

18. **Represent Real-World Problems** A new shoe comes in two colors, black or red, and in sizes from 5 to 12, including half sizes. If a pair of the shoes is chosen at random for a store display, what is the probability it will be red and size 9 or larger? ______________

Work Area

H.O.T. FOCUS ON HIGHER ORDER THINKING

19. **Analyze Relationships** At a diner, Sondra tells the server, "Give me one item from each column." Gretchen says, "Give me one main dish and a vegetable." Who has a greater probability of getting a meal that includes salmon? Explain.

Main Dish	Vegetable	Side
Pasta	Carrots	Tomato soup
Salmon	Peas	Tossed salad
Beef	Asparagus	
Pork	Sweet potato	

____

____

20. The digits 1 through 5 are used for a set of locker codes.

a. **Look for a Pattern** Suppose the digits cannot repeat. Find the number of possible two-digit codes and three-digit codes. Describe any pattern and use it to predict the number of possible five-digit codes.

____

____

____

b. **Look for a Pattern** Repeat part **a**, but allow digits to repeat.

____

____

____

c. **Justify Reasoning** Suppose that a gym plans to issue numbered locker codes by choosing the digits at random. Should the gym use codes in which the digits can repeat or not? Justify your reasoning.

____

____

____

LESSON 13.3

Making Predictions with Theoretical Probability

7.6.13.3

Students will make predictions using theoretical probability.

ESSENTIAL QUESTION

How do you make predictions using theoretical probability?

EXPLORE ACTIVITY Real World

Using Theoretical Probability to Make a Quantitative Prediction

Math On the Spot

my.hrw.com

You can make quantitative predictions based on theoretical probability just as you did with experimental probability earlier.

EXAMPLE 1 **Use proportional reasoning to solve each problem.**

A **You roll a standard number cube 150 times. Predict how many times you will roll a 3 or a 4.**

The probability of rolling a 3 or a 4 is $\frac{2}{6} = \frac{1}{3}$.

Method 1: Set up a proportion.

Write a proportion. The ratio 1 out of 3 is how many out of 150?

$$\frac{\square}{3} = \frac{\square}{150}$$

Since 3 times _______ is 150, multiply 1 by _______ to find the value of x.

$$\frac{\square}{3} \overset{\times \square}{=} \frac{\square}{150}$$

$x =$ _______

Method 2: Set up an equation and solve.

p(rolling a 3 or 4) · Number of events = Prediction

Multiply the probability by the total number of rolls.

$$\frac{\square}{\square} \cdot \square = x$$

Solve for x.

_______ $= x$

You can expect to roll a 3 or a 4 about _______ times out of 150.

EXPLORE ACTIVITY *(cont'd)*

B **Celia volunteers at her local animal shelter. She has an equally likely chance to be assigned to the dog, cat, bird, or reptile section. If she volunteers 24 times, about how many times should she expect to be assigned to the dog section?**

The probability of being assigned to the dog section is $\frac{\square}{\square}$.

Write a proportion. The ratio 1 out of 4 is how many out of 24?

$$\frac{\square}{4} = \frac{\square}{24}$$

Since 4 times _____ is 24, multiply 1 by _____ to find the value of *x*.

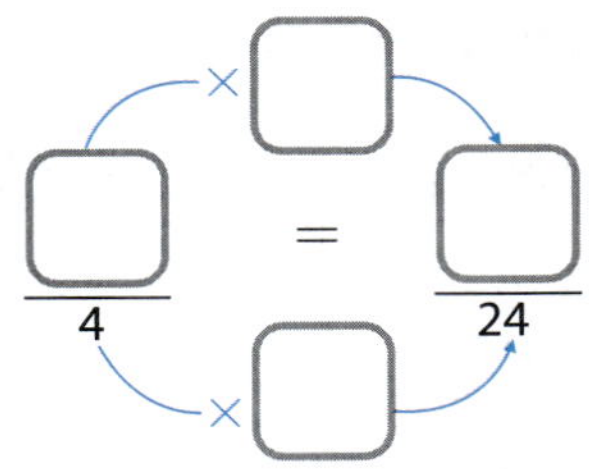

Celia can expect to be assigned to the dog section about _______ times out of 24.

YOUR TURN

1. Predict how many times you will roll a number less than 5 if you roll a standard number cube 250 times.

____

2. You flip a fair coin 18 times. About how many times would you expect heads to appear?

____

Personal Math Trainer
Online Assessment and Intervention
my.hrw.com

Math On the Spot
my.hrw.com

Using Theoretical Probability to Make a Qualitative Prediction

Earlier, you learned how to make predictions using experimental probability. You can use theoretical probabilities in the same way to help you predict or compare how likely events are.

EXAMPLE 2 Real World

A **Herschel pulls a sock out of his drawer without looking and puts it on. The sock is black. There are 7 black socks, 8 white socks, and 5 striped socks left in the drawer. He pulls out a second sock without looking. Is it likely that he will be wearing matching socks to school?**

Find the theoretical probability that Herschel picks a matching sock and the probability that he picks one that does not match.

$P(\text{matching}) = \frac{7}{20}$ $\quad\quad$ $P(\text{not matching}) = 1 - \frac{7}{20} = \frac{13}{20}$

$P(\text{not matching}) = 1 - P(\text{matching})$

The probability that Herschel picks a matching sock is about half the probability that he picks one that does not match. It is likely that he will **not** be wearing matching socks to school.

B **All 2,000 customers at a gym are randomly assigned a 3-digit security code that they use to access their online accounts. The codes are made up of the digits 0 through 4, and the digits can be repeated. Is it likely that fewer than 10 of the customers are issued the code 103?**

Set up a proportion. The probability of the code 103 is $\frac{1}{125}$.

There are 5 possible first numbers, 5 possible second numbers, and 5 possible third numbers. So, the probability of any one code is $\frac{1}{5} \cdot \frac{1}{5} \cdot \frac{1}{5} = \frac{1}{125}$.

$\frac{1}{125} = \frac{x}{2{,}000}$ $\quad$ *Write a proportion. 1 out of 125 is how many out of 2,000?*

$\frac{1}{125} = \frac{16}{2{,}000}$ (× 16) $\quad$ *Since 125 times 16 is 2,000, multiply 1 times 16 to find the value of x.*

It is **not** likely that fewer than 10 of the customers get the same code. It is more likely that 16 members get the code 103.

YOUR TURN

3. A bag of marbles contains 8 red marbles, 4 blue marbles, and 5 white marbles. Tom picks a marble at random. Is it more likely that he picks a red marble or a marble of another color?

____

4. At a fundraiser, a school group charges \$6 for tickets for a "grab bag." You choose one bill at random from a bag that contains 40 \$1 bills, 20 \$5 bills, 5 \$10 bills, 5 \$20 bills, and 1 \$100 bill. Is it likely that you will win enough to pay for your ticket? Justify your answer.

____

____

____

Guided Practice

1. Bob works at a construction company. He has an equally likely chance to be assigned to work different crews every day. He can be assigned to work on crews building apartments, condominiums, or houses. If he works 18 days a month, about how many times should he expect to be assigned to the house crew? (Explore Activity Example 1)

STEP 1 Find the probabilities of being assigned to each crew.

Apartment ☐ Condo ☐ House ☐

The probability of being assigned to the house crew is ________

STEP 2 Set up and solve a proportion.

$\frac{\square}{\square} = \frac{x}{\square}$ $x =$ ______

Bob can expect to be assigned to the house crew about

______ times out of 18.

2. During a raffle drawing, half of the ticket holders will receive a prize. The winners are equally likely to win one of three prizes: a book, a gift certificate to a restaurant, or a movie ticket. If there are 300 ticket holders, predict the number of people who will win a movie ticket.

(Explore Activity Example 1) ________________________________

3. In Mr. Jawarani's first period math class, there are 9 students with hazel eyes, 10 students with brown eyes, 7 students with blue eyes, and 2 students with green eyes. Mr. Jawarani picks a student at random. Which color eyes is the student most likely to have? Explain. (Example 2)

____

____

ESSENTIAL QUESTION CHECK-IN

4. How do you make predictions using theoretical probability?

____

____

____

Name ______________________ Class ______________ Date ______________

13.3 Independent Practice

Personal Math Trainer
Online Assessment and Intervention
my.hrw.com

5. A bag contains 6 red marbles, 2 white marbles, and 1 gray marble. You randomly pick out a marble, record its color, and put it back in the bag. You repeat this process 45 times. How many white or gray marbles do you expect to get?

____

6. Using the blank circle below, draw a spinner with 8 equal sections and 3 colors—red, green, and yellow. The spinner should be such that you are equally likely to land on green or yellow, but more likely to land on red than either on green or yellow.

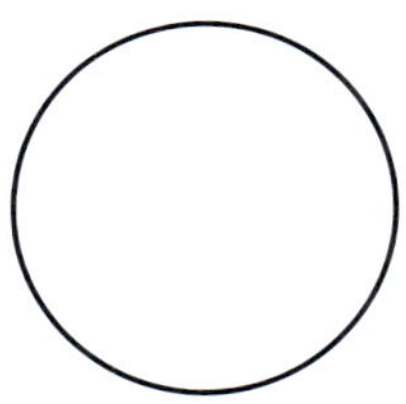

Use the following for Exercises 7–9. In a standard 52-card deck, half of the cards are red and half are black. The 52 cards are divided evenly into 4 suits: spades, hearts, diamonds, and clubs. Each suit has three face cards (jack, queen, king), and an ace. Each suit also has 9 cards numbered from 2 to 10.

7. Dawn draws 1 card, replaces it, and draws another card. Is it more likely that she draws 2 red cards or 2 face cards?

____

____

8. Luis draws 1 card from a deck, 39 times. Predict how many times he draws an ace.

____

9. Suppose a solitaire player has played 1,000 games. Predict how many times the player turned over a red card as the first card.

____

10. John and O'Neal are playing a board game in which they roll two number cubes. John needs to get a sum of 8 on the number cubes to win. O'Neal needs a sum of 11. If they take turns rolling the number cube, who is more likely to win? Explain.

____

____

____

11. Every day, Navya's teacher randomly picks a number from 1 to 20 to be the number of the day. The number of the day can be repeated. There are 180 days in the school year. Predict how many days the number of the day will be greater than 15. ____________

12. Eben rolls two standard number cubes 36 times. Predict how many times he will roll a sum of 4. ______________

13. **Communicate Mathematical Ideas** Can you always show that a prediction based on theoretical probability is true by performing the event often enough? If so, explain why. If not, describe a situation that justifies your response.

____

____

____

____

____

14. **Represent Real-World Problems** Give a real-world example of an experiment in which all of the outcomes are not equally likely. Can you make a prediction for this experiment, using theoretical probability?

H.O.T. FOCUS ON HIGHER ORDER THINKING

Work Area

15. **Critical Thinking** Pierre asks Sherry a question involving the theoretical probability of a compound event in which you flip a coin and draw a marble from a bag of marbles. The bag of marbles contains 3 white marbles, 8 green marbles, and 9 black marbles. Sherry's answer, which is correct, is $\frac{12}{40}$. What was Pierre's question?

16. **Make a Prediction** Horace is going to roll a standard number cube and flip a coin. He wonders if it is more likely that he rolls a 5 **and** the coin lands on heads, or that he rolls a 5 **or** the coin lands on heads. Which event do you think is more likely to happen? Find the probability of both events to justify or reject your initial prediction.

17. **Communicate Mathematical Ideas** Cecil solved a theoretical prediction problem and got this answer: "The spinner will land on the red section 4.5 times." Is it possible to have a prediction that is not a whole number? If so, give an example.

LESSON 13.4

Using Technology to Conduct a Simulation

7.6.13.4

Students will use technology simulations to estimate probabilities.

ESSENTIAL QUESTION

How can you use technology simulations to estimate probabilities?

EXPLORE ACTIVITY Real World

Designing and Conducting a Simulation for a Simple Event

Math On the Spot my.hrw.com

You can use a graphing calculator or computer to generate random numbers and conduct a simulation.

EXAMPLE 1 **A cereal company is having a contest. There are codes for winning prizes in 30% of its cereal boxes. Find an experimental probability that you have to buy *exactly* 3 boxes of cereal before you find a winning code.**

STEP 1 Choose a model to simulate the event.

The probability of finding a winning code is 30% $= \frac{\square}{10}$.

Let 3 out of 10 numbers represent buying a box with a winning code. Use whole numbers from 1 to 10.

Winning: 1, 2, 3 Nonwinning: ______________

STEP 2 Generate random numbers from 1 to 10 until you get one that represents a box with a winning code. Record how many boxes you bought before finding a winning code.

Sample Trial 1: 9, 6, 7, 8, 1

For Trial 1, you got the winning code ____ after buying ____ boxes.

Trial	Numbers generated	Boxes bought
1	9, 6, 7, 8, 1	5
2	2	1
3	10, 4, 8, 1	4
4	4, 10, 7, 1	4
5	2	1
6	4, 3	2
7	3	1
8	7, 5, 2	3
9	8, 5, 4, 8, 10, 3	6
10	9, 1	2

STEP 3 Perform multiple trials by repeating Step ____.

STEP 4 Find the experimental probability of the event.

Circle the trial(s) where you bought exactly ____ boxes of cereal before finding a winning code.

In ____ of 10 trials, you bought exactly 3 boxes of cereal before finding a winning code.

The experimental probability is $\frac{\square}{10}$ or ____ %.

Animated Math my.hrw.com

EXPLORE ACTIVITY *(cont'd)*

YOUR TURN

1. An elephant has a 50% chance of giving birth to a male or a female calf. Use a simulation to find an experimental probability that the elephant gives birth to 3 male calves before having a female calf. (*Hint:* Use 0s and 1s. Let 0 represent a male calf, and 1 represent a female calf. Generate random numbers until you get a 1.)

Trial	Numbers generated	3 Males first
1		
2		
3		
4		
5		

Trial	Numbers generated	3 Males first
6		
7		
8		
9		
10		

____

Personal Math Trainer
Online Assessment and Intervention
my.hrw.com

Math Talk
Mathematical Processes

Could you generate random numbers from a list of more than 2 numbers? Explain.

Math On the Spot
my.hrw.com

Designing and Conducting a Simulation for a Compound Event

You can use random numbers to simulate compound events as well as simple events.

EXAMPLE 2 Real World

Suppose that there is a 20% chance that a particular volcano will erupt in any given decade. Find an experimental probability that the volcano will erupt in at least 1 of the next 5 decades.

STEP 1 Choose a model.

The probability of an eruption is $20\% = \frac{1}{5}$. Use whole numbers from 1 to 5.

Let 1 represent a decade with an eruption.

Let 2, 3, 4, and 5 represent a decade without an eruption.

STEP 2 Generate 5 random numbers from 1 to 5. Record the number of decades with an eruption.

5 numbers generated: 3, 1, 3, 4, 2 Eruption decades: 1

STEP 3 Perform multiple trials by repeating Step 2. Calculate the percent of trials in which there was an eruption in at least 1 of the 5 decades.

Trial	Numbers generated	Eruption decades
1	3, 1, 3, 4, 2	1
2	3, 2, 2, 4, 5	0
3	1, 3, 3, 2, 5	1
4	5, 3, 4, 5, 4	0
5	5, 5, 3, 2, 4	0

Trial	Numbers generated	Eruption decades
6	2, 3, 3, 4, 2	0
7	1, 2, 4, 1, 4	2
8	1, 3, 2, 1, 5	2
9	1, 2, 4, 2, 5	1
10	5, 5, 3, 2, 4	0

In 5 out of the 10 trials, there was an eruption in at least 1 of the 5 decades. The experimental probability of an eruption in at least 1 of the next 5 decades is $\frac{5}{10} = 50\%$.

YOUR TURN

2. Matt guesses the answers on a quiz with 5 true-false questions. The probability of guessing a correct answer on each question is 50%. Use a simulation to find an experimental probability that he gets at least 2 questions right. (*Hint:* Use 0s and 1s. Let 0s represent incorrect answers, and 1s represent correct answers. Perform 10 trials, generating 5 random numbers in each, and count the number of 1s.)

Trial	Numbers generated	Correct answers
1		
2		
3		
4		
5		

Trial	Numbers generated	Correct answers
6		
7		
8		
9		
10		

____

Personal Math Trainer
Online Assessment and Intervention
my.hrw.com

Guided Practice

There is a 30% chance that T'Shana's county will have a drought during any given year. She performs a simulation to find the experimental probability of a drought in at least 1 of the next 4 years.
(Explore Activity Example 1 and Example 2)

1. T'Shana's model involves the whole numbers from 1 to 10. Complete the description of her model.

Let the numbers 1 to 3 represent ______

and the numbers 4 to 10 represent ______

Perform multiple trials, generating ___ random numbers each time.

2. Suppose T'Shana used the model described in Exercise 1 and got the results shown in the table. Complete the table.

Trial	Numbers generated	Drought years
1	10, 3, 5, 1	
2	10, 4, 6, 5	
3	3, 2, 10, 3	
4	2, 10, 4, 4	
5	7, 3, 6, 3	

Trial	Numbers generated	Drought years
6	8, 4, 8, 5	
7	6, 2, 2, 8	
8	6, 5, 2, 4	
9	2, 2, 3, 2	
10	6, 3, 1, 5	

3. According to the simulation, what is the experimental probability that there will be a drought in the county in at least 1 of the next 4 years? ________

ESSENTIAL QUESTION CHECK-IN

4. You want to generate random numbers to simulate an event with a 75% chance of occurring. Describe a model you could use.

____

____

____

____

Name ______________________ Class ______________ Date ______________

13.4 Independent Practice

Personal Math Trainer
my.hrw.com
Online Assessment and Intervention

Every contestant on a game show has a 40% chance of winning. In the simulation below, the numbers 1–4 represent a winner, and the numbers 5–10 represent a nonwinner. Numbers were generated until one that represented a winner was produced.

Trial	Numbers generated
1	7, 4
2	6, 5, 2
3	1
4	9, 1
5	3

Trial	Numbers generated
6	8, 8, 6, 2
7	2
8	5, 9, 4
9	10, 3
10	1

5. In how many of the trials did it take exactly 4 contestants to get a winner? ________

6. Based on the simulation, what is the experimental probability that it will take exactly 4 contestants to get a winner? ________

Over a 100-year period, the probability that a hurricane struck Rob's city in any given year was 20%. Rob performed a simulation to find an experimental probability that a hurricane would strike the city in at least 4 of the next 10 years. In Rob's simulation, 1 represents a year with a hurricane.

Trial	Numbers generated
1	2, 5, 3, 2, 5, 5, 1, 4, 5, 2
2	1, 1, 5, 2, 2, 1, 3, 1, 1, 5
3	4, 5, 4, 5, 5, 4, 3, 5, 1, 1
4	1, 5, 5, 5, 1, 2, 2, 3, 5, 3
5	5, 1, 5, 3, 5, 3, 4, 5, 3, 2

Trial	Numbers generated
6	1, 1, 5, 5, 1, 4, 2, 2, 3, 4
7	2, 1, 5, 3, 1, 5, 1, 2, 1, 4
8	2, 4, 3, 2, 4, 4, 2, 1, 3, 1
9	3, 2, 1, 4, 5, 3, 5, 5, 1, 2
10	3, 4, 2, 4, 3, 5, 2, 3, 5, 1

7. According to Rob's simulation, what was the experimental probability that a hurricane would strike the city in at least 4 of the next 10 years? ________

8. **Analyze Relationships** Suppose that over the 10 years following Rob's simulation, there was actually 1 year in which a hurricane struck. How did this compare to the results of Rob's simulation?

____

____

9. **Communicate Mathematical Ideas** You generate three random whole numbers from 1 to 10. Do you think that it is unlikely or even impossible that all of the numbers could be 10? Explain?

10. Erika collects baseball cards, and 60% of the packs contain a player from her favorite team. Use a simulation to find an experimental probability that she has to buy exactly 2 packs before she gets a player from her favorite team.

H.O.T. FOCUS ON HIGHER ORDER THINKING

Work Area

11. **Represent Real-World Problems** When Kate plays basketball, she usually makes 37.5% of her shots. Design and conduct a simulation to find the experimental probability that she makes at least 3 of her next 10 shots. Justify the model for your simulation.

12. **Justify Reasoning** George and Susannah used a simulation to simulate the flipping of 8 coins 50 times. In all of the trials, at least 5 heads came up. What can you say about their simulation? Explain.

MODULE QUIZ

Ready to Go On?

Personal Math Trainer
Online Assessment and Intervention
my.hrw.com

13.1, 13.2 Theoretical Probability of Simple and Compound Events

Find the probability of each event. Write your answer as a fraction, as a decimal, and as a percent.

1. You choose a marble at random from a bag containing 12 red, 12 blue, 15 green, 9 yellow, and 12 black marbles. The marble is red. ____________

2. You draw a card at random from a shuffled deck of 52 cards. The deck has four 13-card suits (diamonds, hearts, clubs, spades). The card is a diamond or a spade. ____________

13.3 Making Predictions with Theoretical Probability

3. A bag contains 23 red marbles, 25 green marbles, and 18 blue marbles. You choose a marble at random from the bag. What color marble will you most likely choose? ____________

13.4 Using Technology to Conduct a Simulation

4. Bay City has a 25% chance of having a flood in any given decade. The table shows the results of a simulation using random numbers to find the experimental probability that there will be a flood in Bay City in at least 1 of the next 5 decades. In the table, the number 1 represents a decade with a flood. The numbers 2 through 5 represent a decade without a flood.

Trial	Numbers generated	Trial	Numbers generated
1	2, 2, 5, 5, 5	6	4, 2, 2, 5, 4
2	3, 2, 3, 5, 4	7	1, 3, 2, 4, 4
3	5, 5, 5, 4, 3	8	3, 5, 5, 2, 1
4	5, 1, 3, 3, 5	9	4, 3, 3, 2, 5
5	4, 5, 5, 3, 2	10	5, 4, 1, 2, 1

According to the simulation, what is the experimental probability of a flood in Bay City in at least 1 of the next 5 decades? ____________

ESSENTIAL QUESTION

5. How can you use theoretical probability to make predictions in real-world situations?

____

____

MODULE 13 MIXED REVIEW

Assessment Readiness

Personal Math Trainer
my.hrw.com
Online Assessment and Intervention

Selected Response

1. What is the probability of flipping two fair coins and having both show tails?

Ⓐ $\frac{1}{8}$
Ⓑ $\frac{1}{4}$
Ⓒ $\frac{1}{3}$
Ⓓ $\frac{1}{2}$

2. A bag contains 8 white marbles and 2 black marbles. You pick out a marble, record its color, and put the marble back in the bag. If you repeat this process 45 times, how many times would you expect to remove a white marble from the bag?

Ⓐ 9
Ⓑ 32
Ⓒ 36
Ⓓ 40

3. Philip rolls a standard number cube 24 times. Which is the best prediction for the number of times he will roll a number that is even and less than 4?

Ⓐ 2
Ⓑ 3
Ⓒ 4
Ⓓ 6

4. A set of cards includes 24 yellow cards, 18 green cards, and 18 blue cards. What is the probability that a card chosen at random is **not** green?

Ⓐ $\frac{3}{10}$
Ⓑ $\frac{4}{10}$
Ⓒ $\frac{3}{5}$
Ⓓ $\frac{7}{10}$

5. A rectangle made of square tiles measures 10 tiles long and 8 tiles wide. What is the width of a similar rectangle whose length is 15 tiles?

Ⓐ 3 tiles
Ⓑ 12 tiles
Ⓒ 13 tiles
Ⓓ 18.75 tiles

6. The Fernandez family drove 273 miles in 5.25 hours. How far would they have driven at that rate in 4 hours?

Ⓐ 208 miles
Ⓑ 220 miles
Ⓒ 280 miles
Ⓓ 358 miles

7. There are 20 tennis balls in a bag. Five are orange, 7 are white, 2 are yellow, and 6 are green. You choose one at random. Which color ball are you **least** likely to choose?

Ⓐ green
Ⓑ orange
Ⓒ white
Ⓓ yellow

Mini-Task

8. Center County has had a 1 in 6 (or about 16.7%) chance of a tornado in any given decade. In a simulation to consider the probability of tornadoes in the next 5 decades, Ava rolled a number cube. She let a 1 represent a decade with a tornado, and 2–6 represent decades without tornadoes. What experimental probability did Ava find for each event?

Trial	Numbers Generated	Trial	Numbers Generated
1	2, 2, 3, 1, 5	6	4, 5, 2, 2, 4
2	3, 5, 6, 4, 5	7	5, 1, 6, 3, 1
3	1, 3, 3, 2, 2	8	1, 2, 1, 2, 4
4	6, 3, 3, 5, 4	9	1, 4, 4, 1, 4
5	4, 1, 4, 4, 4	10	3, 6, 5, 3, 6

a. That Center County has a tornado in at least one of the next five decades.

____

b. That Center County has a tornado in exactly one of the next five decades.

____

UNIT 6

Study Guide Review

MODULE 12 Experimental Probability

Key Vocabulary

complement *(complemento)*
compound event *(suceso compuesto)*
event *(suceso)*
experiment *(experimento)*
experimental probability *(probabilidad experimental)*
outcome *(resultado)*
probability *(probabilidad)*
sample space *(espacio muestral)*
simple event *(suceso simple)*
simulation *(simulación)*
trial *(prueba)*

ESSENTIAL QUESTION

How can you use experimental probability to solve real-world problems?

EXAMPLE 1

What is the probability of picking a red marble from a jar with 5 green marbles and 2 red marbles?

$P(\text{picking a red marble}) = \frac{\text{number of red marbles}}{\text{number of total marbles}}$

$= \frac{2}{7}$ There are 2 red marbles. The total number of marbles is $2 + 5 = 7$.

EXAMPLE 2

For one month, a doctor recorded information about new patients as shown in the table.

	Senior	Adult	Young adult	Child
Female	5	8	2	14
Male	3	10	1	17

What is the experimental probability that his next new patient is a female adult?

$P\left(\begin{matrix}\text{new patient is a} \\ \text{female adult}\end{matrix}\right) = \frac{\text{number of female adults}}{\text{total number of patients}}$

$P = \frac{8}{60} = \frac{2}{15}$

What is the experimental probability that his next new patient is a child?

$P\left(\begin{matrix}\text{new patient is} \\ \text{a child}\end{matrix}\right) = \frac{\text{number of children}}{\text{total number of patients}}$

$P = \frac{31}{60}$

EXERCISES

Find the probability of each event. (Lesson 12.1)

1. Rolling a 5 on a fair number cube.

____

2. Picking a 7 from a standard deck of 52 cards. A standard deck includes 4 cards of each number from 2 to 10.

____

3. Picking a blue marble from a bag of 4 red marbles, 6 blue marbles, and 1 white marble.

____

4. Rolling a number greater than 7 on a 12-sided number cube.

____

5. Christopher picked coins randomly from his piggy bank and got the numbers of coins shown in the table. Find each experimental probability. (Lessons 12.2, 12.3)

Penny	Nickel	Dime	Quarter
7	2	8	6

a. The next coin that Christopher picks is a quarter. ________________

b. The next coin that Christopher picks is not a quarter. ________________

c. The next coin that Christopher picks is a penny or a nickel. __________

6. A grocery store manager found that 54% of customers usually bring their own bags. In one afternoon, 82 out of 124 customers brought their own grocery bags. Did a greater or lesser number of people than usual bring their own bags? (Lesson 12.4)

____

MODULE 13 Theoretical Probability

Key Vocabulary
theoretical probability
(probabilidad teórica)

ESSENTIAL QUESTION

How can you use theoretical probability to solve real-world problems?

EXAMPLE 1

A. Lola rolls two fair number cubes. What is the probability that the two numbers Lola rolls include at least one 4 and have a product of at least 16?

There are 5 pairs of numbers that include a 4 and have a product of at least 16:

(4, 4), (4, 5), (4, 6), (5, 4), (6, 4)

Find the probability.

$$P = \frac{\text{number of possible ways}}{\text{total number of possible outcomes}} = \frac{5}{36}$$

	1	2	3	4	5	6
1	1	2	3	4	5	6
2	2	4	6	8	10	12
3	3	6	9	12	15	18
4	4	8	12	16	20	24
5	5	10	15	20	25	30
6	6	12	18	24	30	36

B. Suppose Lola rolls the two number cubes 180 times. Predict how many times she will roll two numbers that include a pair of numbers like the ones described above.

One way to answer is to write and solve an equation.

$\frac{5}{36} \times 180 = x$ Multiply the probability by the total number of rolls.

$25 = x$ Solve for x.

Lola can expect to roll two numbers that include at least one 4 and have a product of 16 or more about 25 times.

EXAMPLE 2

A store has a sale bin of soup cans. There are 6 cans of chicken noodle soup, 8 cans of split pea soup, 8 cans of minestrone, and 13 cans of vegetable soup. Find the probability of picking each type of soup at random. Then predict what kind of soup a customer is most likely to pick.

$P(\text{chicken noodle}) = \frac{6}{35}$

$P(\text{split pea}) = \frac{8}{35}$

$P(\text{minestrone}) = \frac{8}{35}$

$P(\text{vegetable}) = \frac{13}{35}$

The customer is most likely to pick vegetable soup. That is the event that has the greatest probability.

EXERCISES

Find the probability of each event. (Lessons 13.1, 13.2)

1. Graciela picks a white mouse at random from a bin of 8 white mice, 2 gray mice, and 2 brown mice.

____

2. Theo spins a spinner that has 12 equal sections marked 1 through 12. It does **not** land on 1.

____

3. Tania flips a coin three times. The coin lands on heads twice and on tails once, not necessarily in that order.

____

4. Students are randomly assigned two-digit codes. Each digit is either 1, 2, 3, or 4. Guy is given the number 11.

____

5. Patty tosses a coin and rolls a number cube. (Lesson 13.3)

   a. Find the probability that the coin lands on heads and the cube lands on an even number.

   ____

   b. Patty tosses the coin and rolls the number cube 60 times. Predict how many times the coin will land on heads and the cube will land on an even number.

   ____

6. Rajan's school is having a raffle. The school sold raffle tickets with 3-digit numbers. Each digit is either 1, 2, or 3. The school also sold 2 tickets with the number 000. Which number is more likely to be picked, 123 or 000? (Lesson 13.3)

____

7. Suppose you know that over the last 10 years, the probability that your town would have at least one major storm was 40%. Describe a simulation that you could use to find the experimental probability that your town will have at least one major storm in at least 3 of the next 5 years. (Lesson 13.4)

Unit 6 Performance Tasks

1. **CAREERS IN MATH** **Meteorologist** A meteorologist predicts a 20% chance of rain for the next two nights, and a 75% chance of rain on the third night.

   a. On which night is it most likely to rain? On that night, is it *likely* to rain or *unlikely* to rain?

   b. Tara would like to go camping for the next 3 nights, but will not go if it is likely to rain on all 3 nights. Should she go? Use probability to justify your answer.

2. Sinead tossed 4 coins at the same time. She did this 50 times, and 6 of those times, all 4 coins showed the same result (heads or tails).

   a. Find the experimental probability that all 4 coins show the same result when tossed.

   b. Can you determine the experimental probability that **no** coin shows heads? Explain.

   c. Suppose Sinead tosses the coins 125 more times. Use experimental probability to predict the number of times that all 4 coins will show heads or tails. Show your work.

UNIT 6 **MIXED REVIEW**

Assessment Readiness

Personal Math Trainer
my.hrw.com
Online Assessment and Intervention

Selected Response

1. A pizza parlor offers thin, thick, and traditional style pizza crusts. You can get pepperoni, beef, mushrooms, olives, or peppers for toppings. You order a one-topping pizza. How many outcomes are in the sample space?

Ⓐ 3
Ⓑ 5
Ⓒ 8
Ⓓ 15

2. A bag contains 9 purple marbles, 2 blue marbles, and 4 pink marbles. The probability of randomly drawing a blue marble is $\frac{2}{15}$. What is the probability of **not** drawing a blue marble?

Ⓐ $\frac{2}{15}$
Ⓑ $\frac{4}{15}$
Ⓒ $\frac{11}{15}$
Ⓓ $\frac{13}{15}$

3. During the month of April, Dora kept track of the bugs she saw in her garden. She saw a ladybug on 23 days of the month. What is the experimental probability that she will see a ladybug on May 1?

Ⓐ $\frac{1}{23}$
Ⓑ $\frac{7}{30}$
Ⓒ $\frac{1}{2}$
Ⓓ $\frac{23}{30}$

4. Ryan flips a coin 8 times and gets tails all 8 times. What is the experimental probability that Ryan will get heads the next time he flips the coin?

Ⓐ 1
Ⓑ $\frac{1}{2}$
Ⓒ $\frac{1}{8}$
Ⓓ 0

5. A used guitar is on sale for $280. Derek offers the seller $\frac{3}{4}$ of the advertised price. How much does Derek offer for the guitar?

Ⓐ $180
Ⓑ $210
Ⓒ $240
Ⓓ $270

6. Jay tossed two coins several times and then recorded the results in the table below.

Coin Toss Results				
Toss 1	Toss 2	Toss 3	Toss 4	Toss 5
H; H	H; T	T; H	T; T	T; H

What is the experimental probability that the coins will land on different sides on his next toss?

Ⓐ $\frac{1}{5}$
Ⓑ $\frac{2}{5}$
Ⓒ $\frac{3}{5}$
Ⓓ $\frac{4}{5}$

7. What is the probability of tossing two fair coins and having exactly one land tails side up?

Ⓐ $\frac{1}{8}$
Ⓑ $\frac{1}{4}$
Ⓒ $\frac{1}{3}$
Ⓓ $\frac{1}{2}$

8. Find the percent change from 60 to 96.

Ⓐ 37.5% decrease
Ⓑ 37.5% increase
Ⓒ 60% decrease
Ⓓ 60% increase

9. A bag contains 6 white beads and 4 black beads. You pick out a bead, record its color, and put the bead back in the bag. You repeat this process 35 times. Which is the best prediction of how many times you would expect to remove a white bead from the bag?

Ⓐ 6
Ⓑ 10
Ⓒ 18
Ⓓ 21

10. A set of cards includes 20 yellow cards, 16 green cards, and 24 blue cards. What is the probability that a blue card is chosen at random?

Ⓐ 0.04
Ⓑ 0.24
Ⓒ 0.4
Ⓓ 0.66

11. Jason, Erik, and Jamie are friends in art class. The teacher randomly chooses 2 of the 21 students in the class to work together on a project. What is the probability that two of these three friends will be chosen?

Ⓐ $\frac{1}{105}$
Ⓑ $\frac{1}{70}$
Ⓒ $\frac{34}{140}$
Ⓓ $\frac{4}{50}$

12. Philip rolls a number cube 12 times. Which is the best prediction for the number of times that he will roll a number that is odd and less than 5?

Ⓐ 2
Ⓑ 3
Ⓒ 4
Ⓓ 6

Hot Tip! **Estimate your answer before solving the problem. Use your estimate to check the reasonableness of your answer.**

13. A survey reveals that one airline's flights have a 92% probability of being on time. Based on this, out of 4000 flights in a year, how many flights would you predict will arrive on time?

Ⓐ 368
Ⓑ 386
Ⓒ 3,680
Ⓓ 3,860

14. Matt's house number is a two-digit number. Neither of the digits is 0 and the house number is even. What is the probability that Matt's house number is 18?

Ⓐ $\frac{1}{45}$
Ⓑ $\frac{1}{36}$
Ⓒ $\frac{1}{18}$
Ⓓ $\frac{1}{16}$

Mini-Tasks

15. Laura picked a crayon randomly from a box, recorded the color, and then placed it back in the box. She repeated the process and recorded the results in the table.

Red	Blue	Yellow	Green
5	6	7	2

Find each experimental probability. Write your answers in simplest form.

a. The next crayon Laura picks is red.

____

b. The next crayon Laura picks is **not** red.

____

16. For breakfast, Trevor has a choice of 3 types of bagels (plain, sesame, or multigrain), 2 types of eggs (scrambled or poached), and 2 juices (orange or apple).

a. Use the space below to make a tree diagram to find the sample space.

b. If he chooses at random, what is the probability that Trevor eats a breakfast that has orange juice?

____

UNIT 1 Selected Answers

MODULE 1

LESSON 1.1

Your Turn

6. −9 **7.** −10 **8.** −60 **9.** −70 **10.** 300 **11.** −145 **12.** −1,650 **13.** −1,000

Guided Practice

1a. 6 **b.** negative **c.** −6 **2a.** 9 **b.** negative **c.** −9 **3.** −7

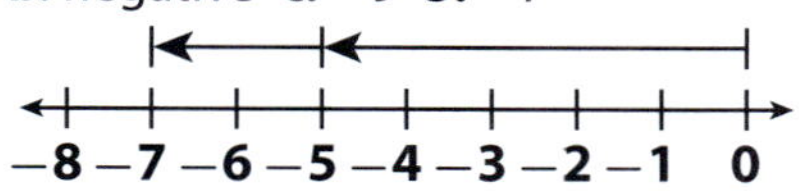

4. −4

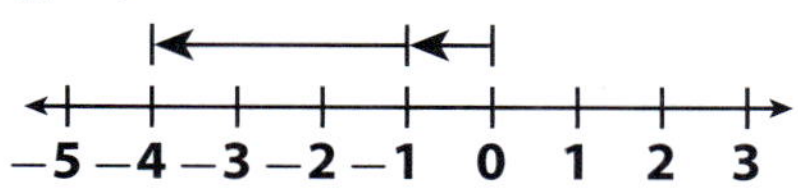

5. −7

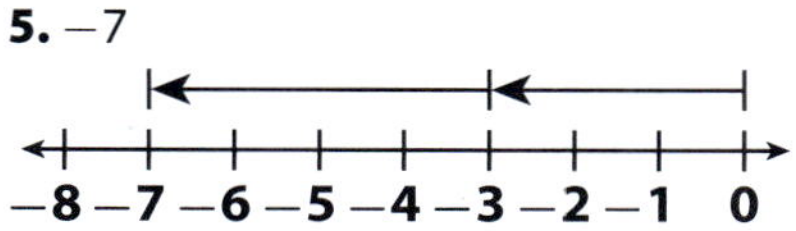

6. −5

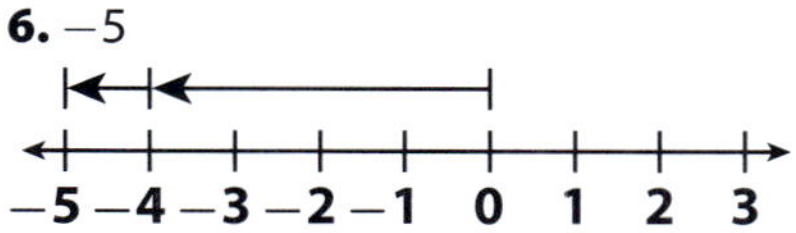

7. −4

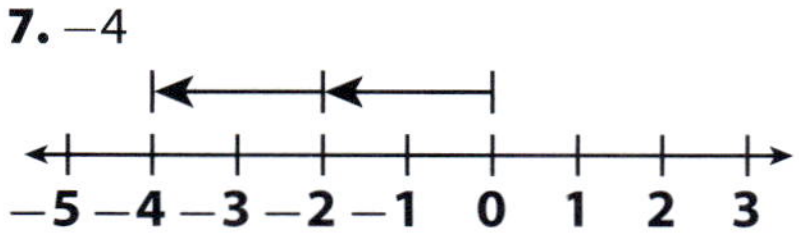

8. −14

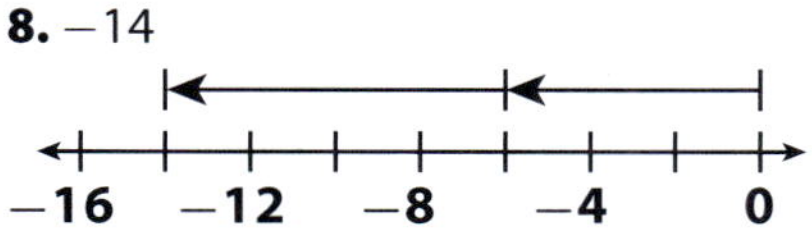

9. −9 **10.** −11 **11.** −10 **12.** −110 **13.** −100 **14.** 203 **15.** −15 **16.** −570

Independent Practice

19. −11 **21.** −54 yards **23.** −100 + (−75) + (−85) = −260

LESSON 1.2

Your Turn

3. 4 **4.** −2 **5.** −6 **6.** −1 **7.** −28 **8.** −8 **9.** 0 **10.** −1

Guided Practice

1. 2

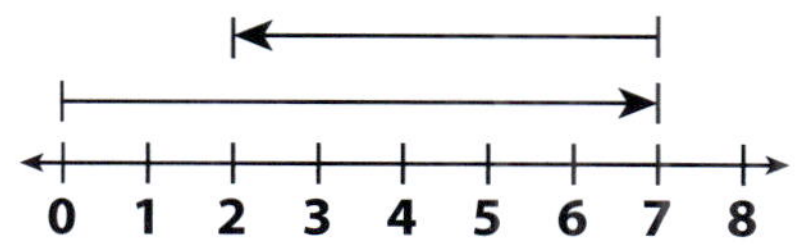

2. 5

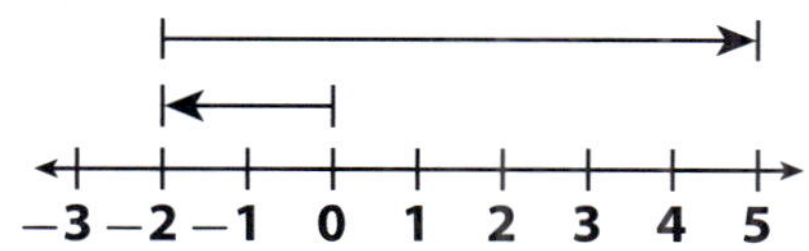

3. −5

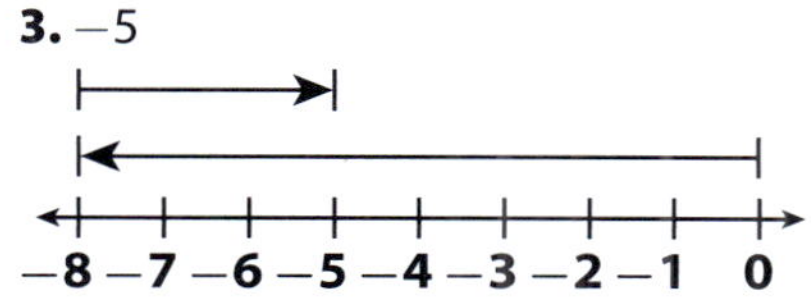

4. −3

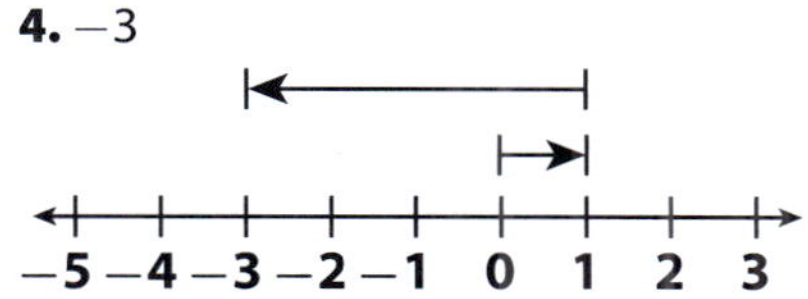

5. 1 **6.** 0 **7.** −3 **8.** 4 **9.** 6 **10.** 2 **11.** −16 **12.** 0 **13.** −5 **14.** 24

Independent Practice

17. −8 **19.** 25 **21.** −95 **23.** −7 **25.** 100 **27.** −55 + 275 = 220. The team's profit was $220.

LESSON 1.3

Your Turn

4. −9 **5.** 2 **6.** −2 **7.** −4

Guided Practice

1. −3 **2.** −2 **3.** (−5); −9 **4.** (−4); −3 **5.** −3 **6.** 2 **7.** −6 **8.** −18 **9.** 5 **10.** 19 **11.** 14 **12.** 42 **13.** 38 **14.** 0

Independent Practice

17. −127 − (−225) = 98 feet **19.** −150 points **21.** Diet Chow **25.** −16, −21, −26

LESSON 1.4

Your Turn

1. −40 − 13 + 18; −35; 35 feet below the cave entrance **3.** −35 + (−45) + 180 = 100; $100 increase **4.** Jim

Guided Practice

1. −15 + 9 − 12 = −18; 18 feet below sea level **2.** −23 + 5 − 7 = −25; −25 °F **3.** 50 − 40 + 87 − 30 = 67 **4.** 24 **5.** −12 **6.** 18 **7.** 21 **8.** 97 **9.** 27 **10.** (−12 + 6 − 4) < (−34 − 3 + 39) **11.** (21 − 3 + 8) > (−14 + 31 − 6)

Independent Practice

13a. 5 − 1 + 6 − 1 = 9 **b.** over par **c.** yes **15.** The Commutative Property does not apply to subtraction. 3 − 6 + 5 = 2 and 3 − 5 + 6 = 4 **17a.** 3:00 to 4:00 **b.** 87 **19.** $24 **23.** The sum of the other two numbers must be greater than the value of the first number.

MODULE 2

LESSON 2.1

Your Turn

4. −15 **5.** 20 **6.** −42 **7.** 0 **8.** 45 **9.** 32

Guided Practice

1. −9 **2.** −28 **3.** 54 **4.** −100 **5.** −60 **6.** 0 **7.** 49 **8.** −135 **9.** −96 **10.** 300 **11.** 0 **12.** −192 **13.** 7(−75) = −525; −$525 **14.** Show 3(−5) on a number line as (−5) + (−5) + (−5); 3(−5) = −15; −15 yards; the team lost 15 yards. **15.** 6(−2) = −12; −12 °F **16.** 4(−5) = −20; −$20; the share price decreased by $20 in 4 days. **17.** 5(−50) = −250; −250 feet

UNIT 1 Selected Answers *(cont'd)*

Independent Practice

19. No **21.** 5(−4) = −20; $20 decrease **23.** 7(−6) = −42; the cost of the jeans decreased by $42 over the 7 weeks. **25.** 7(−8) = −56; 7(−5) = −35; −56 + (−35) = −91. The savings decreased by $91. **27a.** −27 **b.** 27 **c.** −27 **d.** −81 **e.** 81 **f.** −81 **g.** negative; positive

LESSON 2.2

Your Turn

2. 0 **3.** −2 **4.** 13 **5.** Yolanda received the same number of penalties in each game, 5; −25 ÷ (−5) = 5 and −35 ÷ (−7) = 5.

Guided Practice

1. −7 **2.** −7 **3.** −2 **4.** 0 **5.** 9 **6.** −3 **7.** 11 **8.** 1 **9.** 0 **10.** 11 **11.** −12 **12.** −20 **13.** undefined **14.** 3 **15.** −40 ÷ (4) = −10; $10 **16.** −22 ÷ (11) = −2; 2 points **17.** −75 ÷ (−15) = 5; 5 targets **18.** −99 ÷ (−9) = 11; 11 times

Independent Practice

21. Elisa; Elisa made −140 ÷ (−20) = 7 withdrawals; Francis made −270 ÷ (−45) = 6 withdrawals, and 7 > 6. **23.** the first part **27.** False; division by 0 is undefined for any dividend. **29.** 12

LESSON 2.3

Your Turn

1. Reggie earned 110 points; 3(−30) + 200 = −90 + 200 = 110. **2.** −78 − 21 = −99 **4.** 0 **5.** 20 **6.** 22 **7.** −28 **8.** Will **9.** −7; −6; (−28) ÷ 4 + 1 **10.** −5; −6; 42 ÷ (−3) + 9

Guided Practice

1. 42 **2.** −21 **3.** −9 **4.** −32 **5.** −4 **6.** −1 **7.** 7(−5) + 20 = −15; 15 dollars less **8.** 7(−10) + (−100) = −170; 170 fewer points **9.** 6(−4) + 10 = −14; lost 14 points **10.** 4(−12) + 10 = −38; $38 less **11.** > **12.** = **13.** > **14.** <

Independent Practice

17. 4 **19.** 0 **21.** 2 **23.** 5(−4) − 8 = −28 **25a.** 4(−35) − 9 = −149; $149 less **b.** Yes **29.** 80 inches

MODULE 3

LESSON 3.1

Your Turn

4. 0.571428… **5.** 0.333… **6.** 0.45 **7.** 2.75; terminating decimal **8.** 7.333…; repeating decimal

Guided Practice

1. 0.6; terminating **2.** 0.89; terminating **3.** 0.333…; repeating **4.** 0.2525…; repeating **5.** 0.7777…; repeating **6.** 0.36; terminating **7.** 0.04; terminating **8.** 0.14204545…; repeating **9.** 0.012; terminating **10.** 11.166… **11.** 2.9 **12.** 8.23 **13.** 7.2 **14.** 54.2727… **15.** 3.0555… **16.** 3.666… **17.** 12.875

Independent Practice

19. $\frac{5}{11}$; 0.4545…; repeating **21.** $\frac{4}{11}$; 0.3636…; repeating **23.** $\frac{11}{11}$; 1; terminating **25a.** $\frac{39}{8}$ **b.** 4.875 **27.** Ben is taller because 5.3125 > 5.2916… . **29.** When the denominator is 3, 6, 7, or 9, the result will be a repeating decimal. **31.** No; although the digits follow a pattern, the same combination of digits do not repeat.

LESSON 3.2

Your Turn

2. $4\frac{1}{2}$

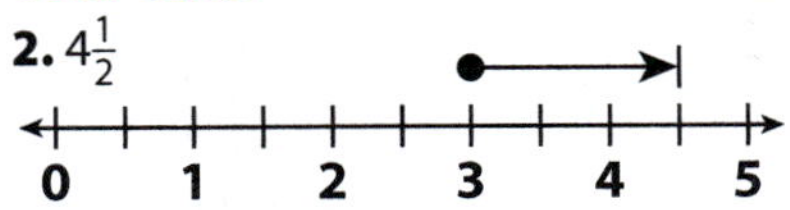

3. −7

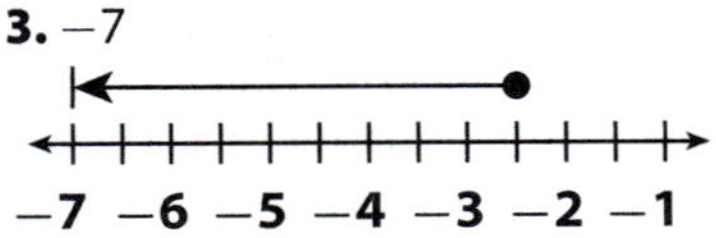

6. −3

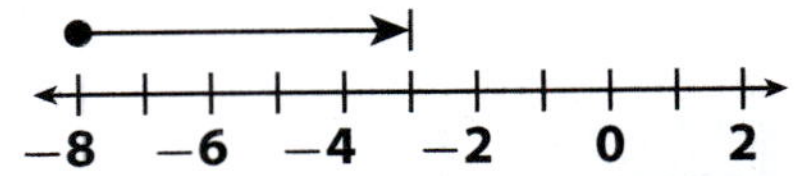

7. $-\frac{1}{4}$

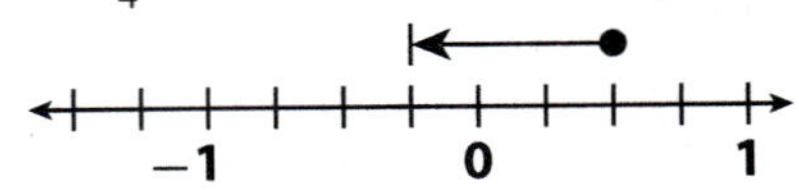

8. 6

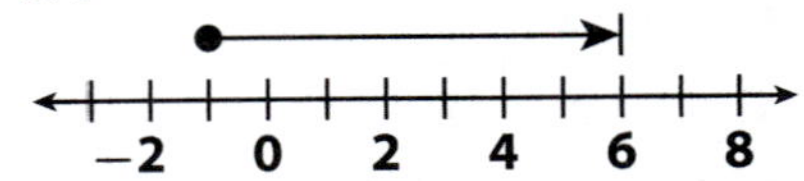

9. 0

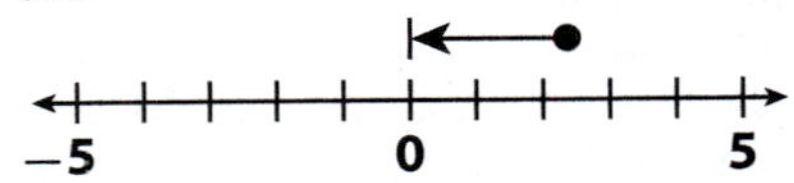

10. 0

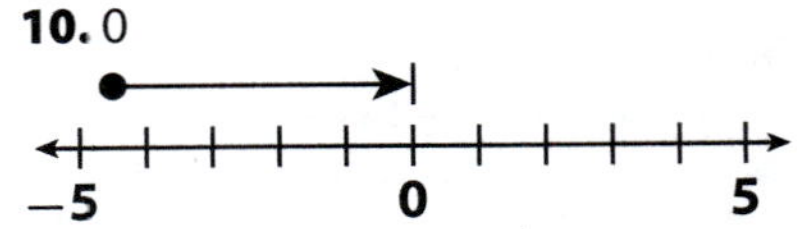

11. 4 **12.** −1 **13.** −1 **14.** 20

Guided Practice

1. −4.5

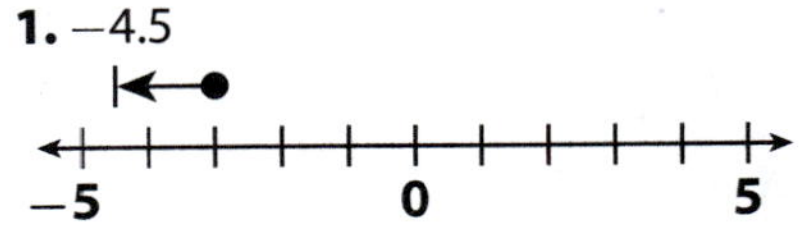

2. 5

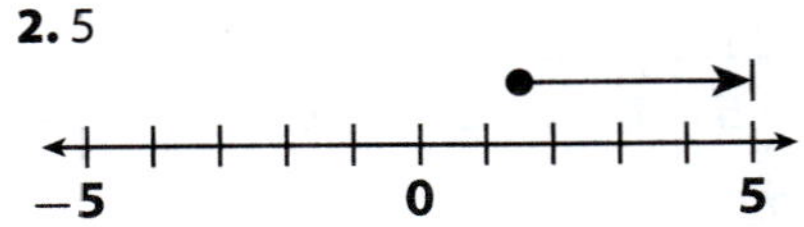

3. $\frac{3}{4}$

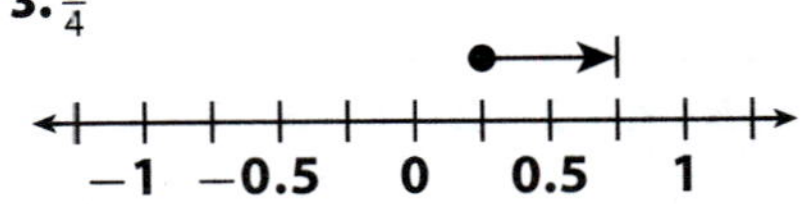

4. −3

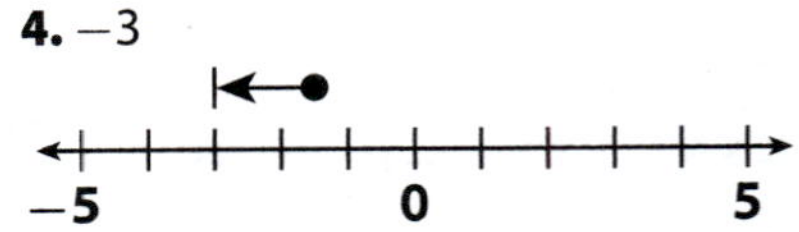

5. −2

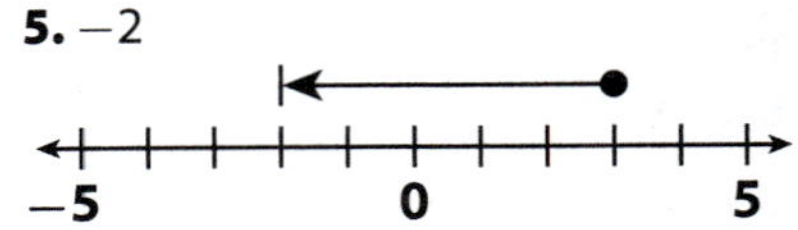

6. 2.5

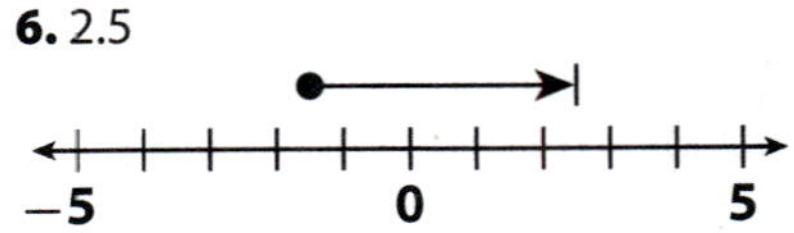

7. $0 **8.** $0 **9.** −4.5 **10.** 1 **11.** −2.2 **12.** 9 **13.** −12 **14.** $-\frac{1}{2}$ **15.** $-2\frac{1}{2}$ **16.** $-9\frac{1}{8}$

Independent Practice

19. \$12.75 **21.** $1\frac{1}{2}$ miles **23.** 30 + 15 + (−25) = 20; the final score is 20 points **25.** June: \$306.77, July: \$301.50, Aug: \$337.88 **27.** opposite or additive inverse

LESSON 3.3

Your Turn

1. −8.5

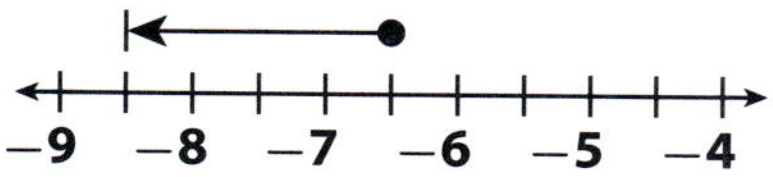

2. $-\frac{1}{2}$

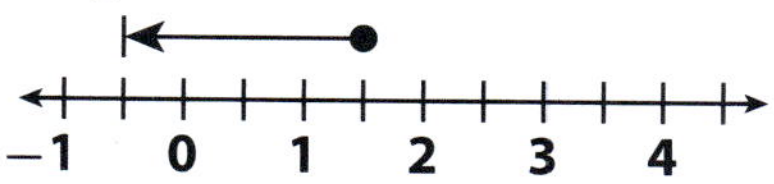

3. −7.75

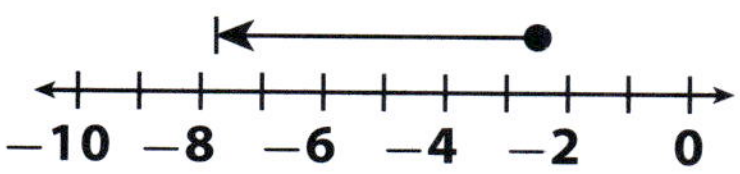

6. 1.75

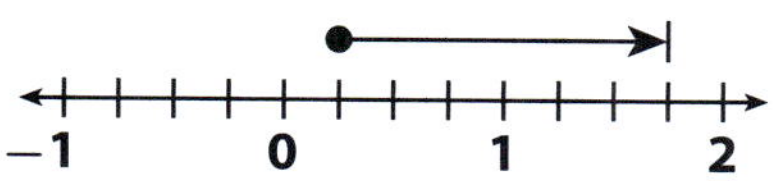

7. $\frac{1}{4}$

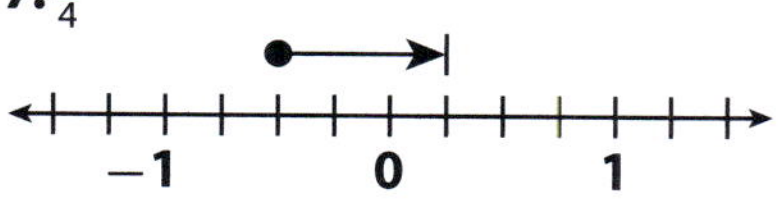

Guided Practice

1. 13

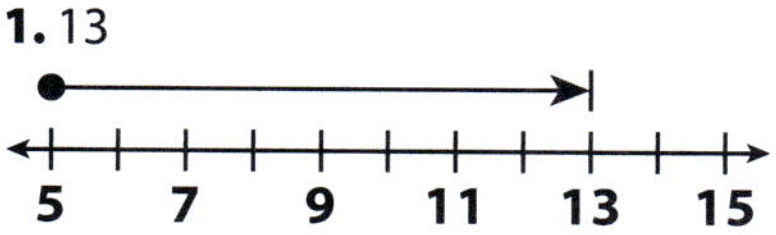

2. −8

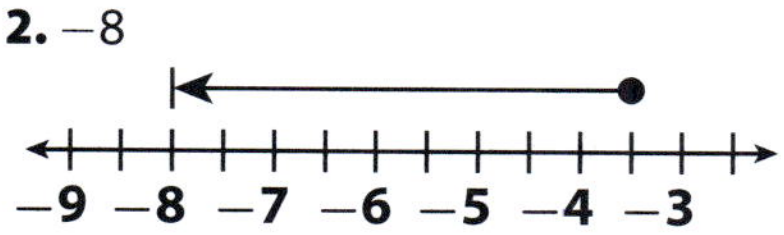

3. −11

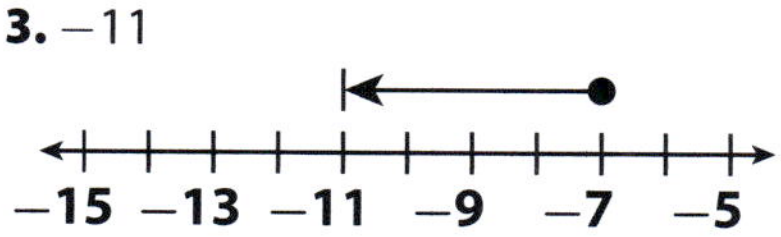

4. −4

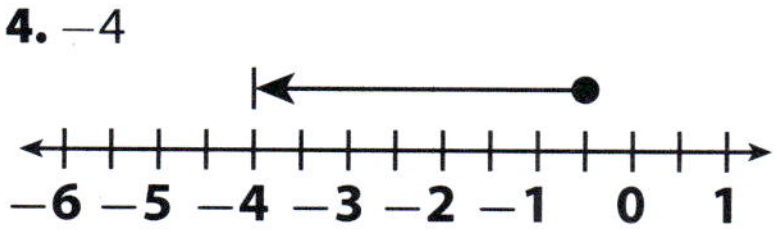

5. −36 **6.** −7.7 **7.** 1 **8.** 79 **9.** $2\frac{7}{9}$ **10.** $78\frac{1}{2}$ **11.** 1.5 meters **12.** $17\frac{1}{2}$ yard loss **13.** 543 feet **14.** $|-7-5|$, or $|5-(-7)|$; 12

Independent Practice

17. −25.65 − 16.5 + 12.45; −29.7 ft; the diver is 29.7 ft below the surface. **19a.** −\$43.30 **b.** −\$68.30 **c.** \$68.30 **21.** 65,233 ft; 96,000 ft; 96,000 ft (Mars); 30,767 ft **23a.** 5 − 7.2 + 2.2 **b.** He is exactly where he started because 5 − 7.2 + 2.2 = 0.

LESSON 3.4

Your Turn

1. −7

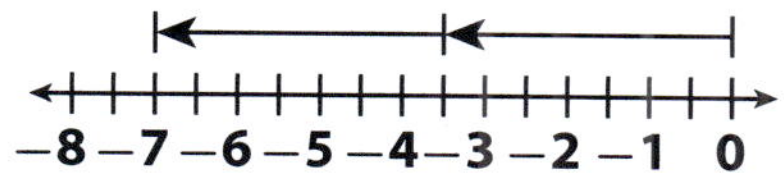

2. 3.75

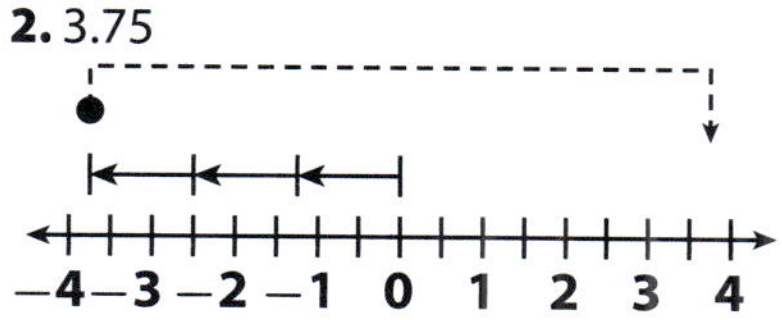

4. $-\frac{2}{7}$ **5.** $\frac{2}{5}$ **6.** $-\frac{1}{2}$

Guided Practice

1. $-3\frac{1}{3}$

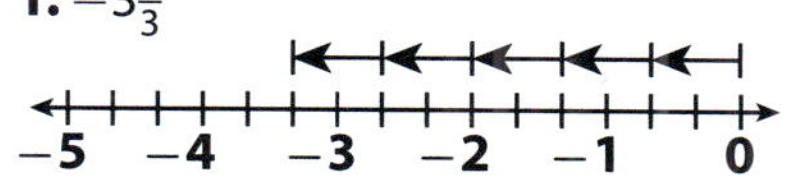

2. $-\frac{3}{4}$

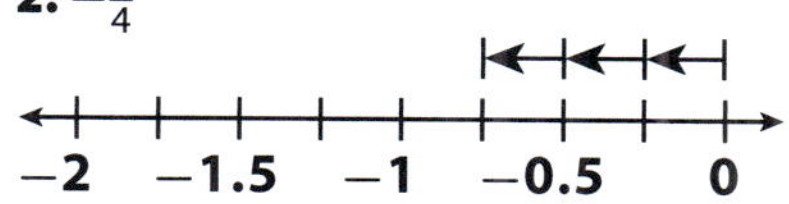

3. $1\frac{5}{7}$

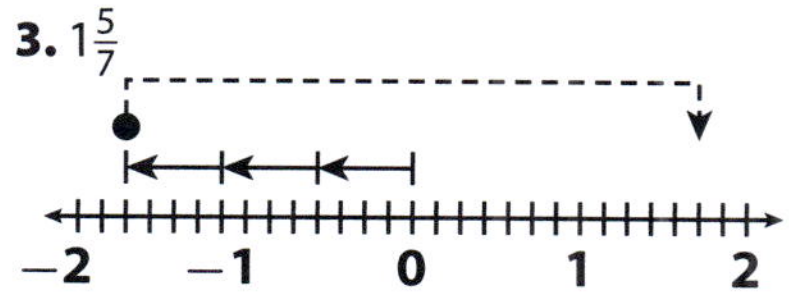

4. 3

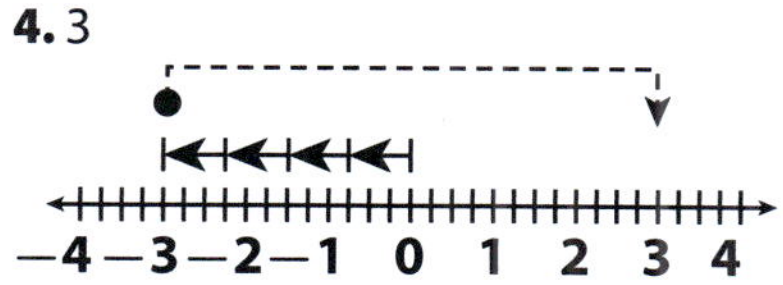

5. −12 **6.** −9 **7.** 6.8 **8.** 4.32 **9.** 6 **10.** −7.2 **11.** $\frac{1}{3}$; $\frac{1}{4}$ **12.** $\frac{12}{35}$; $-\frac{4}{5}$ **13.** $-\frac{5}{12}$ **14.** $\frac{2}{7}$ **15.** 4(−3.50) = −14; The share price decreased by \$14. **16.** 18(−100) = −1,800; The money in the ATM decreased by \$1,800.

Independent Practice

21. The submarine would be 975 feet below sea level, or −975 feet. **25.** 13.5 points

LESSON 3.5

Your Turn

3. −0.7 **4.** 16.6 **5.** −11 **6.** −3.8 feet per minute **7.** $\frac{35}{48}$ **8.** $-\frac{5}{8}$ **9.** $-1\frac{3}{5}$

Guided Practice

1. −0.8 **2.** $-\frac{1}{7}$ **3.** −8 **4.** $-\frac{502}{3}$ **5.** −375 **6.** 7 **7.** $-\frac{4}{21}$ **8.** −400 **9.** −0.875 liter per day **10.** −45.75 ÷ 5 = −9.15; −\$9.15 per day, on average **11.** −0.55 mile per minute

Independent Practice

13. −20 **15.** 20 **17.** −0.1 **19.** $\frac{5}{9}$ **21.** 4.5 **23.** $-1\frac{3}{4}$ yards **25a.** \$250 per day **b.** \$1,050 per day **c.** −\$70 **31.** Yes, since an integer divided by an integer is a ratio of two integers and the denominator is not zero, the number is rational by definition.

LESSON 3.6

Your Turn

1. $5\frac{5}{8}$ min **2.** 12 batches; \$0.29 per batch **3.** \$1,070.72

Guided Practice

1. Step 1: $3\frac{1}{5}$ or 3.2 mi/h, 14.4 mi; Step 2: 14.4 mi, $3\frac{3}{5}$ or 3.6 mi/h, 4 h **2.** Step 1: 25.68 in., −0.02375 in, −0.61 in.; Step 2: 25.68 in., 0.61 in., 25.07 in.

Independent Practice

5. $4\frac{1}{4}$ in. **7.** $29\frac{1}{8}$ yd **9.** 5 more; $88\% = \frac{88}{100} = \frac{44}{50}$ **11.** Yes, because the product is negative and about half of 1.5. **13.** Sample answer: Yes; −0.7343 ≈ −0.75 **15.** Sample answer: (1) Convert the fraction to a decimal and find the sum of 27.6 and 15.9, then multiply the result by 0.37. (2) Convert the fraction, then use the Distributive Property. Multiply both 27.6 and 15.9 by 0.37, then add the products. The first method; there are fewer steps and so fewer chances to make errors.

UNIT 2 Selected Answers

MODULE 4

LESSON 4.1

Your Turn

3. $\frac{1}{6} \div \frac{1}{4} = \frac{1}{6} \times \frac{4}{1} = \frac{4}{6} = \frac{2}{3}$; $\frac{2}{3}$ acre per hour **4.** 4 ounces **5.** Jaylon's unit rate is $3\frac{3}{4}$ cups of water per cup of lime juice. Wanchen's unit rate is 4 cups of water per cup of lime juice. Wanchen's limeade has a weaker lime flavor because $4 > 3\frac{3}{4}$ and the limeade with a greater ratio of water to lime juice will have a weaker flavor.

Guided Practice

2. $2\frac{4}{5}$ miles per hour **3.** $\frac{15}{16}$ page per minute **4.** $\frac{1}{2}$ foot per hour **5.** $2\frac{1}{2}$ square feet per hour **6.** Brand A: 720 mg/pickle, Brand B: 650 mg/pickle; Brand B **7.** C: $\frac{3}{8}$ cup/serving, D: $\frac{4}{9}$ cup/serving; Ingredient C

Independent Practice

9a. On Call: about \$2.86 per hour; Talk Time: \$2.50 per hour **b.** Talk Time; their rate per hour is lower. **c.** Multiply 0.05 times 60 because there are 60 minutes in 1 hour. **d.** The unit rate is \$3 per hour, so it is not a better deal. **11.** $\frac{5 \text{ songs}}{1 \text{ commercial}}$ **13.** Faster; he typed 50 words per minute in his first attempt and 60 words per minute in his second attempt.

LESSON 4.2

Your Turn

3. No; the rates are not equal because her speed changed. **4.** Each rate is equal to $\frac{1 \text{ adult}}{12 \text{ students}}$. The relationship is proportional; $a = \frac{1}{12}s$.

Guided Practice

1. 8; $\frac{49}{7} = 7$; $\frac{52}{8} = 6.5$; $\frac{54}{9} = 6$; the relationship is not proportional. **2.** $k = 5$; $y = 5x$ **3.** $k = \frac{1}{4}$; $y = \frac{1}{4}x$

Independent Practice

5. $y = 18.50x$ **7.** Rent–All has the best deal because it has the lowest rate per day (\$18.50). **9.** The rates have the same unit rate, \$6.25 per hour. **11.** x is the number of hours Steven babysits, and y is the amount he charges; the equation is $y = 6.25x$. **13.** 150 feet per minute; 9,000 feet per hour **15.** Feet per minute

LESSON 4.3

Your Turn

1. No; A line drawn through the points does not go through the origin.

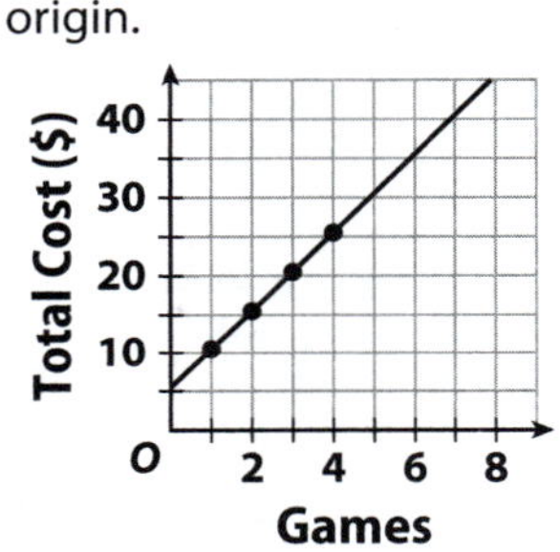

5a. The bicyclist rides 60 miles in 4 hours. **b.** 15 **c.** $y = 15x$

Guided Practice

1. proportional; pages is always 65 times the number of hours; 65 pages/hour. **2.** proportional; earnings are always 7.5 times the number of hours; \$7.50/hour. **3.** not proportional; the line will not pass through the origin. **4.** proportional; the line will pass through the origin. **5.** $y = 3.5x$ **6.** $y = \frac{1}{4}x$

Independent Practice

9. Horse A takes about 4 minutes. Horse B takes about 2.5 minutes. **11.** Horse A: $y = 3$ miles; Horse B: $y = 4\frac{4}{5}$ miles **13.** Yes; A graph of miles traveled compared to number of hours will form a line that passes through the origin.

15a.

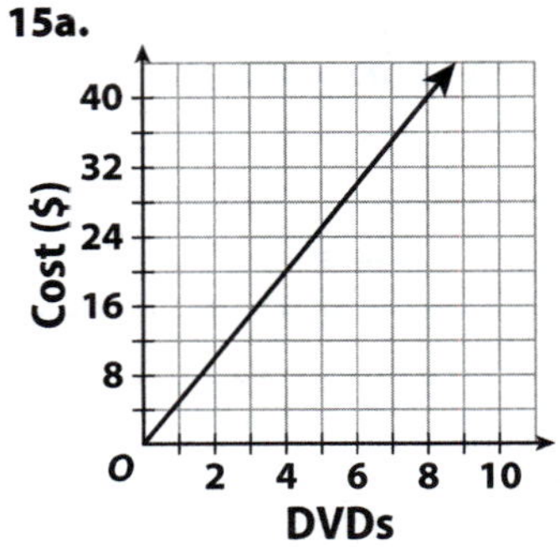

b. Sample answer: (4, 20); 4 DVDs cost \$20. **17.** Yes. The graph is a line that passes through the origin. **21.** If the values in the "Time" column are the same, each value in the "Distance" column for Car 4 will be twice the corresponding value for Car 2.

MODULE 5

LESSON 5.1

Your Turn

2. 23% **4.** 33% **5.** 37.5% **8.** \$548.90 **9.** \$349.30

Guided Practice

1. 60% **2.** 50% **3.** 74% **4.** 11% **5.** 8% **6.** 220% **7.** 78% **8.** 20% **9.** 28% **10.** 50% **11.** 9% **12.** 67% **13.** 100% **14.** 83% **15.** \$9.90 **16.** 36 cookies **17.** 272 pages **18.** 42 members **19.** \$27,840 **20.** 1,863 songs **21.** 26 miles

Independent Practice

25a. Amount of change = 1; percent decrease = $\frac{1}{5} = 20\%$ **27a.** They have the same. \$1,000 + \$100 = \$1,100 and \$1,000 + 10%(\$1,000) = \$1,100. **b.** Sylvia has more. Leroi has \$1,100 + \$100 = \$1,200, and Sylvia has \$1,100 + 10%(\$1,100) = \$1,210.

29. No. The first withdrawal is $60. Each withdrawal after that is less than $60 because it is 10% of the remaining balance. There will be money left after 10 withdrawals.

LESSON 5.2

Your Turn

2a. $1c + 0.1c$; $1.1c$ **b.** $30.80
3a. 200% **b.** $1c + 2c$; $3c$
5a.

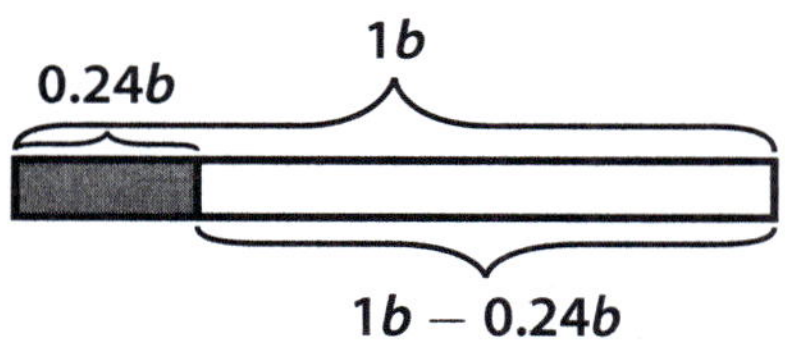

b. $0.76b$ **6a.** $1p - 0.05p$, $0.95p$
b. $14.25

Guided Practice

1a. $0.35s$ **b.** $1s + 0.35s$ or $1.35s$ **c.** $43.20 **d.** $11.20 **2.** $2.70; $20.70 **3.** $9.45; $31.95 **4.** $25.31; $59.06 **5.** $24.75; $99.74 **6.** $48.60; $97.20 **7.** $231.25; $416.25 **8.** $35.10 **9.** $59.63 **10.** $13.43 **11.** $70.00

Independent Practice

13a. $0.46b$ **b.** $1b - 0.46b$ or $0.54b$ **c.** $15.66 **d.** $13.34 **17.** Either buy 3, get one free or $\frac{1}{4}$ off. Either case would result in a discount of 25%, which is better than 20%.
19. No; first change: 20.1% decrease; second change: 25.1% increase. The second percent change is greater.

LESSON 5.3

Your Turn

1. $1; $21 **3.** $4,262; total = 3,300 + 0.0325(29,600) = 3,300 + 962 = 4,262 **5.** $34.13

Guided Practice

1. $1.50 **2.** $10.50 **3.** $0.40 **4.** $33 **5.** $0.80 **6.** $10 **7a.** $3.08 **b.** $47.07 **8.** $120 **9.** $700 **10.** $530.50 **11a.** $18 **b.** $19.53 **12.** $37.86

Independent Practice

15. $82.58 **17.** $75.14 **19.** $4,500
21a. Multiply Sandra's height by 0.10 and add the product to 4 to get Pablo's height. Then multiply Pablo's height by 0.08 and add the product to Pablo's height to get Michaela's height. **b.** about 4 feet 9 inches **23a.** $101.49 **b.** $109.39 **c.** Digital camera; he can save $8. **d.** $109.61

UNIT 3 Selected Answers

MODULE 6

LESSON 6.1

Your Turn

2. $10x - 4$ **3.** $1.25x + 4.4$ **5.** $0.6b - 3c$ **6.** $x + 6$ **7.** $11.8 - 2.6y$ **9.** $2(x + 1)$ **10.** $3(x + 3)$ **11.** $5(x + 3)$ **12.** $4(x + 4)$

Guided Practice

1. Step 1: baseballs: $14 + 12n$, tennis balls: $23 + 16n$; Step 2: $14 + 12n + 23 + 16n$, $14 + 23 + 12n + 16n$, $37 + 28n$, $37 + 28n$ **2.** 289 **3.** $0.5(12m) - 0.5(22n)$, $6m - 11n$ **4.** $2x - 6 - 6x + 4 = 2x + (-6x) + (-6) + 4 = -4x - 2$ **5.** $2(x + 6)$ **6.** $12(x + 2)$ **7.** $7(x + 5)$

Independent Practice

9. $15(100 + 5d) + 20(50 + 7d) = 2{,}500 + 215d$ **11.** 3 and $x + 2$; $3x + 6$ **13.** The area is the product of the length and width (6×9). It is also the sum of the areas of the rectangles separated by the dashed line $(6 \times 5$ and $6 \times 4)$. So, $6(9) = 6(5) + 6(4)$.
15. $2x + 6$ **17.** $x^2 + 5x + 6$
19. (1) Think of 997 as $1{,}000 - 3$. So, $8 \times 997 = 8(1{,}000 - 3)$. By the Distributive Property, $8(1{,}000 - 3) = 8{,}000 - 24 = 7{,}976$. (2) Think of 997 as $900 + 90 + 7$. By the Distributive Property, $8(900 + 90 + 7) = 7{,}200 + 720 + 56 = 7{,}976$.

LESSON 6.2

Your Turn

1. $z = -13.9$ **2.** $r = 12.3$ **3.** $c = -12$ **5.** $x - 1.5 = 5.25$; $x = 6.75$; the initial elevation of the plane is 6.75 miles.
6. $\frac{x}{3.5} = -1.2$; $x = -4.2$; \$4.20
7. $2.5x = 7.5$; $x = 3$; 3 hours

Guided Practice

1. Step 1: the number of degrees warmer the average temperature is in Nov. than in Jan., $x + (-13.4) = -1.7$ or $x - 13.4 = -1.7$; Step 2: 11.7°
2. Step 1: the number of days it takes the average temperature to decrease by 9 °F, $-1\frac{1}{2}x = -9$; Step 2: 6 days **3.** $x = -17$ **4.** $y = 1.4$ **5.** $z = -9$

Independent Practice

7. 29,028.87 ft
9. $28{,}251.31 - x = 11{,}194.21$; $x = 17{,}057.1$; 17,057.1 ft
11. $26\frac{1}{2}$ ft/min
13. 18.8 °C warmer
15. $36\frac{1}{3}$ yards **17.** Sample answer: the elevation is the product of the rate and the time. **19.** (1) The elevations of the diver and the reef; both are below sea level. (2) The change in the plane's elevation; the plane is moving from a higher to a lower elevation.
21. Add the deposits and the withdrawals. Let x represent the amount of the initial deposit. Write and solve the equation x + deposits − withdrawals = \$210.85.

LESSON 6.3

Your Turn

4. $150 - 35x = 45$

Guided Practice

1.

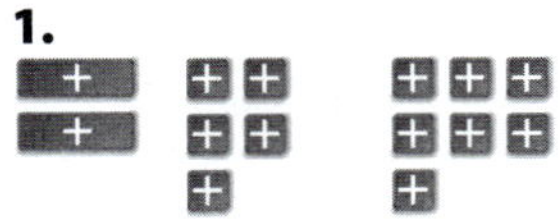

2.

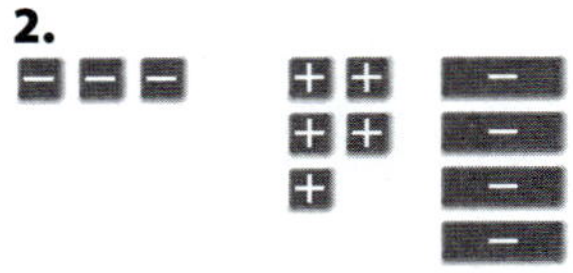

3. $6 + 9a = 78$ **4.** the solution; multiplied by 2; added to $2x$; result

Independent Practice

7. three negative variable tiles and seven +1–tiles on one side of a line and 28 +1–tiles on the other side **9.** $1.25r + 6.75 = 31.75$
11. $\frac{1}{2}n + 45 = 172$ **13.** $500 - 20x = 220$ **15a.** $10 + 5c = 25$ **b.** 3 children **c.** They should choose Kimmi because she charges only \$25. If they chose Sandy, they would pay \$35.
17. Part of the equation is written in cents and part in dollars. All of the numbers in the equation should be written either in cents or in dollars.

LESSON 6.4

Your Turn

1. $x = 3$ **2.** $n = 3$ **3.** $a = -1$
4. $y = 1$ **6.** $3n + 10 = 37$; the triplets are 9 years old.
7. $\frac{n}{4} - 5 = 15$; the number is 80.
8. $-20 = \frac{5}{9}(x - 32)$; −4 °F
9. $120 - 4x = 92$; 7 incorrect answers

Guided Practice

1. one +1–tile from both sides; two equal groups **2.** 4 **3.** $2(18 + w) = 58$; the width is 11 inches
4. $1200 - 25x = 500$; 28 days

Independent Practice

7. $d = 9$ **9.** $k = 42$ **11.** $z = -190$
13. $n = -9$ **15.** $c = 9$ **17.** $t = -9$
19. 13 °F **21.** 12 years old
23. \$188 **25.** $x = 0.4$
27. $k = -180.44$ **29.** Sample answer: $\frac{x}{5} + 10 = 5$
31. The equation says that a number was divided by 4 and that 6 was then subtracted from the quotient, giving the result 2. So, working backward, first add 6 to 2, giving 8. Then multiply 8 by 4, giving $x = 32$; Algebraic: Add 6 to both sides, then multiply by 4, giving $x = 32$. The operations are the same. **33.** $w = \frac{P - 2\ell}{2}$

MODULE 7

LESSON 7.1

Your Turn

4. $y \geq -2$

5. $x < 9$

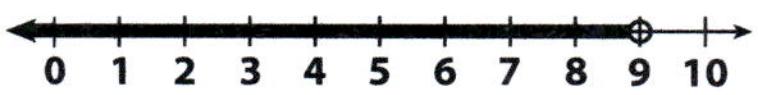

6. $y > -6$

7. $t \geq -42$

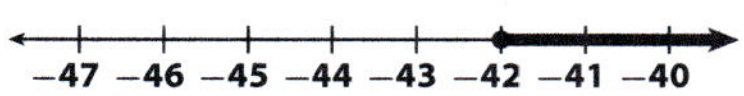

8. $m \leq 9$; Tony can pay for no more than 9 months of his gym membership using this account.

Guided Practice

1. $2 \leq 5$ **2.** $2 > 1$ **3.** $0 > -11$
4. $2 \leq 16$ **5.** $n \geq 3$

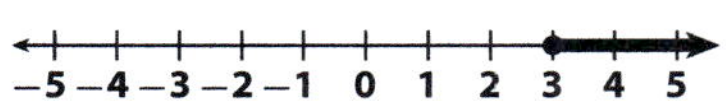

6. $x < 4$

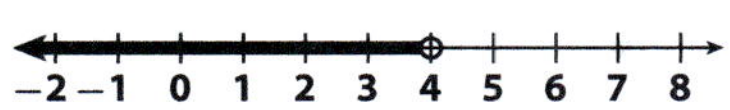

7. $y \geq -2$

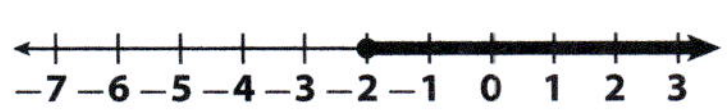

8. $b > -5$

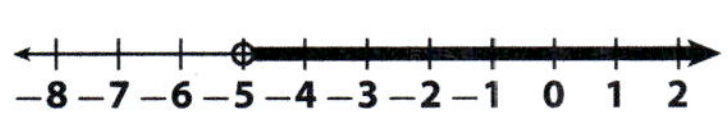

9a. $-4t \geq -80$
b. 20 or fewer hours
c. more than 20 hours

Independent Practice

11. $x > 50$

13. $q \leq 7$

15. $z < 8$ **17.** at most 16 in. **19.** at most 7 in. **21.** at least 11 ft **23.** $3\frac{1}{3}$ lb **25.** No; $1.25x \leq 3$; $x \leq 2.4$ so 2.4 lb of onions is the most Florence can buy. $2.4 < 2.5$, so she cannot buy 2.5 lb. **27.** $x > 9$ for each inequality; in each case the number added to x is 9 less than the number on the right side of each inequality, so $x > 9$ is the solution.

LESSON 7.2

Your Turn

3. $1{,}240 + 45a \geq 6{,}000$
4. $6 + 3n \leq 40$

Guided Practice

1.

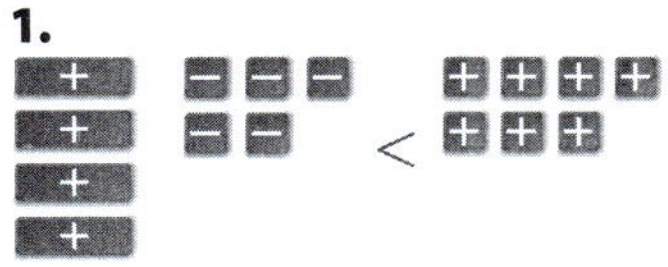

2.

3. \$7,000; \$1,250; 92; $1{,}250 + 92a \geq 7{,}000$ **4.** The solution of the problem; the solution multiplied by 7; 18 is subtracted from $7x$; the result can be no greater than 32.

Independent Practice

7. $3a + 28 > 200$; $a =$ possible amounts each friend earned
9. $4a - 25 \leq 75$; $a =$ the maximum amount each shirt can cost
10. $120 + 32n \leq 720$; $n =$ the number of people in each row
13. $7 + 10c \leq 100$; $c =$ the number of CDs she buys **17.** $\leq$
19. $\leq$ **21.** $\geq$ **25.** $n > \frac{1}{n}$ if $n > 1$; $n < \frac{1}{n}$ if $n < 1$; $n = \frac{1}{n}$ if $n = 1$

LESSON 7.3

Your Turn

1. $x > 2$ **2.** $h \geq 3$ **3.** $p \geq 6$; Joshua has to run at a steady pace of at least 6 mi/h. **4.** $v = 11$ **5.** $h = -3$; $h = -4$; $h = -5$

Guided Practice

1. Remove 4 + 1–tiles from both sides, then divide each side into 3 equal groups; $x < 3$
2. $d < 9$

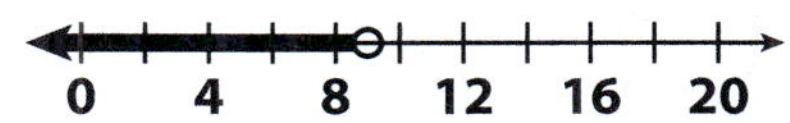

3. $b \geq 4$

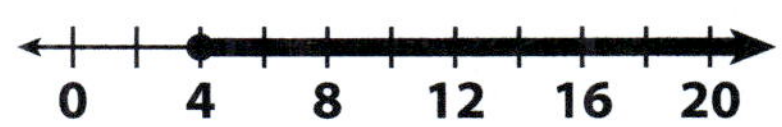

4. $m = -10$ **5.** $y = \frac{1}{2}$; $y = 0$
6. $t \leq 1.25$;

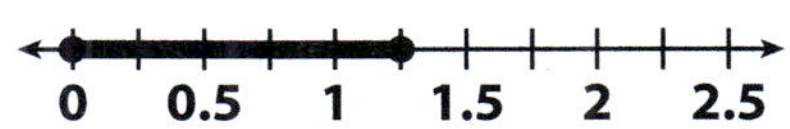

Lizzy can spend from 0 to 1.25 h with each student. No; 1.5 h per student will exceed Lizzy's available time.

Independent Practice

9. $t \leq 10$ **11.** $m < 8$
13. $f < 140$ **15.** $g < -18$
17. $a \geq 16$ **19.** $7n - 25 \geq 65$; $n \geq 12\frac{6}{7}$; Grace must wash at least 13 cars, because n must be a whole number.
21c. There is no number that satisfies both inequalities. **d.** The solution set is all numbers.

UNIT 4 Selected Answers

MODULE 8

LESSON 8.1

Your Turn

4. length: 17.3 feet; width: 13.3 feet; area: 230.1 square feet
5. length: 22 feet; width: 10 feet; area: 220 square feet

Guided Practice

1a. $y = \frac{5}{3}x$ **b.** $16\frac{2}{3}$ feet
c. 1.5 inches **2.** 28 feet; $\frac{1 \text{ inch} \times 14}{2 \text{ feet} \times 14} = \frac{14 \text{ inches}}{28 \text{ feet}}$; 14 feet; 392 square feet **3.** length: 25 meters; width: 15 meters; area: 375 square meters
4a.

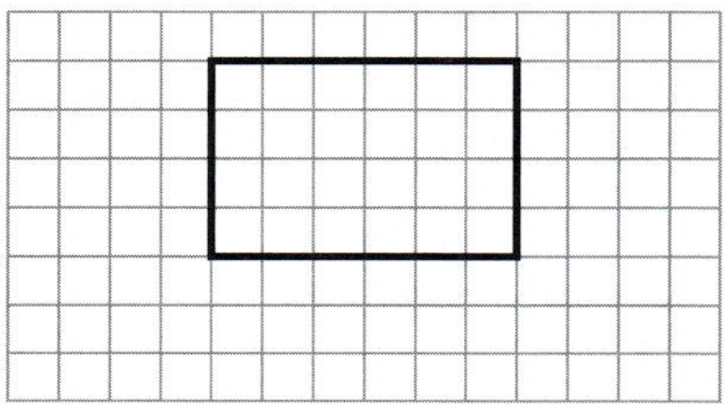

b. Length is 36 m and width is 24 m, using both scales.

Independent Practice

7. The scale drawing is 24 units by 15 units. **9.** Because the scale is 10 cm:1 mm and because 10 cm is longer than 1 mm, the drawing will be larger. **11a.** 6 toothpicks tall **b.** approximately 5 cotton swabs tall

LESSON 8.2

Guided Practice

1. a unique triangle
2. no triangle
3. a unique triangle
4. a unique triangle

Independent Practice

7. The side lengths proposed are 15, 21, and 37 ft, and $15 + 21 < 37$. No such triangle can be created.
9. More than one triangle; two triangles can be created by connecting the top of the 2-in. segment with the dashed line, once in each spot where the arc intersects the dashed line. The triangles are different, but both have sides with lengths of 2 in. and $1\frac{1}{2}$ in., and a 45° angle not included between them.

LESSON 8.3

Guided Practice

1. triangle or equilateral triangle
2. rectangle
3. triangle
4. rainbow-shaped curve

Independent Practice

7. Circles or ovals
9a. It is a circle with a radius of 12 in.
b. The cross sections will still be circles, but their radii will decrease as the plane moves away from the sphere's center.
11. Sample answer: If you think of a building shaped like a rectangular prism, you can think of horizontal planes slicing the prism to form the different floors.

LESSON 8.4

Your Turn

5. Sample answer: $\angle FGA$ and $\angle AGC$ **6.** Sample answer: $\angle FGE$ and $\angle BGC$ **7.** Sample answer: $\angle FGD$ and $\angle DGC$ **8.** Sample answer: $\angle BGC$ and $\angle CGD$
9. 55° **10.** $54° + 3x = 180°$, $x = 42°$, $m\angle JML = 3x = 126°$
11. Sample answer: You can stop at the solution step where you find the value of $3x$ because the measure of $\angle JML$ is equal to $3x$.

Guided Practice

1. complementary **2.** adjacent
3. vertical; 30° **4.** 50°, 30°, $2x$; 80°; 100°; 100° **5.** $3x - 13$, 58°, 45°; 45°, 15°; 15°; 45°; 32°

Independent Practice

7. Sample answer: $\angle SUR$ and $\angle QUR$ **9.** Sample answer: $\angle TUS$ and $\angle QUN$ **11.** $m\angle RUQ$
13. 96° **15.** 28°
17. $m\angle A = 47°$, $m\angle B = 43°$
19. 41 degrees, 33 minutes, 52 seconds **21.** Disagree; the sum of the measures of a pair of complementary angles is 90°. So, the measure of each angle must be less than 90°. But $m\angle A = 119°$, and $119° > 90°$.

MODULE 9

LESSON 9.1

Your Turn

3. about 34.54 cm **6.** about 2 hours

Guided Practice

1. 3.14(9); 28.26 **2.** 7; 44
3. 78.5 m **4.** 30.14 yd **5.** 47.1 in.
6. 66; 66; 21; $21 + 4 = 25$; 25; \$11.25; \$11.25 **7.** 0.5 yd; 1 yd
8. 12.55 ft; 25.10 ft **9.** 1.7 in.; 10.68 in.

Independent Practice

11. 18.53 ft **13.** 110 in.
15. $d = 18.8$ ft; $C \approx 59.0$ ft
17. $r = 9$ in.; $C \approx 56.52$ in.
19. about 2,376 ft
21. about 0.14 mi
23. about \$713.18
25. 12.56 feet **27.** Pool B; about 0.57 m or 1.84 ft

LESSON 9.2

Your Turn

4. 314 ft^2

Guided Practice

1. 153.9 m^2 **2.** 452.2 mm^2 **3.** 314 yd^2 **4.** 200.96 in^2 **5.** 113.04 cm^2 **6.** 132.67 in^2 **7.** 4π square units **8.** 36π square units **9.** $\frac{\pi}{16}$ square units **10.** 16π yd

Independent Practice

13. 803.84 cm^2 **15.** 28.26 square units **17.** 30.96 m^2 **19.** No; the top of the large cake has an area 9 times that of the small cake. The area of the top of the large cake is 144π in^2 and that of the small cake is 16π in^2. **21.** The 18-inch pizza is a better deal because it costs about 8¢ per square inch while the 12-inch pizza costs about 9¢ per square inch. **23.** No; the combined area is $2\pi r^2$ while the area of a circle with twice the radius is $4\pi r^2$. **25.** $\frac{\pi(1.5)^2}{\pi(1.75)^2} = \frac{2.25}{56.25} = \frac{1}{25}$ or 0.04 or 4%

LESSON 9.3

Your Turn

2. 51.5 ft^2 **3.** 139.25 m^2 **4.** \$911.68

Guided Practice

1. rectangle; 4; 15; 15; 4; 15; 15; 34; 34 **2.** Method 1: Divide the figure into a 12 by 9 rectangle and a 20 by 9 rectangle. Method 2: Divide the figure into a 9 by 8 rectangle and a 12 by 18 rectangle. The area is 288 cm^2. **3.** \$97.88

Independent Practice

5. 941.33 in^2

7. 30 square units

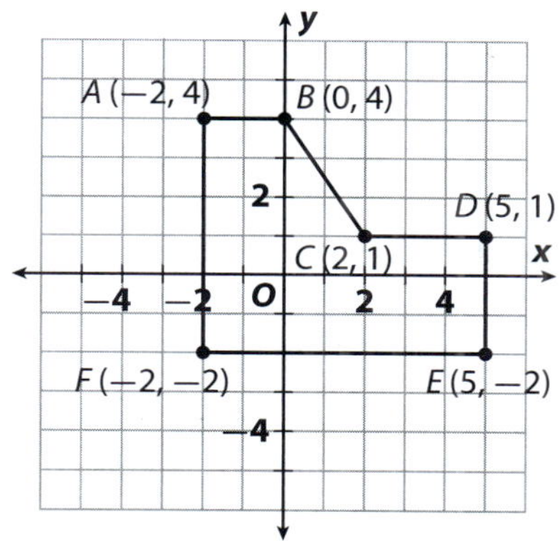

9. 60.56 cm^2 **11.** 5 ft; 32.5 ft^2 − 7.5 ft^2 = 25 ft^2; 25 ft^2 is area of the square, so each side of the square is 5 ft because $5 \times 5 = 25$ **15a.** 2,228 in^2 **b.** 3,016 in^2

LESSON 9.4

Your Turn

3. 69 in^2

4. 976 in^2

Guided Practice

1. 18 ft, 7 ft, 12 ft^2, (18 ft)(7 ft) + 2(12 ft^2), 150 ft^2 **2.** 37.5 m^2, 478 m^2, 6.25 m^2, 37.5 + 478 − 2(6.25), 503 m^2

Independent Practice

5. 3,720 tiles **7.** 66 ft^2

9. 3,264 in^2

11. No; they need 3 cans, which will cost 3(\$6.79) = \$20.37.

13. No; *Ph* doubles, and 2*B* quadruples. *S* more than doubles.

15. 138.2 in^2; 1,440 ft^2 of cardboard

LESSON 9.5

Your Turn

2. 1,848 m^3

5. 2,200 cm^3

7. 6,825 in^3

Guided Practice

1. 12 ft^2; (12×7) ft^3 = 84 ft^3

2. 30 m^2; (30×11) m^3 = 330 m^3

3. 288 ft^3; 72 ft^3; 360 ft^3

4. 40,000 ft^3

5. 385 cm^3

Independent Practice

7. 17.5 in^3

9. 384 ft^3

11. The units for volume are incorrect; the volume is 300 cubic inches.

13. 316.41 m^3

15. Triangular prism; you get 192 in^3 for the same price you would pay for 180 in^3 with the trapezoidal prism.

17. $V = 30(2.5) = 75$ cm^3; mass ≈ 75(8.6) = 645g

19. Sample answers: (1) height of trapezoid = 4 cm, base lengths = 2 cm and 6 cm, height of prism = 7.5 cm (2) height of trapezoid = 2.5 cm, base lengths = 1 cm and 7 cm, height of prism = 12 cm

UNIT 5 Selected Answers

MODULE 10

LESSON 10.1

Your Turn

4. Yes; every employee had an equal chance of being selected. **5.** The question is biased since cats are suggested. **6.** The question is not biased. It does not lead people to pick a particular season.

Guided Practice

2. more; random **3.** less; biased **4.** Yes; Sample answer: What is your favorite color?

Independent Practice

9. It is biased because students who aren't in that class won't be selected. **11.** Yes; the sample is random. **13.** Jae's question is not biased since it does not suggest a type of art to students. **15a.** 60; a random sample **b.** 58%; it appears reasonable because Barbara used a random sample and surveyed a significant percent of the students.

LESSON 10.2

Your Turn

5. 420 damaged MP3s **6.** Sample answer: 6 is a little more than 10% of 50. 10% of 3,500 is 350, and 420 is a little more than that.

Guided Practice

1.

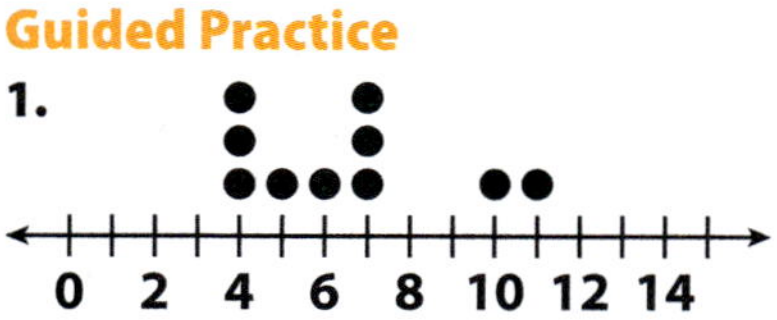

2.

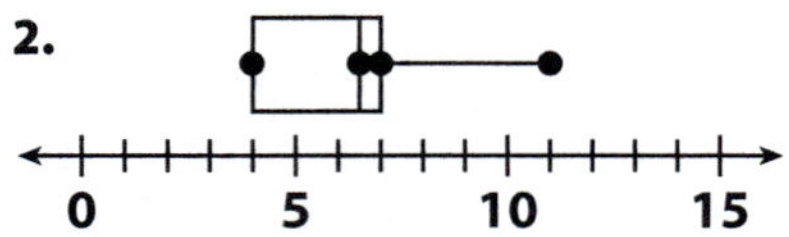

3. 4; 7 **4.** 4; 11 **5.** 6.5 **6.** 280 **7.** 720 elk

Independent Practice

9. 48 people **11.** 240 puppies **13.** Yes, this seems reasonable because 25 is the median of the data. **17.** Kudrey needs to find the median and the lower and upper quartiles and plot those points. He assumed all quartiles would be equally long when each quartile represents an equal number of data values. **19.** a box plot

LESSON 10.3

Guided Practice

1. (1, 600); 20
2. 50; 51, 600
3. No, it has 4 defective batteries, or 20%. For the shipment, $\frac{50}{600}$, or about 8% of the batteries are defective.

Independent Practice

5. Shop A sells 100; Shop B sells 115; Shop C sells 140.
7. Shop A or Shop B; Both samples are large enough to produce a reasonably valid inference. Shop C's sample is too small.
9a. 49.8 palms **b.** about 3,187 palms
11. Sample answer: Roll two six-sided number cubes, with one cube representing the row and the other representing the column. Select the cell represented by the row and column shown on the cubes.

MODULE 11

LESSON 11.1

Your Turn

2. Dot plots for field hockey players and softball players have a similar spread. Center of the field hockey dot plot is less than the center for softball or basketball players. Dot plots for field hockey players and softball players have a similar spread.
3. median: 6 h, range: 10 h; If you remove the outliers, the range is 4 hours. The median is greater than the median for exercise. The range is less than the range for exercise.

Guided Practice

1. Class A: clustered around two areas; Class B: clustered in the middle **2.** Class A: two peaks at 4 and 13 mi; Class B: looks centered around 7 mi **3.** Class A: spread from 4 to 14 mi, a wide gap no data; Class B: spread from 3 to 9 mi **4.** The median for both dot plots is 6 miles. **5.** Range for Class A: 10 mi; range for Class B: 6 mi

Independent Practice

7. The dots have a relatively even spread, with a peak at 8 letters.
9. The dots spread from 3 to 9 letters. **11.** AL: clustered in one small interval with an outlier to the left; VA: relatively uniform in height over the same interval
13. AL: spreads from 1 to 12 days of rain, an outlier at 1; VA: spreads from 8 to 12 days of rain
15. Group A: clustered to the left of size 9; Group B: clustered to the right of size 9 **17.** Group A: range with outlier = 6.5, without outlier = 2.5; Group B: range = 3 **19.** Yes; one group of five students could

have the following number of pets: 1, 2, 3, 4, 5. Another group of five students could have the following number of pets: 1, 3, 3, 3, 5. For both groups of students, the median would be 3 and the range would be 4.

LESSON 11.2

Your Turn

3. Sample: The boxes have similar shapes, although Group B has a shorter box and shorter whiskers. Group B's median is greater than Group A's. Group B's shorter box means the middle 50% of the data are closer together than the middle 50% of Group A's.
4. Sample answer: The shape is similar to Store A's. The median is greater than Store A's and less than Store B's. The interquartile range is about the same as Store A's and longer than B's.

Guided Practice

1. 72; 88 **2.** 79 **3.** 16; 10 **4.** Volleyball players **5.** Hockey players **6.** Both groups

Independent Practice

9. Both cars have ranges of 45 in. Both cars have interquartile ranges of 25 in. **11.** Car A has less variability in the lowest quarter of its data and greater variability in the highest quarter of its data. The variability is reversed for Car B. **13.** City A; $25

LESSON 11.3

Your Turn

1. About 1.1 times the MAD.
2. There is much more overlap between the two distributions.

Guided Practice

1. Class 1: 6, Class 2: 11; Class 1: 3, Class 2: 3 **2.** 1.67 **3.** Both distributions show longer travel times for school A. The distribution of the medians shows less overlap, so is more convincing.

Independent Practice

5. Mean: 50 °F, MAD: 13 °F
7. 35 °F, 13 °F; the mean for City 2 must be 15 °F less than the mean for City 1, and the MAD must be the same.
9. The variation and overlap in the distributions make it hard to make any convincing comparison.
11. 1.75 × range **13.** Ramon's; the larger the sample size, the less variability there should be in the distributions of the medians and means.

UNIT 6 Selected Answers

MODULE 12

LESSON 12.1

Your Turn

3. as likely as not; $\frac{1}{2}$ **4.** $\frac{1}{2}$ **5.** $\frac{1}{3}$ **7.** $\frac{7}{8}$ **8.** $\frac{1}{2}$

Guided Practice

1. 8; 5; 7; 1; 3; 2; 4; 6 **2.** impossible; 0 **3.** as likely as not; $\frac{1}{2}$ **4.** certain; 1 **5.** unlikely; close to 0 **6.** $\frac{2}{5}$ **7.** $\frac{1}{4}$ **8.** $\frac{5}{6}$ **9.** $\frac{2}{3}$ **10.** $\frac{4}{5}$ **11.** $\frac{12}{13}$

Independent Practice

13. $\frac{2}{13}$; The event can occur in 8 ways. There are 52 outcomes in the sample space. $\frac{8}{52} = \frac{2}{13}$ **15.** No, it is unlikely that she will have oatmeal for breakfast. **19a.** $\frac{8}{14} = \frac{4}{7}$ **b.** $8 - 1 = 7$ blue coins and $6 + 3 = 9$ red coins; $\frac{9}{16}$ **c.** $8 + 3 = 11$ blue coins and $6 - 1 = 5$ red coins; $\frac{5}{16}$ **21.** Yes; Because not selecting red means black will be selected, and vice versa. $P(\text{not black}) + P(\text{black}) = P(\text{not black}) + P(\text{not red}) = 1$.

LESSON 12.2

Your Turn

7. red: $\frac{1}{3}$, yellow: $\frac{7}{15}$, blue: $\frac{1}{5}$ **8.** Let 1 and 2 represent red, let 3 and 4 represent white, and let 5 and 6 represent blue. Toss the cube 50 times to determine the experimental probability for each color. Predict that the next ball released will be the color with the greatest experimental probability.

Guided Practice

1. A: $\frac{7}{20}$, 0.35, 35%; B: $\frac{7}{40}$, 0.175, 17.5%; C: $\frac{11}{40}$, 0.275, 27.5%; D: $\frac{1}{5}$, 0.2, 20% **2.** Sample answer: Write "yes" on 6 cards and "no" on 4. Draw a card at random 50 times. Use the number of "yes" cards as her prediction.

Independent Practice

5. Sample answer: Compare the number of wins to the total number of trials; $\frac{1}{6}$. **7.** Yes, because it is based on actual data of weather patterns. **9.** $\frac{2}{5}$; 16 aces; $\frac{2}{5}$ of 40 is 16. **11.** No; there were 40 heads in 100 trials; $P(\text{heads}) = \frac{40}{100}$.

LESSON 12.3

Your Turn

1. $\frac{60}{400} = \frac{3}{20} = 15\%$ **3.** $\frac{12}{75} = \frac{4}{25}$

Guided Practice

1. $\frac{50}{400} = \frac{1}{8}$

Independent Practice

5. $\frac{60}{400} = \frac{3}{20}$ **7.** 12; The total is the product of 3 page count choices and 4 color choices, which is 12. **13.** No, because coins are fair and the probabilities do not appear to be equally likely.

LESSON 12.4

Your Turn

1. 132 customers **3.** No; about 371 e-mails out of 12,372 will come back undelivered. The prediction is high. **4.** 84 customers; Yes, $107 > 84$, so more customers than normal bought two or more pairs.

Guided Practice

1. 15 times **2.** about 55 days **3.** No, about 1,009 candles out of 16,824 will be returned. The prediction is low. **4.** No, about 746 toys out of 24,850 will be defective. The prediction is high. **5.** 39 times; The light-rail's claim is higher than the actual 85%. **6.** 900 students; The college's claim is close to the number actually accepted.

Independent Practice

9. Yes; 6th grade: $\frac{2}{100} = \frac{x}{250} \rightarrow x = 5$; 7th grade: $\frac{4}{100} = \frac{x}{200} \rightarrow x = 8$; 8th grade: $\frac{8}{100} = \frac{x}{150} \rightarrow x = 12$ **11.** 36 clients; more than would be expected on average **13.** He set up the fraction incorrectly; it should be $\frac{1}{3} = \frac{x}{180}$. **15.** 14,700 on-time flights

MODULE 13

LESSON 13.1

Your Turn

2. $\frac{1}{3}$ **3.** The total number of outcomes in the sample space is the denominator of the formula for theoretical probability.

Guided Practice

1.

	Basket A	Basket B
Total number of outcomes	16	20
Number of red balls	3	4
$P(\text{win}) = \frac{\text{number of red balls}}{\text{total number of outcomes}}$	$\frac{3}{16}$	$\frac{4}{20} = \frac{1}{5}$

2. Basket B **3.** odd, 6; sections, 11 **4.** even, 5; sections, 11 **5.** $\frac{2}{6} = \frac{1}{3}$ **6.** Sample answer: No, but it might be reasonably close.

Independent Practice

9. $\frac{2}{3}$, 0.67, 67% **11.** $\frac{1}{2}$, 0.50, 50% **13.** $\frac{3}{5}$, 0.60, 60% **15.** 9 represents the ways the event can occur; 13 represents the number of equally likely outcomes.

LESSON 13.2

Your Turn

3. $\frac{4}{12} = \frac{1}{3}$ **4.** $\frac{6}{12} = \frac{1}{2}$ **5.** $\frac{3}{8}$

Guided Practice

1.

	1	**2**	**3**	**4**	**5**	**6**
1	1	2	3	4	5	6
2	2	4	6	8	10	12
3	3	6	9	12	15	18
4	4	8	12	16	20	24
5	5	10	15	20	25	30
6	6	12	18	24	30	36

2. $\frac{15}{16}$ **3.** $\frac{23}{36}$

4.

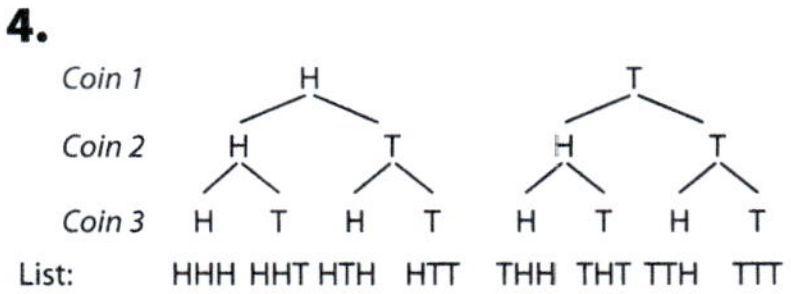

5. 8 **6.** TTT **7.** $\frac{1}{8}$ **8.** 3; HTH, THH ; $\frac{3}{8}$

Independent Practice

11. $\frac{1}{2}$ **13.** $\frac{1}{10}$ **15.** $\frac{2}{9}$ **17.** Because there are 3 choices for the first item and 2 for the second, there are $3 \cdot 2 = 6$ possible outcomes. **19.** Neither

LESSON 13.3

Your Turn

1. about 167 times **2.** about 9 times **3.** more likely that he picks a marble of another color **4.** No

Guided Practice

1. $\frac{1}{3}, \frac{1}{3}, \frac{1}{3}, \frac{1}{3}$; 1, 3, 18, 6, 6 **2.** 50 people **3.** brown; $P(\text{hazel}) = \frac{9}{28}$, $P(\text{brown}) = \frac{10}{28}$, $P(\text{blue}) = \frac{7}{28}$, and $P(\text{green}) = \frac{2}{28}$. The event with the greatest probability is choosing a person with brown eyes.

Independent Practice

5. 15 white or gray marbles **7.** It is more likely that she draws 2 red cards. **9.** 500 times **11.** 45 days **17.** Yes, but only theoretically because in reality, nothing can occur 0.5 time.

LESSON 13.4

Guided Practice

1. years with a drought; years without a drought; 4

2.

Trial	Numbers generated	Drought years
1	10, 3, 5, 1	2
2	10, 4, 6, 5	0
3	3, 2, 10, 3	3
4	2, 10, 4, 4	1
5	7, 3, 6, 3	2

Trial	Numbers generated	Drought years
6	8, 4, 8, 5	0
7	6, 2, 2, 8	2
8	6, 5, 2, 4	1
9	2, 2, 3, 2	4
10	6, 3, 1, 5	2

3. 80%

Independent Practice

5. 1 trial **7.** 20%

Glossary/Glosario

A

ENGLISH	SPANISH	EXAMPLES
absolute value The distance of a number from zero on a number line; shown by | |.	**valor absoluto** Distancia a la que está un número de 0 en una recta numérica. El símbolo del valor absoluto es | |.	$\|5\| = 5$ $\|-5\| = 5$
accuracy The closeness of a given measurement or value to the actual measurement or value.	**exactitud** Cercanía de una medida o un valor a la medida o el valor real.	
acute angle An angle that measures greater than 0° and less than 90°.	**ángulo agudo** Ángulo que mide más de 0° y menos de 90°.	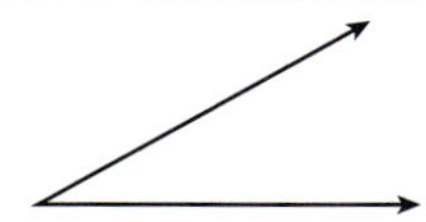
acute triangle A triangle with all angles measuring less than 90°.	**triángulo acutángulo** Triángulo en el que todos los ángulos miden menos de 90°.	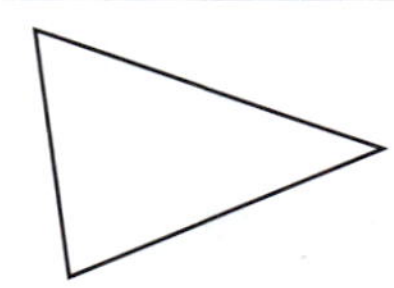
addend A number added to one or more other numbers to form a sum.	**sumando** Número que se suma a uno o más números para formar una suma.	In the expression $4 + 6 + 7$, the numbers 4, 6, and 7 are addends.
Addition Property of Equality The property that states that if you add the same number to both sides of an equation, the new equation will have the same solution.	**Propiedad de igualdad de la suma** Propiedad que establece que puedes sumar el mismo número a ambos lados de una ecuación y la nueva ecuación tendrá la misma solución.	$x - 6 = 8$ $\underline{+6 \quad +6}$ $x = 14$
Addition Property of Opposites The property that states that the sum of a number and its opposite equals zero.	**Propiedad de la suma de los opuestos** Propiedad que establece que la suma de un número y su opuesto es cero.	$12 + (-12) = 0$
additive inverse The opposite of a number.	**inverso aditivo** El opuesto de un número.	The additive inverse of 5 is -5.
adjacent angles Angles in the same plane that have a common vertex and a common side.	**ángulos adyacentes** Angulos en el mismo plano que comparten un vértice y un lado.	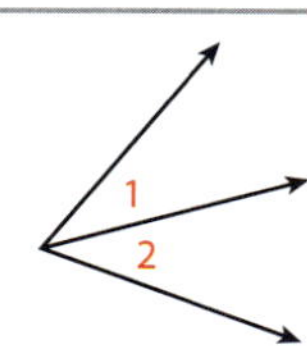 $\angle 1$ and $\angle 2$ are adjacent angles.
algebraic expression An expression that contains at least one variable.	**expresión algebraica** Expresión que contiene al menos una variable.	$x + 8$ $4(m - b)$

ENGLISH	SPANISH	EXAMPLES
algebraic inequality An inequality that contains at least one variable.	**desigualdad algebraica** Desigualdad que contiene al menos una variable.	$x + 3 > 10$ $5a > b + 3$
alternate exterior angles A pair of angles on the outer side of two lines cut by a transversal that are on opposite sides of the transversal.	**ángulos alternos externos** Par de ángulos en los lados externos de dos líneas intersecadas por una transversal, que están en lados opuestos de la transversal.	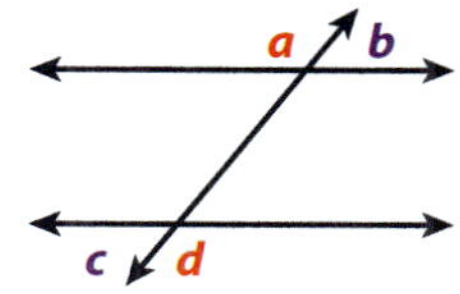 $\angle a$ and $\angle d$ are alternate exterior angles.
alternate interior angles A pair of angles on the inner sides of two lines cut by a transversal that are on opposite sides of the transversal.	**ángulos alternos internos** Par de ángulos en los lados internos de dos líneas intersecadas por una transversal, que están en lados opuestos de la transversal.	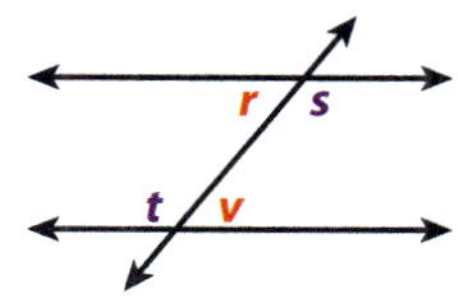 $\angle r$ and $\angle v$ are alternate interior angles.
angle A figure formed by two rays with a common endpoint called the vertex.	**ángulo** Figura formada por dos rayos con un extremo común llamado vértice.	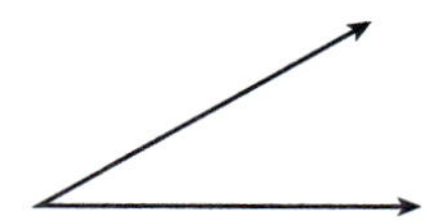
arc A part of a circle named by its endpoints.	**arco** Parte de un círculo que se nombra por sus extremos.	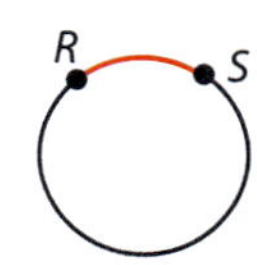
area The number of square units needed to cover a given surface.	**área** El número de unidades cuadradas que se necesitan para cubrir una superficie dada.	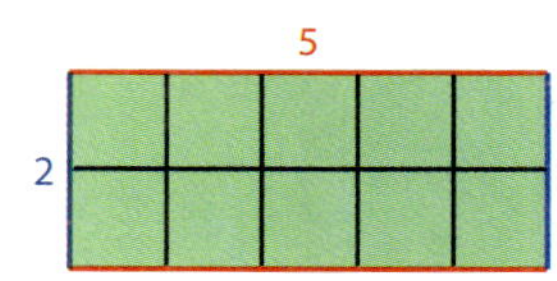 The area is 10 square units.
arithmetic sequence A sequence in which the terms change by the same amount each time.	**sucesíon aritmética** Una sucesión en la que los términos cambian la misma cantidad cada vez.	The sequence 2, 5, 8, 11, 14 ... is an arithmetic sequence.
assets Items a person owns that have monetary value.	**activos** Cosas que posees y que tienen valor monetario.	
Associative Property of Addition The property that states that for all real numbers *a*, *b*, and *c*, the sum is always the same, regardless of their grouping.	**Propiedad asociativa de la suma** Propiedad que establece que para todos los números reales *a*, *b* y *c*, la suma siempre es la misma sin importar cómo se agrupen.	$2 + 3 + 8 = (2 + 3) + 8 = 2 + (3 + 8)$
Associative Property of Multiplication The property that states that for all real numbers *a*, *b*, and *c*, their product is always the same, regardless of their grouping.	**Propiedad asociativa de la multiplicación** Propiedad que para todos los números reales *a*, *b* y *c*, el producto siempre es el mismo sin importar cómo se agrupen.	$2 \cdot 3 \cdot 8 = (2 \cdot 3) \cdot 8 = 2 \cdot (3 \cdot 8)$

Glossary/Glosario

ENGLISH	SPANISH	EXAMPLES

asymmetry Not identical on either side of a central line; not symmetrical.

asimetría Ocurre cuando dos lados separados por una línea central no son idénticos; falta de simetría.

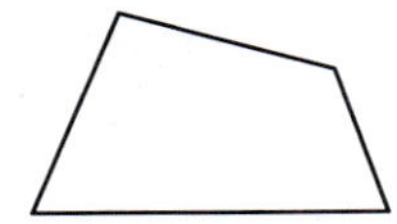

The quadrilateral has asymmetry.

---

axes The two perpendicular lines of a coordinate plane that intersect at the origin.

ejes Las dos rectas numéricas perpendiculares del plano cartesiano que se intersecan en el origen.

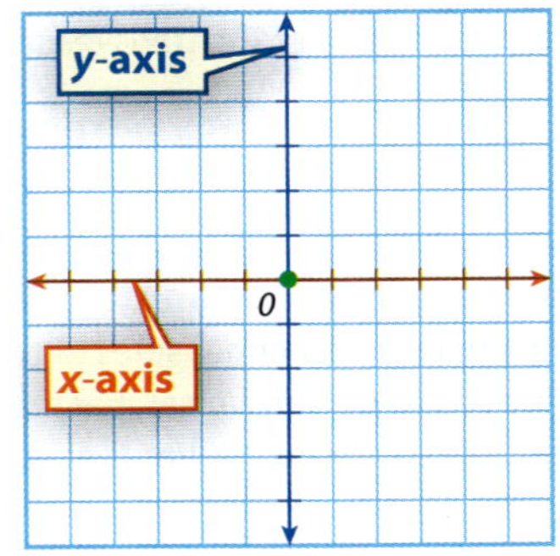

B

bar graph A graph that uses vertical or horizontal bars to display data.

gráfica de barras Gráfica en la que se usan barras verticales u horizontales para presentar datos.

---

base-10 number system A number system in which all numbers are expressed using the digits 0–9.

sistema de base 10 Sistema de numeración en el que todos los números se expresan con los dígitos 0–9.

---

base (in numeration) When a number is raised to a power, the number that is used as a factor is the base.

base (en numeración) Cuando un número es elevado a una potencia, el número que se usa como factor es la base.

$3^5 = 3 \cdot 3 \cdot 3 \cdot 3 \cdot 3$; 3 is the base.

---

base (of a polygon) A side of a polygon.

base (de un polígono) Lado de un polígono.

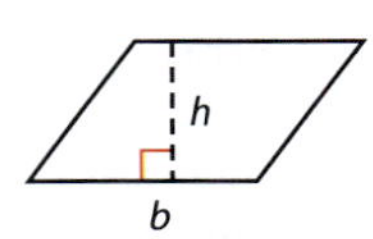

---

base (of a three-dimensional figure) A face of a three-dimensional figure by which the figure is measured or classified.

base (de una figura tridimensional) Cara de una figura tridimensional a partir de la cual se mide o se clasifica la figura.

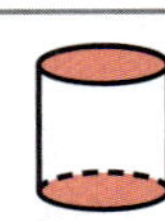

Bases of a cylinder

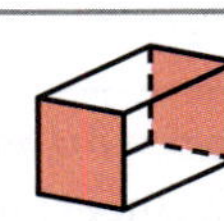

Bases of a prism

Base of a cone

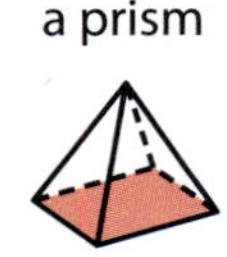

Base of a pyramid

ENGLISH	SPANISH	EXAMPLES
biased sample A sample that does not fairly represent the population.	**muestra no representativa** Muestra que no representa adecuadamente la población.	
bisect To divide into two congruent parts.	**trazar una bisectriz** Dividir en dos partes congruentes.	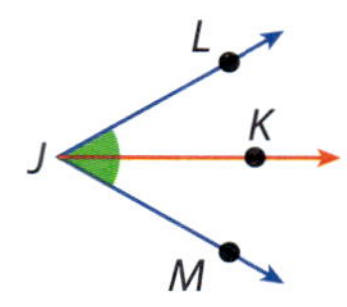 $\overrightarrow{JK}$ bisects $\angle LJM$.
box-and-whisker plot A graph that shows how data are distributed by using the median, quartiles, least value, and greatest value; also called a box plot.	**gráfica de mediana y rango** Gráfica que muestra los valores máximo y mínimo, los cuartiles superior e inferior, así como la mediana de los datos.	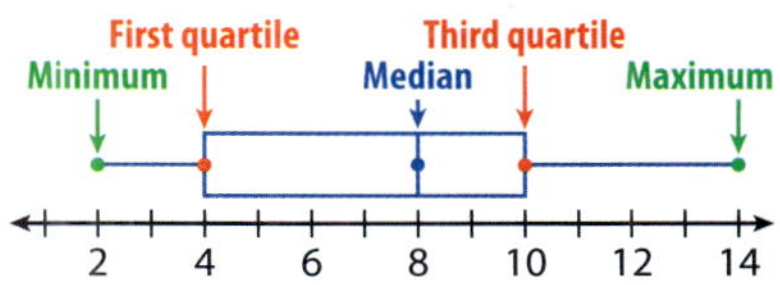
break (graph) A zigzag on a horizontal or vertical scale of a graph that indicates that some of the numbers on the scale have been omitted.	**discontinuidad (gráfica)** Zig-zag en la escala horizontal o vertical de una gráfica que indica la omisión de algunos de los números de la escala.	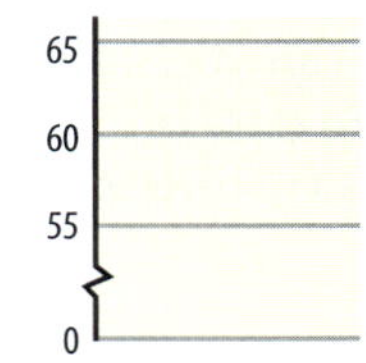
budget A plan to help you reach your financial goals.	**presupuesto** Plan que te ayuda a obtener tus metas financieras.	

C

ENGLISH	SPANISH	EXAMPLES
capacity The amount a container can hold when filled.	**capacidad** Cantidad que cabe en un recipiente cuando se llena.	A large milk container has a capacity of 1 gallon.
Celsius A metric scale for measuring temperature in which 0 °C is the freezing point of water and 100 °C is the boiling point of water; also called *centigrade*.	**Celsius** Escala métrica para medir la temperatura, en la que 0 °C es el punto de congelación del agua y 100 °C es el punto de ebullición. También se llama *centígrado*.	
center (of a circle) The point inside a circle that is the same distance from all the points on the circle.	**centro (de un círculo)** Punto interior de un círculo que se encuentra a la misma distancia de todos los puntos de la circunferencia.	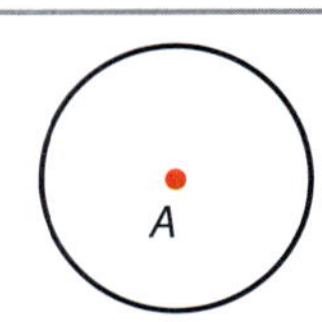
center (of rotation) The point about which a figure is rotated.	**centro (de una rotación)** Punto alrededor del cual se hace girar una figura.	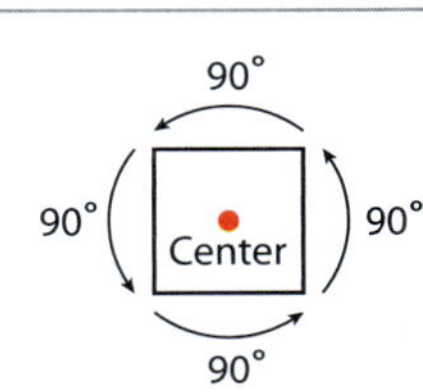

ENGLISH	SPANISH	EXAMPLES

central angle of a circle An angle with its vertex at the center of a circle.

ángulo central de un círculo Ángulo cuyo vértice se encuentra en el centro de un círculo.

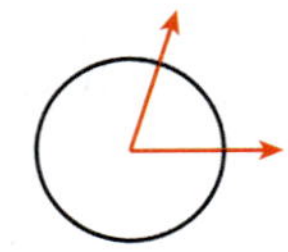

certain (probability) Sure to happen; having a probability of 1.

seguro (probabilidad) Que con seguridad sucederá. Representa una probabilidad de 1.

chord A line segment with endpoints on a circle.

cuerda Segmento de recta cuyos extremos forman parte de un círculo.

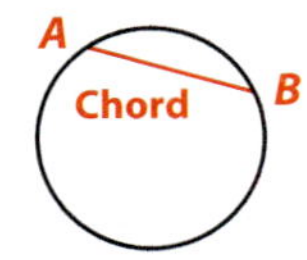

circle The set of all points in a plane that are the same distance from a given point called the center.

círculo Conjunto de todos los puntos en un plano que se encuentran a la misma distancia de un punto dado llamado centro.

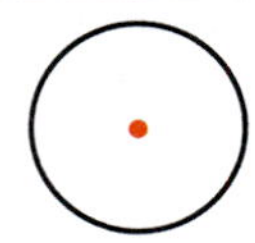

circle graph A graph that uses sectors of a circle to compare parts to the whole and parts to other parts.

gráfica circular Gráfica que usa secciones de un círculo para comparar partes con el todo y con otras partes.

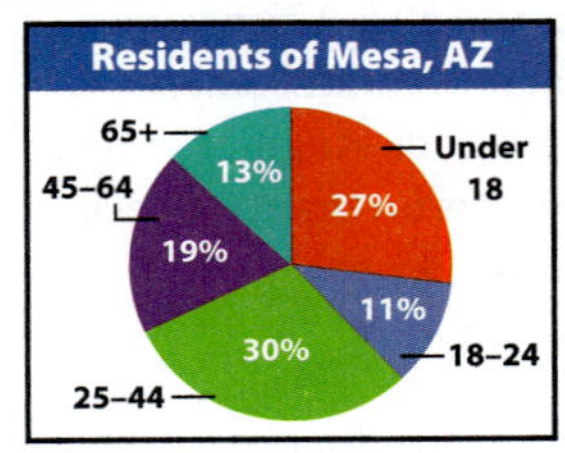

circumference The distance around a circle.

circunferencia Distancia alrededor de un círculo.

clockwise A circular movement in the direction shown.

en el sentido de las manecillas del reloj Movimiento circular en la dirección que se indica.

coefficient The number that is multiplied by the variable in an algebraic expression.

coeficiente Número que se multiplica por la variable en una expresión algebraica.

5 is the coefficient in 5*b*.

combination An arrangement of items or events in which order does not matter.

combinación Agrupación de objetos o sucesos en la cual el orden no es importante.

For objects *A*, *B*, *C*, and *D*, there are 6 different combinations of 2 objects: *AB*, *AC*, *AD*, *BC*, *BD*, *CD*.

commission A fee paid to a person for making a sale.

comisión Pago que recibe una persona por realizar una venta.

commission rate The fee paid to a person who makes a sale expressed as a percent of the selling price.

tasa de comisión Pago que recibe una persona por hacer una venta, expresado como un porcentaje del precio de venta.

A commission rate of 5% and a sale of $10,000 results in a commission of $500.

common denominator A denominator that is the same in two or more fractions.

denominador común Denominador que es común a dos o más fracciones.

The common denominator of $\frac{5}{8}$ and $\frac{2}{8}$ is 8.

ENGLISH	SPANISH	EXAMPLES
common difference In an arithmetic sequence, the nonzero constant difference of any term and the previous term.	**diferencia común** En una sucesión aritmética, diferencia constante distinta de cero entre cualquier término y el término anterior.	In the arithmetic sequence 3, 5, 7, 9, 11, …, the common difference is 2.
common factor A number that is a factor of two or more numbers.	**factor común** Número que es factor de dos o más números.	8 is a common factor of 16 and 40.
common multiple A number that is a multiple of each of two or more numbers.	**múltiplo común** Número que es múltiplo de dos o más números.	15 is a common multiple of 3 and 5.
Commutative Property of Addition The property that states that two or more numbers can be added in any order without changing the sum.	**Propiedad conmutativa de la suma** Propiedad que establece que sumar dos o más números en cualquier orden no altera la suma.	$8 + 20 = 20 + 8$
Commutative Property of Multiplication The property that states that two or more numbers can be multiplied in any order without changing the product.	**Propiedad conmutativa de la multiplicación** Propiedad que establece que multiplicar dos o más números en cualquier orden no altera el producto.	$6 \cdot 12 = 12 \cdot 6$
compatible numbers Numbers that are close to the given numbers that make estimation or mental calculation easier.	**números compatibles** Números que están cerca de los números dados y hacen más fácil la estimación o el cálculo mental.	To estimate 7,957 + 5,009, use the compatible numbers 8,000 and 5,000: 8,000 + 5,000 = 13,000.
complement The set of all outcomes that are not the event.	**complemento** La serie de resultados que no están en el suceso.	When rolling a number cube, the complement of rolling a 3 is rolling a 1, 2, 4, 5, or 6.
complementary angles Two angles whose measures add to 90°.	**ángulos complementarios** Dos ángulos cuyas medidas suman 90°.	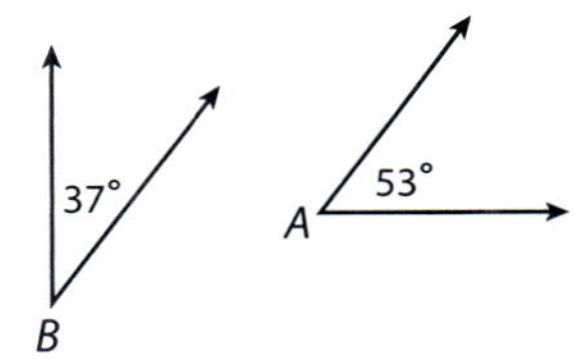
complex fraction A fraction that contains one or more fractions in the numerator, the denominator, or both.	**fracción compleja** Fracción que contiene una o más fracciones en el numerador, en el denominador, o en ambos.	
composite figure A figure made up of simple geometric shapes.	**figura compuesta** Figura formada por figuras geométricas simples.	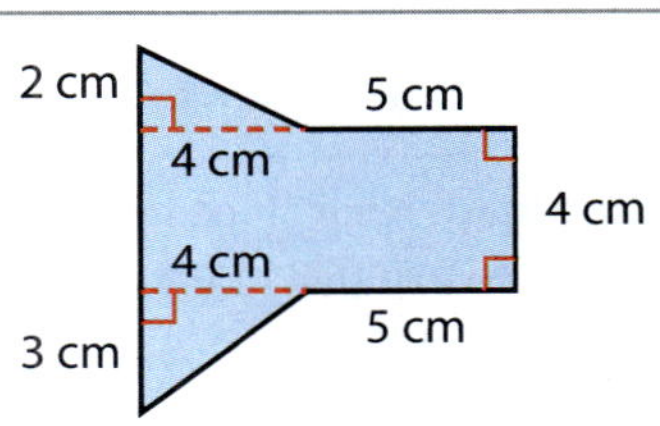
composite number A number greater than 1 that has more than two whole-number factors.	**número compuesto** Número mayor que 1 que tiene más de dos factores que son números cabales.	4, 6, 8, and 9 are composite numbers.

ENGLISH	SPANISH	EXAMPLES
compound event An event made up of two or more simple events.	**suceso compuesto** Suceso que consista de dos o más sucesos simples.	Rolling a 3 on a number cube and spinning a 2 on a spinner is a compound event.
compound inequality A combination of more than one inequality.	**desigualdad compuesta** Combinación de dos o más desigualdades.	$-2 \leq x < 10$
cone A three-dimensional figure with one vertex and one circular base.	**cono** Figura tridimensional con un vértice y una base circular.	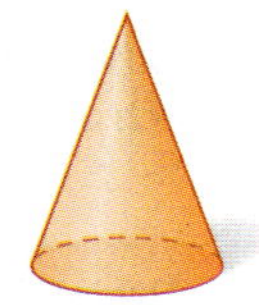
congruent Having the same size and shape; the symbol for congruent is ≅.	**congruentes** Que tiene el mismo tamaño y la misma forma, expresado por ≅.	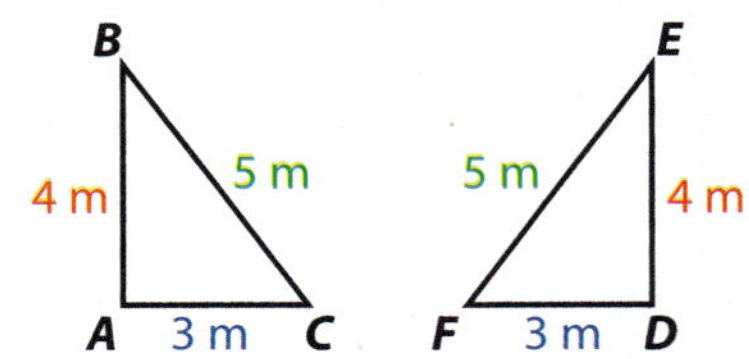 $\triangle ABC \cong \triangle DEF$
congruent angles Angles that have the same measure.	**ángulos congruentes** Ángulos que tienen la misma medida.	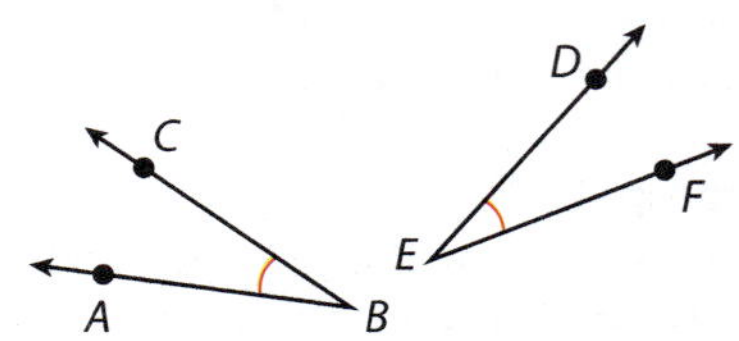 $\angle ABC \cong \angle DEF$
conjecture A statement believed to be true.	**conjetura** Enunciado que se supone verdadero.	
constant A value that does not change.	**constante** Valor que no cambia.	3, 0, π
constant of proportionality A constant ratio of two variables related proportionally.	**constante de proporcionalidad** Razón constante de dos variables que están relacionadas en forma proporcional.	
constant of variation The constant *k* in direct and inverse variation equations.	**constante de variación** La constante *k* en ecuaciones de variación directa e inversa.	$y = 5x$ ↑ constant of variation
convenience sample A sample based on members of the population that are readily available.	**muestra de conveniencia** Una muestra basada en miembros de la población que están fácilmente disponibles.	
coordinate One of the numbers of an ordered pair that locate a point on a coordinate graph.	**coordenada** Uno de los números de un par ordenado que ubica un punto en una gráfica de coordenadas.	
coordinate plane A plane formed by the intersection of a horizontal number line called the *x*-axis and a vertical number line called the *y*-axis.	**plano cartesiano** Plano formado por la intersección de una recta numérica horizontal llamada eje *x* y otra vertical llamada eje *y*.	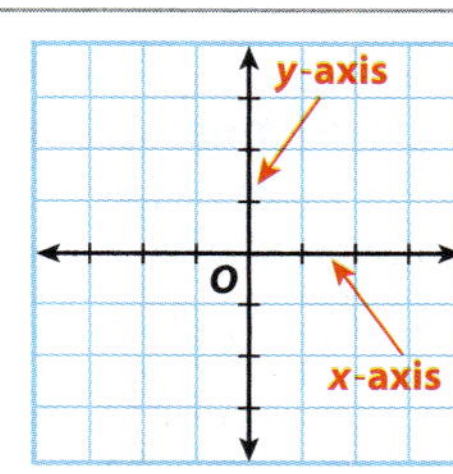

Glossary/Glosario

ENGLISH	SPANISH	EXAMPLES
correlation The description of the relationship between two data sets.	**correlación** Descripción de la relación entre dos conjuntos de datos.	
corresponding angles (for lines) Angles in the same position formed when a third line intersects two lines.	**ángulos correspondientes (en líneas)** Ángulos en la misma posición formaron cuando una tercera línea interseca dos líneas.	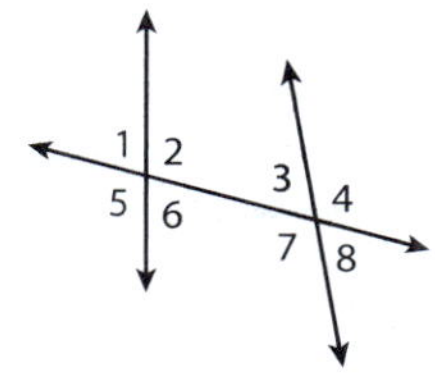 $\angle 1$ and $\angle 3$ are corresponding angles.
corresponding angles (of polygons) Angles in the same relative position in polygons with an equal number of sides.	**ángulos correspondientes (en polígonos)** Ángulos que se ubican en la misma posición relativa en dos o más polígonos.	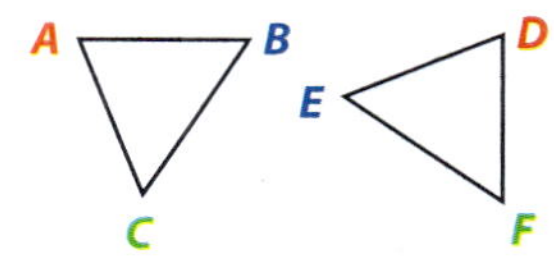 $\angle A$ and $\angle D$ are corresponding angles.
corresponding sides Matching sides of two or more polygons.	**lados correspondientes** Lados que se ubican en la misma posición relativa en dos o más polígonos.	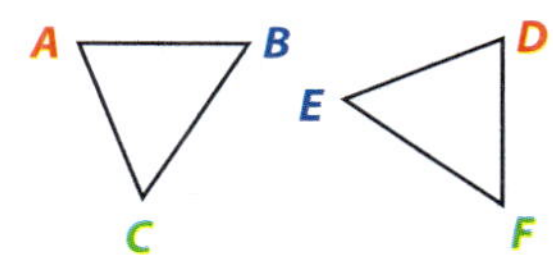 $\overline{AB}$ and $\overline{DE}$ are corresponding sides.
counterclockwise A circular movement in the direction shown.	**en sentido contrario a las manecillas del reloj** Movimiento circular en la dirección que se indica.	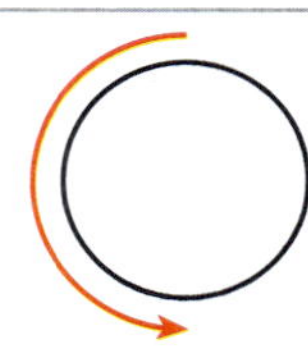
counterexample An example that shows that a statement is false.	**contraejemplo** Ejemplo que demuestra que un enunciado es falso.	
cross product The product of numbers on the diagonal when comparing two ratios.	**producto cruzado** El producto de los números multiplicados en diagonal cuando se comparan dos razones.	 For the proportion $\frac{2}{3} = \frac{4}{6}$, the cross products are $2 \cdot 6 = 12$ and $3 \cdot 4 = 12$.
cross section The intersection of a three-dimensional figure and a plane.	**sección transversal** Intersección de una figura tridimensional y un plano.	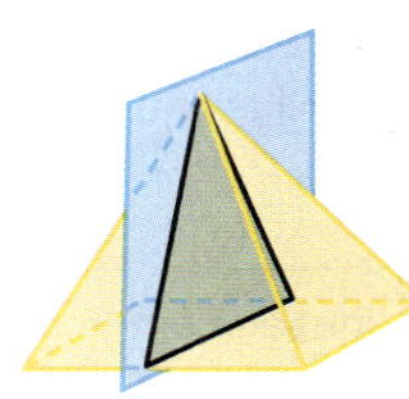
cube (geometric figure) A rectangular prism with six congruent square faces.	**cubo (figura geométrica)** Prisma rectangular con seis caras cuadradas congruentes.	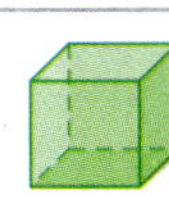
cube (in numeration) A number raised to the third power.	**cubo (en numeración)** Número elevado a la tercera potencia.	$5^3 = 5 \cdot 5 \cdot 5 = 125$

Glossary/Glosario

ENGLISH	SPANISH	EXAMPLES
cumulative frequency The frequency of all data values that are less than or equal to a given value.	**frecuencia acumulativa** La frecuencia de todos los datos que son menores que o iguales a un valor dado.	
customary system of measurement The measurement system often used in the United States.	**sistema usual de medidas** El sistema de medidas que se usa comúnmente en Estados Unidos.	inches, feet, miles, ounces, pounds, tons, cups, quarts, gallons
cylinder A three-dimensional figure with two parallel, congruent circular bases connected by a curved lateral surface.	**cilindro** Figura tridimensional con dos bases circulares paralelas y congruentes, unidas por una superficie lateral curva.	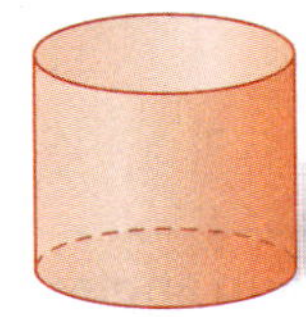

D

ENGLISH	SPANISH	EXAMPLES
decagon A polygon with ten sides.	**decágono** Polígono de 10 lados.	
decimal system A base-10 place value system.	**sistema decimal** Sistema de valor posicional de base 10.	
deductive reasoning Using logic to show that a statement is true.	**razonamiento deductivo** Uso de la lógica para demostrar que un enunciado es verdadero.	
degree The unit of measure for angles or temperature.	**grado** Unidad de medida para ángulos y temperaturas.	
denominator The bottom number of a fraction that tells how many equal parts are in the whole.	**denominador** Número de abajo de una fracción que indica en cuántas partes iguales se divide el entero.	$\frac{3}{4}$ ← Denominator
dependent events Events for which the outcome of one event affects the probability of the second event.	**sucesos dependientes** Dos sucesos son dependientes si el resultado de uno afecta la probabilidad del otro.	A bag contains 3 red marbles and 2 blue marbles. Drawing a red marble and then drawing a blue marble without replacing the first marble is an example of dependent events.
diagonal A line segment that connects two nonadjacent vertices of a polygon.	**diagonal** Segmento de recta que une dos vértices no adyacentes de un polígono.	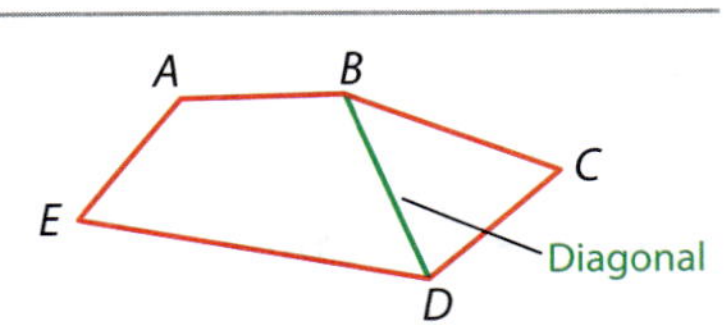
diameter A line segment that passes through the center of a circle and has endpoints on the circle, or the length of that segment.	**diámetro** Segmento de recta que pasa por el centro de un círculo y tiene sus extremos en la circunferencia, o bien la longitud de ese segmento.	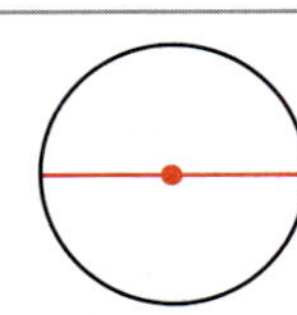
difference The result when one number is subtracted from another.	**diferencia** El resultado de restar un número de otro.	In 16 − 5 = 11, 11 is the difference.

ENGLISH	SPANISH	EXAMPLES
dimension The length, width, or height of a figure.	**dimensión** Longitud, ancho o altura de una figura.	
direct variation A linear relationship between two variables, x and y, that can be written in the form $y = kx$, where k is a nonzero constant.	**variación directa** Relación lineal entre dos variables, x e y, que puede expresarse en la forma $y = kx$, donde k es una constante distinta de cero.	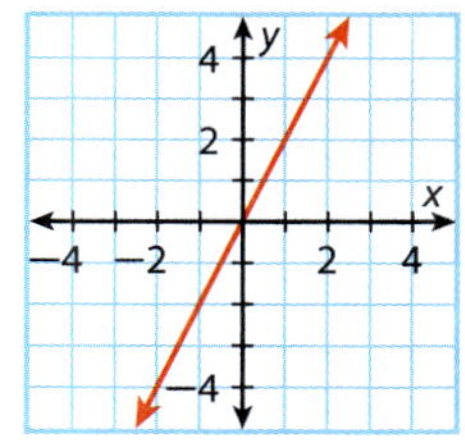 $y = 2x$
Distributive Property For all real numbers, a, b, and c, $a(b + c) = ab + ac$ and $a(b - c) = ab - ac$.	**Propiedad distributiva** Dado números reales a, b, y c, $a(b + c) = ab + ac$ y $a(b - c) = ab - ac$.	$5(20 + 1) = 5 \cdot 20 + 5 \cdot 1$
dividend The number to be divided in a division problem.	**dividendo** Número que se divide en un problema de división.	In $8 \div 4 = 2$, 8 is the dividend.
divisible Can be divided by a number without leaving a remainder.	**divisible** Que se puede dividir entre un número sin dejar residuo.	18 is divisible by 3.
Division Property of Equality The property that states that if you divide both sides of an equation by the same nonzero number, the new equation will have the same solution.	**Propiedad de igualdad de la división** Propiedad que establece que puedes dividir ambos lados de una ecuación entre el mismo número distinto de cero, y la nueva ecuación tendrá la misma solución.	$4x = 12$ $\frac{4x}{4} = \frac{12}{4}$ $x = 3$
divisor The number you are dividing by in a division problem.	**divisor** El número entre el que se divide en un problema de división.	In $8 \div 4 = 2$, 4 is the divisor.
double-bar graph A bar graph that compares two related sets of data.	**gráfica de doble barra** Gráfica de barras que compara dos conjuntos de datos relacionados.	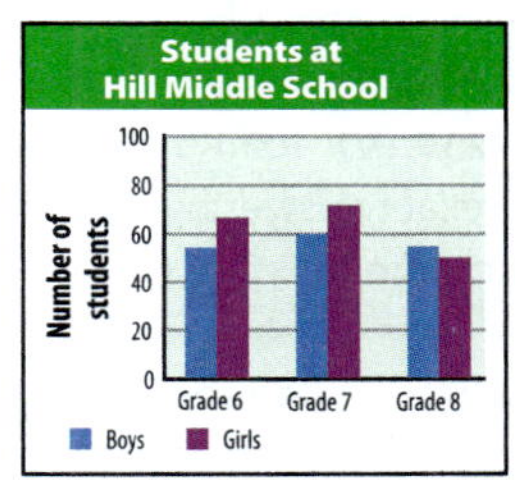
double-line graph A line graph that shows how two related sets of data change over time.	**gráfica de doble línea** Gráfica lineal que muestra cómo cambian con el tiempo dos conjuntos de datos relacionados.	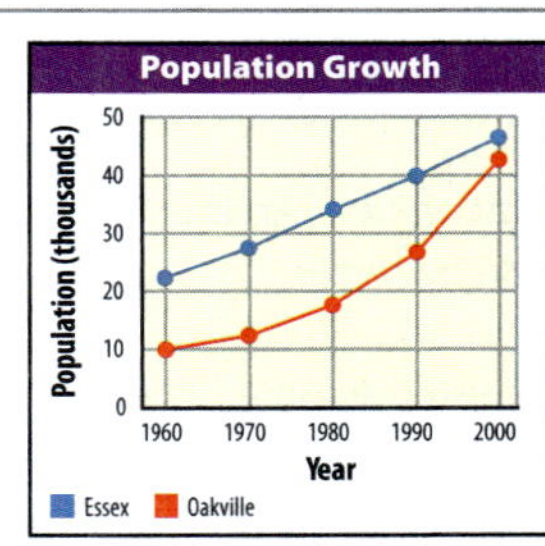

E

ENGLISH	SPANISH	EXAMPLES
edge The line segment along which two faces of a polyhedron intersect.	**arista** Segmento de recta donde se intersecan dos caras de un poliedro.	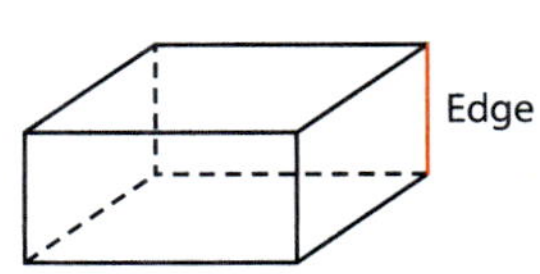

Glossary/Glosario

Glossary/Glosario

ENGLISH	SPANISH	EXAMPLES
endpoint A point at the end of a line segment or ray.	**extremo** Un punto ubicado al final de un segmento de recta o rayo.	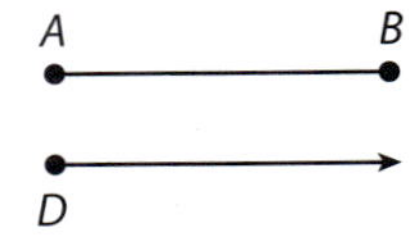
equally likely Outcomes that have the same probability.	**resultados igualmente probables** Resultados que tienen la misma probabilidad de ocurrir.	
equation A mathematical sentence that shows that two expressions are equivalent.	**ecuación** Enunciado matemático que indica que dos expresiones son equivalentes.	$x + 4 = 7$ $6 + 1 = 10 - 3$
equilateral triangle A triangle with three congruent sides.	**triángulo equilátero** Triángulo con tres lados congruentes.	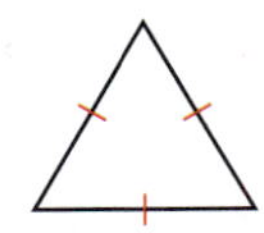
equivalent Having the same value.	**equivalentes** Que tienen el mismo valor.	
equivalent fractions Fractions that name the same amount or part.	**fracciones equivalentes** Fracciones que representan la misma cantidad o parte.	$\frac{1}{2}$ and $\frac{2}{4}$ are equivalent fractions.
equivalent ratios Ratios that name the same comparison.	**razones equivalentes** Razones que representan la misma comparación.	$\frac{1}{2}$ and $\frac{2}{4}$ are equivalent ratios.
estimate (n) An answer that is close to the exact answer and is found by rounding or other methods.	**estimación** Una solución aproximada a la respuesta exacta que se halla mediante el redondeo u otros métodos.	
estimate (v) To find an answer close to the exact answer by rounding or other methods.	**estimar** Hallar una solución aproximada a la respuesta exacta mediante el redondeo u otros métodos.	
evaluate To find the value of a numerical or algebraic expression.	**evaluar** Hallar el valor de una expresión numérica o algebraica.	Evaluate $2x + 7$ for $x = 3$. $2x + 7$ $2(3) + 7$ $6 + 7$ 13
even number An integer that is divisible by two.	**número par** Número entero divisible entre 2.	2, 4, 6
event An outcome or set of outcomes of an experiment or situation.	**suceso** Un resultado o una serie de resultados de un experimento o una situación.	When rolling a number cube, the event "an odd number" consists of the outcomes 1, 3, and 5.
expanded form A number written as the sum of the values of its digits.	**forma desarrollada** Número escrito como suma de los valores de sus dígitos.	236,536 written in expanded form is $200{,}000 + 30{,}000 + 6{,}000 + 500 + 30 + 6$.
experiment In probability, any activity based on chance, such as tossing a coin.	**experimento** En probabilidad, cualquier actividad basada en la posibilidad, como lanzar una moneda.	Tossing a coin 10 times and noting the number of "heads"

ENGLISH	SPANISH	EXAMPLES
experimental probability The ratio of the number of times an event occurs to the total number of trials, or times that the activity is performed.	**probabilidad experimental** Razón del número de veces que ocurre un suceso al número total de pruebas o al número de veces que se realiza el experimento.	Kendra attempted 27 free throws and made 16 of them. Her experimental probability of making a free throw is $\frac{\text{number made}}{\text{number attempted}} = \frac{16}{27} \approx 0.59$.
exponent The number that indicates how many times the base is used as a factor.	**exponente** Número que indica cuántas veces se usa la base como factor.	$2^3 = 2 \cdot 2 \cdot 2 = 8$; 3 is the exponent.
exponential form A number is in exponential form when it is written with a base and an exponent.	**forma exponencial** Se dice que un número está en forma exponencial cuando se escribe con una base y un exponente.	4^2 is the exponential form for $4 \cdot 4$.
expression A mathematical phrase that contains operations, numbers, and/or variables.	**expresión** Enunciado matemático que contiene operaciones, números y/o variables.	$6x + 1$

F

ENGLISH	SPANISH	EXAMPLES
face A flat surface of a polyhedron.	**cara** Superficie plana de un poliedro.	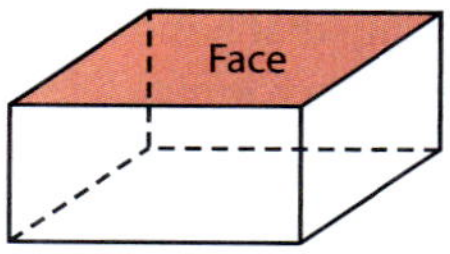
factor A number that is multiplied by another number to get a product.	**factor** Número que se multiplica por otro para hallar un producto.	7 is a factor of 21 since $7 \cdot 3 = 21$.
factor tree A diagram showing how a whole number breaks down into its prime factors.	**árbol de factores** Diagrama que muestra cómo se descompone un número cabal en sus factores primos.	12 $3 \cdot 4$ $2 \cdot 2$ $12 = 3 \cdot 2 \cdot 2$
factorial The product of all whole numbers except zero that are less than or equal to a number.	**factorial** El producto de todos los números cabales, excepto cero que son menores que o iguales a un número.	4 factorial $= 4! = 4 \cdot 3 \cdot 2 \cdot 1$
Fahrenheit A temperature scale in which 32 °F is the freezing point of water and 212 °F is the boiling point of water.	**Fahrenheit** Escala de temperatura en la que 32 °F es el punto de congelación del agua y 212 °F es el punto de ebullición.	
fair When all outcomes of an experiment are equally likely, the experiment is said to be fair.	**justo** Se dice de un experimento donde todos los resultados posibles son igualmente probables.	
federal withholding The amount of an employee's pay that the employer sends to the federal government as partial payment of the employee's yearly income tax.	**retención fiscal federal** Ingresos que descuenta un empleador y que envía al gobierno federal como pago parcial del impuesto sobre el salario anual del empleado.	

ENGLISH	SPANISH	EXAMPLES

first quartile The median of the lower half of a set of data; also called *lower quartile.*

primer cuartil La mediana de la mitad inferior de un conjunto de datos. También se llama *cuartil inferior.*

---

fixed expenses Expenses that occur regularly and stay the same.

gastos fijos Gastos que ocurren con regularidad y se mantienen igual.

---

formula A rule showing relationships among quantities.

fórmula Regla que muestra relaciones entre cantidades.

$A = lw$ is the formula for the area of a rectangle.

---

fraction A number in the form $\frac{a}{b}$, where $b \neq 0$.

fracción Número escrito en la forma $\frac{a}{b}$, donde $b \neq 0$.

---

frequency The number of times the value appears in the data set.

frecuencia Cantidad de veces que aparece el valor en un conjunto de datos.

In the data set 5, 6, 6, 7, 8, 9, the data value 6 has a frequency of 2.

---

frequency table A table that lists items together according to the number of times, or frequency, that the items occur.

tabla de frecuencia Una tabla en la que se organizan los datos de acuerdo con el número de veces que aparece cada valor (o la frecuencia).

Data set: 1, 1, 2, 2, 3, 4, 5, 5, 5, 6, 6, 6, 6
Frequency table:

Data	1	2	3	4	5	6
Frequency	2	2	1	1	3	4

---

function An input-output relationship that has exactly one output for each input.

función Relación de entrada-salida en la que a cada valor de entrada corresponde exactamente un valor de salida.

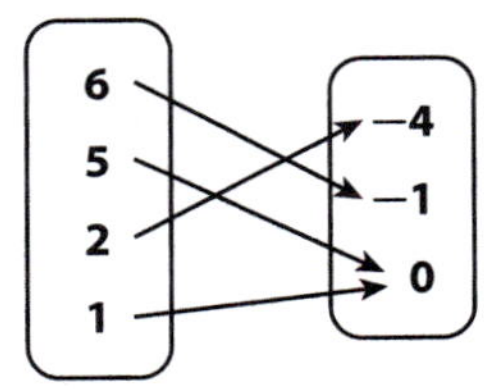

---

function table A table of ordered pairs that represent solutions of a function.

tabla de función Tabla de pares ordenados que representan soluciones de una función.

x	3	4	5	6
y	7	9	11	13

Fundamental Counting Principle If one event has *m* possible outcomes and a second event has *n* possible outcomes after the first event has occurred, then there are $m \cdot n$ total possible outcomes for the two events.

Principio fundamental de conteo Si un suceso tiene *m* resultados posibles y otro suceso tiene *n* resultados posibles después de ocurrido el primer suceso, entonces hay $m \cdot n$ resultados posibles en total para los dos sucesos.

There are 4 colors of shirts and 3 colors of pants. There are $4 \cdot 3 = 12$ possible outfits.

G

geometric sequence A sequence in which each term is multiplied by the same value to get the next term.

sucesión geométrica Una sucesión en la que cada término se multiplica por el mismo valor para obtener el siguiente término.

The sequence 2, 4, 8, 16 ... is a geometric sequence.

---

graph of an equation A graph of the set of ordered pairs that are solutions of the equation.

gráfica de una ecuación Gráfica del conjunto de pares ordenados que son soluciones de la ecuación.

---

greatest common factor (GCF) The largest common factor of two or more given numbers.

máximo común divisor (MCD) El mayor de los factores comunes compartidos por dos o más números dados.

The GCF of 27 and 45 is 9.

ENGLISH	SPANISH	EXAMPLES
gross pay An employee's pay before any deductions are taken.	**paga bruta** Paga de un empleado antes de sustraer cualquier deducción.	

H

height In a pyramid or cone, the perpendicular distance from the base to the opposite vertex.	**altura** En una pirámide o cono, la distancia perpendicular desde la base al vértice opuesto.	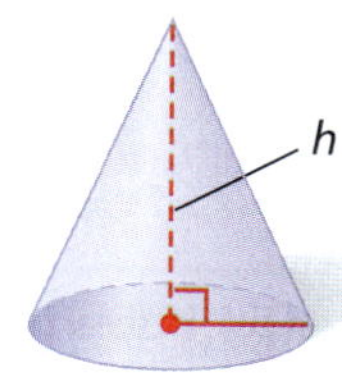
In a triangle or quadrilateral, the perpendicular distance from the base to the opposite vertex or side.	En un triángulo o cuadrilátero, la distancia perpendicular desde la base de la figura al vértice o lado opuesto.	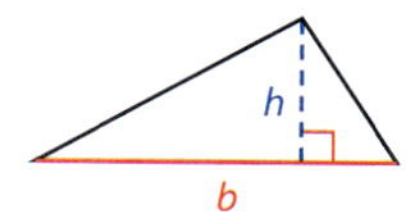
In a prism or cylinder, the perpendicular distance between the bases.	En un prisma o cilindro, la distancia perpendicular entre las bases.	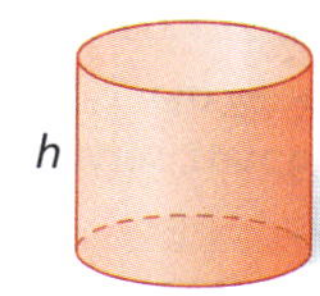
heptagon A seven-sided polygon.	**heptágono** Polígono de siete lados.	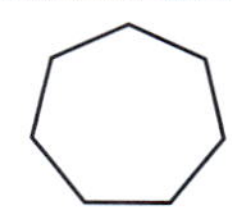
hexagon A six-sided polygon.	**hexágono** Polígono de seis lados.	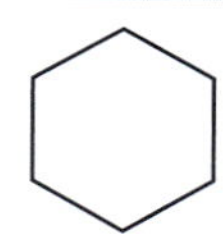
histogram A bar graph that shows the frequency of data within equal intervals.	**histograma** Gráfica de barras que muestra la frecuencia de los datos en intervalos iguales.	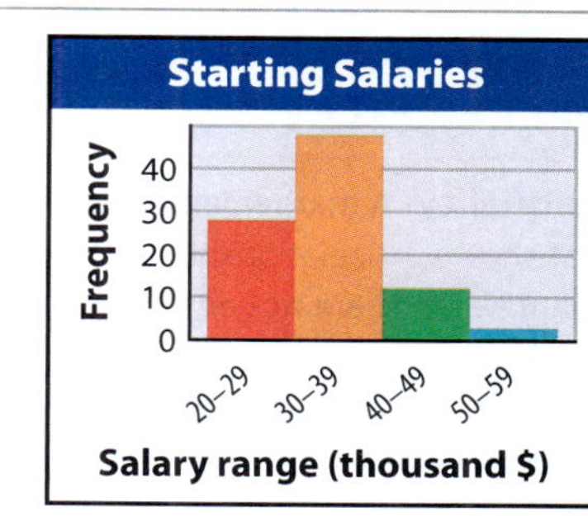
hypotenuse In a right triangle, the side opposite the right angle.	**hipotenusa** En un triángulo rectángulo, el lado opuesto al ángulo recto.	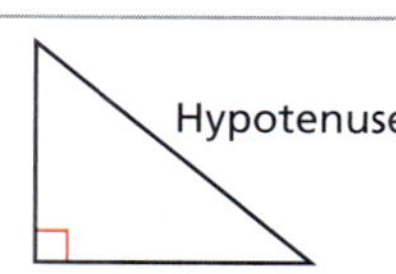

I

Identity Property of Addition The property that states that the sum of zero and any number is that number.	**Propiedad de identidad de la suma** Propiedad que establece que la suma de cero y cualquier número es ese número.	$5 + 0 = 5$ $-4 + 0 = -4$

Glossary/Glosario

ENGLISH	SPANISH	EXAMPLES
Identity Property of Multiplication The property that states that the product of 1 and any number is that number.	**Propiedad de identidad de la multiplicación** Propiedad que establece que el producto de 1 y cualquier número es ese número.	$3 \cdot 1 = 3$ $-9 \cdot 1 = -9$
image A figure resulting from a transformation.	**imagen** Figura que resulta de una transformación.	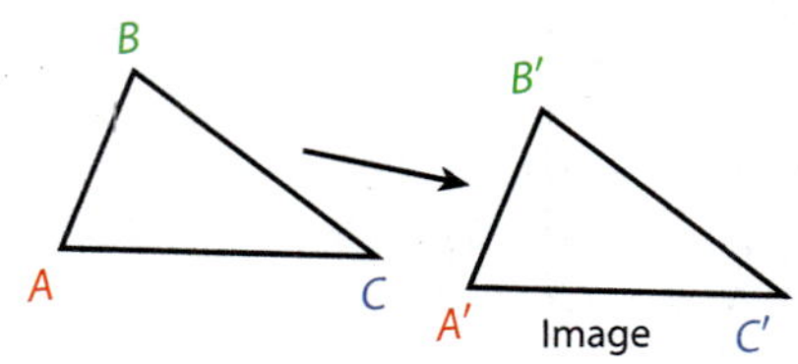
impossible (probability) Can never happen; having a probability of 0.	**imposible (en probabilidad)** Que no puede ocurrir. Suceso cuya probabilidad de ocurrir es 0.	
improper fraction A fraction in which the numerator is greater than or equal to the denominator.	**fracción impropia** Fracción en la que el numerador es mayor que o igual al denominador.	$\frac{5}{5}$ $\frac{7}{4}$
income Money that is paid to a person for goods, services, or investments.	**ingreso** Dinero que se le paga a una persona por bienes, servicios o inversiones.	
independent events Events for which the outcome of one event does not affect the probability of the other.	**sucesos independientes** Dos sucesos son independientes si el resultado de uno no afecta la probabilidad del otro.	A bag contains 3 red marbles and 2 blue marbles. Drawing a red marble, replacing it, and then drawing a blue marble is an example of independent events.
indirect measurement The technique of using similar figures and proportions to find a measure.	**medición indirecta** La técnica de usar figuras semejantes y proporciones para hallar una medida.	
inductive reasoning Using a pattern to make a conclusion.	**razonamiento inductivo** Uso de un patrón para sacar una conclusión.	
inequality A mathematical sentence that shows the relationship between quantities that are not equivalent.	**desigualdad** Enunciado matemático que muestra una relación entre cantidades que no son equivalentes.	$5 < 8$ $5x + 2 \geq 12$
input The value substituted into an expression or function.	**valor de entrada** Valor que se usa para sustituir una variable en una expresión o función.	For the function $y = 6x$, the input 4 produces an output of 24.
integers The set of whole numbers and their opposites.	**enteros** Conjunto de todos los números cabales y sus opuestos.	$\ldots -3, -2, -1, 0, 1, 2, 3, \ldots$
interest The amount of money charged for borrowing or using money, or the amount of money earned by saving money.	**interés** Cantidad de dinero que se cobra por el préstamo o uso del dinero, o la cantidad que se gana al ahorrar dinero.	

ENGLISH	SPANISH	EXAMPLES
interquartile range The difference between the upper and lower quartiles in a box-and-whisker plot.	**rango entre cuartiles** La diferencia entre los cuartiles superior e inferior en una gráfica de mediana y rango.	Lower half: 18, (23), 28; Upper half: 29, (36), 42 Lower quartile: 23; Upper quartile: 36 Interquartile range: $36 - 23 = 13$
intersecting lines Lines that cross at exactly one point.	**líneas secantes** Líneas que se cruzan en un solo punto.	
interval The space between marked values on a number line or the scale of a graph.	**intervalo** El espacio entre los valores marcados en una recta numérica o en la escala de una gráfica.	
inverse operations Operations that undo each other: addition and subtraction, or multiplication and division.	**operaciones inversas** Operaciones que se cancelan mutuamente: suma y resta, o multiplicación y división.	Addition and subtraction are inverse operations: $5 + 3 = 8; 8 - 3 = 5$ Multiplication and division are inverse operations: $2 \cdot 3 = 6; 6 \div 3 = 2$
Inverse Property of Addition The sum of a number and its opposite, or additive inverse, is 0.	**propiedad inversa de la suma** La suma de un número y su opuesto, o inverso aditivo, es cero.	$3 + (-3) = 0; a + (-a) = 0$
irrational number A number that cannot be expressed as a ratio of two integers or as a repeating or terminating decimal.	**número irracional** Número que no puede expresarse como una razón de dos enteros ni como un decimal periódico o finito.	$\sqrt{2}, \pi$
isolate the variable To get a variable alone on one side of an equation or inequality in order to solve the equation or inequality.	**despejar la variable** Dejar sola la variable en un lado de una ecuación o desigualdad para resolverla.	$x + 7 = 22$ $-7 \quad -7$ $x = 15$
isosceles triangle A triangle with at least two congruent sides.	**triángulo isósceles** Triángulo que tiene al menos dos lados congruentes.	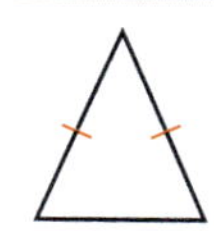

L

lateral area The sum of the areas of the lateral faces of a prism or pyramid, or the area of the lateral surface of a cylinder or cone.

área lateral Suma de las áreas de las caras laterales de un prisma o pirámide, o área de la superficie lateral de un cilindro o cono.

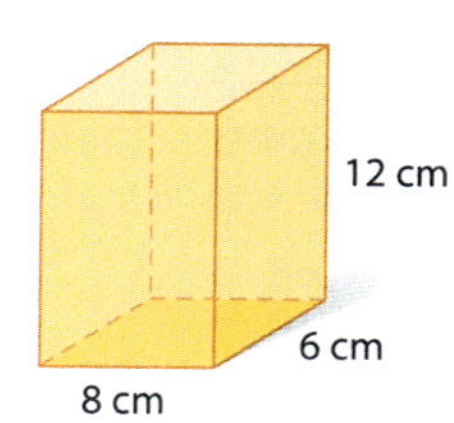

Lateral area $= 12(8)(2) + 12(6)(2)$
$= 336 \text{ cm}^2$

lateral face A face of a prism or a pyramid that is not a base.

Cara lateral Cara de un prisma o pirámide que no es una base.

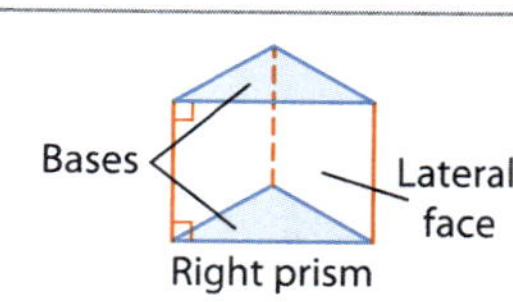

Glossary/Glosario

ENGLISH	SPANISH	EXAMPLES
least common denominator (LCD) The least common multiple of two or more denominators.	**mínimo común denominador (mcd)** El mínimo común múltiplo de dos o más denominadores.	The LCD of $\frac{3}{4}$ and $\frac{5}{6}$ is 12.
least common multiple (LCM) The least number, other than zero, that is a multiple of two or more given numbers.	**mínimo común múltiplo (mcm)** El menor de los números, distinto de cero, que es múltiplo de dos o más números.	The LCM of 10 and 18 is 90.
legs In a right triangle, the sides that include the right angle; in an isosceles triangle, the pair of congruent sides.	**catetos** En un triángulo rectángulo, los lados adyacentes al ángulo recto. En un triángulo isósceles, el par de lados congruentes.	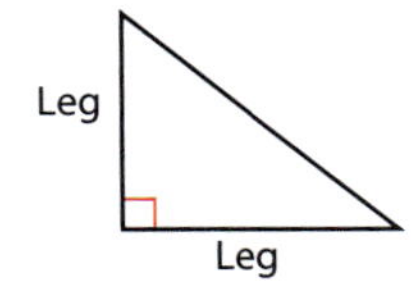
liability Money a person owes.	**pasivo** Dinero que debe una persona.	
like terms Terms with the same variables raised to the same exponents.	**términos semejantes** Términos que contienen las mismas variables elevada a las mismas exponentes.	In the expression $3a^2 + 5b + 12a^2$, $3a^2$ and $12a^2$ are like terms.
line A straight path that has no thickness and extends forever.	**línea** Trayectoria recta que no tiene ningún grueso y que se extiende por siempre.	
line graph A graph that uses line segments to show how data changes.	**gráfica lineal** Gráfica que muestra cómo cambian los datos mediante segmentos de recta.	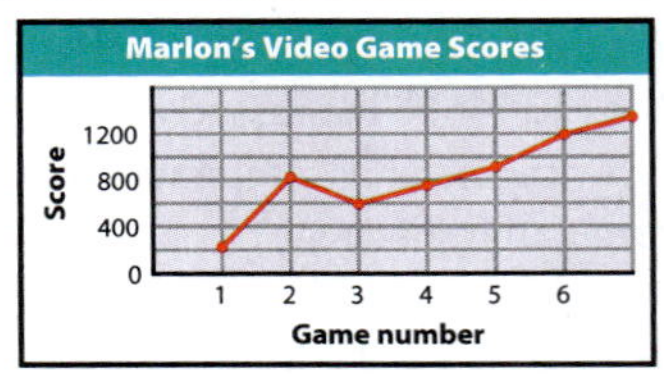
line of best fit A straight line that comes closest to the points on a scatter plot.	**línea de mejor ajuste** la línea recta que más se aproxima a los puntos de un diagrama de dispersión.	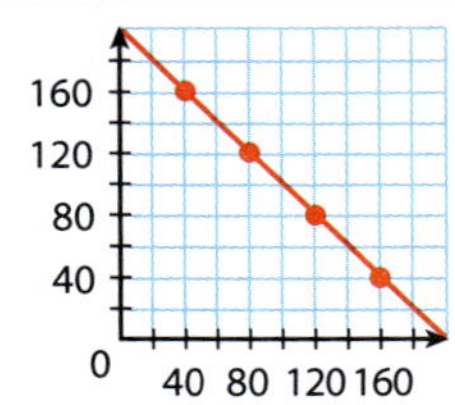
line of reflection A line that a figure is flipped across to create a mirror image of the original figure.	**línea de reflexión** Línea sobre la cual se invierte una figura para crear una imagen reflejada de la figura original.	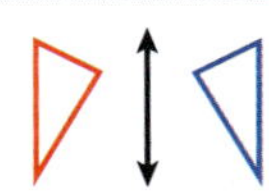 **Line of reflection**
line of symmetry The imaginary "mirror" in line symmetry.	**eje de simetría** El "espejo" imaginario en la simetría axial.	
line plot A number line with marks or dots that show frequency.	**diagrama de acumulación** Recta numérica con marcas o puntos que indican la frecuencia.	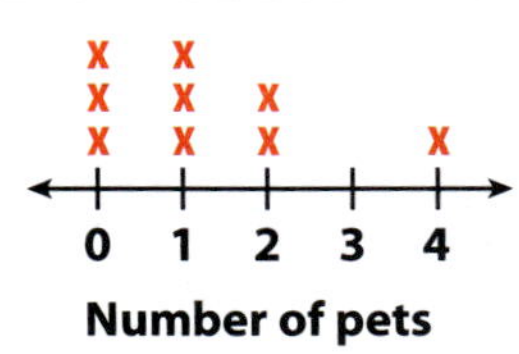

ENGLISH	SPANISH	EXAMPLES
line segment A part of a line made of two endpoints and all points between them.	**segmento de recta** Parte de una línea con dos extremos.	
line symmetry A figure has line symmetry if one-half is a mirror-image of the other half.	**simetría axial** Una figura tiene simetría axial si una de sus mitades es la imagen reflejada de la otra.	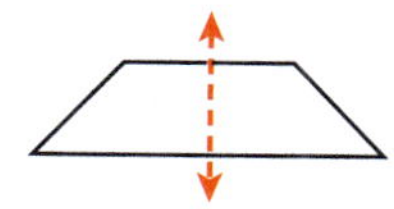
linear equation An equation whose solutions form a straight line on a coordinate plane.	**ecuación lineal** Ecuación cuyas soluciones forman una línea recta en un plano cartesiano.	$y = 2x + 1$
linear function A function whose graph is a straight line.	**función lineal** Función cuya gráfica es una línea recta.	$y = x - 1$ 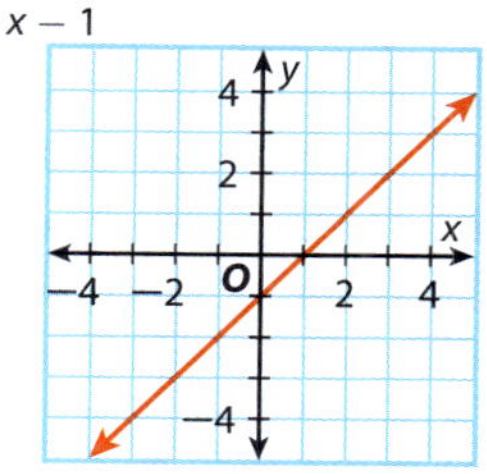
linear relationship A relationship between two quantities in which one variable changes by a constant amount as the other variable changes by a constant amount.	**relación lineal** Relación entre dos cantidades en la cual una variable cambia según una cantidad constante y la otra variable también cambia según una cantidad constante.	
lower quartile The median of the lower half of a set of data.	**cuartil inferior** La mediana de la mitad inferior de un conjunto de datos.	Lower half Upper half 18, (23,) 28, 29, 36, 42 ↑ Lower quartile

M

ENGLISH	SPANISH	EXAMPLES
mean The sum of the items in a set of data divided by the number of items in the set; also called *average*.	**media** La suma de todos loselementos de un conjunto de datos dividida entre el número de elementos del conjunto. También se llama *promedio*.	Data set: 4, 6, 7, 8, 10 Mean: $\frac{4+6+7+8+10}{5} = \frac{35}{5} = 7$
mean absolute deviation (MAD) The mean distance between each data value and the mean of the data set.	**desviación absoluta media (DAM)** Distancia media entre cada dato y la media del conjunto de datos.	
measure of central tendency A measure used to describe the middle of a data set; the mean, median, and mode are measures of central tendency.	**medida de tendencia dominante** Medida que describe la parte media de un conjunto de datos; la media, la mediana y la moda son medidas de tendencia dominante.	
median The middle number, or the mean (average) of the two middle numbers, in an ordered set of data.	**mediana** El número intermedio, o la media (el promedio), de los dos números intermedios en un conjunto ordenado de datos.	Data set: 4, 6, 7, 8, 10 Median: 7

ENGLISH	SPANISH	EXAMPLES
metric system of measurement A decimal system of weights and measures that is used universally in science and commonly worldwide.	**sistema métrico de medición** Sistema decimal de pesos y medidas empleado universalmente en las ciencias y comúnmente en todo el mundo.	centimeters, meters, kilometers, grams, kilograms, milliliters, liters
midpoint The point that divides a line segment into two congruent line segments.	**punto medio** El punto que divide un segmento de recta en dos segmentos de recta congruentes.	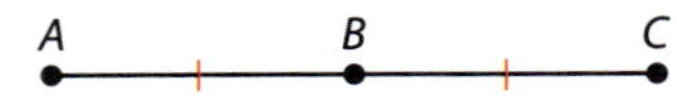 B is the midpoint of $\overline{AC}$.
mixed number A number made up of a whole number that is not zero and a fraction.	**número mixto** Número compuesto por un número cabal distinto de cero y una fracción.	$5\frac{1}{8}$
mode The number or numbers that occur most frequently in a set of data; when all numbers occur with the same frequency, we say there is no mode.	**moda** Número o números más frecuentes en un conjunto de datos; si todos los números aparecen con la misma frecuencia, no hay moda.	Data set: 3, 5, 8, 8, 10 Mode: 8
multiple The product of any number and any nonzero whole number is a multiple of that number.	**múltiplo** El producto de un número y cualquier número cabal distinto de cero es un múltiplo de ese número.	30, 40, and 90 are all multiples of 10.
Multiplication Property of Equality The property that states that if you multiply both sides of an equation by the same number, the new equation will have the same solution.	**Propiedad de igualdad de la multiplicación** Propiedad que establece que puedes multiplicar ambos lados de una ecuación por el mismo número y la nueva ecuación tendrá la misma solución.	$\frac{1}{3}x = 7$ $(3)(\frac{1}{3}x) = (3)(7)$ $x = 21$
Multiplication Property of Zero The property that states that for all real numbers a, $a \times 0 = 0$ and $0 \times a = 0$.	**Propiedad de multiplicación del cero** Propiedad que establece que para todos los números reales a, $a \times 0 = 0$ y $0 \times a = 0$.	$6 \cdot 0 = 0$ $-5 \cdot 0 = 0$
Multiplicative Inverse Property The product of a nonzero number and its reciprocal, or multiplicative inverse, is one.	**Propiedad inversa de la multiplicación** El producto de un número distinto a cero y su recíproco, o inverso multiplicativo, es uno.	$\frac{2}{3} \cdot \frac{3}{2} = 1; \frac{a}{b} \cdot \frac{b}{a} = 1$
mutually exclusive Two events are mutually exclusive if they cannot occur in the same trial of an experiment.	**mutuamente excluyentes** Dos sucesos son mutuamente excluyentes cuando no pueden ocurrir en la misma prueba de un experimento.	

N

ENGLISH	SPANISH	EXAMPLES
negative correlation Two data sets have a negative correlation, or relationship, if one set of data values increases while the other decreases.	**correlación negativa** Dos conjuntos de datos tienen correlación, o relación, negativa, si los valores de un conjunto aumentan a medida que los valores del otro conjunto disminuyen.	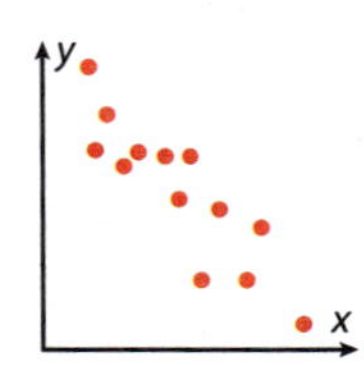
negative integer An integer less than zero.	**entero negativo** Entero menor que cero.	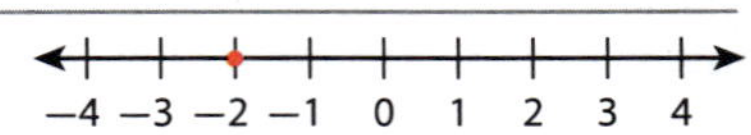 −2 is a negative integer.

ENGLISH	SPANISH	EXAMPLES
net An arrangement of two-dimensional figures that can be folded to form a polyhedron.	**plantilla** Arreglo de figuras bidimensionales que se doblan para formar un poliedro.	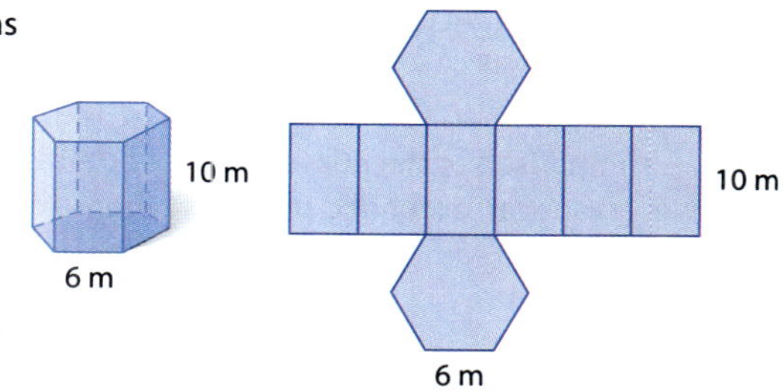
net pay The amount that remains after all deductions are taken from the gross pay.	**paga neta** Cantidad restante después de restar todas las deducciones de la paga bruta.	
net worth The difference between the monetary values of a consumer's assets and liabilities.	**patrimonio neto** Diferencia entre el valor monetario de los activos y pasivos de un consumidor.	
no correlation Two data sets have no correlation when there is no relationship between their data values.	**sin correlación** Caso en que los valores de dos conjuntos de datos no muestran ninguna relación.	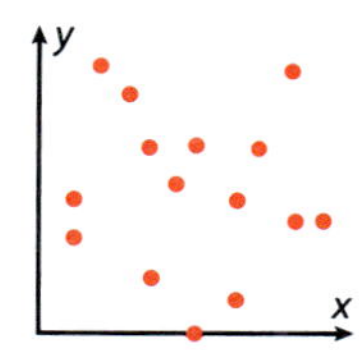
nonlinear function A function whose graph is not a straight line.	**función no lineal** Función cuya gráfica no es una línea recta.	
nonterminating decimal A decimal that never ends.	**decimal infinito** Decimal que nunca termina.	
numerator The top number of a fraction that tells how many parts of a whole are being considered.	**numerador** El número de arriba de una fracción; indica cuántas partes de un entero se consideran.	$\frac{4}{5}$ ← Numerator
numerical expression An expression that contains only numbers and operations.	**expresión numérica** Expresión que incluye sólo números y operaciones.	$(2 \cdot 3) + 1$

O

ENGLISH	SPANISH	EXAMPLES
obtuse angle An angle whose measure is greater than 90° but less than 180°.	**ángulo obtuso** Ángulo que mide más de 90° y menos de 180°.	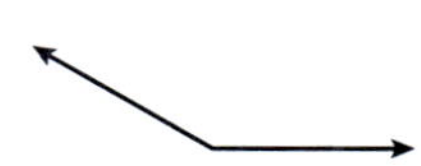
obtuse triangle A triangle containing one obtuse angle.	**triángulo obtusángulo** Triángulo que tiene un ángulo obtuso.	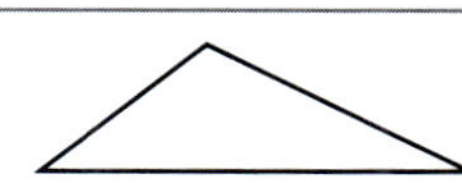
octagon An eight-sided polygon.	**octágono** Polígono de ocho lados.	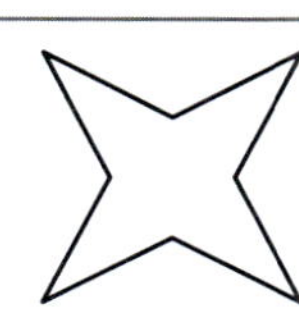

ENGLISH	SPANISH	EXAMPLES
odd number An integer that is not divisible by two.	**número impar** Entero que no es divisible entre 2.	
odds A comparison of the number of ways an event can occur and the number of ways an event can NOT occur.	**posibilidades** Comparación del número de las maneras que puede ocurrir un suceso y el número de maneras que no puede ocurrir el suceso.	
opposites Two numbers that are an equal distance from zero on a number line; also called *additive inverse.*	**opuestos** Dos números que están a la misma distancia de cero en una recta numérica. También se llaman *inversos aditivos.*	5 and −5 are opposites. 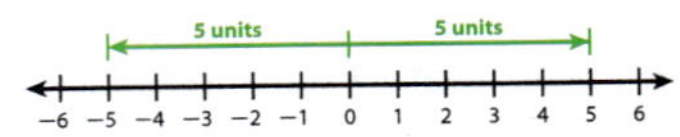
order of operations A rule for evaluating expressions: first perform the operations in parentheses, then compute powers and roots, then perform all multiplication and division from left to right, and then perform all addition and subtraction from left to right.	**orden de las operaciones** Regla para evaluar expresiones: primero se hacen las operaciones entre paréntesis, luego se hallan las potencias y raíces, después todas las multiplicaciones y divisiones de izquierda a derecha y, por último, todas las sumas y restas de izquierda a derecha.	$3^2 - 12 \div 4$ $9 - 12 \div 4$ Evaluate the power. $9 - 3$ Divide. 6 Subtract.
ordered pair A pair of numbers that can be used to locate a point on a coordinate plane.	**par ordenado** Par de números que sirven para ubicar un punto en un plano cartesiano.	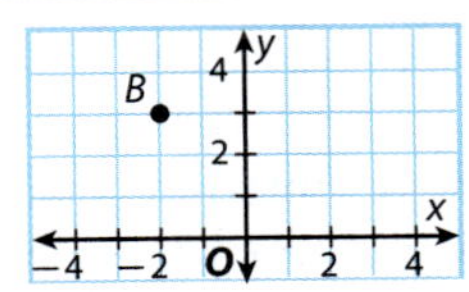 The coordinates of *B* are (−2, 3).
origin The point where the *x*-axis and *y*-axis intersect on the coordinate plane; (0, 0).	**origen** Punto de intersección entre el eje *x* y el eje *y* en un plano cartesiano: (0, 0).	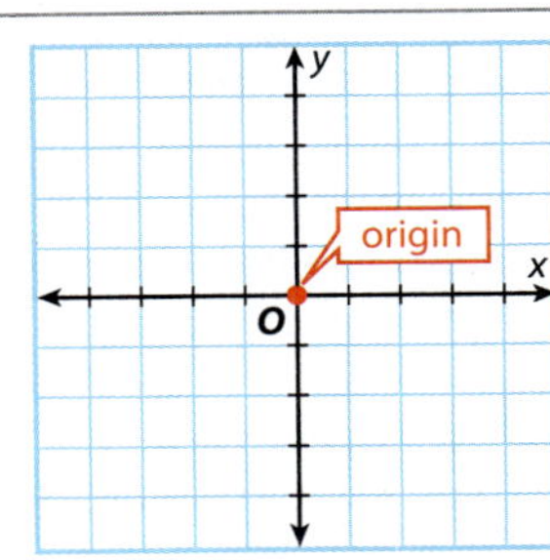
outcome A possible result of a probability experiment.	**resultado** Posible resultado de un experimento de probabilidad.	When rolling a number cube, the possible outcomes are 1, 2, 3, 4, 5, and 6.
outlier A value much greater or much less than the others in a data set.	**valor extremo** Un valor mucho mayor o menor que los demás de un conjunto de datos.	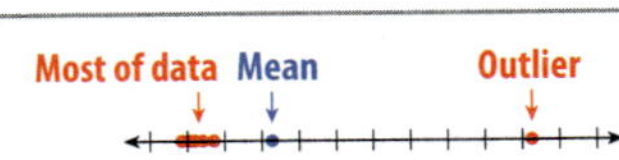
output The value that results from the substitution of a given input into an expression or function.	**valor de salida** Valor que resulta después de sustituir un valor de entrada determinado en una expresión o función.	For the function $y = 6x$, the input 4 produces an output of 24.
overestimate An estimate that is greater than the exact answer.	**estimación alta** Estimación mayor que la respuesta exacta.	100 is an overestimate for the sum $23 + 24 + 21 + 22$.

P

ENGLISH	SPANISH	EXAMPLES
parallel lines Lines in a plane that do not intersect.	**líneas paralelas** Líneas que se encuentran en el mismo plano pero que nunca se intersecan.	
parallelogram A quadrilateral with two pairs of parallel sides.	**paralelogramo** Cuadrilátero con dos pares de lados paralelos.	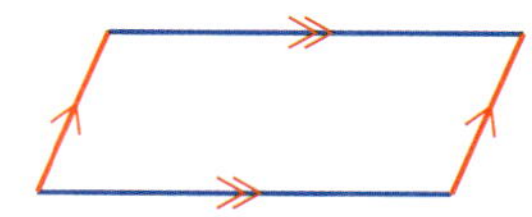
pentagon A five-sided polygon.	**pentágono** Polígono de cinco lados.	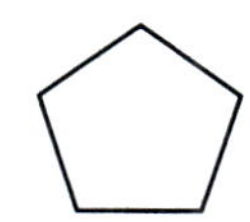
percent A ratio comparing a number to 100.	**porcentaje** Razón que compara un número con el número 100.	$45\% = \frac{45}{100}$
percent of change The amount stated as a percent that a number increases or decreases.	**porcentaje de cambio** Cantidad en que un número aumenta o disminuye, expresada como un porcentaje.	
percent of decrease A percent change describing a decrease in a quantity.	**porcentaje de disminución** Porcentaje de cambio en que una cantidad disminuye.	An item that costs \$8 is marked down to \$6. The amount of the decrease is \$2, and the percent of decrease is $\frac{2}{8} = 0.25 = 25\%$.
percent of increase A percent change describing an increase in a quantity.	**porcentaje de incremento** Porcentaje de cambio en que una cantidad aumenta.	The price of an item increases from \$8 to \$12. The amount of the increase is \$4, and the percent of increase is $\frac{4}{8} = 0.5 = 50\%$.
perfect square A square of a whole number.	**cuadrado perfecto** El cuadrado de un número cabal.	$5^2 = 25$, so 25 is a perfect square.
perimeter The distance around a polygon.	**perímetro** Distancia alrededor de un polígono.	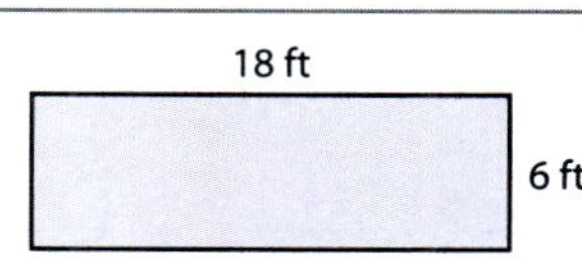 perimeter = $18 + 6 + 18 + 6 = 48$ ft
permutation An arrangement of items or events in which order is important.	**permutación** Arreglo de objetos o sucesos en el que el orden es importante.	For objects *A*, *B*, and *C*, there are 6 different permutations, *ABC*, *ACB*, *BAC*, *BCA*, *CAB*, and *CBA*.
perpendicular bisector A line that intersects a segment at its midpoint and is perpendicular to the segment.	**mediatriz** Línea que cruza un segmento en su punto medio y es perpendicular al segmento.	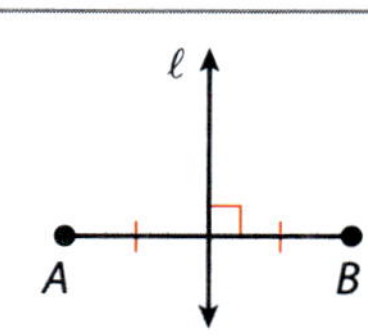

Glossary/Glosario

ENGLISH	SPANISH	EXAMPLES
perpendicular lines Lines that intersect to form right angles.	**líneas perpendiculares** Líneas que al intersecarse forman ángulos rectos.	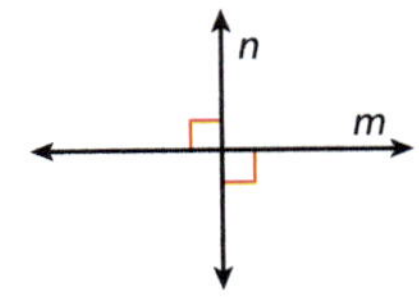
pi (π) The ratio of the circumference of a circle to the length of its diameter; $\pi \approx 3.14$ or $\frac{22}{7}$.	**pi (π)** Razón de la circunferencia de un círculo a la longitud de su diámetro; $\pi \approx$ 3.14 ó $\frac{22}{7}$.	
plane A flat surface that has no thickness and extends forever.	**plano** Superficie plana que no tiene ningún grueso y que se extiende por siempre.	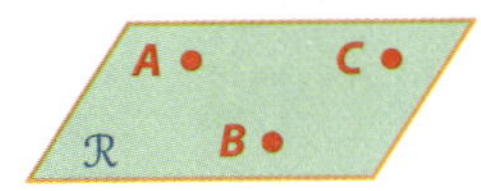 plane *ABC*
point An exact location that has no size.	**punto** Ubicación exacta que no tiene ninqún tamaño.	 point *P*
polygon A closed plane figure formed by three or more line segments that intersect only at their endpoints (vertices).	**polígono** Figura plana cerrada, formada por tres o más segmentos de recta que se intersecan sólo en sus extremos (vértices).	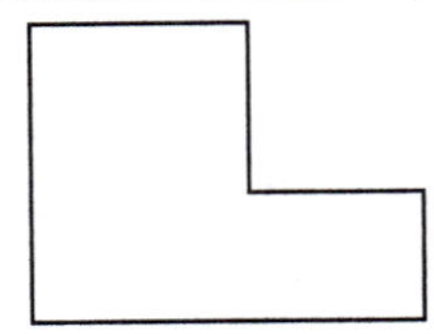
polyhedron A three-dimensional figure in which all the surfaces or faces are polygons.	**poliedro** Figura tridimensional cuyas superficies o caras tienen forma de polígonos.	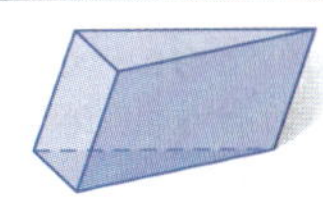
population The entire group of objects or individuals considered for a survey.	**población** Grupo completo de objetos o individuos que se desea estudiar.	In a survey about the study habits of middle school students, the population is all middle school students.
positive correlation Two data sets have a positive correlation, or relationship, when their data values increase or decrease together.	**correlación positiva** Dos conjuntos de datos tienen una correlación, o relación, positiva cuando los valores de ambos conjuntos aumentan o disminuyen al mismo tiempo.	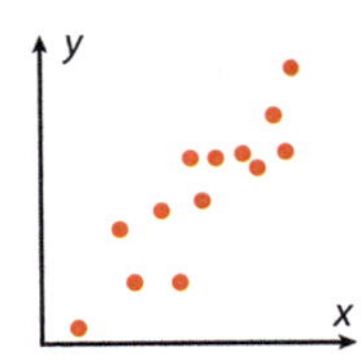
positive integer An integer greater than zero.	**entero positivo** Entero mayor que cero.	
power A number produced by raising a base to an exponent.	**potencia** Número que resulta al elevar una base a un exponente.	$2^3 = 8$, so 2 to the 3rd power is 8.
precision The level of detail of a measurement, determined by the unit of measure.	**precisión** Detalle de una medición, determinado por la unidad de medida.	A ruler marked in millimeters has a greater level of precision than a ruler marked in centimeters.
prediction Something you can reasonably expect to happen in the future.	**predicción** Algo que se puede razonablemente esperar suceder en el futuro.	

ENGLISH	SPANISH	EXAMPLES
preimage The original figure in a transformation.	**imagen original** Figura original en una transformación.	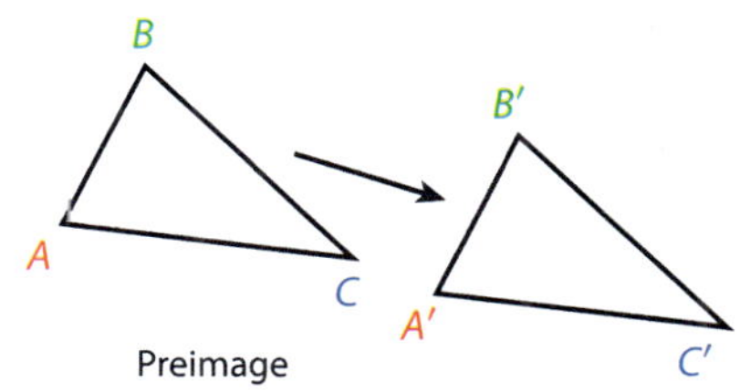
prime factorization A number written as the product of its prime factors.	**factorización prima** Un número escrito como el producto de sus factores primos.	$10 = 2 \cdot 5$ $24 = 2^3 \cdot 3$
prime number A whole number greater than 1 that has exactly two factors, itself and 1.	**número primo** Número cabal mayor que 1 que sólo es divisible entre 1 y él mismo.	5 is prime because its only factors are 5 and 1.
principal The initial amount of money borrowed or saved.	**capital** Cantidad inicial de dinero depositada o recibida en préstamo.	
prism A polyhedron that has two congruent polygon-shaped bases and other faces that are all parallelograms.	**prisma** Poliedro con dos bases congruentes con forma de polígono y caras con forma de paralelogramo.	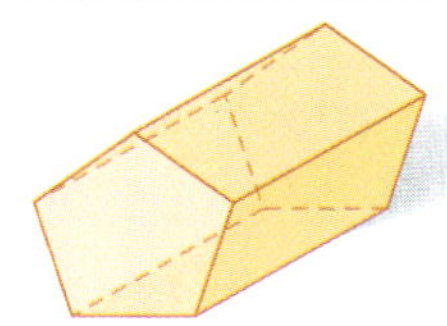
probability A number from 0 to 1 (or 0% to 100%) that describes how likely an event is to occur.	**probabilidad** Un número entre 0 y 1 (ó 0% y 100%) que describe qué tan probable es un suceso.	A bag contains 3 red marbles and 4 blue marbles. The probability of randomly choosing a red marble is $\frac{3}{7}$.
product The result when two or more numbers are multiplied.	**producto** Resultado de multiplicar dos o más números.	The product of 4 and 8 is 32.
proper fraction A fraction in which the numerator is less than the denominator.	**fracción propia** Fracción en la que el numerador es menor que el denominador.	$\frac{3}{4}, \frac{1}{12}, \frac{7}{8}$
proportion An equation that states that two ratios are equivalent.	**proporción** Ecuación que establece que dos razones son equivalentes.	$\frac{2}{3} = \frac{4}{6}$
proportional relationship A relationship between two quantities in which the ratio of one quantity to the other quantity is constant.	**relación proporcional** Relación entre dos cantidades en que la razón de una cantidad a la otra es constante.	
protractor A tool for measuring angles.	**transportador** Instrumento para medir ángulos.	
pyramid A polyhedron with a polygon base and triangular sides that all meet at a common vertex.	**pirámide** Poliedro cuya base es un polígono; tiene caras triangulares que se juntan en un vértice común.	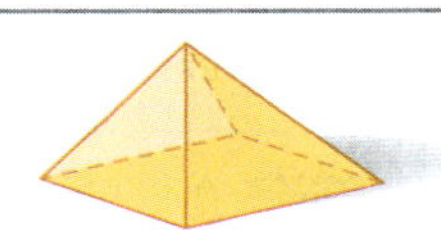

ENGLISH	SPANISH	EXAMPLES
Pythagorean Theorem In a right triangle, the square of the length of the hypotenuse is equal to the sum of the squares of the lengths of the legs.	**Teorema de Pitágoras** En un triángulo rectángulo, la suma de los cuadrados de los catetos es igual al cuadrado de la hipotenusa.	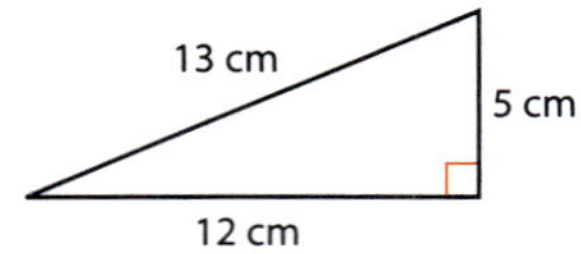 $5^2 + 12^2 = 13^2$ $25 + 144 = 169$

Q

ENGLISH	SPANISH	EXAMPLES
quadrant The x- and y-axes divide the coordinate plane into four regions. Each region is called a quadrant.	**cuadrante** El eje x y el eje y dividen el plano cartesiano en cuatro regiones. Cada región recibe el nombre de cuadrante.	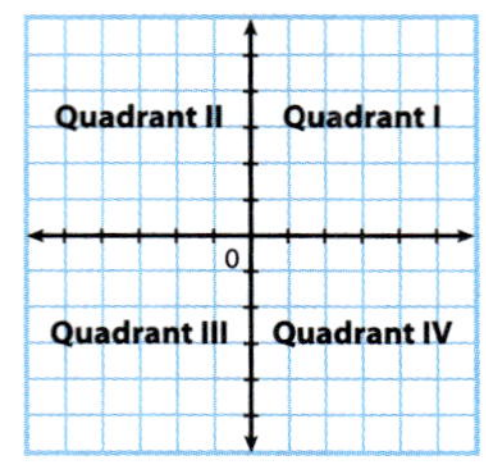
quadratic function A function of the form $y = ax^2 + bx + c$, where $a \neq 0$.	**función cuadrática** Función del tipo $y = ax^2 + bx + c$, donde $a \neq 0$.	$y = 2x^2 - 12x + 10$, $y = 3x^2$
quadrilateral A four-sided polygon.	**cuadrilátero** Polígono de cuatro lados.	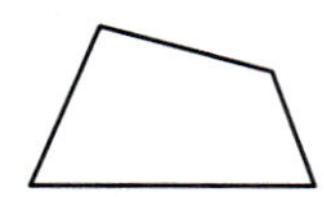
quartile Three values, one of which is the median, that divide a data set into fourths. See also *first quartile, third quartile.*	**cuartiles** Cada uno de tres valores, uno de los cuales es la mediana, que dividen en cuartos un conjunto de datos. Ver también *primer cuartil, tercer cuartil.*	
quotient The result when one number is divided by another.	**cociente** Resultado de dividir un número entre otro.	In $8 \div 4 = 2$, 2 is the quotient.

R

ENGLISH	SPANISH	EXAMPLES
radical sign The symbol $\sqrt{\ }$ used to represent the nonnegative square root of a number.	**símbolo de radical** El símbolo $\sqrt{\ }$ con que se representa la raíz cuadrada no negativa de un número.	$\sqrt{36} = 6$
radius A line segment with one endpoint at the center of a circle and the other endpoint on the circle, or the length of that segment.	**radio** Segmento de recta con un extremo en el centro de un círculo y el otro en la circunferencia; o bien la longitud de ese segmento.	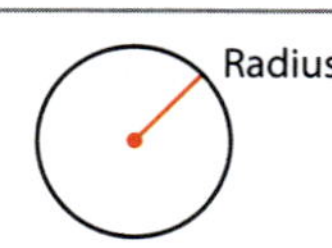
random sample A sample in which each individual or object in the entire population has an equal chance of being selected.	**muestra aleatoria** Muestra en la que cada individuo u objeto de la población tiene la misma oportunidad de ser elegido.	Mr. Henson chose a random sample of the class by writing each student's name on a slip of paper, mixing up the slips, and drawing five slips without looking.

ENGLISH	SPANISH	EXAMPLES
range (in statistics) The difference between the greatest and least values in a data set.	**rango (en estadística)** Diferencia entre los valores máximo y mínimo de un conjunto de datos.	Data set: 3, 5, 7, 7, 12 Range: $12 - 3 = 9$
rate A ratio that compares two quantities measured in different units.	**tasa** Una razón que compara dos cantidades medidas en diferentes unidades.	The speed limit is 55 miles per hour, or 55 mi/h.
rate of change A ratio that compares the amount of change in a dependent variable to the amount of change in an independent variable.	**tasa de cambio** Razón que compara la cantidad de cambio de la variable dependiente con la cantidad de combio de la variable independiente.	The cost of mailing a letter increased from 22 cents in 1985 to 25 cents in 1988. During this period, the rate of change was $\frac{\text{change in cost}}{\text{change in year}} = \frac{25 - 22}{1988 - 1985} = \frac{3}{3}$
rate of interest The percent charged or earned on an amount of money; see *simple interest.*	**tasa de interés** Porcentaje que se cobra por una cantidad de dinero prestada o que se gana por una cantidad de dinero ahorrada; ver *interés simple.*	
ratio A comparison of two quantities by division.	**razón** Comparación de dos cantidades mediante una división.	12 to 25, 12:25, $\frac{12}{25}$
rational number Any number that can be expressed as a ratio of two integers.	**número racional** Número que se puede escribir como una razón de dos enteros.	6 can be expressed as $\frac{6}{1}$. 0.5 can be expressed as $\frac{1}{2}$.
ray A part of a line that starts at one endpoint and extends forever in one direction.	**rayo** Parte de una recta que comienza en un extremo y se extiende infinitamente en una dirección.	
real number A rational or irrational number.	**número real** Número racional o irracional.	
reciprocal One of two numbers whose product is 1; also called *multiplicative inverse.*	**recíproco** Uno de dos números cuyo producto es igual a 1. También se llama *inverso multiplicativo.*	The reciprocal of $\frac{2}{3}$ is $\frac{3}{2}$.
rectangle A parallelogram with four right angles.	**rectángulo** Paralelogramo con cuatro ángulos rectos.	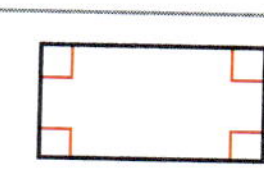
rectangular prism A polyhedron whose bases are rectangles and whose other faces are parallelograms.	**prisma rectangular** Poliedro cuyas bases son rectángulos y cuyas caras tienen forma de paralelogramo.	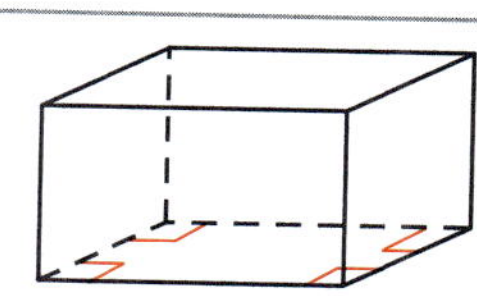
reflection A transformation of a figure that flips the figure across a line.	**reflexión** Transformación que ocurre cuando se invierte una figura sobre una línea.	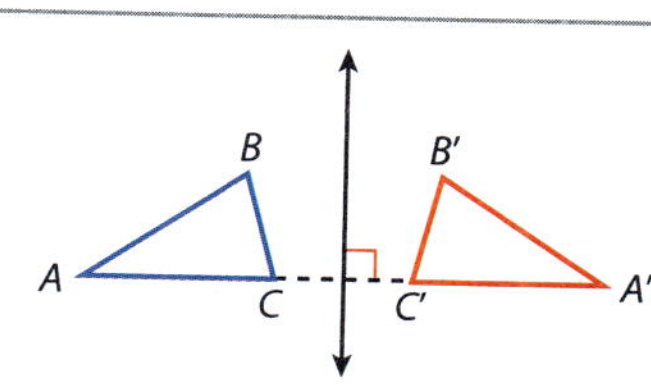
regular polygon A polygon with congruent sides and angles.	**polígono regular** Polígono con lados y ángulos congruentes.	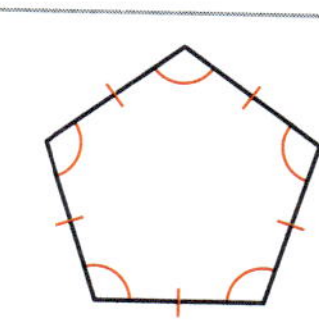

Glossary/Glosario

ENGLISH	SPANISH	EXAMPLES
regular pyramid A pyramid whose base is a regular polygon and whose lateral faces are all congruent.	**pirámide regular** Pirámide que tiene un polígono regular como base y caras laterales congruentes.	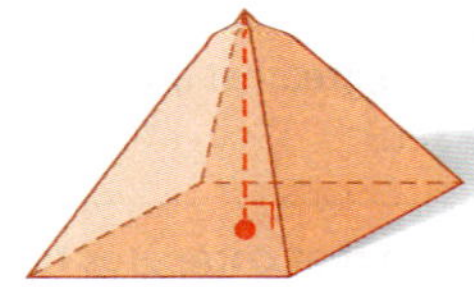
relative frequency The frequency of a data value or range of data values divided by the total number of data values in the set.	**frecuencia relativa** La frecuencia de un valor o un rango de valores dividido por el número total de los valores en el conjunto.	
relatively prime Two numbers are relatively prime if their greatest common factor (GCF) is 1.	**primo relatívo** Dos números son primos relativos si su máximo común divisor (MCD) es 1.	8 and 15 are relatively prime.
repeating decimal A decimal in which one or more digits repeat infinitely.	**decimal periódico** Decimal en el que uno o más dígitos se repiten infinitamente.	$0.757575\ldots = 0.\overline{75}$
rhombus A parallelogram with all sides congruent.	**rombo** Paralelogramo en el que todos los lados son congruentes.	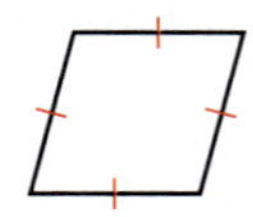
right angle An angle that measures 90°.	**ángulo recto** Ángulo que mide exactamente 90°.	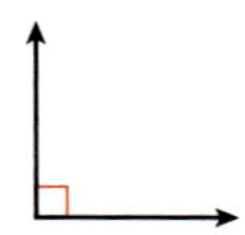
right triangle A triangle containing a right angle.	**triángulo rectángulo** Triángulo que tiene un ángulo recto.	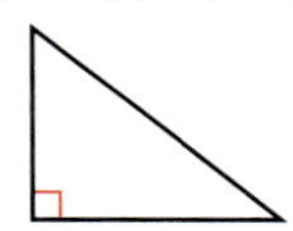
rise The vertical change when the slope of a line is expressed as the ratio $\frac{\text{rise}}{\text{run}}$, or "rise over run."	**distancia vertical** El cambio vertical cuando la pendiente de una línea se expresa como la razón $\frac{\text{distancia vertical}}{\text{distancia horizontal}}$, o "distancia vertical sobre distancia horizontal".	For the points (3, −1) and (6, 5), the rise is 5 − (−1) = 6.
rotation A transformation in which a figure is turned around a point.	**rotación** Transformación que ocurre cuando una figura gira alrededor de un punto.	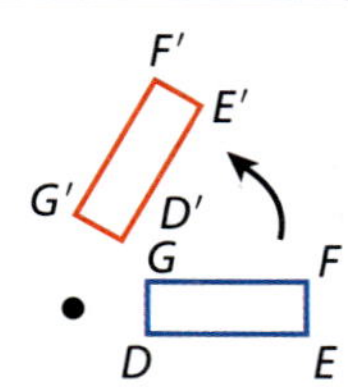
rotational symmetry A figure has rotational symmetry if it can be rotated less than 360° around a central point and coincide with the original figure.	**simetría de rotación** Ocurre cuando una figura gira menos de 360° alrededor de un punto central sin dejar de ser congruente con la figura original.	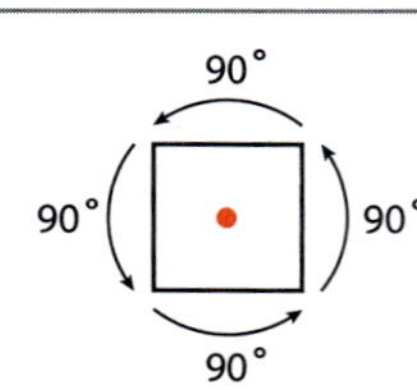
rounding Replacing a number with an estimate of that number to a given place value.	**redondear** Sustituir un número por una estimación de ese número hasta cierto valor posicional.	2,354 rounded to the nearest thousand is 2,000, and 2,354 rounded to the nearest 100 is 2,400.

ENGLISH	SPANISH	EXAMPLES
run The horizontal change when the slope of a line is expressed as the ratio $\frac{\text{rise}}{\text{run}}$, or "rise over run."	**distancia horizontal** El cambio horizontal cuando la pendiente de una línea se expresa como la razón $\frac{\text{distancia vertical}}{\text{distancia horizontal}}$, o "distancia vertical sobre distancia horizontal".	For the points (3, −1) and (6, 5), the run is $6 - 3 = 3$.

S

ENGLISH	SPANISH	EXAMPLES
sales tax A percent of the cost of an item that is charged by governments to raise money.	**impuesto sobre la venta** Porcentaje del costo de un artículo que los gobiernos cobran para recaudar fondos.	
sample A part of the population.	**muestra** Una parte de la población.	In a survey about the study habits of middle school students, a sample is a survey of 100 randomly chosen students.
sample space All possible outcomes of an experiment.	**espacio muestral** Conjunto de todos los resultados posibles de un experimento.	When rolling a number cube, the sample space is 1, 2, 3, 4, 5, 6.
savings Money that is not spent by a consumer currently, but is reserved for later use.	**ahorros** Dinero que un consumidor no gasta en el presente, pero que reserva para uso futuro.	
scale The ratio between two sets of measurements.	**escala** La razón entre dos conjuntos de medidas.	1 cm:5 mi
scale drawing A drawing that uses a scale to make an object smaller than or larger than the real object.	**dibujo a escala** Dibujo en el que se usa una escala para que un objeto se vea mayor o menor que el objeto real al que representa.	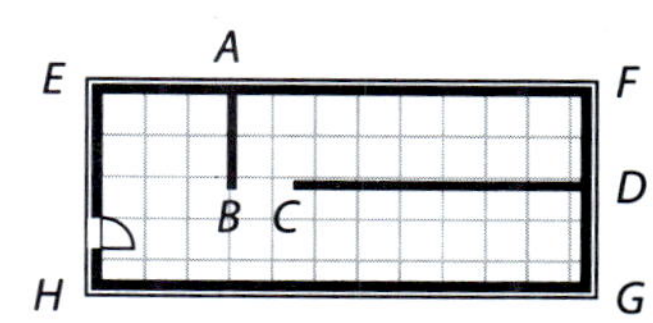 A blueprint is an example of a scale drawing.
scale factor The ratio used to enlarge or reduce similar figures.	**factor de escala** Razón que se usa para agrandar o reducir figuras semejantes.	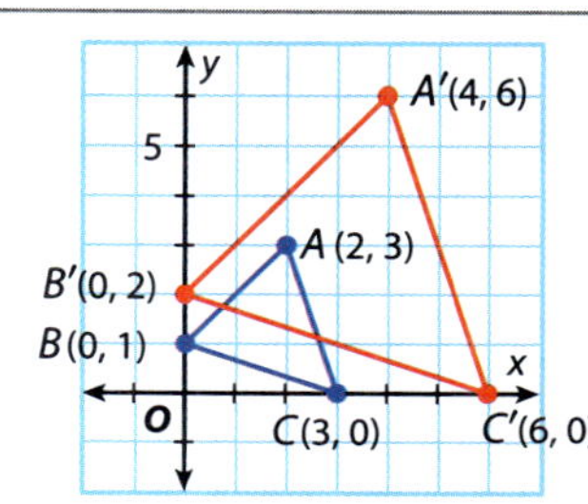 Scale factor: 2
scale model A proportional model of a three-dimensional object.	**modelo a escala** Modelo proporcional de un objeto tridimensional.	
scalene triangle A triangle with no congruent sides.	**triángulo escaleno** Triángulo que no tiene lados congruentes.	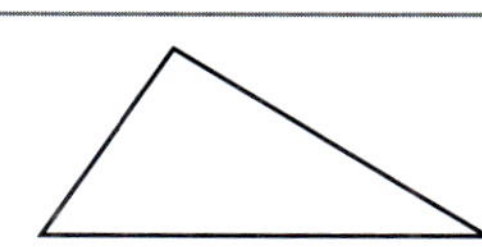

Glossary/Glosario

ENGLISH | **SPANISH** | **EXAMPLES**

scatter plot A graph with points plotted to show a possible relationship between two sets of data.

diagrama de dispersión Gráfica de puntos que se usa para mostrar una posible relación entre dos conjuntos de datos.

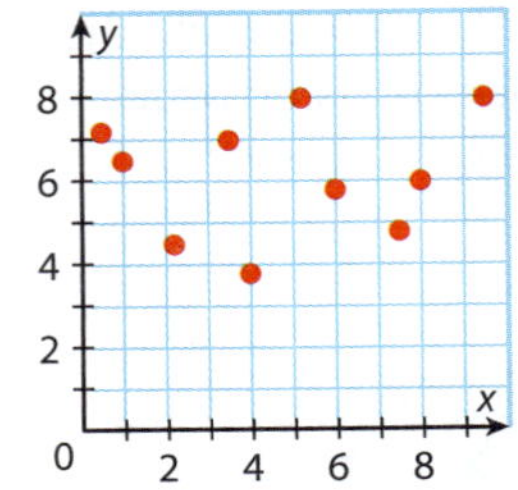

---

scientific notation A method of writing very large or very small numbers by using powers of 10.

notación científica Método que se usa para escribir números muy grandes o muy pequeños mediante potencias de 10.

$12{,}560{,}000{,}000{,}000 = 1.256 \times 10^{13}$

---

sector A region enclosed by two radii and the arc joining their endpoints.

sector Región encerrada por dos radios y el arco que une sus extremos.

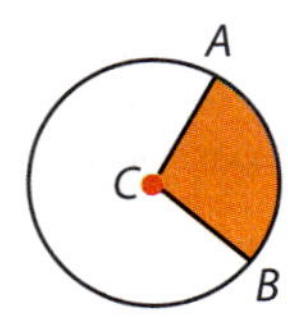

---

sector (data) A section of a circle graph representing part of the data set.

sector (datos) Sección de una gráfica circular que representa una parte del conjunto de datos.

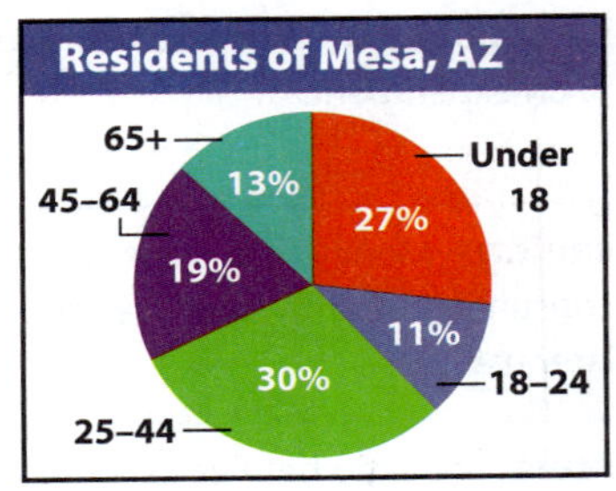

The circle graph has 5 sectors.

---

segment A part of a line between two endpoints.

segmento Parte de una línea entre dos extremos.

---

sequence An ordered list of numbers.

sucesíon Lista ordenada de números.

2, 4, 6, 8, 10, …

---

set A group of terms.

conjunto Un grupo de elementos.

---

side A line bounding a geometric figure; one of the faces forming the outside of an object.

lado Línea que delimita las figuras geométricas; una de las caras que forman la parte exterior de un objeto.

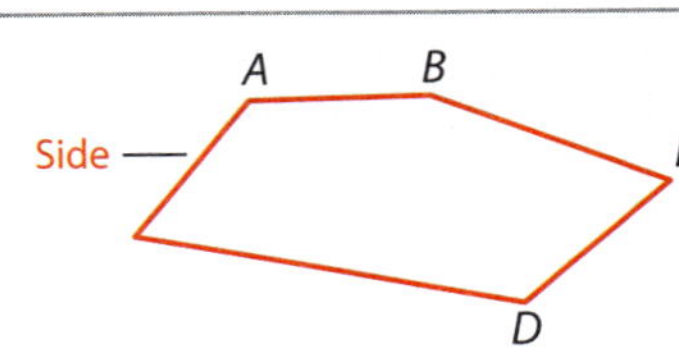

Side-Side-Side (SSS) A rule stating that if three sides of one triangle are congruent to three sides of another triangle, then the triangles are congruent.

Lado-Lado-Lado (LLL) Regla que establece que dos triángulos son congruentes cuando sus tres lados correspondientes son congruentes.

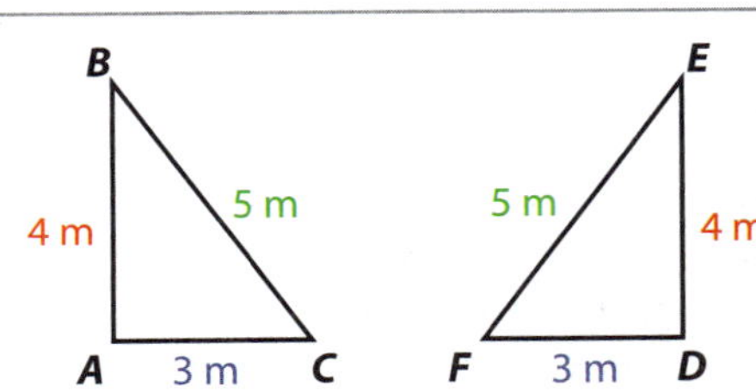

$\triangle ABC \cong \triangle DEF$

ENGLISH	SPANISH	EXAMPLES
significant digits The digits used to express the precision of a measurement.	**dígitos significativos** Dígitos usados para expresar la precisión de una medida.	0.048 has 2 significant digits. 5.003 has 4 significant digits.
similar Figures with the same shape but not necessarily the same size are similar.	**semejantes** Figuras que tienen la misma forma, pero no necesariamente el mismo tamaño.	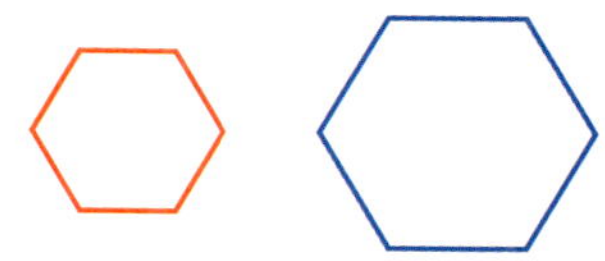
simple event An event consisting of only one outcome.	**suceso simple** Suceso que tiene sólo un resultado.	In the experiment of rolling a number cube, the event consisting of the outcome 3 is a simple event.
simple interest A fixed percent of the principal. It is found using the formula $I = Prt$, where P represents the principal, r the rate of interest, and t the time.	**interés simple** Un porcentaje fijo del capital. Se calcula con la fórmula $I = Cit$, donde C representa el capital, i, la tasa de interés y t, el tiempo.	\$100 is put into an account with a simple interest rate of 5%. After 2 years, the account will have earned $I = 100 \cdot 0.05 \cdot 2 = \$10$.
simplest form A fraction is in simplest form when the numerator and denominator have no common factors other than 1.	**mínima expresión** Una fracción está en su mínima expresión cuando el numerador y el denominador no tienen más factor común que 1.	Fraction: $\frac{8}{12}$ Simplest form: $\frac{2}{3}$
simplify To write a fraction or expression in simplest form.	**simplificar** Escribir una fracción o expresión numérica en su mínima expresión.	
simulation A model of an experiment, often one that would be too difficult or too time-consuming to actually perform.	**simulación** Representación de un experimento, por lo regular de uno cuya realización sería demasiado difícil o llevaría mucho tiempo.	
skew lines Lines that lie in different planes that are neither parallel nor intersecting.	**líneas oblicuas** Líneas que se encuentran en planos distintos, por eso no se intersecan ni son paralelas.	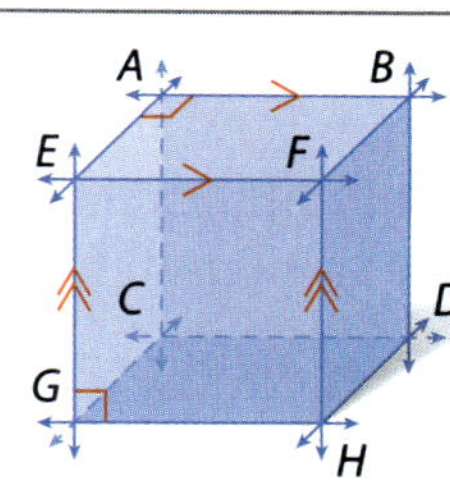 $\overleftrightarrow{AB}$ and $\overleftrightarrow{CG}$ are skew lines.
slant height of a cone The distance from the vertex of a cone to a point on the edge of the base.	**altura inclinada de un cono** Distancia desde el vértice de un cono hasta un punto en el borde de la base.	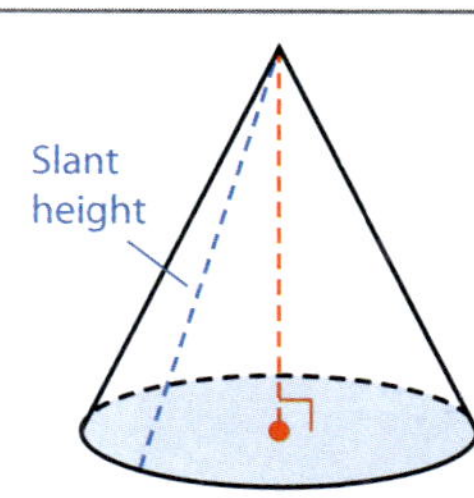
slant height of a pyramid The distance from the vertex of a pyramid to the midpoint of an edge of the base.	**altura inclinada de una pirámide** Distancia desde el vértice de una pirámide hasta el punto medio de una arista de la base.	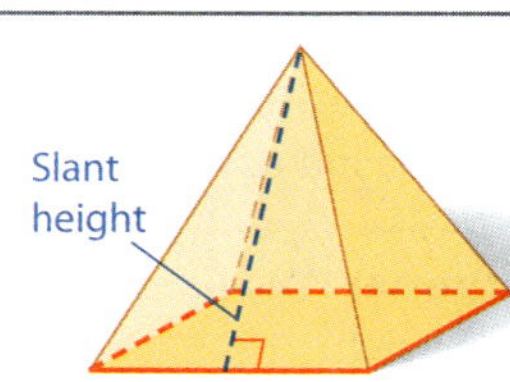

ENGLISH	SPANISH	EXAMPLES
slope A measure of the steepness of a line on a graph; the rise divided by the run.	**pendiente** Medida de la inclinación de una línea en una gráfica. Razón de la distancia vertical a la distancia horizontal.	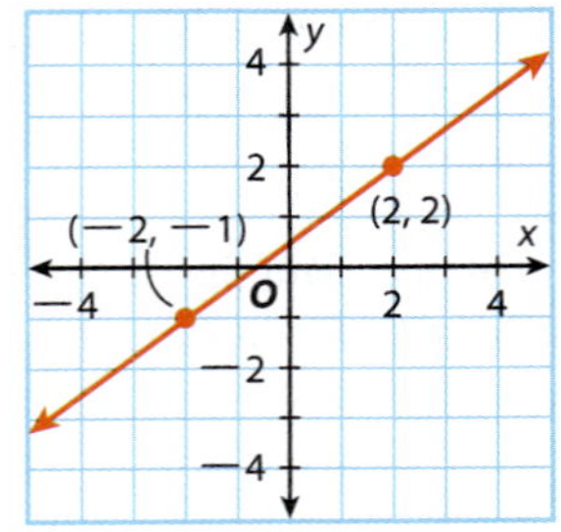 Slope $= \frac{\text{rise}}{\text{run}} = \frac{3}{4}$
slope-intercept form A linear equation written in the form $y = mx + b$, where m represents slope and b represents the y-intercept.	**forma de pendiente-intersecciíon** Ecuación lineal escrita en la forma $y = mx + b$, donde m es la pendiente y b es la intersección con el eje y.	$y = 6x - 3$
solid figure A three-dimensional figure.	**cuerpo geométrico** Figura tridimensional.	
solution of an equation A value or values that make an equation true.	**solución de una ecuación** Valor o valores que hacen verdadera una ecuación.	Equation: $x + 2 = 6$ Solution: $x = 4$
solution of an inequality A value or values that make an inequality true.	**solución de una desigualdad** Valor o valores que hacen verdadera una desigualdad.	Inequality: $x + 3 \geq 10$ Solution: $x \geq 7$
solution set The set of values that make a statement true.	**conjunto solución** Conjunto de valores que hacen verdadero un enunciado.	Inequality: $x + 3 \geq 5$ Solution set: $x \geq 2$ 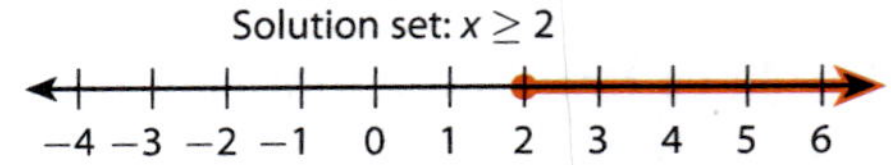
solve To find an answer or a solution.	**resolver** Hallar una respuesta o solución.	
sphere A three-dimensional figure with all points the same distance from the center.	**esfera** Figura tridimensional en la que todos los puntos están a la misma distancia del centro.	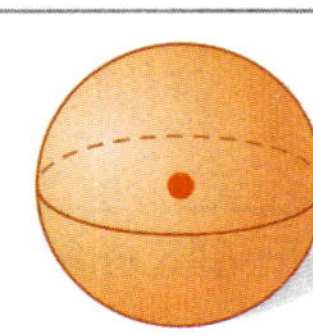
square (geometry) A rectangle with four congruent sides.	**cuadrado** (en geometría) Rectángulo con cuatro lados congruentes.	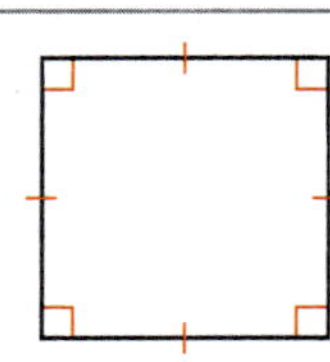
square (numeration) A number raised to the second power.	**cuadrado (en numeración)** Número elevado a la segunda potencia.	In 5^2, the number 5 is squared.
square number The product of a number and itself.	**cuadrado de un número** El producto de un número y sí mismo.	25 is a square number. $5 \cdot 5 = 25$

ENGLISH	SPANISH	EXAMPLES

square root A number that is multiplied by itself to form a product is called a square root of that product.

raíz cuadrada El número que se multiplica por sí mismo para formar un producto se denomina la raíz cuadrada de ese producto.

$\sqrt{16} = 4$ because $4^2 = 4 \cdot 4 = 16$

---

standard form (in numeration) A way to write numbers by using digits.

forma estándar (en numeración) Una manera de escribir números por medio de dígitos.

Five thousand, two hundred ten in standard form is 5,210.

---

stem-and-leaf plot A graph used to organize and display data so that the frequencies can be compared.

diagrama de tallo y hojas Gráfica que muestra y ordena los datos, y que sirve para comparar las frecuencias.

Stem	Leaves
3	2 3 4 4 7 9
4	0 1 5 7 7 7 8
5	1 2 2 3

Key: 3|2 means 3.2

---

straight angle An angle that measures 180°.

ángulo llano Ángulo que mide exactamente 180°.

---

subset A set contained within another set.

subconjunto Conjunto que pertenece a otro conjunto.

---

substitute To replace a variable with a number or another expression in an algebraic expression.

sustituir Reemplazar una variable por un número u otra expresión en una expresión algebraica.

Subtraction Property of Equality The property that states that if you subtract the same number from both sides of an equation, the new equation will have the same solution.

Propiedad de igualdad de la resta Propiedad que establece que puedes restar el mismo número de ambos lados de una ecuación y la nueva ecuación tendrá la misma solución.

$$\begin{aligned} x + 6 &= 8 \\ -6 &\quad -6 \\ x &= 2 \end{aligned}$$

---

sum The result when two or more numbers are added.

suma Resultado de sumar dos o más números.

The sum of $6 + 7 + 1$ is 14.

---

supplementary angles Two angles whose measures have a sum of 180°.

ángulos suplementarios Dos ángulos cuyas medidas suman 180°.

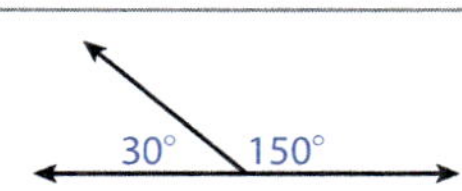

---

surface area The sum of the areas of the faces, or surfaces, of a three-dimensional figure.

área total Suma de las áreas de las caras, o superficies, de una figura tridimensional.

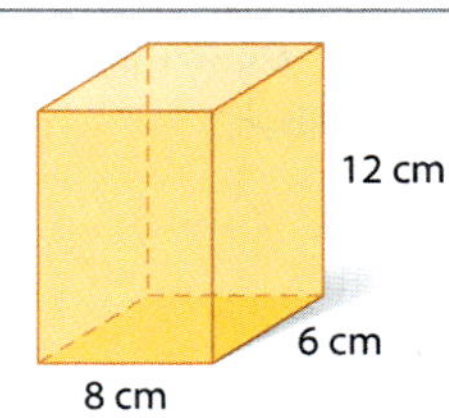

Surface area $= 2(8)(12) + 2(8)(6) + 2(12)(6) = 432 \text{ cm}^2$

T

taxable income The total amount of income minus qualifying deductions.

ingreso sujeto a impuestos Cantidad total de ingresos, menos las deducciones aplicables.

ENGLISH	SPANISH	EXAMPLES

term (in an expression) The parts of an expression that are added or subtracted.

término (en una expresión) Las partes de una expresión que se suman o se restan.

$3x^2 + 6x - 8$ (each of $3x^2$, $6x$, and 8 is a Term)

---

term (in a sequence) An element or number in a sequence.

término (en una sucesión) Elemento o número de una sucesión.

5 is the third term in the sequence 1, 3, 5, 7, 9, …

---

terminating decimal A decimal number that ends, or terminates.

decimal finito Decimal con un número determinado de posiciones decimales.

6.75

---

tessellation A repeating pattern of plane figures that completely covers a plane with no gaps or overlaps.

teselado Patrón repetido de figuras planas que cubren totalmente un plano sin superponerse ni dejar huecos.

---

theoretical probability The ratio of the number of ways an event can occur to the total number of equally likely outcomes.

probabilidad teórica Razón del número de las maneras que puede ocurrir un suceso al número total de resultados igualmente probables.

When rolling a number cube, the theoretical probability of rolling a 4 is $\frac{1}{6}$.

---

third quartile The median of the upper half of a set of data; also called *upper quartile*.

tercer cuartil La mediana de la mitad superior de un conjunto de datos. También se llama *cuartil superior*.

---

transformation A change in the position or orientation of a figure.

transformación Cambio en la posición u orientación de una figura.

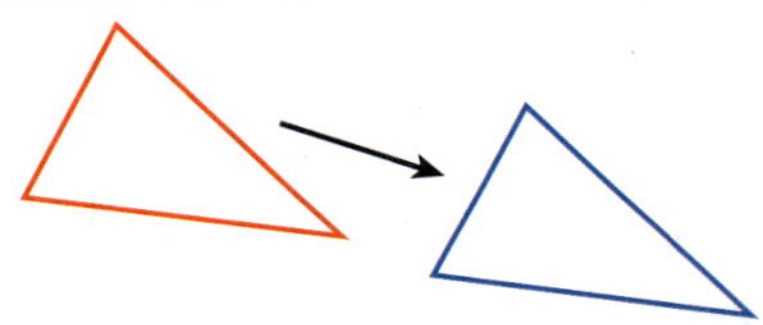

---

translation A movement (slide) of a figure along a straight line.

traslación Desplazamiento de una figura a lo largo de una línea recta.

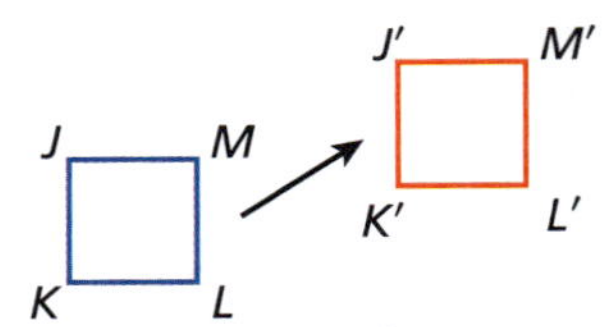

---

transversal A line that intersects two or more lines.

transversal Línea que cruza dos o más líneas.

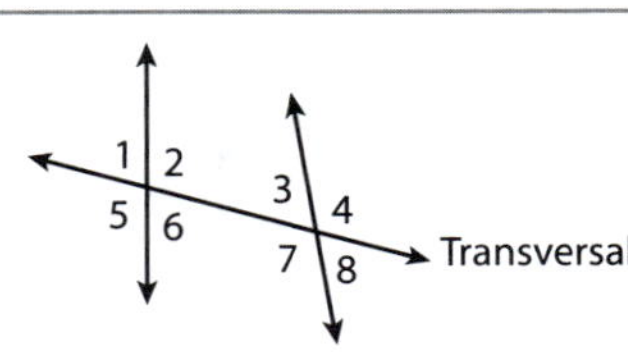

---

trapezoid A quadrilateral with at least one pair of parallel sides.

trapecio Cuadrilátero con al menos un par de lados paralelos.

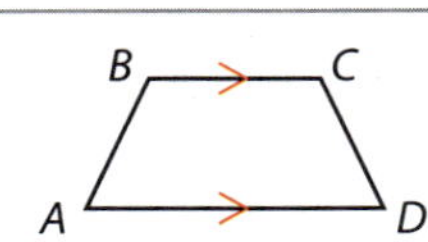

---

tree diagram A branching diagram that shows all possible combinations or outcomes of an event.

diagrama de árbol Diagrama ramificado que muestra todas las posibles combinaciones o resultados de un suceso.

---

trial Each repetition or observation of an experiment.

prueba Una sola repetición u observación de un experimento.

When rolling a number cube, each roll is one trial.

ENGLISH	SPANISH	EXAMPLES
triangle A three-sided polygon.	**triángulo** Polígono de tres lados.	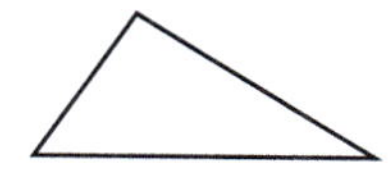
Triangle Sum Theorem The theorem that states that the measures of the angles in a triangle add to 180°.	**Teorema de la suma del triángulo** Teorema que establece que las medidas de los ángulos de un triángulo suman 180°.	
triangular prism A polyhedron whose bases are triangles and whose other faces are parallelograms.	**prisma triangular** Poliedro cuyas bases son triángulos y cuyas demás caras tienen forma de paralelogramo.	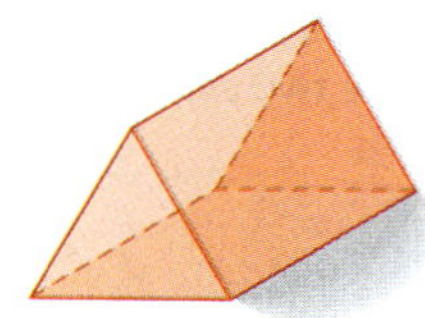

U

ENGLISH	SPANISH	EXAMPLES
underestimate An estimate that is less than the exact answer.	**estimación baja** Estimación menor que la respuesta exacta.	
unit conversion The process of changing one unit of measure to another.	**conversión de unidades** Proceso que consiste en cambiar una unidad de medida por otra.	
unit conversion factor A fraction used in unit conversion in which the numerator and denominator represent the same amount but are in different units.	**factor de conversión de unidades** Fracción que se usa para la conversión de unidades, donde el numerador y el denominador representan la misma cantidad pero están en unidades distintas.	$\frac{60 \text{ min}}{1 \text{h}}$ or $\frac{1 \text{h}}{60 \text{ min}}$
unit price A unit rate used to compare prices.	**precio unitario** Tasa unitaria que sirve para comparar precios.	
unit rate A rate in which the second quantity in the comparison is one unit.	**tasa unitaria** Una tasa en la que la segunda cantidad de la comparación es la unidad.	10 cm per minute
upper quartile The median of the upper half of a set of data.	**cuartil superior** La mediana de la mitad superior de un conjunto de datos.	Lower half: 18, 23, 28, Upper half: 29, (36), 42 — 36 = Upper quartile

V

ENGLISH	SPANISH	EXAMPLES
variable A symbol used to represent a quantity that can change.	**variable** Símbolo que representa una cantidad que puede cambiar.	In the expression $2x + 3$, x is the variable.
variable expense Expenses that occur regularly but may change because the consumer has some control over the amount.	**gasto variable** Gasto que ocurre con regularidad y que es necesario para vivir, pero que puede cambiar debido a que el consumidor tiene algún control sobre la cantidad.	

ENGLISH	SPANISH	EXAMPLES

Venn diagram A diagram that is used to show relationships between sets.

diagrama de Venn Diagrama que muestra las relaciones entre conjuntos.

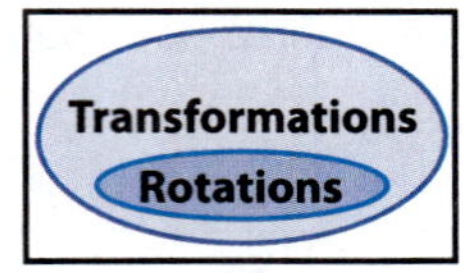

verbal expression A word or phrase.

expresión verbal Palabra o frase.

vertex On an angle or polygon, the point where two sides intersect.

vértice En un ángulo o polígono, el punto de intersección de dos lados.

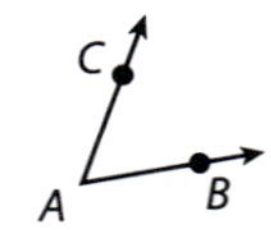

A is the vertex of $\angle CAB$.

vertical angles A pair of opposite congruent angles formed by intersecting lines.

ángulos opuestos por el vértice Par de ángulos opuestos congruentes formados por líneas secantes.

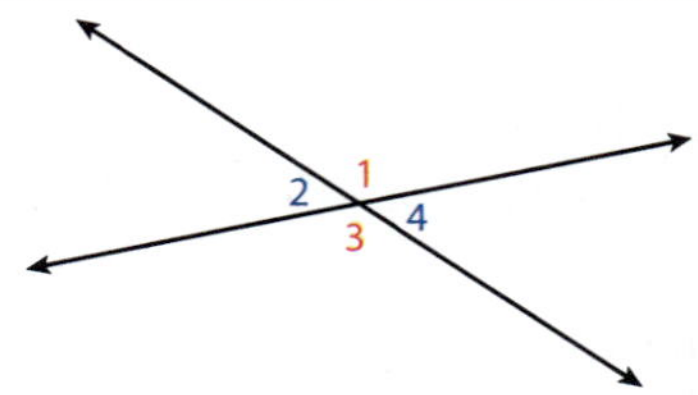

$\angle 1$ and $\angle 3$ are vertical angles.
$\angle 2$ and $\angle 4$ are vertical angles.

volume The number of cubic units needed to fill a given space.

volumen Número de unidades cúbicas que se necesitan para llenar un espacio.

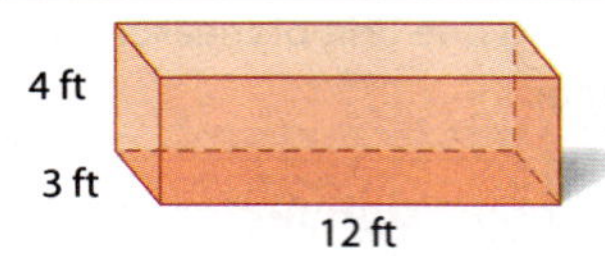

Volume $= 3 \cdot 4 \cdot 12 = 144$ ft^3

X

***x*-axis** The horizontal axis on a coordinate plane.

eje *x* El eje horizontal del plano cartesiano.

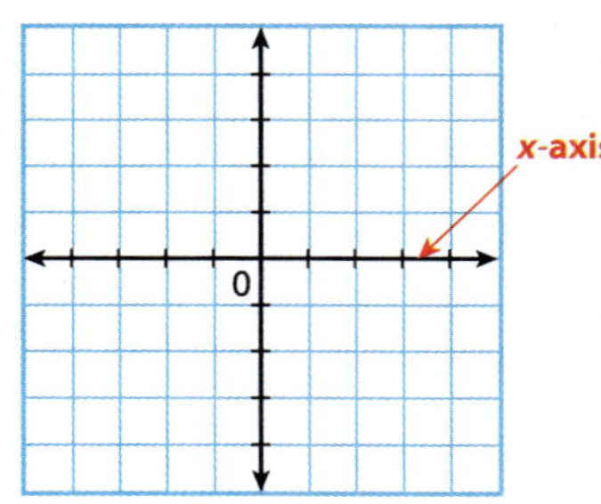

***x*-coordinate** The first number in an ordered pair; it tells the distance to move right or left from the origin, (0, 0).

coordenada *x* El primer número en un par ordenado; indica la distancia que debes avanzar hacia la izquierda o hacia la derecha desde el origen, (0, 0).

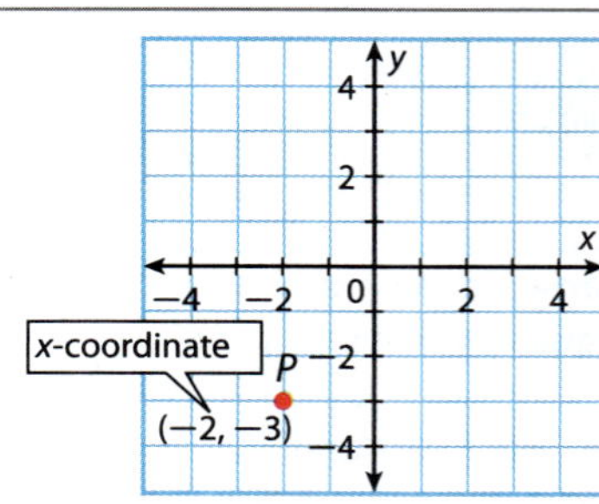

ENGLISH	SPANISH	EXAMPLES

x-intercept The *x*-coordinate of the point where the graph of a line crosses the *x*-axis.

intersección con el eje x Coordenada *x* del punto donde la gráfica de una línea cruza el eje *x*.

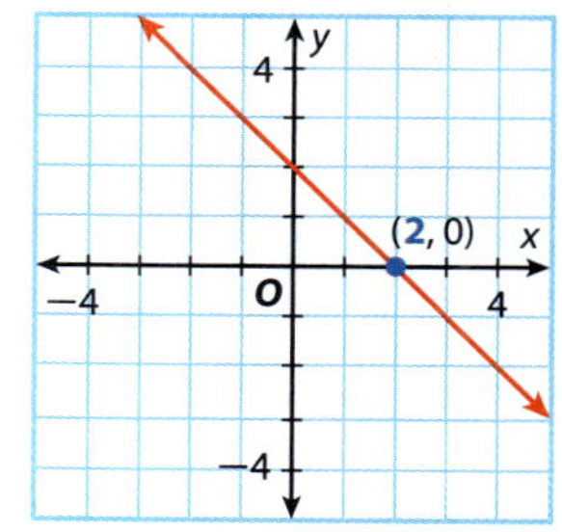

The *x*-intercept is 2.

Y

y-axis The vertical axis on a coordinate plane.

eje y El eje vertical del plano cartesiano.

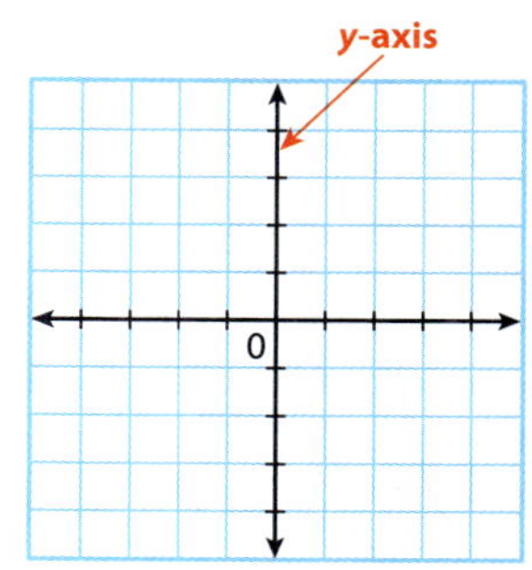

y-coordinate The second number in an ordered pair; it tells the distance to move up or down from the origin, (0, 0).

coordenada y El segundo número de un par ordenado; indica la distancia que debes avanzar hacia arriba o hacia abajo desde el origen, (0, 0).

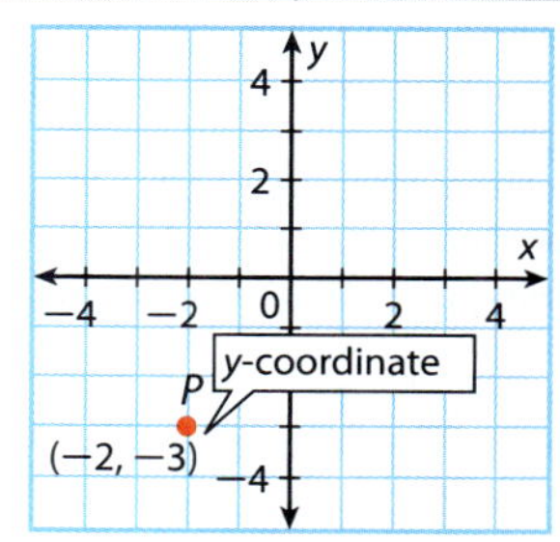

y-intercept The *y*-coordinate of the point where the graph of a line crosses the *y*-axis.

intersección con el eje y Coordenada *y* del punto donde la gráfica de una línea cruza el eje *y*.

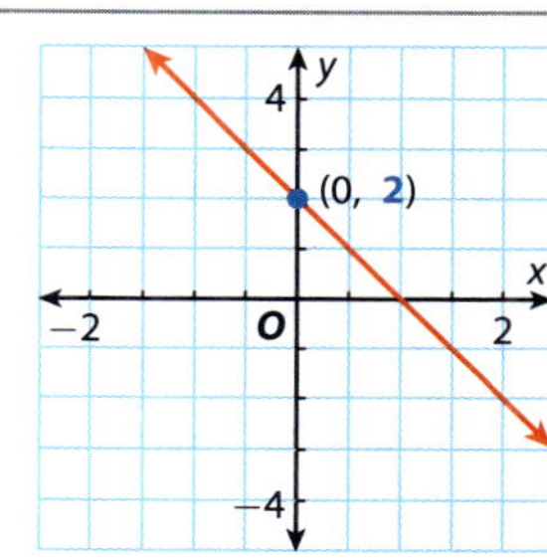

The *y*-intercept is 2.

Index

A

B

C

D

E

Index

F

G

H

I

J

K

L

M

N

O

P

Q

R

Index

S

T

U

V

W

Y

Z

Index

ASSESSMENT REFERENCE SHEET

TABLE OF MEASURES

Length

1 inch = 2.54 centimeters

1 meter ≈ 39.37 inches

1 mile = 5,280 feet

1 mile = 1,760 yards

1 mile ≈ 1.609 kilometers

1 kilometer ≈ 0.62 mile

Mass/Weight

1 pound = 16 ounces

1 pound ≈ 0.454 kilogram

1 kilogram ≈ 2.2 pounds

1 ton = 2,000 pounds

Capacity

1 cup = 8 fluid ounces

1 pint = 2 cups

1 quart = 2 pints

1 gallon = 4 quarts

1 gallon ≈ 3.785 liters

1 liter ≈ 0.264 gallon

1 liter = 1000 cubic centimeters

FORMULAS

Area

Parallelogram	$A = bh$
Circle	$A = \pi r^2$
Triangle	$A = \frac{1}{2}bh$

Volume

General prism	$V = Bh$

Circumference

Circle	$C = \pi d$ or $C = 2\pi r$